A Guide to the Major Trusts

2003/2004 edition

Volume 2
700 further trusts

Alan French
Dave Griffiths
Tom Traynor

DIRECTORY OF SOCIAL CHANGE

A Guide to the Major Trusts
Volume 2
2003/2004 edition

Published by
Directory of Social Change
24 Stephenson Way
London NW1 2DP
Tel. 020 7209 5151; Fax 020 7391 4804
E-mail books@dsc.org.uk
www.dsc.org.uk
from whom further copies and a full books catalogue are available.

Directory of Social Change is a Registered Charity no. 800517

First published 1993
Second edition 1995
Third edition 1997
Fourth edition 1999
Fifth edition 2001
Sixth edition 2003

ISBN 1 903991 31 5

British Library Cataloguing in Publication Data

A catalogue record for this book is available from the British Library

Cover design by Keith Shaw
Text designed by Lenn Darroux and Linda Parker
Typeset by Linda Parker
Printed and bound by Page Bros., Norwich

Other Directory of Social Change departments in London:
Courses and conferences 020 7209 4949
Charity Centre 020 7209 1015
Charityfair 020 7391 4875
Publicity & Web Content 020 7391 4900
Policy & Research 020 7391 4880

Directory of Social Change Northern Office:
Federation House, Hope Street, Liverpool L1 9BW
Courses and conferences 0151 708 0117
Research 0151 708 0136

Contents

Introduction

Welcome to *A Guide to the Major Trusts Volume 2*. This guide contains the 700 major UK trusts which follow on from the 300 largest detailed in Volume 1. The trusts in this book give around £148 million each year, a rise of £20 million from the previous edition. (This total equates to less than 10% of the £1,500 million in Volume 1.)

The guide's main aim is to help people raise money from trusts. We provide as much information as is available to enable fundraisers to locate relevant trusts and produce suitable applications. There is also a secondary aim: to be a survey of the work of grant-making trusts, to show where their money is going and for what purposes.

What trusts do we include?

There has been a minor change to the Major Trusts series since the last edition of the guide. *A Guide to the Major Trusts Volume 3* now covers the trusts we rank 1,001 to 1,500 to give a more comprehensive coverage of the largest UK trusts. (We now produce a separate guide for trusts in Scotland; trusts that give in Northern Ireland are listed on our website at www.dsc.org.uk/; and fundraisers in Wales will be able to consult *The Welsh Funding Guide*, to be published in autumn 2003.)

Trusts in this guide all have the potential to give between £60,000 and £500,000 to UK organisations each year. Some trusts included have given more than £500,000, but do not have large enough income or assets to maintain this level of giving. Others have given less than £60,000, but have the potential to give more. For a full list of the trusts in size order, please see page ix.

What is excluded?

To make this guide as useful to as possible to fundraisers in the UK, we have excluded the following trusts:

- Those which give funding to individuals and have less than £60,000 a year available to organisations. Where a trust is included which gives to individuals, this guide merely mentions the fact and does not provide in-depth information. Our publications *The Educational Grants Directory* and *A Guide to Grants for Individuals in Need* provide detailed information on this subject.
- Those which give to a particular location rather than UK-wide. In general terms, grants must be available throughout England, or to two or more UK countries, to maximise the number of trusts which are relevant to each reader. For trusts which only cover a specific area of England, we have four local trusts guides (London, the midlands, the north and the south).
- Those which support international charities. Details of these can be found in *The International Development Directory*.
- Trusts which are funded by a company as a vehicle for their giving. We see this as corporate money rather than trust money and therefore they are included in *A Guide to UK Company Giving*. (Trusts like The Pet Plan Charitable Trust, which gives clients the option of making a £1 donation with their policy, are included as the funds are coming from a charitable source rather than a slice of corporate profits.)

The layout of this book

The layout of this guide is the same as in previous years, except that we now include the Charity Commission (or Inland Revenue) numbers for the trusts.

We have used the word chair in preference to chairman, unless specifically requested to do so by the trust. We have also rounded off the financial figures to make the guides easier to read, which explains why in some places the totals do not add up exactly.

Indexes

The trusts are listed alphabetically in this guide. For reference, we have included two indexes, which are a useful starting point.

- **Subject index** (page 273). This can be used for identifying trusts with a particular preference for a certain cause. Many trusts have general charitable purposes, but we have not included a general category as it would be too extensive. Trusts with general charitable purposes with a preference for the arts, for instance, could fund any project, but would only be indexed under the arts. For this reason, fundraisers should not look at the list and believe these are the only trusts that would support them.
- **Geographical index** (page 285). Although we have excluded trusts which only fund in a particular area, many trusts will give grants UK-wide but have a preference for a particular area. These are listed in this index. We have only listed the special cases, not trusts that will fund anywhere, so again these are not the only trusts which will fund a particular area.

It is essential to remember that a trust which appears under a particular category may have other criteria which exclude your particular charity from applying. For instance, a trust supporting the arts in England and Wales could not support art organisations in Aberdeen, or educational projects in Aberystwyth. When using the index, please read the entries carefully to identify those trusts which are of the most relevance to you; do not use the index as a mailing list.

It is also important to check through every entry in the guide to find those relevant trusts not included in the index. The main areas of work and geographical restrictions are listed at the start of every entry, so it is often obvious which trusts would not accept an application without reading the full entry.

On a practical note, it may be a good idea to start in the middle of the alphabet. Most people naturally read these types of guides from front to back, and apparently trusts with names beginning with L–Z get fewer applications.

How we compiled this guide

The following are the practical guidelines we followed to produce this guide:

- concentrate on what the trust does in practice rather than the wider objects permitted by its formal trust deed
- provide extensive information which will be of the most use to readers, such as the trust's criteria and guidelines for applicants where available
- include, where available, details of the organisations which have received grants, to give the reader an idea of what the trust supports and the amounts it usually gives
- provide the most up-to-date information at the time of research, including changes expected in coming years
- include all trusts which meet our criteria for inclusion
- comment on instances of good and bad practice in the trust world (something we have paid more attention to than in previous editions).

Availability of information

We create the entries in this guide using the information available to the general public; there is no requirement for any trust to treat our enquiries as a special case. We produce guides such as these so that people can find the relevant information easily rather than contacting hundreds of trusts for their accounts, or wading through files at the Charity Commission.

We believe that trusts are public bodies, not private ones, and that they should be publicly accountable. This view is backed up by the Charity Commission regulations and the SORP (Statement of Recommended Practice).

Many trusts recognise the importance of providing good, clear information about the work they do. However there are some which believe they are private bodies and ignore their statutory obligation to provide information to the public. Sometimes information held at the Charity Commission is out of date and there is no information in the public domain about their work in recent years. (For further information on the legal responsibilities of trusts, please see the introduction to Volume 1.)

Of the 700 trusts in this guide, only 268 replied to our initial requests for information, of which just 192 sent accounts. Charities may make a reasonable charge for sending accounts (for photocopying and postage costs, for instance), although only two did so (which in both cases was £10). We also found, after visiting the Charity Commission, that over 15% of trusts do not provide any details of the grants they make in their accounts, something which is again unacceptable.

Applying to trusts

There is a lot of competition for grants. Many trusts in this guide receive far more applications than they can support. Some of the trusts told us that even though trust directories publish accurate information about their criteria, they receive many applications which are clearly outside of their area of giving. Such applications increase the administration expenses of both the applicant and the trust, and sometimes leads to trusts refusing to accept unsolicited applications, which penalises those charities which fundraise effectively.

The point, therefore, is to do the research: read the trust's criteria carefully and target the right trusts. This can only lead to a higher success rate and save you from spending a lot of time writing applications which are destined only for the bin.

Unsolicited applications

A number of trusts state that they do not want to receive applications (and often, therefore, do not want to appear in this guide). There can be good reasons for this. For example, the trust may do its own research, or support the same list of charities each year. There are some trusts, however, which believe they are a 'private' trust. No registered charity is a private body. We believe trusts should not resent applications but be committed to finding those charities most eligible for assistance.

We include these trusts for two reasons. Firstly, it may be that they state 'no unsolicited applications' simply as a deterrent, in an effort to reduce the number of applications they receive, but will still consider the applications they receive. The second reason relates to the secondary purpose of this guide: to act as a comprehensive survey of grant-making trusts.

If you choose to write to one of these trusts, do so with caution, and only write to those where your organisation very clearly fits the trust's criteria. We would advise you not to include an sae and to state that you do not expect a response unless you are successful. If they do not reply, do not follow it up.

Further information

This introduction aims to follow on from the comments in Volume 1, which we assume most users of this guide will have seen. For further information about how to apply, the role of grantmaking and an overview of the trust world in general, please see the introduction to that guide.

Finally...

The research has been done as fully and carefully as possible. Many thanks to those who have made this easier: trust officers, trustees and others who have helped us. We send draft entries to all the relevant trusts and their comments are noted, although the text and any mistakes within it remain ours and not theirs.

As always, we are also extremely grateful to all at the registration department at the Liverpool office of the Charity Commission who ordered an endless number of files to help us with our research.

We are aware that some of this information is incomplete, or will become out of date. We are equally sure that we will have missed some relevant trusts. We apologise for these imperfections and would be grateful if readers could let us know about any omissions or mistakes so we can correct them in future. Similarly, we are also happy to help find new contact addresses for trusts which move after publication of our guides. We can be contacted at the Research Department of the Liverpool office of DSC, by either e-mailing north@dsc.org.uk or telephoning 0151 708 0136.

We now have a subscription website, *www.trustfunding.org.uk*, which contains all the information that we publish in any of our trust directories. We update as soon as we find new information on any trust, which means the information is available before the printed versions of our guides are published. We also have a quarterly journal, *Funding for Change*, which contains up-to-date information on funding issues, including contributions from leading funders, as well as details of new trusts and changes in trust policies and addresses.

As well as publications, DSC also provides a comprehensive training programme for charities, including an extensive fundraising programme, in conjunction with the Institute of

Fundraising. A comprehensive list of all DSC's publications and training courses can be found at www.dsc.org.uk, or by telephoning 020 7391 4800 for copies of our catalogues.

To end on a positive note, there are more potential funders out there than you think, and some do not receive enough relevant applications. Several trusts in this guide even had unspent surpluses – many complain that they do not receive enough of the sort of applications they enjoy receiving. Finally, it's certainly worth considering this guide contains £20 million more in funding than the last edition, an increase of 15% in just two years. We hope this gives you extra encouragement and wish you success in your fundraising.

How to use this guide

The contents

The entries are in alaphabetical order describing the work of 700 trusts. Most give over £60,000 a year, almost all have the potential to give over £60,000 a year from ordinary income.

The entries are preceded by a listing of the trusts in order of size and are followed by a subject index and geographical index. There is also an alphabetical index at the back of the guide.

Finding the trusts you need

There are three basic ways of using this guide:

(a) You can simply read the entries through from A – Z (a rather time-consuming activity).

(b) You can look through the trust ranking table which starts on page ix and use the box provided to tick trusts which might be relevant to you (starting with the biggest).

(c) You can use the subject or geographical indices starting on pages 273 and 285 respectively. Each has an introduction explaining how to use them.

If you use approaches (b) or (c), once you have identified enough trust to be going on with, read each entry very carefully before deciding whether to apply. Very often their interest in your field will be limited and specific, and may require an application specifically tailored to their needs – or, indeed, no application at all.

Sending off applications which show that the available information has not been read antagonises trusts and brings charities into disrepute within the trust world. Carefully targeted applications, on the other hand, are welcomed by most trusts and usually have a reasonably high rate of success.

A typical trust entry

The Fictitious Trust

Welfare

£50,000 (2001)

Beneficial area UK, with a preference for New Town

The Old Barn, Main Street, New Town ZX48 2QQ

Tel. 020 7209 5050

Correspondent Ms A Grant, Appeals Secretary

Trustees Lord Great; Lady Good; A T Home; T Rust.

CC number 123456

Information available Full accounts were on file at the Charity Commission.

General The trust supports welfare charities with emphasis on disability and homelessness. The trustees will support both capital and revenue projects. 'Specific projects are preferred to general running costs.'

In 2001 it trust had assets of £640,000 and an income of £57,000. Over 70 grants were given totalling £50,000. Grants ranged from £100 to £5,000, with over half given in New Town. The largest grants were to: New Town Disability Group (£5,000), Homelessness Exeter (£4,000) and New Town Family Support Agency (£3,500). There were 10 other grants of £1,000 or more including those to New Town Mobility, Refugee Support Group and 'Tiny Tots' Playgroup.

Smaller grants were given to a range of local charities and local branches of UK charities.

Exclusions No support for minibuses, to individuals or to non-registered charities.

Applications In writing to the correspondent, including a brief decription of the project and a budget. Trustees' meetings are held in March and September.

Name of the Charity

Our summary of the main activities. We state what the trust does in practice rather than what its trust deed allows it to do.

Grant total (not income) for the most recent year available.

Geographical area of grant-giving including where the trust can legally give and where it gives in practice.

Contact address and telephone, fax and minicom numbers, and e-mail and website addresses, if available.

Contact person

Trustees

Sources of information we used and which are available to the applicant.

Background/summary of activities. A quick indicator of the policy to show whether it is worth reading the rest of the entry.

Financial information. We try to note the assets, ordinary income and grant total, and comment on unusual figures.

Typical grants range to indicate what a successful applicant can expect to receive.

Large grants to indicate where the main money is going, often the clearest indication of trust priorities.

Other examples of grants – listing typical beneficiaries, and where possible the purpose of the grant. We also indicate whether the trust gives one-off or recurrent grants.

Exclusions – listing any areas, subjects or types of grant the trust will not consider.

Applications including how to apply and when to submit an application.

Trusts ranked by grant total

☐	£240,000	Norwood & Newton Settlement	Christian	page 177
☐	£239,000	The South Square Trust	General	page 230
☐	£238,000	Morgan Williams Charitable Trust	Christian	page 166
☐	£237,000	The Joseph & Annie Cattle Trust	General	page 42
☐	£237,000	Largsmount Ltd	Jewish	page 134
☐	£237,000	The Norman Whiteley Trust	Evangelical Christianity, welfare, education	page 262
☐	£236,000	The Bernard Kahn Charitable Trust	Jewish	page 128
☐	£236,000	Premierquote Ltd	Jewish, general	page 189
☐	£234,000	The Christopher Laing Foundation	Social welfare, environment, culture, health and medicine; general	page 132
☐	£233,000	The Eleanor Rathbone Charitable Trust	Merseyside, women, unpopular causes	page 198
☐	£232,000	The Ecological Foundation	Environment/conservation	page 67
☐	£232,000	The Russell Trust	General	page 208
☐	£231,000	Seamen's Hospital Society	Seafarers	page 218
☐	£230,000	Highmoor Hall Charitable Trust	Christian mission societies and agencies	page 105
☐	£230,000	The Lillie Johnson Charitable Trust	Children, young people who are blind or deaf, medical	page 127
☐	£230,000	The Williams Family Charitable Trust	Jewish, medical	page 263
☐	£228,000	The Naggar Charitable Trust	Jewish, general	page 172
☐	£228,000	The Wixamtree Trust	General	page 264
☐	£227,000	The Kasner Charitable Trust	Jewish	page 129
☐	£227,000	The Edwina Mountbatten Trust	Medical	page 170
☐	£227,000	REMEDI	Research into disability	page 200
☐	£226,000	The Thomas Sivewright Catto Charitable Settlement	General	page 43
☐	£226,000	The Emmandjay Charitable Trust	Social welfare, medicine, youth	page 70
☐	£225,000	The John Swire (1989) Charitable Trust	General	page 238
☐	£224,000	Servite Sisters' Charitable Trust Fund	Women, refugees	page 221
☐	£223,000	The Cross Trust	Christian work	page 57
☐	£222,000	DG Charitable Trust	General	page 64
☐	£222,000	The Thornton Trust	Evangelical Christianity, education, relief of sickness and poverty	page 244
☐	£220,000	The Ward Blenkinsop Trust	Medicine, social welfare, general	page 255
☐	£218,000	The Clive Richards Charity Ltd	Disability, poverty	page 202
☐	£218,000	The Jean Sainsbury Animal Welfare Trust	Animal welfare	page 210
☐	£217,000	Brushmill Ltd	Jewish	page 35
☐	£217,000	The Three Oaks Trust	Welfare	page 244
☐	£216,000	The A B Charitable Trust	Promotion and defence of human dignity	page 1
☐	£216,000	Access 4 Trust	Children, welfare	page 2
☐	£216,000	The Children's Research Fund	Child health research	page 46
☐	£216,000	The Cecil Rosen Foundation	Welfare, especially older people, infirm, people who are mentally or physically disabled	page 207
☐	£215,000	The Batchworth Trust	Medical, social welfare, general	page 22
☐	£215,000	R G Hills Charitable Trust	General	page 108
☐	£214,000	Gordon Cook Foundation	Education and training	page 52
☐	£212,000	Sue Hammerson's Charitable Trust	Medical research, relief in need	page 97
☐	£212,000	The Whitaker Charitable Trust	Education, environment, music, personal development	page 261
☐	£211,000	Grimmitt Trust	General	page 94
☐	£210,000	The Saintbury Trust	General	page 214
☐	£209,000	The Scouloudi Foundation	General	page 218
☐	£209,000	The Bassil Shippam and Alsford Trust	Older people, health, education, Christian	page 224

☐	£121,000	**The Peter Beckwith Charitable Trust**	Medical, welfare	page 24
☐	£121,000	**The Peter Minet Trust**	General	page 163
☐	£121,000	**The Schapira Charitable Trust**	Jewish	page 216
☐	£120,000	**The Blair Foundation**	General	page 27
☐	£120,000	**Hospital Saturday Fund Charitable Trust**	Medical, health	page 113
☐	£120,000	**Marchig Animal Welfare Trust**	Animal welfare	page 154
☐	£120,000	**Triodos Foundation**	Overseas development, organics, community development	page 247
☐	£119,000	**The Hope Trust**	Temperance, reformed protestant churches	page 113
☐	£119,000	**The Lynn Foundation**	General	page 149
☐	£118,000	**The Rose Flatau Charitable Trust**	Jewish, social welfare	page 78
☐	£118,000	**Stuart Hine Trust**	Evangelical Christianity	page 109
☐	£118,000	**Ranworth Trust**	General	page 197
☐	£118,000	**Rosalyn and Nicholas Springer Charitable Trust**	Welfare, Jewish, education, general	page 233
☐	£117,000	**The Anglian Water Trust Fund**	Money advice provision/individuals in need	page 10
☐	£117,000	**The George Elias Charitable Trust**	Jewish, general	page 68
☐	£117,000	**The Gibbs Charitable Trusts**	Methodism, international, arts	page 87
☐	£117,000	**The Weinstein Foundation**	Jewish, medical, welfare	page 258
☐	£116,000	**The Magen Charitable Trust**	Education, Jewish	page 153
☐	£116,000	**The Peggy Ramsay Foundation**	Writers and writing for the stage	page 196
☐	£116,000	**The Steinberg Family Charitable Trust**	Jewish, health	page 234
☐	£115,000	**The Mayfield Valley Arts Trust**	Arts, especially chamber music	page 160
☐	£114,000	**The Francis Coales Charitable Foundation**	Historical	page 49
☐	£114,000	**The Sir Edward Lewis Foundation**	General	page 142
☐	£114,000	**Matliwala Family Charitable Trust**	Islam, general	page 159
☐	£114,000	**Dame Violet Wills Charitable Trust**	Evangelical Christianity	page 264
☐	£114,000	**The Worshipful Company of Chartered Accountants General Charitable Trust**	General, education	page 267
☐	£113,000	**The Simon Whitbread Charitable Trust**	Education, family welfare, medicine, preservation	page 261
☐	£112,000	**The Primrose Trust**	General	page 190
☐	£111,000	**David Charitable Trust**	Health, welfare, children, older and infirm people, educational institutions, the arts	page 60
☐	£111,000	**Golden Charitable Trust**	Preservation, conservation	page 88
☐	£111,000	**The Stone Foundation**	Research into addiction, medical research, welfare	page 235
☐	£111,000	**Wychdale Ltd**	Jewish	page 268
☐	£110,000	**William Geoffrey Harvey's Discretionary Settlement**	Animal welfare and bird life	page 100
☐	£110,000	**The Inland Waterways Association**	Inland waterways	page 116
☐	£110,000	**The Lambert Charitable Trust**	Health, welfare, Jewish, arts	page 134
☐	£110,000	**The Janet Nash Charitable Trust**	Medical, general	page 172
☐	£110,000	**The Samuel & Freda Parkinson Charitable Trust**	General	page 183
☐	£110,000	**SEM Charitable Trust**	Disability, general, Jewish	page 220
☐	£110,000	**The Stanley Foundation Ltd**	Older people, medical, education, social welfare	page 233
☐	£109,000	**The Acacia Charitable Trust**	Jewish, education, general	page 2
☐	£108,000	**The Bacta Charitable Trust**	General	page 19
☐	£108,000	**The Laurence Misener Charitable Trust**	Jewish, general	page 164
☐	£108,000	**The Willie & Mabel Morris Charitable Trust**	Medical, general	page 167
☐	£108,000	**Oppenheim Foundation**	General	page 181
☐	£108,000	**The Westcroft Trust**	International understanding, overseas aid, Quaker, Shropshire	page 260
☐	£106,000	**The Sir Jeremiah Colman Gift Trust**	General	page 51
☐	£73,000	**The C L Loyd Charitable Trust**	General	page 147

☐	£106,000	Macdonald-Buchanan Charitable Trust	General	page 152
☐	£106,000	The Victor Mishcon Charitable Trust	Jewish, social welfare	page 164
☐	£106,000	Penny in the Pound Fund Charitable Trust	Hospitals, health-related charities	page 184
☐	£106,000	Trust Sixty Three	Disability, overseas aid, famine relief, general	page 249
☐	£105,000	Airways Charitable Trust Limited	Welfare, health	page 4
☐	£105,000	The Birmingham Hospital Saturday Fund Medical Charity & Welfare Trust	Medical	page 25
☐	£105,000	The Graham Kirkham Foundation	General	page 130
☐	£105,000	George A Moore Foundation	General	page 165
☐	£105,000	The Rainford Trust	Social welfare, general	page 195
☐	£105,000	The Shipwrights Company Charitable Fund	Maritime or waterborne connected charities	page 224
☐	£104,000	The Marjorie Coote Animal Charity Fund	Wildlife and animal welfare	page 54
☐	£104,000	The Late St Patrick White Charitable Trust	General	page 213
☐	£103,000	Rokach Family Charitable Trust	Jewish, general	page 205
☐	£103,000	The Seedfield Trust	Christian, relief of poverty	page 219
☐	£103,000	Blyth Watson Charitable Trust	Humanitarian causes in the UK	page 256
☐	£102,000	Krattiger Rennison Charitable Trust	AIDS, education	page 132
☐	£101,000	The J G Hogg Charitable Trust	Welfare, animal welfare, general	page 111
☐	£101,000	The Lawlor Foundation	Social welfare, education, general	page 136
☐	£101,000	The Seven Fifty Trust	Christian	page 221
☐	£100,000	Barclays Stockbrokers Charitable Trust	Welfare	page 20
☐	£100,000	The Dumbreck Charity	General	page 65
☐	£100,000	The R J Larg Family Charitable Trust	Education, health, medical research, arts – particularly music	page 134
☐	£100,000	The Stanley Charitable Trust	Jewish	page 233
☐	£100,000	The Thomson Corporation Charitable Trust	People who are physically, mentally and socially disadvantaged	page 243
☐	£99,000	The Dorothy Gertrude Allen Memorial Fund	General	page 8
☐	£99,000	Hinchley Charitable Trust	Mainly evangelical Christian	page 108
☐	£99,000	The Kyte Charitable Trust	Medical, disadvantaged and socially isolated people	page 132
☐	£98,000	The Chamberlain Foundation	General	page 44
☐	£98,000	The Lyndhurst Trust	Christian	page 148
☐	£98,000	Morris Leigh Foundation	Jewish, general	page 140
☐	£98,000	The Helen Roll Charitable Trust	General	page 206
☐	£98,000	The Thriplow Charitable Trust	Higher education and research	page 245
☐	£98,000	The Treeside Trust	General	page 247
☐	£97,000	The Dent Charitable Trust	Jewish, general	page 63
☐	£97,000	The Dinam Charity	International understanding, general	page 64
☐	£97,000	The Eventhall Family Charitable Trust	General	page 72
☐	£97,000	The Huggard Charitable Trust	General	page 114
☐	£97,000	The Jenour Foundation	General	page 124
☐	£97,000	The Jephcott Charitable Trust	Alleviation of poverty in developing countries, general	page 125
☐	£97,000	The Leach Fourteenth Trust	Disability, general	page 139
☐	£97,000	The Schreiber Charitable Trust	Jewish	page 217
☐	£96,000	The Beaverbrook Foundation	General	page 24
☐	£96,000	May Hearnshaw's Charity	General	page 102
☐	£96,000	The Langdale Trust	Social welfare, Christian, medical, general	page 134
☐	£96,000	The N Smith Charitable Trust	General	page 227
☐	£95,000	The Charlotte Bonham-Carter Charitable Trust	General	page 28
☐	£95,000	The Oliver Morland Charitable Trust	Quakers, general	page 166

The 1970 Trust

Disadvantaged minorities

£70,000 (2001)

Beneficial area UK, with an interest in Scotland.

c/o C W Pagan, Messrs Pagan Osborne, 12 St Catherine Street, Cupar, Fife KY15 4HN

Tel. 01334 653777 **Fax** 01334 655063

Email enquiries@pagan.co.uk

Website www.pagan.co.uk

Correspondent The Trustee

Trustee *David Rennie.*

CC Number SC008788

Information available Information was supplied by the trust.

General The trust states it supports small UK charities 'doing innovative, educational, or experimental work in the following fields:

- civil liberties (e.g. freedom of information; constitutional reform; humanising work; children's welfare)
- the public interest in the face of vested interest groups (such as the advertising, alcohol, road, war, pharmaceuticals and tobacco industries)
- disadvantaged minorities, multiracial work, prison reform
- new economics ('as if people mattered' – Schumacher) and intermediate technology
- public transport, pedestrians, bicycling, road crash prevention, traffic-calming, low-energy lifestyles
- preventative health'.

Grants are usually of between £300 and £2,000 and for between one and three years, but they can sometimes cover longer periods. In 2001 the trust's assets totalled £1.5 million, its income was £50,000 and grants were made totalling £70,000. Beneficiaries included Earth Resources, Make Votes Count and Roadpeace (£3,000 each), Backcare, BADAC, Parent to Parent Adoption, Parents for Children and The Pestices (£2,000 each) and Concern (£1,500).

Exclusions No support for larger charities, those with religious connections, or individuals (except in rare cases – and then only through registered charities or educational bodies). No support to central or local government agencies.

Applications In writing to the correspondent. Proposals should be summarised on one page with one or two more pages of supporting information. The trust states that it regrettably only has time to reply to the very few applications it is able to fund and that it is fully committed for the next two years.

The A B Charitable Trust

Promotion and defence of human dignity

£216,000 (2000/01)

Beneficial area UK and developing world.

12 Addison Avenue, London W11 4QR

Correspondent T M Denham, Secretary

Trustees *Y J M Bonavero; D Boehm; Mrs A G M-L Bonavero; Miss C Bonavero; Miss S Bonavero.*

CC Number 1000147

Information available Accounts were on file at the Charity Commission.

General The trust gives grants for the promotion and defense of human dignity. It is the trust's aim to make 'medium-sized' grants for a three-year period, subject to satisfactory reports and reapplication to the trustees.

In 2000/01 it had an income of £278,000 mainly from Gift Aid and other donations. Grants totalled £216,000 and the balance at the year end stood at £200,000.

From 534 applications received, grants to 59 organisations were made generally ranging from £1,000 to £5,000. The two exceptions were £12,000 to Prison Reform Trust and £6,000 to Richmond Fellowship. The 19 organisations which received £5,000 included Bethany Project, Catholic Housing Aid Society, Comeback, Holy Cross Centre Trust, New Horizon Youth Centre, Prisoners Abroad, Prisoners of Conscience, Respond, Women's Therapy Centre and Youth at Risk.

Other beneficiaries included Alcohol and Drug Abstinence Service, Cellar Project, Disabled Young Adults Centre, Good Shepherd Outreach Trust, North Brixton Trust, Open Door and Quaker Social Action.

To mark its tenth anniversary, the trust established a three-year fellowship at the Prison Reform Trust. It was agreed that £36,000 will be contributed over three years from March 2001.

Exclusions No support for medical research, animal welfare, expeditions, scholarships, conservation and environment.

Applications In writing to the secretary, up to a maximum of four A4 pages if appropriate, plus the most recent detailed audited accounts. The trustees meet on a quarterly basis in March, June, September and December. Applications should be from UK registered charities only.

The Henry & Grete Abrahams Second Charitable Foundation

Jewish, medical welfare, general

£62,000 (1998/99)

Beneficial area UK.

Hill Dickinson, 66–67 Cornhill, London EC3V 3RN

Tel. 020 7695 1048 **Fax** 020 7695 1001

Correspondent D Maislish, Trustee

Trustees *Grete Abrahams; David Maislish; Mark Gluckstein.*

CC Number 298240

Information available Full accounts were on file at the Charity Commission.

General Established in 1987 by Henry and Grete Abrahams, the foundation supports a variety of medical and health organisations. In the past there has also been a preference for Jewish and London-based organisations. In 1998/99 it had an income of £58,000 and gave grants totalling £62,000 to 18 organisations, 4 of which were supported in the previous year.

Grants ranging from £250 to £20,000 were awarded. The largest went to Royal Star & Garter Home (£20,000), Wizo Charitable Foundation (£13,000), with £10,000 each to St John's Hospice, and Wingate Youth Trust, £3,000 to Gurkha Welfare Trust, £2,000 to Nightingale House and £1,000 to Evelina Children's Hospital Appeal. Grants of £250 were given to 10 organisations including British Epilepsy

Association, Mudchute Park and Farm and Pavilion Opera Educational Trust.

Exclusions No grants to individuals or non-registered charities.

Applications The trust states: 'We are fully committed to a number of charities for the next few years, therefore cannot undertake any more appeals'. The trustees meet in November.

The Acacia Charitable Trust

Jewish, education, general

£109,000 (2000/01)

Beneficial area UK and Israel.

5 Clarke's Mews, London W1G 6QN

Tel. 020 7486 1884 **Fax** 020 7487 4171

Correspondent Mrs Nora Howland, Secretary

Trustees *K D Rubens; Mrs A G Rubens; S A Rubens.*

CC Number 274275

Information available Information was provided by the trust.

General In 2000/01 the trust had assets of £1.6 million and an income of £87,000. Grants were given in the categories of education, overseas aid, UK charities and Jewish charities (other than education), and totalled £109,000. Grants ranged from £20 to £36,000, although most were for under £1,000, and were given to 37 organisations. About half of the grants were recurrent.

The largest beneficiary continued to be University of Reading, which received £36,000 to provide a lectureship in Land Management. Other larger grants were to ORT Trust (£27,000), World Jewish Relief (£12,000), Community Security Trust (£10,000), Jewish Museum (£9,000), Centre for Theology and Society and Jewish Care (£2,000 each) and Spanish and Portuguese Jews Congregation (£1,600). Grants of £1,000 each went to British Museum Development Trust, Institute for Jewish Policy Research, Norwood Ltd, JJCT, NSPCC, Royal National Theatre and Spanish and Portugese Jews' Home for the Aged.

Beneficiaries receiving £500 or less included British Friends of Haifa University, Big Issue Foundation, St John's Hospice, Nightingale House, Care

International, Shelter and Jewish Women's Week.

Exclusions No grants to individuals.

Applications In writing to the correspondent.

Access 4 Trust

Children, welfare

£216,000 (2000/01)

Beneficial area UK and newly developing countries.

Slater Maidment, 7 St James's Square, London SW1Y 4JU

Tel. 020 7930 7621

Correspondent C Sadlow

Trustees *Miss S M Wates; J R F Lulham.*

CC Number 267017

Information available Full accounts were on file at the Charity Commission.

General Most grants, as in previous years, were to assist families in need and their children with funds going overseas to developing countries.

The assets in 2000/01 stood at £422,000. The income was £82,000, of which £26,000 was from donations; grants totalled £216,000. The trust listed 31 grants of £1,000 and above in the accounts, of which 16 were recurrent from the previous year. The largest grants over £10,000 each were £24,000 to Entebbe All Christian Womens Association, £23,000 to Post Adoption Centre, £20,000 to TRAX Programme Support and £11,000 each to Actionaid and Friends of the Centre of the Rehabilitation of the Paralysed.

Other larger grants included those to Dharka Ashsania Mission (£7,500), Rains Appeal – Ghana (£7,000) and Bartimeus Fund – Ghana, British Agencies for Adoption and Fostering, Commonwork Land Trust and UNIFAT School – Uganda (£5,000 each).

Grants ranging from £1,000 to £4,000 included those to AVP – London, Girls Growth and Development, International Care & Relief, Liverpool Family Service, Oxfam and WISH.

Exclusions No grants to individuals.

Applications In writing to the correspondent.

Achiezer Association Ltd

Jewish

£405,000 (1999/2000)

Beneficial area Worldwide.

132 Clapton Common, London E5 9AG

Tel. 020 8800 5465

Correspondent David Chontow, Trustee

Trustees Mrs J A Chontow; D Chontow; S S Chontow; M M Chontow.

CC Number 255031

Information available Accounts were on file at the Charity Commission.

General This trust mainly supports Jewish organisations; in previous years a few small grants have also been given to medical and welfare charities. In 1999/2000 it had assets of £1.3 million and an income of £410,000, most of which was from donations received. Grants ranging from £50 to £50,000 were made to 175 organisations and totalled £405,000.

Nine organisations received grants of over £10,000 each. Beneficiaries were: JET (£50,000); Gerurch Ari Torah Ac Trust (£48,000); Menorah Grammar Schoool (£36,000); Achisomoch Aid (£35,000); Ohel Shimon Chaim (£30,000); Be'er Yitzchock Kollel (£20,000); Beth Jacob Grammar School (£15,000); Stamford Hill Beth Hamedrash and Torah Teminah Primary School (£12,000 each).

Other grants included those to Chested Le Yisroel Trust (£7,200), Beis Malka (£5,000), Orthodox Council of Jerusalem (£1,000), Kollel Shomrie Hachomoth and Whitefield Community Kollel (£250 each), Saatchi Synagogue (£100) and Initiation Society (£50).

Applications The trust states that funds are already committed to existing beneficiaries for the next two years. Unsolicited applications are therefore very unlikely to be successful.

The ADAPT Trust

Access for people who are disabled and older to arts and heritage venues

£137,000 (2000)

Beneficial area UK.

Wellpark, 120 Sydney Street, Glasgow
G31 1JF

Tel. 0141 556 2233 **Fax** 0141 556 7799

Email adapt.trust@virgin.net

Website www.adapttrust.co.uk

Correspondent Stewart Coulter

Trustees *Michael Cassidy, Chair; Elizabeth Fairbairn; Gary Flather; John C Griffiths; Alison Heath; Trevan Hingston; Robin Hyman; C Wycliffe Noble; Maurice Paterson; Rita Tushingham.*

CC Number SC020814

Information available A detailed annual report, including full accounts, was provided by the trust.

General The ADAPT (Access for Disabled People to Arts Premises Today) Trust aims to improve accessibility for disabled and older people to arts and heritage venues. It does this in several ways. It encourages broader consideration of access at the planning stage of buildings by providing a consultancy service and carrying out disability awareness training. It gives grants to adapt existing facilities through a number of schemes, and awards for excellence, described below. It also seeks to influence government policies and regulations by contributing to relevant committees and commenting on new strategies.

During the year the trust piloted a student award competition at the Glasgow School of Art. The students were given training in disability issues and they then produced innovative designs that were fully inclusive. The trust plans to expand this area by providing further training and awards for students throughout the UK.

In 1999 the trust had assets of £440,000 and an income of £323,000. It gave grants totalling £120,000.

	1999	(1998)
ADAPT – General	£2,500	(£1,300)
Scottish Grants Scheme	£9,800	(£1,000)
British Gas Awards	–	(£7,500)
Capital Access	£6,625	(£56,000)
Sightline Millennial Grants	£38,598	(£36,000)
Railtrack Museum Grants	£38,970	(£26,000)
Millennial Awards	£21,000	(£21,000)
Hugh Fraser Founation	£2,500	(–)
Total	£120,000	(£149,000)

- Sightline Millennial Grants is funded by Guide Dogs for the Blind Association (GDBA) and administered by ADAPT Trust. Grants are given to performing arts venues to help improve access for people who are visually impaired. Applicants must operate an 'open doors' policy for accompanying guide dogs. The maximum grant is £4,500 and can cover 75% of costs. During the year 12 grants were given, of £1,000 to £4,500. Beneficiaries included Blue Coat Arts Centre, Liverpool; Norwich Arts Centre; Theatre Royal, Windsor; Traverse Theatre, Edinburgh; and Yorkshire Dance Centre, Leeds. Closing dates for these applications are 31 March and 30 September.

- ADAPT Millennial Awards
  These awards are made to recognise good practice venues where access has been designed for the benefit of all users. The awards were made in seven categories:
  – Cinema sponsored by Richard Attenborough Charitable Trust
  – Concert Halls sponsored by the John S Cohen Foundation
  – Galleries
  – Heritage Venues
  – Museums all sponsored by RailTrack PLC
  – Libraries sponsored by Carnegie United Kingdom Trust
  – Theatres sponsored in memory of Teddy and Freda Mautner.

  Seven awards were made, they went to Film and Television – Bradford; Kidderminster Library; National Museum of Photography; National Railway Museum – York; Paxton House – Berwick upon Tweed; Potteries Museum and Art Gallery – Stoke-on-Trent; and Snape Maltings Concert Hall – Aldeburgh.

  Applications are invited from venues (in these categories) that have facilities for people who are disabled that can be looked upon as role models. Main awards of £32,500 are made in each category, with additional certificates for Highly Commended entries. The closing date for entries is the end of June.

- Adapt General
  A grant of £2,500 was made to Walk the Plank, Salford.

Information on the funding given by The Hugh Fraser Foundation was not given in the trust's annual report.

The trust also gave grants in three categories that have now been discontinued. Railtrack Grants for Museums gave grants ranging between £1,000 and £3,500 to 31 museums to tackle physical, sensory and intellectual barriers and put in place a programme to make their buildings and displays widely accessible. The Scottish Grants Scheme gave three grants to Scottish organisations. Two capital access grants totalling £6,700 were also given.

During the year the trust organised another one-day conference on the theme Access v Aesthetics in Glasgow. At this conference it launched its new guide *Open Sesame – The Magic of Access*. The guide is a CD-ROM aimed at everyone involved in the design process and is intended to ensure that inclusive design becomes the norm. The guide was funded as part of a Railtrack PLC sponsorship.

Exclusions No grants to: stately homes, heritage centres and crafts centres; halls designed and used for other purposes such as church halls, hospitals or educational establishments even though they sometimes house the arts; or festivals, unless at a permanent arts venue.

Applications Guidelines and application details are available from the ADAPT office. Applicants for grants have to demonstrate that all aspects of access have been considered, including parking, publicity and staff training.

Adenfirst Ltd

Jewish

£136,000 (2000)

Beneficial area Worldwide.

479 Holloway Road, London N7 6LE

Tel. 020 7272 2255

Correspondent I M Cymerman, Governor

Trustees *Mrs H F Bondi; I M Cymerman; Mrs R Cymerman.*

CC Number 291647

Information available Information was on file at the Charity Commission, but with no financial statements.

General The trust supports mostly Jewish organisations, with a preference for education and social welfare. In 2000 grants totalled £136,000.

Awards over £1,000 each were made to 33 organisations and were listed by the trust. The largest were: £10,000 each to Beis Rachel D'Satmar, Beis Yaakov Institutions, Friends of Harim Establishments and Yesodei Hatorah Grammar School.

Other beneficiaries included Yad Eliezer (£9,000), Emuno Educational Centre Ltd (£8,500), Ezer Layeled (£8,000), Gur Trust Building Fund and Keren Hatorah (£5,000 each), Torah Study Group (£3,000) and Beth Chasidim Gur (£1,000). Miscellaneous payments of less than £1,000 each totalled £4,200.

Applications In writing to the correspondent.

The Adint Charitable Trust

Children, medical and health

£342,000 (2001/02)
Beneficial area UK.

BDO Stoy Hayward, 8 Baker Street, London W1U 3LL
Correspondent D R Oram, Trustee
Trustees *Anthony J Edwards; Mrs Margaret Edwards; D R Oram; Brian Pate.*
CC Number 265290
Information available Accounts were provided by the trust.

General Most of the grants made by this trust are for £5,000 or £10,000 to a range of health and welfare charities, many concerned with children.

In 2001/02 the trust had assets of £5.2 million, which generated an income of £332,000. Management, administration and professional costs were low at £25,000. Grants totalling £342,000 were made to 63 organisations, only 8 of which were also supported in the previous year.

The largest grants were £16,000 to UCL and £10,000 each to Cancer Bacup, Crisis, Disabled Living Foundation, NCH Action for Children, NSPCC, Queens Park Family Service Unit, Scope and Winged Fellowship.

Grants of £5,000 each went to 45 organisations. Beneficiaries included AFASIC, Alone in London, British Lung Foundation, Dementia Relief Trust, Home Warmth for the Aged Benevolent Fund, International Spinal Research Trust, Marie Curie Cancer Care, National Association of Clubs for Young People, National Autistic Society, National Playbus Association, Re-Solve, Royal Marsden Hospital Cancer Fund, Surrey Association for Youth Culture, Surrey Care Trust and Westminster Pastoral Foundation.

Other grants went to Tuberous Sclerosis Association and Wessex Healthy Living Foundation (£2,500 each), Guide Dogs for the Blind and Sound Around (£1,000 each), ROYAD (£620) and A Nolan Memorial Trust (£250).

Exclusions Grants can be made to registered charities only and in no circumstances to individuals.

Applications To the correspondent, in writing only. There is no particular form in which applications are required; each applicant should make its own case in the way it considers best. The trust notes that it cannot enter into correspondence.

Airways Charitable Trust Limited

Welfare, health

£105,000 (1999/2000)
Beneficial area UK.

The Gate House, 2 Park Street, Windsor, Berkshire SL4 1LU
Tel. 01753 753900 **Fax** 01753 753901
Email sandra.fletcher@actg.co.uk
Website www.actg.co.uk
Correspondent Sandra Fletcher, Grants Coordinator
Trustees *E P Gostling, Chair; D P Dugard; J J O'Sullivan; D N Taylor; M Street; P Nield.*
CC Number 1068617
Information available Accounts were on file at the Charity Commission.

General The charity has several wholly owned trading subsidiaries. The companies donate profits to the charity under the Gift Aid scheme. The trust's assets total some £30 million.

The trust stated in 2002 that it had pledged a grant totalling £4 million, to be made over three or more years, towards building sheltered accommodation.

In 1999/2000 the trust's income was £1.5 million. Grantmaking is only a small part of its work. The trust's priority is to help people to maintain independence within their own home, for example, through providing residential accommodation, and welfare and health services and amenities.

Grants totalling £105,000 were made to organisations, and £46,000 was given to 19 individuals. Grants to organisations included £27,000 to Shepperton Parish Church, £15,000 to Woodlands School, Guildford, £10,000 to CONNECT, £9,800 to Spelthorne Farm, £9,000 to Royal Schools for the Deaf, £5,000 to Age Concern, £4,100 to Guildford Voluntary Services, £4,000 to Hillington Autistic Care and Support and £3,500 to National Benevolent Fund for the Aged.

Applications In writing to the correspondent, stating: the name of your organisation and what you do; what you want the grant for; how much you want; how much of the grant total you have already raised; and who else you are approaching for funds. Individual applicants should contact the correspondent to request an application form.

The Sylvia Aitken Charitable Trust

Medical research and welfare, general

£141,000 (2000/01)
Beneficial area UK, with a preference for Scotland.

Fergusons Chartered Accountants, 24 Woodside, Houston, Renfrewshire PA6 7DD
Tel. 01505 610412 **Fax** 01505 614944
Correspondent Jim Ferguson, Trust Administrator
Trustees *Mrs S M Aitken; Mrs M Harkis; J Ferguson.*
CC Number SC010556
Information available Full accounts were provided by the trust.

General Whilst this trust has a preference for medical projects, it has general charitable purposes, making small grants to a wide range of small local organisations throughout the UK, particularly those in Scotland.

In 2000/01 the trust had assets of £3.9 million, which generated an income of £214,000. Grants were made to 58 organisations totalling £141,000. A payment of £20,000 was paid to a firm of chartered accountants, of which one of the trustees is a partner, for 'day to day management of the trust and professional advice'. Even though wholly legal, these editors always regret such payments unless, to use the words of the Charity Commission, 'there is no realistic alternative'.

The largest grants were £12,000 to Respiratory Diseases, £10,000 each to Royal Zoological Society of Scotland, National Counselling Services and Stirling University, £7,000 to Paths for All Partnerships, £6,000 to Shabbos Youth Club and £5,000 each to National Missing Persons Helpline and Shelter Scotland.

Other grants included those to Turning Point (£2,100), NCDL and Scottish Ballet (£2,000 each), St Peter's Church (£1,500), L'Arche Inverness and The Waterway's Trust (£1,000 each), Rainbow Trust (£750), with £500 each to Homeless Alliance, Honeycombe Community Project, Positive Help, South Sudanese Community Association in the UK and Visual Impairment Services South East Scotland.

Exclusions No grants to individuals: the trust can only support UK registered charities.

Applications In writing to the correspondent. Applicants should outline the charity's objectives and current projects for which funding may be required. The trustees meet at least twice a year, usually in March/April and September/October.

The Ajahma Charitable Trust

Health and social welfare
£475,000 (2000/01)
Beneficial area Worldwide.

4 Jephtha Road, London SW18 1QH
Correspondent Suzanne Hunt, Administrator

Trustees *Jennifer Sheridan; Elizabeth Simpson; James Sinclair Taylor; Michael Horsman.*

CC Number 273823

Information available Full accounts and funding guidelines were provided by the trust.

General The trust generally supports established charities. It aims to balance its donations between international and UK charities.

The trust considers grants in the following areas:

- development
- health
- disability
- poverty
- women's issues
- family planning
- human rights
- social need.

It has also favoured applications from new groups and those which may have difficulty finding funds from traditional sources are particularly encouraged.

In 2000/01 the trust had assets of £4.7 million and an income of £195,000. Grants totalled £475,000, of which 50% went to charities working overseas and 50% to charitable work in the UK. A total of 59 grants were given ranging from £1,500 to £35,000. Local Headway groups have continued to receive substantial support from the trust, with grants totalling £59,000.

The largest grants went to Oxfam (£35,000), Action on Disability & Development (£23,000), Sudanese Victims of Torture Group (£19,000), CAMFED, International Care & Relief and Health Unlimited (£15,000 each). There were 14 beneficiaries of £10,000 each, including Anti-Slavery International, APT Enterprise Development, Cambodia Trust, Changing Faces, One Parent Families, Who Cares? Trust and Youth at Risk.

Other beneficiaries included Education for Choice (£8,000), Toynbee Hall (£7,000), Ugandan Society for Disabled Children (£6,000), Speakability (£5,000), Respond (£4,000) and Action on Elder Abuse (£2,500).

The Headway Groups which received support, of up to £6,500, were Ayrshire, Cardiff, East Kent, Jersey, Greater Manchester Headway House Project, Milton Keynes, North East Worcestershire, Nottingham, Somerset, Surrey, Tayside, West Midlands and Wirral.

Exclusions Large organisations with a turnover above £4 million will not normally be considered, nor will applications with any sort of religious bias or those which support animal rights/welfare, arts, medical research, buildings, equipment, local groups or overseas projects where the charity income is less than £500,000 a year. Applications for grants or sponsorship for individuals will not be supported.

Applications The trustees meet in May and November, the closing dates for

applications are mid-March and mid-September. Information about applying should be sought first from the administrator.

The Alchemy Foundation

Health and welfare, famine relief overseas
£366,000 (2000/01)
Beneficial area UK and overseas.

Trevereux Manor, Limpsfield Chart, Oxted, Surrey RH8 0TL
Correspondent Annabel Stilgoe

Trustees *Richard Stilgoe; Annabel Stilgoe; Rev. Donald Reeves; Esther Rantzen; Alex Armitage; Andrew Murison; Holly Stilgoe; Jack Stilgoe; Rufus Stilgoe; Joseph Stilgoe; Dr Jemima Stilgoe.*

CC Number 292500

Information available Full accounts were provided by the foundation.

General This foundation was established in 1985 as The Starlight Foundation. It receives most of its income from a share of the royalties from the works of Richard Stilgoe and changed its name in 1987. It provides support for all forms of welfare, ranging from the material, mental and spiritual welfare of children, older people and people with disabilities or mental, physical or terminal illnesses to assisting those affected by famine. It also supports medical research. It shares the same board of trustees with The Orpheus Trust, a connected charity, which regularly receives large grants from this foundation.

In 2000/01 the total income was £806,000, of which £737,000 came from donations received and just £69,000 was generated from the assets, which totalled £2.4 million. After low management and administration expenditure of £8,200, grants were made totalling £366,000, broken down as follows:

Donations to The Orpheus Trust	£300,000
46 grants to organisations	£46,000
144 grants to individuals	£21,000

Details of 10 grants to unconnected charities were listed in the accounts, the largest was £19,000 to Bridgets. The others were £6,000 to Weston Spirit, £5,000 to MERU, £2,000 each to Chicken Shed Theatre Company and Sight Savers International, £1,000 each to Apex Trust, Marlborough Brandt Group, Starting

Point and Surrey Care Trust and £750 to Exeter Family Trust.

Applications In writing to the correspondent.

Alexandra Rose Day

Fundraising partnerships with 'people-caring' charities

About £150,000

Beneficial area UK.

2A Ferry Road, London SW13 9RX

Tel. 0870 770 0275 **Fax** 0870 770 0276

Email enquiries@alexandraroseday.org.uk

Website www.alexandraroseday.org.uk

Correspondent Alan Leng, National Director

Trustees *The Council: Rt Hon. Lord Wakeham, Chairman; Andrew Mitchell; Lady Grade; Lady Heald; Lord King of Wartnaby; Mrs Aubrey Beckham; Peter Beckham; Ms Cecily Engle; Stephen King; Mrs Katheryn Langridge; Mrs Morton Neal; Sir Ian Rankin; Peter Russell-Wood; Raymond Salisbury-Jones; Mrs Diane Sillem; Mrs Domonic Tayler.*

CC Number 211535

Information available Information was provided by the trust.

General This charity offers partnership in fundraising and other forms of support for smaller, people-caring charities. Its activities include an annual national Flag Day (Alexandra Rose Day) and regular raffles.

For Flag Days, this charity makes the arrangements and supplies equipment whilst the partner charity provides the flag sellers. Alexandra Rose Day makes an immediate grant to the partner equivalent to 70% of its gross collection. For raffles, Alexandra Rose Day organises the prizes and prints the tickets, which the partner charity sells and receives 70% of all gross sales.

Small charities are also offered access to value-for-money insurance, printing and other services. The Rose Ball is the largest of the two or three major fundraising events the charity organises each year, the surplus of which is donated through the special appeal fund, an annual

programme of grants designed to bring immediate, practical benefits to people-caring charities and voluntary groups.

In 2000/01 the trust had an income of £400,000 and a total expenditure of £499,000. In 1998/99, when the income was similar, a total of £150,000 was donated to beneficiaries.

Exclusions Only participants in Flag Days or raffles are eligible to apply. Grants are not made to individuals or charities operating overseas.

Applications In writing to the correspondent.

All Saints Educational Trust

Education, Anglican religious work, home economics

£180,000 to organisations

(2001/02)

Beneficial area Mostly UK.

St Katherine Cree Church, 86 Leadenhall Street, London EC3A 3DH

Tel. 020 7283 4485 **Fax** 020 7621 9758

Email enquiries@aset.org.uk

Website www.aset.org.uk

Correspondent R Poulton, Clerk

Trustees *The Rt Revd & Rt Hon. Richard Chartres, Bishop of London, Chair; Revd Prebendary Swan; Mrs M R Behenna; P Chandler; T L Guiver; Revd Canon P Hartley; Dr D W Lankshear; Ms D McCrea; Miss A Philpott; Revd K G Riglin; Mrs A Rose; D Trillo; Ven C Chessun; Mrs B Harvey; J K Hoskin; G King.*

CC Number 312934

Information available Full accounts were provided by the trust, including a detailed narrative report.

General This trust was established from the proceeds of the closure of two teacher training colleges in London, one of which worked within a Christian framework and the other of which specialised in domestic science (now home economics and technology). Keeping in line with the former colleges, the trust's objects are advancing higher or further education by:

- allowing individuals to attend a further education institute, or otherwise pursue a course of study to enable them to gain teaching qualifications
- promoting in other ways education and training
- promoting research and development of education, particularly in religious studies and home economics and similar subjects.

It achieves these aims by providing financial assistance to 'institutions that seek to undertake imaginative projects that enhance higher and further education', with the trustees distributing their grants in the way they feel will make the maximum possible difference to the institutions and their respective communities or spheres of influence. (For further information on the grants made to individuals and how to apply, please see *The Educational Grants Directory*, also published by DSC.)

In 2001/02 the trust had assets totalling £8.7 million (£11 million in 2000/01), which generated an income of £431,000. Grants to 14 organisations totalled £179,000, and to 60 individuals £281,000.

The largest grants were £35,000 each to RSA 'Focus on Food' Campaign for an issue of a new magazine to be distributed free to 28,000 schools in the UK and Association of Church College Trusts for an extention to the RETRI project, and £33,000 to The Patrick V Saxton Fellowship Award for a University of Stirling student to continue her research.

Other large grants went to: The Society for Promoting Christian Knowledge for the final year towards the establishment of a website to provide updated Christian material for use in school assemblies (£15,000); The Wulugu Project for an educational project in Northern Ghana which involved 'twinning' with UK schools and establishing a science curriculum which is relevant to girls in a developing country (£10,000); Guildhall School of Music and Drama for bursary funds to be awarded to two students selected by the school on a postgraduate music therapy course (£9,000); London Diocesan Board for Schools for the final of three grants for a 'Preparation for Headship' course for staff in church schools (£8,600); and Exchange for the continuation of a research and communication network (£8,500).

Smaller grants included those to: The National Society for the final year of an on-going grant for a project to set up a website (£7,500); Southwark Cathedral Education Trust towards the salary and associated costs of an educational officer

(£5,000 for three years); Churches' Action for Racial Equality as the last of three grants to enable research and the preperation of teaching materials on 'holy people of the African diaspora' (£3,000); and Ockenden International to provide textbooks, training materials and other supplies to 240 teachers in Sudan (£2,500).

Exclusions The trust cannot support:

- schools by providing grants for buildings, equipment or supplies
- the general funds of any organisation
- public appeals
- the establishment of courses or departments in universities and colleges, which is a prime responsibility of the institutions themselves
- chaplaincies
- applicants which have already been supported by the trust.

Grants are not made retrospectively.

Applications For applications from organisations (not individuals): applicants are invited to discuss their ideas informally with the clerk before requesting an application form. In some cases, a 'link trustee' is appointed to assist the organisation in preparing the application and who will act in a liaison role with the trust. Completed applications are put before the awards committee in February or May, with final decisions made in June.

The trust normally responds to all written enquiries received, but in order to reduce administration costs, the trust will not be able to reply to letters seeking assistance in respect of projects detailed in Exclusions above.

Allavida

International development

£185,000 (2001/02)
Beneficial area Currently south east Europe and East Africa.

55 Bondway, London SW8 1SJ
Tel. 020 7735 8006 **Fax** 020 7735 7608
Email enquiries@allavida.org
Website www.allavida.org
Correspondent Andrew Kingman, Director
Trustees *David Carrington, Chair; Steven Burkeman; Duncan Grant; Christine*

Forrester; Barry Knight; David Bonbright; Bisi Adelaye-Fayemi.
CC Number 1089984
Information available The organisation was due publish its first annual report in late 2002.

General Allavida (Alliances for Voluntary Initiatives and Development) was formed after merging Charity Know How (CKH) with the Charities Aid Foundation's International Department, and was registered with the Charity Commission in January 2002. The charity states: 'Allavida will retain the mission and objectives that we have pursued through CKH over the years; i.e. we will continue to offer our support in strengthening formal and informal voluntary and non-profit organisations as they seek to address key issues in the daily life of individuals and their communities … we will continue to focus grantmaking on developing skills and learning in voluntary and non-profit organisations, encouraging the spread of learning and developing mutually supportive partnerships wherever we work.'

Allavida continues to operate a range of grants programmes in south east Europe, and is about to launch an East Africa programme. In 2001/02 it made grants to 25 organisations totalling £185,000. Grants ranged from £1,000 to £15,000.

Examples of projects which received funding during the year are as follows:

Applicant: Field Studies Council
Partner: Roza Vetrov & Donetsk Youth Debate Centre
Countries of Benefit: Russia and Ukraine
Grant: £15,000

The grant was made to help develop Roza Vetrov's organisational capacity so that it can effectively run a newly established environmental information centre in Tomsk.

Applicant: DISC
Partner: Mother's Union
Country of Benefit: Russia
Grant: £10,000

Funding was awarded to cover three alternating training visits between the UK and Russia to build the organisational capacity of Mother's Union as a non-governmental organisation (NGO) and as a provider of effective services to drug users.

Applicant: Children in Crisis
Partner: AVEC Charitable Fund
Country of Benefit: Ukraine
Grant: £7,600

This project involved a six-week study visit to the UK by two Ukrainian educators in order to adapt the methodologies of the CiC drugs education programme 'd:side' and deliver a version in the Ukraine.

Applicant: West Devon Environmental Network
Partner: Albanian Ecological Club
Countries of Benefit: Albania and India
Grant: £7,000

Funding for a one-week visit to Albania by the partners, as part of West Devon Environmental Network's Rural Links Programme aimed to increase capacity within rural communities. This grant also covers the publication of two newsletters, plus website development costs.

Applicant: Ukrainian Family Planning Association
Partner: Latvian Family Planning Association
Countries of Benefit: Ukraine and Latvia
Grant: £7,000

Funding was awarded for two exchange visits between each organisation to allow for training in sexual and reproductive health issues, exchange of best practice and the development of a mutual partnership strategy.

Applications must include at least two organisations from different countries working in partnership. The transfer of skills between NGOs known to CKH in countries of Central & Eastern Europe and the Newly Independent States is also eligible for support and therefore both applicant and partner can be from these countries without the involvement of a UK charity. State-run organisations and institutions, professional associations, private schools, universities and organisations aimed primarily at promoting a specific religion are not themselves eligible for funding, although NGOs using their facilities may still apply.

The following activities are considered for funding:

- Exploratory work aimed at further activity that includes a significant element of the transfer of know-how.
- Visits to any eligible countries or to the UK to enable NGO sectoral and organisational learning and development.

- Training programmes for NGO staff and volunteers, usually in areas such as financial management, strategic planning, lobbying, volunteer management, governance, fundraising, public relations and so on, rather than in specific professional skills such as nursing techniques, artistic skills or journalism, although all capacity-building initiatives will be considered. Training programmes funded tend to be workshops and seminars (and very occasionally conferences) or short-term placements within organisations.
- Professional advice visits from charity or NGO representatives to assist with organisational aspects of an individual NGO, coordinating bodies or the sector as a whole.
- Translation and adaptation of training or information materials for NGOs.

Exclusions Grants are not normally available for the following:

- teaching of English as a foreign language
- costs of offices, salaries or equipment (including fax machines and other communications equipment)
- building or capital cost
- transporting humanitarian aid or medical equipment
- attendance at conferences where the benefit to NGO development is not clearly demonstrated
- administration of schemes for UK volunteers (e.g. working holidays)
- core funding in the region or the UK
- full professional fees for any consultancy (although some replacement costs may be considered)
- activities considered by the grants committee to be for personal rather than institutional development
- youth, artistic or cultural exchanges
- promotion of a specific religion or sectarian belief
- applications from individuals
- student programmes or scholarships
- retrospective grants.

Applications There is a clear application form to which other material can be attached, together with comprehensive guidance notes for applicants. The grants committee meets four times a year, in March, June, September and December, and there is a published deadline for receipt of applications for grants about six weeks in advance of these meetings. Potential applicants should first read the 'Guidelines for Applicants' available from Allavida.

The Dorothy Gertrude Allen Memorial Fund

General
£99,000 (2001)
Beneficial area UK.

Teigncombe Barn, Chagford, Devon TQ13 8ET
Tel. 01647 433235
Email dgallen.memorialfund@btinternet.com
Correspondent Peter B Shone, Trustee
Trustees *Miss Heather B Allen; Peter B Shone.*
CC Number 290676
Information available Full accounts were on file at the Charity Commission.

General In 2000/01 this trust had assets of £733,000 and an income of £75,000, including £43,000 received from Gift Aid. Grants were made to 45 organisations totalling £99,000. The trust pointed out that its core income excluding Gift Aid, which is not guaranteed to continue, falls in the range of £30,000 to £35,000 per year.

Grants were in the range of £1,000 to £5,000 and can be recurring or one-off, and for revenue or capital purposes. The trust also states that they have no restrictions as to the kinds of project or the areas supported, and are generally prepared to consider any field. Intending applicants should note that organisations that have received grants in the past should not be taken as indicative of a geographical or other bias.

Grants were broken down into the following categories:

	No.	Total
Arts	2	£3,000
Blindness	3	£6,000
Carers/elderly	3	£6,000
Children/young people	6	£16,000
Deafness	1	£3,000
Disability	4	£4,000
Environment/wildlife	11	£28,000
General community	5	£7,000
Housing/homelessness	1	£3,000
Medical/research/hospitals	7	£12,000
Mental disability	1	£2,000
Overseas aid/international	3	£9,000

Beneficiaries of grants of £5,000 each were Childhope, International Otter Survival Fund, RSPB, Scottish Wildlife Trust and Send a Cow. Other grants were either for £1,000, £2,000 or £3,000 each and

included those to Books Abroad, CALIBRE, Canine Partners for Independence, Changing Faces, Marwell Zoological Park, Plantlife, Prisoners Abroad, Rural Youth Trust, Sussex Snowdrop Trust, Thames Salmon Trust, Understanding Industry and Wildfowl and Wetlands Trust.

Exclusions No grants to individuals (including gap-year students) or to organisations which are not UK-registered charities.

Applications In writing to the correspondent. Applications should be received by October for consideration in November/December. Due to an increasing number of appeals (the amount has doubled in the last few years) the trustees do not acknowledge them. Applicants are contacted usually only when they are successful or where further information is required.

The Almond Trust

Christian
£406,000 (1999/2000)
Beneficial area UK and worldwide.

111 Dulwich Village, London SE21 7BJ
Correspondent J L Cooke, Trustee
Trustees *J L Cooke; Barbara H Cooke.*
CC Number 328583
Information available Full accounts were on file at the Charity Commission.

General The trust's aims are the support of evangelistic Christian projects, Christian evangelism and the translation, reading, study and teaching of the Bible.

In 1999/2000 the trust had an income of £426,000, virtually all of which was comprised of donations. After making grants totalling £406,000, the trust had a balance at the year end of £247,000.

The trust made 16 grants of which a number were recurrent. The largest were £100,000 each to All Saints Crawborough and Oasis Trust.

Other grants included those to: Christian Youth and Sports Charitable Company (£27,000); London Insitute for Contemporary Christianity (£25,000); Counselling, Consulting Training and Leadership (£22,000); St Barnabas PCC (£20,000); Christians in Sport and St Peter's Trust (£10,000 each); Freemantle

PCC (£7,000); Agape (£5,000); and Great Whyte Baptist Church (£3,000).

Applications In writing to the correspondent, but please note that the trust states it rarely responds to uninvited applications.

The Altajir Trust

Islam, education, science and research

£199,000 to organisations (2000)
Beneficial area UK and Arab or Islamic states.

11 Elvaston Place, London SW7 5QG
Tel. 020 7581 3522 **Fax** 020 7584 1977
Correspondent A C Duncan, Director
Trustees *Sir John Moberly, Chair; Peter Tripp; Prof. Alan Jones; Dr Roger Williams; Dr Charles Tripp.*
CC Number 284116
Information available Accounts were on file at the Charity Commission.

General This trust makes grants for the advancement of science, education and research which is beneficial to the community in Britain or any Arab or Islamic state. Support is also given to students at universities in the UK, USA and Bahrain, and conferences and exhibitions are sponsored which promote understanding and the study of Islamic culture and arts throughout the world. Grants are made to both individuals and organisations.

In 2000 the trust had assets of £262,000 and an income of £651,000. Direct charitable expenditure totalled £568,000 of which £199,000 went to organisations, £168,000 on student fees, £148,000 on student maintenance and £54,000 on the Ottoman Jerusalem project costs.

The accounts listed seven grants made to organisations; beneficiaries were Arab Women's Association (£60,000), School of Oriental and African Studies – Research Fellowship (£40,000), Learning Centre – Adu Daubi (£30,000), Dar Al Hekma (£24,000), St Catherine's – Cumberland Lodge (£20,000) and Jubilee Sailing Trust and Royal Collection Trust (£5,000 each). Other unlisted grants totalled £14,000.

Applications The trust states that its resources are fully used without receiving applications.

AM Charitable Trust

Jewish, general

£59,000 (1999/2000)
Beneficial area UK and overseas.

Kleinwort Benson Trustees Ltd, The Trustees Department, 10 Fenchurch Street, London EC3M 3LB
Tel. 020 7475 5086 **Fax** 020 7475 5558
Correspondent The Secretary
Trustees *Kleinwort Benson Trustees Ltd.*
CC Number 256283
Information available Full accounts were on file at the Charity Commission.

General This trust supports a range of causes, particularly Jewish organisations but also medical, welfare, arts and conservation charities. Certain charities are supported for more than one year, although no commitment is usually given to the recipient.

In 1999/2000 the trust's assets stood at £1.6 million and it had an income of £73,000. Grants were made to 50 organisations totalling £59,000. Grants were in the range of £100 to £10,000 but were mainly for £250 or less. Larger donations were £10,000 each to Jerusalem Foundation and World Jewish Relief and £5,000 each to British ORT, British Technion Society and Friends of the Hebrew University of Jerusalem. Other beneficiaries of grants of over £1,000 each included Friends of Boys Town Jerusalem (£3,000), Joint Jewish Charitable Trust (£2,500), Weizmann Institute Foundation (£2,200) and British Heart Foundation, Cancer Research Campaign and Norwood Ltd (£2,000 each).

Beneficiaries of smaller grants included Artists' General Benevolent Institution, Care International, Iris Fund, Kent Wildlife Trust, League of Friends of Alder Hey Children's Country Holidays Fund, Splash, Volunteer Reading Help and Water Aid.

Exclusions No grants to individuals.

Applications Unsolicited applications are not welcomed. The trust stated that its funds are fully committed and only a small percentage of its income is allocated to new beneficiaries. Only successful applications are notified of the trustees' decision. Trustees meet in March and applications need to be received by January.

Viscount Amory's Charitable Trust

Welfare, older people, education

£388,000 to organisations (2001/02)
Beneficial area UK, primarily in Devon.

The Island, Lowman Green, Tiverton, Devon EX16 4LA
Tel. 01884 254899 **Fax** 01884 255155
Correspondent The Trust Secretary
Trustees *Sir Ian Heathcoat Amory; Sir John Palmer; Mrs D Cavender.*
CC Number 204958
Information available Accounts, with a schedule of grants but only a brief narrative report, were provided by the trust.

General This trust has a strong preference for organisations in Devon, many of which receive recurrent grants. Local organisations in the south west of England are also supported and a variety of UK charities. (Grants are also made to individuals, for further information please see *The Educational Grants Directory*, or *A Guide to Grants for Individuals in Need*, both published by DSC.)

In 2001/02 the trust had assets of £9.1 million. Total income was £316,000, including £3,200 in donations received. Grants were made totalling £399,000, broken down as follows:

Category	Individuals	Institutions	Total
Educational	£11,000	£192,000	£202,000
Religious	–	£13,000	£13,000
General	£580	£183,000	£184,000
Total	£11,000	£388,000	£399,000

The largest grants were £73,000 to London Sailing Project and £46,000 to Blundell's School. Other large grants were £20,000 to Blundell's Foundation, £19,000 to Eton College and £10,000 each to Mid Devon Show and Sight Savers International.

The grants list included many educational establishments. These included Queen's College (£7,400), Sands School and Wellington School (£7,000 each), Grenville College (£6,700), Edge Hill College (£3,900), Tower House School (£3,200), University of Newcastle (£2,700), University of Bristol (£2,600), St Margaret's School (£2,100), Italia Conti

Academy (£1,700), Shebbear College (£1,200) and Ellen Tinkham School and School of Oriental and African Studies (£1,000 each).

Among the other beneficiaries were many organisations in Devon, particularly Tiverton. These included Mid Devon Enterprise Agency (£4,000), Tiverton Market Centre (£3,000), Tiverton Senior Citizens Association (£2,000), Shaldon Sailing Club (£1,500) with £1,000 each to Age Concern – Okehampton and Torridge, Carn Brea Methodist Church, Chevithorne PCC, East Budleigh with Bicton Village Hall, Exmoor Search and Rescue, North Devon Hospice, St George's Church – Tiverton, Sheldon Courtyard Development, Tiverton & District Community Transport Association and Torbay Coast & Countryside Trust.

Other grants included £2,000 to ViRSA, £1,200 to Disability Aid Fund and £1,000 each to Abbeyfield Wellington (Somerset) Society Ltd, Bruised Reed Trust, Discovery Dockland Trust, Motability, National Blind Children's Society and Police Convalescence and Rehabilitation Trust.

Exclusions No grants to individual applications from outside south west England.

Applications In writing to the correspondent, giving general background information, total costs involved, amount raised so far and details of applications to other organisations.

The Ampelos Trust

General
£80,000 (1998/99)
Beneficial area UK.

9 Trinity Street, Colchester, Essex CO1 1JN
Tel. 01206 544434
Correspondent G W N Stewart, Secretary
Trustees *G W N Stewart; Baroness Rendell of Babergh; A M Witt.*
CC Number 1048778
Information available Full accounts were on file at the Charity Commission.

General In 1998/99, the trust's assets totalled £20,000 and it had an income of £53,000, including £40,000 from Gift Aid

donations. There was a deficit of expenditure over income of £27,000.

Grants totalled £80,000 and went to 19 organisations. Only six received less than £1,000. The larger grants were £25,000 to Refuge, £10,000 to Bexley NSPCC, £7,000 to Ethiopiaid and £6,000 to The Smith Institute. There were five grants of £5,000 each and four of £1,000 each. Grants for £5,000 were received by Dorah Makoena Charitable Trust, John Aspinal Appeal Fund, London Women's Health Action, MacMillan Cancer Relief and RefAid, and those for £1,000 were received by Anti Slavery International, Limegrove Appeal, Westminster City Library and VVF Clinic.

Applications In writing to the correspondent.

The Andrew Anderson Trust

Christian, social welfare
£279,000 (2000/01)
Beneficial area UK and overseas.

84 Uphill Road, Mill Hill, London NW7 4QE
Correspondent The Trustees
Trustees *Miss A A Anderson; Miss M S Anderson; Revd A R Anderson; Mrs M L Anderson.*
CC Number 212170
Information available Full accounts were provided by the trust.

General The trust states in its trustees' report that it provides support to a wide range of charitable causes. Most of its money appears to go to evangelical organisations and churches, but it also makes a large number of small grants to health, disability and social welfare charities.

In 2000/01 the assets of the trust stood at just over £8 million generating an income of £281,000. Grants were made totalling £279,000, categorised by the trust as follows (previous years' figures in brackets):

UK and overseas charitable organisations £226,000 (£251,000) Individuals currently involved and the dependants of individuals formerly involved in charitable activities £42,000 (£57,000) Individuals following theological study courses £11,500 (£7,000)

Almost 300 grants were made to charities during the year, about 50 of which were for £1,000 or more including only 4 of over £5,000. These larger grants went to St John's Downshire Hill Trust (£25,000), Street Baptist Church (£10,000), Cornhill Training Course (£9,100) and Kensington Baptist Church, Bristol (£7,500). Virtually all the other grants of more than a few hundred pounds went to similar evangelical causes such as Bible Club Movement, Christian Medical Fellowship, Evangelical Fellowship of Asia, OMS International, Rock Foundation and Scripture Union. Various local Christian churches and causes were also supported.

The numerous smaller grants were given to a range of causes, local as well as larger well-known charities.

Exclusions Individuals should not apply for travel or education.

Applications In writing to the correspondent. The trust states 'we prefer to honour existing commitments and initiate new ones through our own contacts rather than respond to applications'.

The Anglian Water Trust Fund

Money advice provision/ individuals in need
£117,000 to organisations (2001/02)
Beneficial area Anglian Water region, i.e. Cambridgeshire, Lincolnshire, North East Lincolnshire, Norfolk, Suffolk, Peterborough, Milton Keynes and Hartlepool plus parts of Bedford, Buckinghamshire, Essex, Hertfordshire, Leicestershire, Northamptonshire, North Lincolnshire and Rutland.

PO Box 42, Peterborough PE3 8XH
Tel. 01733 331177 **Fax** 01733 334344
Email admin@awtf.org.uk
Website www.awtf.org.uk
Correspondent Paul Hobbs, Administrator
Trustees *Barbara Ruffell, Chair; Graham Blagden; Norman Guffick; Elizabeth Ingram; Stuart de Prochnow; John Sansby; Stephen Harrap; Valerie Mansfield.*

CC Number 1054026

Information available Full annual report and accounts, including guidelines, were provided by the trust.

General The trust's main activity, worth about £1.1 million a year, is to help individuals and families in hardship who are customers of Anglian Water plc (or Hartlepool Water since its purchase by Anglian Water plc in 1997) with their water and sewerage debts, and to assist with general welfare support, such as help with other priority debts or the purchase of essential household equipment. A secondary programme aims to improve and increase the provision of independent money advice services in the Anglian and Hartlepool Water regions, typically by paying for the salaries, over three years, of advice workers at Citizen's Advice Bureaux.

The trust fund receives an income of £1 million a year from Anglian Water plc, £12,000 from Tendring Hundred Water and £7,000 from Three Valleys Water. The trust primarily assists individuals and families in need. In addition, grants to organisations during 2001/02 totalled £117,000 (£267,000 in 2000/01). Grants are given to voluntary organisations to enable them to:

- establish or extend debt counselling services
- provide education in the prevention of debt.

The trust supported organisations to deliver front-line money advice, some of which were receiving support for either their second or third year. The trust states that 'in their second or third year of support, organisations must raise balancing funding from other sources to complement tapered decreases in [support from the trust]'.

Awards by the trust were broken down as follows:

County Court Help Desks
The following awards were made to assist organisations in providing helpdesks at County Courts: Great Yarmouth CAB (£6,500), Huntingdon Independent Advice Centre (£4,000), Lowestoft CAB (£3,500) and Buckingham CAB (£500).

Partnership Innovation Budget
In partnership with the Legal Services Commission the following organisations were awarded grants to provide money management/training. The amount listed accounts for a quarter of the total cost of each project: Wymondham/Norwich CAB and Norfolk Money Advice (£19,000), Basildon CAB (£3,500),

Welfare Rights Advice Service – Northampton (£3,000), Castle Point CAB (£2,500).

Debt Advice
The following organisations received funding towards providing advice on debt and money management: Castle Point CAB (£13,500), Brandon CAB (£10,500), Dereham CAB (£10,000), Marham CAB (£5,500), Lowestoft CAB (£3,500), Mid Suffolk CAB (£2,500), Peterborough Family Care and West Lindsey CAB (£2,000 each).

A grant of £31,500 was given to NACAB to improve training and networking for money advisers throughout the regions covered by Anglian and Hartlepool Water. NACAB received a further £10,000 to enable them to produce a pack containing personal and business debt information for small traders affected by rural crises.

Two further organisations were also supported which were to deliver money advice and money management education projects to young people, especially those who were leaving, or had recently left, the care system. These organisations were NCH Action for Children – Norfolk/Suffolk (£31,000) and Mancroft Advice Project – Norwich (£29,000).

Exclusions No grants for: fines for criminal offences; educational needs; debts to central government departments; medical equipment, aids and adaptations; holidays; business debts; catalogues; credit cards; personal loans; deposits for secure accommodation; overpayment of benefits.

Applications Organisational grants: Unfortunately, the trust states that until further notice no applications from organisations can be considered due to commitments to individuals and families. Up-to-date information can be found on the trust's website.

Individual grants: applications can be submitted throughout the year. Applications must be made on a standard application form which can be obtained from local advice centres such as citizens advice bureaux or by writing to the trust.

The Animal Defence Trust

Animal welfare
£82,000 (2000/01)
Beneficial area UK.

c/o Butler Associates, 10 Wales Street, Kings Sutton, Banbury, Oxfordshire OX17 3RR

Tel. 01295 811888

Email ba@kingssuttonfreeserve.co.uk

Correspondent A A Meyer, Trustee

Trustees *Marion Saunders; Alan A Meyer; Vivien McIrvine; Carole Bowles; Paddy Newton.*

CC Number 263095

Information available Accounts were on file at the Charity Commission.

General The trust makes grants for capital projects purely to animal welfare charities. In 2000/01 it had assets totalling £1.5 million and an income of £52,000, including £21,000 from donations and legacies. Grants were made to 27 organisations, including 16 that have previously been supported, totalling £82,000.

Grants of £6,000 each were made to Celia Hammond Animal Trust, International League for the Protection of Horses – Glenda Spooner Farm, Ferne Animal Sanctuary and Thoroughbred Rehabilitation Centre. Other beneficiaries included Society for the Welfare of Horses and Ponies (£4,000), Dartmoor Livestock Protection Society, Brooke Hospital for Animals, Cat Abuse Treatment Society, International Otter Foundation, People and Dogs Society and Essex Horse and Pony Protection Society (£2,500), Devon Horse and Pony Sanctuary (£2,000), Prevent Unwanted Pups (£1,500) and Birmingham Dogs Home (£500).

Exclusions No grants to individuals.

Applications In writing to the correspondent.

The Annandale Charitable Trust

Major UK charities

£69,000 (1999/2000)

Beneficial area UK.

HSBC Trust Services, Norwich House, Nelson Gate, Commercial Road, Southampton SO15 1GX

Tel. 023 8072 2244

Correspondent A T Fryers, Trust Officer

Trustees *Mrs S M Blofeld; Mrs A Lee; HSBC Trust Company (UK) Ltd.*

CC Number 1049193

Information available Full accounts were provided by the trust.

General The trust supports a range of major UK charities. In 1999/2000 it had assets of £3.4 million and an income of £512,000, which included £441,000 transferred to the assets by the settlor and £71,000 from investment income. It made grants totalling £69,000 to 28 organisations. The largest went to the following: Victim Support (£7,000), Oxfam and Macmillan Cancer Relief (£6,000 each), British Red Cross (£4,300) and Age Concern, Imperial Cancer Research and RSPCA (£4,000 each). Other larger grants of £2,000 or £3,000 included those to National Canine Defence League (£3,000) and International League for Protection of Horses (£2,000).

Applications In writing to the correspondent. The trust stated that it has an ongoing programme of funding for specific charities and all its funds are fully committed.

Anpride Ltd

Not known

£243,000 (1998/99)

Beneficial area Not known.

99 Geldeston Road, London E5 8RS

Tel. 020 8806 1011

Correspondent C Benedikt, Trustee

Trustees *C Benedikt; G L Benedikt; I M Halpern.*

CC Number 288978

Information available Accounts were on file at the Charity Commission, but without a list of grants or a narrative report.

General In 2000/01 this trust had a income of £24,000 and a total expenditure of £33,000. This information was taken from the Charity Commission database as unfortunately no further details were available for this year.

In 1998/99 the trust's income was £17,000. Its expenditure far exceeded this, with the trust making grants totalling £243,000. The trust's assets totalled £19,000 at the year end. In the previous year the income had been £126,000, its grants £232,000 and assets £257,000. Unfortunately a list of grant beneficiaries was not available for either of these years.

Exclusions Grants to state-aided institutions will generally not be considered.

Applications In writing to the correspondent.

The Archbishop of Canterbury's Charitable Trust

Christianity, welfare

£199,000 to individuals and organisations (2000)

Beneficial area Worldwide.

1 The Sanctuary, Westminster, London SW1P 3JT

Tel. 020 7222 5381

Correspondent P F B Beesley, Registrar

Trustees *Archbishop of Canterbury; Miss Sheila Cameron; Rt Revd Richard Llewellin; Jeremy Harris.*

CC Number 287967

Information available Accounts were on file at the Charity Commission, but without a list of grants.

General This trust was established in 1983 by the former Archbishop of Canterbury, Lord Runcie, to advance the Christian religion and Christian education, in particular the objects and principles of the Church of England, as well as supporting individuals working towards these goals. The trust deed states that trustees should hold particular interest towards:

- people training for the ministry and church work
- ministers, teachers and the church workers who are in need, and their dependants

- the extension of education in, and knowledge of, the faith and practice of the Church of England
- the development of work of any church, union of churches, denominations or sects which will further the Christian religion generally.

A proportion of the trust's funds are distributed through the Archbishop of Canterbury Trinity Church Fund, which can give support worldwide to Anglican projects at the discretion of the Archbishop of Canterbury. However, the correspondent states that there is much call on these funds and therefore the success rate of applications is very small.

There are also three smaller, restricted funds which are administered as part of this trust. The Michael Ramsey Chair Fund finances the Michael Ramsey Chair in Anglican and Ecumenical Theology at the University of Kent. Dick and Sheila Stallard Fund supports church-related work in China and the Far East, rarely supporting work in the Middle East. Living Memory Rogers Harrison Lozo Relief Fund supports British-born retired Anglican bishops and priests, and their wives and widows living in England, as well as supporting people who are poor, blind, elderly or disabled in Greater London.

In 2000 the trust had assets of £2.5 million. The total income was £283,000, including £176,000 in donations received. After very low management and administration expenses of just £3,300, grants were made totalling £199,000. No information on beneficiaries was provided in the accounts, although they were broken down as follows:

General fund	£185,000
Dick and Sheila Stallard Fund	£6,000
Living Memory Rogers Harrison Lozo Relief Fund	£5,400
The Michael Ramsey Chair Fund	£2,800

Applications Funds are allocated for several years ahead, therefore no new applications can be considered.

The Armourers and Brasiers' Gauntlet Trust

Organisations benefiting young adults, academics, research workers and students; general

£172,000 (2001/02)

Beneficial area UK, with some preference for London.

Armourers' Hall, 81 Coleman Street, London EC2R 5BJ

Tel. 020 7374 4000 **Fax** 202 7606 7481

Correspondent The Secretary

Trustees *Ven. C J H Wagstaff, Chair; Revd P E de D Warburton; R A Crabb; R N Lay; A M R Pontifex.*

CC Number 279204

Information available Full accounts were provided by the trust.

General The trust, which provides the charitable outlet for the Worshipful Company of Armourers and Brasiers, was set up in 1979. Three-quarters of charitable giving is directed towards materials science education, supporting students and also teachers. The remaining funds are therefore quite limited and are directed towards 'people' rather than 'things', with the emphasis on youth and community projects. Grants are given in single payments, not on an ongoing basis. However organisations can still apply for grants each year.

In 2001/02 the trust had assets of £5.1 million and an income of £336,000, including £163,000 in donations received. Grants totalling £172,000 were broken down as follows:

Armed services: prizes – 7 grants totalling £3,700 The largest was £1,900 to Royal Armoured Corps for silver statuettes. Other beneficiaries included Royal Air Force and Royal Marines (£200 each).

Armed services: grants – 2 grants totalling £600 £300 each went to Inns of Court & City Yeomanry and VC & GC Association.

Youth – 2 grants totalling £3,300 STA received £2,800 for voyages and £500 as a donation.

City of London – 6 grants totalling £4,100 Guildhall School of Music received £1,700 for a bursary and £600 for brass prize and an accompanist. Other beneficiaries included Lord Mayor's

Charity (£1,000), Sheriffs' and Recorder's Fund (£200) and United Guilds Service (£130).

Other – 2 grants totalling £530 These both went to an individual, for an award and new medals.

Hospices – 4 grants totalling £2,500 Dove Cottage Day Hospice and Tapping House Hospice both received £750 while The Children's Hospice and St Luke's Hospice each received £500.

Community and Social Care – 26 grants totalling £11,000 The largest grants were £1,000 to St Mary's Convent and Nursing Home, £820 to Salvation Army and £750 to Listening Books. Other grants included £500 each to 3H Fund, Aidis Trust, Cruse Bereavement Care and Tower Hamlets Mission, £400 to Tower Hamlets Old People's Welfare Trust, £300 to New Bridge and £250 each to Fishermen's Mission and Guideposts Trust.

Children/youth – 20 grants totalling £7,800 Beneficiaries included Save the Children (£780), Bromley Hall School and The Foyer Foundation (£500 each), Alone in London and Dundee Young Women's Centre (£300 each) and Handicapped Children's Outing (£50).

Education – 5 grants totalling £2,000 Recipients were Link House Trust (£610), Volunteer Reading Help (£500) and EDUCATION, Memorial Gates Trust and Pumphouse Educational Museum (£300 each).

The arts – 2 grants totalling £750 These went to St Lawrence Jewry (£500) and Friends of St Paul's Cathedral (£250).

Medical/health – 17 grants totalling £6,800 These included £600 to St Luke's Hospital for the Clergy, £500 each to ACET, Autism London, Mental Aid Projects and National Society for Mental Health and Deafness, £400 to DEBRA, £250 to Rehab UK and £190 to Royal School for the Deaf Development Trust.

Arms and armour – 1 grant of £2,000 This went to an individual for leather/metal research.

Armed forces – 3 grants totalling £1,500 £500 each went to British Commonwealth Ex-Services League, 'Not Forgotten' Association and Royal Air Force and Dependants Disabled Holiday Trust.

Spiritual renewal – 3 grants totalling £1,500 £500 each went to Assumption Priory, Derby Cathedral Development Trust and Oxford Centre for Mission Studies.

School level – 8 grants totalling £13,000 A total of £5,100 was spent on primary school projects while £3,500 went to

Royal Society of Chemistry for teachers materials training. Other grants included £900 for the sixth form scholarship scheme in England and Wales and £48 to secondary schools for CD-Roms.

Undergraduate level – 8 grants totalling £8,100 Recipients of funds for bursaries included Sheffield Hallam University (£1,400 for general scholarships and £1,200 for forensic engineering scholarships), Cambridge A&B Newton (£1,500), University of Wales (£1,200) and Liverpool University.

University medals and awards for excellence – 19 grants totalling £4,900 Universities to benefit included Imperial College (£500), Southampton (£375), Cambridge (£300), Birmingham (£250) and Liverpool (£100).

Research student level – 3 grants totalling £4,600 These were for bursaries at Oxford (£2,600) and Cambridge (£2,000) universities and for conference grants (£40).

Undergraduate permanent industrial experience awards – 5 grants totalling £8,500 Recipients included UTCS/Rolls Royce (£4,800), Birmingham/Morgan Technology (£1,000) and Nottingham/ Luxfer (£750).

Technical level – 1 grant of 600 This went to City and Guilds of London Institute.

Professional institutions – 4 grants totalling £3,700 Beneficiaries were Royal Society Award (£2,600), Institute of Materials for a lecture competition (£700), LOGVEC (£300) and London Materials Society for prizes (£100).

Cutlers' Company, Hallamshire – 1 grant of £4,500 This went to the Sheffield Scheme Awards.

The trust also gave £55,000 through the Armourers' Alcan Scheme to schools and university students and £20,000 through the Armourers' Corus Scheme.

Exclusions In general grants are not made to:

- organisations or groups which are not registered
- individuals
- organisations or groups whose main object is to fund or support other charitable bodies which are in direct relief of any reduction of financial support from public funds
- charities with a turnover of over £4 million
- charities which spend over 10% of their income on fundraising activities
- organisations whose accounts disclose substantial financial reserves.

Nor towards general maintenance, repair or restoration of buildings, including ecclesiastical buildings, unless there is a long standing connection with the Armourers and Brasiers' Company or unless of outstanding importance to the national heritage.

Applications In writing to the correspondent, with a copy of the latest annual report and audited accounts. Applications are considered quarterly.

The Ove Arup Foundation

Construction – education and research

£136,000 (2000/01)
Beneficial area Unrestricted.

13 Fitzroy Street, London W1T 4BQ
Tel. 020 7755 3298
Email keithdavid@aol.com
Website www.theovearupfoundation.com
Correspondent K D Dawson
Trustees P Ahm; P Dowson; B Perry; M Shears; D Michael; R F Emmerson; R B Haryott.
CC Number 328138
Information available Full accounts were provided by the trust.

General The trust was established in 1989 with the principal objective of supporting education in matters associated with the built environment, including construction-related academic research. The trustees are appointed by the board of the Ove Arup Partnership. It gives grants for research and projects, including start-up and feasibility costs.

In 2000/01 the trust had assets of £2.5 million, invested in 'units' which do not generate income but vary in value from day-to-day. Donations and interest generated a total income of £48,000. Grants were made to 10 organisations and institutions totalling £136,000; a reduction of 36% on the previous year.

By far the largest grant during the year was £100,000 given to the London School of Economics towards maintaining a new department which the foundation helped to establish. Imperial College also received £18,000 towards funding a professor.

The remaining beneficiaries were The Edge and Institute of Directors (around £3,500 each), The Arkwright Scholarships

(£3,000), The Tavistock Institute of Human Relations (£2,500), Tower Hamlets Education Business Partnership, Space Link Learning Foundation (£2,000 each), The Anglo-Danish Society (£1,200) and Housing and Hazards (£200).

Exclusions No grants to individuals, including students.

Applications In writing to the correspondent, with brief supporting financial information. Trustees meet quarterly to consider applications (March, June, September and December).

The AS Charitable Trust

Chrisitan, development, social concern

£41,000 (2000/01)
Beneficial area UK and the third world.

Bixbottom Farm, Bix, Henley-on-Thames RG9 6BH
Tel. 01491 577745
Correspondent The Administrator
Trustees R Calvocoressi; C W Brocklebank.
CC Number 242190
Information available Full accounts were on file at the Charity Commission.

General This trust makes grants in particular to projects which combine the advancement of the Christian religion, with Christian lay leadership, with third world development, with peacemaking and reconciliation or with other areas of social concern.

In 2000/01 the trust's assets stood at £6.6 million and it had an income of £167,000. Grants to eight organisations were made totalling £41,000. The largest grant was £30,000 to Christian International Peace Service. A grant of £1,500 went to War on Want with £1,100 each going to Barnabas Fund and St Matthew Housing. The remaining four grants were of £1,000 each and went to Christian Engineers in Development, Corrymeela Community, St Michael's Church – Chester Square and Traidcraft Exchange.

Exclusions Grants to individuals or large charities are very rare. Such applications are discouraged.

Applications In writing to the correspondent.

Ashburnham Thanksgiving Trust

Christian

£100,000 to organisations and individuals (2000/01)
Beneficial area UK and worldwide.

Agmerhurst House, Ashburnham, Battle, East Sussex TN33 9NB
Email att@lookingforward.biz
Correspondent The Trustees
Trustees Mrs M Bickersteth; Mrs E M Habershon; E R Bickersteth; R D Bickersteth.
CC Number 249109
Information available Full accounts were on file at the Charity Commission.

General The trust supports a wide range of Christian mission organisations and other Christian organisations which are known to the trustees, in the UK and worldwide. Individuals are also supported.

In 2000/01 the trust's assets, including properties owned, totalled £4.1 million, and generated an income of £137,000. A total of £100,000 was distributed, of which £66,000 went to organisations. Further monies were distributed in restricted grants and grants to individuals.

The 91 grants of over £50 each were listed in the accounts. By far the largest was £11,000 to Lawrence Barham Memorial Trust. There were 18 other grants over £1,000 each including £5,200 to Evangelical Alliance, £4,000 to Genesis Arts Trust, £3,000 to Penhurst Retreat Centre, £2,400 to Ashburnham Village Jubilee Millennium Fund, £2,000 to Wycliffe Bible Translators, £1,800 to Interserve, £1,400 to Oak Hill Bursary Fund and £1,000 to Catalyst Ministry.

Beneficiaries of smaller grants included All Nations Christian College, Lambeth Partnership, London City Mission, Scripture Union, Sisters of Mercy, Tearfund, Timothy Trust and United Mission to Nepal.

Exclusions No grants for buildings.

Applications By e-mail only, potential applicants should not send anything by post. The trust has stated that its funds are fully committed to current beneficiaries. Unfortunately it receives far more applications than it is able to deal with.

The Ashe Park Charitable Trust

Possible preference for hospitals

£194,000 (2000)

Beneficial area UK.

Ashe Park, Steventon, Basingstoke, Hampshire RG25 3AZ

Tel. 01256 771689

Correspondent Mrs Jan Scott

Trustees *P J Scott; Mrs J M T Scott.*

CC Number 297647

Information available Accounts were on file at the Charity Commission, but without a detailed description of its grant-making policy.

General In 2000 the trust had assets totalling £8,500 and an income of £276,000, mainly derived from fundraising events. The main fundraising event was The Ashe Park Polo Challenge which raised £193,000. Three grants were made totalling £194,000.

After fundraising costs of £81,000, grants were made to Rose Road Children's Appeal and NSPCC Full Stop Appeal (£66,000 each) and Leonard Children's Cancer Fund (£62,000).

Applications In writing to the correspondent.

The Laura Ashley Foundation

Art and design, higher education, local projects in mid-rural Wales

£166,000 to organisations (2000/01)

Beneficial area England and Wales.

3 Cromwell Place, London SW7 2JE

Tel. 020 7581 4662

Email info@laf.uk.net

Website www.laf.uk.net

Correspondent The Administrator

Trustees *Jane Ashley, Chair; Prof. Susan Solombok; Martyn C Gowar; Martin Jones; Emma Shuckburgh; Marquis of Queensbury; Helena Appio.*

CC Number 288099

Information available Accounts were provided by the trust; guidelines are available on the foundation's website.

General The foundation was set up in 1986 in memory of Laura Ashley by her family. It has a strong commitment to art and design and also to Wales, particularly Powys, where the Laura Ashley business was first established.

The foundation is constantly reviewing its funding policies. Very few unsolicited applications receive funding. Potential applicants are advised to check the website for the latest details.

The main areas of activity are:

Projects in mid-rural Wales
- to enhance the lives of families
- rural regeneration such as Farmer's Markets
- adult education
- music or art & design projects.

Education
Special bursaries have been set up through institutions of the trustees' choice:

- music conservatoires – bursaries for talented musicians
- LSE – scholarship for a mature anthropology MA student
- Royal College of Art – scholarship for mature textile student.

Fellowship Awards
This initiative was launched in 1999. Awards are made to two individuals per year of around £12,000 to £25,000. They are given to people aged 30 and above, usually working in the fields of art or science, who have outstanding ideas which need funding to develop.

The Arts in London
A pilot project set up by Jane Ashley called SLATE – a network of documentary film makers to encourage wider use of their talents.

In 2000/01 the trust had an income from investments of £277,000. Out of a total expenditure of £582,000, grants totalling £166,000 were made to organisations, with £45,000 going to nine individuals. A further £224,000 was paid in committed grants.

Examples of beneficiaries in 2001/02, taken from the trust's website, include: Royal Society of Arts Summer School (£20,000 to sponsor costs); The Bracken Trust, Llandrindod Wells (£15,000 towards the salary of a respite care nurse at this health practice); Royal Welsh College of Music and Drama (£11,000 to the student hardship fund); Family Welfare Association (£10,000 grant to the Educational Grants Advisory Service); Honeypot House – New Forest (£10,000); Learning for Life – India and Pakistan (£10,000 towards teacher training colleges); Mid-Wales Opera (£5,000 touring grant); Festival of the Great Outdoors – Rhayader (£5,000 development grant); Llani Weaver, Llanidloes (£1,600 for production costs); and Sheepmusic Festival – Presteigne (£1,000 ongoing grant to provide salary for an administrator).

Exclusions The foundation does not fund the following:

- individuals
- new buildings
- medical research
- overseas travel/exchange visits
- private education
- purchase cost of property/land
- restoration of historic buildings or churches
- university or similar research
- projects concerned with domestic violence
- penal affairs
- sport
- youth clubs/projects concerned with 'youth at risk'
- general funds
- taking projects into schools
- outward bound type courses
- newspapers/journals/publications/information packs
- video projects
- safety devices
- theatre, dances, shows/touring
- internet-related projects.

Applications Potential applicants are encouraged to telephone the trust to discuss eligibility before submitting an application. An initial application should be made in writing to the correspondent. It should include a summary of your activities and work, outline the actual project and for what specific purpose the grant is required and what funds have already been raised. It should be typed on one side of headed note paper.

The Ashworth Charitable Trust

Welfare

£129,000 to organisations

(2000/01)

Beneficial area UK and worldwide, with some preference for certain specific needs in Ottery St Mary, Honiton and Sidmouth in Devon.

Foot Anstey Sargent, 4–6 Barnfield Crescent, Exeter, Devon EX1 1RF

Tel. 01392 411221 **Fax** 01392 218554

Email ajt@foot-ansteys.co.uk

Correspondent Alison Tancock, Administrative Correspondent

Trustees *C F Bennett, Chair; Miss S E Crabtree; Mrs K A Gray; G D R Cockram.*

CC Number 1045492

Information available Full accounts were on file at the Charity Commission.

General The trust currently supports:

- Ironbridge Gorge Museum Trust
- people living in the areas covered by the medical practices in Ottery St Mary, Honiton and Sidmouth – such grants are to be paid only for particularly acute needs
- humanitarian projects.

In 2000/01 the trust had assets of £3.5 million and an income of £132,000. Grants ranged from £200 to £10,000 and were made to 65 organisations and 13 individuals totalling £134,000. About half of all grants to organisations were for £2,000.

As in the previous year the largest grants of £10,000 each went to Ironbridge Gorge Museum Trust and Hospiscare. Other larger grants included those made to Exeter Women's Aid and Angels International (£4,000 each), The Esther Benjamins Trust and Action on Water (£3,000 each) and Red Rose Children's Appeal (£2,500). Other beneficiaries included Action on Addiction, Chooselife, Coldingley Welfare Fund, Contact the Elderly, Deafblind UK, Relief Fund for Romania, Richmond Fellowship International and Young Minds (£2,000 each), Pathway Project (£1,500), Charnwood Shelter Project, Macmillan Cancer Relief – Exeter and Torbay, Sanctuary – South Devon and Somerset Croston Trust (£1,000 each), Cot Death Society (£800), Handicapped Children's Action Group (£500) and PHAB Club (£200).

The grants to individuals, totalling £4,700, were given from the designated fund to help those under the second category above.

Exclusions No grants for:

- research-based charities
- animal charities
- 'heritage charities' such as National Trust or other organisations whose aim is the preservation of a building, museum, library and so on (with the exception of the Ironbridge Gorge Museum)
- 'faith-based' charities, unless the project is for primarily humanitarian purposes and is neither exclusive to those of that particular faith or evangelical in its purpose.

Grants to individuals are strictly limited to the geographical area and purpose specified in the general section.

Applications In writing to the correspondent.

The Ian Askew Charitable Trust

General

£72,000 to organisations

(2000/01)

Beneficial area UK with preference for Sussex, and overseas.

Baker Tilly, Spectrum House, 20–26 Cursitor Street, London EC4A 1HY

Tel. 020 7405 2088

Correspondent Christine Wilson

Trustees *J R Rank; Mrs C Pengelley; R A R Askew; R J Wainwright; G B Ackery.*

CC Number 264515

Information available Accounts were on file at the Charity Commission.

General The property owned by the trust includes an SSSI (Site of Special Scientific Interest) and maintenance of this comes out of the trust income. In 2000/01 it had assets of £5.3 million, an income of £214,000 and a total expenditure of £194,000. Maintenance and support of the SSSI cost £61,000, while management and administration costs totalled £57,000. Grants totalled £72,000.

Grants are distributed through three funds: Estate Fund; Education Fund; and Conservation Fund. During the year separate grants were made to a wide

variety of organisations. The majority were for amounts of £500 or less, with 20 for £1,000 or more. These included £12,000 to Middle East Relief, £2,500 to Ringmer Village Hall Fundraising Appeal, £2,000 to St Peter and St James Hospice Anniversary Appeal and £1,500 to Ringmer Parochial Church Council. Beneficiaries receiving £1,000 each included The Salvation Army, British Brain and Spine Foundation, Carl Grace Memorial Foundation, David Tolkien Trust for Stoke Manderville Hospital, The Kingswood Trust, PDSA and Sussex Heritage Trust.

Beneficiaries receiving grants of £500 or less included British Deaf Association, Brunswick Older People's Project, The Cot Death Society, Fight for Sight, Glyndebourne Arts Trust, Mission to Seamen, NSPCC, Royal Academy Trust, Snowdon Award Scheme, Sussex Record Society, West Sussex Society for the Blind and YWCA – Hove.

The Conservation Fund mainly donates money for the upkeep or restoration of churches and old houses.

Exclusions No grants to individuals.

Applications In writing to the correspondent. Applications are considered monthly.

The Association of Colleges Charitable Trust

Further education colleges

£122,000 (2001/02)

Beneficial area UK.

5th Floor, Centre Point, 103 New Oxford Street, London WC1A 1RG

Tel. 020 7827 4600 **Fax** 020 7827 4645

Email alice_thiagaraj@aoc.co.uk

Website www.feonline.net

Correspondent Alice Thiagaraj, Trust Manager

Trustees *Association of Colleges.*

CC Number 1040631

Information available Full accounts and a prospectus were provided by the trust.

General This trust is responsible for administering four programmes. The largest of these is the Beacon Awards, which provide monetary grants to specific initiatives within further education (FE) colleges. The other programmes that operate within the trust are the Gold Awards, the Work Shadowing Scheme and the International Churchill Society for Fine Art Painting.

Established in 1994, the Beacon Awards recognise and promote the interdependence of further education colleges and business, professional and voluntary sector organisations to their mutual advantage. Its aims are to:

- give recognition annually to outstanding teaching and learning practice across the further education curriculum
- highlight the breadth and quality of further education throughout the UK
- support learning and continuous improvement through the dissemination of award-bearing practice
- raise awareness and increase understanding of the colleges' contribution to and role within the UK economy.

The following general criteria must be fulfilled:

- the application may be for a programme, course, or project or for some other aspect of college provision – teaching, learning, guidance or support
- institutions can only submit one application to a specific award each year, but may apply for as many of the different award programmes as are relevant
- it must meet the criteria of the particular award
- it must be subject to evaluation and quality assurance
- it must have been running for at least one academic session before the deadline
- it must promote effective teaching and learning
- it must benefit one or more groups of students or trainees who should be identified and described in the application
- it must have wider relevance and applicability to other colleges as an example of good practice and innovation.

Each award has separate criteria in the interests of the area of work of the sponsor. They range from broad educational development to the promotion of particular courses or subjects, covering most aspects of further education. Programmes in 2002/03 included:

- The Basic Skills Agency Award for ESOL/EAL, which is open to all departments in further education colleges in England and Wales demonstrating best practice in the development and management of ESOL/EAL programmes that meet a range of local needs
- The Churches' Award for Sustainable Community Development, which supports the college in the UK which has been seen as most effectively fostering a broad and sustainable sense of self-worth in a marginalised group, whilst recognising the diversity and opportunities in the locality
- The Edexcel Award for Lifelong Learning, which supports sixth form and further education colleges with effective and imaginative approaches of motivating adults back into education
- The Protocol Professional Award for Art and Design, which is open to all educational institutions providing training in art and design, media studies, publishing, journalism, design and crafts or fine art which encourage students' creativity, learning and transferable skills.

Other schemes operated by the trust are: The Gold Awards for Further Education Alumni, which reward former members of further education colleges who have since excelled in their chosen field or profession; the International Churchill Society Awards for Fine Art Painting, which are given to promising students nominated by their college; and The Work Shadowing Scheme, which provides an opportunity for senior managers to update their skills by spending time in industry.

In 2001/02 the trust had assets of £151,000. Total income was £199,000, of which £108,000 came from Beacon Awards donations received and a further £87,000 from Beacon Awards administrative donations. Total expenditure for the year was £299,000, including £48,000 spent on generating the income. Fine Art Awards were made to four individual students totalling £9,500.

In 2001/2002 there were 33 Beacon Awards made to 32 colleges totalling £122,000. (Telford College of Arts and Technology received two awards.) Of these awards, 25 were for £4,200, the others ranged from £2,800 to £4,100. It is welcome to see the beneficiaries were spread widely across the UK, including colleges in Aberdeen, Bridgwater, Chichester, Hartlepool and Llandrillo.

Applications Potential applicants are advised to look at the Beacon Awards zone at the Association of Colleges website.

Applications should be made in writing to the correspondent, with three copies of each application sent. There is an annual deadline, usually in early summer. Contact should be made solely with the trust's office; the individual sponsors should never be approached.

The following is taken from the 2002/03 Beacon Awards Prospectus:

'Your application should address all of the criteria and should be made in a statement of no more than 3,000 words. The statement should be made by a senior member of staff who has had close contact with the initiative. Written evidence from beneficiaries should be included in the word limit. You may make reference to other materials (i.e. multimedia material, college documents etc.) which the assessors can request, should they wish to do so.

'Your submissions should be structured, as far as possible, under the following headings:

- The Project: Planning and Purpose – include a description of the initiative and how it was set up or developed. Also include a clear description of target group, including numbers.
- Aims and Objectives – outline how aims and objectives were established and how the initiative evolved to meet them.
- Monitoring Procedures – demonstrate how quality assurance was used to improve the initiative.
- Outcomes and Benefits – show how the initiative has benefited the students/trainees and others involved with the project – this should be supported by written evidence from beneficiaries who may be students, trainees, employers or, in some cases, parents.
- Dissemination and the Future – indicate how the initiative could be of benefit to other colleges and how you perceive it developing in the future.

'The statement needs to be accompanied by a completed application form [available on the back of the prospectus or the website] and must be signed by the principal/chief executive.

'All applications will be treated as strictly confidential by the steering group, assessors and Beacon Awards manager. Material from any application will only be made public with the express approval of the college concerned.

'Each application will be sent an acknowledgement addressed to the principal/chief executive. Your college will be subsequently contacted only if the project is shortlisted.'

The Astor Foundation

General

£148,000 (2000/01)
Beneficial area UK.

2 Kew Gardens, Shalbourne, Wiltshire
SN8 3QW

Correspondent Mrs Pam Garraway,
Secretary

Trustees *Sir William Slack; J R Astor,
Chair; Lord Astor of Hever; Dr H Swanton;
R H Astor; C Money-Coutts.*

CC Number 225708

Information available Full accounts
were on file at the Charity Commission.

General The trust supports a variety of
causes, particularly disability, health and
medical research. The grants list also
shows some preference for conservation
projects. In the past the trust has not
favoured giving large grants for building
projects although they are not excluded.

In 2000/01 the trust had an income of
£161,000. After management and
administration costs of £25,000, the sum
of £148,000 was distributed in 93 grants.
The assets at the year end stood at £3.4
million. By far the largest grant was
£25,000 to Royal Free University College
Medical School. Other grants included
those to League of Friends – Middlesex
Hospital (£4,500), Help the Hospices
(£3,500), Samaritans (£3,000) and Aidis
Trust, Jubilee Sailing Trust, RNLI and
Royal National College for the Blind
(£2,500 each).

The remainder of grants were mainly for
amounts of £2,000, £1,500, £1,000 or
£500 each. Beneficiaries included: Born
Free Foundation, Demand, Gurkha
Welfare Trust and Memorial Gates Trust
(£2,000 each); British Stammering
Association, British Wheelchair Sports
Foundation, Catholic Housing Aid
Society, DEBRA and National Library for
the Blind (£1,500 each); Action for Kids,
Children's Country Holidays Fund, Fight
for Sight and Memorial Gates Trust
(£1,000 each); and Age Concern,
Greenwich Healthcare Trust, National
Eye Research Centre and Pelican Centre
(£500 each).

Exclusions No grants to individuals or
towards salaries. Grants are given to
registered charities only.

Applications There are no deadline
dates; applications should be in writing to
the correspondent. If the appeal arrives

too late for one meeting it will
automatically be carried over for
consideration at the following meeting.
The trustees meet twice a year, in March
and October. A reply will always be sent
irrespective of whether an appeal is
successful.

This entry was not confirmed by the trust,
but is correct according to information on
file at the Charity Commission.

The Atlantic Foundation

Education, medical, general

£75,000 (2000/01)
Beneficial area Worldwide, though
with some preference for Wales.

7–8 Raleigh Walk, Atlantic Wharf, Cardiff
CF10 4LN

Tel. 029 2046 1651

Correspondent Mrs B L Thomas, Trustee

Trustees *P Thomas; Mrs B L Thomas.*

CC Number 328499

Information available Full accounts
were on file at the Charity Commission.

General This trust relies on covenanted
donations each year for its income, which
totalled £61,000 in 2000/01. It supports a
range of causes, with a strong interest in
Wales. Grants totalled £75,000 and were
categorised by the trust as follows:

		No. of grants
Independent schools and colleges	£28,000	24
Registered charities	£23,000	38
Community aid	£13,000	34
Medical appeals and support	£5,500	13
Local authority support	£3,000	6
Religious foundations	£1,200	3
International appeals	£1,200	2

The main beneficiaries in this category
were Welsh College of Music and Drama
(£2,800), Royal Academy of Music
(£2,400), Royal Academy of Dramatic Art
(£2,200), London Academy of Music and
Dramatic Art and Italia Conti Academy of
Theatre Arts Ltd (£2,000 each), Bristol
Old Vic Theatre School (£1,800) and
Hereford Theatre School Ltd (£1,600).

Registered charities
Beneficiaries included The Variety Club
(£3,300), Deaf Blind UK (£2,000), Live
Music Now – Wales (£1,300), Weston

Spirit and Welsh Initiative for Conductive
Education (£1,000 each), RUKBA,
National Museums and Galleries of Wales
and Vision Trust (£500 each).

Community aid
Grants included those to Gibbonsdown
Children's Centre and Vale View
Allotment Association (£1,000 each),
Bluebird Football Club – Merthyr Tydfil
and The Piano Fund (£800 each), The
Guides Association (£600), Streets Youth
Project and Tae Kwon Do Cymru (£500
each), Welsh Salmon and Trout Angling
Association (£400).

Medical appeals & support
Beneficiaries included Caerphilly
Borough Council (£1,250), Alzheimers
Research Trust and Whizz Kidz (£1,000),
Arthritis Care in Wales (£300), Drugs and
Family Support Group and Pontypool
Pacers Heart Support Club (£200 each).

Local authority
Beneficiaries included Llanishen Fach
Primary School and Storey Arms Outdoor
Educational Centre (£1,000 each),
Willows High School Cardiff Bay (£750)
and Brecon High School (£500).

Religious foundations
Grants were given to Woodville Baptist
Church and Llanrhian Parish Church
(£500 each) and St David's RC Sixth Form
College (£200).

International appeals
Two grants were given in this category.
Beneficiaries were Sirigu Children's
Home – Ghana (£1,000) and Convoy of
Hope – Croatia (£200).

Applications In writing to the
correspondent. Applications are
considered throughout the year.

The Richard Attenborough Charitable Trust

Acting, human rights, overseas, general

£89,000 (2000/01)
Beneficial area UK and developing
world with some preference for
South Africa.

Beaver Lodge, Richmond Green, Surrey
TW9 1NQ

Tel. 020 8940 7234

Correspondent Lady Attenborough, Trustee

Trustees *Lady Attenborough; Lord Attenborough.*

CC Number 259186

Information available Full accounts were provided by the trust.

General This trust not surprisingly focuses much of its grant-making towards acting-related organisations. It also makes a number of grants to overseas and human rights organsiations.

In 2000/01 the trust had assets of £326,000 and an income of £4,100. Grants totalling £90,000 were made to 38 organisations, of which 15 were also supported in the previous year.

The largest grants were £28,000 to Royal Academy of Dramatic Art and £14,000 to Waterford School, both of which also received substantial grants in the previous year.

Other beneficiaries included Bretton Hall (£10,000), Waterford Kamhlaba (£9,800), Royal Academy of Arts (£5,000), Adapt Trust (£3,000), Orange Tree Theatre (£2,000), Muscular Dystrophy (£1,700), Chicken Shed Theatre Company (£1,500), Prisons Video Trust and Emile Litter Foundation (£1,000 each), Zimbabwe Democracy Trust (£500), Whitechapel Art Gallery (£350), British Heart Foundation (£250), Relate (£100) and Friends of RADA (£70).

Applications The funds of this trust are donated principally to charities with which the trustees are associated. They greatly regret, therefore, that they are unable to reply to any external applications.

The Aurelius Charitable Trust

Conservation of culture and the humanities

£88,000 (2001)

Beneficial area Generally UK only.

Briarsmead, Old Road, Buckland, Betchworth, Surrey RH3 7DU

Tel. 01737 842186 **Fax** 01737 842186

Email haynes@knowall.co.uk

Correspondent P E Haynes, Trustee

Trustees *W J Wallis; P E Haynes.*

CC Number 271333

Information available Full accounts were on file at the Charity Commission.

General During the settlor's lifetime, the income of the trust was distributed broadly to reflect his interests in the conservation of culture inherited from the past, and the dissemination of knowledge, particularly in the humanities field. Since Dr Marc Fitch's death in April 1994, the trustees have continued with this policy.

Grants are for seed-corn or completion funding not otherwise available. Grants are usually one-off and range from £500 to £3,000.

In 2001 the trust's income was £82,000, it made grants totalling £88,000 and its assets at the year end were £2 million. Grants included: £11,000 to Ruskin Diaries; £10,000 to The British Academy; £5,000 each to The London Library, National Coal Mining Museum for England and The Sixteens' Endowment Fund; and £4,300 to The CABI Trust. Other grants ranged from £500 to £3,500.

Exclusions No grants to individuals.

Applications In writing to the correspondent. Grants are generally made on the recommendation of the trust's board of advisors. Unsolicited applications will only be responded to if an sae is included. Trustees meet twice a year, in January and July, and applications need to be received by May and November.

The Avenue Charitable Trust

General

£348,000 (1999/2000)

Beneficial area Worldwide.

c/o Messrs Sayers Butterworth, 18 Bentinck Street, London W1U 2AR

Tel. 020 7935 8504 **Fax** 020 7487 5621

Correspondent Sue Brotherhood

Trustees *R D L Astor; The Hon. Mrs B A Astor; S G Kemp.*

CC Number 264804

Information available Accounts were on file at the Charity Commission.

General In 1999/2000 the trust had assets of £596,000. The total income was £6,500, down on the previous year when the trust received donations totalling £762,000. Grants were made to 85 organisations totalling £348,000.

Anna Freud Centre received by far the largest grant, of £103,000. Other large grants were £20,000 to Brandon Centre, £17,000 to Progressive Farming Trust, £15,000 to Prisoners Advice, £14,000 to Prisoners Abroad and £10,000 each to Adventure Playground, Lincoln Trust, Youth at Risk and Waterford School.

Other beneficiaries included Asylum Aid (£9,000), Centre for Research into Adolescent Breakdown and Young Vics Theatre Co. (£5,000 each), Anti-Slavery International (£3,000), Virginia House Settlement (£2,300), Royal National Theatre (£1,400), Arab Association for Human Rights and Northern Ireland Voluntary Trust (£1,000 each), Parkinson's Disease Society (£700), Shelter and Women in Prisons (£500 each), Runnymede Trust (£350), Cobden Trust (£20) and Council for the Protection of Rural England (£18).

Applications The trust has previously stated that all available income is now committed to existing beneficiaries.

The Bacta Charitable Trust

General

£108,000 (1999/2000)

Beneficial area UK.

Bacta House, Regents Wharf, 6 All Saints Street, London N1 9RQ

Tel. 020 7713 7144 **Fax** 020 7713 0446

Correspondent Linda Malcolm, Clerk

Trustees *Robert Higgins, Chair; Sonia Meaden; Charles Henry; Simon Thomas; Mark Horwood.*

CC Number 328668

Information available Information was provided by the trust.

General The trust only supports charities recommended by Bacta members. Bacta is the Trade Association for the Coin Operated Amusement Industry.

The trust's principal fundraising takes place at the annual Bacta Charity Ball through a prize raffle and pledges made by guests. In 1999 the trust received over £60,000 from this event. Bacta and individual members of the association continued to make requests to the trust for funds for particular charities they supported, which were considered by the trust.

In 1999/2000 the trust made 20 grants, totalling £108,000. Beneficiaries have included Bobath Cymru, CPA Dalmore House Appeal, Children's Hospice South West, Fairbridge, Gordon House Association, William C Harvey School, Macmillan Cancer Relief, Andrew Marvell Community Youth Centre and NSPCC.

Exclusions No grants for overseas charities or religious purposes.

Applications In writing to the correspondent, but via a Bacta member. Applications should be submitted by January, April or August, for trustees' meetings in February, May or September.

The Balcombe Charitable Trust

Education, environment, health and welfare

£410,000 (2000/01)

Beneficial area UK.

c/o Citroen Wells, Devonshire House, 1 Devonshire Street, London W1W 5DR

Tel. 020 7304 2000

Correspondent J Prevezer, Trustee

Trustees *R A Kreitman; P M Kreitman; Mrs S I Kreitman.*

CC Number 267172

Information available Full accounts were on file at the Charity Commission.

General This trust generally makes grants in the fields of education, the environment and health and welfare. It only supports registered charities.

In 2000/01 the trust had assets of £8.2 million and an income of £257,000. Grants totalled £410,000. A total of 36 organisations received grants ranging from £1,000 to £25,000, of these, 20 had been supported in the previous year.

The largest grants were: £50,000 to Brook Advisory Centres; £25,000 each to British Red Cross, ChildLine, Durrell Wildlife Conservation Trust and NSPCC; £20,000 to World Wildlife Fund UK; £15,000 to BACUP, Crisis and Parentline; and £10,000 each to Friends of the Earth, MIND, Princess Royal Trust for Carers, Samaritans and Who Cares Trust.

Beneficiaries of smaller grants included Body and Soul, British Trust for Conservation Volunteers, Galopagos

Conservation Trust, Womankind and Youth Access.

Exclusions No grants to individuals or non-registered charities.

Applications In writing to the correspondent.

The Barber Charitable Trust

Evangelical Christian causes, churches

£72,000 (2000/01)

Beneficial area UK with some preference for West Sussex, and overseas.

Tortington Cottage, Tortington, Arundel, West Sussex BN18 0BG

Tel. 01903 882337 **Fax** 01903 882337

Correspondent E E Barber, Trustee

Trustees *E E Barber; Mrs D H Barber.*

CC Number 269544

Information available Full accounts were on file at the Charity Commission.

General The trust makes grants to churches and Christian charities for evangelical Christian causes and also makes a few grants to individual missionaries and Christian workers personally known to the trustees.

In 2000/01 the trust's assets totalled £46,000 and it had an income of £71,000, mostly from donations. Grants totalled £72,000, with over 50 organisations and churches supported, principally for evangelical causes, in the UK and overseas.

Grants over £1,000 were made to 23 organisations, 19 of which received grants the year before, although of different amounts. Beneficiaries included Scripture Union International (£9,000), Arundel Baptist Church (£7,500), Hope Now Ministries (£5,500), Gideons International (£4,500), Africa Inland Mission (£4,000), Western Province Baptist Association – South Africa (£3,000) and Christian Ministries (£2,900). Ten organisations received £2,000 each, including SASRA, Missionary Aviation Fellowship, Worldshare and Scripture Gift Mission.

Projects supported included:

- Bible distribution in the British Isles and overseas

- Christian workers in Africa, Madagascar, Romania and Albania (personally known to the trustees)
- training of Christian leaders in developing countries
- training of students in Bible colleges (personally known to the trustees)
- a mission hospital, two hospices and site development for children's work in Madagascar
- ministry and evangelism in the UK, Ukraine and South Africa.

Exclusions Requests from individuals are not considered unless personally known by the trustees. Requests from non-registered charities are not considered. Requests for building construction or renovation are not considered.

Applications In writing to the correspondent. Funds tend to be committed several years in advance and therefore unsolicited appeals are unlikely to be considered or acknowledged.

Barclays Stockbrokers Charitable Trust

Physical and mental disability, ill health, relief of suffering, poverty, homelessness, family and social welfare, education and training, children, young people and older people

About £100,000 each year

Beneficial area UK.

Barclays Bank Trust Co. Ltd, Estates and Trusts, Osbourne Court, Gadbrook Park, Northwich, Cheshire CW4 7UE

Tel. 01606 313173 **Fax** 01606 303000

Correspondent Miss M Y Bertenshaw, Trust Officer

Trustees *Barclays Bank Trust Co. Ltd.*

CC Number 1093833

Information available Information was provided by the trust.

General This new trust was set up in July 2002 with the purpose of making one-off grants to registered and exempt charities working with disability/vulnerable groups (such as people who are ill or elderly and children and young people), addressing a range of needs including health, homelessness, poverty and education and training.

The trust states that 'preference will be given to small/medium charities or self-sufficient local branches of larger national charities as opposed to the large well-endowed national charities. Where possible, the trustees will, when exercising their discretion, attempt to "make a difference".

Grants will be categorised as small, medium and large, and will be in the range of £10,000 to £50,000. In practice, the trust aims to make 'small' grants of around £10,000, medium grants of £25,000 and large grants of £50,000.

Support will only be given for capital projects and specific programmes rather than funding core or revenue costs.

Exclusions The trust will generally not consider funding individuals, schools, colleges or universities, religious buildings, overseas projects, medical research or animal welfare. Expenses that have already been incurred will not be considered.

Applications Initially in writing to the correspondent for consideration in February, May, August and November. If eligibility is established an application form will then be sent.

The Barnabas Trust

Evangelical Christianity

£363,000 to organisations
(2000/01)

Beneficial area UK and overseas. Overseas projects are supported only if they are personally known by the trustees.

63 Wolsey Drive, Walton-on-Thames, Surrey KT12 3BB

Tel. 01932 220622

Correspondent Mrs Doris Edwards, Secretary

Trustees *N Brown; K C Griffiths, Chair; D S Helden.*

CC Number 284511

Information available Full accounts were on file at the Charity Commission.

General In 2000/01 the trust had assets of £4.7 million generating an income of £208,000. Grants to 108 organisations totalled £363,000, to 16 individuals for education £13,000, with a further £7,000 to six individuals for Christian missionary work. Grants were split into the following categories:

Community welfare – 29 grants totalled £90,000.
Grants were given to local, UK and international medical institutions and charities concerned with the welfare of children, older people, prisoners, people experiencing poverty and the general community. Beneficiaries included Shaftesbury Society (£12,000), Princess Alice Hospice (£8,000), Medical Missionary News and Yeldall Manor (£6,000 each), Bethany Children's Trust and International Fellowship of Evangelical Students (£5,000 each) and Torch Trust for the Blind (£2,500).

Educational – 33 grants to organisations totalled £65,000.
Grants were given to establishments in the UK and overseas, and general educational charities, including religious education. Beneficiaries included Schools Outreach and Haggai Institute (£6,000 each), Redcliffe College (£4,000), National Bible Society of Scotland (£2,500), Danoka Training College – Kenya and Medina Valley Centre (£2,000 each) and National Bible Study Group (£1,000).

Christian mission overseas – 23 grants to organisations totalled £146,000.
The largest grants were £90,000 to SGM International. Other grants were of £1,000 to £6,000 (although one grant of £75 was also given) and beneficiaries included Echoes of Service, High Adventure Ministries, Naval, Military and Air Force Bible Society, Nigeria Evangelical Missionary Institute, SGM International – Pavement Project (£5,000 each) and Operation Mobilisation and Latin Link (£3,000 each).

Christian mission in the UK – 27 grants totalled £43,000.
Grants included £5,000 each to Counties Evangelical Trust and Message to Schools Trust, £3,000 to Scripture Union, £1,500 each to Manchester City Mission and Careforce and £1,000 each to Campaigners Scotland, Warrington Youth for Christ and St Mary's Church, Lemmington Spa. Smaller grants were also given.

Exclusions 'The trust is no longer able to help with building, refurbishment or equipment for any church, since to be of any value grants need to be large.' On-going revenue costs such as salaries are not supported.

Applications In writing to the correspondent, giving as much detail as possible, and enclosing a copy of the latest audited accounts, if applicable. The trust states: 'Much of the available funds generated by this trust are allocated to existing donees. The trustees are willing to consider new applications, providing they refer to a project which is overtly evangelical in nature'. If in doubt about whether to submit an application, please telephone the secretary to the trust for guidance.

The trustees meet four times a year, or more often as required, and applications will be put before the next available meeting.

Lord Barnby's Foundation

General

£162,000 (2000/01)

Beneficial area Unrestricted.

PO Box 71, Plymstock, Plymouth PL8 2YP

Correspondent Mrs J A Lethbridge, Secretary

Trustees *Sir John Lowther; Lord Newall; Sir Michael Farquhar; Hon. George Lopes; Countess Peel.*

CC Number 251016

Information available Accounts were available at the Charity Commission, with only a brief narrative report.

General The foundation has established a permanent list of charities that it supports each year, with the remaining funds then distributed to other charities. The grants list does not indicate which charities are on the permanent list.

Its priority areas include the the following:

- heritage; the preservation of the environment; and the countryside and ancient buildings, particularly the 'great Anglican cathedrals'
- charities benefiting people who are ex-service and service, Polish, disabled or refugees
- welfare of horses and people who look after them

- youth and other local organisations in Ashtead – Surrey, Blyth – Nottinghamshire and Bradford – Yorkshire
- technical education for the wool industry.

In 2000/01 the trust had assets of £4.8 million and an income of £136,000. After high management and administration costs of £25,000, a total of £162,000 was distributed in 64 grants. By far the largest donation was £40,000 to Therfield School. Beneficiaries of other grants over £5,000 each included Country Trust (£15,000), Atlantic College (£14,000) and Animal Health Trust, Ashtead Rotary Club, Fairbridge, Ghurkha Welfare Trust, Langford Trust, Royal Commonwealth Society for the Blind and Volunteer Reading Help (£5,000 each).

Smaller grants in the range of a few hundred pounds to £2,000 included those to Raleigh International, Royal Star and Garter Home (£2,000 each), All Hallows Development Trust and Racing Welfare Charities (£1,000 each), Cedar Trust, Sick Children's Trust, Teenage Cancer Trust and Tetbury Hospital Trust (£500 each), Game Conservancy Trust (£400) and Spinal Research Trust (£250).

Exclusions No grants to individuals.

Applications Applications will only be considered if received in writing accompanied by a set of the latest accounts. Appeals are considered three times a year, in February, June and November.

The Misses Barrie Charitable Trust

Medical, general

£188,000 (2001/02)
Beneficial area UK.

Messrs Raymond Carter & Co, 1b Haling Road, South Croydon CR2 6HS
Tel. 020 8686 1686
Correspondent Raymond Carter, Trustee
Trustees *R G Carter; R S Waddell; R S Ogg.*
CC Number 279459
Information available Full accounts were on file at the Charity Commission.

General In 2001/02 the income of the trust was £219,000 and grants totalled £188,000; assets stood at £4.9 million.

By far the largest grant was £15,000 to University of Dundee for research support. Other larger grants went: to Princess Royal Trust for Carers (£5,000); Age Concern – Edinburgh and Leith (£4,000); Surrey Cricket Board (£3,200); Company of Hackney Carriage Drivers, Eden Project, Over the Wall Gang and Worcestershire County Cricket Board (£3,000 each); and SSAFA (£2,500).

Remaining donations were for £2,000 (50 grants), £1,000 (46) or £500 (1). Beneficiaries included All Saints Church Organ Appeal – Warlingham, Brighton & Hove Parents' and Children's Group, Broadway Garden Club, Cruse Bereavement Care, Fight for Sight, Iris Murdoch Centre, Parkinsons Disease Society, Quaker Social Action, Rainbow Trust – Leatherhead, Remedi, Spirit – Manchester, Starlight Childrens Foundation, Warwickshire Association of Boys Clubs and Willow Trust – Cirencester.

Exclusions No grants to individuals.

Applications In writing to the correspondent. Trustees meet four times a year.

The Batchworth Trust

Medical, social welfare, general

£215,000 (2001/02)
Beneficial area Worldwide.

33–35 Bell Street, Reigate, Surrey RH2 7AW
Tel. 01737 221311
Correspondent M R Neve, Administrative Executive
Trustees *Lockwell Trustees Ltd.*
CC Number 245061
Information available Full accounts were on file at the Charity Commission.

General The trust mainly supports nationally-recognised charities, in the categories shown below. In 2001/02 it had assets of £7.9 million and an income of £2.5 million. It made 36 grants totalling £215,000, broken down as follows:

Category	2001/02 %	2000/01 %
Social welfare	48	44
Medical	22	20
Foreign aid	15	22
Youth & education	13	13
Environment	2	1

Grants ranged from £2,000 to £10,000, but were mainly for amounts of £5,000 or less. The largest, £15,000, went to International Red Cross with eight grants of £1,000 each going to Alzheimer's Society, Médicins Sans Frontiéres, New Hall College, Prisoners of Conscience, RNID, Restore, Royal Commonwealth Society for the Blind and Schizophrenia Research.

Smaller grants included those to Action for Kids, Anchor Society, Farm Africa, Garsington Opera, Haddo Arts Trust, Royal Agricultural Benevolent Trust, Waterside Trust and Youth Clubs UK.

Exclusions No applications from individuals can be considered.

Applications In writing to the correspondent. An sae should be included if a reply is required.

The Bay Tree Charitable Trust

Development work, general

£155,000 (2001)
Beneficial area UK and overseas.

10 New Square, London WC2A 3QG
Correspondent c/o Payne Hicks Beach
Trustees *I M P Benton; Miss E L Benton; P H Benton.*
CC Number 1044091
Information available Accounts were provided by the trust.

General In 2001 the trust had assets of £2.9 million, an income of £106,000 and gave grants totalling £155,000. A total of six grants were made to: Crusaid (£56,000); Tree Aid and Wateraid (£25,000 each); Brtish Red Cross (£20,000); Fair Trial Abroad (£19,000); and Save the Children (£10,000).

Other previous beneficiaries include Cotswold Riding for the Disabled, Médecins Sans Frontières and Youth Care Initiative.

Exclusions No grants to individuals.

Applications In writing to the correspondent. No acknowledgements will be made to unsuccessful applications.

Bear Mordechai Ltd

Jewish
£619,000 (2000/01)
Beneficial area Worldwide.

136 Holmleigh Road, London N16 5PY
Correspondent Mrs Leah Benedikt, Secretary
Trustees Y Benedikt; C Benedikt; E S Benedikt.
CC Number 286806
Information available Accounts were on file at the Charity Commission with only a brief report and no grants list.

General Grants are made to Jewish organisations. The trust states that religious, educational and other charitable institutions are supported.

In 2000/01 this trust had assets of £833,000 and an income of £382,000, of which £301,000 came from donations. Grants totalled £619,000.

The accounts listed grants made over £2,000 each, of which there were 15 in 2000/01. The largest grants were £219,000 to Kollel Bear Mordechy and £131,000 to Agudat Yad Yemin Jerusalem. Other beneficiaries included Kolel Shomrei Hachomoth (£88,000), Almat Limited (£26,000), Yedokoh Bechol (£15,000), Orthodox Council of Jerusalem Ltd (£10,000), United Talmusical Associates (£4,000) and Arpride Limited (£2,000).

Smaller unlisted grants totalled £2,700.

Applications In writing to the correspondent.

This entry was not confirmed by the trust but was correct according to information on file at the Charity Commission.

The Beaufort House Trust

Christian, education
£79,000 (2001)
Beneficial area UK.

Beaufort House, Brunswick Road, Gloucester GL1 1JZ
Tel. 01452 528533
Website www.allchurches.co.uk
Correspondent Mrs R J Hall, Company Secretary
Trustees Sir Alan McLintock; M R Cornwall-Jones; B V Day; Viscount Churchill; Revd D G Shelgrove; W H Yates; Mrs S Homersham; N Assheton.
CC Number 286606
Information available Full accounts were provided by the trust.

General The trustees make grants to promote the furtherance of education and Christian religion. Appeals are considered from schools, colleges, universities or any other charitable body involved in this work. It receives an annual payment from the Ecclesiastical Insurance Group plc.

In 2001 the trust had assets of £111,000 and an income of £676,000 including £625,000 from their school fees scheme. After school fees were paid totalling £611,000, the sum of £79,000 was given in grants.

Donations over £1,000 each were: £20,000 to Be Your Best Foundation – Sussex; £5,000 to Queen Margaret School – York; £2,000 to Worshipful Company of Insurers; and £1,500 each to St John's College – Nottingham and St Williams Foundation – York.

Beneficiaries of smaller grants included Balancraig School – Perth, Diocese of Southwark, Evangelical Theological College of Wales – Bridgend, Friends of Fosse Way School – Bath, Irish School of Ecumenicas – Belfast, Leeds Faith in Schools, Northenden Primary School – Manchester, St Martin's School Classroom Appeal – Newbury and Shaftesbury Society – London.

Exclusions No grants are made to organisations with political associations, national charities or individuals.

Applications In writing to the correspondent detailing: charity number; the objectives of the charity; the appeal target; how the funds are to be utilised; funds raised to date; and previous support

received from the trust. If available the application should be accompanied by supporting literature and an annual report.

Beauland Ltd

Jewish
£196,000 (2000/01)
Beneficial area Worldwide, possibly with a preference for the Manchester area.

4 Cheltenham Crescent, Salford M7 4FP
Correspondent The Trustees
Trustees F Neuman; H Neuman; M Friedlander; H Roseman; J Bleir; R Delange; M Neuman; P Neuman; E Neuman; E Henry.
CC Number 511374
Information available Accounts were on file at the Charity Commission.

General The trust's objects are the advancement of the Jewish religion in accordance with the Orthodox Jewish faith and the relief of poverty. It gives grants to 'religious, educational and similar bodies'.

In 2000/01 it had assets of £1.4 million and an income of £205,000. Grants totalled £196,000, mostly given to Jewish organisations.

There were 80 grants in the year, the largest of which was £29,000 to Chesed L'Yisroel. Other beneficiaries included Torah V'emunah Charitable Trust (£17,000), Tomchei Shaarei Zion (£15,000), Jewish High School (£11,000), Beis Yakov Institutions and Yeshivas Nitra (£10,000 each), Bnos Yisovel School (£8,800) and Kehilla Centre and MALA (£5,000 each).

Applications In writing to the correspondent.

This entry was not confirmed by the trust but was correct according to information on file at the Charity Commission.

The Beaverbrook Foundation

General

£96,000 to organisations
(1999/2000)

Beneficial area UK and Canada.

11 Old Queen Street, London SW1H 9JA

Tel. 020 7222 7474 **Fax** 020 7222 2198

Website
www.beaverbrookfoundation.org

Correspondent Jane Ford, General
Secretary

Trustees *Lord Beaverbrook, Chair; Lady
Beaverbrook; Lady Aitken; T M Aitken;
Laura Levi; J E A Kidd; M F Aitken.*

CC Number 310003

Information available Accounts were on
file at the Charity Commission with an
inadequate report and without a list of
grants.

General In 1999/2000 the trust had
assets of £18 million and an income of
£519,000. Grants to organisations totalled
£96,000. Other expenditure included
£209,000 on management and
administration, presumably related to
managing the trust's properties and
£466,000 on renovations to Cherkley
Court, which is owned by the trust.

Very little is known about the work of this
trust. It has not provided any information
on its activities since 1993 when, from an
income of £477,000, donations of
£332,000 were made in 49 grants.
Examples of the largest included:
Beaverbrook Canadian Foundation
(£100,000); National Association of Boys
Clubs (£32,000); Reading University
(£14,000); and £10,000 each to National
Association for the League of Hospital
Friends, Raleigh International, Cartoon
Art Trust, Isle of Wight Youth Trust, St
Thomas Hospital – Tommy Campaign
and ReSolve.

Exclusions Only registered charities are
supported.

Applications In writing to the
correspondent with an sae. Trustees meet
in May and November.

The Peter Beckwith Charitable Trust

Medical, welfare

£121,000 (2000/01)

Beneficial area UK.

Hill Place House, 55a High Street,
Wimbledon Village, London SW19 5BA

Tel. 020 8944 1288

Correspondent P M Beckwith, Trustee

Trustees *P M Beckwith; Mrs P Beckwith;
Mrs A Peppiatt.*

CC Number 802113

Information available Accounts were on
file at the Charity Commission but
without a list of grants.

General This trust was established in
1989. In 2000/01 it received an income of
£137,000 mostly from donations. Assets
at the year end totalled £84,000.
Unfortunately, no list of grants was
included with the accounts that were on
file at the Charity Commission.

In previous year beneficiaries have
included Burnbake Trust, Cara Trust,
Carousel, Dartington International
Summer School, Handy Aid to
Independent Living, Queen Elizabeth
Foundation for Disabled People, REAC,
Royal School for Deaf Children and
Rugby Mayday Trust.

Applications In writing to the
correspondent.

Belljoe Tzedoko Ltd

Jewish

£72,000 (2000)

Beneficial area UK.

27 Fairholt Road, London N16 5EW

Tel. 020 8800 4384

Correspondent H J Lobenstein, Trustee

Trustees *H J Lobenstein; Mrs B
Lobenstein; D Lobenstein; M Lobenstein.*

CC Number 282726

Information available Accounts were on
file at the Charity Commission, but
without a list of grants.

General The trust's objects are 'the
advancement of religion in accordance
with the orthodox Jewish faith and the
relief of poverty'.

In 2000 the trust had assets of just £2,300;
its income of £68,000 came mainly from
covenants. Grants totalled £72,000, no
further details were available.

The most recent grants list available in the
Charity Commission file was for 1995
when grants totalled £76,000. They
ranged from £10 to £8,600 and were made
to 87 Jewish organisations. The three
largest were £8,600 to Marbeh Torah
Trust, £7,500 to Society of Friends of the
Torah and £5,500 to Yesodey Hatorah
School.

Applications In writing to the
correspondent.

The Benham Charitable Settlement

Youth, general

£178,000 (2001/02)

Beneficial area UK, with a special
emphasis on Northamptonshire.

Hurstbourne, Portnall Drive, Virginia
Water, Surrey GU25 4NR

Correspondent Mrs M Tittle, Managing
Trustee

Trustees *Mrs M M Tittle; Lady Hutton; E
N Langley.*

CC Number 239371

Information available Full accounts
were on file at the Charity Commission,
together with a narrative report.

General The settlement was founded in
1964 by the late Cedric Benham and his
wife Hilda, then resident in
Northamptonshire, 'to benefit charities
and for divers' good causes and
considerations'.

'The object of the charity is the support of
registered charities working in many
different fields – including charities
involved in medical research, disability,
elderly people, children and young
people, disadvantaged people, overseas
aid, missions to seamen, the welfare of ex-
servicemen, wildlife, the environment,
and the arts. The trust also supports the
Church of England, and the work of
Christian mission throughout the world.
Special emphasis is placed upon those

churches and charitable organisations within the county of Northamptonshire.'

'In recent years the settlement has made a series of substantial donations, exceeding £1.6 million, to the Northamptonshire Association of Youth Clubs.' These donations were principally for the purchase of a freehold site and to facilitate the financing and construction of an indoor sports arena. The trust stated its intention to continue to support certain operations of the association on a selected basis.

In 2001/02 the trust had assets of £4.6 million which generated an income of £141,000. A total of £178,000 was given in 227 grants. These ranged from £50 to £35,000, although most were for £600 or less. Northamptonshire Association of Youth Clubs received the largest grant, of £35,000. Other larger grants included £12,000 to The Lambeth Partnership, £8,000 to Coworth Park School, £5,000 each to St George's School – Ascot and St Jude's Church – Plymouth, £2,000 to Northampton Symphony Orchestra and £900 to Holy Trinity Church towards a pension fund.

Beneficiaries receiving £600 or less included Boddington Parish Church Appeal Fund, 8th Northampton Scout Group, Boughton Church Appeal Fund, Chelmsford Cathedral, Coventry Cathedral Development Trust, Friends of Northampton General Hospital, Grange Community School – Kettering, Moreton Pinkney Village Hall, Northampton Festival of Dance, Northampton Festival of Music and Drama, The Abbey Centre, IBS Research Appeal, Hearing Dogs for the Deaf, Friends of St Peter's Hospital, National Eye Research Centre and Ethiopiaid.

Exclusions No grants to individuals.

Applications In writing to the correspondent. The trust regrets that it cannot send replies to all applicants, nor will they accept telephone calls. 'Applications will be dealt with promptly at any time of year (no application forms necessary), but no charity will be considered more than once each year (repeated applications are automatically ignored for twelve months).'

The Billmeir Charitable Trust

General, health and medical
£169,000 (2000/01)

Beneficial area UK, with a preference for the Surrey area, specifically Elstead, Tilford, Farnham and Frensham.

Messrs Moore Stephens, 1 Snow Hill, London EC1A 2EN

Tel. 020 7334 9191

Correspondent T T Cripps, Accountant

Trustees *B C Whitaker; M R Macfadyen; S Marriott; J Whitaker.*

CC Number 208561

Information available Full accounts were provided by the trust.

General The trust states it supports a wide variety of causes. About a quarter of the grants are given to health and medical charities and about a third of the grants are given to local organisations in Surrey, especially the Farnham, Frensham, Elstead and Tilford areas.

In 2000/01 the trust's assets were £3.8 million and it had an income of £123,000. Donations were given to 44 charities totalling £169,000, of those supported, 29 had received a grant in the previous year.

The two largest grants went to Elstead United Reform Church (£20,000) and Reeds School – Cobham (£10,000). Remaining grants were in the range of £1,000 to £6,000 and included those to Arundel Castle Cricket Foundation, British Home and Hospital for Incurables, Cancer Vaccine Institute, Counsel & Care of Elstead and Farnham, Farnham Youth Choir, Homestart, Marlborough College, Old Kiln Museum Ltd, RNIB, RNLI, Southmead Research Foundation, Woodlarks Campsite Trust and Youth Sport Trust.

Applications The trust states that it does not request applications and that its funds are fully committed.

The Birmingham Hospital Saturday Fund Medical Charity & Welfare Trust

Medical
£105,000 (2001)

Beneficial area UK, but mostly centred around the Birmingham area.

Gamgee House, 2 Darnley Road, Birmingham B16 8TE

Tel. 0121 454 3601

Correspondent Kate Bradshaw, Appeals Administrator

Trustees *Dr R P Kanas; S G Hall; E S Hickman; M Malone; D J Read; J Salmons.*

CC Number 502428

Information available Full accounts and guidelines were provided by the trust.

General The objects of this trust are the advancement and promotion of medical science and medical research, as well as the relief of sickness.

In 2001 the trust had assets of £928,000. Total income was £914,000, of which £875,000 came from convalescence centre accommodation charges. A total of £867,000 was then spent on running costs for the convalescence centre. Grants were made to 45 hospitals and medical charities totalling £105,000.

The largest grants were: £5,100 to West Midlands NHS Trust for three travel scholarships for nurses; £5,000 each to Age Concern for a minibus and Foundation for Nursing Studies – London for the Patient Involvement in Care awards scheme for nurses; £4,700 to Friends of Stourbridge Education Centre for computer equipment; £4,500 to City of Birmingham Special Olympics for 2001 Midlands Regional Games; £4,300 each to Abbeyfield Stafford Society for air conditioning for a new conservatory and Institute of Ageing and Health for the Excellent Care Award and desk top publishing equipment; and £4,000 to The Extra Care Charitable Trust for equipment for a dementia project.

Other beneficiaries in the West Midlands included: Birmingham Medical Institute for the 2001 and 2002 Gamgee Lectures and library books (£3,600); Institute of Occupational Health at Birmingham University for a MSc scholarship for student nurses (£2,800); British Dyslexics – Cheshire for information packs for parents and schools in the Birmingham area (£2,500); St John Ambulance for equipment for the refurbished training centre at the Birmingham headquarters (£2,300); Birmingham Rathbone for equipment for two residential homes (£2,000); Birmingham Disability Resource Centre for travelling expenses for a blind volunteer counsellor (£1,600); KIDS West Midlands for a family support creche for children with special needs or disabilities (£1,500); Dodford Children's Farm for special equipment (£600); and Brain and Spinal Injury Charity for telephone running costs for the Birmingham branch (£200).

Grants given elsewhere in the UK included those to The Aidis Trust – Dorset for a specialist laptop computer for library for people with disabilities (£3,700); NHS Executive South West for two travel scholarships for nurses (£3,400); Cheltenham Old People's Housing Society Ltd for a specialist wheelchair (£2,600); Moorlands Charitable Trust for equipment for a hydrotherapy pool (£1,500); Mercia MS Therapy Centre for two physiotherapy couches (£1,300); Tiny Tim Centre for ice therapy machines (£760); Bourneville Day Centre – Weston-super-mare for hall hire for exercise classes for older people (£580); and British Retinitis Pigmentosa Society for a finger-speller interpreter project (£320).

Exclusions The trust will not generally fund: administration expenditure including salaries; bank loans/deficits/mortgages; items or services which should normally be publicly funded; large general appeals; vehicle operating costs; or motor vehicles for infrequent use and where subsidised vehicle share schemes are available to charitable organisations.

Applications On a form available from the correspondent. The form requires basic information and should be submitted with financial details. Evidence should be provided that the project has been adequately considered through the provision of quotes or supporting documents, although the trust dislikes applications which provide too much general information or have long-winded descriptions of projects.

The Bisgood Charitable Trust (registered as The Miss Jeanne Bisgood's Charitable Trust)

Roman Catholic purposes, older people

£173,000 (2001/02)

Beneficial area UK, overseas and locally in Bournemouth and Dorset, especially Poole.

12 Waters Edge, Brudenell Road, Poole BH13 7NN

Tel. 01202 708460

Correspondent Miss J M Bisgood, Trustee

Trustees *Miss J M Bisgood; P Schulte; P J K Bisgood.*

CC Number 208714

Information available The information for this entry was provided by the trust. Full accounts were on file at the Charity Commission.

General This trust has emerged following a recent amalgamation of The Bisgood Trust with The Miss Jeanne Bisgood's Charitable Trust. Both trusts had the same objects. It now operates a sub-fund, The Bertram Fund (see below).

The General Fund has the following priorities:

1. Roman Catholic charities
2. Charities benefiting people in Poole, Bournemouth and the county of Dorset
3. National charities for the benefit of older people.

No grants are made to local charities which do not fall under categories 1 or 2. Many health and welfare charities are supported as well as charities working in relief and development overseas.

The trust was given 12 paintings to be held as part of the trust funds. Most of the paintings were sold and the proceeds were placed in a new fund, The Bertram Fund, established in 1998, the income of which is purely for Roman Catholic causes. It is intended that it will primarily support major capital projects.

In 2001/02 the trust had total assets of £4.9 million and an income of £172,000. Grants totalled £173,000.

The largest grants made from the general fund were: £2,000 each to Intermediate Technology, Impact, Medical Foundation for the Victims of Torture, the Passage, Sight Savers International and the De Paul Trust; and £1,500 each to St Francis Leprosy Guild, Intercare, Shaftesbury Society – Poole and St Barnabas Society.

Most of The Bertram Fund grants are made anonymously.

Exclusions Grants are not given to local charities not fitting categories 1 or 2, see above. Individuals and non-registered charities are not supported.

Applications In writing to the correspondent, quoting the UK registration number and registered title of the charity. A copy of the most recent accounts should also be enclosed. Applications should NOT be made directly to the Bertram Fund. Applications for capital projects 'should provide brief details of the main purposes, the total target and the current state of the appeal'. The trustees regret that they are unable to acknowledge appeals. The trustees normally meet in late February/early March and September.

The Bertie Black Foundation

Jewish, general

£77,000 (2000/01)

Beneficial area UK, Israel.

Abbots House, 198 Lower High Street, Watford WD17 2FG

Correspondent Mrs I R Broido, Trustee

Trustees *I B Black; Mrs D Black; H S Black; Mrs I R Broido.*

CC Number 245207

Information available Full accounts were on file at the Charity Commission.

General The trust tends to support organisations which are known to the trustees or where long-term commitments have been entered into. Grants can be given over a three-year period towards major projects.

In 2000/01 the trust had assets of £2.6 million and an income of £140,000. Grants totalled £77,000. The major beneficiary was Magen David Adom – UK which received two grants totalling £25,000. Others included: Child Resettlement Fund (two grants totalling £6,000); Bournemouth Jewish Day School, Community Security Trust,

Lanaido Hospital and Norwood (£5,000 each); Friends of Lubavitch UK and Jewish National Fund (£2,000 each); and Bournemouth Hebrew Congregation and Jewish Music Institute (£1,000 each).

Applications In writing to the correspondent, but please note, the trust states it 'supports causes known to the trustees'.

The Blair Foundation

General

£120,000 (2000/01)

Beneficial area UK and overseas.

Smith & Williamson, 1 Bishops Wharf, Walnut Tree Close, Guildford, Surrey GU1 4RA

Tel. 01483 407100 **Fax** 01483 407194

Correspondent Graham Healy, Trustee

Trustees *Robert Thornton; Jennifer Thornton; Graham Healy; Alan Thornton; Philippa Thornton.*

CC Number 801755

Information available Full accounts were provided by the trust, with a detailed narrative report

General This foundation was originally established to create environmental conditions in which wildlife can prosper, as well as improving disability access to such areas. However, it has since widened its scope and aims to provide at least £100,000 to other charities in addition to its wildlife work.

In 2000/01 the foundation had assets of £1.4 million and an income of £206,000, including £98,000 in donations received. Total expenditure was £166,000, including £39,000 in other direct expenditure and £6,400 in management and administration. Grants totalled £120,000, including 30 grants of £1,000 or more totalling £118,000.

The 2000/01 annual report contained a detailed narrative report which mentioned that the trustees had advanced with a 200-acre development near another site in Culzean. It also mentioned that the trust had done much work in Kent, clearing dead wood and brambles to enable new trees to become established as well as clearing paths to enable visitors to enjoy the wildlife.

The largest grant during the year was £51,000 to Ayrshire Wildlife Services, which received £79,000 in the previous

year. (There was no explanation of how this grant was to be used in the narrative report.)

Queen Elizabeth Foundation for the Disabled is a regular beneficiary of large grants from the foundation, receiving £17,000 during the year to improve wheelchair access to outdoor areas.

Other larger grants were £5,000 each to Dailly Amateur Football Club and Surrey Community Development Trust, £4,000 to Sense, £2,500 each to Help the Aged and National Trust for Scotland for Culzean Castle, £2,000 to Ayrshire Fiddler Orchestra, Manx Wildlife Trust, Royal Navy Museum and Wells Cathedral School. Grants of £1,000 each included those to Erskin 2000, Guide Posts Trust, RSPB, RYA Sailability, Wildlife Conservation Research Unit and The Wildlife Trusts.

Exclusions Charities that have objectives the trustees consider harmful to the environment are not supported.

Applications In writing to the correspondent, for consideration at trustees' meetings held twice a year. A receipt for donations is requested from all donees. The correspondent stated: 'I have been inundated with appeals for help, which far exceed the resources available … the costs of administration are now becoming disproportionate to the funds available.'

Blatchington Court Trust

Education of people under 31 who are blind and partially sighted

£1.1 million (1998/99)

Beneficial area UK, preference for Sussex.

Ridgeland House, 165 Dyke Road, Hove, East Sussex BN3 1TL

Tel. 01273 727222 **Fax** 01273 722244

Email enquiries@blatchington-court.co.uk

Website www.blatchington-court.co.uk

Correspondent Dr Geoff Lockwood, Chair

Trustees *Dr Geoffrey Lockwood, Chair; Roger Jones; Dr Geoffrey Lockwood; Richard Martin; Lady Helen Trafford; Bruce McCleod; Colin Finnerty; Ms Georgina James.*

CC Number 306350

Information available Full accounts were on file at the Charity Commission.

General This trust's initial income arose from the sale of the former Blatchington Court School for people who are partially sighted at Seaford. Its aim is the 'the promotion of education and employment (including social and physical training) of blind and partially sighted persons under the age of 31 years'. There is a preference for Sussex.

In fulfilling its objects, the trust's aims are to:

- develop as a distinct trust with a primary role of an independent facilitator
- focus its resources on clearly defined needs and to avoid any duplication of provision
- listen to, and further the interests of, people who are visually impaired relevant to its objects
- initiate and develop working partnerships with statutory and voluntary organisations concerned with the care of the young people who are visually impaired
- provide professional specialist service to people up to 31 years who are visually impaired
- make grants in pursuance of its objectives.

In 1998/99 the trust has assets of £11.5 million and an income mainly from investments of £494,000. Grants were exceptionally high totalling £1.1 million (in 1997/98 grants totalled £308,000), in addition, expenditure on counselling was about £225,000. The two largest grants went to SeeABILITY for different projects: £525,000 towards the residential unit and day centre for visually impaired children and young adults at Barclay House (the trust, which owns the building, has leased it to the organisation for 99 years); and £300,000 towards the construction of a centre for children with Battnes Disease in Hampshire.

Other grants included £40,000 to Dorton House School Distance Learning Project, £17,000 to LOOK for the provision of advocacy services and the costs of producing a newsletter, £6,200 to Eastnet Project, £6,000 to Scope and £5,500 to West Sussex Association for the Blind. Smaller grants included those to Berkshire County Blind Association, Bibles for Children, Brighton Society for the Blind, Peter Pan Nursery at Selby and Understanding Industry. Grants to individuals of £1,000 or under totalled £148,000.

Applications In writing to the correspondent from whom individual or corporate/charity grant application forms can be obtained. Applications can be considered at any time. An application on behalf of a registered charity should include audited accounts and up-to-date information on the charity and its commitments.

The Neville & Elaine Blond Charitable Trust

Jewish, education, general

£125,000 (2001/02)

Beneficial area Worldwide.

c/o H W Fisher & Co, Chartered Accountants, Acre House, 11–15 William Road, London NW1 3ER

Tel. 020 7388 7000

Correspondent The Trustees

Trustees *Dame Simone Prendergast; Peter Blond; Mrs A E Susman; S N Susman; Mrs J Skidmore.*

CC Number 206319

Information available Full accounts were on file at the Charity Commission.

General In 2001/02 the trust had assets of £1.4 million and an income of £74,000. Grants totalling £125,000 were made to 13 organisations, 11 of which had been supported in the previous year. The main beneficiary was British WIZO which received £55,000. Other larger grants were £30,000 to JPAIME and £10,000 each to Weizmann Institute Foundation and World Jewish Relief.

The remaining grants were in the range of £1,000 to £7,000 and included those to GRET (£7,000), Halle Orchestra (£4,000) and Jerusalem Foundation (£2,500). Five grants of £1,000 each were made to British ORT, Chicken Shed Theatre, Fulcrum Challenge, Institute of Child Health, Jewish Lads and Girls Brigade and Westminster Children's Society.

Exclusions Only registered charities are supported.

Applications In writing to the correspondent. Applications should arrive by 31 January for consideration in late spring.

The Bluston Charitable Settlement

Jewish, general

£151,000 (1999/2000)

Beneficial area Mostly UK.

BDO Stoy Hayward, 8 Baker Street, London W1U 3LL

Tel. 020 7486 5888

Correspondent The Trustees

Trustees *Edward Langton; M D Paisner.*

CC Number 256691

Information available Full accounts were on file at the Charity Commission.

General The trust has general charitable purposes, although in practice most grants are given to Jewish organisations.

The trust had assets of £225,000 in 2000/01, which included 505,000 ordinary shares in Bluston Securities Ltd. The income for the year was £126,000 and three grants were made totalling £151,000. Beneficiaries were Jewish Free School (£100,000), Variety Club Children's Charity (£50,000) and British Friends of the Ohel Sarah (£1,000).

Exclusions No grants to individuals.

Applications In writing to the correspondent. The trustees meet annually in March.

The Charlotte Bonham-Carter Charitable Trust

General

£95,000 (2000/01)

Beneficial area UK, with some emphasis on Hampshire.

66 Lincoln's Inn Fields, London WC2A 3LH

Tel. 020 7917 7331 **Fax** 020 7831 6301

Correspondent Sir Matthew Farrer, Trustee

Trustees *Sir Matthew Farrer; Norman Bonham-Carter; Nicolas Wickham-Irving.*

CC Number 292839

Information available Full accounts were provided by the trust.

General The trust is principally concerned to support charitable bodies and purposes which were of particular concern to Lady Bonham-Carter during her lifetime or are within the county of Hampshire.

In 2000/01 the trust had assets of £3.6 million and an income of £100,000. It gave £96,000 in 72 grants, ranging from £100 to £15,000. The largest went to National Trust (£15,000), Canine Partners for Independence, Fitzwilliam Museum and Tate Gallery (£5,000 each). Other recipients included Ashmolean Museum (£3,000), British Museum and International Merv Project (£2,500 each), Ballet Rambert, Romsey Hospital Appeal and Sports Trust's Refit 2001 Appeal (£2,000 each) and Milestone Museum and Gilbert White Museum (£1,500 each).

Grants of £1,000 or less included those to Brighton Festival Society, Foundling Museum, Friends of the County Youth Orchestra, Hampshire Archives Trust, Holy Island Project, Meningitis Research Association, Royal Academy of Arts, SCOPE, Sustrans, Thornley Hill Community, Winchester Carers Project and Youth Clubs of Hampshire and Isle of Wight.

Of the grants made, 13 were recurrent from the previous year.

Exclusions No grants to individuals or non-registered charities.

Applications In writing to the correspondent, although the trust states that 'unsolicited general applications are unlikely to be successful and only increase the cost of administration'. There are no application forms. Trustees meet in January and July; applications need to be received by May or November.

Charles Boot Trust

General

£89,000 (2000/01)

Beneficial area UK, with a preference for Oxfordshire.

Meadow Cottage, Church Street, Beckley, Oxford OX3 9UT

Correspondent Miss E J Reis, Trustee

Trustees *John S Reis; Simon C Hogg; Miss Elizabeth J Reis.*

CC Number 802050

Information available Basic accounts were provided by the trust.

General The trust supports large UK charities, many of which are regular beneficiaries. It would prefer to give new grants to locally-based organisations in Oxfordshire.

In 2000/01 the trust's income was £97,000 including £61,000 from investments, all of which are held in Henry Boot & Sons Plc, and £15,000 from Gift Aid donations. Grants were made totalling £89,000.

Beneficiaries were Age Concern, Brainwave, Coventry Cathedral to benefit local disadvantaged people, Extracare, IMPS, Mental Health Foundation, NSPCC, Prison Phoenix Trust, RNID, Save The Children, Sense, Shelter, Sight Savers International, Smart and Trax to combat car-crime by re-educating offenders.

Exclusions No grants to individuals.

Applications In writing to the correspondent. The trust states that it does not consider unsolicited applications.

Salo Bordon Charitable Trust

Jewish, some health-related

£163,000 (2000/01)
Beneficial area Worldwide.

78 Corringham Road, London NW11 7EB
Tel. 020 8458 5842
Correspondent S Bordon, Trustee
Trustees *S Bordon; Mrs L Bordon; M Bordon; D Bordon; M Bordon.*
CC Number 266439
Information available Full accounts were on file at the Charity Commission.

General This trust makes grants mainly to Jewish organisations, for social welfare and religious education. In 2000/01 it had assets amounting to £6.7 million and an income of £219,000. Grants were made totalling £163,000.

Grants of over £1,000 each were listed in the accounts. The largest were £8,500 each to Agudas Israel Housing Association Ltd and MIR Charitable Trust, £5,300 to Gateshead Foundation for Torah and £5,000 each to Gateshead Jewish Primary

School, North West London Communal Mikvah and Shaarei Torah Buildings Ltd. Other listed beneficiaries included Golders Green Beth Hamedrash Congregation (£4,900), Institute for Higher Rabbinical Studies (£4,300), Parsha Ltd (£4,400), Yad Eliezer (£3,000), Talmudic Research Centre (£2,000) and AB Foundation (£1,000).

Applications In writing to the correspondent.

The A Bornstein Charitable Settlement

Jewish

£186,000 (2000/01)
Beneficial area UK and Israel.

HLB AV Audit plc, 66 Wigmore Street, London W1H 2HQ
Tel. 020 7467 4000 **Fax** 020 7467 4040
Correspondent Peter Musgrave
Trustees *N P Bornstein; M Hollander.*
CC Number 262472
Information available Accounts were on file at the Charity Commission.

General In 2000/01 the trust had assets of £780,000 and an income of £244,000. Grants were given to nine beneficiaries totalling £186,000.

The largest grant was given to Shaare Zedek Hospital in Israel, which received £115,000. Other beneficiaries were British Olim Society Charitable Trust (£23,000), UJA Federation (£15,000), Friends of Care of the Needy of Jerusalem (£12,500), Friends of Yad Sarah (£7,500), National Foundation for Jewish Culture (£5,000), Chabad House (£2,000) and Chai Lifeline Cancer Care (£500). Six of these beneficiaries were supported in the previous year.

Exclusions No grants for non-Jewish organisations.

Applications In writing to the correspondent.

The Harry Bottom Charitable Trust

Religion, education, medical

£137,000 (2000/01)
Beneficial area UK, with a preference for Yorkshire and Derbyshire.

Westons, Queen's Buildings, 55 Queen Street, Sheffield S1 2DX
Tel. 0114 273 8341 **Fax** 0114 272 5116
Correspondent D R Proctor
Trustees *J G Potter; J M Kilner; H F Woods.*
CC Number 204675
Information available Accounts were on file at the Charity Commission.

General The trust states that support is divided roughly equally between religion, education and medical causes. Within these categories grants are given to:

- religion – small local appeals and cathedral appeals
- education – universities and schools
- medical – equipment for hospitals and charities concerned with disability.

In 2000/01 the trust had assets of £3.5 million. It had an income of £167,000, of which £75,000 came from investments and £90,000 from rent. After administration costs of £36,000 and property expenditure of £24,000 grants totalled £137,000 and were broken down as follows:

Medical
21 grants ranging from £100 to £25,000 totalled £61,000
Beneficiaries included Sheffield Kidney Research (£10,000), University of Sheffield Children's Hospital (£7,500), University of Sheffield School of Medicine (£5,500), Wishbone Trust (£5,000), St Luke's Hospice (£4,500), Arthritis Care (£1,000), Mind (£500) and Sheffield Women's Aid (£250).

Religious
5 grants ranging from £100 to £25,000 totalled £32,000
Beneficiaries included South Yorkshire Baptist Association (£25,000), Cemetery Road Baptist Church (£5,000), St Mary's 2000 (£1,000), Industrial Mission of South Yorkshire (£500) and St Helen's Church – Treeton (£100).

Education and other

34 grants ranging from £300 to £4,500 totalled £44,000
Beneficiaries included RNLI (£4,500), Cherry Tree Children's Home and Innovations Project (£3,000 each), Whirlow Hall Farm (£1,500), Yorkshire Residential School for the Deaf and YMCA (£1,000 each), Share Psychotherapy (£750), Disability Aid Fund and Trinity Day Care Trust (£500 each) and St Chad's Church Holiday Fund (£300).

Exclusions No grants to individuals.

Applications In writing to the correspondent.

The A H & E Boulton Trust

Evangelical Christian

£138,000 (2000/01)
Beneficial area Worldwide.

Moore Stephens, 47–49 North John Street, Liverpool L2 6TG
Tel. 0151 236 9044
Correspondent J Glasby
Trustees Mrs J R Gopsill; F P Gopsill.
CC Number 225328
Information available Accounts were on file at the Charity Commission.

General The trust mainly supports the erection and maintenance of buildings to be used for preaching the Christian gospel, and teaching its doctrines. The trustees can also support other Christian institutions, especially missions in the UK and developing world.

In 2000/01 the trust had assets of £3.1 million and an income of £166,000. Grants totalled £138,000.

The largest beneficiaries were Echoes of Service (£45,000), Liverpool City Mission (£30,000), Bridge Street Chapel and Charles Thompson Mission (£20,000). Other beneficiaries included Salvation Army (£4,000), Open Air Mission, Leprosy Mission and Home Evangelism (£3,000 each) and Gideons International (£2,000).

A number of smaller grants were also made totalling £8,200.

Applications In writing to the correspondent. The trust tends to support a set list of charities and applications are very unlikely to be successful.

The P G & N J Boulton Trust

Christian

£166,000 (2000/01)
Beneficial area Worldwide.

28 Burden Road, Moreton, Wirral, Merseyside CH46 6BQ
Email email@boultontrust.org.uk
Website www.boultontrust.org.uk
Correspondent Miss N J Boulton, Trustee
Trustees *Miss N J Boulton, Chair; Miss L M Butchart; A L Perry; Mrs S Perry.*
CC Number 272525
Information available Accounts were on file at the Charity Commission.

General The trust gives a substantial proportion of its support to Christian missionary work. It also supports the areas of poverty relief, medical research, healthcare and disability. Preference is given to smaller charities where 'a relatively small gift can make a significant difference'.

In 2000/01 the trust had assets of £1.6 million and an income of £98,000. Grants were given to 71 beneficiaries totalling £166,000. The largest grant of £65,000 was given to Shalom Christian Fellowship. Other grants were broken down as follows:

Christian missionary work	39%
Specialised Christian ministries	24%
Combined Christian missionary/ relief work	16%
Poverty/disaster relief (overseas)	7%
Disability relief and care of elderly	5%
Medical research and healthcare	4%
Poverty relief (UK)	2%
Other	3%

Grants of £1,000 or more were given to Elim Pentecostal Mission Fund and Intercessors for Britain (£16,000 each), British Red Cross (£6,500), Just Care (£4,900), Mission Aviation Fellowship (£3,000), Open Doors (£2,900), Elam Ministries (£2,500), Ebenezer Aid Fund and Operation Mobilisation (£2,400 each), Christian Friends of Israel (£1,800), International Gospel Outreach and Southeast Asian Outreach (£1,600 each), Samaritan's Purse International (£1,500), Life for the World Trust, Messianic Testimony and Prayer for Israel (£1,400 each) and Teen Challenge (£1,000).

Smaller grants to other beneficiaries totalled £32,000.

Exclusions No grants to individuals, environment/conservation, heritage or animal welfare.

Applications In writing to the correspondent. Owing to the number of applications received the trustees cannot acknowledge all of them. Successful applicants will be contacted within two months.

The Bowerman Charitable Trust

General

£263,000 to organisations (2000/01)
Beneficial area UK, with a preference for West Sussex.

Champs Hill, Coldwatham, Pulborough, West Sussex RH20 1LY
Tel. 01798 831205
Correspondent D W Bowerman, Trustee
Trustees *D W Bowerman; Mrs C M Bowerman; Mrs J M Taylor; Miss K E Bowerman; Mrs A M Downham; J M Capper.*
CC Number 289446
Information available Accounts were on file at the Charity Commission, but without a written report.

General The trust makes grants towards:

- church activities
- the arts, particularly music
- medical charities
- youth work
- charities concerned with relief of poverty and the resettlement of offenders.

In 1999/2000 the trust had assets of £10.1 million and an income of £124,000. Grants were made totalling £263,000.

The accounts listed the largest 22 grants, of over £1,000 each. The largest was £78,000 to Elgar Foundation. Other larger grants included those to English Chamber Orchestra and Music Society (£49,000), University of St Andrews (£25,000), St Margaret's Trust (£21,000), Chichester Cathedral Trust (£17,000), British Youth Opera (£12,000) and London Handel Society (£10,000).

Smaller grants included those to Royal College of Music (£6,000), Titus Trust (£5,000), Arundel Festival (£3,500) and Petworth Cottage Hospital (£1,000).

Applications In writing to the correspondent. The trustees said that they are bombarded with applications and unsolicited applications will not be considered.

The Bowland Charitable Trust

Young people, education, general

£148,000 (1999)

Beneficial area UK, with a preference for north west England.

TDS House, Whitebirk Estate, Blackburn, Lancashire BB1 5TH

Tel. 01254 676921 **Fax** 01254 676950

Correspondent Mrs Carol Fahy

Trustees *H A Cann; R A Cann; D Walmsley.*

CC Number 292027

Information available Full accounts were on file at the Charity Commission.

General The trust has general charitable purposes but focuses its support on the 'promotion of educational character-forming activities for young people'. It has stated that its grants are 'almost entirely' given in north west England.

In 2001 this trust had an income of £56,000 and a total expenditure of £119,000. This information was taken from the Charity Commission database, unfortunately no further details were available for this year. In 1999 the trust had an income of £93,000 and gave grants totalling £148,000. The largest was £91,000 to Lancaster University. Other beneficiaries included Brantwood (£27,000), Unitarian Millennium Appeal (£10,000), Nazareth Unitarian Chapel (£9,700), Christie's Hospital (£2,500) and Blackburn Cathedral and Ribblesdale Scouts (£1,300). There were also two grants to individuals totalling £1,500.

Applications In writing to the correspondent, to be considered at any time.

Bramble Charitable Trust

General

£312,000 (2001/02)

Beneficial area UK, with a preference for south west England.

Bramble Cottage, Dinghurst Road, Churchill, Winscombe BS25 5PJ

Tel. 01934 852589

Correspondent Caroline Smallwood, Trustee

Trustees *Caroline Smallwood; Glenys Parkinson; Graeme Varley.*

CC Number 1028751

Information available Accounts were provided by the trust, but without a narrative report.

General The main area of support is organisations working with young people who are disadvantaged. The trust usually supports work which benefits people in the Bristol/Weston-super-Mare area, although this includes national organisations for work in the region. In previous years the trust has made a couple of substantial grants and a few smaller donations, but its general policy is to make grants of between £250 and £5,000.

In 2001/02 the trust gave 10 grants totalling £312,000. This included two substantial grants, £250,000 to North Somerset Council for Churchill Primary School and £51,000 to Knightstone Housing for a foyer.

Other grants were £4,000 to Greater Bristol Foundation for summer activities, £2,000 to Winged Fellowship Trust, £1,000 each to Bristol Children's Help Society, NCH Action for Children and Windmill City Farm and £500 each to Network Counselling, Salvation Army and Wheels Project.

In the previous year the trust had assets of £208,000 and an income of £423,000, including £409,000 from donations received. Grants totalling £428,000 were made to 17 organisations, including two substantial grants. The list of smaller grants was very similar to that for 2001/02.

Applications In writing to the correspondent.

The British Council for Prevention of Blindness

Prevention and treatment of blindness

£302,000 (2000/01)

Beneficial area Worldwide.

296 Montague Street, London WC1B 5BH

Tel. 020 7631 5100

Correspondent Stephen Silverton

Trustees *Prof. Andrew Elkington; Rolf Blach; William Weisblatt; Mark Thompson; Prof. Alistair Fielder; Lady Wilson; Richard Porter; Jackie Boulter; Raymond Hazan.*

CC Number 270941

Information available Full accounts were on file at the Charity Commission.

General The BCPB's mission statement is 'to help prevent blindness and restore sight in the UK and developing world by:

- funding research in UK hospitals and universities into the causes and treatments of the major eye diseases
- supporting practical treatment programmes and research in the developing world
- promoting vital skills, leadership, awareness and demand for the expansion of community eye health in the developing world through the education of doctors and nurses within communities.'

The trust's policy is to divide its support equally between projects in the UK and abroad. Grants are given to hospitals, universities and health centres both in the UK and in developing countries. Grants are also given to individuals through the Boulter Fellowship Awards, see below. Grants are usually for a maximum of £40,000 and given for a maximum of three years.

In 2000/01 the trust had assets of £226,000. It had an income of £415,000, from donations (including Gift Aid), legacies and a Community Fund grant of £126,000. Grants totalled £302,000 to 10 organisations, including two Community Fund funded projects.

The beneficiary of the largest grant was International Centre for Eye Health. This organisation recieved £97,000 funded by the Community Fund. Four grants were made to International Centre for Eye Health for work related to: rapid diagnosis of corneal ulcers (£45,000); rapid pregnancy and childbirth risk factors for cateracts in women (£34,000); factors influencing the outcome of surgery for childhood cateracts in developing countries (£29,000); and evaluation of costs of tele-ophthalmology in South Africa (£15,000).

Other beneficiaries included: Queens University – Belfast (£29,000 funded by the Community Fund); University of Liverpool (£29,000); and British Ophthalmology Surveillance Unit (two grants of £5,000).

£15,000 was given to the Boulter Fellowship Awards to enable individuals from developing countries to study community eye health.

Exclusions All except projects directly concerned with research into blindness prevention or restoration of sight. 'We do NOT deal with the individual welfare of blind people in the UK.'

Applications Application forms are available from the correspondent. An initial proforma must be completed prior to submission of the formal application and must be received no later than the first Monday in June. The deadline for completed applications is the last Friday in July.

All projects are subject to a review process and a shortlist made at a meeting in October. All successful grants are awarded in February, unless otherwise stated.

British Record Industry Trust

Musical education
£762,000 (1999)
Beneficial area UK.

BPI, Riverside Building, County Hall, Westminister Bridge Road, London SE1 7JA
Tel. 020 7803 1300
Website www.brittrust.co.uk
Correspondent Maggie Crowe
Trustees *S Alder; P Burger; J Craig; R Perry; R Dickins; Andrew Yeates.*
CC Number 1000413
Information available Information was provided by the trust.

General The trust was established in 1989 and is entirely funded by contributions from the music industry and related organisations in the UK. Its mission is 'to encourage young people in the exploration and pursuit of educational, cultural or therapeutic benefits emanating from music'.

In 2000 grants were given to BRIT School for Performing Arts, British Medicine Performing Arts Trust, Chicken Shed, Drugscope, Heart 'n' Soul, Music in Prisons, Nordoff Robbins Music Therapy Centre and The Princes Trust. Further information was not yet available.

In 1999 the trust had assets of £2 million. Income totalled £1.1 million made up of: Gift Aid donations of £850,000 from BRIT Awards Limited, including £200,000 from their Abbamania project; other donations from music organisations totalling £193,000; and an interest and investment income of £45,000. Administration and management fees were very low at £22,000. Grants totalling £762,000 were given to seven organisations, four of which were supported in the previous year. Grants were given as follows (1998 figures in brackets where applicable):

Brit School for the Performing Arts and Technology £260,000 (£120,000) Nordoff Robbins £260,000 (£80,000) National Foundation of Youth Music £200,000 Institute for the Study of Drug Dependency £25,000 (£25,000) Heart 'n' Soul £7,200 Avenues Youth Project £5,000 (£2,000) Fairbridge in Kent £5,000

Several of the trustees are directors of organisations which donated large sums to the trust; several were also directors or organisations which received large grants.

Exclusions No bursaries or grants to individual. No capital funding projects are considered. Only registered charities are supported.

Applications By application form. Applications which match the trust's mission statement are welcomed.

The Britten-Pears Foundation

Promotion of the work of Benjamin Britten and Peter Pears, the arts, particularly music by living composers, education, the environment and humanitarian causes
£263,000 to organisations
(2000/01)
Beneficial area UK, with a preference for East Anglia.

The Red House, Golf Lane, Aldeburgh, Suffolk IP15 5PZ
Tel. 01728 452615
Email e.gibson@btinternet.com
Correspondent Dr E Gibson
Trustees *Lord Justice Carnwath, Chair; Dr Colin Matthews; Noel Periton; Hugh Cobbe; Peter Carter; Michael Berkeley; Mark Fisher; Stephen Oliver; Janice Susskind; John Evans.*
CC Number 295595
Information available Accounts were provided by the foundation.

General The foundation was set up 'to promote public knowledge and appreciation of the musical works and writings of Benjamin Britten and Peter Pears and the tradition and principles of musical education and performance developed by them.' It aims to promote the arts in general, particularly music, by way of grants to other charities or those whose objects are of charitable intent, for commissions, live performances and, occasionally, recordings and innovatory musical education projects. It also makes grants to educational, environmental and peace organisations. Grants normally range from £100 to £2,500.

The foundation owns and finances the Britten-Pears Library at Aldeburgh, and supports the Britten-Pears School for Musical Studies at Snape and the annual Aldeburgh Festivals in June and the autumn. Its annual income largely derives from the royalties from the performance worldwide of the works of Benjamin Britten, and is channelled to the foundation through its trading subsidiary, the Britten Estate Ltd, by deed of covenant.

In 2000/01 the foundation had assets of £12.5 million and an income of £520,000 (£388,000 being the net income from the trading subsidiary). Management and administration costs amounted to £100,000. In total, 26 organisations were supported during the year. Direct charitable expenditure totalled £446,000 (down from £768,000 in 1999/2000), broken down as follows:

Grants	£263,000
Britten-Pears Library	£139,000
Red House Complex	£45,000

Grants included £145,000 in total to Aldeburgh Productions (£94,000 for B P School Subvention, £40,000 for Contemporary Music Festival and £11,000 for a musical advisor), and £30,000 to English National Opera. Jubilee Hall received a grant of £22,000 for further redevelopment of the building as part of an ongoing funding programme.

Other beneficiaries included Welsh National Opera, Aldeburgh Cinema, and SPNM (£5,000 each), London Sinfonietta and Richardson Institute (£3,000 each), Nancy Evans Bursary, John Cross Bursary, Britten/Keller Concerts, Lennox Berkeley Society, Scottish Opera and Aldeburgh County Primary School (£2,000 each). Recipients of £1,000 each included Musicians Benevolent Fund, Bath Festivals Trust, Cheltenham Arts Festival, Darlington International Summer Festival, The Gogmagogs and RCNM.

The trust also paid £19,000 in total in grants of less than £1,000.

Exclusions No grants for: general charitable projects; general support for festivals other than Aldeburgh; requests from individuals for bursaries and course grants other than for Britten-Pears School; travel costs; or purchase or restoration of musical instruments or equipment, and of buildings other than at Snape Maltings/Aldeburgh.

The foundation does not consider applications for support for performances or recordings of the works of Benjamin Britten, of whose estate it is the beneficiary. Subsidy for works by Britten which, in the estate's view, need further promotion, can be sought from The Britten Estate Ltd, which is a subsidiary trading company.

Applications In writing to the correspondent. Trustees meet in January, May and October. Applications should be sent for consideration by the middle of the preceding month. Five copies of any application should be sent. Applications should be addressed to Dr Elizabeth Gibson (Tel: 01728 451709; e-mail: e.gibson@britten-pears.co.uk).

The Broadfield Trust

Education
About £200,000
Beneficial area UK.

c/o Baker Tilly, Elgar House, Holmer Road, Hereford HR4 9SF

Tel. 01432 352222

Correspondent Ann Sheldon, Accountant

Trustees *Hon. E R H Wills; J R Henderson; Sir Ashley Ponsonby; P N H Gibbs; C A H Wills; P J H Wills.*

CC Number 206623

Information available Full accounts were on file at the Charity Commission but only up to 1994/95.

General In 2000/01 the trust had an income of £229,000 and an expenditure of £238,000. This information was available on the Charity Commission's database but unfortunately the accounts were not yet in the public file.

The main beneficiary of this trust has been the Farmington Trust. In fact in 1994/95 it received £208,000 out of a grant total of £210,000. However, in previous years substantial grants have also been given to other organisations.

In 1993/94 the Farmington Trust received £238,000 with £40,000 given to the Roberts Centre, £7,000 to Balliol College, £3,500 to Our Lady's Convent Senior School and £2,000 to Manchester College.

The assets of the trust stood at £3.9 million in 1994/95.

Exclusions No grants to individuals.

Applications In writing to the correspondent.

The Bromley Trust

Human rights, conservation
£315,000 (2001/02)
Beneficial area Worldwide.

Ashley Manor, King's Somborne, Stockbridge, Hampshire SO20 6RQ

Tel. 01794 388241 **Fax** 01794 388264

Correspondent Keith Bromley, Trustee

Trustees *Keith Bromley; Anna Home; Peter Edwards; Anne Lady Prance; Ann Lady Wood; Anthony Roberts; Michael Ingall; Bryan Blamey.*

CC Number 801875

Information available Full accounts were provided by the trust.

General The aims and objects of the trust are to make grants to charitable organisations which:

'a) combat violations of human rights, and help victims of torture, refugees from oppression and those who have been falsely imprisoned

b) help those who have suffered severe bodily or mental hurt through no fault of their own, and if need be their dependants, try in some small way to offset man's inhumanity to man

c) oppose the extinction of the world's fauna and flora and the destruction of the environment for wildlife and for mankind worldwide.'

The trust's objectives are narrow and it hardly ever departs from them. By far the greater part of the income goes to charities that are concerned with human rights; a comparatively small proportion is given to charities concerned with the preservation of the world environment. In general, conservation interests are limited to the preservation of rainforests and national and international conservation issues, not local projects. One-off grants are occasionally made, but are infrequent. Grants are given to UK-registered charities only.

The trust's declared policy is to give larger amounts to fewer charities rather than spread its income over a large number of small grants. Consequently the trust is slow to add new charities to its list. The trust's mainstream charities normally receive their grants in two half-yearly payments for a period of not less than three years, barring unforeseen circumstances.

The mainstream charities (as at April 2002): Medical Foundation for the Care of Victims of Torture; The Redress Trust; Amnesty International (UK Section) Charitable Trust; Institute of Psychiatry – Istanbul Human Rights Centre; Kurdish Human Rights Project; Anti-Slavery International; Survival International; Prisoners of Conscience Appeal Fund; Ockenden International; Karuna Trust; Womankind Worldwide; Marie Stopes International; Find Your Feet; Asylum Aid; Prisoners Abroad; Prison Reform Trust; Prisoners' Education Trust; The New Bridge; The Hardman Trust; Penrose Housing Association; Inside Out Trust; Koestler Awards Trust; Writers & Scholars Educational Trust; Minority Rights Group; Justice; Childhope; International Childcare Trust; Greenpeace Environmental Trust; Birdlife International; Durrell Wildlife Conservation Trust; Wildfowl & Wetlands Trust; Wildlife Conservation Research Unit; Marine Conservation Society; Tree Aid; Rio Atlantic Forest Trust; Butterfly Conservation; Manic Depression Fellowship; Aldeburgh Productions; Orchard Vale Trust.

The trust predicted its 2002/03 income would be between £300,000 and £35,000 and therefore it would be difficult to support organisations not on its list of regular beneficiaries.

In 2001/02 it had assets of £7.9 million and its income totalled £1.9 million, including £875,000 from donations. Grants totalled £315,000, of which £275,000 was given to the regular beneficiaries above. One-off donations were given to nine organisations: Jubilee Plus (£20,000), Farm Africa, Healing Hands Network, Impact Foundation and Tapol (£3,000 each) and Esther Benjamin's Trust, Black Women's Health and Family Support, Tigre Trust and World Pheasant Association (£2,000 each).

Exclusions Grants are only given to UK-registered charities. No grants to non-registered charities and individuals, or for expeditions or scholarships, or anything outside the stated objectives.

Applications In writing to the correspondent in the form of a short letter setting out objectives and achievements as with a copy of summarised accounts. The trustees meet twice a year in April and October, applications should be received the previous month. Urgent appeals may be dealt with at any time.

The David Brooke Charity

Youth, medical

£77,000 (2000/01)

Beneficial area UK.

Windmill House, 37–39 Station Road, Henley-on-Thames, Oxfordshire RG9 1AT

Correspondent D J Rusman, Trustee

Trustees D Brooke; D J Rusman; P M Hutt; N A Brooke.

CC Number 283658

Information available Accounts were on file at the Charity Commission.

General The trust supports youth causes, favouring disadvantaged young people, particularly through causes providing self-help programmes and outdoor activity training. Grants are also given to medical organisations.

In 2000/01 the trust had assets of £1.9 million generating an income of £85,000. After administration and management costs of £15,000, grants were given to 30 organisations and totalled £77,000.

Grants were given to a variety of UK and local groups concerned with children's welfare, the largest of which was £4,500 to Finchdale Training College. Other grants were in the range of £500 to £4,000 and included those to Barnardos, British Stammering Association, Camphill Village Trust, Children's Society, Fortune Centre of Riding Therapy, Great Ormond St Hospital, Kennet & Avon Canal Trust, NSPCC, RNIB, RNLI, Salvation Army, Unicef and Who Cares Trust.

Applications The correspondent stated that the trust's annual income is not for general distribution as it is committed to a limited number of charities on a long-term basis.

The Roger Brooke Charitable Trust

General

£206,000 (2000/01)

Beneficial area UK, with a preference for Hampshire.

Withers, 16 Old Bailey, London EC4M 7EY

Correspondent J P Arnold, Trustee

Trustees J P Arnold; C R E Brooke; N B Brooke; J R Rousso; S H R Brooke.

CC Number 1071250

Information available Accounts were on file at the Charity Commission.

General Established in 1998, this trust has general charitable purposes, including medical research, support for carers and social action.

in 2000/01 this trust had assets of £1 million and an income of £35,000. Grants were made totalling £206,000. Unfortunately there were no further details on the size or number of beneficiaries.

Exclusions In general, individuals are not supported.

Applications In writing to the correspondent. Applications will only be acknowledged if successful.

The Palgrave Brown Foundation

Education, medical

£361,000 (2000/01)

Beneficial area UK, with a preference for the south of England.

c/o PB Forestry Lands Ltd, 24 Bedford Row, London WC1R 4EH

Tel. 020 7831 6393

Correspondent D Dooley, Trustees' Correspondent

Trustees A P Brown; I P Brown.

CC Number 267848

Information available Accounts were on file at the Charity Commission, with a brief narrative report.

General Grants are given primarily to educational and medical organisations.

In 2000/01 the trust had assets of £3.4 million which generated an income of £1.7 million. Grants totalled £361,000. After management and administration costs of £3,300 and an income tax liability of £70,000, the total expenditure was £434,000.

The largest grant was £200,000 to Shrewsbury School Foundation, which has often been supported in previous years. Other large grants were £50,000 to The Fettes Foundation and £10,000 each to Macmillan Cancer Relief, Prostate Cancer Charity and Tapping House Hospice.

A total of 24 grants of £1,000 or more were listed in the accounts. These included £5,000 each to British Limbless Ex-Servicemen's Association, Marie Curie Cancer Care, Greensleeves House Trust, and Norfolk Heart Trust. Smaller grants totalled £105.

Exclusions No grants to individuals.

Applications Unsolicited applications are not supported.

Bill Brown's Charitable Settlement

Health, social welfare

£84,000 (2000/01)
Beneficial area UK.

Payne Hicks Beach, 10 New Square, Lincoln's Inn, London WC2A 3QG
Tel. 020 7465 4300
Correspondent G S Brown, Trustee
Trustees *P W E Brown; G S Brown; A J Barnett.*
CC Number 801756
Information available Full accounts were on file at the Charity Commission.

General This settlement support health and welfare causes, including those for older people.

In 2000/01 the trust had assets of £1.2 million generating an income of £71,000. Grants totalling £84,000 were made to 18 organisations, a number of which were recurrent. Administration and management costs totalled £11,000.

There were three grants of £10,000 each given to Macmillan Cancer Relief, Leonard Cheshire Foundation and Salvation Army.

Beneficiaries of other grants included Imperial Cancer Research Fund (£7,500), Alzheimer's Disease Society (£6,000), National Association for Colitis and Crohn Disease and Princess Alice Hospice (£5,000 each), John Chilton Charitable Trust (£4,000), Lindon Lodge Charitable Trust (£3,000), Barnardos and Twickenham & District Mental Health Association (£2,000 each) and DEBRA and Make-a-Wish Foundation UK (£1,000 each).

Applications In writing to the correspondent, including as much detail as possible. Applications are considered every six months. The trust states that nearly all of its funds are allocated to charities known to the trust and new applications have little chance of receiving grants.

Brushmill Ltd

Jewish

£217,000 (1995/96)
Beneficial area Worldwide.

Cohen Arnold, 13–17 New Burlington Place, Regent Street, London W1S 2HL
Tel. 020 8731 0777
Correspondent Stanley Davis
Trustees *J Weinberger; Y Getter; Mrs E Weinberger.*
CC Number 285420
Information available Full accounts were on file at the Charity Commission up to 1991/92, since when the accounts have not included a list of grants.

General In 2000/01 this trust had an income of £281,000 and a total expenditure of £261,000. This information was taken from the Charity Commission database although unfortunately no further details were available for this year. In 1995/96 the trust had an income of £134,000, virtually all from Gift Aid. Grants totalled £217,000, but no grants list was available.

In 1991/92 the trust had an income of £158,000, down from £283,000 the previous year. Grants totalled £186,000, a slight rise from £167,000 the previous year. All the recipients were Jewish organisations with the largest grants going to Bais Rochel (£34,000), Friends of Yeshivas Shaar Hashomaim (£15,000) and Holmleigh Trust (£14,000).

Applications In writing to the correspondent.

Buckingham Trust

Christian, general

£132,000 to organisations
(1998/99)
Beneficial area UK and worldwide.

Messrs Foot Davson & Co., 17 Church Road, Tunbridge Wells, Kent TN1 1LG
Correspondent The Secretary
Trustees *D J Hanes; D G Benson; R W D Foot; P R Edwards.*
CC Number 237350
Information available Full accounts were on file at the Charity Commission.

General In 2001 the trust had assets of £838,000 and an income of £221,000. A total of £155,000 was given in 56 grants.

In 1998/99 grants to over 200 charities totalled £84,000, grants to 43 churches £48,000 and to more than 35 individuals £6,600. Grants to charities were given to UK Christian organisations or similar local groups in London. Beneficiaries included Tearfund (£8,400), Watford New Hope (£2,300) and The Gideons (£1,500). Grants were also given to churches all over the country, including Lancaster (£4,500), Cambridge (£3,400) and Llandrindod (£2,700).

Applications In writing to the address below. However, generally funds are allocated to known organisations and limited funds are available for unsolicited applications. Please enclose an sae.

The Bulldog Trust

Arts, medical, youth, general

£152,000 (2000/01)
Beneficial area Worldwide, with a preference for the south of England.

Messrs Hoare Trustees, 37 Fleet Street, London EC4P 4DQ
Correspondent Richard Hoare, Trustee
Trustees *Richard Hoare; Messrs Hoare Trustees; Martin Rupert Riley.*
CC Number 326292
Information available Full accounts were provided by the trust.

General The objects of the trust are general, but it focuses on education and the arts, the environment and the support of excellence and enterprise, particularly in the young.

The total income for the year 2000/01 was almost £2.4 million, with £1.9 million being donated to the endowment funds. The assets stood at amost £6.6 million at the year end. Ordinary income came from several sources: donations (£210,000), trading activities (£162,000), rent (£60,000) and investments (£47,000).

Expenditure totalled £567,000, of which £152,000 was given in grants. These were classified as follows: Education £77,000; Performing arts £18,000; Medical £5,000; Social welfare £49,000; Sport £1,200; Religion £2,000

The largest grants were £22,000 to Chamraj Children's Home (India), £15,000 to Royal British Legion, £14,000 to Hampshire County Council Project Tahir and £10,000 to Hampshire Gardens Trust. A further 38 causes received £1,000 to £5,000 including nine schools (from Rugby School to St Mary's Primary), and three universities. Others to receive grants in this range included Army Benevolent Fund, Chicken Shed Theatre Company, National Theatre, Rescue a Child, Royal Veterinary College, Trinity College of Music and Winchester Music Festival. Smaller grants of less than £1,000 totalled almost £15,000.

Exclusions No grants are given to individuals or to unsolicited applications.

Applications In writing to the correspondent; there are no application forms. However, please note that unsolicited applications are not acknowledged and are unlikely to be successful.

The E F Bulmer Benevolent Fund

Relief of poverty or sickness

£380,000 to individuals and organisations (2001/02)

Beneficial area Preference for west Midlands, particularly Herefordshire.

The Old Rectory, Stoke Lacy, Nr Bromyard, Herefordshire HR7 4HH

Tel. 01432 820272 **Fax** 01432 820959

Email jcaiger@lineone.net

Correspondent John Caiger, Administrator

Trustees *G M Bulmer; J Bulmer; Wilma Bulmer; A Patten; Jocelyn Harvey Wood.*

CC Number 214831

Information available Accounts were provided by the trust.

General The fund was established for the benefit of people who have been employees of H P Bulmer Holdings Plc or its subsidiary companies for a period of not less than one year, or their dependants who are in poverty, and to others for the relief of sickness and poverty. The fund prefers to support causes in Herefordshire.

In 2001/02 the fund had assets of £9 million generating an income of £453,000. Grants during the year totalled £380,000, with £284,000 of this awarded to 120 organisations and individuals not related to H P Bulmer Holdings Plc. Management and administration costs totalled £35,000.

The fund listed 20 organisations which received grants over £5,000 each. All were in Hereford or Herefordshire unless stated otherwise. They were: Mind, NSPCC, CAN, Workmatch, WRVS, Royal Orthopaedic Hospital Oswestry, Herefordshire Education Action Zone, Primrose Hospice, Relate, Hereford Hospital Radio, St Michael's Hospice in Bartestree, Holly Bush Family Centre, Hereford Cathedral School, Hope in Bromyard, Plynlimon Trust (Dial-a-Ride), Newton Farm Community Association, St John Ambulance Herefordshire and Worcestershire, Family Mediation, Centre for Independent Living and Community Care Alliance.

Exclusions Large UK charities are unlikely to be supported.

Applications In writing to the correspondent, although an application form is available and will be sent if requested. Applications should be accompanied by a copy of the latest report and accounts. All applications will be acknowledged. The administrator is very happy to discuss applications by telephone prior to the application being submitted. The trustees usually meet in January, April, July and August; applications should be received the previous month.

The Burden Trust

Christian, welfare, medical research, general

£177,000 (2001/02)

Beneficial area UK and overseas.

Little Clandon, West Clandon, Surrey GU4 7ST

Tel. 01483 222561 **Fax** 01483 224187

Correspondent Malcolm Tosh, Hon. Secretary

Trustees *Dr M G Barker, Chair; R E J Bernays; A C Miles; Prof. G M Stirrat; Bishop of Southwell; M C Tosh; Mrs Caroline Baker.*

CC Number 235859

Information available Full accounts were provided by the trust.

General The trust operates in accordance with various trust deeds dating back to 1913. These deeds provide for grants for medical research, hospitals, retirement homes, schools and training institutions, homes and care for the young and people in need. The trust operates with an adherence to the tenets and principles of the Church of England.

In 2001/02 the trust had assets of £3.9 million and an income of £170,000. A total of £177,000 was given in 23 grants.

The largest was £45,000 to Burden Neurological Institute, regularly the major beneficiary. Other grants over £10,000 went to Trinity College, Bristol (£17,500), Langham Research Scholarships (£15,000), Oxford Centre for Mission Studies (£12,000), Theological College, Vaux-sur-Seine (£10,000) and Association for Theological Education by Extension, Bangalore (£10,000). The remaining grants ranged between £1,000 and £9,000. The organisations to benefit were Union Biblical Seminary, Pune (£9,000), Home Farm Trust (£6,000), Research into Ageing, All Nations Christian College, Dean Close School and Monkton Combe School (£5,000 each), Easton Christian Family Centre (£4,000), St Mark's College Trust, St Paul's Divinity College, Kenya and Julian House, Bath (£3,000 each), Studylink (£2,500), Evangelical Literature Trust, Batemans Trust and SPACE Trust, Bristol (£2,000 each), Banstead Place, St Loye's College Foundation and Universal Beneficent Society (£1,000 each).

In addition to the above grants, the trust made provision in 1999 for £500,000 to be paid towards funding research costs of the Burden Chair in Clinical Neurosciences at the University of Bristol; £100,000 of this was paid in 2001/02. The remaining £225,000 will be paid by year end 2005.

The report highlighted that in addition to those causes supported during 2001/02 about 520 applications for grants were received, 76 of which were not eligible.

Exclusions No grants to individuals.

Applications In writing to the correspondent to be received before 31 March each year. Financial information is required in support of the project for which help is requested. No application is responded to without an sae.

Recipients of recurring grants are notified each year that grants are not automatic and must be applied for annually.

Applications are considered at the annual trustees meeting.

Burdens Charitable Foundation

General
£506,000 (2000/01)

Beneficial area UK, but mostly overseas, with special interest in West Africa.

St George's House, 215–219 Chester Road, Manchester M15 4JE

Tel. 0161 832 4901 **Fax** 0161 835 3668

Correspondent A J Burden, Trustee

Trustees *Arthur Burden; Godfrey Burden; Hilary Perkins; Sally Schofield.*

CC Number 273535

Information available Full report and accounts, with a list of the top 65 grants, were provided by the foundation.

General The foundation was created in 1977 by Mr and Mrs W T Burden, who endowed it with shares in the business Mr Burden had created in 1929, WTB Group Ltd. This is a private company which employs about 800 people, many of whom also own shares in the company.

The application of the foundation's priorities has recently led to funds being distributed roughly equally between the UK and overseas to less developed countries where its aim, to relieve 'human suffering, impairment and economic deprivation', are most frequently encountered. The likely effect of the foundation's planned development is that UK grants will diminish quite substantially as a proportion of the whole in order to enable more to be distributed to, for example, Sub Saharan Africa and India.

Priorities overseas are:

- the geographical area of West Africa, although consideration will be given to projects in other parts of Africa and other less developed countries
- projects involving the provision of clean water, sanitation and combating visual impairment.

Priorities in the UK are:

- small local groups rather than large national/international charities
- social outreach projects of local churches
- groups where volunteers play a key role in the service delivered
- low-cost umbrella agencies designed to facilitate the above.

Grants can relate to core costs, salaries, capital assets and so on without any exclusions in principle, save only that they really do make a difference. Large charities/projects and causes using professional fundraising costs to any substantial extent do not generally score particularly well.

In keeping with the present policy regarding less privileged parts of the world, this tenet also applies within the UK. For instance the trustees perceive the south of England to be economically better placed than northern Britain, and London to have a resource of charitable grant-making trusts larger per capita than elsewhere. Whilst not always readily capable of precise measurement, the trustees endeavour to assist where the need is greatest and alternative resources are the least.

In 2000/01 the foundation had assets of £11 million, an income of £354,000 and a total expenditure of £508,000. Grants made directly by the foundation during the year totalled £477,000, of which £234,000 was given in total to 156 charities working abroad. In the previous year, the foundation gave a grant of £25,000 to Community Foundation for Greater Manchester for distribution to charities. A similar donation being made by a third party, which the foundation retained the disbursement rights for and during the 2000/01 financial year a total of £28,000 was distributed. Including these grants, a total of £272,000 was given to 295 charities in the UK.

The average grant in the UK was reduced compared to the previous year from £1,000 to about £920, while the average grant overseas increased from £1,300 to £1,500. The foundation states that it only responded positively to 25% of applications, with a further 21% still under consideration at its year-end. However, as the foundation is hoping to increase its support in poorer countries, it appears the UK success rates may fall significantly over the next few years.

The largest grants given in the UK were to Easton Christian Family Centre (£16,000), William Hulme Grammar School (£11,000), Gaddum Centre – Manchester, Salford Methodist Mission and Scottish Churches Community Trust (£5,000 each), Care and Share Foundation and Youth Link NI (£4,000 each), M13 Youth for Christ Urban Action (£3,500), Impact Schools Team, Royal National Eisteddfod of Wales and National Library for the Blind (£3,000 each). A further 11 beneficiaries received £2,500 each, with the remaining 273 beneficiaries receiving less than £2,500, totalling £154,000 in small grants.

The largest grants given overseas were to Merlin, a healthcare organisation (£9,000) and International Foundation for Dermatology (£6,000). A further 12 organisations received £5,000 each, including Accedes, Busoga Trust, Church Relief International, Computeraid, Harvest Help, Hope and Homes for Children, Karenaid, Kings World Trust for Children, National Library for the Blind – Books Around the World, ROKBA, Royal Commonwealth Society for the Blind and Wesley Guild – Nigeria Health Care Project. Three beneficiaries received £3,500 each, six received £3,000, with a further 19 receiving £2,500 each. Smaller overseas grants were given to 113 beneficiaries totalling £79,000.

Exclusions Causes which rarely or never benefit include animal welfare (except in less developed countries), the arts and museums, political activities, most medical research, preservation etc. of historic buildings and monuments, individual educational grants and sport, except sport for people with disabilities. No grants are made to individuals.

Applications In writing to the correspondent, accompanied by recent, audited accounts and statutory reports, coupled with at least outline business plans where relevant. Trustees usually meet in March, June, September and December.

The Clara E Burgess Charity

Children

£590,000 (2000/01)

Beneficial area UK and worldwide.

The Royal Bank of Scotland plc, Trust and Estate Services, Capital House, 2 Festival Square, Edinburgh EH3 9SU

Tel. 0131 556 8555 **Fax** 0131 228 9889

Correspondent Eileen Kidd, Administrator

Trustees *The Royal Bank of Scotland plc.*

CC Number 1072546

Information available The information for this entry was provided by the trust.

General Registered in 1998, this trust makes grants to registered charities where children are the principal beneficiaries of the work. Grants are towards 'the provision of facilities and assistance to enhance the education, health and physical well-being of children particularly (but not exclusively) those under the age of 10 years who have lost one or both parents'. Within these boundaries grants can be made to the following causes: education/training, overseas projects, disability, social welfare, hospitals/hospices, medical/health and medical research.

In 2000/01 the trust had assets of £10 million and an income of £659,000 from bank interest, investments and legacies from the estate of the late Douglas Burgess. The accounts include the sum of £94,000 listed as 'trustees fees – direct charitable matters', which 'represents time directly occupied on charitable matters, including the receipt and consideration of applications for assistance and the subsequent granting of assistance to successful applicants'. A further £25,000 was listed in the accounts as 'trustees fees – general and administration'. In total, the sum of £119,000 was paid during the year on 'trustees fees'. A total of 68 grants were made to organisations totalling £590,000. Some beneficiaries have previously been supported, while some organisations received more than one grant during the year.

Grants of £10,000 or more were made to 22 organisations, including Winston's Wish, which received two grants totalling £93,000. Other beneficiaries of large grants were Cheltenham & Gloucester College of Further Education (two grants totalling £39,000), After Adoption (two grants totalling £39,000), St Francis Children's Society: The Anancy Project (£35,000), International Care & Relief (£28,000), Little Haven Children's Hospice, Barnardo's Orchard Project Newcastle and NCH Action for Children (£25,000 each), Mildmay Mission Hospital (£20,000), British Agencies for Adoption and Fostering (£18,000), DEBRA – Gene Therapy Project and World Medical Fund (£15,000 each), Save the Children Fund (£12,000), The Royal Schools for the Deaf – Manchester, The Rainbow Trust Children's Charity, Le Jeune Clinic, BREAK, Sierra Leone War Trust for Children, The Royal Wolverhampton School: The Orphan Foundation, Hope & Homes for Children and The Rainbow Centre (£10,000 each).

Other beneficiaries included Wigan Mencap (£8,000), Richard House Trust – Children's Hospice (£7,500), Acorns Children's Hospice, Family Service Units, Children's Aid Direct and Relief Fund for Romania (£5,000 each), Wirral Autistic Society (£3,000), Cwm Cynon Women's Aid Children's Playscheme and Motability (£2,000 each), KIND, Berwick Family Centre and Befriend a Child Scheme (£1,000 each), Seaton Delavla Pre-School Playgroup (£750) and Reach (£500).

Exclusions No grants to non-registered charities.

Applications On a form available from the correspondent. The trustees meet to consider grants in February, May, August and November and applications should be received in the month before those meetings. The trust states that applications should be as brief as possible: the trustees will ask for any further information they require.

The Arnold James Burton 1956 Charitable Settlement

General

£252,000 (2000/01)

Beneficial area UK and overseas, with preferences for Yorkshire and Israel.

Trustee Management Ltd, 19 Cookridge Street, Leeds LS2 3AG

Correspondent Keith Pailing

Trustees *A J Burton; J J Burton; M T Burton.*

CC Number 1020986

Information available Full accounts were on file at the Charity Commission.

General Although donations are made at the discretion of the trustees, special consideration will be given to registered institutions relating to Jewish charities, medical research, education, social welfare and heritage.

In 2000/01 the trust had assets of £4.6 million which generated an income of £199,000. Grants totalled £252,000.

The largest grant made was £52,000 to UJIA. Other larger grants went to Marie Curie Cancer Care and Lubavitch Centre (£10,000), JNF Foundation (£8,600) and Arthritis Research and Care (£6,000).

Among the other beneficiaries were a large number of Jewish and Israeli organisations. These included Beth Shalom (£5,500), British ORT (£2,000) and £1,000 each to British Friends of Haifa University, British Friends of Sarah Hertzog Memorial Hospital, Friends of Israel Education Trust, Jewish Care and Oxford Centre for Hebrew and Jewish Studies.

There was also a noticeable preference for Yorkshire. Beneficiaries included Yorkshire Air Museum (£5,000), York Millennium Mystery Plays (£4,000), AbilityNet York Centre (£2,000), Leeds College of Music (£1,200) with £1,000 each to Leeds Jewish Welfare Board, Yorkshire and Humberside Arts, Yorkshire Association for Disabled People and Yorkshire Dales Trust.

Other beneficiaries included Cambridge Expeditions (£5,500), Caring for Life and Sustrans (£5,000 each), Learning Partners (£3,500), YMCA (£2,800), National Deaf Children's Society (£2,500), BTCV (£2,000) with £1,000 each to I Can, National Association of Clubs for Young People, Sight Savers International, Survival International and Variety Club of Great Britain.

Exclusions No grants to individuals.

Applications In writing to the trust managers. The trust states that its funds are fully committed to charities already known to the trustees and new applications are not invited. Unsuccessful appeals will not necessarily be acknowledged.

The R M 1956 Burton Charitable Trust

Jewish charities, social welfare, education, the arts

£84,000 (2000/01)

Beneficial area England, with a preference for the Yorkshire and Humber area, particularly Leeds; also Israel.

c/o Trustee Management Ltd, 19 Cookridge Street, Leeds LS2 3AG

Correspondent The Trustees

Trustees *Raymond M Burton; Arnold Burton.*

CC Number 253421

Information available Full accounts were on file at the Charity Commission.

General The trust has general charitable purposes, with particular interests in Jewish charities, social welfare, education and the arts, particularly in Yorkshire. Grants are given to national and international organisations as well as local charities in Yorkshire and London. Many of the beneficiaries appear on the grants list each year, with the trust not wishing to add organisations to the list which provide the same services as those that have received funding in the past.

In 2000/01 the trust had assets of £1.2 million and an income of £124,000. Grants made to organisations totalled £84,000. There was also £500,000 spent on 'Capital appropriated', comprised of £250,000 each to Harriet Burton Charitable Trust and The Calmcott Trust.

The largest grant made was £10,000 to Dean and Chapter of York. Other large grants went to Community Security Trust (£5,500) and Harrogate Community House Trust and Yorkshire Archaeological Society (£5,000 each).

Other grants in the Yorkshire area included £2,000 to Yorkshire and Humberside Arts and £1,000 each to Boothby Road Community Project, Hull Jewish Community Care, Leeds Jewish Welfare Board and St George's Crypt.

Other beneficiaries elsewhere included Weizmann Institute (£3,500), The Woodland Trust (£2,000), Royal Opera House Trust (£1,500) with £1,000 each to Aidis Trust, British Heart Foundation, Norwood, Prince's Trust, RNIB, St John Ambulance, Textile Industry Children's Trust, UJIA and University of Cambridge.

Exclusions Grants are not given to local charities outside Yorkshire or London, individuals or to new charities where their work overlaps with already established organisations that are supported by the trust.

Applications In writing to the correspondent at any time. The trustees try to make a decision within a month. Negative decisions are not necessarily communicated.

The Bill Butlin Charity Trust

General

£76,000 (2000/01)

Beneficial area UK.

Eagle House, 110 Jermyn Street, London SW1Y 6RH

Tel. 020 7451 9000

Correspondent The Secretary

Trustees *R F Butlin; Lady Sheila Butlin; P A Hetherington; T Watts; F T Devine; S I Meaden; T H North.*

CC Number 228233

Information available Full accounts were on file at the Charity Commission.

General This trust was established by Sir William E Butlin in 1963. It has a preference for organisations working with children, especially those with disabilities and older people. The trust has a list of regular beneficiaries, to which only a few charities may be added each year. In 2000/01, 13 of the 19 groups receiving a grant had been supported in the previous year.

In 2000/01 the trust had assets of £2.3 million and an income of £100,000. After management and administration costs of £9,400, grants were made totalling £76,000.

The largest grants were £20,000 to Canadian Veteran's Association UK and £10,000 each to Crowndale Recreational Association and Jessie May Trust. Other grants included: £5,000 each to Home Farm Trust, Liver Research Trust and NSPCC – Full Stop Appeal; £2,500 each to Cup of Kindness Fund and Tresco and Bryher Educational Foundation; £2,000 each to Grand Order of Water Rats, Saints & Sinners Club of London, South Buckinghamshire Riding for the Disabled and Victims of Violence; £1,000 each to Bud Flanagan Leukaemia Fund and Marine Conservation Society; and £500 to Royal Marsden Hospital.

Grants are available to individuals for welfare purposes.

Applications In writing to the correspondent. Trustees usually meet twice a year.

The C J M Charitable Trust

Social entrepreneurship

£72,000 (1998/99)

Beneficial area UK and overseas.

Messrs Farrer and Co., 66 Lincoln's Inn Fields, London WC2A 3LH

Tel. 020 7242 2022

Correspondent Mrs Jane Leighton

Trustees *Christopher James Marks; Timothy John Marks; William Robert Marks; Rupert Philip Marks; Mary Elizabeth Falk.*

CC Number 802325

Information available Accounts were on file at the Charity Commission.

General In 2000/01 this trust had an income of £23,000 and a total expenditure of £66,000. This information was taken from the Charity Commission database; unfortunately, no further details were available for this year. In 1998/99 the trust had an income of £33,000 and net assets of £474,000. Grants totalling £72,000 were given to Network Foundation (£63,000), Ashoka (UK) Trust (£8,000) and Falkland Community Trust (£1,000).

Applications In writing to the correspondent.

The Edward & Dorothy Cadbury Trust (1928)

Health, education, arts

£79,000 (2001/02)

Beneficial area Preference for the West Midlands area.

Tel. 0121 472 1838 **Fax** 0121 472 7013

Correspondent Miss Susan Anderson, Trust Manager

Trustees *Mrs P A Gillett, Chair; Dr C M Elliott; Mrs P S Ward.*

CC Number 221441

Information available Full accounts were on file at the Charity Commission.

General The trust supports registered charities only, with a special preference for health, education and the arts in the West Midlands area. The size of grant varies but most are within the range of £500 to £1,000. Ongoing funding commitments are rarely considered.

In 2001/02 the trust's assets stood at £3.8 million and it had an income of £114,000. A total of 122 grants were made totalling £79,000. They were caregorised by the trust as follows:

Children's charities	£7,600	(11)
Community projects	£7,200	(16)
Compassionate support	£10,000	(16)
Conservation	£8,200	(9)
Creative arts	£21,000	(14)
Disability and special needs support	£8,700	(27)
Ecumenical mission	£2,400	(2)
International aid	£500	(2)
Research	£3,400	(8)
Society of Friends	£5,500	(2)
Youth	£5,500	(15)

Donations were in the range of £350 to £10,000 although the majority of grants were under £1,000. Grants of £1,000 and above were given to 18 organisations, the largest of which was £10,000 to Huntingdon Hall.

Other recipients of larger grants included Age Concern – Bromsgrove (£5,000), Fauna and Flora (£4,000), Bromsgrove Festival (£3,800), Acorns Children's Trust and Black and White Christian Partnership (£2,000 each), Birmingham Settlement (£1,500) and Avoncroft, Children Nationwide, CORD Blood Charity, Coventry Cathedral, Hippodrome Theatre Rebuilding Project, Macmillan Cancer Relief – Birmingham and Worcester Three Choirs Festival 2001 (£1,000 each).

Smaller grants under £1,000 each included those to Birmingham Centre for Art Therapies, Birmingham Foster Care Association, Birmingham Settlement, Diabetes UK, Foundation for Conductive Education, Home Start – Northfield, Relate – Birmingham, Sandwell Community and Caring Trust, Soil Association, Victim Support – South West Birmingham and Whizz Kids.

Applications In writing to the correspondent, giving clear, relevant information concerning the project's aims and its benefits, an outline budget and how the project is to be funded initially and in the future. Up-to-date accounts and annual reports, where available, should be included.

Applications can be submitted at any time but three months should be allowed for a response.

Applications that do not come within the policy as stated above may not be considered or acknowledged.

The George Cadbury Trust

General

£256,000 (2001/02)

Beneficial area Preference for the West Midlands, Hampshire and Gloucestershire.

New Guild House, 45 Great Charles Street, Queensway, Birmingham B3 2LX

Tel. 0121 212 2222 **Fax** 0121 212 2300

Correspondent Roger Harriman, Trust Administrator

Trustees *Peter E Cadbury; Annette L K Cadbury; R N Cadbury; Sir Adrian Cadbury; Roger V J Cadbury.*

CC Number 1040999

Information available Full accounts were on file at the Charity Commission.

General The trust was set up in 1924 and maintains a strong financial interest in the Cadbury company. In 2001/02 the trust had assets of £8.3 million and an income of £300,000. Grants were made to 225 beneficiaries totalling £256,000. The largest grants went to The Michael Cadbury Children's Orthopaedic Assessment Centre (£25,000), National Youth Ballet (£20,000) and St John Ophthalmic Hospital (£11,500).

Other larger grants of £8,000 each went to Bower Trust and a number of

grantmaking trusts: PHG Cadbury Charitable Trust, RVJ Cadbury Charitable Trust, RA & VB Reekie Charitable Trust, Sarnia Charitable Trust and C James Cadbury Charitable Trust.

A further 37 grants were made of less than £5,000 each, and 168 grants of under £1,000 each. Many beneficiaries have been supported in previous years.

Exclusions No support for individuals for projects, courses of study, expeditions or sporting tours. No support for overseas appeals.

Applications In writing to the correspondent to be considered quarterly. Please note that very few new applications are supported due to ongoing and alternative commitments.

The George W Cadbury Charitable Trust

Population control, conservation, general

£270,000 (2001/02)

Beneficial area Worldwide.

New Guild House, 45 Great Charles Street, Queensway, Birmingham B3 2LX

Tel. 0121 212 2222 **Fax** 0121 212 2300

Correspondent Roger Harriman, Trust Administrator

Trustees *Mrs C A Woodroffe; Mrs L E Boal; P C Boal; Mrs J C Boal; N B Woodroffe; Mrs J L Woodroffe.*

CC Number 231861

Information available Full accounts were on file at the Charity Commission.

General In 2000/01 the trust had assets of £5.6 million generating an income of £212,000. Grants totalled £270,000, given in the following geographical areas:

UK	47%	(£128,000)
USA	46%	(£124,600)
Canada	7%	(£17,500)

The trust has general charitable purposes with a bias towards population control and family planning, welfare causes and conservation.

Altogether 91 grants were given, with 20 of £5,000 and above. The largest were £25,000 to World Development Movement, £20,000 to Friends of the Earth, £14,000 each to Westchester

Childrens Association, Professional Children's School and New York City Combinations Ballet Fund and £11,000 for Food for Survival.

Exclusions No grants to individuals or non-registered charities, or for scholarships.

Applications In writing to the correspondent. However, it should be noted that trustees' current commitments are such that no unsolicited applications can be considered at present.

The D W T Cargill Fund

General

£196,000 (2000/01)

Beneficial area UK, with a preference for the West of Scotland.

Miller Beckett & Jackson, 190 St Vincent Street, Glasgow G2 5SP

Tel. 0141 204 2833

Correspondent Norman A Fyfe, Trustee

Trustees *A C Fyfe; W G Peacock; N A Fyfe; Mirren Elizabeth Graham.*

CC Number SC012703

Information available Accounts were provided by the trust.

General This trust has the same address and trustees as two other trusts, W A Cargill Charitable Trust and W A Cargill Fund, although they all operate independently.

This trust supports 'any hospitals, institutions, societies or others whose work in the opinion of the trustees is likely to be beneficial to the community'.

In 2000/01 it had assets of £6.3 million and an income of £194,000. Grants to organisations totalled £196,000, broken down as annual grants and appeals.

Annual – 35 grants totalling £161,000 The largest grants, as in the previous year, were £35,000 to Ardgowan Hospice and £15,000 to RUKBA. Other notable grants included £9,000 to Marie Curie Cancer Care – Hunter's Hill, £8,000 to Greenock Medical Aid Society, £7,500 to City of Glasgow Society of Social Service, £7,000 to Quarriers Village and £6,000 to Glasgow and West of Scotland Society for the Blind.

Other beneficiaries included Scottish Maritime Museum – Irvine and Scottish Episcopal Church – Eventide Homes

(£5,000 each), The Thistle Foundation, Muscular Dystrophy Group and Enable (£4,000 each), Colquhoun Bequest Fund for Incurables (£3,000), Glasgow City Mission and Scottish Motor Neurone Disease Association (£2,000 each) and Bethesda Nursing Home and Hospice – Stornoway and Earl Haig Fund (£1,000 each).

Appeals – 11 grants totalling £35,000
David Cargill House received four grants, £20,000 for operating deficits, £1,300 for residents' Christmas outings, £1,100 for staff Christmas outing and £1,000 for staff gift vouchers. Other beneficiaries were Kilmacolm Community Transport New Bus Fund (£3,000), David Cargill Club (£2,000 for rewiring), St Mary's Episcopal Cathedral, Lead Scotland, Three Towns Blind Bowling/Social Club, North Glasgow Community Forum, Crathie Opportunity Holidays and The Pavillion Youth Cafe (£1,000 each), Alzheimer Scotland Action on Dementia and Kennyhill School (£500 each).

Exclusions No grants are made to individuals.

Applications In writing to the correspondent, supported by up-to-date accounts. Trustees meet quarterly.

Carlee Ltd

Jewish

£182,000 to organisations and individuals (2000/01)

Beneficial area Worldwide.

6 Grangecourt Road, London N16 5EG

Correspondent The Secretary

Trustees *H Grunhut; Mrs P Grunhut.*

CC Number 282873

Information available Accounts were on file at the Charity Commission, with only a very brief narrative report.

General In 2000/01 the trust had assets of £799,000 and an income of £194,000, comprised of rental income and donations received. Grants totalled £182,000. The trust supports Jewish causes and individuals in need, for example, Talmudical scholars, widows and their families.

Grants were made to 45 beneficiaries and ranged from £8 to £26,000. Half of all grants were for under £1,000.

The largest grants went to YHTC (£26,000) and Rav Chesed (£20,000). Other beneficiaries included Tevini

(£17,000), UTA (£13,000), Telz Academy (£12,500), Gur Trust (£10,000), Gevurath Trust and Egerton Road Building Trust (£9,500 each), Bais Yacob Institution and YHTS (£8,000 each).

Smaller grants listed included those to Bais Rishim Trust, HHT, Mimar, Ponovitz and Yetev Lev.

Applications In writing to the correspondent.

This entry was not confirmed by the trust, but the address was correct according to the Charity Commission database.

The Carpenters' Company Charitable Trust

Education, general

£264,000 to organisations and individuals (2000/01)

Beneficial area UK.

Carpenters' Hall, 1 Throgmorton Avenue, London EC2N 2JJ

Tel. 020 7588 7001

Correspondent The Clerk

Trustees *V F Browne; M R Francis; P C Osborne.*

CC Number 276996

Information available Full accounts were on file at the Charity Commission.

General This trust's income is mainly comprised of donations from the Carpenters' Company. In 2000/01 it had an income of £1.2 million and made grants totalling £264,000 to organisations and individuals.

The trust makes grants in the areas listed below:

Education
Building crafts college and technical education £126,000

Educational grants, scholarships and prizes* £47,000

Other charitable
Richard Wyatt's Almshouses – Other donations and gifts* £90,000

Masters' Gift £750

Grantmaking to general charitable organisations is covered in the two categories marked with an asterisk, and descriptions of these follow.

Educational grants, scholarships and prizes

These totalled around £47,000, broken down as follows: 'Craft grants' were given to 26 individuals and totalled £41,000, about half of which was given to individuals at Building Crafts College. Four organisations also received support; City of London Schools (£3,000), King Edward's School, Witley (£2,000), Osbourne Fund – an annual award for a student at the Guildhall School of Music and Drama (£1,000) and Exchange Scholarships (£177).

Other donations and gifts

These totalled almost £90,000. The largest grant was to Carpenters and Dockland Centre, which received £20,000, and is supported each year. The trust made 30 grants of £2,000 each, including those to St Paul's Cathedral, Metropolitan Society for the Blind, The PACE Centre, Neonatal Unit at St George's Hospital, Starlight Children's Foundation, Carers First, The Lord Mayor's Appeal, Royal British Legion, Arthritis Care, Sports Aid London and Stepping Stones Farm.

Nine grants of £1,000 each were made, including those to Wall Trust, Tunbridge Wells Mental Health Association, Chichester Cathedral Restoration and Development Fund and Dame Henrietta Barnett Fund.

There were also 12 grants of £800 and under, including those to Cot Death Society, Tools with a Mission, Royal Marines National Memorial, Wimbledon Guild, 999 Club, Bellfields Publications and Macmillan Cancer Relief.

Applications In writing to the correspondent, although the trust states that unsolicited applications are not invited.

The Leslie Mary Carter Charitable Trust

Conservation/ environment, welfare

£195,000 (2000)

Beneficial area UK, with a preference for Norfolk and Suffolk.

Birketts, 24–26 Museum Street, Ipswich IP1 1HZ

Tel. 01473 232300

Correspondent S R M Wilson

Trustees *Miss L M Carter; S R M Wilson.*

CC Number 284782

Information available Accounts were on file at the Charity Commission.

General The trust has a preference for nature conservation and wildlife, it also supports welfare organisations. It favours organisations in Norfolk or Suffolk. Grants generally range from £500 to £5,000.

In 2000 the trust had an income of £161,000 and gave grants totalling £195,000. Further information was not available.

In the previous year, when grants totalled £67,000, the largest grants were £6,000 each to Alzheimer's Research Trust and Multiple Sclerosis Society and £5,000 each to Action Research, Broughton House Home, Field Studies Council, KGFS, RNIB for Talking Books, RSPB for Dingle Marshes, St Johns Church – Clacton and WRNS Benevolent Fund.

Exclusions No grants to individuals.

Applications In writing to the correspondent. Telephone calls are not welcome. There is no need to enclose an sae unless applicants wish to have materials returned.

The Cattanach Charitable Trust

'Community deprivation'

£241,000 (2001)

Beneficial area UK, with a preference for Scotland.

Royal Bank of Scotland plc, Private Trust and Taxation, 2 Festival Square, Edinburgh EH3 9SU

Tel. 0131 523 2648 **Fax** 0131 228 9889

Email don.henderson@rbs.co.uk

Correspondent Don Henderson

Trustees *Royal Bank of Scotland plc; Colette Douglas Home; Lord MacLay; F W Fletcher; Adam Thomson; William Syson.*

CC Number SC020902

Information available Information was provided by the trust.

General For the five years from December 2002 to 2007 the trustees wish to concentrate on one individual theme, 'community deprivation', helping deprived communities to help themselves. This covers the full spectrum of community life, including health and employment issues, childcare, drug misuse, homelessness and disability.

The trustees welcome appeals from charities working in Scottish communities, including rural communities and small towns. They prefer to make a significant contribution to the funding of a distinct project that they feel will have a beneficial impact on the relevant community, rather than make a small contribution to a large project.

In addition, the trust will consider any appeals from charities named in the trust deed and any appeals they consider particularly compelling.

Exclusions Only registered charities can receive support. Grants will not be given to fund salaries of staff already in post; the trustees also prefer not to commit to permanent funding of any long-term project.

Applications A standard application form is available from the correspondent.

The trustees meet at the end of June and December and applications together with the charity's latest report and annual accounts must be received not less than three months before each meeting. Applications received after this deadline will only be considered if they are extraordinary, in which case they should be received not less than seven days prior to the meeting at which they are to be considered.

Applications are acknowledged upon receipt. The trust may contact the applicant for further information prior to the trustees' meeting. All applicants are informed of the trustees' decision and, if sucessful, any conditions attached to it.

The Joseph & Annie Cattle Trust

General

£237,000 to organisations (1998/99)

Beneficial area Worldwide, with a preference for Hull and East Yorkshire.

Morpeth House, 114 Spring Bank, Hull HU3 1QJ

Tel. 01482 211198 **Fax** 01482 219772

Correspondent R C Waudby, Administrator

Trustees *J A Collier; M T Gyte; P A Robins.*

CC Number 262011

Information available Full accounts were on file at the Charity Commission.

General The object of the charity is to provide for general charitable purposes by making grants, principally to applicants in the Hull area. Older people and people who are disabled or underprivileged are assisted wherever possible, and there is a particular emphasis on giving aid to children with dyslexia.

In 2000/01 the trust had an income of £281,000 and a total expenditure of £264,000. This information was taken from the Charity Commission database; unfortunately no further details were available for this year.

In 1998/99 the trust's investment income increased by 8% to £368,000 and the assets rose to £7.4 million. The total income was £396,000, which included a donation of £28,000. Administration expenses were very low at £5,200. Under the terms of the trust deed, 20% of net income (£73,000, this year) is capitalised. 526 applications for grants were received during the year, of which 248 were approved totalling £298,000.

£237,000 of this went to organisations and £61,000 to individuals. 75 grants of £1,000 or more were listed in the accounts, one was given to an individual and three to organisations on behalf of individuals. At least half the grants were given in Hull and the surrounding area. The largest grants were £21,000 to Hull & East Riding Institute for the Blind for a minibus, £20,000 to Brocklehurst Neurosurgical Fund, £10,000 each to Holy Trinity Appeal and Sobriety Project and £6,000 to Godfrey Robinson Home for the Disabled. Grants of £5,000 each went to British Red Cross for Crisis in Central America Appeal, Cottingham Tigers RLFC, Disability Aid for Abilitynet, Hull Compact Ltd and St Mark's Scout Group, with Riding for the Blind receiving £4,500.

The remaining grants listed were for £1,000 to £3,000, including those to Children with Leukaemia, Depression Alliance, Help an Orphan Ministries in Malawi, Hull CVS, Hull Fish Trades Boys' Club, North Bransholme Community Association, Pooh Bear Reading Association Society, Royal National Mission to Deep Sea Fishermen, Sailors Families Society, Samaritans, St Nicholas Parish Withernsea and Sick Children's Trust.

Exclusions No grants to individuals, national societies (except for work in North Humberside area) or professional appeals (where agents and appeal staff are employed or paid).

Applications In writing to the correspondent. Meetings are usually held on the third Monday of each month.

The Thomas Sivewright Catto Charitable Settlement

General

£226,000 (2000/01)

Beneficial area Unrestricted, for UK-based registered charities.

Clarebell House, 5–6 Cork Street, London W1S 3NX

Correspondent Miss Ann Uwins

Trustees *Mrs Olivia Marchant; Lord Catto; Miss Zoe Richmond-Watson.*

CC Number 279549

Information available Full accounts were provided by the trust.

General This trust has general charitable purposes, making a large number of smaller grants to a wide range of organisations and a few larger grants of up to £20,000. Despite the large number of grants made, there appears to be no strong preference for any causes or geographical areas.

In 2000/01 the trust had assets of £3.9 million, almost entirely composed of shares in Yule Catto & Co. plc, which produced an income of £267,000. Grants were made to 173 organisations and totalled £226,000.

The largest grants were £20,000 to Oxfam Partners Against Poverty, £10,000 each to King Edward VII's Hospital and London Immunotherapy Cancer Trust and £5,000 each to Disasters Emergency Committee for the Indian Earthquake, Elizabeth Finn Trust, Minchinhampton Centre for the Elderly, Royal Hospital for Neuro-Disability, Royal Scottish Academy of Music and Westbourne House School.

Other grants included: £3,000 to Royal Scottish National Orchestra for a chair endowment; £2,000 each to British Museum for the Great Court Project,

Children with Leukaemia for the Lifelife Centre appeal and University College London for a drug treatment project; £1,000 each to Edinburgh Leith Age Concern, Haddo House Choral and Operatic Society, Erskine Hospital – Renfrewshire, Link Africa, Soil Association and Wiltshire Air Ambulance; £500 each to Centrepoint, Gloucestershire Wildlife Trust, Missions for Seafarers, National Trust for Scotland, Prison Reform Trust, Royal Liverpool Philarmonic Society, Scottish Native Woods and Tools for Self Reliance; and £250 for National Subtitling Library for Deaf People.

Exclusions The trust does not support non-registered charities, expeditions, travel bursaries and so on, or unsolicited applications from churches of any denomination. Grants are unlikely to be considered in the areas of community care, playschemes and drug abuse, or for local branches of national organisations such as scout groups.

Applications In writing to the correspondent, including an sae.

The Wilfrid & Constance Cave Foundation

Conservation, animal welfare, health, welfare

£181,000 (2000/01)

Beneficial area UK with preference for Berkshire, Cornwall, Devon, Dorset, Hampshire, Oxfordshire, Somerset, Warwickshire and Wiltshire.

New Lodge Farm, Drift Road, Winkfield, Windsor SL4 4QQ

Correspondent Mrs Lorraine Olsen, Secretary

Trustees *F Jones, Chair; Mrs T Jones; Mrs J Pickin; M D A Pickin; Mrs N Thompson; Mrs J Archer; R Walker; Mrs M Waterworth.*

CC Number 241900

Information available Full accounts were on file at the Charity Commission.

General The trust supports local and UK organisations for general charitable purposes.

In 2000/01 the trust had assets of £1.9 million generating an income of £107,000. Grants to 68 organisations totalled £181,000. Grants were mainly for £1,000 or £2,000.

The largest grants were given to Exford First School (£25,000), Royal Agricultural Benevolent Institution (£15,000) and British Red Cross (£11,000). Other beneficiaries included The Farmer's Club Pinnacle Award (£8,000), Nuneaton Equestrian Centre (£7,500), Titirheleni Primary School (£6,000), Dulverton Town Hall, Lifeline, The Fortune Centre for Riding Therapy and Devon Air Ambulance (£5,000 each).

Smaller grants included those to Marie Curie Cancer Care, Treloar Trust, British Blind Sport, Theatre Royal Plymouth, Mary Ann Evans Hospice, Heartline, The Project Hospice and Prostate Cancer Research.

Exclusions No grants to individuals.

Applications In writing to the correspondent a month before trustees' meetings held twice each year, in May and October.

The B G S Cayzer Charitable Trust

General

£88,000 (1999/2000)
Beneficial area UK.

Cayzer House, 30 Buckingham Gate, London SW1E 6NN
Tel. 020 7802 8080
Correspondent Ms Jeanne Cook
Trustees *Peter N Buckley; Peter R Davies.*
CC Number 286063
Information available Full accounts were on file at the Charity Commission.

General In 1999/2000 the trust had assets of £2.2 million. The total income was £88,000, all of which was given in grants. There were 22 grants of £1,000 or over listed in the accounts, with a total of £3,400 given in smaller grants.

The largest grant was £25,000 to Feathers Club Association, which received £35,000 in the previous year. Tinsbury Youth Club and Westerkirk Parish Trust both received £10,000.

Other grants included £5,000 each to Game Conservancy Trust, Romsey Hospital Appeal and Tabor Tree

Methodist Church, £3,000 to Christchurch, £2,500 to Clan McQuarrie Memorial Hall, and C Waller Memorial Trust and £2,300 to PSP Association.

Exclusions No grants to organisations outside the UK. Unsolicited appeals will not be supported.

Applications In writing to the correspondent, although the trust tends to support only people/projects known to the Cayzer family or the trustees.

The Chamberlain Foundation

General

£98,000 to organisations
(1998/99)
Beneficial area UK with a preference for London and the south east and eastern regions.

3c Wilson Street, London N21 1BP
Tel. 020 8886 0965
Correspondent C Elmer
Trustees *Mrs M J Spears; Mrs G M Chamberlain; G R Chamberlain; A G Chamberlain; Mrs S J Kent; Mrs C M Lester; Mrs L A Churcher.*
CC Number 1033995
Information available Full accounts were on file at the Charity Commission.

General In 2000/01 the trust had an income of £711,000 and a total expenditure of £262,000. This information was taken from the Charity Commission database; unfortunately no further details were available for this year.

In 1998/99 the trust's assets totalled £3.1 million (up from £2.8 million the year before). It had an unusually high income of £415,000 from investments and grants totalled £161,000. In 1997/98, which was a more typical year, the trust had an income of £119,000 and gave grants of £113,000, broken down as follows.

Individuals
Gifts were made to 25 individuals totalling £49,000.

Donations
Grants were given to 37 organisations and 2 individuals, totalling £98,000. It gave an exceptional gift of £50,000 to The Farmhouse in Bucquoy. Ten grants were

given ranging from £1,500 to £3,800 including those to Parkinson's Disease Society, The Ripple Down House Trust, Seven Rivers Cheshire Home, Tourette Syndrome Association Headquarters, Winged Fellowship and Worshipful Company of Needlemakers. Grants of £1,000 each went to 15 organisations, including Pace Centre, National Institute of Conductive Education, Boys' Brigade in Enfield 10th Company, Tools for Self Reliance – Middlesbrough and Young Minds. Smaller grants included those to Brainwave, CRUSE and Morning Star Trust. Two grants totalling £5,500 were made to individuals.

Education
A limited number of education grants were given, totalling £13,000. Six grants were given to individuals with the only grants to organisations being £5,000 to Birdham Church of England School and £500 to Christ's Hospital.

Applications In writing to the correspondent. However, the trust states that it is proactive in choosing beneficiaries and the amount available for unsolicited applications is limited. Unsolicited applications are not acknowledged. The trustees meet at least twice a year.

The Chapman Charitable Trust

Welfare, general

£185,000 (2001/02)
Beneficial area Eastern and south east England, including London, and Wales.

Messrs Crouch Chapman, 62 Wilson Street, London EC2A 2BU
Tel. 020 7782 0007 **Fax** 020 7782 0939
Email cct@crouchchapman.co.uk
Correspondent Roger S Chapman, Trustee
Trustees *Roger S Chapman; Richard J Chapman; Bruce D Chapman; Guy J A Chapman.*
CC Number 232791
Information available Full accounts were provided by the trust.

General Established in 1963 with general charitable purposes, the trust mainly supports culture and recreation, education and research, health, social

THE CHAPMAN CHARITABLE TRUST
Grants in 2001/02

	Local total	no.	National total	no.	Total total	no.
Culture and recreation	£8,000	10	£23,000	6	£31,000	16
Education and research	£5,000	1	£1,000	1	£6,000	2
Health	–	–	£13,000	15	£13,000	15
Social services	£44,000	31	£78,000	53	£122,000	84
Environment and heritage	£2,000	4	£500	1	£2,500	5

services, environment and heritage causes.

In 2001/02 the trust had assets of £5.2 million, which generated an income of £172,000. Grants were made totalling £174,000, broken down as shown in the table, above.

The largest grants were £20,000 to Aldeburgh Productions and £10,000 each to Methodist Homes – MHA Care Group, NCH Action for Children, Pesticide Action Network UK, Queen Alexandra Hospital Home and St Bridget's Cheshire Home. All these grants were made in two payments.

Other large grants were £5,000 each to A Rocha, Harington Scheme, Kings Cross Furniture Projects and Leys and St Faith Foundation, £4,000 to Fragile X Society, £2,500 each to Wesley Church – Cambridge and Winged Fellowship, £2,000 each to Tower Theatre and Yateley Industries and £1,500 to National Asthma Campaign.

There were also 43 grants of £1,000 each and 53 grants of £500 each. Beneficiaries of £1,000 included Alcohol Recovery Project, Breast Cancer Campaign, Bridget's Trust for Students with a Disability, Children's Hospital for Wales, Goring Methodist Church, Hearing Research Trust, I-Can, Lupus UK, Migraine Trust, Phoenix Cinema, Prostate Cancer Charity, RNID, RUKBA, UK Youth and Weston Spirit. Recipients of £500 included Action on Addiction, Bat Conservation Trust, Canine Partners for Independence, Carousel, Centre 404, Disability Law Service, Fair Play for Children, Museum of Garden History, Penrose Housing Trust, Pitlochry Festival Theatre, Porthmadog Maritime Museum, SeeAbility, Streatham Youth Centre, Surrey Wildlife Trust, Sussex Autistic Society, Victim Support London, Welshpool Community Transport and Winged Fellowship Trust.

Exclusions No grants to or for the benefit of individuals, local branches of UK charities, animal welfare, sports tours or sponsored adventure holidays.

Applications In writing at any time. The trustees currently meet to consider grants twice a year at the end of September and March. They receive a large number of applications and regret that they cannot acknowledge receipt of them. The absence of any communication for six months would mean that an application must have been unsuccessful.

The Charities Advisory Trust

See below

£397,000 (2000/01)

Beneficial area UK and overseas.

Radius Works, Back Lane, London NW3 1HL

Tel. 020 7794 9835 **Fax** 020 7431 3739

Email charities.advisory.trust@ukonline.co.uk

Website www.charitiesadvisorytrust.org.uk

Correspondent Hilary Blume, Director

Trustees Dr Cornelia Navari; Dr Carolyne Dennis; Prof. Bob Holman; Ms Dawn Penso.

CC Number 1040487

Information available Annual report and accounts.

General The Charities Advisory Trust is a registered charity which helps other charities with their trading. The Trust was set up nearly 20 years ago (originally under the name The Charity Trading Advisory Group), with home office funding, to provide an impartial source of advice on all aspects of trading for charities. Much of the trust's work has been directed to providing practical help to charities to help them trade more efficiently. The trust carries out research into all aspects of charity trading with the aim of providing reliable information on the sector, striving to provide practical help through 'bench-marking' and

'comparability' so charities can assess their performances and set realistic targets. The CARD AID chain of charity Christmas card shops – the largest in London – sell cards for over 100 good causes at locations as diverse as the Barbican centre, St Mary le Bow and the Royal Festival Hall. It also publishes a wide range of books and has a comprehensive training programme.

The trust's website offers the following guidelines for applicants: 'We are willing to consider applications for any charitable purpose: we have given money to buy a canoe for young disabled people in Wiltshire, and have bought a tea plantation for tribal people in South India; we have paid for books for village libraries and supported research into early detection of cancer.

'In 2001/2002, the main areas of interest to which funds have already been committed are:

- peace and reconciliation projects, particularly in the Middle East
- the early detection of cancer through saliva sampling
- research into the prevention and control of diabetes
- an ongoing programme of tree planting in London
- libraries and projects to encourage reading
- homelessness.

'Smaller amounts have been committed to:

- the establishment of a fulfilment and warehousing project through a sheltered workshop
- arts access, particularly for school age children
- museums and galleries'.

In 2000/01 the trust had assets of £1.3 million. Total income was £1.2 million, including £805,000 from donated cards and gift tags and £254,000 from other Card Aid income. Direct charitable expenditure was £1.3 million, of which £397,000 was given in grants.

The largest grants were £61,000 to Trees for London, £35,000 to New Israel Fund for nominated projects and £30,000 to Whittington Hopsital for research into cancer. Other large grants went to Friends of Feltham Hardship Fund (£20,000), Ducane Housing Association (£19,000), ACCORD Tea Co-operative – India (£17,000), MS Research Trust and Vridavan – Gujerat (£12,000 each) and NCH Action for Children (£9,000).

Other beneficiaries included Shelter (£5,200), SOS Childrens Villages (£5,100), Groundswell – Tower Hamlets (£5,000), Medical Foundation for the

Care of Victims of Torture (£4,200), Portugal Prints (£3,500), Oxfam (£3,200), Cancer Research Campaign (£2,900), Resurrection Self Build (£2,500), Terrence Higgins Trust and People's Education Trust (£2,000 each), Roma Refugees (£1,800), Edinburgh Young Carers and National Literacy Trust (£1,500 each), BBC Children in Need and RUKBA (£1,300 each) and Blue Cross Animal Welfare and Trinity Hospice (£1,200 each).

Exclusions 'We do not have an application form and we accept applications throughout the year. Nearly all our grants are made because we have prior knowledge of the project or area of concern. In most cases the idea for the project comes from us; we work with suitable organisations to achieve our objectives.

'We rarely respond to unsolicited applications for projects of which we know nothing. In such cases where support is given, the amounts are usually £200 or less.

'We do not consider grants to individuals in need. Neither do we give to individuals going on gap year trips to the developing world.

'We are unlikely to give to large fund-raising charities.

'We do not give for missionary work.'

Applications 'To apply simply send us details of your proposal (no more than two pages in length) in the form of a letter. You might try to include the following information:

1. the aims and objectives of your organisation
2. the project for which you need money
3. who benefits from the project and how
4. breakdown of the costs and total estimated costs
5. how much money you need from us
6. other funding secured for the project
7. a summary of your latest annual accounts

'If we refuse you it is not because your project is not worthwile - it is because we do not have sufficient funds, or it is simply outside our current area of interest.

'Applications should be addressed to the Director. Good luck! '

Charitworth Limited

Jewish causes

£1.2 million (2000/01)
Beneficial area UK.

c/o Cohen Arnold, Regent Street, 13–17 New Burlington Place, London W1S 2HL
Tel. 020 7734 1362
Correspondent D Halpern, Trustee
Trustees *D M Halpern; Mrs R Halpern; S Halpern; S J Halpern.*
CC Number 286908
Information available Accounts were on file at the Charity Commission.

General This trust was set up in 1983 and its objects are the advancement of the Jewish religion, relief of poverty and general charitable purposes. It is particularly interested in supporting religious and educational charities.

In 1998/99 the trust had an income of £2.3 million, which boosted its assets. In 2000/01 the trust had assets of £8.6 million and an income of £346,000. Grants to organisations increased to £1.2 million (£562,000 in 1998/99).

The largest grants were made to Cosmon (Belz) Limited (£317,000), a charity which promotes the advancement of the Jewish Orthodox faith, Friends of Beis Yaacov (£250,000), Yeshiva Ohel Shimon Trust (£190,000) and Friends of Horim (£120,000).

Other grants were given to Zichron Nachum (£70,000), Dushinsky Trust (£40,000), Mercaz Chasidei Buhush (£32,000), Beth Hayeled Trust (£30,000) and SOFT (£28,000).

Grants to charities of less than £25,000 each, which were not listed in the accounts, totalled £95,000.

Applications In writing to the correspondent.

The Children's Research Fund

Child health research

£216,000 (1998/99)
Beneficial area UK.

668 India Buildings, Water Street, Liverpool L2 0RA
Tel. 0151 236 2844 **Fax** 0151 258 1606
Website www.crfund.org
Correspondent H Greenwood, Chair
Trustees *H Greenwood, Chair; G W Inkin; Dr G J Piller; H E Greenwood; Prof. J Lister; Lord Morris; Elizabeth Theobald.*
CC Number 226128
Information available Full accounts were on file at the Charity Commission.

General The trust supports research into children's diseases, child health and prevention of illness in children, carried out at institutes and university departments of child health. The policy is to award grants, usually over several years, to centres of research. It will also support any charitable project associated with the wellbeing of children.

In 2000/01 the trust had an income of £219,000 and a total expenditure of £234,000. This information was taken from the Charity Commission database; unfortunately no further details were available for this year. In 1998/99 it had assets of £1.3 million and an income of £198,000. A total of £216,000 was given in 11 grants. The largest grants were £45,000 to University of Liverpool – Department of Paediatrics, £32,000 to Great Ormond Street Hospital and £25,000 each to the Great Ormond Street Hospital Institute of Child Health and University of Southampton – Therapist course. The remaining grants were all to different UK universities, ranging from £650 to £23,000. Five of the grants were recurrent.

Exclusions No grants for capital projects.

Applications Applicants from child health research units and university departments are invited to send in an initial outline of their proposal; if it is eligible they will then be sent an application form. Applications are considered in March and November.

The Childs Charitable Trust

Christian

£287,000 (2000/01)
Beneficial area Worldwide.

2–4 Saffrons Road, Eastbourne, East Sussex BN21 1DQ
Tel. 01323 417944
Email childs@charitabletrust.fsnet.co.uk

Correspondent D Martin, Trustee

Trustees *D N Martin; R H Williams; A B Griffiths.*

CC Number 234618

Information available Full accounts were on file at the Charity Commission.

General The objects of the trust are the furtherance of Christian Gospel, education, the relief of poverty and other charitable causes. The principal object is the furtherance of the Christian Gospel and the trustees are actively involved in supporting and encouraging Christian charities to achieve this goal. There is a preference for large-scale projects in the UK and abroad and ongoing support is given to some long-established Christian organisations.

In 2000/01 the trust had assets of £7.7 million and an income of £367,000. Grants totalled £287,000.

The largest grants were £54,000 to Home Evangelism and £32,000 to Mission Aviation Fellowship, both of which have received larger grants in previous years.

Other larger grants went to Latin Link (£20,000), Echoes of Service and Mustard Seed Trust (£13,000 each), Counties Evangelistic Work and Russian Ministries (£12,000 each), Scripture Gift Mission and Words of Life Ministry (£11,000 each) and Medical Missionary News (£10,000).

Other grants included those to Redcliffe College (£8,000), Penhurst Retreat (£6,000), Questscope and Vision International (£5,000), East to West Trust (£3,500), Sandhurst Baptist Church (£2,000), Moorlands College (£1,500) and St Anthony's Church (£1,300).

Applications In writing to the correspondent. The trust stated that its funds are fully committed and further applications are not welcomed.

The Chownes Foundation

General

£75,000 to organisations (1998/99)

Beneficial area UK.

The Courtyard, Beeding Court, Shoreham Road, Steyning, West Sussex BN44 3TN

Tel. 01903 816699

Email sjs.russellnew@btconnect.com

Correspondent Sylvia Spencer, Secretary

Trustees *Charles Stonor; the Abbot of Worth; Mrs U Hazeel.*

CC Number 327451

Information available Full accounts were on file at the Charity Commission.

General The objectives of this trust are the advancement of religion, the advancement of education among the young, the amelioration of social problems, and the relief of poverty amongst older people and the former members of Sound Diffusion PLC who lost their pensions when the company went into receivership.

In 2001/02 this trust had an income of £70,000 and a total expenditure of £90,000. This information was taken from the Charity Commission database; unfortunately no further details were available for this year. In 1998/99 it had assets of £34,000 and an income of £115,000 from Gift Aid donations from the company's directors. Grants totalled £98,000, including six grants to individuals totalling £23,000. No grants list was provided. In the past most beneficiaries have been based in the south of England.

Exclusions Applicant organisations must fit into the above criteria.

Applications In writing to the correspondent.

CLA Charitable Trust

Disabled facilities and training

£67,000 (2000/01)

Beneficial area England and Wales only.

Caunton Grange, Caunton, Newark, Nottinghamshire NG23 6AB

Tel. 01636 636171 **Fax** 01636 636171

Website www.clacharitabletrust.org

Correspondent Peter Geldart

Trustees *A Duckworth-Chad; A H Duberly; G E Lee-Strong; G N Mainwaring.*

CC Number 280264

Information available Full accounts were provided by the trust.

General The trust was founded in 1980. Its work includes support for education projects in the countryside (a) to provide

sport and recreation facilities for disabled people, and (b) for children and young people with learning difficulties or who are disadvantaged.

It prefers to support smaller projects where a grant from the trust can make a 'real contribution to the success of the project'. It gives grants for specific projects or items rather than for ongoing running costs.

In 2000/01 the trust had assets of £310,000 and an income of £90,000. Grants totalled £67,000; the largest were £3,000 to Essex Association of Boys Clubs, £2,500 to Yvonne Arnaud Theatre, £2,000 each to Dwyryd Anglers Ltd and Nancy Oldfield Trust, £1,800 to West Norfolk Riding for the Disabled and £1,000 each to Living Springs, and Royal Bath and West Show.

Exclusions No grants to individuals.

Applications In writing to the correspondent. Trustees meet four times a year.

J A Clark Charitable Trust

Health, education, peace, preservation of the earth, the arts

£134,000 (2000/01)

Beneficial area UK, with a preference for south west England.

PO Box 1704, Glastonbury, Somerset BA16 0YB

Tel. 01458 842374 **Fax** 01458 842022

Email jactrust@ukonline.co.uk

Correspondent Mrs P Grant, Secretary

Trustees *Lancelot Pease Clark; John Cyrus Clark; Thomas Aldham Clark; Caroline Pym; Aidan J R Pelly.*

CC Number 1010520

Information available Full accounts were on file at the Charity Commission.

General The trust was established in 1992. It is concerned with projects oriented towards social change in areas of health, education, peace, preservation of the earth and the arts. Quaker organisations are also well supported. The trustees are particularly interested in supporting the work of small, new or innovative projects.

In 2000/01 the trust had assets of £8.5 million and an income of £397,000 (£254,000 in 1999/2000). Grants were given to 30 beneficiaries totalling £134,000 (£169,000 in 1999/2000).

As in previous years, the largest grant went to Cyrus Clark Charitable Trust (£27,000). Other larger grants went to Inner City Scholarship Fund (£14,000), QPS (£12,000) and ASHOKA (£10,000).

Other beneficiaries included Watershed Arts Trust (£6,500), Quaker Peace Studies (£5,500), Addiction Recovery Agency, CJC Bursary and Street Theatre Workshop Trust (£5,000 each), Dance United and Jubilee 2000 Coalition (£4,000 each), Take Art Ltd (£3,000), British Red Cross, New Economics Foundation and Drop The Debt (£2,000 each), Children's Classic Concerts and Hareclive Football Club (£1,000 each) and Guild of Psychotherapy (£800).

Exclusions No support for independent schools (unless they are for special needs), conservation of buildings or for individuals.

Applications The trust is fundamentally restructuring itself towards the objective of supporting exclusively one or two innovative projects, and so is 'absolutely unable to respond to any unsolicited appeals at this point in time'.

The Cleopatra Trust

Health and welfare, disability, homelessness, addiction, underprivileged children, environment

£162,000 (2000)
Beneficial area Mainly UK.

Charities Aid Foundation, King's Hill, West Malling, Kent ME19 4TA

Tel. 01732 520083 **Fax** 01732 520001

Correspondent Mrs Sue David, Donor Grants Officer

Trustees *Charles Peacock; Mrs Bettine Bond; Dr Clare Sellers.*

CC Number 1004551

Information available Full accounts were on file at the Charity Commission.

General The trust has common trustees with two other trusts, Dorus Trust and

Epigoni Trust (see separate entries), with which it also shares the same aims and polices. All three trusts are administered by Charities Aid Foundation. Generally the trusts support different organisations each year.

The trust makes grants in the following areas:

- mental health
- cancer welfare/education – not research
- diabetes
- physical disability – not research
- homelessness
- addiction
- underprivileged children.

There is also some preference for environmental causes. It only gives grants for specific projects and does not give grants for running costs or general appeals. Generally support is given to organisations with a UK-wide remit.

In 2000 the trust had assets of £3.1 million and an income of £162,000, all of which was given in 29 grants. These ranged from £500 to £16,000.

The largest grant of £16,000 went to Sight Savers International. Grants of £10,000 each went to seven organisations, Brick by Brick London Home Activity Group, Cancer Link, Couple Counselling Scotland, Heal Cancer Charity Ltd, Royal Blind Asylum & School, St Mungo Community Housing Association and Tommy's Campaign.

Other larger grants included those to Medical Foundation for the Care of Victims of Torture and Claire House (£8,000 each), Cruse Bereavement Care Swindon, Habitat for Humanity Belfast and Fairtrade Foundation (£5,000 each), Help the Hospices (£3,000), Inspire (£2,500) and St Giles Hospice (£2,000).

Exclusions No grants to individuals, expeditions, research, scholarships, charities with a local focus, local branches of UK-wide charities or towards running costs.

Applications On a 'funding proposal form' available from the correspondent. Applications should include a copy of the latest audited annual report and accounts. They are considered twice a year in mid-summer and mid-winter. Organisations which have received grants from this trust, Dorus Trust or the Epigoni Trust should not reapply in the following two years. Usually, funding will be considered by only one of these trusts.

The Clifton Charitable Trust

General
£702,000 (2000)
Beneficial area UK and overseas, preference for south west England.

KPMG, 100 Temple Street, Bristol BS1 6AG

Tel. 0117 905 4000

Correspondent Lisa Mirams

Trustees *Avon Executor and Trustee Company.*

CC Number 285564

Information available Full accounts were provided by the trust.

General The trust was set up as a vehicle to receive the company's partners and its clients' Gift Aid payments. Towards the end of each year they nominate the charities that will receive the money.

In 2000 the trust had assets of £1.8 million and an income of £897,000, mainly from Gift Aid payments received from the partners and clients. During the year the trust made 37 grants to organisations totalling £702,000. Grants were in the range of £200 to £50,000, with an exceptional grant of £102,000 to Fry Abbots Leigh 2000 Trust, although most were for £10,000 and above.

The largest beneficiaries were Bristol Cathedral, Bristol Foyer Project, Dorothy House, Farm America, Julian House, Royal United Hospital Charitable Fund, South Mead MRI Scanner Appeal and Welsh National Opera, which each received £50,000.

Other notable beneficiaries include: National Eye Research Centre and RNLI (£25,000 each); Theatre Royal Bath – Ustinov Campaign (£17,000); Camphill School and Ovingdean Hall School (£15,000 each); and Actors Benevolent School, Bath Philharmonia, Bristol Mediation, Holburne Museum, National Trust, RADA and Royal Opera House Trust (£10,000 each).

Organisations receiving £1,000 or less include Alzheimer's Support West, Botton Village Appeal, British Legion, CPRE, Friends of the Earth, High Peak Theatre Trust, International Horse Protection League, The Marine Society, Royal Naval Museum, Shuttleworth Trust, UNICEF and Yorkshire Air Museum.

The trust also comprises The Craig Fund, which in 2000 gave grants of £32,000 each to the Salvation Army and Barnardos.

Applications In writing to the correspondent. Unsolicited applications cannot be considered.

Clover Trust

Older people, young people

£330,000 (2000)

Beneficial area UK and overseas, with a slight preference for West Dorset.

c/o Suite 7, Messrs Herbert Pepper and Rudland, Accurist House, 44 Baker Street, London W1U 7BD

Tel. 020 7486 5535

Correspondent Nicholas C Haydon, Trustee

Trustees *N C Haydon; S Woodhouse.*

CC Number 213578

Information available Full accounts were provided by the trust.

General This trust supports organisations concerned with health, disability, children and Catholic activities. However, most grants are given to a 'core list' of beneficiaries and the trust states: 'the chances of a successful application from a new applicant are very slight, since the bulk of the income is earmarked for the regular beneficiaries, with the object of increasing the grants over time rather than adding to the number of beneficiaries.'

Grants are given towards general charitable running costs, although no grants are given towards building work. Unsolicited applications which impress the trustees are given one-off grants, although only a tiny percentage of the many applications are successful.

In 2000 the trust had assets of £4.9 million and an income of £275,000. Grants to 65 organisations totalled £330,000. Grants were in the range of £1,000 to £30,000, but were mainly for amounts under £5,000. Those over £10,000 were: £30,000 to Downsize Settlement; £15,000 each to Action Research for the Crippled Child, National Society for the Prevention of Cruelty to Children and Friends of Orphanages in Romania; £13,000 to 999 Club; and £10,000 each to British Red Cross Society and Cotswold Care.

Other donations included £5,000 each to Blandford RC Parish and Dorset Association for the Disabled and £3,000 to Parkinsons Disease – West Dorset.

Exclusions The arts, monuments and non-registered charities are not supported.

Applications In writing to the correspondent. Replies are not given to unsuccessful applications.

Clydpride Ltd

Jewish charities, general

£287,000 (1997/98)

Beneficial area UK.

1003 Finchley Road, London NW11 7HB

Tel. 020 8731 7744 **Fax** 020 8731 8373

Correspondent L Faust, Secretary to the Trustees

Trustees *L Faust; D Faust; T Faust.*

CC Number 295393

Information available Accounts up to 1997/98 only, and then without a grants list or a narrative report, were on file at the Charity Commission.

General In 2000/01 this trust had an income of £1.3 million and a total expenditure of £299,000. This information was taken from the Charity Commission database; unfortunately no further details were available for this year. In 1997/98, when the trust had a rental income of £248,000, grants totalled £287,000. It is not known how much was given in grants in 1998/99.

The objectives are to 'advance religion in accordance with the Jewish Orthodox faith, relief of poverty and general charitable causes'.

Little information is available. The trust has previously stated that 'it is not company policy to give any information' and 'we give grants in too many areas to tell you, write in and we will consider it'.

Applications The trust states that unsolicited applications are not entertained.

The Francis Coales Charitable Foundation

Historical

£114,000 (2001)

Beneficial area UK, with a preference for Bedfordshire, Buckinghamshire, Hertfordshire and Northamptonshire.

The Bays, Hillcote, Bleadon Hill, Weston-super-Mare, Somerset BS24 9JS

Tel. 01934 814009 **Fax** 01934 814009

Email fccf45@hotmail.com

Correspondent T H Parker, Administrator

Trustees *J Coales, Chair; H G M Leighton; A G Harding; Revd B H Wilcox; H M Stuchfield.*

CC Number 270718

Information available An information leaflet was provided by the trust. Full accounts were on file at the Charity Commission.

General The 2001 trustees report stated: 'In 1885 Francis Coales and his son, Walter John Coales, acquired a corn merchant's business in Newport Pagnell, Buckinghamshire. Over the years similar businesses were acquired, but after a major fire it was decided to close down the business. From the winding-up was established The Francis Coales Charitable Trust in 1975.

'The nature of the foundation is to assist with grants for the repair of old buildings which are open to the public, for the conservation of monuments, tombs, hatchments, memorial brasses, etc., also towards the cost of archaeological research and related causes, the purchase of documents or items for record offices and museums, and the publication of architectural and archaeological books or papers. Assistance for structural repairs is normally given to churches and their contents in Buckinghamshire, Bedfordshire, Northamptonshire and Hertfordshire where most of the business of Francis Coales and Son was carried out with farmers. However, no territorial restriction is placed upon church monuments, etc.'

In 2001 the foundation had assets of £1.7 million. The total income was £100,000. Grants were approved totalling £114,000.

The largest grant was £25,000 to Northamptonshire VCH Trust for research, with £5,000 each to Higham Ferrers – Northamptonshire for repairs to its tower, Sawbridgeworth – Hertfordshire to repair the dry rot in the nave roof, Stoneleigh – Warwickshire to conserve a monument and Thorpe Malsor – Northamptonshire to repairs its tower and spires.

Other beneficiaries included: Marsham – North Yorkshire for the Danby Monument (£4,000); Drayton Parslow – Buckinghamshire for general structural repairs (£3,000); British Archaeological Association for publication proceedings for the Windsor Conference (£2,000); Buckinghamshire Record Office to buy two maps of Whaddon Chase (£1,000); Cranfield – Bedfordshire to rehang bells (£75); Wolverton and District Archaeological Society to copy the photographic collections (£300); and Northamptonshire Records Office for a document (£34).

Exclusions No grants for buildings built after 1875, hospitals or hospices. Ecclesiastical buildings cannot receive grants for 'domestic' items such as electrical wiring, heating, improvements or re-ordering.

Applications On a form available from the correspondent.

Applications should include a quotation for the work or the estimated cost, details of the amount of funds already raised and details of funds applied for and other bodies approached. Applications for buildings or contents should include a copy of the relevant part of the architect/conservator's specification showing the actual work proposed. 'Photographs showing details of the problems often speak louder than words.'

The trust also states that receiving six copies of any leaflet or statement of finance is helpful so that each trustee can have a copy in advance of the meeting. Trustees normally meet three times a year to consider grants.

John Coates Charitable Trust

Arts, children, environment, medical, general

£307,000 (2001/02)

Beneficial area UK, mainly southern England.

40 Stanford Road, London W8 5PZ

Tel. 020 7938 1944 **Fax** 020 7938 2390

Correspondent Mrs P L Youngman, Trustee

Trustees *Mrs McGregor; Mrs Kesley; Mrs Lawes; Mrs Youngman.*

CC Number 262057

Information available Full accounts were provided by the trust.

General This trust has general charitable purposes. Grants are made to large UK-wide charities, or small charities of personal or local interest to the trustees.

In 2001/02 the trust had assets of £8.7 million, which generated an income of £286,000. Management and administration charges were very high at £53,000, largely due to a stockbroker's management fee of £46,000. Grants totalling £307,000 were made to 59 organisations, of which 31 were also supported in the previous year.

The largest grants were £15,000 each to OPTIMA and South Bank Centre for the Royal Festival Hall. Grants of £10,000 each went to British Wheelchair Sports Foundation, Cleft Lip and Palate Association, English National Opera, Girton College – Cambridge, Handel House Museum, Jubilee Sailing Trust, NASS, National Trust, NSPCC, Painshill Park Trust, Royal Albert Hall Trust, Royal Hospital for Neuro-disability, Scope, Shakespeare Globe Trust and Tommy's The Baby Charity.

Other beneficiaries included Dulwich Picture Gallery and St Bride's Church (£5,000 each), Canine Partners for Independence and The Sixteen (£3,000 each), National Back Pain Association (£2,500), Wey and Arun Canal Trust (£2,000), Queen Elizabeth's Foundation (£1,500), High School of Dundee (£1,500), Chichester Cathedral Trust and Worldwide Volunteering for Young People (£1,000 each), Barn Owl Trust and RNLI (£500 each) and All Saints Church – Fulham (£50).

Exclusions Grants are given to individuals only in exceptional circumstances.

Applications In writing to the correspondent. Small local charities are visited by the trust.

The Andrew Cohen Charitable Trust

Jewish

£90,000 (2001/02)

Beneficial area UK.

c/o Wood Hall Securities Ltd, Wood Hall Lane, Shenley, Hertfordshire WD7 9AA

Tel. 01923 289999

Email alc@woodhall.com

Correspondent Mr & Mrs Cohen

Trustees *Andrew L Cohen; Wendy P Cohen.*

CC Number 1033283

Information available Basic accounts were on file at the Charity Commission, without a grants list or a narrative report.

General In 2000/01 the trust had assets of £259,000 and an income of £11,000. Grants totalled £119,000. In 2001/02 these figures had fallen to an income of £6,500 and a total expenditure of £90,500. Most of its expenditure is usually given in grants.

A recent grants list was unavailable, although in the past grants have been given to JIA, Oxford University L'Chaim Society, Scope Jewish Trust and Imperial Cancer Research.

Applications The trust does not respond to unsolicited applications. It states that its funds are fully committed for the next couple of years and that generally grants are made to organisations that have been previously supported. New applications are unlikely to be successful.

The Vivienne & Samuel Cohen Charitable Trust

Jewish, education, health and welfare

£180,000 (2000/01)

Beneficial area UK and Israel.

9 Heathcroft, Hampstead Way, London NW11 7HH

Correspondent Dr Vivienne Cohen, Trustee

Trustees *Dr Vivienne Cohen; M Y Ben-Gershon; G Cohen; D H J Cohen; J S Lauffer.*

CC Number 255496

Information available Full accounts were on file at the Charity Commission.

General The majority of the trust's support is to Jewish organisations.

In 2000/01 the trust had assets of £2.4 million and an income of £104,000. Grants totalled £180,000. Only the seven largest grants were listed in the accounts. All but one of the beneficiaries were Jewish organisations. The largest donation was £75,000 to London School of Jewish Studies. Maaleh Nievo Synagogue received £31,000. The other grants listed were £6,000 to Be'er Hatarah School, £5,000 each to Maaleh Hatorah School and Variety Club, £3,500 to B'Nei B'Rith and £2,000 to Machanim.

Smaller grants totalled £53,000 but no information was available on the beneficiaries.

Exclusions No grants to individuals.

Applications In writing only, to the correspondent.

This entry was not confirmed by the trust, but the address was correct according to the Charity Commission database.

The Sir Jeremiah Colman Gift Trust

General

£106,000 (2001/02)

Beneficial area UK, with a preference for Hampshire especially Basingstoke.

Malshanger, Basingstoke, Hampshire RG23 7EY

Correspondent Sir Michael Colman, Trustee

Trustees *Sir Michael Colman; Lady Judith Colman; Oliver J Colman; Cynthia Colman; Jeremiah M Colman.*

CC Number 229553

Information available Accounts were provided by the trust.

General The trust has special regard to:

- advancement of education and literary scientific knowledge
- moral and social improvement of people

- maintenance of churches of the Church of England and gifts and offerings to the churches
- financial assistance to past and present employees/members of Sir Jeremiah Colman at Gatton Park, J & J Colman Ltd or other clubs and institutions associated with Sir Jeremiah Colman.

In 2001/02 the trust had assets of £2.1 million and an income of £93,000. Grants totalled £106,000 and were broken down as follows:

Annual grants	£55,000
Extra grants	£300
Special grants	£51,000

The largest grant was given to Ark Facility, which received a final installment of £5,000 (£25,000 in total over the last five years); The Margaret Mee Fellowship Programme received £3,000. All other grants were for £2,500 or less, with most under £1,000.

The trust made 165 'annual' grants, with all the beneficiaries being supported in the previous year. Of these, just eight were for £1,000 or more. These were to National Art Collections Fund (£2,000), Basingstoke & North Hampshire Medical Trust and Church of England Pensions Fund (£1,500 each), Bridges International (£1,300), and National Trust, Skinners Company School for Girls, Wootton St Lawrence Church and Youth for Christ (£1,000 each). Other beneficiaries included Action Research, Age Concern – Basingstoke & Dean, Basingstoke Samaritans, British Deaf Association, British Sailors Society, Careforce, Children's Society – Southern, Divert Trust, Endeavour Training, Family Welfare Association, Gatton Park Educational Trust, Hamilton Lodge School for Deaf Children, Handicapped Adventure Playground Association, Independent Adoption Society, Living Waters, Multiple Sclerosis Society, National Council for One Parent Families, Prison Reform Trust, Royal Naval Museum, Spinal Injuries Association and YWCA.

During the year, 43 'special' grants were made, including nine which were part of a long-term payments scheme. Examples of 'special' grants include those to The Anvil and Basingstoke Sports Centre (£2,500 each), CARE (£1,000), The Grub Institute and UK Youth Parliament (£750 each), and YMCA Norwich and YWAM – Restore (£500 each).

Just one 'extra' grant was awarded during the year to MNDA Schroder (£300).

Exclusions Grants are not made to individuals requiring support for personal

education, or to individual families for welfare purposes.

Applications 'The funds of the trust are fully committed and any unsolicited applications are most unlikely to be successful.'

The Colt Foundation

Occupational and environmental health research

£366,000 to organisations (2001)

Beneficial area UK.

New Lane, Havant, Hampshire PO9 2LY

Tel. 023 9249 1400 **Fax** 023 9249 1363

Email jackie.douglas@uk.coltgroup.com

Website www.coltfoundation.org.uk

Correspondent Mrs Jacqueline Douglas

Trustees *Mrs Patricia Lebus, Chair; Jerome O'Hea; Timothy Ault; Mrs Clare Gilchrist; Walter McD Morison; Alan O'Hea; Peter O'Hea; Prof. David Coggon. Prof. D Denison and Prof. A J Newman Taylor act as Scientific Advisors.*

CC Number 277189

Information available Report and accounts with grants list and narrative explanation of grants and grant-making policy.

General The foundation makes grants to support organisations and post-graduate students for research into occupational and environmental health. It is particularly interested in work aimed at discovering the causes of illnesses arising from conditions in the workplace. Donations to organisations vary from a few thousand pounds to over £100,000 and may be repeated over two to five years. Beneficiaries are well-established research institutes (awards to individuals are made through such).

In 2001 it had assets totalling £11.3 million from which £352,000 was generated in income. After management and administration costs of £53,000, grants amounting to £502,000 were made to 14 organisations and a total of £136,000 was awarded to an unspecified number of students. Of the organisations, nine had been supported in the previous year and most have long-term funding relationships with the trust.

Grants included those to National Heart and Lung Institute (£86,000), Napier University (£69,000), Hearing Research Trust (£33,000), University of Southampton (two grants totalling £32,000), Silsoe Research Institute (£31,000), University of Manchester (£30,000), University Of Edinburgh (£25,000) and British Occupational Health Research Foundation (£15,000).

Exclusions Grants are not made for the general funds of another charity or projects overseas.

Applications In writing to the correspondent. Trustees meet in May and November and applications may be submitted at any time.

The Comino Foundation

Education
£552,000 (2000/01)
Beneficial area UK.

29 Hollow Way Lane, Amersham, Buckinghamshire HP6 6DJ
Tel. 01494 722595
Email enquire@cominofoundation.org.uk
Website www.cominofoundation.org.uk
Correspondent A C Roberts, Administrator
Trustees *Anna Comino-Jones; J A C Darbyshire; Dr W Eric Duckworth; Prof. John Tomlinson; Mike Tomlinson; Simon Bailey; J E Slater.*
CC Number 312875
Information available Full accounts were on file at the Charity Commission.

General The Comino Foundation is an educational charity and has two main purposes:

- to promote awareness that industry and commerce produce the basic goods, services and resources on which wellbeing and quality of life depend
- to promote a clearer understanding of the basic processes involved in getting results, and thus improve people's power and will to create opportunities and achieve their purposes.

The foundation's vision is: 'that people in Britain should live more fulfilled lives within a prosperous and responsible society. The foundation contributes to the

realisation of this vision through its educational activities by:

a) encouraging and enabling groups and individuals to motivate and empower themselves and to develop progressively their potential for the benefit of themselves and others, and
b) encouraging a culture which affirms and celebrates both achievement and responsible practice in industry and commerce.'

In 2000/01 the foundation had assets of £7 million and an income of £268,000. After management and administration expenses of £99,000, grants totalled £552,000.

The largest grants were £30,000 each to six institutions that have actively promoted the GRASP approach during the year. GRASP (Getting Results and Solving Problems) is a registered trademark of the Comino Foundation and offers a structure for thinking about getting high-quality results. 'It introduces pattern design and method into this thinking. It helps to develop a clearer understanding of the process of achieving results and a more creative way of operating to enable the achievement of those results.' The institutions supported were Dudley Education Services, King Alfred's College – Winchester, Liverpool John Moores University, Sheffield Hallam University, University of Warwick and Wigan Borough Partnership, all of which were also supported in the previous year.

Other larger grants went to Institute for Global Ethics UK Trust (£25,000), RSA (£23,000), Brunel University (£15,000), SATRO (£12,000), Potential Trust (£9,000), CCTL (£5,000), Campaign for Learning (£3,000), Foundation for Science and Technology (£2,000) and National Parenting Institute (£1,500).

Exclusions No grants to individuals or general appeals.

Applications By letter, including full details of proposed project and finances. There is no formal application form. Applications are considered at four formal meetings of the trustees each year.

Gordon Cook Foundation

Education and training
£214,000 (2000)
Beneficial area UK.

Hilton Place, Aberdeen AB24 4FA
Tel. 01224 283704 **Fax** 01224 485457
Email i.b.brown@norcol.ac.uk
Website www.norcol.ac.uk
Correspondent Irene B Brown, Foundation Secretary
Trustees *D A Adams, Chair; Prof. B J McGettrick; Dr P Clarke; Dr W Gatherer; J Marshall; C P Skene; D S C Levie.*
CC Number SC017455
Information available Full accounts and guidelines were provided by the trust.

General This foundation was set up in 1974 and is dedicated to the advancement and promotion of all aspects of education and training which are likely to promote 'character development' and 'citizenship'. The following information is taken from the foundation's own leaflet.

'In recent years, the foundation has adopted the term 'Values Education' to denote the wide range of activity it seeks to support. This includes:

- the promotion of good citizenship in its widest terms, including aspects of moral, ethical and aesthetic education, youth work, cooperation between home and school, and coordinating work in school with leisure time pursuits
- the promotion of health education as it relates to values education
- supporting relevant aspects of moral and religious education
- helping parents, teachers and others to enhance the personal development of pupils and young people
- supporting developments in the school curriculum subjects which relate to values education
- helping pupils and young people to develop commitment to the value of work, industry and enterprise generally
- disseminating the significant results of relevant research and development.'

The view of the trustees is that the work of the foundation should:

- invest in people and in effective organisations
- have an optimum impact on the educational and training system, and consequently on children and young people in life and work.

In 2000 assets stood at £9 million generating an income of around £285,000 each year. The foundation states that it currently supports a number of projects, including 'Consultations' organised by Institute of Global Ethics, Professional Ethics, Business Ethics, Enterprise Ethics and Values Education in the Four Home Nations.

Grants to 28 projects totalled £214,000. They ranged from £1,000 to £30,000. Lager grants included those to Norham Foundation (£30,000), Health Education Board for Scotland (£20,000), Citizen Foundation (£14,000) and North Lanarkshire Council and Northern College (£10,000 each).

Exclusions Individuals are unlikely to be funded.

Applications The trustees are proactive in looking for projects to support; however, unsolicited applications may be considered if they fall within the foundation's criteria and are in accordance with current programmes. Forms may be obtained from the correspondent.

The Mansfield Cooke Trust

Evangelical Christian work
£86,000 (2000/01)
Beneficial area Worldwide.

PO Box 201, West Malling, Kent ME19 5RS
Correspondent Nigel A M Cooke, Trustee
Trustees *N A M Cooke; B O Chilver.*
CC Number 244493
Information available Full accounts were provided by the trust.

General Nearly all grants are for some form of evangelical work – missions, youth work, scripture and so on. Grants are given locally, to UK charities and overseas, to causes with which the trustees have personal contact. Other applications are not considered.

In 2000/01 the trust had assets of £120,000 and an income of £143,000, mainly from donations. A total of £86,000 was given in 48 grants ranging from £100 to £19,000. The largest grants went to Worthing Tabernacle (£19,000), Operation Mobilisation (£9,000), Haggai

Institute (£7,500), Tearfund (£5,000), Luis Palau Evangelistic Association, Care Trust and Christians in Overseas Services Trust (£2,500 each). A further 20 organisations received grants ranging between £1,000 and £2,000, including Africa Inland Mission, Latin Link, Action Partners, Dayspring Trust, South Asia Concern, Philo Trust and U F M Worldwide.

Beneficiaries receiving under £1,000 included Elim Pentecostal Church in Harare, Cystic Fibrosis Trust, Keswick Convention, John Grooms Association, Interhealth and Christian Research Association.

Applications The correspondent states that the trust is 'established for specific purposes related to the personal contacts of the trustees' and that 'funds are fully committed and that applicants should not waste their time or ours by writing'. There would therefore seem little point in applying to this trust unless you have personal contact with a trustee.

The Cooks Charity

Catering, general
£178,000 (2000/01)
Beneficial area UK and London.

The Old Deanery, Deans Court, London EC4V 5AA
Tel. 020 7593 5043 **Fax** 020 7248 3221
Correspondent M C Thatcher, Clerk and Solicitor
Trustees *M V Kenyon; A W Murdoch; H F Thornton.*
CC Number 297913
Information available Accounts were on file at the Charity Commission.

General The trust was established in 1989 to support educational and welfare projects concerned with people involved in catering, and then any charitable purposes in the City of London. In 2000/01 it had assets of £3 million and an income of £224,000, of which £80,000 came from investments and £62,000 from Gift Aid.

Grants were given to Hackney College (£98,000) and Bournemouth University (£51,000), both of which appear to be receiving ongoing support. Other beneficiaries were Academy of Culinary Arts (£20,000), Cooks Benefactors

Charity (£7,500), St Lawrence Jewry (£1,000) and City of London Sea Cadets (£800). In previous years other beneficiaries have included British Heart Foundation, Broderers Trust, Constable Trust, Friends of Highgate Cemetery, HCBA, St John Ambulance and PM Club.

Applications In writing to the correspondent. Applications are considered in spring and autumn.

The Cooper Charitable Trust

Medical, disability, Jewish
£128,000 (2000/01)
Beneficial area UK.

c/o Portrait Solicitors, 1 Chancery Lane, London WC2A 1LF
Tel. 020 7320 3890
Correspondent Miss J S Portrait, Trustee
Trustees *Mrs S Roter; Miss Judith Portrait; Ms M Hockley.*
CC Number 206772
Information available Accounts were on file at the Charity Commission with a very brief narrative report.

General The trust was originally endowed with shares in Lee Cooper plc, which was taken over by Vivat Holdings plc. These shares were sold in 1990/91 and the assets of the trust are now invested in government stocks.

In 2000/01 the trust had assets of £2 million and an income of £145,000. Grants were given to 18 beneficiaries totalling £128,000. One large grant of £108,000 was made to British Heart Foundation, with a further three grants of £2,000 each given to Elimination of Leukaemia Fund, Heathlands Village and Motor Neurone Disease Association.

A further 14 grants of £1,000 each were given to Aidis Trust, Aspire, Children's Hospitals Appeals Trust, Disabled Young and Adults Centre, Dystonia Society, Guideposts Trust, Handicapped Children's Action Group, International Spinal Research Trust, Jewish Blind and Disabled, Kidscape, Movement Foundation, Muscular Dystrophy Group, Side by Side and Thrive.

Exclusions No grants to individuals.

Applications In writing to the correspondent; applications are not acknowledged.

The Alice Ellen Cooper-Dean Charitable Foundation

General

£337,000 (2000/01)

Beneficial area UK, with a preference for Dorset.

Hinton House, Hinton Road, Bournemouth BH1 2EN

Tel. 01202 292424

Correspondent D J Neville-Jones, Trustee

Trustees *Miss S A M Bowditch; Rupert J A Edwards; Douglas J E Neville-Jones; Miss E J Bowditch.*

CC Number 273298

Information available Full accounts were provided by the trust.

General This trust aims to relieve poverty, distress and sickness, and advance education and religion and other charitable purposes of benefit to the community. Donations are only made to registered charities, which includes UK charities, but primarily go to local organisations.

The trust had assets of £6.6 million generating an income of £459,000 in 2000/01. Audit, accountancy and administration, legal and agents fees totalled £84,500. The foundation made 88 grants totalling £337,000.

The largest grants went to St John Ambulance – Dorset Branch (£28,000) and Bournemouth University (£25,000). Seven other beneficiaries received £10,000 or more; these were The West of England School (£15,000), Breakthrough Breast Cancer Appeal, Dorset (£12,000) and Hyped Project for Homeless Young People in East Dorset, Prama Care Attendant Scheme, Save the Children Fund – Ethiopia Appeal, Save the Children Fund – India Appeal and Sheltered Work Opportunities Project (£10,000 each).

Eventide Homes – Bournemouth received £6,000. All other grants were for between £1,000 and £5,000. Beneficiaries included Age Concern Bournemouth, Bournemouth Guide Camp Association, Bournemouth Sport Forum for the Disabled, Bournemouth War Memorial Homes, CancerCare Dorset, Devon & Dorset Regiment Museum Development Fund, Dorset County Association for the Blind, Dorset Opera, Green Island Holiday Trust, Hospital Radio Bedside, Salisbury Cathedral, Stable Family Home Trust and Youth Cancer Trust.

Exclusions No grants to individuals.

Applications In writing to the correspondent. The trust has stated that its funds are fully committed and that unsolicited applications have little chance of success.

The Marjorie Coote Animal Charity Fund

Wildlife and animal welfare

£104,000 (2000/01)

Beneficial area Worldwide.

Barn Cottage, Lindrick Common, Worksop, Nottinghamshire S81 8BA

Correspondent Sir Hugh Neill, Trustee

Trustees *Sir Hugh Neill; Mrs J P Holah; N H N Coote.*

CC Number 208493

Information available Full accounts were on file at the Charity Commission.

General The trust was established in 1954 for the benefit of five named charities and any other charitable organisation which has as its main purpose the care and protection of horses, dogs or other animals or birds. The trustees concentrate on research into animal health problems and on the protection of the species, whilst applying a small proportion of the income to general animal welfare, including sanctuaries.

In 2000/01 the trust had assets of £2.9 million generating an income of £111,000. It made 17 recurrent grants totalling £77,000 and 9 one-off grants totalling £27,000.

The largest recurrent grants went to Animal Health Trust (£25,000), PDSA (£7,000), Friends of Conservation (£6,000), Worldwide Fund for Nature (5,500), Frame and Guide Dogs for the Blind (£5,000 each), Devon Wildlife Trust and Whitley Wildlife Conservation Trust (£3,500 each) and Dian Fossey Gorilla Fund (£2,500).

The largest one-off grant was £20,000 to Langford Trust. Other one-off grants were for either £500 or £1,000 each and beneficiaries included Brecknock Wildlife Trust, Environmental Investigation Agency, International Otter Survival Fund and University of Oxford for the department of zoology.

Exclusions No grants to individuals.

Applications In writing to the correspondent. Applications should reach the correspondent during September for consideration in October/November. Urgent one-off applications for a specific project can be considered between meetings, although most applications are held over until the next meeting.

The Coppings Trust

General

£389,000 (2000/01)

Beneficial area UK.

44a New Cavendish Street, London W1G 8TR

Tel. 020 7486 4663

Correspondent Clive M Marks, Trustee

Trustees *Clive Marks; Dr R M E Stone; T P Bevan.*

CC Number 1015435

Information available Full accounts were on file at the Charity Commission.

General This trust does not respond to unsolicited applications as its funds are fully allocated in advance.

The trust states: 'The principle aims and objectives ... are centred around human rights, be it for immigrants' aid, the welfare of prisoners, or the victims of torture and anti-personnel mines. Family welfare therapy, care for disadvantaged youths, the aged and refugees are also the concern of the trustees. The trust also supports the literary and educational interests of the late settlor.'

In 2000/01 the trust had assets of £1.7 million and an income of £67,000. After high administration and management costs of £16,000, grants to 23 organisations totalled £389,000, up from £159,000 in 1999/2000.

The largest grants over £20,000 each were: £51,000 to Power; £50,000 to Prisoners Abroad; £35,000 each to 1990 Trust and Friends of Hebrew University of Jerusalem; £25,000 to London Jewish Cultural Centre; and £20,000 each to

Uniting Britain Trust and Ebony Steel Band Trust.

Other grants included Brighton Islamic Mission, Conciliation Resources and Yakar Educational Foundation – London (£15,000 each), Community Security Trust (£5,000), Amadeus Scholarship Fund (£2,000), Family Welfare Association (£500) and MTL Trust (£250).

Applications The trust has previously stated: 'The trustees are at present considering a number of applications already placed before them. Because of the heavy existing demands made, the trustees are concentrating on those projects already known to them'. The trust has previously stated: 'As funds are not available for new projects, the trustees do not feel justified in allocating administrative costs to responding to applications.'

The Duke of Cornwall's Benevolent Fund

General

£184,000 to organisations (2000/01)

Beneficial area UK.

10 Buckingham Gate, London SW1E 6LA

Tel. 020 7834 7346 **Fax** 020 7931 9541

Correspondent Robert Mitchell

Trustees *Hon. James Leigh-Pemberton; W R A Ross.*

CC Number 269183

Information available Full accounts were on file at the Charity Commission.

General The fund receives donations from the Duke of Cornwall (Prince Charles) based on amounts received by the Duke as Bona Vacantia (the causal profits of estates of deceased intestates dying domiciled in Cornwall without kin) after allowing for costs and ex-gratia payments made by the Duke in relation to claims on any estate.

The fund's objectives are:

- the relief of people in need
- provision of almshouses
- homes of rest
- hospitals and convalescent homes
- advancement of education

- advancement of religion
- advancement of the arts
- preservation for the benefit of the public of lands and buildings.

In 2000/01 the trust had assets of £2.5 million and an income of £98,000. Grants to organisations totalled £184,000. Grants were also given to three individuals totalling £12,000. The fund had administration and management costs of £1,400.

Support was given to environmental, conservation and medical groups. The accounts listed 22 grants of over £1,000, of which the largest single donation was £100,000 to Prince of Wales Charitable Foundation. Other beneficiaries of £5,000 or more included: Soil Association (£16,000), Trustees of Edington Foundation (£5,500), Isles of Scilly Environmental Trust (£5,300) and Brownsword Hall Charity and Hereford Cathedral Perpetual Trust (£5,000 each).

Other grants included those to Church of the Archangel Michael and St Piron (£4,200), Cornwall Macmillan Service, National Trust and University of Reading (£2,000 each) and Cornwall Children's Hospital Appeal (£1,500). There were 11 grants of £1,000 each, including those to Dorchester Arts Centre, Exeter Health Care Arts, Marine Conservation Society, New Connection Project, Somervale School and Westcountry Rivers Trust.

Unlisted grants of less than £1,000 each totalled £24,000.

Applications In writing to the correspondent. Applicants should give as much detail as possible, especially information on how much money has been raised to date, what the target is and how it will be achieved. Applications can be made at any time.

The Sidney & Elizabeth Corob Charitable Trust

General

£268,000 (2000/01)

Beneficial area UK.

62 Grosvenor Street, London W1K 3JF

Correspondent Stephen Wiseman, Trustee

Trustees *S Corob; E Corob; C J Cook; J V Hajnal; Ms S A Wechsler; S Wiseman.*

CC Number 266606

Information available Full accounts were on file at the Charity Commission.

General The trust has general charitable purposes, supporting a range of causes including education, arts, welfare and Jewish charities.

In 2000/01 the trust had assets of £1.7 million and an income of £87,000. Grants totalled £268,000, of which 43, of £1,000 or more, were listed in the accounts. By far the largest was £90,000 to Oxford Centre for Hebrew and Jewish Studies.

Other beneficiaries of grants over £10,000 included University College London (£27,000), Jewish Care (£15,000) and British Museum Development Trust (£11,000).

Remaining listed grants ranged from £1,000 to £8,500 and included those to British Technion Society (£8,500), Community Security Trust (£7,300), Pegasus Scholarship Trust (£6,000), Royal National Theatre (£5,400), Chief Rabbinate Charitable Trust (£5,000), Hampstead Theatre (£3,000), National Trust (£2,500), Live Music Now! (£1,500), B'nai Brith Hillel Foundation and RNIB (£1,300 each) and Family Welfare Association, Holocaust Education Trust, Jewish Book Council and Scopus Jewish Education Trust (£1,000 each).

Sundry donations of less than £1,000 each totalled £30,000.

Exclusions No grants to individuals or non-registered charities.

Applications Due to funds being fully committed the trust cannot accept any further applications for at least the next 12, possibly 24 months.

The Cotton Trust

Relief of suffering, elimination and control of disease, people who are disabled and disadvantaged

£190,000 (2001/02)

Beneficial area UK and overseas.

PO Box 6895, Earl Shilton, Leicester LE9 8ZE

Correspondent Mrs J B Congdon, Trustee

Trustees *Mrs J B Congdon; Mrs T E Dingle; Ms E S Cotton.*

CC Number 222995

Information available Accounts were provided by the trust, but without a narrative report or a list of grants.

General The trust's policy is: the relief of suffering; the elimination and control of diseases; and helping people of any age who are disabled or disadvantaged. Grants are given for defined capital projects (excluding building construction and the purchase of new buildings). Running costs can be funded where there are identified projects. About 70 to 80 grants are awarded each year, ranging between £500 and £2,500.

In 2001/02 the trust had assets of £5.3 million and an income of £216,000. Grants totalled £190,000. Management and administration costs amounted to £41,000. No information was available on the beneficiaries.

Exclusions Grants are only given to UK-registered charities that have been registered for at least one year. No grants to animal charities, individuals, students, further education, travel, expeditions, conservation, environment, arts, new building construction or the purchase of new buildings.

Applications In writing to the correspondent with latest accounts, evidence of charitable status, detailed budget, timetable and details of funds raised.

Guidelines are available with an sae. Deadlines for applications are the end of July and the end of January, with successful applicants being notified within three months of these dates. It is regretted that only successful applications can be answered. The trustees only accept one application in a 12-month period.

The Augustine Courtauld Trust

General

£93,000 (2000/01)

Beneficial area UK, with a preference for Essex.

Red House, Colchester Road, Halstead, Essex CO9 2DZ

Website www.augustinecourtauldtrust.org

Correspondent Richard Long, Clerk

Trustees Lord Bishop of Chelmsford; Revd A C C Courtauld; Lord Braybrooke; Col. N

A C Croft; J Courtauld; Lord Tanlaw; Lady Braybrooke; Derek Fordham.

CC Number 226217

Information available Accounts were on file at the Charity Commission.

General This trust was founded in 1956 by Augustine Courtauld, an Arctic explorer who was proud of his Essex roots. His charitable purpose was simply: 'my idea is to make available something that will do some good.' Among the main areas of work supported before his death in 1959 were young people, people with disabilities, the countryside, certain churches, Arctic exploration and the RNLI. The current guidelines are to support organisations that are:

- working within the historical boundaries of the county of Essex
- involved in expeditions to the Arctic and Antarctic regions
- known to one of the trustees.

Within Essex, the preference is to support disadvantaged young people, conservation projects and certain charities that the founder specifically wanted to help. Grants range from £500 to £2,000 for projects and core costs and can be for multiple years, but only if the charity applies for a grant in consecutive years.

In 2000/01 the trust had assets of £1.5 million, which generated an income of £103,000. Grants were given to 78 organisations and totalled £93,000. Administration costs were very low at only £4,600.

The largest grants were £10,000 to Friends of Essex Churches, £7,000 to Gino Watkins Memorial Fund, £5,000 to Chelmsford Cathedral, £4,000 to Essex Association of Boys Clubs, £3,000 to Saffron Walden Church, £2,500 each to Bishop of Chelmsford's Discretionary Fund, Lord Lieutenant's Discretionary Fund and YMCA Chelmsford, £2,000 each to Cirdan Trust, Dawn Hall Trust and Prader-Willi Syndrome and £1,500 to Little Haven Children's Hospice.

Recipients of £1,000 each included Age Concern Essex, Essex Clergy Charity Corporation, Essex Community Foundation, Essex Heritage Trust, Mildmay Mission Hospital, MS Society, Royal Geographical Society and St Luke's Church – Upminster. Smaller grants included £750 to Clergy Orphan Corporation (Chelmsford Diocesan Fund), £500 each to Camping Holidays for Inner City Kids, Cancer Campaign in Suffolk, Daybreak, Fairbridge Drake Society, Hearing Help Trust, Keston College, National Association of Swimming Clubs for the Handicapped,

Thomas Phillips Price Trust and Southend YMCA and £250 to Clockwise Centre – Clacton-on-sea.

Exclusions No grants to individuals. No grants to individual churches for fabric repairs or maintenance.

Applications In writing to the correspondent, or online via the trust's website. Applications are considered in spring.

The Sir William Coxen Trust Fund

Orthopaedic hospitals or other hospitals or charities doing orthopaedic work

£74,000 (2001/02)

Beneficial area England.

The Town Clerk's Office, Corporation of London, PO Box 270, Guildhall, London EC2P 2EJ

Tel. 020 7332 1432

Email david.haddon@corpoflondon.gov.uk

Correspondent David Haddon, Clerk to the Trustees

Trustees Six Aldermen appointed by the Court of Aldermen, together with the Lord Mayor.

CC Number 206936

Information available Accounts were on file at the Charity Commission.

General This trust was established following a bequest from the late Sir William Coxen in 1940. Expenditure is mainly applied for the support of orthopaedic hospitals or other hospitals or charities doing orthopaedic work.

In 2001/02 the trust had assets of £1.6 million and an income of £66,000. Grants were made to nine organisations totalling £74,000. By far the largest grant was £34,000 to St Bartholomew's Foundation to fund a fellowship. The remaining eight beneficiaries each received £5,000; these were Brittle Bones Society, Claire House, Jennifer Trust, Medical Engineering Resource Unit, Osteopathic Centre for Children, Handicapped Children's Action Group, Brainwave and Simon Paul Foundation.

Exclusions No grants to individuals or non-charitable institutions.

Applications In writing to the correspondent.

The Craignish Trust

Arts, education, environment, general

£82,000 (2000/01)

Beneficial area UK, with a preference for Scotland.

Messrs Geoghegan & Co., 6 St Colme Street, Edinburgh EH3 6AD

Tel. 0131 225 4681 **Fax** 0131 220 1132

Correspondent The Secretaries

Trustees *Clifford Hastings; Ms Caroline Younger; Ms Margaret Matheson.*

CC Number SC016882

Information available Full accounts were provided by the trust.

General Established in 1961 by the late Sir William McEwan Younger, the 2000/01 accounts summarised the funding criteria as follows:

- no large national charities
- Scottish bias, but not exclusively
- arts, particularly where innovative and/or involved in the community
- education
- environment
- of particular interest to a trustee.

In 2000/01 the trust had assets of £4.1 million, which generated an income of £151,000. From a total expenditure of £117,000, grants were given to 48 organisations totalling £82,000. Nine of the beneficiaries were also supported in the previous year.

The largest grants were £5,000 each to Henley Symphony Orchestra and Institute of Economic Affairs, £4,000 to Autonomic Disorders Association and £3,500 to John Muir Trust Appeal. Other grants included £2,500 each to Boilerhouse Theatre Group, Drug Prevention Group, Edinburgh Common Purpose and Friends of the Earth Scotland, £2,000 each to Edinburgh Cyrenians and Sustrans, £1,500 to Cannongate Youth Project, £1,000 each to Braendam Link, ChildLine Scotland, Edinburgh Youth Orchestra Society, Reality at Work in Scotland and Visible Fictions Theatre Company, £500 each to

Edinburgh Sitters and Working for Environmental Community Action and £250 to Orcadia Creative Learning Centre.

Exclusions Running costs are not normally supported.

Applications There is no formal application form; applicants should write to the correspondent. Details of the project should be included together with a copy of the most recent annual report and accounts.

The Craps Charitable Trust

Jewish, general

£200,000 (2001/02)

Beneficial area UK, Israel.

3rd Floor, Bryanston Court, Selden Hill, Hemel Hempstead, Hertfordshire HP2 4TN

Correspondent The Trustees

Trustees *J P M Dent; C S Dent; L R Dent.*

CC Number 271492

Information available Full accounts were on file at the Charity Commission.

General This trust supports mostly Jewish charities, although medical and other organisations are also supported. There is a list of eight charities mentioned in the trust deed, although not all of these are supported every year and other groups in the UK and overseas can be supported.

In 20001 the trust had assets of £3.3 million, which generated an income of £264,000. Grants totalling £200,000 were made during the year.

The largest grants were: £30,000 to British Technion Society; £20,000 to Jewish Care; £16,000 each to Friends of the Federation of Women Zionists and Home for Aged Jews; £10,000 each to Joint Jewish Charitable Trust and the New Israel Fund; £4,000 each to Amnesty International, Ben-Gurian University Foundation, Friends of the Earth, British Friends of Haifa University, Friends of Israel Educational Trust, and Revelswood Foundation.

Applications The trust states that 'funds of the trust are fully committed and the trust does not invite applications for its funds'.

The Cross Trust

Christian work

£251,000 to organisations
(2000/01)

Beneficial area UK and overseas.

Cansdales, Bourbon Court, Nightingale Corner, Little Chalfont, Buckinghamshire HP7 9QS

Tel. 01494 765428

Correspondent The Trustees

Trustees *M S Farmer; Mrs J D Farmer; D J Olsen.*

CC Number 298472

Information available Full accounts were on file at the Charity Commission

General The trust's objects are:

- work for the furtherance of religious and secular education
- advancement of the Christian faith in the UK and overseas
- relief of Christian workers, their dependants, and other people who are poor, sick, elderly or otherwise in need
- support for any religious or charitable institution.

In 2000/01 the assets of the trust totalled £370,000. Total income was £675,000, nearly all of which came from donations received. Grants were made to nine organisations totalling £251,000, and to 14 individuals totalling £92,000.

The largest grant was £150,000 to Aeropagus Trust for general work. Other large grants were £50,036 to George Whitefield Theological Training College for the new building fund, £25,000 to Rock Foundation and £10,000 to Cornhill Training Courses for overseas students' fees.

The other organisations supported were E Ivor Hughes Education Foundation (£5,500), Girls' Day School Trust (£3,300), Emmanuel College, and Gujarat Appeal (£3,000 each) and Met Clinic (£1,500).

Applications No unsolicited applications are supported, with funds already fully committed.

Cuby Charitable Trust

Jewish

£123,000 (1999/2000)

Beneficial area UK.

16 Mowbray Road, Edgware, Middlesex HA8 8JQ

Tel. 020 7563 6868

Correspondent S S Cuby, Chair

Trustees *S S Cuby; Mrs C B Cuby.*

CC Number 328585

Information available Accounts are on file at the Charity Commission, but without a list of grants.

General This trust states that it supports Jewish causes. In 1999/2000 it received an income totalling £133,000 and grants totalled £123,000. The trust's assets totalled £1,000. A list of beneficiaries was not included with the accounts.

Applications In writing to the correspondent.

The Dennis Curry Charitable Trust

Conservation, general

£90,000 (2000/01)

Beneficial area UK.

Messrs Alliotts, 5th Floor, 9 Kingsway, London WC2B 6XF

Tel. 020 7240 9971

Correspondent N J Armstrong, Secretary to the Trust

Trustees *M Curry; Mrs A S Curry; Mrs M Curry-Jones; Mrs P Edmond.*

CC Number 263952

Information available Accounts were on file at the Charity Commission with a very brief narrative report.

General The trust has general charitable objects with special interest in the environment and education; occasional support is given to churches and cathedrals.

In 2000/01 the trust had assets of £3.1 million and an income of £125,000. A total of £90,000 was given in 19 grants.

The largest grants were of £10,000 each and went to three organisations: Council for National Parks, Durrell Wildlife Conservation Society and Galopagos Trust. Other grants included: £9,400 to Earth Science Teachers' Association; £5,000 each to Friends of Ludlow Museum, National Youth Wind Orchestra of Great Britian and South Buckinghamshire NHS Trust; £2,000 to Forest Stewardship Council; £1,000 to Project Trust; and £500 each to International Scientific Support Trust and Rainforest Concern.

Applications In writing to the correspondent.

The Roald Dahl Foundation

Haematology, neurology, literacy

£453,000 (2000/01)

Beneficial area UK.

92 High Street, Great Missenden, Bucks HP16 0AN

Tel. 01494 890465 **Fax** 01494 890459

Website www.roalddahlfoundation.org

Correspondent Linda Lazenby, Deputy Director

Trustees *Felicity Dahl, Chair; Martin Goodwin; Roger Hills.*

CC Number 1004230

Information available Guidelines for applicants. Exceptionally clear, complete and well-written annual report and accounts.

General This foundation aims to provide support to three areas that were of personal interest and significance to Roald Dahl: neurology, haematology and literacy. Within these areas, its current policy and criteria as follows:

Neurology and haematology

In these fields the foundation is keen to help children and young people up to the age of 25 (and their families) with, in the case of haematology: haemophillia, sickle cell disease and thalassaemia and some rare blood disorders which are not cancer related; and in the case of neurology: epilepsy, acquired brain injury and neurodegenerative conditions in which there is progressive intellectual and neurological deterioration. Specifically, grants may be made for:

- pump-prime funding of specialist paediatric nursing care, especially where there is an emphasis on community care, for a maximum of two years (the trust will require information about the source of permanent funding after the two-year period)
- provision of information and/or support to children and young people who come into the above medical categories and their families
- assistance to residential and day care centres for children and young people who come into the above medical categories (such grants would normally be awarded on a project basis)
- small items of medical equipment that will allow the patient to be cared for in the home, with community care/ hospital back-up.
- individual grants of £50 to £500 to the children in the above categories from families that are suffering financial hardship, for specified needs.

Literacy

Through its association with Readathon, the national sponsored reading event, the foundation is already actively involved in promoting literacy throughout the UK. Currently it is interested in making grants for:

- specific literacy work to improve poor literacy skills among children and young people, and their families, in out-of-school clubs and centres for young people (aged 16–25)
- computer/technological and other assistance to enable children and young people who are visually impaired or head-injured to access the written word.

Applications concerning dyslexia are not currently considered. Before he died, Roald Dahl with the foundation's president, Quentin Blake, donated a large sum to the Dyslexia Institute through the auction of their book *The Vicar of Nibbleswicke.*

In general, the foundation aims to provide help to organisations to whom funds are not readily available. It prefers to help small or new organisations rather than long-established, large or national organisations.

The range of grants given is wide. At the moment, the individual grants vary from £50 to £500 and those to organisations from £500 to £25,000; the largest grants are made to pump-prime new nursing posts.

Potential applicants are strongly advised to telephone the foundation to obtain a copy of the current guidelines, and to discuss a potential application, before making an application for funding.

In 2000/01 the foundation had assets of £1.5 million and an income of £674,000 including £41,000 in general donations and £556,000 from the proceeds of the annual Readathon (whose proceeds are shared with Sargent Cancer Care for Children). Grants totalled £453,000 and were categorised as follows, shown with examples of beneficiaries:

Neurology – £223,000
There were 25 grants listed in this category, of which 8 were over £10,000. Included in these grants were seven part-payments of grants to pump-prime new nursing posts: £34,000 to Glan Hafren NHS Trust – Newport, £7,100 to National Hospital for Neurology and Neurosurgery, £6,000 to Leeds Teaching Hospitals NHS Trust and £2,000 to Surrey Sussex NHS Trust.

Other grants included those to National Hospital for Neuro-disability (£25,000), Headway Belfast (£10,000), Different Strokes (£6,300), Fund for Epilepsy – London (£5,000), Children's Acquired Brain Injury Interests Group (£4,000), Royal Belfast Hospital for Sick Children (£1,600), Queens Medical Centre – Nottingham (£500) and Royal Liverpool Children's Hospital Trust (£200).

Haematology – £86,000
There were eight grants listed in this category, the largest of which was £25,000 to University College London. One grant was a part-payment of a two-year pump-priming grant to fund a new post at North Middlesex Hospital (£2,000). Other beneficiaries included Haemophilia Society UK (£13,000 in two grants), Primary Immunodeficiency Association UK (£12,000), Oxford Radcliffe Hospital Trust (£9,000), Tower Hamlets Sickle Cell & Thalassaemia Centre (£5,000) and Francis Barber Pupil Referral Unit at St George's Hospital – London (£280).

Literacy – £110,000
There were 39 grants listed in this category, the largest of which was £10,000 to AbilityNet – Scotland to enable them to assess the computer needs of children with disabilities. Other beneficiaries included Henshaws Society for Blind People – Harrogate, Newcastle Literacy Trust and YMCA Training – Croydon (£5,000 each), Cardinal Hume Centre – London, Impact Community Developments – Bradford and REACH (£4,000 each), Ethiopian Advice and Support Centre – London (£3,800), Manchester Settlement (£2,500), Parenting 2000 – Southport (£1,500), Templemore Secondary School –

Londonderry (£1,200), Moneynenna After School Club – County Derry (£1,000), Deeplish CP School – Rochdale (£500) and Cuttleslowe Community Centre Homework Club – Oxford (£180).

Small, unlisted grants, mainly to individuals were distributed across the three categories totalling £73,000. Those distributed in the literacy category were given via AbilityNet and Disability Aid Fund.

Exclusions The foundation does not consider grant applications for:

- general appeals from large, well-established charities or national appeals for large building projects
- research in any field
- any organisations which do not have charitable status or exclusively charitable aims
- statutory bodies
- outside the UK
- school or higher education fees.

Applications On the straightforward form provided, with a covering letter if necessary.

Applications are considered throughout the year. Decisions on smaller sums can take as little as a few weeks. Applications for grants of several thousand pounds may take several months to be considered.

The Daiwa Anglo-Japanese Foundation

Anglo-Japanese relations
£314,000 to organisations and individuals (1999/2000)
Beneficial area UK, Japan.

Daiwa Foundation, Japan House, 13/14 Cornwall Terrace, London NW1 4QP

Tel. 020 7486 4348 **Fax** 020 7486 2914

Email office@dajf.org.uk

Website www.dajf.org.uk

Correspondent Prof. Marie Conte-Helm, Director General

Trustees *Sir David Wright; Yoshitoki Chino; Lady Adrian; Prof. Sir Alec Broers; Lord Carrington; Nicholas Clegg; Hiroaki Fujii; Tomoaki Kusuda; Lord Roll of Opsden.*

CC Number 299955

Information available An information leaflet was available from the foundation.

Full accounts were on file at the Charity Commission.

General The foundation was established in 1988, through a donation made by Daiwa Securities, to promote understanding between the UK and Japan in the cultural, professional, academic and artistic fields.

The foundation has three objectives:

- advancement of UK and Japanese citizens' understanding of each other's peoples and culture
- award of scholarships and maintenance allowances for UK or Japanese students to travel abroad to pursue education
- grants to institutions involved in promoting education in the UK or Japan, or research into cultural, historical, medical and scientific subjects and publication of such research.

In 1999/2000 the trust had assets of £40 million and an income of £1.6 million. Charitable expenditure totalled £1.1 million and administration and management fees £234,000, spent on the centre's library and holding seminars and conferences. Grants totalled £314,000.

The grants list was divided into the following catergories:

Grants given in the UK
Japanese Language
£12,000 in four grants, including £5,000 to Association for Language and Learning (ALL) to fund the first two years of the newly established Japanese Language Committee and £1,500 to British Association for Teachers of Japanese (BATJ) to cover the costs of printing the BATJ journal.

Japanese Studies
£97,000 in 20 grants, the largest was £15,000 to Birbeck College, London, towards a lectureship in Japanese History (last instalment of a five-year grant). There were 14 grants of £1,000 each for annual student exchanges at schools. The foundation has entered into an arrangement with Connect Youth International (part of the British Council), which now processes applications for school and youth exchanges related to Japan.

Professional and academic exchanges
£56,000 in 18 grants, including £7,500 to the UK/Japan Research and Development Group for Ageing, Disability and Rehabilitation (RADGADAR) in order to advance areas of development in relation to ageing and £5,000 to Links Japan towards the costs of a week long visit by a delegation from the Shimin (civil) Forum 21 Non Profit Organisation centre to

study the structure of the voluntary sector in the UK.

Art

£53,000 in 31 grants, including £2,000 each to Tate Gallery towards the costs of a pilot scheme to send two British Artists on three month residencies in Japan, to World Haiku Festival and to West Country Craftsmen of UK–Japan for members to travel to Japan to put on an exhibition in Okayama and to acquire experience of Japanese traditional crafts.

Grants given in Japan

Professional and academic exchanges: £63,000 in 27 grants of between £1,000 and £3,000, to allow Japanese citizens to visit the UK for academic or medical research.

Art

£32,000 in 15 grants, including £1,000 each towards the visit a Kabuki actor to London for a public discussion at the Globe Theatre and to Theatre Planning Network Kansai to hold a workshop on the Alexander Technique.

The foundation also awards the Daiwa Adrian Prizes every three years to joint teams of British and Japanese scientists engaged in collaborative research. (In December 1998 four prizes totalled £50,000.)

Applications Forms are available online at www.dajf.org.uk. Deadlines for applications are 31 March and 30 September.

Applications originating from the UK should be sent to the address shown. Applications originating from Japan should be sent to The Daiwa Anglo-Japanese Foundation, TBR Bldg. 810, Nagat-cho2-10-2, Chiyoda-ku, Tokyo 100-0014.

Oizer Dalim Trust

General

£147,000 (1998/99)
Beneficial area UK.

68 Osbaldeston Road, London N16 7DR
Correspondent M Cik
Trustees *B Berger; M Freund; N Weinberger.*
CC Number 1045296
Information available Accounts were on file at the Charity Commission, but without a list of grants.

General The trust has previously supported a wide range of charities throughout the UK, but without having been able to see a recent grants list we are unable to confirm this is still true.

In 2000/01 it had an income of £172,000 and a total expenditure of £171,000. This information was taken from the Charity Commission database; unfortunately no further details were available for this year. In 1998/99 its assets totalled only £7,200, while it received an income of £141,000. Grants were made totalling £147,000; a list of beneficiaries was not available.

Applications In writing to the correspondent.

This entry was not confirmed by the trust but was correct according to information on file at the Charity Commission.

David Charitable Trust

Health, welfare, children, older and infirm people, educational institutions, the arts

£111,000 (2001)
Beneficial area UK.

Payne Hicks Beach, Solicitors, 10 New Square, Lincoln's Inn, London WC2A 3QG
Tel. 020 7465 4300
Correspondent The Trustees
Trustees *B J David; C M David; G S Brown.*
CC Number 1015509
Information available Full accounts were on file at the Charity Commission.

General The trust makes grants towards health and welfare, children, older and infirm people, educational institutions and the arts. In 2001 it had assets of £386,000 and an income of £13,000. In 2000 the income was £471,000 due to the receipt of a donation of investments from a trustee.

Grants were made to seven organisations: Lady Hoare Trust (£75,000), Home Farm Trust and Prisoners of Conscience (£10,000 each), Martlet Hospice, Trestle Theatre Company Ltd and Trinity Hospice (£5,000 each) and National Endometriosis Society (£500).

Exclusions No grants to individuals.

Applications In writing to the correspondent, accompanied by latest annual report and accounts.

Davidson Charitable Trust

Jewish

£64,000 (1999/2000)
Beneficial area UK.

58 Queen Anne Street, London W1G 8HW
Tel. 020 7224 1030
Correspondent Mrs E Winer, Trustee
Trustees *G A Davidson; M Y Davidson; Mrs E Winer.*
CC Number 262937
Information available Accounts were on file at the Charity Commission.

General This Jewish charity had an income in 1999/2000 of £108,000, mainly derived from Gift Aid donations. Grants totalled £64,000, but a grants list was not included in the trust's annual report for that year. The trust's assets totalled £75,000 at the year end.

The most recent grants list available at the Charity Commission was for 1997/98, when £25,000 was donated in 35 grants. The largest grants were £5,300 to Norwood Ravenswood, £3,000 to British Friends of CBI, £2,700 to Joint Jewish Charitable Trust, £2,500 to Imperial War Museum's Holocaust Project and £1,700 to World Jewish Relief.

The remaining grants ranged between £100 and £1,000. Non-Jewish beneficiaries of these small grants included Barnardos, British Heart Foundation, Child Resettlement Fund, London University and The Progressive Supranuclear Palsy Association.

Applications In writing to the correspondent.

This entry was not confirmed by the trust, but the information was correct according to the Charity Commission file.

The Gwendoline & Margaret Davies Charity

Arts, general

£274,000 (2001/02)

Beneficial area UK, with particular favour given to Wales.

The Offices, Plas Dinam, Llandinam, Powys SY17 5DO

Tel. 01686 689172 **Fax** 01686 689172

Correspondent Mrs S Hamer

Trustees *Dr J A Davies; Lord Davies; Dr D Balsom.*

CC Number 235589

Information available Accounts and a separate list of grants were supplied by the trust.

General In 2001/02 the trust had assets of £5.8 million generating an income of £310,000. After administration expenses of £30,000, grants totalled £274,000.

The largest of these were £65,000 to MCRA, £50,000 to Wales Millennium Centre, £30,000 to Bethshan Nursing Home and £20,000 to University of Wales (re Gregynog). Wales Video Gallery received £12,000 with five grants of £10,000 including those to Coleg Y Bala, Llanelli/Dinefwr General Charitable Trust and Shooting Star Appeal.

A further 50 grants ranged from £50 to £5,000 and were given to a range of organisations including Beaumaris Festival, Gwynnedd Hospice at Home, Machynlleth Tabernacle Trust, Montgomery Area Scout Council, National Museums and Galleries of Wales, North Powys Youth Orchestra and Swansea Samaritans.

Details were provided in the trustees' report of nine grants totalling £242,000 that had been committed for the following year. As can be seen by comparison with the list above, most are recurrent grants. These were £100,000 to MCRA for a gallery, £50,000 to Millennium Centre, £30,000 to Bethshan Nursing Home, £20,000 to University of Wales, £12,000 to Wales Video Press, £10,000 each to Institute of Orthopaedics and North East Wales NHS Trust and £5,000 each to Powys Challenge Trust and University of Wales.

Exclusions Grants are made to registered charities only.

Applications The trustees consider appeals on an individual basis. There are no application forms as the trustees prefer to receive letters from applicants setting out the following information:

- whether the organisation is a registered charity
- details of the reason for the application – the type of work and so on
- the cost
- how much has been raised so far towards the cost
- the source of the sums raised
- a copy of the last audited accounts if available
- any other information that the applicant may consider would help the application.

Unsuccessful appeals are not informed unless an sae is enclosed.

The Dawe Charitable Trust

Homelessness, young people over the age of 16

£181,000 (2000/01)

Beneficial area Primarily East Anglia.

East View, 5 Coles Lane, Oakington, Cambridge CB4 5BA

Tel. 01223 237700 **Fax** 01223 235870

Email lisa@dawemedia.co.uk

Correspondent Lisa Baldwin

Trustees *Peter Dawe; Lindsay Dawe.*

CC Number 1060314

Information available Accounts were on file at the Charity Commission.

General Founded in 1997, this trust is primarily concerned with homelessness and young people over the age of 16. As well as supporting organisations, it has a nine-bedroom house running a working and living project for young people in Norfolk who are homeless.

In 2000/01 the trust had assets of £4.6 million and an income of £243,000. Grants were made to six organisations totalling £181,000. Total expenditure was £302,000.

Grants were £100,000 to Centrepoint, £50,000 to Order of St Ethelreda, £10,000 each to Access Partnership, Break and Motability and £1,000 to Camsight.

Applications In writing to the correspondent, outlining ideas and needs.

Peter De Haan Charitable Trust

Youth, general

£174,000 (2000/01)

Beneficial area UK.

3 Eurogate Business Park, Ashford, Kent TN24 8XW

Tel. 01233 652010

Correspondent Peter Charles De Haan, Trustee

Trustees *Peter Charles De Haan; Katherine Cockburn De Haan; Sallie Donaldson; David Peter Davies.*

CC Number 1077005

Information available Accounts were on file at the Charity Commission.

General As well as having general charitable purposes, this trust makes a number of grants to charities connected with children and young people. In 2000/01 it had assets of £1.3 million and an income of £297,000. After management and administration costs of £20,000, grants to 28 organisations totalled £174,000.

By far the largest grants were £40,000 to Brandon Centre, £30,000 to Rainbow Centre, £25,000 to National Missing Persons Helpline, £20,000 to CHAS Housing Aid Centre and £15,000 to Kids Company.

Other grants included £8,000 to League of Friends of Hazelhurst Resource Centre, £5,000 each to Apex Leicester and Tenterden Day Care Centre, £4,800 to KCA, £2,500 to Princes Trust and £2,000 to Demelza House.

Smaller grants in the range of £50 to £1,000 included those to Children's Aid Direct, Anthony Nolan Bone Marrow Trust, Victoria Hospital League of Friends and Youth Call Centre.

Applications In writing to the correspondent.

The Leopold De Rothschild Charitable Trust

Arts, Jewish, general
£79,000 (1996/97)
Beneficial area UK.

Rothschild Trust Corporation Ltd, New Court, St Swithin's Lane, London EC4P 4DU

Correspondent Miss Norma Watson
Trustees *Rothschild Trust Corporation Ltd.*
CC Number 212611
Information available Accounts were on file at the Charity Commission.

General The trust gives most of its support to the arts and has some preference for Jewish organisations, with limited support to other causes covering heritage, welfare, medical and children.

In 2000/01 this trust had an income of £45,000 and a total expenditure of £193,000. This information was taken from the Charity Commission database; unfortunately no further details were available for this year.

In 1996/97 the income was £62,000 and grants totalled £79,000, with the largest to English Chamber Orchestra and Music Society (£25,000). Other larger grants included £5,200 to American Museum in Britain and £5,000 each to Child Southbank Foundation, Jewish Childs Day and Saddlers Wells. Most grants were for £1,000 or less.

Applications In writing to the correspondent.

The Debmar Benevolent Trust

Jewish
£359,000 (1999/2000)
Beneficial area UK.

3rd Floor, Manchester House, 86 Princess Street, Manchester M1 6NP
Tel. 0161 236 4107
Correspondent M Weisz, Secretary
Trustees *M Weisz; G Klein; H Olsberg.*

CC Number 283065
Information available Full accounts were on file at the Charity Commission.

General Grants are given towards the advancement of the orthodox Jewish faith and the relief of poverty. In 1999/2000 the trust had assets of £1.9 million and an income of £440,000. Grants to 70 organisations totalled £359,000.

The largest grants were given to Square Foundation (£25,000) and Gevuras Ari Academy Trust and Telz Talmudical College (£23,000 each). Two of these were also major beneficiaries in the previous year.

Other grants included £10,000 each to Ahavas Torah Kollel – Jerusalem, Breslor Research Institute, Dushinsky Trust, Ohel Shimon – Jerusalem, Oizer Dalim Trust, Torah V'emurah – Jerusalem and Yeter Lev.

Applications In writing to the correspondent.

The Dellal Foundation

General, Jewish
£1.2 million (2000/01)
Beneficial area UK.

14th Floor, Bowater House, 68 Knightsbridge, London SW1X 7LT
Tel. 020 7299 1400
Correspondent S Whalley, Administrator
Trustees *J Dellal; E Azouz; J Azouz; G Dellal.*
CC Number 265506
Information available Full accounts were on file at the Charity Commission, but with only a brief narrative report.

General The trust states that it continues to give 'a significant proportion of the grants towards charities whose aim is the welfare and benefit of Jewish people'.

In 2000/01 the trust had assets of £2.3 million and an income of £245,000. Management and administration costs were very low at £1,600. A total of £1.2 million was given in 60 grants, up from £634,000 in the previous year.

There were two exceptionally large grants, of £500,000 to Somerset House Arts Fund and £400,000 to Tate Gallery. Other grants of £20,000 or more went to St

John's Hospice (£50,000), Tel Aviv Foundation (£35,000), Hineni Heritage Centre (£33,000), Institute for Policy Research and Westminster Synagogue (£25,000 each) and Community Security Trust (£20,000, plus a smaller grant of £5,000). There were seven grants of £10,000 each including those to Charity Challenge, Leukaemia Research Fund and Norwood Ltd.

Smaller grants of £500 to £6,000 included those to UNICEF (£6,000), Rescue a Child (£5,000), Focus and Salomon Sasson Foundation (£3,000 each), Imperial Cancer Research Fund and Magen David Yeshirah (£2,000 each), Parents for Children (£1,000) and Centrepoint (£500).

Exclusions No grants to individuals.

Applications In writing to the correspondent.

The Delves Charitable Trust

Environment, conservation, medical, general
£240,000 (2000/01)
Beneficial area UK.

New Guild House, 45 Great Charles Street, Queensway, Birmingham B3 2LX
Tel. 0121 212 2222 **Fax** 0121 212 2300
Correspondent Roger Harriman, Trust Administrator
Trustees *Mary Breeze; John Breeze; George Breeze; Dr Charles Breeze; Elizabeth Breeze; Roger Harriman.*
CC Number 231860
Information available Full accounts were on file at the Charity Commission.

General This trust has a list of 40 organisations that receive an annual subscription from the trust, and also provides a small number of grants to other organisations.

In 2001/02 the trust had assets of £5.6 million, which generated an income of £204,000. Management and administration for the year totalled £20,000. Grants totalled £251,000, broken down as follows:

Subscriptions – 40 totalling £223,000
The largest were £25,000 to British Heart Foundation, £10,000 each to Intermediate

Technology, Macmillan Cancer Relief, Sequel WaterAid, Liverpool School of Tropical Medicine and Quaker Peace and Service, and £5,000 to Survival International.

Donations – 25 totalling £28,000
Survival International received £5,000 from this category as well as £5,000 from the subscriptions list. The only other donations over £2,500 were to St Luke's – Oxford, Selby Oak Nursery School and Avoncroft Museum of Buildings, which received £3,000 each.

Exclusions The trust does not give sponsorships or personal educational grants.

Applications 'The funds of the trust are currently fully committed and no unsolicited requests can therefore be considered by the trustees.' Trustees meet in July and applications should therefore be received by the end of May.

The Dent Charitable Trust

Jewish, general
£97,000 (2000/01)
Beneficial area Worldwide.

c/o RSM Robson Rhodes, 186 City Road, London EC1V 2NU
Tel. 020 7251 1644
Correspondent J P M Dent, Trustee
Trustees *Miss C S Dent; J P M Dent; Miss L Dent.*
CC Number 271512
Information available Full accounts were on file at the Charity Commission.

General The trust has a list of eight Jewish organisations that it prefers to support. After this it will consider other charities in the UK and elsewhere, especially those concerned with agriculture, arts, children and medicine.

In 2000/01 the trust had assets of £1.6 million and an income of £98,000. Grants totalled £97,000.

The main grants were given to British Technion Society (£30,000), Friends of the Hebrew University (£14,000) and JNF Charitable Trust and Jerusalem Foundation (£10,000 each), all of which are regularly supported. Other grants included: £5,000 each to CBF World Jewish Relief, Sarah Herzog Memorial

Hospital and Shaare Zedek Medical Centre; £3,000 each to British ORT, Mind and Save the Children Fund; and £1,000 each to Holocaust Education Trust, Medical Foundation for the Care of Victims of Torture and Soho Theatre Company.

Applications The trust has previously stated that 'no further applications for funds can be considered'.

This entry was not confirmed by the trust, but it is correct according to information on file at the Charity Commission.

The Richard Desmond Charitable Trust

General
About £130,000 (2001)
Beneficial area Worldwide.

The Northern and Shell Tower, Ludgate House, 245 Blackfriars Road, London SE1 9UX
Tel. 020 7579 4580
Correspondent Gary Suckling
Trustees *R C Desmond; Mrs J Desmond.*
CC Number 1014352
Information available Information was provided by the trust

General The trust gives one-off and recurrent grants for core, capital and project funding for general charitable purposes, especially for the relief of poverty and sickness amongst children.

In 2001 the trust had an income of £144,000 and gave £138,000 in grants. Beneficiaries included Disability Foundation, Variety Club Educational Trust and World Jewish Relief.

Applications In writing to the correspondent.

The Duke of Devonshire's Charitable Trust

General, especially in Derbyshire
£245,000 (2001/02)
Beneficial area UK, with a preference for Derbyshire.

Currey & Co, 21 Buckingham Gate, London SW1E 6LS
Tel. 020 7802 2700 **Fax** 020 7828 5049
Correspondent The Trustee Manager
Trustees *Marquess of Hartington; Sir Richard Beckett; Nicholas W Smith.*
CC Number 213519
Information available Full accounts were provided by the trust.

General This trust has general charitable purposes giving grants ranging from £50 to £60,000 to a wide range of organisations, with a preference for those working in Derbyshire.

In 2001/02 the trust had assets of £9.4 million, which generated an income of £254,000. Grants were made to 106 organisations totalling £245,000. Management and administration expenditure was high at £32,000, including £14,000 in administration fees to a firm of solicitors in which one of the trustees is a parter. Whilst wholly legal, these editors always regret such payments unless, in the words of the Charity Commission, 'there is no realistic alternative'.

As in the previous year, the largest grant was £60,000 to Chatsworth House Trust. Other large grants went to Macmillan Cancer Relief (£25,000), Pilsley Church of England School (£20,000), Bolton Abbey for the vicar's house (£14,000) with £10,000 each to Cavendish Disabled Sailing Group, Craven Trust, Duke's Barn Trust and Myasthenia Gravis Association.

Grants in Derbyshire included £1,000 each to Belper Community Hall, Bolsover and District CVS, Chesterfield Action for Access, Derbyshire Children's Holiday Centre, Derbyshire Dales Careline, Hillstown Miners Welfare Scheme and Willington Old School.

Other beneficiaries included Abbeyfield Ilkley Society and Countryside Foundation for Education (£5,000), Eastbourne College Development Fund and Sheffield Childrens Hospital (£2,500 each), British Wireless for the Blind Fund

(£2,000), Challenger Disabled Sailing Group and St Leonard's Hospice – York (£1,000),

Exclusions Grants are only given to registered charities and not to individuals.

Applications In writing to the correspondent.

DG Charitable Trust

General

£222,000 (1998/99)
Beneficial area UK.

PO Box 62, Heathfield, East Sussex TN21 8ZE

Tel. 01435 867604 **Fax** 01435 863287

Correspondent Joanna Nelson

Trustees D J Gilmour; P Grafton-Green; Ms P A Samson.

CC Number 1040778

Information available Full accounts are on file at the Charity Commission.

General This trust makes regular donations to a fixed list of charities. In 2000/01 it had an income of £561,000 and a total expenditure of £390,000. This information was taken from the Charity Commission database; unfortunately no further details were available for this year.

At the end of 1998/99 its assets totalled £643,000. During the year it received an income of £513,000 and made grants totalling £222,000.

In 1998/99 grants ranged between £500 and £50,000, with the largest as follows: £50,000 to Amnesty International, which also received a second grant of £25,000 during the year; £27,000 to Terrence Higgins Trust; £25,000 each to Crisis and Diane Fossey Gorilla Fund; £15,000 to Petworth Cottage Nursing Home; £10,000 each to Great Ormond Street Hospital and St Richard's Hospital Appeal; £8,000 to The Weald; and £1,600 to Prince of Wales Charitable Foundation.

Applications This trust does not consider unsolicited applications.

The Dinam Charity

International understanding, general

£97,000 (1999/2000)
Beneficial area Worldwide.

Thomas Eggar, The Corn Exchange, Baffins Lane, Chichester, West Sussex PO19 1GE

Tel. 01243 786111

Correspondent Amanda King-Jones

Trustees Hon. Mrs M M Noble; Hon. Mrs G R J Cormack; Mrs A C Weston; Mrs M A M Lovegrove; R D Noble.

CC Number 231295

Information available Accounts were on file at the Charity Commission.

General In 1999/2000 the trust had assets of £2.7 million and an income of £86,000. Grants totalled £97,000, including £92,000 to David Davies Memorial Institute, regularly the main beneficiary.

A further 25 grants were made ranging from £30 to £1,000. Beneficiaries included St Andrew's Evangelical Mission (£1,000), Edinburgh Direct Aid (£600), Jubilee Action, Kurdish Disaster Fund, Medical Foundation and NSPCC (£500 each), Christian Aid (£400), Seafront Trust (£300), Friends of the Earth – Scotland (£200), World Development Movement (£150), Free Tibet Campaign and UNA Trust (£100 each) and Second Trust (£30).

Exclusions Grants are only given to registered charities. No grants to individuals.

Applications Applications can be made at any time. Unsuccessful applicants will not be notified unless an sae is enclosed with the application.

The Dorus Trust

Health and welfare, disability, homelessness, addiction, underprivileged children, environment

£168,000 (2000)
Beneficial area Mainly UK.

Charities Aid Foundation, King's Hill, West Malling, Kent ME19 4TA

Tel. 01732 520083 **Fax** 01732 520001

Correspondent Mrs Sue David, Donor Grants Officer

Trustees C H Peacock; Mrs Bettine Bond; A M Bond.

CC Number 328724

Information available Full accounts were on file at the Charity Commission.

General The trust has common trustees with two other trusts, The Cleopatra Trust and The Epigoni Trust (see separate entries) with which it also shares the same aims and polices. All three trusts are administered by Charities Aid Foundation. Generally the trusts support different organisations each year.

The trust makes grants in the following areas:

- mental health
- cancer welfare/education – not research
- diabetes
- physical disability – not research
- homelessness
- addiction
- underprivileged children.

There is also some preference for environmental causes. It only gives grants for specific projects and does not give grants for running costs or general appeals. Generally support is given to organisations with a UK-wide remit.

In 2000 the trust had assets of £3.1 million and an income of £161,000. Administration costs were low at £588. The trust gave 27 grants totalling £168,000. The largest was £18,000 to Royal Commonwealth Society for the Blind. Six grants of £10,000 each went to Carers National Association, Contact the Elderly, Independent Panel for Special Education Advice, Mentor Foundation (UK) for the Prevention of Substance Abuse, Refuge and Scottish Council on Alcohol.

Other grants included those to Children's Liver Disease Foundation (£8,000), Association of Wheelchair Children (£7,000), Action Cancer and Epilepsy

Association of Scotland (£6,000 each), Deafblind UK, Kidsactive and Young Minds Trust (£5,000 each) and REACH (£1,000).

Exclusions No grants to individuals, expeditions, research, scholarships, charities with a local focus, local branches of UK charities or towards running costs.

Applications On a 'funding proposal form' available from the correspondent. Applications should include a copy of the latest audited annual report and accounts. They are considered twice a year in mid-summer and mid-winter. Organisations which have received grants from this trust, The Cleopatra Trust or the Epigoni Trust should not reapply in the following two years. Usually, funding will be considered from only one of these trusts.

The Dumbreck Charity

General

£100,000 (2001/02)

Beneficial area Worldwide, especially the Midlands.

Church House, North Piddle, Worcestershire WR7 4PR

Correspondent A C S Hordern, Trustee

Trustees *A C S Hordern; H B Carslake; Mrs J E Melling.*

CC Number 273070

Information available Full accounts were on file at the Charity Commission.

General In 2001/02 the charity had assets of £3.2 million and an income of £98,000. Grants to 144 organisations totalled £100,000, and were of between £500 and £3,000. Although the trust gives worldwide, new grants are generally made in the Midlands.

Animal welfare/conservation
International/UK
13 grants totalled £12,000, including Brooke Hospital for Animals – Cairo (£3,000), International League for Protection of Horses (£2,000), People's Dispensary for Sick Animals (£750) and RSPB and World Wildlife Fund (£500 each).

Local
15 grants totalled £9,500, including Birmingham Dogs Home (£1,000), Rugby Animal Trust (£750), Avon Cats Home

and Warwickshire Nature Conservation Trust (£500 each) and Greyhound Rescue West of England (£250).

Children's welfare
UK
Six grants totalled £4,500, including NSPCC and Save the Children Fund (£1,000 each) and Childline and Farms for City Children (£500 each).

Local
21 grants totalled £13,000, including Leamington Boy's Club, Noah's Ark Trust and NSPCC (£1,000 each), Barnardos – West Midlands and West Midlands Autistic Society (£500 each) and BUGS (£250).

Elderly people and people with mental/physical disabilities
International/UK
15 grants totalled £9,300, including Motability (£1,000), National Listening Library (£750) and Deafblind UK, Electronic Aids for the Blind and Royal Star and Garter Home (£500 each).

Local
29 grants totalled £21,000, including Myton Hospice (£2,000), Warwickshire Association for the Blind (£1,500), Dogs of Disabled and Riding for the Disabled Association (£1,000 each), TOCH (£750) and Birmingham Settlement, Coventry and Warwickshire Association for the Deaf, Mencap – Warwick and Warwick Old People's Friendship Circle (£500 each).

Medical
UK
Six grants totalled £3,500, including Alzheimer's Research Trust (£1,000) and Breast Cancer Campaign, Iris Fund and MIND – Foot and Mouth Appeal (£500 each).

Local
14 grants totalled £11,000 including British Red Cross Association – Hereford and Worcester Branch and County Air Ambulance (£1,000 each), National Association for Crohns and Colitis and Stoke Mandeville Hospital Charitable Fund (£750 each) and Coventry Hospitals Charity, Dyslexia Institute – West Midlands and Meningitis Trust (£500 each).

Miscellaneous
International/UK
Nine grants totalled £5,300, including British Field Sports Association and Countryside Alliance (£1,000 each), Leonard Cheshire Foundation (£750) and Hunt Servants Benefit Society and SSAFA (£500 each).

Local
16 grants totalled £12,000, including ARC Addington Fund, Elgar School of Music and Worcester Cathedral Appeal (£1,000), Mayor of Leamington Christmas Fund and Worcester Farming and Wildlife Advisory Group (£750 each), Ironbridge Gorge Museum Development Trust and Relate – Worcester (£500 each) and Birmingham Pen Trade Heritage Association (£250).

Exclusions No grants to individuals.

Applications In writing to the correspondent. The trustees meet annually in April/May. Unsuccessful applications will not be acknowledged.

The Dyers' Company Charitable Trust

General

£240,000 (1999/2000)

Beneficial area UK.

Dyers Hall, Dowgate Hill, London EC4R 2ST

Tel. 020 7236 7197

Correspondent The Clerk

Trustees *The court of The Dyers' Company.*

CC Number 289547

Information available Full accounts were on file at the Charity Commission.

General In 1999/2000 the trust had assets of £3.4 million generating an income of £204,000. Grants to 81 organisations totalled £240,000 and were given in the following categories:

Crafts
Eight grants of between £600 and £10,000 totalled £81,000. They were given towards education and training in the crafts and included £10,000 to Textile Conservation Centre, £9,000 over three years to Heriot-Watt University, £3,000 over three years to UMIST, £2,100 to City & Guild of London Institute, £1,000 to Society of Dyers and Colourists and £300 to Royal School of Needlework.

Education and young people
13 grants of between £500 and £123,000 totalled £135,000. Support was given towards the development of young people, largely in the form of grants to

educational establishments and youth organisations. These included: £133,000 to Norwich School; £2,500 to Hyde Park Nursery School Charitable Trust; £1,000 each to Centre 70, Outward Bound Association – Merseyside and Deeside Branch and Princes's Youth Business Trust; £750 to Young Enterprise; and £500 to Connection.

Health and welfare

23 grants of between £50 and £2,000 totalled £22,000. Recipients included League of Friends of Buckingham Hospital and Lord Mayor's Appeal – Barnardos (£2,000 each), Camphill Village Trust (£1,500), Newport Cottage Hospital – Shropshire, Surgery Research Trust and Wessex Children's Hospice Trust (£1,000 each), Listening Library (£750), PACE Centre (£500) and British Heart Foundation (£50).

Local community city/inner London

18 grants of between £50 and £8,300 totalled £28,000. Larger grants were given to educational establishments including Boutcher CE Primary School – Bermondsey (£8,300), St Saviour's and St Olave's Secondary School – Southwark (£6,000) and Homerton House School – Hackney. Other grants included those to Stepping Stones Farm – Stepney (£1,000), College of Arms Trust (£750), London Wildlife Trust (£500), Dreamwork Youth and Arts (£250) and City of London Police Widows and Orphans Fund (£50).

The arts

16 grants of between £250 and £2,500 totalled £14,000. Support was given towards musical development and museums, including National Maritime Museum (£2,500), Chelsea Opera Group and Grange Park Opera (£1,000), British Performing Arts Medicine Trust and Ironbridge Gorge Museum Development Trust (£750 each), Young Concert Artists Trust (£500) and Florence Nightingale Museum Trust (£250).

Services

One grant of £2,500 was given to Reserve Forces Ulysses Trust.

The church

Two grants were made to All Saints – Datchworth (£1,000) and Historical Churches Preservation Trust (£500).

Exclusions No grants to individuals.

Applications The trust does not welcome unsolicited applications.

The Sir John Eastwood Foundation

Social welfare, education, health, in Nottinghamshire

£394,000 (2000/01)

Beneficial area UK, but mainly Nottinghamshire in practice.

Burns Lane, Warsop, Mansfield, Nottinghamshire NG20 0QG

Tel. 01623 842581 **Fax** 01623 847955

Correspondent Gordon Raymond, Chair

Trustees *G G Raymond, Chair; Mrs D M Cottingham; Mrs V A Hardingham; Mrs C B Mudford; P M Spencer.*

CC Number 235389

Information available Accounts were on file at the Charity Commission.

General The charity makes grants to registered charities benefiting Nottinghamshire, although other applications are considered. Priority is given towards people with disabilities, older people and children with special needs.

The 2000/01 accounts stated: 'The charity supports a number of registered charities on a regular basis by making donations each year to those particular charities. The prime target of the trustees each year is to ensure the continuance of these regular donations. Once these have been ensured the trustees consider special projects' applications and then other individual applications. These are reviewed and donations made as the trustees deem appropriate out of surplus income'.

In 2000/01 the trust had assets of £11.2 million and an income of £443,000, including £100,000 from its trading subsidiary, Adam Eastwood & Sons Limited. Total expenditure was £410,000, including £394,000 given in 179 grants. Despite being a large trust, it has previously been among the very small number to charge for a copy of its accounts, asking for the 'reasonable' postage and printing costs of £15.

By far the largest grant was £100,000 given to Nottingham City Hospital General Fund for their Breast Unit Fund; the majority of other grants were for £2,000 or less. Examples of larger grants included Nottingham Hospice (£22,000 in total), Royal Life Saving Society Meden School,

Newark & Nottingham Agricultural Society, Fountaindale School Trust and Warsop & District Mentally Handicapped Association (£10,000 each), Jenny Farr Centre (£10,000 in total), Yeoman Park School Fund (£9,000), Leonard Cheshire (£6,000), Friends of Bramcote School and Disabilities Living Centre (£5,000 each).

Warsop United Charities and Royal Life Saving Society received £3,000 each. All other grants were for £2,500 or less, including those to Mansfield Area Society for the Deaf, St Saviours Church PCC, Rosehill School Association, Starlight Children's Foundation and Ashfield Home Safety Project.

A number of beneficiaries received more than one grant during the year, most notably Nottingham Hospice which received £2,000 almost every month.

Exclusions No grants to individuals.

Applications In writing to the correspondent.

The Ebenezer Trust

Evangelical Christianity, welfare

£68,000 (1998/99)

Beneficial area UK and overseas.

31 Middleton Road, Shenfield, Brentwood, Essex CM15 8DJ

Correspondent N T Davey, Trustee

Trustees *Nigel Davey; Ruth Davey.*

CC Number 272574

Information available Full accounts were provided by the trust.

General The trust gives grants to Evangelical Christian charities for education, medical, religion and welfare purposes.

In 1998/99 the trust had assets of £465,000 and an income of £380,000. Grants totalled £68,000. Although grants ranged from £42 to £20,000, 34 of the 50 grants were of less than £1,000.

The largest grant was £20,000 to Brentwood Baptist Church, with £6,700 also given to Tearfund. Other grants were given to Pilgrims Hatch Baptist Church (£3,300), Scripture Union (£2,200), Servants Fellowship International (£1,600), Medical Foundation for the

Victims of Torture (£300), Word of Life (£250) and Treasures in Heaven Trust (£50).

Exclusions No grants to individuals.

Applications The trust states that they 'are most unlikely to consider unsolicited requests for grants'.

The Ecological Foundation

Environment/ conservation

£232,000 (2001)
Beneficial area Worldwide.

Lower Bosneives, Withiel, Bodmin, Cornwall PL30 5NQ
Tel. 01208 831236 **Fax** 01208 831083
Email ojfaull@gn.apc.org
Correspondent J Faull, Director
Trustees *Marquis of Londonderry; R Hanbury-Tenison; Edward Goldsmith.*
CC Number 264947
Information available Full accounts were on file at the Charity Commission.

General The foundation supports projects which it either has set up itself or chosen to sponsor. Income is raised from donations for the specific projects and is therefore all restricted. In 2001 the trust had an income of £181,000 and gave grants totalling £232,000. The largest grant of £110,000 went to Trade Investment and Environment Project. Other larger grants went to Eden Bequest (£35,000), World Rainforest Project (£30,000), Outsider's Guide (£23,000), Global Commons Institute (£21,000), Chapter Seven (£8,000) and Rural Futures (£5,100). Other grants totalled £880.

Applications Unsolicited applications are not entertained, as the foundation has no unrestricted funds.

The Gilbert & Eileen Edgar Foundation

General – see below

£71,000 (1999)
Beneficial area UK (and a few international appeals).

c/o Chantrey Vellacott DFK, Prospect House, 58 Queens Road, Reading RG1 4RP
Tel. 0118 952 4700
Website www.cvdfk.com
Correspondent Penny Tyson
Trustees *A E Gentilli; J G Matthews.*
CC Number 241736
Information available Full accounts were on file at the Charity Commission.

General The settlor expressed the desire that preference be given to the following objects:

- the promotion of medical and surgical science in all forms
- helping people who are young, old or in need
- raising artistic taste of the public in music, drama, opera, painting, sculpture and the fine arts
- the promotion of education in the fine arts
- the promotion of academic education
- the promotion of religion
- the promotion of conservation and heritage, facilities for recreation and other leisure-time activities.

There is a preference for smaller organisations 'where even a limited grant may be of real value'. The majority of grants are around £500 each. Many of the organisations supported are regular beneficiaries.

In 2001 the trust had an income of £91,000 and a total expenditure of £85,000. This information was taken from the Charity Commission database; unfortunately no further information was available for this year.

In 1999 it had assets of £1.8 million and an income of £92,000. A total of £71,000 was given in 113 grants. These were broken down as follows:

Category	No. of grants	Total £
Medical and surgical research	22	10,000
Care and support	63	27,000
Fine arts	9	6,800
Education in fine arts	3	19,000
Academic education	4	2,500
Religion and recreation, including conservation and heritage	12	6,500

Care and support was further broken down:

Children and young people:	21 grants totalling	£8,800
Older People:	5 grants totalling	£1,800
People with special needs:	37 grants totalling	£16,000

This category receives the most applications. Its areas of support are quite broad and can include disability, people with chronic medical disorders, refugees and people who have experienced war, homelessness, natural disasters or poverty.

Examples of grants given under each category are shown below.

Medical and surgical research
Most grants were for £500 each, including those to Breast Cancer Campaign and Leukaemia Research Fund. Smaller grants included Cardiac Fund – Battle Hospital (£300) and Meningitis Research Foundation (£250). 13 grants were recurrent from the previous year.

Care and support
Children and young people
15 grants of £500 each included those to Aberlour Childcare Trust, ChildLine and Women Caring Trust for Children in Northern Ireland. The remaining grants were £250 each, for example, to Breakout Children's Holidays. All but three of the grants were recurrent.

Older people
Grants ranging from £250 to £500 included those to Alzheimers Scotland, Counsel and Care for the Elderly and New Horizon Trust.

People with special needs
One grant of £1,000 went to Disasters Emergency Committee – Kosovo Crisis. 24 grants of £500 each included those to Action for Blind People and DEMAND – Design & Manufacture for Disability. The remaining grants were of £250 each, beneficiaries included Arthritis Care and Disability Law Service.

Fine Arts
Larger grants were given under this category with £3,000 to Royal National Theatre and £1,000 to English National Ballet. Smaller grants of £250 or £500

included those to Artists General Benevolent Institution and Music for the Blind.

Education in fine arts

Scholarships were given, one of £9,000 and the others for £5,000 each. They were given to three Royal Academies: of the arts; dramatic art and music. All of the grants were recurrent.

Academic education

Four grants went to Wolverhampton Grammar School (£1,500), Royal National College for the Blind (£500) and £250 each to St Loye's College Foundation and Royal School for the Blind, Leatherhead. They were all recurrent.

Religion and recreation, including conservation

The largest grant was £2,000 to Holy Cross Church in Ramsbury. Seven grants of £500 each included those to Atlantic Salmon Trust, Camp Mohawk and Survival for Tribes People. Four grants of £250 each included those to Jubilee Sailing Trust and Northamptonshire Association of Youth Clubs.

Exclusions Grants for education in the fine arts are made by way of scholarships awarded by academies and no grants are made directly to individuals in this regard.

Applications In writing to the correspondent. There are no application forms.

The Edinburgh Trust, No 2 Account

Education, service, scientific expeditions

£66,000 (1999/2000)

Beneficial area UK and worldwide.

Buckingham Place, London SW1A 1AA

Tel. 020 7930 4832

Correspondent P Hughes, Secretary

Trustees *Sir Brian McGrath; C Woodhouse; M Hunt-Davis.*

CC Number 227897

Information available Full accounts were on file at the Charity Commission.

General We were advised by the trust that for 1999/2000 its income was £64,000

and that grants totalled £66,000. No further details were provided.

In 1998/99 the trust's assets totalled £1.4 million and it had an income of £68,000, mostly from investments. Grants totalled £61,000, of which £15,000 was given towards the armed services with the remainder towards education. The trust also makes grants towards 'scientific expeditions'. The trust appears to favour the areas of wildlife and nature conservation, preservation of historic buildings, youth and outdoor pursuits, and in some cases medical and health-related causes.

Donations were listed under the following headings:

Civilian – annual

Grants were given to 32 organisations, of which 28 were between £200 and £300. The largest grants were £2,700 to Edwina Mountbatten Trust, £1,500 to Royal Life Saving Society and £1,300 to Romsey Abbey. Other beneficiaries included British Red Cross Society, LEPRA Children's Account and Galapagos Conservation Trust.

Service organisations

A total of 24 grants were made. The largest were £2,500 each to British Commonwealth Ex-Serviceman's League, King George Fund for Sailors and Royal Marines General Fund, £1,750 to King Edward VII Hospital for Officers and £1,500 to SSAFA No. 1 Account. The other grants were all for between £200 and £300.

Non-annual

Grants were given to 26 organisations. The largest, of £2,500 each, were given to The Award Scheme, London Federation of Clubs for Young People, Outward Bound Trust and PPT for Windsor and Maidenhead, followed by a grant of £2,000 to St George's House and International Sacred Literature Trust. Most of these grants were recurrent from the previous year. Nine other grants were of £1,500, with the majority of the remainder for £100 to £500, including 14 grants towards scientific expeditions.

Exclusions No grants to individuals, only scientific expeditions are considered with the backing of a major society. No grants to non-registered charities.

Applications In writing to the correspondent. The trustees meet to consider grants in April each year, and applications must be submitted by January.

The W G Edwards Charitable Foundation

Care of older people

£201,000 (2001/02)

Beneficial area UK.

Wedge Property Co. Ltd, 123a Station Road, Oxted, Surrey RH8 0QE

Tel. 01883 714412 **Fax** 01883 714433

Correspondent Janet Brown, Clerk to the Trustees

Trustees *Mrs Margaret E Offley Edwards; Prof. Wendy D Savage; Mrs G Shepherd Coates.*

CC Number 293312

Information available Accounts were on file at the Charity Commission, without a list of grants.

General The foundation assists with the provision of care for older people through existing charities, principally with capital projects but also supporting schemes involved in ongoing care.

In 2002 grants were made to around 30 charities totalling £201,000. No further information was available on the size of grants given or who received them.

In 2000/01 the foundation had an income of £82,000 and a total expenditure of £40,000.

The foundation has previously made large donations to Lillian Faithful Homes, Age Concern in Tower Hamlets and Friends of the Elderly.

Exclusions No grants to individuals.

Applications In writing to the correspondent.

The George Elias Charitable Trust

Jewish, general

£117,000 (2000/01)

Beneficial area Some preference for Manchester.

Elitex House, Moss Lane, Hale, Altrincham, Cheshire WA15 8AD

Tel. 0161 928 7171

Correspondent N G Denton, Charity Accountant

Trustees *G H Elias; Mrs D Elias; E C Elias; S E Elias.*

CC Number 273993

Information available Accounts were on file at the Charity Commission.

General This trust states it gives grants to charities supporting educational needs and the fight against poverty as well as organisations promoting the Jewish faith. In practice, grants are only given to Jewish groups.

In 2000/01 the trust had assets of £313,000 and an income of £67,000, of which £40,000 came from Gift Aid. Grants totalled £117,000. The accounts listed 37 grants of over £200 each. By far the largest grants were £27,000 to Bet Hatfusot and £10,000 to South Manchester Mikva Trust.

Other grants included those to Hoba (£8,700), Yad Eli Ezer (£8,500), Parkhill Charity Trust (£6,500), Association Chested (£4,500), Ponovez Congregation (£4,000), Aish Hatorah (£2,300), Manchester Jewish Federation (£2,000), YSCCR (£1,800), Neve Jerusalem (£1,500), Manchester Charitable Trust (£500) and Manchester Beth Din (£300).

Applications In writing to the correspondent. Trustees meet monthly.

The Ellinson Foundation Ltd

Jewish

£186,000 (2000/01)

Beneficial area Worldwide.

Messrs Robson Laidler & Co, Fernwood House, Fernwood Road, Jesmond, Newcastle upon Tyne NE2 1TJ

Tel. 0191 281 8191

Email ellinsonestates@aol.com

Correspondent Gerry Crichton

Trustees *C O Ellinson; Mrs E Ellinson; A Ellinson; A Z Ellinson; U Ellinson.*

CC Number 252018

Information available Full accounts were on file at the Charity Commission.

General The trust supports hospitals, education and homelessness in the UK and overseas, usually with a Jewish teaching aspect. The trust regularly supports organisations such as boarding schools for boys and girls teaching the Torah.

In 2000/01 the trust had assets of £552,000 and an income of £295,000. Grants totalled £186,000. The accounts listed 17 grants of over £1,000 each.

The largest were to North West London Communal Mikvah (£50,000), Friends of United Institution of Arad and Ruzin Sadagora Trust (£20,000 each), Friends of Neve Yerusholayim Seminary Trust (£18,000) and Friends of Yeshivas Brisk (£12,000).

Other grants included British Friends of the Chazon Ish Institutions (£7,000), Friends of Ohr Elchonon (£6,000), Talmud Torah Chavos Da'as (£5,000), Etz Chaim Yeshiva (£3,000), Institute for Higher Rabbinical Studies (£2,500) and Friends of Toras Chaim Moscow (£1,000).

Exclusions No grants to individuals.

Applications In writing to the correspondent. However, the trust generally supports the same organisations each year and unsolicited applications are not welcome.

Elman Charitable Trust

Jewish charities

£177,000 (2000/01)

Beneficial area UK and Israel.

Laurence Homes Eastern Limited, 14 Ruskin Close, Chilton Hall, Stowmarket, Suffolk IP14 1TY

Tel. 01449 771177

Correspondent Kenneth Elman, Trustee

Trustees *Charles Elman; Kenneth Elman; Colin Elman.*

CC Number 261733

Information available Basic accounts but no narrative report on file at the Charity Commission.

General The majority of the grants are given in Israel to organisations such as schools and hospitals. Jewish charities in the UK are also supported. In 2000/01 the trust gave 26 grants totalling £177,000.

By far the largest grants were £50,000 to Wish Care and £25,000 to Friends of Assaf Harofeh Medical Care.

Other beneficiaries included Save a Child's Heart (£17,000), Emunah National Religious Women's organisation in Israel (£12,000), Atidenu Fund

(£10,000), Shai Society for Rehabilitation and Support of Handicapped Children (£7,000), Norwood Ltd (£6,000), Friends of the Israel Opera and Holocaust Educational Trust (£5,000 each), Tel Aviv University (£3,000), Institute for the Advancement of Education in Jaffa (£1,000) and British Friends of Ezer Mitzion (£500).

Exclusions Grants are not usually given to individuals.

Applications In writing to the correspondent.

Elshore Ltd

Jewish

£87,000 (2000/01)

Beneficial area Worldwide.

10 West Avenue, London NW4 2LY

Tel. 020 8203 1726

Correspondent H Lerner, Trustee

Trustees *H M Lerner; A Lerner; S Yanofsky.*

CC Number 287469

Information available Accounts were on file at the Charity Commission, but without a full written report or a grants list.

General This trust appears to make grants solely to Jewish organisations. In 2000/01 it had an income of £112,000. Out of a total expenditure of £88,000 grants were made totalling £87,000 (£220,000 in 1999/2000). A grants list was not included with the accounts for this year.

Further information has been unavailable since 1994/95, when grants to 40 beneficiaries totalled £178,000. The larger grants were £26,000 to Eminor Educational Centre and £20,000 to Cosmon Belz. Grants of £10,000 were given to 10 organisations, including Gur Trust and Marbe Torah Trust. Most other grants were less than £1,000, although some were for up to £8,000.

Applications In writing to the correspondent.

The Vernon N Ely Charitable Trust

Christian, welfare, disability, children and youth, overseas

£90,000 (2000/01)

Beneficial area Worldwide, with a preference for London borough of Merton.

Grosvenor Gardens House, 35–37 Grosvenor Gardens, London SW1W 0BY

Tel. 020 7828 3156 **Fax** 020 7630 7451

Correspondent Derek Howorth, Trustee

Trustees *J S Moyle; D P Howorth; R S Main.*

CC Number 230033

Information available Accounts were on file at the Charity Commission, but without a list of grants.

General The trust makes grants to Christian, welfare, disability, children, youth and overseas charities. Its 1997/98 annual report stated that the trust's policy had been reviewed during the year and it had been decided that the number of beneficiaries each year would be reduced, with larger grants being made.

In 2000/01 the trust had assets of £1.3 million and an income of £93,000. Grants were made totalling £90,000. Unfortunately no further information was available on the size or number of beneficiaries for this year.

In 1995/96, before the trust had reviewed its policy, it made 69 grants including 58 of less than £1,000. Grants show a preference for Merton and included £6,100 to Cottage Homes, £3,700 to London Playing Fields Association, £2,100 to Merton Voluntary Association for the Blind, £1,200 to British Red Cross Society and £1,000 each to Oxfam, Royal Marsden Cancer Appeal and Save the Children Fund. Beneficiaries of smaller grants included Merton WelCare Association, RSPCA Wimbledon and District, Second Hook Scout Group and Wimbledon Community Association.

Exclusions No grants to individuals.

Applications In writing to the correspondent. Please note that the trust has previously stated that no funds are available.

This entry was not confirmed by the trust but is correct according to information on file at the Charity Commission.

The Emerton-Christie Charity

Health, welfare, disability, arts

£71,000 (1998/99)

Beneficial area UK.

c/o Cartmell Shepherd, Viaduct House, Carlisle CA3 8EZ

Tel. 01228 516666

Correspondent The Trustees

Trustees *A F Niekirk; D G Richards; Dr N A Walker.*

CC Number 262837

Information available Full accounts were provided by the trust.

General The Emerton Charitable Settlement was established in 1971 by Maud Emerton, with additional funds subsequently added by Vera Bishop Emerton. In April 1996, it became the Emerton-Christie Charity following a merger with another trust, The Mrs C M S Christie Will Trust.

In 1998/99 it had assets totalling £2.4 million and an income of £68,000. Grants totalled £71,000 and were given to 35 organisations. The largest grant was £10,000 to Harnhill Centre for Christian Learning to reduce the interest-free loan that the organisation had borrowed from the trust. Most grants were to health, welfare and disability causes, with a couple to arts organisations.

Other larger grants included Royal College of Music (£5,000), RNLI (£4,000), BACUP and Woodlands Hospice Charitable Trust (£3,000 each) and Save the Children Fund (£2,500).

Two-thirds of the grants were between £1,000 and £1,500. Examples included Canine Partners for Independence, Disability Aid Foundation, Helen Arkell Dyslexia Centre, The Farm in the Forest Respice, NSPCC, Second Chance and Sense.

About 10 grants were recurrent from the previous year.

Exclusions Generally no grants to: individuals; religious organisations; restoration or extension of buildings; start-up costs; animal welfare and

research; cultural heritage; or environmental projects.

Applications In writing to the correspondent. A demonstration of need based on budgetary principles is required and applications will not be acknowledged unless accompanied by an sae. Trustees normally meet once a year in the autumn to select charities to benefit.

The Emmandjay Charitable Trust

Social welfare, medicine, youth

£226,000 (2000/01)

Beneficial area UK, with a special interest in West Yorkshire.

PO Box 88, Otley, West Yorkshire LS21 3TE

Correspondent Mrs A E Bancroft, Administrator

Trustees *Mrs Sylvia Clegg; John A Clegg; Mrs S L Worthington; Mrs E A Riddell.*

CC Number 212279

Information available Full accounts were on file at the Charity Commission, but without a grants list.

General The trust was established in 1962 by Frederick Moore, his wife Elsie, and their daughter and son-in-law, Sylvia and John Clegg 'as a token of gratitude for the happiness given to them by their late daughter and grand-daughter'. It is a time charity: all remaining capital will be distributed to the descendants of the family in 50 years from 1962, or 21 years from the death of the last survivor of the descendants of George V, whichever is the sooner.

The trust gives 'most particularly to help disadvantaged people, but many different projects are supported – caring for the disabled, physically and mentally handicapped and terminally ill, work with young people and medical research. The trust likes projects which reach a lot of people. The trustees are keen that grants are actually spent'.

In 2000/01 the trust had assets of £2.6 million generating an income of £265,000. Grants totalled £226,000.

No grants list was included in the accounts, although it contained a breakdown of the areas in which it gives grants as follows (1999/2000 figures in brackets):

Hospices, terminally		
ill, care	£70,000	(£62,000)
Youth activities, schools	£17,000	(£37,000)
Medical research	£17,000	(£36,000)
National charities	£47,000	(£32,000)
Special overseas appeals	£5,000	(£25,000)
Special schemes,		
workshops, disability	£12,000	(£23,000)
Homeless	£15,000	(£15,000)
Local community groups	£11,000	(£9,200)
Hospital appeals	£3,300	(£7,000)
Social services, probation		
services	£4,600	(£4,800)
Counselling services	£1,100	(£3,100)
Children's charities		
and care	£11,000	(£2,000)
Housing associations	£10,000	(£500)
Advice centres	£600	(£450)
Church, religious activities	£1,500	(£150)

Exclusions 'The trust does not pay debts, does not make grants to individual students, and does not respond to circulars.' Grants are only given, via social services, to individuals if they live in Bradford.

Applications In writing to the correspondent.

The Englefield Charitable Trust

General

£319,000 (2000/01)

Beneficial area UK, with a special interest in Berkshire.

Englefield Estate Office, Theale, Reading RG7 5DU

Tel. 0118 930 2504 **Fax** 0118 932 3748

Email benyon@englefields.co.uk

Correspondent A S Reid, Secretary to the Trustees

Trustees *Sir William Benyon; James Shelley; Lady Elizabeth Benyon; Richard H R Benyon; Mrs Catherine Haig.*

CC Number 258123

Information available Report and accounts with full grants list were provided by the trust.

General The trust was founded in 1968 by the settlor, and current trustee, Sir William Benyon. In 2000/01 it had assets of £10 million and an income of £367,000. Grants totalled £319,000. In addition to grantmaking, the trust also provides low-cost and retirement housing. The latter cost the trust £30,000 in the year.

Out of about 300 applications received in the year, a total of 116 grants were made to registered charities, most of them based in Berkshire. Grants varied from £100 up to £31,000, with most in the range of £1,000 to £5,000. A wide variety of causes are supported including a number of Christian, health and welfare organisations.

The largest grant of £31,000 was given to Englefield PCC and Fabric Fund. A further five sizeable donations over £10,000 were made to ARC Addington Fund (£20,000), Burghfield Church Hall and Spire Trust (£15,000 each) and Brightwalton Millennium Project and Douglas Martin Trust (£10,000 each).

Other grants included Berkshire Community Foundation (£9,000), Watermill Theatre – Education Programme West Berkshire Schools (£,7,000), Home-Start – West Berkshire (£5,000), Common Purpose – Reading (£2,500), Multiple Sclerosis – Reading Branch (£2,400), St Mary's PCC – Kensworth (£2,000), Newbury YMCA (£1,600), MS Therapy Centre – Reading (£1,500), Berkshire Association of Young People – Project 2000 (£1,200) and £1,000 each to Bibles for Children, Holy Brook School – Reading, League of Friends at Reading Hospital and Parkinson's Disease Society – Newbury Branch. Smaller grants included £700 to Age Concern – Berkshire and £500 each to NSPCC – Newbury District, Reading Christian Viewpoint and Reading Disabled Society.

Exclusions Individual applications for study or travel are not supported.

Applications In writing to the correspondent stating the purpose for which the money is to be used and accompanied with the latest accounts. All applicants should have charitable status. Applications are considered in March and September.

The Epigoni Trust

Health & welfare, disability, homelessness, addiction, underprivileged children, environment

£163,000 (2000)

Beneficial area Mainly UK.

Charities Aid Foundation, King's Hill, West Malling, Kent ME19 4TA

Tel. 01732 520083 **Fax** 01732 520001

Correspondent Mrs Sue David, Donor Grants Officer

Trustees *H Peacock; Mrs Bettine Bond; A M Bond.*

CC Number 328700

Information available Full accounts were on file at the Charity Commission.

General The trust has common trustees with two other trusts, Cleopatra Trust and Dorus Trust (see separate entries) with which it also shares the same aims and policies. All three trusts are administered by Charities Aid Foundation. Generally the trusts support different organisations.

The trust makes grants in the following areas:

- mental health
- cancer welfare/education – not research
- diabetes
- physical disability – not research
- homelessness
- addiction
- underprivileged children.

There is also some preference for environmental causes. It only gives grants for specific projects and does not give grants for running costs or general appeals. Generally support is given to organisations with a UK-wide remit.

In 2000 the trust had assets of £3.2 million and an income of £165,000. It gave £165,000 in 27 grants. Administration charges were low at £588. The largest grants was £14,000 to Royal Commonwealth Society for the Blind. Five grants of £10,000 each went to New Bridge, St Richard's Hospital Charitable Trust, St Wilfrid's Hospice – Chichester, Council of Milton Abbey School Ltd and Who Cares Trust.

Other grants included £9,700 to Shelter – Work Opportunities Project, £8,000 to Womankind Worldwide, £7,500 to Schizophrenia Association of Great Britain, £6,000 to Tree Aid, £5,000 to Church Education Corporation Ltd, £3,000 to Ryder Cheshire Foundation and £1,500 each to Aspire and Lambeth Accord.

Exclusions No grants to individuals, expeditions, research, scholarships, charities with a local focus, local branches of UK charities or towards running costs.

Applications On a 'funding proposal form' available from the correspondent. Applications should include a copy of the latest audited annual report and accounts. They are considered twice a year in mid-summer and mid-autumn. Organisations which have received grants from this trust, Cleopatra Trust or Dorus Trust should not reapply in the following two years. Usually, funding will be considered from only one of these trusts.

The Equity Trust Fund

Welfare of professional performers and stage managers

£340,000 (1999/2000)

Beneficial area UK.

222 Africa House, 64 Kingsway, London WC2B 6AH

Tel. 020 7404 6041 **Fax** 020 7831 4953

Email keith@equitytrustfund.freeserve.co.uk

Correspondent Keith Carter, Secretary

Trustees *Hugh Manning; Milton Johns; Jeffrey Wickham; Nigel Davenport; Gillian Raine; Peter Plouviez; Derek Bond; Frank Williams; Ian McGarry; John Barron; Colin Baker; Barbara Hyslop; Roy Marsden; Annie Bright; Graham Hamilton; Harry Landis; Frederik Pyne; Rosalind Shanks; Johnny Worthy; Frank Hitchman; James Bolam; Imogen Claire; Peter Finch; John Rubinstein; Ian Talbot; Josephine Tewson.*

CC Number 328103

Information available Accounts were on file at the Charity Commission, but without a full list of grants.

General The fund is a benevolent fund for professional performers and stage managers and their dependants. It offers help with welfare rights, gives free debt counselling and information and can offer financial assistance to those in genuine need. It also has an education fund to help members of the profession with further training provided they have at least 10 years' professional adult experience.

Professional theatre venues and theatre companies can approach the fund to see if they are eligible for consideration. It is not general policy to help with production costs. Projects that are going to provide long-term benefits to members of the profession are more likely to be considered.

In 1999/2000 the assets of the trust were £9.2 million, the income was £405,000

and direct charitable expenditure was £258,000. This was broken down as follows (1998/99 figures in brackets):

Theatre grants	£37,000	(£39,000)
Education grants	£124,000	(£101,000)
Welfare and benevolence	£86,000	(£52,000)
Loans – provisions and write-offs	£6,100	(£28,000)

No further details of grants were given in the accounts, but a list of the current outstanding loans was included in the 1998/99 accounts. The main loan was £113,000 to the Actors' Centre, with others ranging from £700 to £15,000 to theatres throughout the UK.

Exclusions No grants to non-professional performers, drama students, non-professional theatre companies, multi arts venues, community projects or projects with no connection to the professional theatre.

Applications In the first instance please call the office to ascertain if the application is relevant. Failing that, submit a brief letter outlining the application. A meeting takes place about every six to eight weeks. Ring for precise dates. Applications are required at least two weeks beforehand.

The Alan Evans Memorial Trust

Preservation, conservation

£130,000 (2000/01)

Beneficial area UK.

Coutts & Co., Trustee Department, 440 Strand, London WC2R 0QS

Tel. 020 7663 6758

Correspondent The Trust Manager

Trustees *Coutts & Co.; D J Halfhead; Mrs D Moss.*

CC Number 326263

Information available Full accounts were on file at the Charity Commission.

General The objects of the trust 'are to promote the permanent preservation, for the benefit of the nation, of lands and tenements (including buildings) of beauty or historic interest and as regards land, the preservation (so far as practicable) of the natural aspect, features and animal and plant life'.

In 2000/01 the trust had assets of £3.2 million and an income of £105,000. After administration and management costs of £18,000, grants totalled £130,000 and were categorised as follows:

Land and buildings	£21,000
Churches	£67,000
Environment	£42,000

A total of 45 grants were made in the year. Grants ranged from £1,000 to £6,000 and were given to various UK and local countryside, environmental and restoration organisations. Beneficiaries included Northumberland Wildlife Trust (£6,000), Essex Wildlife Trust (£5,000), Gaia Trust and John Muir Birthplace Trust (£4,000 each), Lincolnshire Wildlife Trust (£3,500), Yorkshire Wildlife Trust (£3,000), National Trust (£2,300) and Ironbridge Gorge Museum Trust and Woodland Trust (£2,000 each).

Over half the grants made were for £1,000; beneficiaries included Advent Church Appeal, Cambridgeshire Wildlife Trust, Ramsay Heritage Trust and Ripon Museum Trust. Grants were also given to a number of churches and cathedrals throughout the country.

Exclusions No grants to individuals or for management or running expenses, although favourable consideration is given in respect of the purchase of land and restoration of buildings. Grants are given to registered charities only. Appeals will not acknowledged.

Applications There is no formal application form, but appeals should be made in writing to the correspondent, stating why the funds are required, what funds have been promised from other sources (for example, English Heritage) and the amount outstanding. Trustees normally meet four times a year, although in urgent cases decisions can be made between meetings.

The Eventhall Family Charitable Trust

General

£97,000 (2000/01)

Beneficial area Preference for north west England.

PO Box 194, Sale M33 5XA

Correspondent L H Eventhall, Chair

Trustees *Leon Eventhall; Corinne Eventhall; David Eventhall.*

CC Number 803178

Information available Accounts were on file at the Charity Commission, but without a grants list.

General In 2000/01 the trust had assets of £1.4 million and an income of £294,000. Grants to 144 charities totalled £97,000. The trust supported Nave Michael's Home for Abandoned Children in Israel and the annual report stated that further potential funds have been earmarked for this project in the future. No further details were available.

In previous years other beneficiaries have included Aish Hatorah, ChildLine, Clitheroe Wolves Football Club, Community Security Trust, Greibach Memorial, Guide Dogs for the Blind, Heathlands Village, International Wildlife Coalition, JJCT, MB Foundation Charity, Only Foals and Horses Sanctuary, Red Nose Day, RNLI, Sale Ladies Society, Shelter and South Manchester Synagogue.

Exclusions No grants to students.

Applications In writing to the correspondent, however, please note that the trust stated it only has a very limited amount of funds available. Telephone calls are not accepted by the trust. Trustees meet monthly to consider grants. A pre-addressed envelope is appreciated (stamp not necessary). Unsuccessful applicants will not receive a reply.

The Beryl Evetts & Robert Luff Animal Welfare Trust

Animal welfare

£182,000 (2000/01)

Beneficial area UK.

294 Earls Court Road, London SW5 9BB

Tel. 020 8954 2727

Correspondent Ms R Jessop

Trustees *Sir R Johnson; Revd M Tomlinson; Mrs J Tomlinson; R P J Price; B Nicholson; Lady Johnson; Ms G Favot.*

CC Number 283944

Information available Full accounts were on file at the Charity Commission.

General The principal objective of the trust is the funding of veterinary research and the care and welfare of animals. It appears to make substantial commitments to a few organisations over several years, whether to build up capital funds or to establish fellowships. The trust gives priority to research projects and bursaries. In practice, the trust supports the same beneficiaries each year.

In 2000/01 the trust had assets of £1.5 million and an income of £80,000. After administration costs of £15,000, six grants were made totalling £182,000 (£62,000 in 1999/2000). By far the largest was £100,000 to Blue Cross. Other beneficiaries were Animal Health Trust (£35,000 in two grants), Royal Veterinary College (£26,000), ARC Addington and Eden Animal Rescue (£10,000 each) and National Equine Defence League (£1,000).

Applications 'No applications, thank you.' The trust gives grants to the same beneficiaries each year and funds are often allocated two years in advance.

The Exilarch's Foundation

Jewish

£408,000 (2000)

Beneficial area Mainly UK.

4 Carlos Place, Mayfair, London W1K 3AW

Tel. 020 7399 0850 **Fax** 020 7399 0860

Correspondent His Highness the Exilarch

Trustees *N E Dangoor; D A Dangoor; E B Dangoor; R D Dangoor; M J Dangoor.*

CC Number 275919

Information available The information for this entry was provided by the trust.

General In 2000 the trust's assets totalled £17 million (£14 million in the previous year) and it had an income of £2.1 million, comprised mainly of donations (£1.5 million) and investment income (£600,000). Expenditure totalled £488,000, including £12,000 spent on publications and £7,600 in management and administration costs. Charitable expenditure totalled £408,000, which was given in grants to other organisations. The trust is connected with Carmel College Estate which focuses in particular on Jewish education. Information on grant beneficiaries was not available.

Applications The trust stated that it does not respond to unsolicited applications for grants.

The Family Foundations Trust

(also known as Mintz Family Foundation)

General, Jewish

£163,000 (2000/01)

Beneficial area UK.

Gerald Edelman, 25 Harley Street, London W1G 9BR

Tel. 020 7299 1400

Correspondent Simon Hosier, Accountant to the Trustees

Trustees *R B Mintz; P G Mintz.*

CC Number 264014

Information available Full accounts were on file at the Charity Commission.

General In 2000/01 the trust's assets totalled £593,000 and it had an income of £141,000. Grants to 50 organisations totalled £163,000. Beneficiaries were mainly Jewish organisations.

The largest grants were £50,000 to JFS General Charitable Trust, £21,000 to Jewish Care and £20,000 to United Jewish Israel Appeal.

Other larger grants included £6,800 to Children of the East, £5,900 to Norwood Ltd, £5,800 to Roundhouse Trust, £5,500 to National Autistic Society, £5,000 each to Community Development Trust and University of Jerusalem, £3,500 to British ORT, £1,700 to World Jewish Relief and £1,000 each to Board of Deputies of British Jews, Joint Jewish Charitable Trust and King Solomon High School.

There were 27 grants made of under £1,000 each, including those to Brighton and Hove New Synagogue, Holocaust Educational Trust, Lolev Charitable Trust, Nightingale House, Spiro Institute, WIZO and Yesoday Hatorah Schools.

Applications In writing to the correspondent.

Famos Foundation Trust

Jewish

£66,000 (1998/99)

Beneficial area UK and overseas.

4 Hanover Gardens, Salford, Lancashire M7 4FQ

Correspondent Rabbi S M Kupetz, Trustee

Trustees *Rabbi S M Kupetz; Mrs F Kupetz.*

CC Number 271211

Information available Accounts were on file at the Charity Commission, but without a grants list and only a very brief narrative report.

General In 2000/01 this trust had an income of £63,000 and a total expenditure of £85,000. This information was taken from the Charity Commission database; unfortunately no further information was available for this year.

In 1998/99 the trust's assets totalled £738,000, it had an income of £69,000 and grants totalled £66,000. Grants of up to £5,000 were given. The trust supports a wide range of Jewish organisations, including those concerned with education and the relief of poverty. Many grants are recurrent. Unfortunately further information was not available.

Exclusions No grants to individuals.

Applications In writing to the correspondent, at any time. The trust does not accept telephone enquiries.

The Lord Faringdon Charitable Trust

Medical, general

£156,000 (2000/01)

Beneficial area UK.

The Estate Office, Buscot Park, Oxfordshire SN7 8BU

Tel. 01367 240786 **Fax** 01367 241794

Correspondent J R Waters, Secretary to the Trustees

Trustees *H S S Trotter; A D A W Forbes; Hon. J H Henderson; R P Trotter.*

CC Number 1084690

Information available Accounts were provided by the trust.

General This trust was formed in 2000 by the amalgamation of the Lord Faringdon first and second trusts.

The trust supports:

- educational objectives
- hospitals and the provision of medical treatment for the sick
- purchase of antiques and artistic objects for museums and collections that have public access
- care and assistance of people who are elderly or infirm
- development and assistance of arts and sciences, physical recreation and drama
- research into matters of public interest
- relief of poverty
- support of matters of public interest
- maintaining and improving the Faringdon Collection.

In 2000/01 it had assets of £6.1 million and an income of £154,000. It gave £156,000 in 51 grants. The three largest were £15,000 to Oxfordshire Youth Music Trust and £10,000 each to St Ethelburga's Appeal and the Prayer Book Society.

Grants in the range of £1,000 to £7,000 were made to 42 organisations, including MS Society (£7,000); Royal Opera House (£6,300); Brighton Dome Appeal, Countryside Foundation, Jubilee Sailing Trust, Oxfordshire Community Trust, Prior's Court and St John's Ambulance (£5,000 each); Action for Kids (£4,000); Alzheimer's Research Trust (£3,000); Sea Cadets (£2,500); Abbeyfield, Friends of the Elderly, National Association of Youth Clubs, Sobell House Hospice Trust and Thames Salmon Trust (£2,000 each); Headway Oxford (£1,500); and Act Against Allergy, Helen Rollason Cancer Care Centre, St Mungo's, Swindon Railway Museum, Willow Trust and Wonderful Beast Company (£1,000 each).

Smaller grants under £1,000 were made to six organisations: Air Cadets – Nicaragua, Faces in Focus, Highgrove School, Millennium Bike Path – Thames and Oxfordshire, New English Art and Tree Register.

Applications In writing to the correspondent.

The Farmers Company Charitable Fund

Agriculture research and education

£78,000 (1999)

Beneficial area UK.

Worshipful Company of Farmers, Chislehurst Business Centre, 1 Bromley Lane, Chislehurst, Kent BR7 6LH

Tel. 020 8467 2255 **Fax** 020 8467 2666

Correspondent The Clerk

Trustees *The Court of Assistants of the Worshipful Company of Farmers.*

CC Number 258712

Information available Full accounts were on file at the Charity Commission, up to those for 1999.

General The trust works towards the promotion of agricultural research and education, including: scholarships; providing relief to members of the Farmers' Company in hardship or distress; providing funds for UK students travelling abroad to study agriculture; and environmental issues.

In 2000/01 this trust had an income of £134,000 and a total expenditure of £102,000. This information was taken from the Charity Commission database; unfortunately no further up-to-date information was available for this year.

In 1999, the last year for which accounts were available in the public files, its income was £98,000 and it made grants totalling £78,000. Assets totalled £1.1 million. Grants normally range from £100 to £2,000.

Grants included: £42,000 to Wye College for the agricultural management course; £5,000 to Seale Hayne College for the agricultural management course; £2,000 to Royal Agricultural Benevolent Institution to assist farmers in need; and £1,000 to Lord Mayor's Appeal for various city charities.

Applications In writing to the correspondent.

The Thomas Farr Charitable Trust

General

£164,000 (2000/01)

Beneficial area UK, especially Nottinghamshire.

Rathbones Trust Co., 159 New Bond Street, London W1S 2UD

Tel. 020 7399 0807 **Fax** 020 7399 0013

Correspondent Kevin Custis, Administrator

Trustees *H J P Farr; Mrs E M Astley-Arlington; Mrs P K Myles; Mrs A M Chisholm; Rathbones Trust Co.*

CC Number 328394

Information available Full accounts were on file at the Charity Commission.

General This trust makes grants mainly for general charitable purposes in Nottinghamshire, but occasionally supports causes in other parts of the UK. Grants range from £250 to £25,000, although most are for under £5,000.

In 2000/01 the trust had assets of £5.5 million and an income of £209,000. After £19,000 spent on management and administration fees, the trust gave £164,000 in 82 grants.

The largest grants were £25,000 to Nottingham High School for Girls, £10,000 to Macmillan Cancer Relief – Nottinghamshire appeal and £8,000 to Edwards Lane Community Centre – Nottingham. Four grants of £5,000 each went to Bramcote Hills Comprehensive School, National Trust – Greet Workhouse, Sargent Cancer Care for Children – Nottingham and Sports Aid East Midlands – Loughborough.

Other grants included those to National Association of Child Contact Centres – Nottingham (£4,500), Friends of Moorfields Eye Hospital, Nottingham Community Transport and REACT – Richmond (£3,000 each), Brainwave – Somerset, Derbyshire Association for the Blind and Parentline – Nottingham (£2,000 each), Family First – Nottingham and NSPCC – Nottingham (£1,000 each) and RUKBA – York (£500).

Support was also given to a number of churches.

Exclusions No grants to individuals.

Applications In writing to the correspondent. Applications are considered in March and September.

Farthing Trust

Christian, general

£128,000 to organisations (2000/01)

Beneficial area UK and overseas.

48 Ten Mile Bank, Littleport, Ely, Cambridgeshire CB6 1EF

Correspondent Heber Martin, Trustee

Trustees *C H Martin; Mrs E Martin; Miss J Martin; Mrs A White.*

CC Number 268066

Information available Accounts were on file at the Charity Commission, but without a list of grants.

General In 2000/01 the trust had assets of £2 million. Total income was £344,000, including £98,000 in donations (which were transferred to assets). After management and administration expenses of £11,000, grants totalled £191,000, broken down as follows:

Education (UK)	£13,000
Education (overseas)	£7,500
UK churches	£38,000
UK Christian causes	£16,000
UK general charities	£2,400
Local	£7,234
Christian workers (active)	£29,000
Christian workers (retired)	£14,000
Individuals in need (UK)	£12,000
Individuals in need (overseas)	£8,900
Overseas Christian missions	£22,000
Overseas Christian causes	£19,000
Overseas general charities	£3,000

There was no indication in the accounts as to which particular charities and projects were supported.

Applications Applications and enquiries should be made in writing to the correspondent. Applicants, and any other requests for information, will only receive a response if an sae is enclosed. There would seem little point in applying unless a personal contact with a trustee is established.

The Fawcett Charitable Trust

Disability

£160,000 (2000/01)

Beneficial area UK, but preference given to Hampshire and West Sussex.

Blake Lapthorn, Harbour Court, Compass Road, North Harbour, Portsmouth, Hampshire PO6 4ST

Tel. 023 9222 1122

Correspondent Sandra Evans

Trustees *D J Fawcett; Mrs F P Fawcett; D W Russell.*

CC Number 1013167

Information available Full accounts were on file at the Charity Commission.

General The trust was set up in 1991 by Derek and Frances Fawcett with an endowment of shares in their company with an initial value of £1.6 million. In recent years the annual income from the fund has averaged about £100,000. In 2000/01 the trust had assets of £1.9 million, an income of £93,000 and made donations totalling £160,000.

According to the trust, it supports work aimed at increasing the quality of life of disabled people by facilitating and providing recreation opportunities. Preference is normally given to organisations and projects located in Hampshire and West Sussex. Outstanding deserving UK initiatives are also supported such as Sense.

The trust is, however, currently devoting a large proportion of its charitable support to RYA Sailability, which received £150,000 in the year. A further grant of £10,000 was made to St Richard's MRI Appeal. In 1999/2000 grants totalled just £10,000, all of which was given to Rowan's Hospice.

Exclusions Large national charities are excluded as a rule.

Applications Until further notice the trust is closed to new applications for the reasons given in the general section.

The Fidelity UK Foundation

General

£344,000 (2000)

Beneficial area Particular preference is given to projects in Kent, Surrey, London and Continental Europe, where Fidelity Investments has an office.

Oakhill House, 130 Tonbridge Road, Hildenborough, Tonbridge, Kent TN11 9DZ

Tel. 01732 361144 **Fax** 01732 838300

Correspondent Miss Jacqueline Guthrie

Trustees *Edward C Johnson; Barry Bateman; Anthony Bolton; Martin*

Cambridge; Robert Milotte; Richard Millar.

CC Number 327899

Information available Guidelines for applications and accounts without a grants list were provided by the trust.

General The trust aims to encourage the highest standards of management and long-term self-reliance in non-profit organisations. It gives to registered charities and some exempt charities, such as certain schools. Particular preference is given to projects in Kent, Surrey, London and Continental Europe, where Fidelity Investments has an office. Giving is primarily allocated to the following sectors: community development, health, arts and culture, and education.

The trust seeks to support projects undertaken by organisations to increase proficiency, achieve goals and reach long-term self-sufficiency. Most often this entails major projects such as capital improvements, technology upgrades, organisational development and planning initiatives. The trust will assess an organisation to determine whether its collaboration and investment can add value. Among the factors considered are:

- the organisation's financial health
- the strength of its management team and board
- evidence of an overall strategic plan.

It also looks at the size and scope of an organisation, evaluating its position within the context of its market and the needs of the constituents it serves. The trust ultimately seeks to understand the potential returns of a project and seeks evidence of:

- instrumental commitment to the project on behalf of the organisation's board
- a realistic project budget
- a thorough implementation plan, including a plan for performance measurement
- net value to the organisation and the community it serves
- significant support from other funders.

In 2000 the trust had assets of £10.5 million up from £5.7 million in the previous year. The income, mainly from donations, totalled £6.3 million and grants totalled £344,000. A grants list was not provided.

Exclusions Grants are not made for:

- sponsorships or benefit events
- scholarships
- corporate membership
- advertising and promotional projects
- exhibitions.

Grants are not generally made to:

- start-up, sectarian, or political organisations
- private schools and colleges or universities
- individuals.

Generally grants are not made for running costs, but may be considered on an individual basis through the foundation's small grant scheme. Grants will not normally cover the entire cost of a project, or support an organisation in successive years.

Applications In writing to the correspondent. Applications should include the Fidelity UK summary form, organisation history and objectives, itemised project budget, a list of other funders and the status of each request, a list of directors and trustees with their backgrounds, current operating budget and most recently audited financial statements. A description of the request and rationale should also be included addressing the following:

- how the project fits into the larger strategic plan of the organisation
- what a grant will allow the organisation to achieve
- how a grant will change or improve the long-term potential of the organisation
- what the implementation plan and timeline for the project is and who is responsible
- how the project will be evaluated.

Applications will receive an initial response within three months.

The foundation receives many more applications for grants than it is able to fund so not all applications that fall within the guidelines will receive grants.

The Doris Field Charitable Trust

General

£208,000 (2000/01)

Beneficial area UK, with a preference for Oxfordshire.

Morgan Cole Solicitors, Buxton Court, 3 West Way, Oxford OX2 0SZ

Tel. 01865 262183 **Fax** 01865 200962

Correspondent Helen Fanyinka

Trustees N A Harper; J Cole; Mrs W Church.

CC Number 328687

Information available Full accounts were on file at the Charity Commission.

General One-off and recurrent grants are given to large UK organisations and small local projects for a wide variety of causes. The trust states that it favours groups in Oxfordshire.

In 2000/01 the trust had assets of £4.9 million and an income of £252,000, of which £191,000 came from rent. Grants to 99 organisations totalled £208,000 and ranged from £50 to £50,000, but were mainly for £5,000 or less. By far the largest was £50,000 to Sobell House Hospice. Other grants over £10,000 each were £34,000 to Nuffield Orthopaedic Centre and £13,000 to Cystic Fibrosis Trust. A grant of £14,000 was made for work on a memorial field.

Remaining grants were in the range of £50 to £5,000 and included those to: Headway Oxford (£5,000), Sixteen Ltd (£2,500), Witney Enterprise for Local Learning (£2,000), Family Links and Oxfordshire Association for the Blind (£1,500 each), Prince's Trust (£1,100), Jubilee Sailing Trust (£1,000), Homestart – Oxford and Wood Farm Youth Club (£500 each), Witney Families Together (£400) and Shires Spectrum Support Group (£50).

Exclusions It is unlikely that grants would be made for overseas projects or to individuals for higher education.

Applications On a form available from the correspondent. Applications are considered three times a year.

The Finnart House School Trust

Jewish children and young people in need of care

£138,000 (2000/01)

Beneficial area Worldwide.

5th Floor, 707 High Road, North Finchley, London N12 0BT

Tel. 020 8445 1670 **Fax** 020 8446 7370

Email finnart@anjy.org

Correspondent Peter Shaw, Clerk

Trustees Dr Louis Marks, Chair; Robert Cohen; Lady Grabiner; Hilary Norton; David Fobel; Lilian Hochhauser; Jane

Leaver; Dr Amanda Kirby; Mark Sebba; Linda Peterson; Sue Leifer.

CC Number 220917

Information available Full accounts were provided by the trust.

General The trust supports the relief of children and young people who are of the Jewish faith and aged 21 and under. Particularly those who are: disaffected; disadvantaged socially and economically, through illness or neglect; or in need of care and education.

In 2000/01 the trust had assets of £4.5 million and an income of £160,000. In the year 27 grants of £2,000 to £10,000 were made totalling £138,000.

The three largest donations were £10,000 each to Ashalim Children's Village, Institute for the Advancemnt of Eduation in Jaffa and King Solomon High School.

Other beneficiaries included Gimmel Foundation (£9,000), Alut, Cosgrove Care, Esra Community Fund and Hasmonean High School (£5,000 each), Jewish Deaf Association (£3,500), Mercaz Harmony (£3,000), Association for the Advancement of the Ethiopian Family and Defence for Children International (£2,500 each) and Association of Jewish Sixth Formers (£2,000).

Applications There is an application form, which needs to be submitted together with a copy of the latest annual report and accounts.

The Sir John Fisher Foundation

General

£305,000 (2000/01)

Beneficial area UK, with a preference for the Furness peninsula and Merseyside.

8–10 New Market Street, Ulverston, Cumbria LA12 7LW

Tel. 01229 583291

Correspondent R F Hart Jackson, Trustee

Trustees *D P Tindall; R F Hart Jackson; Mrs D S Meacock.*

CC Number 277844

Information available Full accounts were on file at the Charity Commission.

General The trust states that it gives grants to charities concerned with the Furness peninsula and local branches of UK charities. Grants are also made to national and international groups concerned with the shipping industry, medicine, the navy or military and music or theatre.

In 1999/2000 it had assets of £6.9 million and an income of £441,000. Grants totalled £305,000, broken down as follows:

Local – 99 grants totalling £197,000

The largest grants of £5,000 or more went to Lancaster University for The Sir John Fisher Chair (£25,000), Friends of Wordsworth Trust and Hospice of St Mary of Furness (£20,000 each), Brewery Arts Centre (£10,000), Downdales School (£8,000), Furness Drug and Alcohol Concern and Samaritans – Furness (£6,500 each), Abbot Hall and Croft Care Trust (£5,000).

Remaining grants were in the range of £100 to £2,500. Beneficiaries included: Furness Falcons Wheelchair Basketball Club and Lakeland Sinfonia Concernt Society (£2,500 each); Hospital Equipment Fund for Furness and YMCA Lakeside Centre (£2,000 each), Lake District Summer Music School, Lakeland Horticultural Society and Windermere Steamboat Museum (£1,000 each); Coniston Mountain Rescue Team and YHA Hawkshead (£500 each); Barrow Chrysanthemum Society (£100); and Furness War Veterans Benevolent Fund (£50).

Liverpool – 9 grants totalling £28,000

By far the largest donation was £20,000 to Merseyside Maritime Museum. Other larger grants went to Merchant Taylors School (£2,500), Frontline Project (£2,000) and Claire House Children's Hospice (£1,000). Remaining grants were £500 each and went to Breast Cancer Campaign, Claire House Children's Hospice, Liverpool School of Tropical Medicine, River Mersey Inshore Rescue and Royal School for the Blind.

National – 45 grants totalling £80,000

The largest grants were £12,000 to Worshipful Company of Shipwrights and £10,000 to Foundation of Coagulation and Thrombosis – Dundee University. Other beneficiaries of larger grants included Handel House Trust Ltd and Imperial Cancer Research Fund (£5,000 each), Prince's Trust (£2,500), Jubilee Sailing Trust (£2,000), Cancer Bacup, National Children's Home and Royal Star and Garter Home (£1,000 each). Grants under £1,000 each included those to

Actor's Benevolent Fund, British Kidney Patient Assoication, Church Army – Cumbria, Drama Trust, Mencap – Blue Sky Appeal, New Bridge, Royal British Legion and RUKBA.

Exclusions Grants are not given to students.

Applications In writing to the correspondent. Trustees usually meet in May and November.

Marc Fitch Fund

Humanities

£150,000 to organisations and individuals (2001/02)

Beneficial area UK.

10 Market Street, Charlbury OX7 3PH

Tel. 01608 811944

Email admin@marcfitchfund.org.uk

Website www.marcfitchfund.org.uk

Correspondent Elaine M Paintin, Executive Secretary

Trustees *A S Bell, Chair; Hon. Nicholas Assheton; Prof. J P Barron; A J Camp; Prof. C R Elrington; Dr J I Kermode; Prof. D M Palliser; J Porteous; Dr J Blair; Dr H Forde; A Murison; Dr G Worsley.*

CC Number 313303

Information available Information was provided by the trust.

General The trust makes grants for 'publication of research in archaeology, historical geography, history of art and architecture, heraldry, genealogy, surnames, catalogues of and use of archives (especially ecclesiastical), conservation of artefacts and other antiquarian, archaeological or historical studies'.

In 2001/02 the fund had assets of almost £4 million and an income of £288,000. The fund made grants to organisations and individuals totalling £150,000.

Examples of beneficiaries were Manorial Documents Register (£28,000), AHRB Centre for North-east England History (£5,000), Bowes Museum (£3,000), Oxford Archaeology (£2,100) and St Albans Architectural and Archaeological Society (£1,000).

Exclusions No grants are given towards: foreign travel or for research outside Great Britain, unless the circumstances are very exceptional; or people reading full-time higher degrees.

Applications In writing to the correspondent. The trustees meet twice a year to consider applications.

The Earl Fitzwilliam Charitable Trust

General

£81,000 (2000/01)

Beneficial area UK, with a preference for areas with historical family connections, chiefly in Cambridgeshire, Northamptonshire and Yorkshire.

Estate Office, Milton Park, Peterborough PE6 7AH

Tel. 01733 267740

Correspondent J M S Thompson, Secretary to the Trustees

Trustees *Sir Philip Naylor-Leyland Bart; Lady Isabella Naylor-Leyland.*

CC Number 269388

Information available Full accounts were provided by the trust.

General The trust tends to favour charities that benefit rural communities, especially those with a connection to Cambridgeshire, Peterborough, South Yorkshire and Malton in North Yorkshire where the Fitzwilliam family have held their landed estates for many centuries.

It was established in 1975 by the Rt Hon. Earl Fitzwilliam and has since had various capital sums and property gifted to it. Assets totalled £3.9 million in 2000/01, with an income of £163,000 and grants totalling £81,000. Other expenditure totalled £134,000, including £63,000 in legal and professional fees, £36,000 on upkeep of the estate and £18,000 as a share of general overheads.

A total of 34 grants ranging from £1,000 to £5,000 are listed in the accounts. Well over half of these show an obvious connection to one of the places mentioned above. Examples include Brathay Hall Trust, Cambridgeshire Life Education Centre, High Sherriff's Award Scheme, National Autistic Society, Peterborough Diocesan Family Care, Rural Minds, Sheffield Galleries and Museum Trust and The Wildside Trust.

Exclusions No grants to individuals.

Applications In writing to the correspondent. Trustees meet about every three months.

The Rose Flatau Charitable Trust

Jewish, social welfare

£118,000 (2000/01)

Beneficial area UK.

5 Knott Park House, Wrens Hill, Oxshott, Leatherhead KT22 0HW

Tel. 01372 843082

Correspondent M E G Prince, Trustee

Trustees *M E G Prince; A E Woolf; N L Woolf.*

CC Number 210492

Information available Full accounts were on file at the Charity Commission.

General The trust supports Jewish organisations and charities concerned with health and older people.

In 2000/01 the trust had assets of £1.3 million, which generated an income of £60,000. Grants were made to 30 organisations totalling £119,000.

The largest grants were £15,000 to Norwood, £10,000 to Cherry Trees and £5,000 each to Anglo-Jewish Association, Cancer Research Campaign, Crisis, Jewish Aged Needy Pension Trust, Jewish Blind and Disabled, Jewish Care, Jewish Children's Day, Multiple Sclerosis Society, Queen Elizabeth Foundation for the Disabled, Queen Mary's Clothing Fund, Royal Hospital for Neuro-disability, Samaritans, United Israel and Winged Fellowship.

Other grants included £2,500 each to BTCV and New Horizon Youth Centre, £2,000 each to Blond McIndoe Medical Research, Motability and St Mungo's, £1,500 to Royal Masonic Benevolent Association, £1,000 to Anthony Nolan Bone Marrow Trust and £110 to United Synagogue.

Exclusions No grants to individuals.

Applications The trust states: 'No further applications can be accepted as the income available is fully committed.'

The Ian Fleming Charitable Trust

Disability, medical

£130,000 (2000/01)

Beneficial area UK.

Haysmacintyre, Southampton House, 317 High Holborn, London WC1V 7NL

Tel. 020 7969 5500

Correspondent A A I Fleming, Trustee

Trustees *A A I Fleming; N A M McDonald; A W W Baldwin; A H Isaacs.*

CC Number 263327

Information available Accounts were on file at the Charity Commission.

General This trust's income is allocated equally between: (a) UK charities actively operating for the support, relief and welfare of men, women and children who are disabled or otherwise in need of help, care and attention, and charities actively engaged in research on human diseases; and (b) Music Education Awards under a scheme administered by the Musicians Benevolent Fund and advised by a committee of experts in the field of music.

In 2000/01 it had assets of £2.3 million and an income of £110,000. A total of £130,000 was distributed in grants of which £61,000 was distributed from the general fund and £69,000 from the designated fund for the Musicians Benevolent Fund.

Grants made from the general fund were listed in the accounts. A total of 35 donations were made, mainly in the range of £1,000 to £3,000. Beneficiaries included: Breakthrough Breast Cancer (£3,000); SSAFA Forces Help (£2,500), British Heart Foundation, Council for Music in Hospitals, Help the Hospices, Multiple Sclerosis Trust and Royal Star and Garter Home (£2,000 each); Action Research, British Brain and Spine Foundation, Disability Living Foundation and Warchild (£1,500 each); and Rainbow Trust (£1,000).

Exclusions No grants to individuals except under the Music Education Award Scheme. No grants to purely local charities.

Applications In writing to the correspondent.

Florence's Charitable Trust

Education, welfare, sick and infirm

£142,000 (2000/01)

Beneficial area UK, with a preference for Rossendale in Lancashire.

E Suttons & Sons, PO Box 2, Riverside, Bacup, Lancashire OL13 0DT

Tel. 01706 874961 **Fax** 01706 879268

Email ronnie@esutton.co.uk

Correspondent R Barker, Secretary to the Trustees

Trustees *C C Harrison, Chair; R Barker; A Connearn; G D Low; J Mellows; R D Uttley; K Duffy.*

CC Number 265754

Information available Full accounts were on file at the Charity Commission.

General In 2000/01 the trust had assets of £1.4 million and an income of £100,000. Grants totalled £142,000 and were mainly recurrent.

Grants are categorised under three main headings: education (£68,000), sick and infirm (£24,000) and general public benefits (£40,000). Four grants totalling £9,500 were given under the category 'Aged'. A further £1,500 was given to individuals in death grants.

There were 34 grants given in the 'education' category. The largest grant went to Britannia Country Primary School (£7,100). Other beneficiaries included All Saints School and Life Education Trust for Lancashire (£3,000 each), Lancaster Royal Grammar School (£2,500), Rossendale School Referral (£2,000) and Young Enterprise (£350).

The 'sick and infirm' category included 20 grants with the largest being £7,500 to Cardiac Services. Other grants went to Burnley Health Trust (£3,400), Stafford University (£2,500), British Red Cross (£2,000), British Heart Foundation (£1,000), DEBRA (£500), East Lancashire Deaf Society (£250) and Rossendale Hospice (£200). A few small grants were given to individuals for disability aids.

In the 'other public benefits' category 35 grants were made, the largest of which was £15,000 to Rossendale Borough Council. Other grants were mostly for £750 or less and included those to Bowland Pennine Mountain Rescue, Get Kids Going, Lancashire Badger Group, Rawtenstall Youth Club and Todmorden Amateur Operatic and Drama Society.

Five local branches of the Samaritans were also supported.

Exclusions No grants to individual, educational costs, exchange visits or gap year activities.

Applications In writing to the correspondent. The trust stated that funds are fully committed until 2006. To save on administration costs, unsuccessful applications will not be acknowledged even if an sae is provided.

The Football Association National Sports Centre Trust

Play areas, community sports facilities

£356,000 (2001)

Beneficial area UK.

25 Soho Square, London W1D 4FA

Tel. 020 7745 4589 **Fax** 020 7745 5589

Email mike.appleby@TheFA.com

Correspondent Mike Appleby, Secretary to the Trustees

Trustees *K St J Wiseman, Chair; W T Annable; A W Brett; A D McMullen; E M Parry.*

CC Number 265132

Information available Full information is available from the Charity Commission.

General In 2001, the trust had assets of £770,000 and an income of £231,000. Grants totalled £356,000 for the year, but no further details of beneficiaries was available.

In 1996 the trust's assets totalled £2.7 million and income was £1.4 million, mainly from Gift Aid donations from the Football Association. Grants were made totalling £663,000.

The trust's 1996 annual report states that the principle activity of the trust is 'the preservation and protection of the physical and mental health of the community; and the provision, in the interests of social welfare and with the object of improving the conditions of life for the persons for whom the facilities are primarily intended, of facilities for recreation and other leisure time occupations which shall be available to members of the public at large'.

In practice the trust appears to make grants in two areas:

a) towards hard surface play areas
b) to 'grassroots' football clubs.

Grants were given to 16 hard surface play areas in 1996, with applicants including councils, sports clubs and community associations. These grants totalled £294,000.

The remaining grants, totalling £369,000 were given in grants up to £5,000, to football clubs.

Applications In writing to the correspondent.

The Football Association Youth Trust

Sports

£1.7 million (2001/02)

Beneficial area UK.

Football Association Ltd, 25 Soho Square, London W1D 4FA

Tel. 020 7745 4589 **Fax** 020 7745 5589

Email mike.appleby@thefa.org

Correspondent M Appleby, Secretary

Trustees *W T Annable; R G Berridge; B W Bright; G Thomson; M Armstrong.*

CC Number 265131

Information available Information was provided by the trust.

General The principal activity of the trust continues to be the organisation or provision of facilities which will enable pupils of schools and universities in the UK to play association football or other games and sports including the provision of equipment, lectures, training colleges, playing fields or indoor accommodation. In addition, the trust has organised or provided facilities for physical recreation in the interests of social welfare in the UK for people under 21 who need such facilities. Schools and in particular, the English Schools Football Association and the Universities and City Football Associations are major beneficiaries. A range of projects and events have been supported, an increasing number of which have been small donations to schools and clubs. Beneficiaries must be under 21 unless they are in full-time education.

In 2001/02 the trust had assets of £10 million and an income of £1.1 million. Grants totalled £1.7 million.

The main beneficiaries were: TOPS Football Programme (£789,000 in various grants providing equipment for primary schools); Mini School Projects (£773,000, of which £339,000 was for goal posts); and English Schools FA (£200,000).

Applications In writing to the correspondent. Grants are made throughout the year. There are no application forms, but a copy of the most recent accounts should be sent.

The Forbes Charitable Trust

Adults with learning disabilities

£72,000 (2000/01)
Beneficial area UK.

9 Weir Road, Kibworth, Leicestershire LE8 0LQ
Tel. 0116 279 3225 **Fax** 0116 279 6384
Email jbscarecentral@freeuk.com
Correspondent J B Shepherd, Secretary to the Trustees
Trustees *Colonel R G Wilkes, Chair; Major Gen. R L S Green; J C V Lang; E J Townsend; N J Townsend; C G Packham; J M Waite.*
CC Number 326476
Information available Full accounts were on file at the Charity Commission.

General The foundation was set up 'to make long-term provision for adults with learning disabilities'. In 2000/01 its assets totalled £1.7 million and it had an income of £73,000. Grants to nine organisations were made totalling £72,000. By far the largest was £50,000 to CARE Fund, which has also received major support in previous years.

Other grants were £10,000 to Downs Syndrome Association, £5,000 to L'Arche, £2,000 to Hansel Foundation and £1,000 each to Brainwave, Break, Holm, Anthony Toby Holmes Trust and Merseyside Tuesday and Thursday Club.

Applications In writing to the correspondent.

The Oliver Ford Charitable Trust

Mental disability, housing

£89,000 to organisations and individuals (2000/01)
Beneficial area UK.

Messrs Macfarlanes, 10 Norwich Street, London EC4A 1BD
Tel. 020 7831 9222
Correspondent Matthew Pintus
Trustees *Derek Hayes; Lady Wakeham; Martin Levy.*
CC Number 1026551
Information available Information was provided by the trust.

General The objects of the trust are to educate the public and advance knowledge of the history and techniques of interior decoration, the designs of fabric and other decorative materials and landscape gardening with particular reference to Oliver Ford's own work. Income not used for these purposes is used for the Anthroposophical Society of Great Britain, Camphill Village Trust, Ravenswood Foundation or any other village or home for people with mental disabilities which is not state-subsidised.

Grants are given each year to students on the Victoria and Albert Museum/Royal College of Art MA course in the History of Design. From 2003 a grant is to be given to students on the Wisley Diploma in Practical Horticulture run by Royal Horticultural Society.

In 2000/01 the trust's assets stood at £1.6 million and it had an income of £95,000. A total of £89,000 was distributed in 40 grants.

Grants included those to Cambridge Mencap (£5,800), Aldingbourne Trust (£5,500), Camphill Communities East Anglia and Wirral Autistic Society (£5,000 each), Network (£4,000), Stockdales (£3,000), Autism Independent UK and Yarrow Housing Ltd (£2,000 each), L'Arche (£1,300) and Norman Laud Association (£1,000).

Applications In writing to the correspondent. Trustees meet in March and October.

Fordeve Ltd

Jewish, general

£414,000 (1999/2000)
Beneficial area UK.

c/o Gerald Kreditor & Co., Tudor House, Llanvanor Road, London NW2 2AQ
Tel. 020 8209 1535 **Fax** 020 8209 1923
Correspondent J Kon, Trustee
Trustees *J Kon; Mrs H Kon.*
CC Number 1011612
Information available Accounts were on file at the Charity Commission but without a grants list.

General The trust makes grants to Jewish causes and for the relief of need. In 1999/2000 it had assets of £469,000 and an income of £305,000, mainly from donations. Grants totalled £305,000. Unfortunately further information was not available about the size or number of grants made.

Applications In writing to the correspondent.

Four Acre Trust

Respite care and holidays, vocational guidance, health disability, social housing

£418,000 (2001/02)
Beneficial area Worldwide.

56 Leslie Grove, Croydon CR0 6TG
Tel. 020 8680 3100
Email info@fouracretrust.org.uk
Website www.fouracretrust.org.uk
Correspondent The Trustees
Trustees *Mary A Bothamley; Jennifer J Bunner; John P Bothamley; Robert L Carruthers.*
CC Number 1053884
Information available Accounts were provided by the trust including a list of the top 50 grants.

General The trust has several guiding principles, these are to:

- give preference to areas which are disadvantaged
- favour projects which will contribute to the preservation and development of a free and stable society

- give preference to projects which are innovative, developmental, designed to make a practical impact on a particular problem or need and reflect the principles of market forces; especially in the case of local projects, preference is given to those which demonstrate active local participation and support self-help
- attach importance to the assessment and dissemination of the results of work it has funded, so that others may benefit.

The trust makes grants under four specific categories:

Repsite care and holidays
Support for: holidays, holiday centres, refuges, carer support and respite, subsidised holidays

Guidance in choice of vocation
Support for: counselling for work training, employment generation, vocational guidance

Relief of health disability at low unit cost
Support for: cataract operations, immunisation programmes, prosthesess

Social housing
Support for: provision of land and premises for social housing.

The trust states that it has continued to support many recipients (114 in 2001/02), and does not necessarily restrict its funding to just three years. There is an emphasis on supporting small charities mainly operating in the UK.

The trust was formed in 1995 and a large part of its income is derived from a company within the construction industry. In 2001/02 the assets totalled £2.8 million and the income was £412,000. This comprised £280,000 from donations and gifts, £125,000 property income and £7,000 from investments.

Direct charitable expenditure totalled £396,000 made up of £275,000 in grants, £122,000 in rental income foregone and £23,000 in depreciation of property used for charitable purposes.

'A major project for the trust was the purchase of Ardale, a former community home, in Thurrock, Essex. This will be updated, converted and extended into a new community in partnership with a number of leading and local charities.'

The project aims to provide sites and buildings for registered charities at 'highly discounted prices'. The project has been delayed, it appears because of Thurrock Council taking a long time to deal with the planning application. The trust states that new guidlelines by the Charity Commission (which the trust welcomes), make rural and urban regeneration and the relief of unemployment clearly charitable objects. The trust can now show the project's costs as charitable expense in future accounts. It states: 'A large part of the trust's expenditure in the coming year is likely to be made on this project as well as continuing support of other charities.'

The largest grants given were £25,000 to Princess Royal Trust HQ, £10,000 each to Ashoka and Youth Hostels Association and £6,000 to Northam Lodge. There were six recipients of £5,000, Abel Charitable Trust, Alzheimer Scotland, Brittle Bone Society, Church Pastoral Aid Society, National Benevolent Fund for Aged and Raleigh International. Other beneficiaries of £2,000 or more included Belfast Central Mission, Disability Challengers, Green Space, Nepal Leprosy Trust, Ocean Youth Trust, Shepherds Bush Families Project, Stroud & District Mencap and Youth Hostels Association.

Exclusions The trust does not support the following:

- animal welfare
- arts
- basic services (as opposed to imaginative new projects) for people who are disabled or elderly
- commercial publications
- conferences or seminars
- direct replacement of statutory funding
- establishing funds for scholarships or loans
- expeditions
- general appeals
- heritage
- hospices
- individuals
- individual parish churches
- large UK-charities which enjoy wide support, including local branches of UK-charities
- medical (including research), general healthcare or costs of individual applicants
- night shelters
- overseas travel, conference attendance or exchanges
- performances, exhibitions or festivals
- projects concerning drug abuse or alcoholism
- religious activities
- science
- sports
- stage, film or television production costs
- university or similar research.

The trust does not make loans, or give grants retrospectively. Grants are not given towards any large capital, endowment or widely distributed appeal.

It would consider a specific item, or project, making part of a large appeal.

Applications In writing to the correspondent. Trustees meet in March, June, September and December. Applications should be kept brief and received two months before the meeting. The trust does not welcome telephone calls.

The Fox Memorial Trust

General
£77,000 to organisations
(2000/01)
Beneficial area UK.

Hangover House, 3 Burford Lane, East Ewell, Surrey KT17 3EY

Correspondent Mrs C Hardy, Administrator

Trustees *Mrs S M F Fitton; Mrs F M F Le Masurier; Miss A M Fox.*

CC Number 262262

Information available Accounts were provided by the trust.

General The trust was established in 1970 with general charitable purposes. It does not describe its work in its annual report; however, the grants list shows a preference for education and health and welfare causes. Mainly UK organisations are supported.

In 2001/02 the trust had assets of £1.5 million and an income of £129,000. Grants to 146 organisations totalled £77,000 with a further £42,000 given in 72 grants to individuals.

The accounts only listed the two grants over £1,000. Beneficiaries were City of London Sinfonia (£5,000) and Follifoot Park Disabled Riders Group (£1,400).

In previous years other beneficiaries have included: Association of Wheelchair Children, Cardon Housing Youth Project, Disabled Living Foundation, Discovery Dockland Trust, Fight for Sight, Forget Me Not Cancer Appeal, Go to the Nations Ministry, International Spinal Research Trust, Muscular Dystrophy Group, NCDL, Oasis Children's Venture, St John's Hospice, Samaritans, Victim Support, WWF and York Minster Fund.

Applications In writing to the correspondent. Initial telephone calls are not necessary. An sae will guarantee a response.

The Timothy Franey Charitable Foundation

Children, health, education, arts

£82,000 (2001/02)

Beneficial area Mainly UK although approximately 10% goes on overseas support. There is a small preference for south east London.

32 Herne Hill, London SE24 9QS

Email info@franeyfoundation.com

Correspondent T Franey, Trustee

Trustees *Timothy Franey; Wendy Ann Franey; Samantha Richmond.*

CC Number 802189

Information available Information was provided by the trust.

General The trust helps children who are sick or underprivileged and supports causes in south east London concerned with health, education and the arts.

In 2001/02 it had assets of £393,000 and an income of £29,000, down from £43,000 in the previous year. After administration and management costs of £5,300 grants totalled £82,000.

No grants list was included in the accounts, although the narrative report stated that a grant of £44,000 was given to Anita Goulden Trust to assist them in their work in Peru caring for children who are underprivileged or disabled.

Previous beneficiries have included NCH Action for Children, Dulwich College Bursary Appeal, Hope and Homes for Children, Kings Appeal and Malcolm Sargent Cancer Fund for Children.

The trust has decided that, because of the large amount of applications it receives and the resulting administration burden and costs, it will now only support charities which it has worked with in the past.

Exclusions No grants to individuals. The trust stated 'we mainly support registered charities, or work with them in funding specific situations and projects'.

Applications Application by e-mail only. Further information will be requested by the trust if required. Applications in writing or by phone will not be considered.

The Jill Franklin Trust

Overseas, welfare, prisons, church restoration

£72,000 (2000/01)

Beneficial area Worldwide.

78 Lawn Road, London NW3 2XB

Tel. 020 7722 4543 **Fax** 020 7722 4543

Email lawnroad@blueyonder.co.uk

Correspondent N Franklin, Trustee

Trustees *Andrew Franklin; Norman Franklin; Sally Franklin; Sam Franklin; Tom Franklin.*

CC Number 1000175

Information available Full accounts were provided by the trust.

General The trust states it has about £70,000 a year to spend, including committed funds. Grants are given in the following areas:

- advice, training, employment and self-help groups to support people with a mental illness or learning difficulties, and their carers
- respite care and holidays (UK only). Grants for holidays are only given where there is a large element of respite care, and are given to registered charities only, not individuals
- special development projects in the Commonwealth with low overheads
- organisations helping and supporting refugees coming to, or already in, the UK
- the restoration (not improvement) of churches of architectural importance and occasionally to other buildings of architectural importance.

Grants are also given towards the resettlement of offenders including young offenders, and work with prisoners and their families. Grants of up to £200 are also given towards the education and training of prisoners. For these grants, the prisoners themselves should apply.

In 2000/01 the trust had an income of £71,000. Grants totalled £72,000 and were broken down as follows:

	No of grants
£200 or less to prisoners	138
£499 or less	5
£500	71
£1,000	8
over £1,000	1

Beneficiaries of grants greater than £500 each included: Camden City Islington and Westminister Bereavement Services (£9,000); Asylum Aid, BIA/Quaker Social Action, Live Music Now!, Oxfam, Refugee Council and Scottish Refugee Council (£1,000 each); Book Aid International, British Red Cross, Camfed, Kings Cross Housing Project, Leisure for Autism, Manic Depression Fellowship, Matthew Trust, Stuart Low Trust and Sefton Children's Trust (£500 each).

Exclusions Grants are not given to:

- both branches of a UK organisation and its centre (unless it is a specific grant, probably for training in the branches)
- building appeals or endowment funds
- encourage the 'contract culture', particularly where authorities are not funding the contract adequately
- religious organisations set up for welfare, education and so on, of whatever religion, unless the users of the service are from all denominations, and there is no attempt whatsoever to conduct any credal propaganda or religious rituals
- restoration
- 'heritage schemes'
- animals
- students or any individuals or for overseas travel
- medical research.

Applications In writing to the correspondent, including the latest annual report, accounts and budget, and a clear statement of purpose. The trustees tend to look more favourably on an appeal which is simply and economically prepared rather than glossy, 'prestige' and mailsorted brochures. Many worthy applications are rejected simply due to a lack of funds. No acknowledgement is given to unsolicited enquiries, except where an sae is enclosed.

The Gordon Fraser Charitable Trust

Children, young people, environment, arts

£149,000 (2001/02)

Beneficial area UK, with some preference for Scotland.

Holmhurst, Westerton Drive, Bridge of Allan, Stirling FK9 4QL

Correspondent Mrs M A Moss, Trustee

Trustees *Mrs M A Moss; W F T Anderson.*

CC Number 260869

Information available Full accounts were provided by the trust.

General Currently the trustees are particularly interested in supporting children/young people in need, the environment and visual arts (including performance arts). Most grants are given within these categories. The trust states that 'applications from or for Scotland will receive favourable consideration, but not to the exclusion of applications from elsewhere'.

In 2001/02 the trust had assets of £2.5 million and an income of £100,000. A total of £149,000 was given in 201 grants, ranging from £100 to £12,000. Most grants were for less than £1,000, with 27 for £1,000 or more.

The largest grant was given to the Dulwich Picture Gallery (£12,000). Others included those to Ballet West and MacRobert Arts Centre (£6,000 each), Scottish Museums Council and Lochaber Music Charitable Trust (£5,000 each), National Library of Scotland (£4,000), Royal Botanic Garden Edinburgh and Royal Scottish National Orchestra (£3,000 each), Scottish Opera (£2,000), Queen Margaret University College, Scottish National Portrait Gallery and Waverley Care Trust (£1,000 each).

Smaller grants of less than £1,000 were given to a wide range of charities, both national and local throughout Scotland. Beneficiaries included Aberdeen International Youth Festival, Alone in London Service, Baby Life Support Systems, Boys and Girls Welfare Society, Canniesburn Research Trust, Drumchapel Law and Money Advice Centre, Edinburgh Sitters, Glasgow Children's Holiday Scheme, John Muir Trust, Motor Neurone Disease Association and Scout Association.

Exclusions No grants are made to organisations which are not recognised charities, or to individuals.

Applications In writing to the correspondent. Applications are considered in January, April, July and October. Grants towards national or international emergencies can be considered at any time. All applicants are acknowledged, an sae would therefore be appreciated.

The Joseph Strong Frazer Trust

General

£644,000 (2000/01)

Beneficial area England and Wales only.

Scottish Provident House, 31 Mosley Street, Newcastle Upon Tyne NE1 1HX

Tel. 0191 232 8065 **Fax** 0191 222 1554

Correspondent The Correspondent

Trustees *Sir William A Reardon Smith, Chair; D A Cook; R M H Read; W N H Reardon Smith.*

CC Number 235311

Information available Accounts were provided by the trust.

General In 2000/01 the trust had assets of £9.3 million and an income of £813,000. After management and administration costs of £56,000, grants totalled £644,000.

Recipients cover a wide variety of fields and are based all over England and Wales (the trust appears to be one of a very guide in this book to have a specific interest in Wales). The awards were categorised as follows:

Children	£65,000	(48 grants)
Youth	£29,000	(30)
Older people	£17,000	(9)
Hospitals and homes	£52,000	(38)
Deaf and blind	£46,000	(30)
Disability	£31,000	(26)
Mental disability	£11,000	(8)
Medical and other research	£101,000	(67)
Maritime	£37,000	(27)
Armed forces	£6,000	(5)
Caring organisations	£70,000	(51)
Other	£95,000	(50)
Schools and colleges	£22,000	(14)
Leisure activities, animals and wildlife	£35,000	(22)
Religious bodies	£29,000	(25)

Grants of over £3,000 went to 70 organisations totalling £303,000, most organisations received more than one grant.

The largest grants were given to Royal Agricultural Benevolent Institution (£30,000) and Children's Hospice in Wales Appeal Limited (£10,000). After grants of £8,000 to Royal Merchant Navy School Foundation, £6,000 each to Bearwood College Charitable Bursary

Fund and Boar Bank Nursing Home and £5,500 to MHOSLJ Charitable Trust. Remaining listed beneficiaries included 5 organisations receiving £5,000 each, 37 receiving £4,000 each and 22 receiving £3,000 each.

Beneficiaries included: Arkwright Scholarships, Army Benevolent Fund, Douglas Bader Foundation, Paul Bevan Home, Contact – London, Hill Homes, Iris Fund, Mencap, National Association for Gifted Children, National Botanic Garden of Wales, National Eczema Society, Piccadilly Advice Centre, Prostate Cancer Charity, Research into Ageing, RSPCA, Scope, Treloar Trust, Welsh Epilepsy Unit Support Fund, Welsh Sports Aid and Wildfowl and Wetlands Trust.

A total of £241,000 was distributed in 312 grants under £3,000 each.

Exclusions No grants to individuals.

Applications In writing to the correspondent. Trustees meet twice a year, usually in March and September. Application forms are not necessary but it is helpful if applicants are concise in their appeal letters, which must include an sae if acknowledgement is required.

The Charles S French Charitable Trust

Community projects, disability, children and youth

£177,000 (2000/01)

Beneficial area UK, in practice north east London and south west Essex.

169 High Road, Loughton, Essex IG10 4LF

Tel. 020 8502 3575

Correspondent R L Thomas, Trustee

Trustees *W F Noble; R L Thomas; D B Shepherd.*

CC Number 206476

Information available Accounts were on file at the Charity Commission, but without a grants list.

General Established by Charles S French in 1959 the trust has a policy of supporting primarily local charities, which have continued to be mainly in north east London and south west Essex, specifically for children and the local community.

In 2000/01 the trust had assets of £5.9 million and an income of £201,000. Grants totalled £177,000.

The grants, although not detailed by beneficiary, were categorised as follows:

community	27%
youth and children	23%
medical	17%
education and sport	11%
arts and music	11%
disability	8%
older people	3%

Exclusions Registered charities only.

Applications In writing to the correspondent, including a copy of the latest accounts.

Friends of Wiznitz Limited

Jewish education

£288,000 (1999/2000)

Beneficial area UK and overseas.

8 Jessam Avenue, London E5 9UD

Correspondent E Gottesfeld

Trustees *H Feldman; E Kahan; R Bergmann; S Feldman.*

CC Number 255685

Information available Grants were on file at the Charity Commission.

General This trust supports major educational projects being carried out by orthodox Jewish institutions. In 1999/2000 it had assets of £308,000 and an income of £410,000. Grants to three organisations totalled £288,000. Beneficiaries were Yeshivat Wiznitz (£220,000), Ahavas Israel Synagogue (£46,000) and CMA Trust (£22,000).

Applications In writing to the correspondent.

This entry was not confirmed by the trust but was correct according to information on file at the Charity Commission.

The Frognal Trust

Older people, disability, blindness/ ophthalmological research, environmental heritage

£77,000 (2001/02)

Beneficial area UK.

Charities Aid Foundation, King's Hill, West Malling, Kent ME19 4TA

Tel. 01732 520083 **Fax** 01732 520001

Correspondent Mrs Sue David, Donor Grants Officer

Trustees *Philippa Blake-Roberts; J P Van Montagu; P Fraser.*

CC Number 244444

Information available Full accounts were provided by the trust.

General The trust particularly supports charities working in the fields of residential facilities and services, cultural heritage, hospices/nursing homes, ophthalmological research, conservation/heritage, parks and community services. Its current policy is to make smaller grants to as many qualifying charities as possible.

In 2001/02 the trust had assets of £1.8 million which generated an income of £54,000. Grants were made to 91 organisations totalling £77,000. Administration costs of £17,000 were high for a trust of this size, although this may be due to the large number of small grants.

The largest grants were £3,500 to Climb, £3,000 to Camphill Community Clanabogan, £2,600 to Cystic Fibrosis Trust, £2,000 each to Enham Trust, Norman Laud Association and Who Cares Trust, £1,600 each to Herefordshire Nature Trust Ltd and Rockingham Forest Trust and £1,500 each to Arthritis Care, Demand, Eric Liddell Centre Ltd, Multiple Sclerosis Society, RUKBA and Umbrella.

Most grants ranged from £200 to £1,000, with nearly half of them of £500 to £600. Recipients of £500 included Age Concern Scotland, Avon Wildlife Trust, Disability Advice and Welfare Network, Dyslexic Computer Training, Listening Books, Norfolk Wildlife Trust, Queen Elizabeth's Foundation for Disabled People, Springboard, Talkback Magazine Service for the Blind, Wearside Mobility and Write Away.

Exclusions The trust does not support:

- any animal charities
- the advancement of religion
- charities for the benefit of people outside the UK
- educational or research trips
- branches of national charities
- general appeals
- individuals.

Applications In writing to the correspondent. Applications should be received by January, April, August or October, for consideration at the trustees' meeting the following month.

The Patrick Frost Foundation

General

£202,000 (2000/01)

Beneficial area Worldwide, but only through UK charities.

c/o Trowers & Hamlins, Sceptre Court, 40 Tower Hill, London EC3N 4DX

Tel. 020 7423 8000 **Fax** 020 7423 8001

Correspondent Mrs H Frost, Trustee

Trustees *Mrs Helena Frost; Donald Jones; Luke Valner; John Chedzoy.*

CC Number 1005505

Information available Full accounts were provided by the foundation.

General The foundation makes general welfare grants to organisations and grants to help small charities that rely on a considerable amount of self-help and voluntary effort.

In 2000/01 the assets totalled £1.4 million. Income was £175,000, including £128,000 in donations received. Grants were made to 27 organisations totalling £202,000. Management and administration fees were high for the year at £28,000, including £18,000 in legal and professional fees to a firm in which one of the trustees is a partner. Even though wholly legal, these editors regret such payments unless, to use the words of the Charity Commission, 'there is no realistic alternative'.

The largest grants were £15,000 each to Acorn Christian Foundation, Family Holiday Association and Universities Settlement in East London for Toynbee Hall and £10,000 each to Action for Blind People, Intermediate Technology,

Lifestyle for Humberside Police, Medical Foundation for the Care of Victims of Torture, Naomi House, Opportunity International and Tools for Self Reliance. Camphill Village Trust also received £10,000, in two grants of £5,000 each.

Apart from £1,000 given to Normandy Veterans Pilgrims Club and £500 to Romanian Appeal Kilearn – England, the other 15 beneficiaries each received £5,000. They included AbilityNet, Demand, Fforest Uchaf Horse and Pony Rehabilitation Centre, John Grooms Association for Disabled People, London Narrow Boat Project, Speakability, Tree Aid and Ty-Agored Animal Sanctuary.

Exclusions No grants to individuals or non-UK charities.

Applications In writing to the correspondent, accompanied by the last set of audited accounts. The trustees regret that due to the large number of applications they receive, they are unable to acknowledge unsuccessful applications.

The Fulmer Charitable Trust

Developing world, general
About £80,000 a year
Beneficial area Worldwide, especially the developing world and Wiltshire.

Estate Office, Street Farm, Compton Bassett, Calne, Wiltshire SN11 8SW
Tel. 01249 760410
Correspondent J S Reis, Chair
Trustees S A Reis; C M Mytum.
CC Number 1070428
Information available Accounts were on file at the Charity Commission, but without a narrative report.

General Most of the support is given in the developing world, although UK charities are also supported, especially those working in Wiltshire.

In 2000/01 the trust had assets of £1.6 million and an income of £110,000. Grants to 64 organisations totalled £118,000. They ranged from £500 to £5,000, although 53 of the grants were of between £1,000 and £3,000.

The largest grants were £5,000 to European Children's Trust, £3,500 to Ethiopiaid, £3,300 to UFM and £3,000 to Jacorander Home Appeal.

Other grants in the developing world included £2,800 each to ITDG, Sight Savers International, Tearfund and UNICEF, £1,500 to Traidcraft and £1,000 to Send a Cow.

Four organisations in Wiltshire were supported during the year. These were Wiltshire Community Foundation (£2,800), Wiltshire Air Ambulance and Youth Action Wiltshire (£1,000 each) and Wiltshire Ambulance Service Trust.

Other grants included those to Childhope (£2,800), Action for Blind People and British Heart Foundation (£1,500 each), Abbeyfield Homes and Christian Concern – Crewe (£1,000 each) and Age Concern and Church Housing Trust (£500 each).

Exclusions No support for gap year requests.

Applications In writing to the correspondent.

Worshipful Company of Furniture Makers Charitable Fund

Furniture industry
£82,000 (1999/2000)
Beneficial area UK.

Painters' Hall, 9 Little Trinity Lane, London EC4V 2AD
Tel. 020 7248 1677 **Fax** 020 7248 1688
Email clerk@furituremkrs.co.uk
Website www.furituremkrs.co.uk
Correspondent Mrs J A Wright
Trustees Patrick V Radford; R B C Waring; Sir John Perring.
CC Number 270483
Information available Full accounts were on file at the Charity Commission.

General This fund distributes around £50,000 each year to causes directly connected to furniture, such as running high quality courses to bring together and train people in the industry, funding design competitions, prototypes and visits to exhibitions or factories and offering bursaries to students at colleges.

In 1999/2000 the fund had assets of £1.2 million and a total income of £168,000.

Grants and scholarships were made totalling £82,000.

From the designated fund, £34,000 was given to the furniture makers' walk and visitor centre within the Castle Howard Arboretum and to other individuals and institutions connected to the furniture industry.

Other donations included £10,000 to Wallace Collection Design Prize, £8,500 to Retail Management Development Course, £7,000 to Student Industrial Tour, £4,100 to Rycote College Residential Course for young manufacturers, £3,300 to Craft Guildmark Seminar, £2,500 to Hans Jourdan Management Course for Manufacturing Excellence, £2,000 towards a seminar for guildmark holders, £1,500 to London Guildhall University for a travel award and £1,000 each to Design Trust and Gunton Formica Award.

Applications In writing to the correspondent.

Gableholt Limited

Jewish
£71,000 (1999/2000)
Beneficial area UK.

115 Craven Park Road, London N15 6BL
Correspondent M A Vemitt, Governor
Trustees S Noe; Mrs E Noe; C Lerner; P Noe.
CC Number 276250
Information available Accounts were on file at the Charity Commission.

General Set up as a limited company in 1978, the trust gives practically all of its funds to Jewish institutions, particularly those working in accordance with the orthodox Jewish faith. In 1999/2000 it had assets of £3.5 million and an income of £344,000, of which £194,00 came from donations. Grants to organisations and individuals totalled £71,000.

Unfortunately no information on grants was included with the trust's accounts that were on file at the Charity Commission. In previous years beneficiaries have included: Afula Society; Child Resettlement; Friends of Harim Establishment; Friends of the Sick; Gur Trust; Mengrah Grammar School; Rachel

Charitable Trust; and Torah Venchased Le'Ezra Vasad.

Applications In the past this trust has stated that "in the governors' view, true charitable giving should always be coupled with virtual anonymity" and for this reason they are most reluctant to be a party to any publicity. Along with suggesting that the listed beneficiaries might also want to remain unidentified, they also state that the nature of the giving (to orthodox Jewish organisations) means the information is unlikely to be of much interest to anyone else. Potential applicants would be strongly advised to take heed of these comments.

Garrick Charitable Trust

Probably arts, children in London
Perhaps £300,000 a year
Beneficial area UK.

15 Garrick Street, London WC2E 9AY
Tel. 020 7836 1737 **Fax** 020 7379 5966
Correspondent The Secretary
CC Number 1071279
Information available Information was provided by the trust.

General The trust was established by the members of the Garrick Club in London in 1998. It was expected to be endowed with about £4 million from the proceeds of selling the Winnie the Pooh copyright to the Disney organisation.

The trust is able to spend interest on capital and it is expected that it will support institutions which are seeking to further theatre (including dance), literature or music.

Since it was established the trust has been receiving applications so there is likely to be high competition for funds.

Applications Initial approaches should be made in writing to the correspondent.

Garvan Limited

Jewish
£170,000 (2000/01)
Beneficial area UK.

Flat 9, Windsor Court, Golders Green Road, London NW11 9PP
Correspondent S Ebert
Trustees *A Ebert; L Ebert.*
CC Number 286110
Information available Accounts were on file at the Charity Commission, but without a list of grants.

General This trust makes grants to Jewish organisations. In 2000/01 it had assets of £339,000 and an income of £236,000, of which £221,000 came from donations. Grants totalled £170,000. Unfortunately, no further information was available on the size or number of beneficiaries for this year.

Applications In writing to the correspondent.

Gederville Ltd

Jewish, general
£300,000 (2000/01)
Beneficial area UK.

40 Fontayne Road, London N16 7DT
Correspondent Y Benedikt
Trustees *Joseph Benedikt; C Benedikt; Jacob Benedikt.*
CC Number 265645
Information available Accounts were on file at the Charity Commission, but without a list of grants.

General In 2000/01 the trust's assets totalled £219,000 and it received an income of £62,000, including £29,000 from donations. Grants totalled £300,000. The trust's accounts stated that it works for the advancement of the orthodox Jewish faith and for general charitable purposes. Examples of grants made were not included with the accounts.

Applications In writing to the correspondent.

Jacqueline and Michael Gee Charitable Trust

Health, education (including Jewish)
£72,000 (2000/01)
Beneficial area UK.

Flat 27, Berkeley House, 15 Hay Hill, London W1J 8NS
Tel. 020 7493 1904 **Fax** 020 7499 1470
Email trust@sherman.co.uk
Correspondent Michael J Gee, Trustee
Trustees *M J Gee; J S Gee.*
CC Number 1062566
Information available Accounts were provided by the trust.

General This charity's policy is to benefit almost exclusively health and educational charities. In practice this includes many Jewish organisations.

It was created in 1997 by the settlement of £50 from the Archie Sherman Charitable Trust. In 2000/01 the income of almost £96,000 included £95,000 in donations from the same trust. Grants totalled £72,000 and the balance was £38,000 at the year end.

A total of 38 grants were made, only 14 of which were for over £1,000. The largest was £10,000 to Purcell School. In addition to health and educational charities, several arts organisations received support from the trust, including Children's Classic Concerts and Garsington Opera (£6,000 each), Royal Opera House (£2,000) and Highgate Choral Society (£500). Other beneficiaries included British ORT (£6,700), Dementia Relief Trust (£2,500), Nightingale House (£3,900) and UJIA (£2,000).

Applications In writing to the correspondent.

The Gertner Charitable Trust

Jewish

£1.6 million to organisations
(2000/01)

Beneficial area Worldwide.

Fordgate House, 1 Allsop Place, London NW1 5LF

Tel. 020 7224 1234

Correspondent Mrs Michelle Gertner, Trustee

Trustees *Moises Gertner; Mrs Michelle Gertner; Mendi Gertner; Michael Wechsler; Simon Jacobs.*

CC Number 327380

Information available Full accounts were on file at the Charity Commission.

General In 2000/01 the trust's assets totalled £1 million and its income, mainly from donations, totalled £1.6 million. Grants to organisations totalled £1.6 million.

The accounts listed the top 50 grants, the largest of which was £250,000 to Kingsley Way Charitable Trust. Other beneficiaries included Yesodey Hatorah – Beth Jacob (£87,000), RS Trust (£66,000), American Friends of Yad Aharon (£55,000), Amuta Lekidum Emtzei Lemida (£40,000), Friends of Mir (£32,000), Mosdos Ohr Hatorah (£30,000), Craven Walk Charitable Trust (£21,000), Ponvenecz (£15,000), Edgware Yeshiva Trust (£12,000), UTA (9,000), Shaarei Torah (£7,000) and CMZ Trust (£6,200).

A further £77,000 went to individuals.

Applications In writing to the correspondent.

The Gibbs Charitable Trusts

Methodism, international, arts

£117,000 (2001/02)

Beneficial area UK, particularly Avon and South Wales, and overseas.

8 Victoria Square, Clifton, Bristol BS8 4ET

Tel. 0117 973 6615 **Fax** 0117 974 4137

Correspondent Dr James M Gibbs, Trustee

Trustees *Mrs S M N Gibbs; Dr J N Gibbs; A G Gibbs; Dr J M Gibbs; W M Gibbs; Dr J E Gibbs; Mrs C Gibbs; Mrs E Gibbs; Mrs P Gibbs; Ms R N Gibbs; Ms J F Gibbs; J W K Gibbs.*

CC Number 207997

Information available Full accounts were provided by the trust.

General The trust supports innovative Methodist work, other Christian causes (especially those of an ecumenical nature) and creative arts, education and international causes.

In 2001/02 the trust had assets of £2.2 million, which generated an income of £77,000. The trust aims to keep its administration and management costs to a minimum (welcomely sending us a copy of its accounts on reused paper), spending just £380 during the year, including subscription fees to the Association of Charitable Foundations. Grants were made to 56 organisations totalling £117,000, broken down as follows:

Methodist Churches, Circuits and Districts – 17 grants totalling £15,000
The largest grants went to Penarth and Dinas Powys Circuit (£3,000), Clubland – Walworth Methodist Church and Victoria Road Methodist Church – Sheffield (£2,000 each) and Dome Mission – Brighton and Temple Methodist Church – Taunton (£1,000 each). Other grants were all of £500 each and included those to Methodist churches in Derby, Huddersfield, Penzance, Redruth and Telford.

Other Methodist initiatives – 11 grants totalling £18,000
Recipients included Cliff College (£5,000), Jasperian Theatre Company (£3,000), Engelsea Brook Museum of Primitive Methodism (£2,000), Oxford Institute of Methodist Theological Studies (£1,500), Museum of Methodism (£1,000) and MIH – Manchester and Penarth Live at Home Scheme (£500 each).

Other Christian initiatives – 4 grants totalling £3,800
These went to Fellowship in Christian Apologetics – Durham (£2,000), Riding Lights (£1,000), SCM Conference (£500) and Art and Christian Enquiry (£250).

International – 12 grants totalling £38,000
Christian Aid received £18,000. Other large grants went to Traidcraft Exchange – Malawi (£5,000), Child to Child (£4,500), Hope and Homes for Children (£3,000), International Planned Parenthood Federation (£2,600) and African Initiatives and Interact (£1,000 each). Smaller grants included those to Tree Aid (£800), Ghana School Aid (£500) and World Write (£300).

Other – 11 grants totalling £13,000
These were £5,000 to Genesis, £1,000 each to Bulith Wells Community Play, Corrymeela, Intercultural Community Arts – Cardiff, Theatr Brycheiniog, Theatre Royal – Stratford East and Wales National Opera and £500 each to Cornwall Arts Centre Trust, Langley House Trust, Prisoner's Trust Video Magazine and West Midlands Post Adoption Service.

There was also £30,000 paid from the designated fund to the Methodist Church Fund for the training of Methodist ministers.

Exclusions A large number of requests are received by the trust from churches undertaking improvement, refurbishment and development projects, but only a few of these can be helped. In general, Methodist churches are selected, sometimes those the trustees have particular knowledge of.

Individuals and animal charities are not supported.

Applications The trust has no application forms; requests should be made in writing to the correspondent. The trustees meet three times a year, at Christmas, Easter and late summer. Unsuccessful applicants are not normally notified. The trustees do not encourage telephone enquiries or speculative applications. They also state that they are not impressed by applicants that send a huge amount of paperwork.

The GNC Trust

General

£142,000 (2001)

Beneficial area UK, with preferences for Midlands, Cornwall and Hampshire.

c/o Messrs PricewaterhouseCoopers, Temple Court, Bull Street, Birmingham B4 6JT

Tel. 0121 265 5000 **Fax** 0121 265 5450

Correspondent R Hardy, Agent to the Trustees

Trustees *R Hardy; G T E Cadbury; Mrs J E B Yelloly.*

CC Number 211533

Information available Full accounts were on file at the Charity Commission.

General In 2001 this trust had assets of £2.4 million generating an income of £88,000. A total of £142,000 was given to 66 organisations.

Beneficiaries of the largest grants were National Institute of Conductive Education (£40,000 in two grants), Charney Manor – Society of Friends (£33,000) and Sibford School (£10,000).

Other beneficiaries of grants over £1,000 each included: Reece School (£7,000 in two grants), British Kidney Patients Association, Refugee Council and Squire Resource (£5,000 each), UNICEF (£2,500), Association for Spina Bifida and Hydrocephalus and Symphony Hall Organ Fund (£2,000 each), Birmingham Royal Ballet Trust and Hampshire Wildlife Trust (£1,500 each), Sail Training Association and Research into Ageing (£1,000 each).

Beneficiaries of smaller grants in the range of £10 and £750 included Action Aid, Action for Blind People, Cancer Bacup, Children's Society, Galapagos Conservation Trust, Hampshire Field Club and Archaeology Society, Maritime Trust, Oakhaven Hospice, Treloar Trust and Worcester Festival Choral Society.

Exclusions Only very occasionally are grants made to individuals. National appeals are not favoured, nor are most London-based charities.

Applications In writing to the correspondent. There is no application form. Applications are not acknowledged.

The Golden Bottle Trust

General

£506,000 (2000/01)

Beneficial area UK.

C Hoare & Co, 37 Fleet Street, London EC4P 4DQ

Tel. 020 7353 4522

Correspondent The Secretariat

Trustees *Messrs Hoare Trustees.*

CC Number 327026

Information available Accounts were on file at the Charity Commission, but without a grants list.

General In 2000/01 the trust had assets of £6.4 million and an income of £973,000, including £745,000 in donations received. The income varies each year, dependent on the donations received. After administration expenses of just £2,000, grants were made totalling £506,000.

No grant information has been included in the trust's accounts since those for 1993/94, when a wide range of organisations were supported, mostly in a large number of small grants of less than £1,000 each.

Exclusions No grants for individuals or organisations that are not registered charities.

Applications In writing to the correspondent, who stated 'trustees meet on a monthly basis, but the funds are already largely committed and, therefore, applications from sources not already known to the trustees are unlikely to be successful'.

Golden Charitable Trust

Preservation, conservation

£111,000 (2001/02)

Beneficial area UK, preference for West Sussex.

Little Leith Gate, Angel Street, Petworth, West Sussex GU28 0BG

Tel. 01798 342434

Correspondent Lewis Golden, Secretary to the Trustees

Trustees *Mrs S J F Solnick; J M F Golden.*

CC Number 263916

Information available Full accounts were on file at the Charity Commission.

General The trust appears to have a preference in its grantmaking for organisations in West Sussex in the field of the preservation and conservation of historic articles and materials.

In 2001/02 the trust had assets of £390,000 and an income of £100,000, including £84,000 from donations. After minimal expenses of £118, grants were made to 13 organisations totalling £111,000. By far the largest was £100,000 to Westminster Synagogue. Other beneficiaries included British ORT (£5,000), Petworth Festival (£1,500),

Friends of King Edward Hospital – Midhurst (£1,400), National Trust (£1,000), Chichester Cathedral Restoration and Development Trust (£700), Whizz-Kidz (£500) and Petworth Cottage Nursing Home (£450).

Exclusions No grants to individuals.

Applications In writing to the correspondent.

The Teresa Rosenbaum Golden Charitable Trust

Medical research

£400,000 (2001/02)

Beneficial area UK.

140 High Street, Edgware, Middlesex HA8 7LW

Tel. 020 8952 1414 **Fax** 020 8952 2424

Email goldentrust@regentsmead.com

Correspondent John Samuels, Trust Administrator

Trustees *T Rosenbaum; R A Ross; R M Abbey.*

CC Number 298582

Information available Excellent accounts were provided by the trust.

General The trust produces an information leaflet, which states: 'The T R Golden Charitable Trust makes most of its charitable donations to medical research, because it wants to support cutting-edge medical research over a wide spectrum of first-class projects. The trustees give preference to projects that offer a realistic prospect of practical results which will lead to new or improved therapies or drugs to benefit patients.

'The trustees are completely independent, having no link with any pharmaceutical or other commercial company engaged in the medical field, and their objective in making substantial donations for medical research is the successful outcome of the research programmes, leading to effective practical treatments. Usually, the trustees start with relatively small grants, but as the reporting progresses and a good working relationship develops between the trust and the researchers these grants are steadily increased and over a period of years can build up to substantial sums.'

In 2001/02 the trust had assets of £741,000. Total income was £886,000, of which £855,000 came from donations received. Grants were made totalling £400,000. After the costs of generating the funds, there was a surplus for the year of £468,000.

A substantial grant of £61,000 was given to The Tissue Engineering Centre at Imperial College – Chelsea, and Westminster and Hammersmith Hospitals to fund a researcher in a specific area of developing bone cells.

Other grants included: £25,000 to Research into Ageing for five different projects; £21,000 to Kings Medical Research Trust for a clinical trial into the treatment of advanced liver cancer; £15,000 to Oncology Trust at Royal Free Hospital into clinical trials in patients using new antibodies; £10,000 to Hearing Research Trust for research at Institute of Otology – London and Institute of Hearing Research – Nottingham into regenerating hair cells and understanding more about possible self-repair mechanisms by studying reptiles and birds; £7,000 to Muscular Dystrophy Campaign for a follow-up project into implanting skin cells into damaged muscles; £6,000 to MS Society for a project to carry out a comprehensive analysis of auto reactive T-cells in multiple sclerosis; £3,000 to Brain and Spine Foundation for a Belfast-based project to block enzymes thought to be responsible for the spread of brain tumours; and £2,000 to Lasers for Life for research into the use of lasers in the treatment and early diagnosis of cancer.

A number of organisations received more than one grant during the year. Alzheimer's Society, for instance, received £10,000 for a fellowship studying the role of TAU protein in the development of tangles leading to the death of brain cells, £5,000 each for a fellowship studying the mechanism of cell death in specific areas of the brain and a fellowship studying protein accumulation and the death of brain cells, and £3,000 to a speculative research project to develop a saliva test to diagnose Alzheimer's disease. Similarly, Royal College of Surgeons received four grants of £2,500 each, for a study into chemotherapy and blood clotting and for fellowships into the role of bacteria in the non-healing of leg fractures following pinning, improvements in knee replacement design to enhance the beneficial effects of surgery and an investigation into how low temperatures could protect the gut in babies and children with severe digestive disorders.

Exclusions No support for individuals, or for non-medical research.

Applications In writing to the correspondent. 'The trustees are not medical experts and require short clear statements in plain English setting out the particular subject to be researched, the objects and likely benefits, the cost and the time-scale. Unless a charity will undertake to provide two concise progress reports each year, they should not bother to apply as this is a vital requirement. It is essential that the trustees are able to follow the progress and effectiveness of the research they support.'

The Jack Goldhill Charitable Trust

Jewish, general
£84,000 (1999)
Beneficial area UK.

85 Kensington Heights, Campden Hill Road, London W8 7BD
Correspondent Jack Goldhill, Trustee
Trustees *G Goldhill; J A Goldhill.*
CC Number 267018
Information available Accounts were on file at the Charity Commission.

General In 1999 the trust had assets of £596,000 and an income of £80,000, including £25,000 in donations received. Grants totalled £84,000.

The largest grants were £27,000 to Jack Goldhill Award Fund and £18,000 to Jewish Care, both of which are regularly supported by the trust.

Other grants included £3,500 to CST, £3,000 to Royal London Hospital, £2,300 to Joint Jewish Charitable Trust, £2,000 each to Inclusion, Tate Gallery and Tricycle Theatre Co., £1,500 to West London Synagogue and £1,000 each to Atlantic College, City and Guilds of London School of Art, JNF Charitable Trust, Nightingale House and Royal Academy of Arts.

Exclusions No support for individuals or new applications.

Applications The trustees have a restricted list of charities to whom they are committed and no unsolicited applications can be considered.

The Golsoncott Foundation

The arts
£60,000 (2000/01)
Beneficial area UK.

31 Danes Road, Exeter EX4 4LS
Tel. Tel & Fax: 01392 252855
Correspondent Hal Bishop, Administrator
Trustees *Penelope Lively, Chair; Josephine Lively; Stephen Wick; Diana Hinds; Dr Harriet Harvey Wood.*
CC Number 1070885
Information available Full accounts were on file at the Charity Commission.

General The trust states its objects as follows: 'to promote, maintain, improve and advance the education of the public in the arts generally and in particular … the fine arts and music. The fostering of the practice and appreciation of the arts, especially amongst young people and new audiences, is a further specific objective.

'Grants vary according to context and are not subject to an inflexible limit, but they are unlikely to exceed £5,000 and are normally given on a non-recurrent basis.'

In 2000/01 the foundation's income was £64,000 and it made grants totalling £60,000. The assets totalled £1.8 million.

Larger grants were: £5,000 each to Horniman Museum, National Youth Orchestra, Royal National Theatre – Education Department, London Suzuki Group and Haringey Young Musicians; £4,100 to Jessie's Fund, £4,000 to London Sinfonietta; £3,900 to the Rachel Reckitt retrospective exhibition; and £3,000 to Pandit Ram Sahai Sangit Vidyalaya. Further grants ranging from £25 to £2,700 were made to 16 organisations.

Exclusions No grants to individuals.

Applications The trustees meet quarterly to consider applications, in February, May, August and November. Applications should be sent to the correspondent by the end of the month preceding the month of the trustees meeting. They should include the following:

- A clear and concise statement of the project, whether the award sought will be for the whole project or a component part. Is the applicant organisation of charitable status?
- Evidence that there is a clear benefit to the public, i.e. does the project conform with the declared object of the trust.

- The amount requested should be specified, or a band indicated. Is this the only source of funding being sought? All other sources of funding should be indicated, including those that have refused funding.
- If the grant requested is part of the match-funding required by the Heritage Lottery Foundation (HLF) following an award, state the amount of that award and the percentage of match-funding required by the HLF and the completion date.
- Wherever possible an annual report and accounts should accompany the application, as may other supporting information deemed relevant.

The Good Neighbours Trust

People with mental or physical disabilities

£70,000 (2001)

Beneficial area UK, with preference for Bristol, Somerset and Gloucestershire.

16 Westway, Nailsea, Bristol BS48 2NA

Correspondent P S Broderick, Secretary

Trustees *G V Arter, Chair; J C Gurney; R T Sheppard; P S Broderick.*

CC Number 201794

Information available Accounts were on file at the Charity Commission.

General The present policy of the trust is to principally support activities which benefit people who are physically or mentally disabled. It mainly gives one-off grants for low-cost specific projects such as purchase of equipment or UK holidays for people with disabilities.

In 2001 the trust had assets of £2.2 million and an income of £82,000. A total of £70,000 was given in grants. They were divided into local grants (which were mainly given in the Greater Bristol area) and UK grants (which were given mostly to locally based groups throughout the UK).

UK grants totalled £51,000 with support going to 105 organisations. The largest grant was £3,000 to Help the Hospices. There were nine grants of £1,000 each made to Ataxia – Telangiectasia Society, Centre 81, Deafblind UK, Eyeless Trust,

Fiveways School, Mark Way School, Pearson's Holiday Fund, Philip Green Memorial School and Rainbow Trust. Remaining grants were in the range of £250 to £500 and included those to Ace Centre, Caring for Life, ENABLE, Cambridge Mencap, Glasgow and West of Scotland Society for the Blind, Kent Adventure Club for the Disabled, Merseyside Thursday Club, RNIB Scotland, Sussex Autistic Society and Vision Foundation.

Local grants went to 39 organisations and totalled £19,000. The largest grants of £1,000 each went to BIME, Children's World, National Eye Research Centre – Bristol Eye Hospital and St Peter's Hospice. Smaller grants in the range of £250 to £500 include those to Action for Blind People, Anchor Society – Bristol, Brainwave, Bristol Care and Repair, Dolphin Society, HCPT, St Peter's Hospice and Willow Trust.

Exclusions Support is not given for:

- overseas projects
- general community projects*
- individuals
- general education projects*
- religious and ethnic projects*
- projects for unemployment and related training schemes*
- projects on behalf of offenders and ex-offenders
- projects concerned with the abuse of drugs and/or alcohol
- wildlife and conservation schemes*
- general restoration and preservation of buildings, purely for historical and/or architectural.

* If these projects are mainly or wholly for the benefit of people who have disabilities then they will be considered.

Ongoing support is not given, and grants are not usually given for running costs, salaries, research and items requiring major funding. Loans are not given.

Applications The trust does not have an official application form, appeals should be made in writing to the secretary, at any time.

The trust asks that the following is carefully considered before submitting an application:

Appeals must:

- be from registered charities
- include a copy of the latest audited accounts available (for newly registered charities a copy of provisional accounts showing estimated income and expenditure for the current financial year)

- show that the project is 'both feasible and viable' and, if relevant, give the starting date of the project and the anticipated date of completion
- include the estimated cost of the project, together with the appeal's target-figure and details of what funds have already been raised and any fundraising schemes for the project.

The trustees state that 'where applicable, due consideration will be given to evidence of voluntary and self-help (both in practical and fundraising terms) and to the number of people expected to benefit from the project'. They also comment that their decision is final and 'no reason for a decision, whether favourable or otherwise, need be given' and that 'the award and acceptance of a grant will not involve the trustees in any other commitment'.

Nicholas & Judith Goodison's Charitable Settlement

Arts, arts education

£167,000 (2001/02)

Beneficial area UK.

PO Box 2512, London W1A 5ZP

Correspondent Sir N Goodison, Trustee

Trustees *Sir Nicholas Goodison; Lady Judith Goodison; Miss Katharine Goodison.*

CC Number 1004124

Information available Accounts were on file at the Charity Commission.

General The trust supports registered charities in the field of the arts and arts education. Grants are also given to institutions in instalments over several years towards capital projects.

In 2001/02 the charity had assets totalling £1.2 million and an income of £280,000, mainly from donations received. Management and administration costs were just £588. The charity made 36 grants totalling £167,000, ranging from £200 to £40,000, although most grants were for £2,000 or less.

The largest grant of £40,000 was given to Marlborough College Appeal (making £100,000 in total) towards the new

Performance Centre for music and drama. Other large grants were given to English National Opera and Tate Gallery (£25,000 each) as part of redevelopment programmes. Both these beneficiaries will receive further sums totalling £75,000 and £100,000 respectively.

Other larger grants were made to Victoria and Albert Museum (£15,000 towards earlier donations to support the new British Galleries), Courtauld Institute (£11,000 in total), Handel House Trust and Fitzwilliam Museum (£10,000 each). The Fitzwilliam Museum also received four smaller grants during the year for craft purchases totalling £8,000.

Other beneficiaries include Cambridge Foundation, National Art Collections Fund, English National Opera, Royal Academy, Francis Haskell Memorial Fund, Albanian Musician's Trust, World Monuments Fund, Miriam Dean Refugee Trust, Clockmaker's Company and King Edward VII Hospital.

Exclusions No grants to individuals.

Applications The trust states that it cannot respond to unsolicited applications.

The Gough Charitable Trust

Youth, Episcopal and Church of England, preservation of the countryside, social welfare

£169,000 available (2000/01)

Beneficial area UK, with a possible preference for Scotland.

Lloyds TSB Private Banking Ltd, UK Trust Centre, 22–26 Ock Street, Abingdon OX14 5SW

Correspondent Mrs E Osborn-King, Trust Manager

Trustees *Lloyds Bank plc; N de L Harvie.*

CC Number 262355

Information available Full accounts were on file at the Charity Commission.

General In 2000/01 the trust had an income of £48,000 and an expenditure of £45,000. The trust says the grant total varies. According to the accounts, the balance available for distribution in 2000

was just under £169,000. Charitable payments totalling £40,000 were made, leaving over £128,000 carried forward to the following year. The trust has previously shown a preference for Scotland, however it is not clear if this is still the case.

Beneficiaries included St Luke with Holy Trinity Charlton (£15,000), RNLI (£10,000), Wykeham Crown and Manor Trust and 999 Club (£5,000 each). Small grants of £100 to £200 were given to National Army Development Trust, Lifeboat Service, Trinity Hospice, Household Brigade Lodge Benevolent Fund, The Prince of Wales Lodge Benevolent Fund, Irish Guards Fund, Lloyds Benevolent Fund and Lloyds Charities Fund.

Exclusions No support for non-registered charities and individuals including students.

Applications In writing to the correspondent at any time. No application forms are available, no acknowledgements are sent. Applications are considered quarterly.

The Grace Charitable Trust

Christian

£368,000 (2000/01)

Beneficial area UK.

Rhuallt House, Rhuallt, St Asaph, Sir Ddinbych LL17 0TG

Fax 01745 585243

Correspondent Mrs G J R Payne, Trustee

Trustees *Mrs G J R Payne; E Payne; Mrs G M Snaith; R B M Quayle.*

CC Number 292984

Information available Accounts were on file at the Charity Commission, but without a list of grants.

General In 2000/01 the trust had assets of £5.1 million and an income of £313,000, mostly from investments. After management and administration costs of £1,300, grants to organisations totalled £368,000.

As in recent years, no grants were listed in the accounts, although in the past grants have ranged from £1,000 to £6,800 and been given generally with a preference for Christian organisations.

Applications The trust states: 'Grants are made only to charities known to the settlors and unsolicited applications are, therefore, not considered.'

The Reginald Graham Charitable Trust

Children, medical, education

£62,000 (1997/98)

Beneficial area UK.

Bircham Dyson Bell, 50 Broadway, London SW1H 0BL

Tel. 020 7227 7000

Correspondent Michael Wood, Trustee

Trustees *Reginald Graham; Mrs Melanie Boyd; George Josselyn; Michael Wood.*

CC Number 212428

Information available Full accounts were on file at the Charity Commission.

General In 2000/01 the trust had an income of £62,000 and a total expenditure of £78,000. Unfortunately we were unable to obtain any further information for this year.

In 1997/98 grants totalled £62,000 and went to 61 organisations. By far the largest grant was £30,000 to Pembroke College which also received £16,000 the previous year. Recipients of grants in the range £1,000 to £5,000 were Education Trust, King Edward VII's Hospital for Officers, King George Fund for Sailors, NSPCC, Oxford University Tennis Club, Pyschiatric Rehabilitation Association, Prince's Trust, Royal Academy Trust, Royal British Legion and Wellbeing; seven of these had also received a grant the previous year. Smaller grants ranged from £25 upwards and were given to a wide range of beneficiaries.

Exclusions No grants to individuals, only charitable organisations are supported.

Applications The trust stated that it currently has a number of charities which receive regular support and they are not considering new applications at present. It is anticipated was January 2003 that no new grants would be made in the next two years.

91

The Grahame Charitable Foundation

Jewish

£279,000 (2001)

Beneficial area UK and worldwide.

5 Spencer Walk, Hampstead High Street, London NW3 1QZ

Tel. 020 7794 5281 **Fax** 020 7794 0094

Correspondent Mrs S Brooks

Trustees *Gitte Grahame; Jeffrey Greenwood.*

CC Number 259864

Information available Accounts were on file at the Charity Commission, but without a grants list.

General The trust's objects are to advance education, relieve poverty and advance religion anywhere in the world. In practice, it appears to make grants to these ends mainly to Jewish charities. Each year small grants are made to a handful of non-Jewish welfare and medical charities.

In 2001 the trust's assets totalled £361,000. It had an income of £345,000, including £275,000 in covenants and donations and £65,000 in rent. Grants totalled £279,000. Unfortunately, for several years now, the trust has not provided a grants list.

The last information available on grants related to 1996, when the trust made 120 grants totalling £81,000. The largest grants were £15,000 to Child Resettlement Fund, £10,000 to Jerusalem College and £5,000 each to Bais Ruzin Trust and Share Zedek. Most grants were for £500 or less. The only non-Jewish beneficiaries were Operation Wheelchairs (£150) with £100 each to Sue Harris Bone Marrow Transplant, The Samaritans and Scope.

Exclusions No grants to individuals.

Applications In writing to the correspondent.

The Grand Order of Water Rats Charities Fund

Theatrical, medical equipment

£88,000 (2000/01)

Beneficial area UK.

328 Gray's Inn Road, London WC1X 8BZ

Tel. 020 7407 8007 **Fax** 020 7403 8610

Email gowr4adrian@aol.com

Correspondent John Adrian, Secretary

Trustees *Wyn Calvin; Declan Cluskey; Roy Hudd; Paul Daniels; Keith Simmons.*

CC Number 292201

Information available Accounts were provided by the trust but without a list of grants.

General The trust was established to assist members of the variety and light entertainment profession and their dependants who, due to illness or age, are in need. The fund also buys medical equipment for certain institutions and also for individuals who have worked with or who have been closely connected with the same profession.

In 2000/01 the trust had an income of £132,000 and a total expenditure of £137,000. The income mainly comes from the profit gained from functions organised by the members of the Grand Order of Water Rats. The assets at the year-end stood at £896,000. Grants totalled £88,000, which included £48,000 listed as donations, £38,000 in monthly allowances, grants and gifts, and £2,700 for fruit and flowers.

In 1997, the last year in which grant information was available, the largest grants went to Cause for Hope (£11,000), Bud Flanagan Leukaemia Fund (£6,700) and Queen Elizabeth Hospital for Children (£3,000). There were six grants of between £1,000 and £2,000 including those to Actors Church Union, British Legion Wales and Northwick Park Hospital.

Exclusions No grants to students.

Applications In writing to the correspondent. The trustees meet once a month.

The Great Britain Sasakawa Foundation

Links between Great Britain and Japan

£346,000 (2001)

Beneficial area UK, Japan.

Dilke House, 1 Malet Street, London WC1E 7JN

Tel. 020 7436 9042 **Fax** 020 7355 2230

Email grants@gbsf.org.uk

Website www.gbsf.org.uk

Correspondent The Administrator

Trustees *Council: Prof. Peter Mathias, Chair; Hon. Yoshio Sakurauchi; Michael French, Treasurer; Baroness Brigstocke; Jeremy Brown; Baroness Park of Monmouth; Earl of St Andrews; Kazuo Chiba; Prof. Harumi Kimura; Yohei Sasakawa; Akira Iriyama; Prof. Shoichi Watanabe; Sir John Boyd.*

CC Number 290766

Information available Accounts and report were provided by the foundation, including a full list of grants.

General Each year grants are given for initiatives that 'improve relations between the UK and Japan by furthering a better understanding between the peoples of both nations'. Fields supported include 'arts and culture, humanities and social sciences, youth exchange including schools and education, Japanese language, science and technology, medicine and health, environment and conservation and sport'. Grants are normally for amounts between £500 and £5,000, rarely for more than £10,000. Roughly three quarters of the beneficiaries are based in the UK and few receive recurrent awards.

The foundation was established following a meeting in 1983 when the late Ryoichi Sasakawa, a shipbuilding tycoon, and the late Robert Maxwell met a number of senior British politicians to discuss Anglo-Japanese relations. The foundation was inaugurated two years later with a gift of £9.5 million from the Japan Shipbuilding Industry Foundation (now called The Nippon Foundation). It has offices in both Tokyo and London.

In 2001 the foundation had assets of £19.4 million, generating an income of £766,000. Management and administration costs totalled £304,000, with grants totalling a below average sum of £346,000 (£512,000 in 2000). This reduced charitable expenditure was 'considered prudent in view of the risk to the reserves (of the foundation) during the year'. Although the foundation's grant total was less than in previous years, the number of grants made increased to 180.

The foundation aims to advance the education of the citizens of Great Britain and Japan in many fields to develop mutual appreciation and understanding of the institutions, people and history, language and culture of the two nations, to promote research and to publish the useful results of such research.

The foundation has supported a wide range of projects including:

- visits between Japan and Great Britain by public servants, leading figures, writers and academics, students, teachers, journalists, artists, and former prisoners of war, their captors and others
- work in the visual or performing arts, translation and publication of books serving foundation aims, and the teaching of the Japanese language in the United Kingdom
- research in the fields of education, the arts, history, medicine and sociology and environmental studies.

In addition the foundation may conduct seminars, meetings and lectures and undertake other activities to encourage understanding between the peoples of Japan and the United Kingdom.

The foundation makes grants under eight headings, the first three having accounted for nearly three quarters of charitable expenditure up to 2001:

- arts and culture
- humanities and social sciences (including Japanese Studies)
- youth exchange (including schools and education)
- Japanese language
- science and technology
- medicine and health
- environment and conservation
- sport.

During 2001 the foundation mainly concentrated its grant-giving on projects and events related to 'Japan 2001', a UK-wide festival celebrating Japanese culture.

Examples of beneficiaries include:

British Association for Japanese Studies (£13,000), as part of a three-year commitment for UK-Japan research initiatives, including workshops and publications on regional governance and the Japanese political economy; London Sinfonietta (£4,000), towards the UK premiere of one act music theatre work

'Hagoromo'; Asia House, London (£3,000), to fund six free lectures on contemporary Japan, looking at design, architecture, film, society and lifestyle; Cardiff Japanese Studies Centre (£3,000), for a one-day conference on Japanese railways; St Catherine's College, Oxford (£2,000), for four speakers to travel to the Oxford-Kobe seminar on language change and historical linguistics in Kobe; Tokei Martial Arts Centre, London (£1,000), to enable members to participate in the International Karate Championships in Tokyo.

In 2001 the foundation established The Butterfield Awards to commemorate the achievements of Lord Butterfield, a medical researcher, clinician and academic administrator, and former chair of the foundation. The awards aim to 'encourage exchanges and collaborations between researchers and practitioners in medicine and health'. Four awards were made of £5,000 each for medical research to individuals working in the UK.

Exclusions Grants are not made to individuals applying on their own behalf. The foundation can, however, consider proposals from organisations that support the activities of individuals, provided they are citizens of the UK or Japan.

No grants can be made for the construction, conservation or maintenance of land and buildings.

The foundation will not support activities involving politics, legislation or election to public office.

Grants are not normally made for medical research.

Applications In advance of formal applications, foundation staff welcome telephone enquiries or personal visits to their office to discuss eligibility. The awards committee meets in London in February, May and October. Applications should be received by December, March and August. Awards meetings in Tokyo are held in April and October, with applications to be submitted by February and September. Applicants should request an application form either from the London headquarters or from the Tokyo liaison office; however, the foundation expresses a strong preference for e-mailed applications. A form will be e-mailed on request, and is also available on their website. Applications should contain the following information:

- a summary of the proposed project and its aims, including its likely impact and long-term benefits
- total cost of the project and the amount of the desired grant, together with a

note of other expected sources of funds, including estimated period for research projects, visits or study
- a description of the applicant's organisation and, where relevant, brief career details of the main participants in any project, and where appropriate the ages of those individuals who may be the recipients.

Applicants are expected to make a careful calculation of all costs of a project before seeking a grant. Where a grant is approved no application for an increase will be accepted after approval, except in very special circumstances.

The foundation will not consider making a further grant to an applicant until at least two years after a successful application. Organisations applying should be registered charities, recognised educational institutions, local or regional authorities, churches, media companies, publishers or such other bodies as the foundation may approve.

School applicants are requested to first file an application with Connect Youth International, Japan Exchange Programme, 10 Spring Gardens, London SW1A 2BN (which is part of the British Council), to which the foundation grants external finance, aimed at encouraging exchanges (both ways) for schools in Great Britain and Japan (their website is www.connectyouthinternational.com).

All applicants are notified shortly after each Awards Committee meeting of the decisions of the trustees. Those offered grants are asked to sign and return an acceptance form and are given the opportunity to say when they would like to receive their grant.

The Constance Green Foundation

Social welfare, medicine, health, general

£389,000 (2001/02)

Beneficial area England, with a preference for West Yorkshire.

ASL Management Services, Bel Royal House, Hilgrove Street, St Helier, Jersey JE2 4SL

Tel. 01534 726506 **Fax** 01534 720625

Email management@asl-jersey.com

Trustees *M Collinson; Col. H R Hall; Mrs M L Hall; Mrs S Collinson.*

CC Number 270775

Information available Report and accounts were provided by the trust.

General The foundation makes grants mainly in the fields of social welfare and medicine. In 2001/02 it had assets of £7.5 million generating an income of £363,000. Out of 798 applications received, 48 grants were made to organisations totalling £389,000. Of these, over 90% were made to assist special projects, rather than to provide core funding.

Charities operating in various parts of Yorkshire received 77% of total funds distributed, with 15% going to other UK organisations and 8% to those working overseas. Giving was broken down as follows:

Medical and social care, including terminal care for children and young people	71%
People who are disabled, both physically and mentally	4%
People who are homeless	5%
Children and young people, including those who are disadvantaged	7%
Medical, including facilities and equipment	11%
Church and community projects	2%

The major beneficiary was Martin House Hospice in Wetherby, which received two grants of £125,000 each; this organisation has also received substantial funding in previous years. Other grants included: £5,000 each to BLESMA, Croft Community – Camphill Vilage Trust, MERLIN, ORBIS Charitable Trust, Royal Agricultural Benevolent Institution, Salvation Army, Shelter and YMCA – England; £3,000 to Hope and Homes for Children and York Minster Fund; £2,000 to Children of the Andes; £1,000 each to Dream Holidays, the Guide Association, One Voice and Pathfinders; and £800 to the Childrens Adventure Farm Trust.

Exclusions Sponsorship of individuals is not supported.

Applications At any time in writing to the correspondent (no special form of application required). Applications should include clear details of the need the intended project is designed to meet, plus an outline budget. All applications meeting the foundation's criteria are acknowledged.

The Barry Green Memorial Fund

Animal welfare

£68,000 (2000/01)

Beneficial area UK, with a preference for Yorkshire and Lancashire.

Claro Chambers, Horsefair, Boroughbridge, York YO51 9LD

Correspondent The Clerk to the Trustees

Trustees *Richard Fitzgerald-Hart; Mark Fitzgerald-Hart.*

CC Number 1000492

Information available Full accounts were on file at the Charity Commission.

General The trust was created under the Will of Mrs E M Green. It supports animal welfare charities concerned with the rescue, maintenance and benefit of cruelly-treated animals and also the prevention of cruelty to animals. There is a preference for small charities.

In 2000/01 the trust had assets of £1.5 million and an income of £170,000. Management and administration costs totalled £55,000 – mostly investment property expenses and legal fees. Grants to 49 organisations were made totalling £68,000, including 10 that were supported in the previous year. The grant total was significantly down from the previous year when £112,000 was given.

Of grants made, 36 were for £1,000 or more including: £5,000 to Winslade Wildlife Sanctuary; £3,000 each to Assisi Animal Sanctuary and Wildlife in Need; £2,500 each to Widewalls Animal Sanctuary and Royal Veterinary College – North Mymms; £2,000 each to Berwick Swan and Wildlife Trust, Cats Paws Sanctuary, Mare and Foal Sanctuary, Mid Cheshire Animal Welfare and Thoroughbred Rehabilitation Centre; £1,500 to Home a Dog Association; and £1,000 each to Border Collie Trust, Capricorn Animal Rescue and Hydestile Wildlife Hospital.

The remainder of grants were either for amounts of £750, £500 or £250 and included those to Animals in Need, Feral Cat Care, Reptile Centre, Rescue Centre, Sussex Horse Rescue Trust and West Midlands Animal Welfare Service.

This trust has stated that a large proportion of the applications it receives bear no relation to the objects of the charity.

Exclusions No expeditions, scholarships, work outside the UK or individuals.

Applications In writing to the correspondent including a copy of the accounts.

Grimmitt Trust

General

£211,000 (2000/01)

Beneficial area Birmingham and district and areas where trustees have a personal interest.

c/o Grimmitt Holdings, Woodgate Business Park, Kettles Wood Drive, Birmingham B32 3GH

Tel. 0121 421 7000 **Fax** 0121 421 9848

Correspondent Catherine E Chase

Trustees *P W Welch; Mrs M E Welch; P B Hyland; M G Fisher; C Hughes Smith; C Humphreys; Dr C Kendrick; Dr D Owen.*

CC Number 801975

Information available Full accounts were on file at the Charity Commission.

General Grants are given to organisations in the Birmingham area. Local branches of UK organisations are supported, but larger UK appeals are not.

In 2000/01 the trust had assets of £564,000 and an income of £270,000, including donations of £132,000 from Grimmitt Holdings Limited. Grants totalled £211,000 and were broken down as follows (1999/2000 figures in brackets):

Cultural and educational	£60,000	(£81,000)
Community	£43,000	(£38,000)
Children and youth	£49,000	(£26,000)
Medical and health	£19,000	(£18,000)
Elderly	£4,000	(£6,000)
Overseas	£30,000	(£14,000)
Benevolent	£2,000	(£2,000)
Other	£5,000	(£0)

Grants over £2,000, of which there were 22, were listed in the accounts. Four were for £10,000 to each of Birmingham Rathbone Society, Methodist Relief Fund, Roger Hooker Memorial and WaterAid. Two of these also received a grant the previous year, together with five other causes which again received over £2,000, including Bartley Green School, Magic Carpet Playbus Association and Symphony Hall Organ Appeal.

Other new recipients of grants over £2,000 included Dorrington Primary

School, Manchester Science Museum, Primrose Hospice Cancer Help and Sutton Arts Theatre.

Management and administration of the trust is carried out by employees of Grimmitt Holdings Ltd for which no charge is made.

Applications In writing to the correspondent.

The GRP Charitable Trust

Jewish, general
£202,000 (2000/01)
Beneficial area UK.

Kleinwort Benson Trustees Ltd, PO Box 191, 10 Fenchurch Street, London EC3M 3LB
Tel. 020 7475 5086 **Fax** 020 7475 5558
Correspondent The Secretary
Trustees *Kleinwort Benson Trustees Ltd.*
CC Number 255733
Information available Full accounts were on file at the Charity Commission.

General The G R P of the title stands for the settlor, George Richard Pinto, a London banker who set up the trust in 1968. Virtually all the grants are given to Jewish organisations.

In 2000/01 the trust had assets of £4.8 million and an income of £213,000, of which £100,000 came from donations. A total of £202,000 was given in 35 grants.

The largest grant was £125,000 to Oxford Centre for Hebrew and Jewish Studies, which has also received a large proportion of the grant total in previous years. After other sizeable grants of £24,000 to Jerusalem Foundation and £10,000 to Jewish Care, other grants mainly ranged from between £50 and £5,000. Beneficiaries included: Anglo-Israel Association (£7,700); Council of Christians and Jews and National Gallery Trust (£5,000 each); Friends of Boys Town Jerusalem (£3,000); Community Security Trust and World London Synagogue (£2,500 each); Royal Opera House Trust (£2,000); Israel Diaspora Trust (£1,500); Roundhouse Trust and Scopus (£1,000 each); Ben Gurion University Foundation (£500); Chicken Shed Theatre Company (£350); Community Centre in Israel Project (£250); and World Jewish Relief (£50).

Exclusions No grants to individuals.

Applications In writing to the correspondent. However, the trustees prefer to provide medium-term support for a number of charities already known to them, and unsolicited applications are not acknowledged. Trustees meet annually in March.

The Walter Guinness Charitable Trust

General
£122,000 (1998/99)
Beneficial area UK and overseas, with a preference for Wiltshire and Hampshire.

Biddesden House, Andover, Hampshire SP11 9DN
Correspondent The Secretary
Trustees *Hon. F B Guinness; Hon. Mrs R Mulji; Hon. Catriona Guinness.*
CC Number 205375
Information available Accounts were on file at the Charity Commission.

General The trust was established in 1961 by Bryan Walter, the second Lord Moyne, in memory of his father, the first Lord Moyne. Most grants are given to a number of charities which the trust has been consistently supporting for many years.

The assets of the trust stood at £3.9 million in 1998/99 generating an income of £143,000. A total of £122,000 was given in 163 grants, ranging from £50 to £10,000. The largest grants were £10,000 each to Enham Trust and St James' Church Ludgershall Restoration Fund. Other larger grants went to UNIPAL (£9,000), Marlborough College Appeal (£5,000), Project Ability (£3,000) and Royal Academy Trust (£2,500). Grants from £1,000 to £2,000 included those to Asylum Aid, Disasters Emergency Committee (Sudan Crisis), Global Cancer Concern, NCH Action for Children, Queen Elizabeth's Foundation for Disabled People, Raleigh International and Wiltshire Community Foundation.

Smaller grants ranging from £50 to £800, but mostly of £500, included those to Anti-Slavery International, British Red Cross, Drug and Alcohol Foundation, Help the Aged, Lytham St Anne's & Fylde

YMCA, Prison Reform Trust, Royal Academy of Music, Scottish Wildlife Trust, Victim Support in Wiltshire and Yately Industries for the Disabled.

Previously the trust has stated: 'We are unlikely to be able to support anything unless there is a personal connection, a local connection or unless the organisation has previously been supported by our trust.'

Exclusions No grants to individuals.

Applications In writing to the correspondent. Replies are only sent when there is a positive decision. Initial telephone calls are not welcome. There are no application forms, guidelines or deadlines. No sae is required.

The Gunter Charitable Trust

General
£61,000 (2000/01)
Beneficial area UK.

c/o Forsters, 67 Grosvenor Street, London W1K 3JN
Correspondent Miss L J Fay
Trustees *J de C Findlay; H R D Billson.*
CC Number 268346
Information available Full accounts were on file at the Charity Commission.

General The trust gives grants to a wide range of local and UK organisations, including countryside, medical and wildlife causes.

In 2000/01 the trust had assets of £2.3 million generating an income of £102,000. After management and administration costs of £13,000, grants were given to 45 organisations totalling £61,000.

The largest grant was £9,500 to Liverpool School of Tropical Medicine. Other grants over £1,000 included those to Dandelion Trust (£5,100), Hunter Trust (£4,000), VSO (£3,800), Scottish Wildlife Trust (£2,400), Refugee Council (£2,200), Marie Stopes International, New Bridge and Sustrans Ltd (£2,000 each) and Jesus College Oxford, Multiple Sclerosis Society and Oxfam (£1,000 each).

Beneficiaries of smaller grants, mainly for £500 or less, included Acorn Children's Hospice, Concern Worldwide, Council for Music in Hospitals, Hearing Dogs for the Deaf, Help the Aged, Shelter, SOS

Children's Villages, Woodland Trust and Women's Environmental Network.

Exclusions No support for unsolicited applications.

Applications No unsolicited applications are accepted by the trustees. All such applications are immediately returned to the applicant.

The H P Charitable Trust

Orthodox Jewish

£133,000 (1999/2000)

Beneficial area UK.

26 Lingwood Road, London E5 9BN

Tel. 020 8806 2432

Correspondent Aron Piller, Trustee

Trustees *A Piller; Mrs H Piller.*

CC Number 278006

Information available Accounts were on file at the Charity Commission, but without a grants list.

General The H P Charitable Trust was created by Hannah Piller in 1979 and makes grants to orthodox Jewish charities. In 1999/2000 its assets totalled £1.1 million and it had an income of £372,000 including £269,000 from donations. Grants totalled £133,000, the recipients were not specified in the accounts.

Applications In writing to the correspondent.

The Hadley Trust

Social welfare

£925,000 (1998/99)

Beneficial area UK, especially London.

Gransmuir, Hadley Green Road, Barnet, Hertfordshire EN5 5QE

Correspondent P Hulme, Trustee

Trustees *Mrs J Hulme; P W Hulme.*

CC Number 1064823

Information available Accounts were on file at the Charity Commission.

General The trust was formed in 1997. Its objects allow it to 'assist in creating opportunities for people who are disadvantaged as a result of environmental, educational or economic circumstances or physical or other handicap to improve their situation, either by direct financial assistance, involvement in project and support work, or research into the causes of and means to alleviate hardship'.

In 2000/01 the trust had an income of £2.5 million and a total expenditure of £1.2 million. This information was taken from the Charity Commission database; unfortunately further information was not available.

In 1998/99, when the trust had an income of £2 million and a total expenditure of £942,000, grants to 61 organisations totalled £925,000. The trust stated in its report that it has successfully identified and established relationships with a number of registered charities which have objectives consistent with its own.

Applications In writing to the correspondent.

This entry was not confirmed by the trust, but the address is correct according to the Charity Commission database.

The Edith Winifred Hall Charitable Trust

General

£390,000 (1999/2000)

Beneficial area UK.

Shoosmiths, 52–54 The Green, Banbury, Oxfordshire OX16 9AB

Tel. 01295 267971

Correspondent D Endicott, Trustee

Trustees *D Reynolds; D Endicott; J R N Lowe.*

CC Number 1057032

Information available Full accounts were on file at the Charity Commission.

General This trust has stated that it wants its funds to make a difference. It prefers to make a small number of large grants. In 1999/2000 it had an income of £131,000 derived from investments and made grants totalling £390,000. The trust's assets totalled £3.6 million at the year end.

Grants were: £150,000 each to Loros and Peterborough Cathedral; £50,000 to Shaftesbury; £20,000 to Friends of St Paul's Church Bedford; £19,000 to St Marys Little Harrowden Heritage Trust and £1,000 for computer equipment to Maplefields School.

Applications In writing to the correspondent.

The Hamamelis Trust

Ecological conservation, medical research

£86,000 (2000/01)

Beneficial area UK, but with a special interest in the Godalming and Surrey areas.

c/o Penningtons, Highfield, Brighton Road, Godalming, Surrey GU7 1NS

Tel. 01483 791800

Correspondent Mrs Joanne Baddeley

Trustees *Michael Fellingham; Dr A F M Stone; Mr R Rippengal.*

CC Number 280938

Information available Accounts were on file at the Charity Commission.

General The trust was set up in 1980 by John Ashley Slocock and enhanced on his death in 1986. The main areas of work are medical research and ecological conservation. Grants are distributed to these areas of work equally. Occasionally grants are made to other projects. Preference is given to projects in the Godalming and Surrey areas.

In 2000/01 the trust had assets of £2.1 million and an income of £75,000. A total of £86,000 was given in grants, the largest of which was £10,000 to Chase. Other beneficiaries included Association for Spina Bifida and Hydrocephalus, BTCV, DEBRA, Defeating Blindness, Dorset Wildlife Trust, Gaia Trust, Help the Hopsices, Woodland Trust and Yorkshire Wildlife Trust.

Exclusions Projects outside the UK are not considered. No grants to individuals.

Applications In writing to the correspondent. All applicants are asked to include a short summary of the application along with any published material and references. Unsuccessful appeals will not be acknowledged.

Medical applications are assessed by Dr Adam Stone, one of the trustees, who is medically qualified.

The Helen Hamlyn 1989 Foundation

Older people, health

£322,000 (2000/01)
Beneficial area UK.

PO Box 7747, London SW3 6XF
Correspondent The Trustees
Trustees *Lady Hamlyn; Lord Owen; Prof. Kevin M Cahill.*
CC Number 802628
Information available Full accounts were on file at the Charity Commission.

General The trust makes grants to enable people who are elderly, sick and 'infirm' to 'live full and satisfying lives in the community'. Related to Helen Hamlyn's profession as a designer, grants are given to organisations which use design skills to improve the environment of older people.

In 2000/01 the trust had assets of £4.7 million and an income of £180,000. Grants to eight organisations totalled £322,000, by far the largest of which was £310,000 to RCA – Helen Hamlyn Research Centre. Remaining grants went to Royal Hospital for Neuro-disability (£5,000), Progress Care Housing Association (£3,800), Extra Care Charitable Trust and UBS (£1,000 each), St Mungo's (£500), Listening Books (£380) and LIFRA (£200).

Exclusions No grants to individuals.

Applications In writing to the correspondent.

This entry was not confirmed by the trust but the address was correct according to information on file at the Charity Commission.

Sue Hammerson's Charitable Trust

Medical research, relief in need

£212,000 (2000/01)
Beneficial area UK.

H W Fisher & Co, Acre House, 11–15 William Road, London NW1 3ER
Tel. 020 7388 7000
Correspondent T D Brown
Trustees *Sir Gavin Lightman; A J Thompson; A J Bernstein; Mrs P A Beecham; D B Hammerson; P S Hammerson.*
CC Number 235196
Information available Information was provided by the trust.

General The objects of this trust are to advance medical learning and research and the relief of sickness and poverty; it also supports a range of other charities including a number of Jewish and arts organisations. In 2000/01 it had assets of £7.5 million and an income of £260,000. After management and administration expenditure of £21,000, 273 grants were made totalling £212,000.

The trust gives special consideration to the needs of the Lewis W Hammerson Memorial Home, which received a substantial donation of £108,000. A further 19 grants were made of £1,000 or more. Beneficiaries included Royal Academy Trust (£5,700), Alzheimer's Disease Society and Royal Opera House Trust (£5,300 each), English National Opera (£4,400), National Theatre (£3,000), West London Synagogue (£2,600), Limmud and Oxford Synagogue Rebuilding Fund (£2,000 each), New Shakespeare Co. Ltd (£1,300) and Carrot Trust, City of London School for Girls, Institute for Jewish Policy Research and Roundhouse Trust (£1,000 each).

The remaining grants ranged from £100 and £950, with most being for less than £500. Beneficiaries included Action on Addiction, Age Concern, Barbican Arts Centre, Brighton Dome, British Tinnitus Association, Cheltenham Hebrew Congregation, Dulwich Picture Gallery, Friends of Marylebone Music, Iris Fund, King's College Medical School, London Festival Ballet, National Art Collections Fund, National Kidney Research Fund, National Schizophrenia Fellowship, Norwood Ltd, Notting Hill Housing

Trust, Oxfam, Royal Academy of Arts, Royal College of Surgeons, Scope, Spinal Injuries Association, Tommy's Campaign, West London Synagogue, Winged Fellowship Foundation, World Jewish Relief, Young Vic Company and Zoological Society of London.

Exclusions No grants to individuals.

Applications In writing to the correspondent. The trust states, however, that its funds are fully committed.

The Handicapped Children's Aid Committee

Equipment for children with disabilities

£271,000 (2000)
Beneficial area Worldwide.

Flat D, Mount Tyndal, Spaniards Road, Hampstead NW3 7JH
Correspondent Mrs B Emden
Trustees *J Bonn; R Adelman; P Maurice.*
CC Number 200050
Information available Accounts were on file at the Charity Commission, but without a list of grants.

General 'The trust's objects are to promote the welfare of handicapped children.'

In 2000 the trust had assets of £864,000 and an income of £124,000, including £61,000 in donations received. Of the 97 applications received, 42 were successful, receiving grants totalling £271,000. A further 21 appeals were still awaiting a final decision.

The 2000 accounts contained no information on which organisations benefited. However, the narrative report stated: 'During the year, applications for help were received from hospitals, homes, special schools and from families and social workers on behalf of individual children. Appeals are investigated and once validity is established and approval given by the committee, money is allocated to purchase requirements. The trust does not give financial support, but purchases equipment directly for and on behalf of the donee.'

Exclusions Building projects, research grants and salaries will not be funded.

Applications Initial telephone calls from applicants are not welcome. Application forms and guidelines are available from the correspondent.

The Haramead Trust

Welfare, children's welfare, health education

£284,000 (1998/99)

Beneficial area UK and overseas with a preference for Leicestershire.

Park House, Park Hill, Gaddesby, Leicestershire LE7 4WH

Tel. 01664 840908

Correspondent M J Linnett, Trustee

Trustees Mrs W M Linnett; M J Linnett; R H Smith; D L Tams.

CC Number 1047416

Information available Accounts were on file at the Charity Commission.

General In 2000/01 this trust had an income of £345,000 and a total expenditure of £503,000. This information was taken from the Charity Commission database, unfortunately no further information was available for this year.

The trust's income has varied considerably. In 1997/98 it had an income of £986,000, mostly from donations, and grants totalling £284,000 were given using both income and capital funds. In 1998/99 the income was only £16,000. Grants for that year totalled £284,000 using both income and capital funds. The assets fell to £120,000 by the year end.

In 1998/99 the trust had assets totalling £120,000 down from £389,000 in the previous year. It had an income of £16,000 from investments, in 1997/98 the trust had an income of £986,000, mostly from donations. Grants totalling £284,000 were given using both income and capital funds.

The trust gives grants for people in need, children's welfare and education about health. During 1998/99 it supported 19 organisations with grants ranging from £1,000 to £50,000. The largest grant of £50,000 went to DePaul Trust. Other large grants went to Leicester YMCA (£33,000), British Red Cross (£25,000)

with four grants of £20,000 each to Shelter, Crisis, Rainbows and NSPCC.

Six grants ranging from £10,000 to £15,000 included those to 28th Leicester Wigston Scout Group, Menphys and Save the Children. Six grants ranging from £1,000 to £7,000 included those to Age Concern, Help the Aged and Intercare. Of all the grants given, five were recurrent from the previous year.

Applications In writing to the correspondent.

The Harbour Charitable Trust

General

£179,000 (2000/01)

Beneficial area UK.

c/o Blevins Frank, Barbican House, 26–34 Old Street, London EC1V 9QQ

Tel. 020 7935 7422

Correspondent The Trustees

Trustees Mrs B B Green; Mrs Z S Blackman; Mrs T Elsenstat; Mrs E Knobil.

CC Number 234268

Information available Accounts were on file at the Charity Commission, but without a list of grants.

General The trust makes grants for the benefit of childcare, education and health research and to various other charitable organisations. In 2000/01 it had assets of £3 million and an income of £277,000. After management and administration costs of £40,000, grants were made totalling £179,000. These were categorised by the trust as follows:

Healthcare	£36,000
Joint Jewish Charitable Trust	£29,000
Education	£77,000
Other	£35,000
Childcare	£2,900

No further information was available on the charities supported.

Exclusions Grants are given to registered charities only.

Applications In writing to the correspondent.

The Harbour Foundation

Jewish, general

£93,000 (1999/2000)

Beneficial area Worldwide with a preference for London.

The Courtyard Building, 11 Curtain Road, London EC2A 3LT

Tel. 020 7456 8180

Correspondent The Trustees

Trustees S R Harbour; A C Humphries; Mrs Z S Blackman; S Green; B B Green.

CC Number 264927

Information available Accounts were on file at the Charity Commission, but without a grants list.

General The principal activities of the trust are providing relief among refugees and people who are homeless, advancement of education learning and research, and to make donations to any institution established for charitable purposes throughout the world.

The following is taken from the 1999/2000 trustee's report:

'The main thrust of the foundation's current and future charitable programme comprises two areas of activities which are, to some extent, complementary.

'The first is the support and development of technology-based education for the community. This support is directed both to university level and to those who have been failed by the educational system especially in the inner boroughs of London. Rapid and continual innovation in this field and the attraction and retention of highly qualified teaching staff necessitate a high level of financial support on a consistent and ongoing basis. A carefully phased release of donations by the foundation to education providers at the leading edge acts as an incentive for them to maximise performance and enables them to plan ahead with some degree of confidence. It is therefore essential to continue to build up reserves of the foundation to a level sufficient to ensure a reliable high level of financial support to such providers.

'The second strand of activity is also mainly aimed at the inner boroughs of London where it is intended to provide funds to improve the physical environment in deprived areas. This will be directed to the development of run down space, both open and constructed, for community use. Again this activity will require a high level of financial support and, therefore, also necessitates an expansion of the foundation's reserves.'

In 1999/2000 the trust had assets of £6.5 million and an income of £308,000 (£1.2 million in 1998/99). Grants totalled £93,000, with management and administration costs high at £51,000, although the trust receives a rental and trading income which may account for this large figure.

Despite having a detailed and comprehensive narrative report, the trust provides no grants list or details of type or size of grants in their accounts.

Applications In writing to the correspondent. Applications need to be received by February, as trustees meet in March.

The Harebell Centenary Fund

General, education, medical research, animal welfare

£83,000 (2002)

Beneficial area UK.

50 Broadway, London SW1H 0BL

Tel. 020 7227 7000

Correspondent Ms P J Chapman

Trustees *J M Denker; M I Goodbody; F M Reed.*

CC Number 1003552

Information available Information was provided by the trust. Full accounts were on file at the Charity Commission.

General Established in 1991, this trust provides funding towards the promotion of neurological and neurosurgical research and the relief of sickness and suffering amongst animals, as well as helping young people to further their education.

The current policy of the trustees is to concentrate on making donations to charities that do not receive widespread public support and to keep administrative expenses to a minimum. For this reason the trustees have decided to make donations only to registered charities and not to individuals.

In 2002 grants were made to 20 organisations and totalled £83,000. Hebridean Trust received £7,500 for the Treshnish Idles while £5,000 each went to

AbilityNet, The Blackie Foundation, Canine Partners for Independence, DEMAND, Ferriers Barn, Motor Neurone Disease Society, National Library for the Blind, REMAP and Royal Hospital for Neuro-disability – Putney.

All the other grants were of £3,000 each, to Fair Havens Christian Hospice, Little Haven's Children's Hospice, Message in a Bottle, The Nordoff Robins Music Centre, The Rachel Hospice, St Christopher's Hospice, St Helen's House Hospice, St Joseph's Hospice – Hackney, St Raphael's Hospice and Trinity Hospice.

In 2000 the assets totalled £2.6 million and generated an income of £81,000. Grants were made totalling £89,000 to 21 organisations, including 11 which were also supported in the previous year. Administration costs were very high at £32,000, which equates to 40% of the trust's income. This included £12,000 in administration fees and £5,800 for legal advice to a firm in which one of the trustees is a partner, and £10,000 for broker's fees to a company another trustee works for. Even though wholly legal, these editors always regret such payments unless, to use the words of the Charity Commission, 'there is no realistic alternative'.

Exclusions No grants are made towards Infrastructure or to individuals.

Applications In writing to the correspondent. Unsolicited applications are not requested, as the trustees prefer to make donations to charities whose work they have come across through their own research. As trustees meet in March and November, any applications made need to be received by February or October.

Harnish Trust

Christian

£85,000 (2000/01)

Beneficial area Worldwide.

The Cottage, 21 St Mary Street, Chippenham, Wiltshire SN15 3JW

Correspondent Jill Dann, Trustee

Trustees *Jill Dann; Jennifer R Paynter.*

CC Number 293040

Information available Full accounts were on file at the Charity Commission.

General The trust supports Christian activity and education worldwide, including charities, voluntary organisations and individuals.

The assets in 2000/01 totalled £348,000. Total income was £14,000, including £6,000 in donations received. Grants were made to 62 organisations totalling £85,000.

The largest grants were £15,000 to St Mary's Church – Ealing and £10,000 to Lambeth Partnership. Other large grants included £4,700 to All Nations, £4,300 to Scripture Union, £3,400 to Jerusalem 2000, £2,500 to Lacock Church PCC, £2,000 each to Church Pastoral Aid Society, Jubilee Centre, Open Theological Seminary and Pakistan Fellowship of Evangelical Students and £1,500 each to Church Urban Fund and John Reay Initiative.

Six branches of Interserve received grants ranging from £290 to £1,200 and totalling £3,400. Other recipients of smaller grants included SAT7 and Tearfund (£1,000 each), Christians in Sport and Wayfarer Trust (£500 each), UFM Worldwide (£400), Goodwill Children's Home (£360) and Crosslinks (£250).

Applications Unsolicited applications are not considered.

The R J Harris Charitable Settlement

General

£113,000 to organisations (2000/01)

Beneficial area UK, with a preference for west Wiltshire, with particular emphasis on Trowbridge, north Wiltshire, south of the M4, and Bath and environs.

Messrs Thring Townsend, Midland Bridge, Bath BA1 2HQ

Tel. 01225 340099

Correspondent J J Thring, Secretary

Trustees *H M Newton-Clare, Chair; T C M Stock; J L Rogers; A Pitt.*

CC Number 258973

Information available Accounts were provided by the trust, but without a list of grants or a full narrative report. A brief information sheet for applicants was also provided.

General This trust has general charitable purposes, supporting both individuals and organisations. Support is focused on

99

west Wiltshire, with particular emphasis on Trowbridge, North Wiltshire south of the M4 merging into the environs of Bath. The main areas of work are social welfare, the arts, education, medical, mental health, conservation, environmental and youth organisations and projects.

In 2000/01 the trust had assets of £1.7 million and an income of £153,000, of which £100,000 came from donations received. Management and administration totalled £12,000. Grants were made to 84 organisations totalling £113,000, including two grants paid out of the capital totalling £61,000. Grants to 16 individuals totalled £3,800. No grants information was included in the accounts, nor any indication as to why grants were made from its assets. However, they did state that £95,000 had been committed by the trustees in grants not paid by the end of the financial year.

Applications In writing to the correspondent. Trustees meet three times each year. An sae is required.

Gay & Peter Hartley's Hillards Charitable Trust

General welfare, social education, disability, medical

£81,000 (2001)

Beneficial area Areas served by a former Hillards store, mainly the north of England, especially Yorkshire.

400 Shadwell Lane, Leeds LS17 8AW

Correspondent Mrs Julia J Peers, Secretary to the Trustees

Trustees *P A H Hartley; Mrs R C Hartley; S R H Hartley; Miss S J H Hartley; A C H Hartley.*

CC Number 327879

Information available Information was provided by the trust.

General The main priority is to support registered charities in areas that were served by a Hillards store, supporting people who are poor, sick or otherwise in need. Churches (with a definite outreach factor), community centres and schools

are also supported, with preference for those with charitable status. Grants generally range from £500 to £1,000, although two grants of £10,000 are awarded each year on merit.

In 2001 the trust gave 90 grants totalling £81,000. Over 40 organisations were visited during the year.

In July 2001 the trust donated its second lifeboat to RNLI. Other beneficiaries included Age Concern Lincolnshire and Sycamore Project – Bolton (£1,000 each) and Dial-a-Ride Scarborough and Leeds Women's Aid (£500 each).

Exclusions No grants were made to:

- unregistered charities
- national charities unless with own autonomy in a relevant area
- animal welfare and wildlife causes
- trips/holiday schemes
- individuals for education, holidays or any other purposes
- activities that receive substantial support from statutory sources
- local authority day centres and health centres
- community-based projects run or managed by local authority workers
- uniformed groups (such as dance troupes and bands)
- musical/artistic productions or touring companies (including as sponsorship)
- medical research
- minibuses (unless shared transport, or occasional maintenance or driver training)
- major capital projects, such as building works (unless all other funding has been obtained and a small identifiable part of the project is apparent)
- church roof/spire restoration.

Applications On a form available from the correspondent, upon written request. Completed forms must be returned by 31 December for consideration in the following spring. Applications are not acknowledged, and if no reply has been received by 1 May applicants should assume they have been unsuccessful.

William Geoffrey Harvey's Discretionary Settlement

Animal welfare and bird life

£110,000 (2001/02)

Beneficial area Some preference for north west England.

1A Gibsons Road, Stockport, Cheshire SK4 4JX

Tel. 0161 432 8307

Correspondent F A Sherring, Trustee

Trustees *F R Shackleton; F A Sherring; G J Hull.*

CC Number 800473

Information available Full accounts were on file at the Charity Commission.

General The trust supports animal and bird welfare charities, supporting the same organisations each year with varying amounts, and it is not expected that any new charities will be funded. In 2001/02 it had assets of £3.7 million and an income of £109,000. Grants to four organisations totalled £110,000. Beneficiaries were: Three Owls Bird Sanctuary & Reserve (£35,000); National Canine Defence League and People's Dispensary for Sick Animals (£30,000 each); and Wildfowl & Wetlands Trust (£15,000).

Applications Please note, the trustees state that the settlor Mrs Harvey gave them 'a clear indication of the causes she favoured and [they] are guided by that for the moment at least'. New applicants will not be considered.

The M A Hawe Settlement

General

£327,000 (1999/2000)

Beneficial area UK, with a preference for the north west of England, particularly the Flyde coast area.

94 Park View Road, Lytham St Annes, Lancashire FY8 4JF

Tel. 01253 796888

Correspondent M A Hawe, Trustee

Trustees *M A Hawe; Mrs G Hawe; Marc G Hawe.*

CC Number 327827

Information available Full accounts are on file at the Charity Commission.

General In 1999/2000 the trust had assets of £5.4 million generating an income of £291,000. After management and administration charges of £25,000, grants to 28 charities totalled £327,000.

As usual, the largest grant was to Kensington House Trust Ltd, which received £320,000. This company was established to run a property bought by the trust in 1993, as accommodation on a short-stay basis for young homeless people. It now also provides furniture and equipment to people in need, shelter for victims of domestic violence and holidays for children who are deprived.

Other beneficiaries included Holy Cross Church and Soup Kitchen (£1,200), Women's Refuge (£860), DVU (£550), Change for Charity (£500), Mereside School (£270) and Foetal Anti-Convulsent Syndrome Association and Home-Start (£250 each).

Applications In writing to the correspondent.

The Hawthorne Charitable Trust

General

£140,000 (2000/01)

Beneficial area UK, especially Hereford and Worcester.

c/o Messrs Baker Tilly, 2 Bloomsbury Street, London WC1B 3ST

Tel. 020 7413 5100

Correspondent Roger Clark, Trustee

Trustees *Mrs A S C Berington; R J Clark.*

CC Number 233921

Information available Full accounts were on file at the Charity Commission.

General The trust supports a wide range of organisations, particularly health and welfare causes but also charities concerned with animal welfare, disability, heritage and young people.

In 2000/01 the trust had assets of £5.9 million generating an income of £170,000. From a total expenditure of £161,000, grants totalling £144,000 were given to 67 organisations.

Donations were in the range of £500 to £5,300, but were mainly for £2,500 or less. Grants included £5,300 to Birmingham Hippodrome Theatre Development Trust; £3,000 each to Avoncroft Museum, Downside Abbey Trustees for St Wulstan's, Friends of Little Malvern Priory, Malvern Festival Theatre Trust Limited and Worcester Association for the Blind; £2,500 each to Ability Net, Canine Partners for Independence, National Deaf Children's Society, Prince's Trust, St Michael's Hospice – Hereford and Toynbee Hall; £1,500 to CLA Charitable Trust; £1,300 each to St Richard's Hospice, Vale Wildlife Rescue and Weston Spirit; £1,000 each to Herefordshire Headway, National Canine Defence League and Worcester Farming & Wildlife Advisory Group; and £500 to Malvern District Scout Council.

Exclusions Grants are given to registered charities only. No grants to individuals.

Applications In writing to the correspondent, including up-to-date accounts. Applications should be received by October for consideration in November.

The Haydan Charitable Trust

Jewish, general

£136,000 (2000)

Beneficial area UK.

4th Floor, 1 Knightsbridge, London SW1X 7LX

Tel. 020 7823 2200

Correspondent Neil Bradley

Trustees *Christopher Smith; Irene Smith; Anthony Winter.*

CC Number 1003801

Information available Full accounts were on file at the Charity Commission.

General This trust was set up in 1990 and it has a clear relationship with its namesake company, Haydan Holdings Ltd. In 2000 it had assets of just £450 with its income of £158,000 coming mainly from Gift Aid. Grants totalled £136,000. The charity expected to receive a Gift Aid donation from Haydan Holdings Ltd in the period to 30 June 2001.

The trust states that it gives recurrent grants to a few organisations and does not invite applications. In 2000 the three largest grants were £50,000 to Nordoff Robbins Music Therapy Centre, £25,000 to Cedar School and £10,000 to Tommy's Campaign. A further 15 grants were listed in the accounts including those to Babes in Arms (£8,000), Wessex Children's Heart Circle, Wessex Heartbeat and Whizz Kidz (£5,000 each), Children with Leukaemia, Leukaemia Research Fund and Nightingale House (£2,500 each) and Beating Bowel Cancer and Sheffield Children's Hospital (£1,000 each). Unlisted miscellaneous grants totalled £3,000.

Exclusions No grants are given for projects overseas.

Applications Unsolicited applications are not considered.

The Haymills Charitable Trust

Education, medicine, welfare, youth

£85,000 to organisations and individuals (2000/01)

Beneficial area UK, but particularly the west of London and Suffolk, where the Haymills group is sited.

Wesley House, 1–7 Wesley Avenue, London NW10 7BZ

Tel. 020 8951 9823

Correspondent I W Ferres, Secretary

Trustees *E F C Drake; I W Ferres; A M H Jackson; K C Perryman; J A Sharpe; J L Wosner; W G Underwood.*

CC Number 277761

Information available Accounts were on file at the Charity Commission, but without a list of grants.

General 'The trustees regularly review their policy, aiming to make the best use of the funds available by donating varying amounts to projects which they believe are not widely known and thus are likely to be inadequately supported. Their main support is to registered charities operating in areas known to them, especially those lying in and to the west of London and in Suffolk.

'Grants fall into four main categories:

Education: grants to schools, colleges and universities

Medicine: grants to hospitals and associated institutions and to medical research

Welfare: primarily to include former Haymills' staff, and to those who are considered to be 'in necessitous circumstances' or who are otherwise distressed or disadvantaged

Youth: support for training schemes to assist in the education, welfare and training of young people.

'No personal applications for support will be considered unless endorsed by a university, a college or other appropriate authority. Each year, a limited number of applicants can be considered who can show that they are committed to further education and training preferably for employment in the construction industry.'

In 2000/01 assets stood at £1.9 million and the income was £162,000, including £89,000 in Gift Aid donations. Grants totalled £85,000 and were broken down as follows:

Education	£11,000
Medical	£22,000
Youth and welfare	£53,000

Unfortunately no list of grants was included with the accounts on file at the Charity Commission. In 1999/2000 beneficiaries in the three categories included the following.

Educational

Grants were given to various educational establishments, especially towards bursaries, prizes and scholarships. Grants included those to: Merchant Taylor's Company for the Dudley Cox Bursary Fund and the Dudley Cox Awards for engineering, design and technology; Anglia Polytechnic University for the Haymills Building Management Scholarship; Suffolk College; and Hammersmith and West London College.

Medical

Grants were mainly given to hospitals and hospital appeals, although grants were also given towards research. Beneficiaries included Central Middlesex Hospital League of Friends, Ealing Hospital League of Friends, Great Ormond Street Children's Hospital and Royal London Hospital.

Youth and welfare

Beneficiaries included Children's Hospice Eastern Region, East Suffolk Association for the Blind, Dyslexia Association, Friends of Samaritans – Ealing, Greater London Central Scout County, London Bible College, Macmillan Cancer Relief, Middlesex Young People's Clubs, Queen Elizabeth Hospital Children's Fund and West London Action for Children.

Exclusions No personal applications will be considered unless endorsed by a university, college or other appropriate authority.

Applications In writing to the correspondent, but note the comments in the general section. Trustees meet at least twice a year, usually in March and October. Applications are not acknowledged.

May Hearnshaw's Charity

General

£96,000 (2000/01)
Beneficial area UK, particularly north Midlands and South Yorkshire.

35–47 North Church Street, Sheffield S1 2DH

Tel. 0114 275 2888 **Fax** 0114 273 0108

Correspondent David Law, Trustee

Trustees *David Law; Jack Rowan.*

CC Number 1008638

Information available Full accounts were on file at the Charity Commission.

General This trust was set up by the will of the late May Hearnshaw who died in 1988. It was her wish that the trust be used for the promotion of education, advancement of religion and relief of poverty and sickness.

The trust supports UK charities or local charities working in the South Yorkshire or north Midlands area. It mainly supports organisations, with a limited number of grants given to individuals recommended by known charities.

In 2000/01 it had assets of £2 million generating an income of £92,000. Grants to 42 organisations, totalled £96,000; about half were recurrent. Grants were broken down as follows:

Relief of poverty and sickness – 28 grants totalling £58,000

Beneficiaries included Children's Appeal (£7,000 in two grants), Ashgate Hospice (£3,600 in two grants), Cavendish Centre (£4,000), Home for Incurables, Neurodegenerative Support Group and St John's Ambulance (£3,000 each), British Red Cross – Sheffield and Mencap (£2,000 each), Well Being (£1,000) and British Geriatrics Society (£500).

Other – 14 grants totalling £39,000

Beneficiaries included Masonic Trust for Boys and Girls (£10,000), NCH Action for Children and RNIB (£5,000 each), National Trust and NSPCC (£3,000 each), RNLI (£2,000), Sheffield Galleries and Museums (£1,000) and Victim Support (£500).

Promotion of education – Nil

Beneficiaries in the previous year were Kids Together Club – Sheffield (£1,000) and Charlton Park School (£500).

In 1998/99 a grant was made to Methodist Homes under the category of 'advancement of religion'.

Exclusions No grants to individuals, except those recommended by known charities.

Applications 'The trustees usually decide on and make grants to charitable organisations twice a year but may decide to make grants at any time. They do not include in their consideration appeals received direct from individuals.'

Heathside Charitable Trust

General, Jewish

£395,000 (2000)
Beneficial area UK.

Hillsdown House, 32 Hampstead High Street, London NW3 1QD

Tel. 020 7431 7739

Correspondent Sir Harry Solomon, Trustee

Trustees *Sir Harry Solomon; Lady Judith Solomon; G R Jayson; R C Taylor.*

CC Number 326959

Information available Full accounts were on file at the Charity Commission.

General This trust has general charitable purposes, with a preference for Jewish organisations.

In 2000 it had assets of £3.5 million, which generated an income of £83,000. Grants totalled £395,000. Management and administration charges were high at £9,800, including £1,700 to a firm in which one of the trustees is a partner. Whilst wholly legal, these editors always regret such payments unless, in the words of the Charity Commission, 'there is no realistic alternative'.

By far the largest grant was £141,000 to Joint Jewish Charitable Trust. Large grants also went to Raft (£35,000), Jewish Education Defence Trust (£25,000), Community Security Trust (£25,000), Jewish Care (£15,000), with £10,000 each to British Friends of Jaffa Institute, GRET and Motivation.

Other beneficiaries included Holocaust Educational Trust (£8,500), First Cheque 2000 and Royal London Institute (£5,000 each), Royal National Theatre (£4,500), Jewish Museum (£3,300), Cancerkin and King Solomon High School (£2,500), Babes in Arms (£2,000) and Marie Curie Cancer Care and Weitzmann Institute (£1,000 each).

Applications In writing to the correspondent, at any time.

The Michael & Morven Heller Charitable Foundation

University and medical research projects, the arts
£153,000 (2000/01)
Beneficial area Worldwide.

8–10 New Fetter Lane, London EC4A 1NQ
Tel. 020 7415 5000 **Fax** 020 7415 0611
Correspondent The Trustees
Trustees *Michael Heller; Morven Heller; Pearl Livingstone.*
CC Number 327832
Information available Accounts and a separate grants list were on file at the Charity Commission.

General This trust was established in 1972, and funds specific projects relating to medical research, science and educational research. This usually involves making large grants to universities for research purposes, particularly medical research. In practice, there appears to be some preference for Jewish organisations.

In 2000/01 the trust had assets of £2.4 million and an income of £220,000. Grants totalled £153,000, with 30 grants of over £1,000 each being listed in the accounts. St Catherine's College received four grants totalling £29,000. Other recipients of awards over £10,000 each were Hampstead Theatre and London Jewish Cultural Centre (£15,000 each) and Norwood Ltd (£12,000).

Other beneficiaries included Beth Shalom (£7,500), Community Security Trust and Jewish Marriage Council (£5,000 each), Ben Uri Gallery (£2,500), Sense (£2,000), New End Theatre (£1,500), Institute for Jewish Policy Research, Royal Academy of Art and Sheffield Jewish Congregation (£1,000 each).

Exclusions No support for individuals.

Applications In writing to the correspondent.

The Simon Heller Charitable Settlement

Medical research, science and educational research
£192,000 (2000/01)
Beneficial area Worldwide.

8–10 New Fetter Lane, London EC4A 1NQ
Tel. 020 7415 5000 **Fax** 020 7415 0611
Correspondent The Trustees
Trustees *M A Heller; Morven Heller; W S Trustee Company Limited.*
CC Number 265405
Information available Accounts were on file at the Charity Commission.

General This trust was established in 1972, and funds specific projects relating to medical research, science and educational research. This usually involves making large grants to universities for research purposes, particularly medical research. In practice, there appears to be some preference for Jewish organisations.

In 2000/01 the trust had assets of almost £4 million and an income of £325,000. Grants totalled £192,000 and were broken down by the trust as follows:

Education	£67,000
Research	£50,000
Humanitarian	£75,000

The accounts listed 19 grants over £1,000 each. UJIA received the largest single grant of £35,000 with Institute for Jewish Policy Research receiving the same amount in two grants of £25,000 and £10,000. Other major beneficiaries were Jewish Care (£30,000), Aish Hatora (£15,000 in two grants), Spiro Institute (£13,000), Scopus (£12,000 in two grants) and Chief Rabbinate Charitable Trust (£10,000).

Other beneficiaries were British ORT, Common Denominator and Community Charity Trust (£5,000 each), Shvut Ami (£2,500) and Israel Diaspora Trust (£2,000).

Exclusions No grants to individuals.

Applications In writing to the correspondent.

Help the Homeless Ltd

Homelessness
£80,000 (2001/02)
Beneficial area UK.

5th Floor, Babmaes House, 2 Babmaes Street, London SW1Y 6HD
Tel. 020 7925 2725 **Fax** 020 7925 2583
Correspondent T Kenny
Trustees *F J Bergin; T S Cookson; L A Bains; M McIntyre; T Rogers; R Reed.*
CC Number 271988
Information available Full accounts were provided by the trust.

General The trust makes small grants to smaller or new voluntary organisations, who are registered charities, for items of capital expenditure directly related to the provision of housing for people who are single and homeless.

In 2001/02 the trust had assets of £1.05 million and an income of £58,000. Grants were made to 28 beneficiaries totalling

103

£80,000. Management and administration costs totalled £17,000.

The largest beneficiary during the year was St Mungo's (£33,333), the largest homelessness organisation in London. Other major grants were: £25,000 to Emmaus UK; £2,000 each to Chester Aid to the Homeless, Finsbury Park Street Drinkers, Kennet Action for Single Homeless, Lighthouse Outreach, Parish of East Ham, and St Edmund's Society; £1,982 to Bedford Housing Link; £1,964 to Good Shepherd Trust.

Exclusions Charities with substantial funds are not supported. No grants for revenue expenditure such as ongoing running costs or salaries, etc.

Applications The trust states 'you need to provide us with information about your organisation, its aims, how it works and how it intends to continue to meet those aims in the future. You will also be asked to send us a copy of your most recent audited reports and accounts'.

Trustees meet to consider grants four times a year. There should be a minimum period of two years between the receipt of a grant and a subsequent application.

Help the Hospices

Hospices
£1.1 million (2000/01)
Beneficial area UK.

34–44 Britannia Street, London WC1 9JG
Tel. 020 7520 8200 **Fax** 020 7278 1021
Email grants@helpthehospices.org.uk
Website www.helpthehospices.org.uk
Correspondent David Praill, Chief Executive
Trustees *Rt Hon. Lord Newton of Braintree, Chair; Ron Giffin; John Cherry; Dr Helen Clayson; Ms Suzy Croft; Robin Eve; Dr Andrew Hoy; Mrs Ann Lee; Ms Terry Maggee; Miss Agnes Malone; Mrs Hilary McNair; George Miall; Hugh Scurfield.*
CC Number 1014851
Information available Full accounts and guidelines were provided by the trust.

General The objects of the charity are to:

- help hospices deliver high standards of care, relief and treatment of terminally ill patients, and support for their families and carers

- support the development and sustainability of independent voluntary hospices
- facilitate working relationships and shared expertise amongst providers and other supports of palliative care, both in the UK and overseas
- promote public education about end of life issues
- raise public support, resources and sufficient funds to enable the achievement of, and add value to, the strategic objectives.

These objectives are met by providing education and training as well as funding hospices and palliative care units through the following programmes:

Major grants
The major grants programme provides financial support for special projects in independent voluntary hospices on an annual basis. Funding for these awards is usually received from other charitable trusts and therefore specific criteria apply each year. Details of current awards can be found on the trust's website.

In 2002 two major grants were available. Ellerman Awards were first given in 2000 following a donation of £100,000 from The John Ellerman Foundation, with a further £150,000 a year given in 2001 to 2005. Awards were given to a maximum of £10,000 to independent voluntary hospices to make a difference to patients, their families and carers, units and palliative care generally.

Rank Foundation Awards were provided for by a grant of £100,0000 to support special capital projects (but not renovations) of between £10,000 and £20,000, especially in hospices which experience difficulty in raising funds.

Regional and outreach training awards
These are available to individual hospices or groups of hospices, as well as professional associations, to help subsidise the cost of their education and training initiatives which:

- encourage increased collaboration, sharing of knowledge and good practice amongst palliative care staff
- satisfy unmet education and training needs cost-effectively within hospices' immediate or wider 'region' (such as a loose geographical area not related to health regions)
- develop closer local control of specialist education and training provision and its evaluation
- improve patient care.

The trust has an information leaflet, which describes the support available thus: 'the typical niche of hospice education, that of short, half-day, one- or

two-day courses, which does not lend itself to national health or social-education funding. The grants allow palliative-care services to take forward new ideas and develop staff either locally or regionally and to recoup expenses. They also allow the development of education based on small, experiential groups, which would otherwise be economically unviable.'

No more than 25% of participants should consist of staff from the host hospice. Grants of up to 50% of the total costs for regional training, and up to 66% for outreach work, can be awarded to an organisation, to a maximum of £1,500 per project, or £5,000 per hospice per year. Hospices can receive awards up to eight times a year, allowing, for instance, a series of workshops on palliative care in nursing homes, although applicants cannot receive funding to repeat sessions that have previously received funding from the programme. Eligible expenses include trainers' fees, home hire, accommodation and travel, even when using internal trainers and rooms in certain cases.

Emergency fund
Applications for emergency funding urgently needed by hospices can be given, upon application directly to the chief executive.

Bursary awards
These are to help support individuals' continuing professional development. Staff and volunteers in independent voluntary hospices are eligible for funding towards attending courses, conferences and study days across a wide range of disciplines. Funding for staff in NHS units, other voluntary hospices or in nursing homes is exclusively for training in palliative care.

In 2000/01 the charity had assets of £3.5 million. Total income was £2.2 million, of which £1.3 million came from donations received, including grants from Bridge House Estates Trust and Community Fund. Direct charitable expenditure was £2 million, including £1.1 million given in grants, broken down as follows:

Education and training – £177,000
This included 88 regional and outreach training awards, totalling £91,000, which went to 37 hospices and 3 professional associations, which typically helped 10 to 15 participants whose course fees were reduced by the subsidy. It also included the subsidised training provided directly by Help the Hospices, which saw 772 delegates attending 51 courses.

Bursary awards – 750 totalling £252,000

These were mostly given for nursing (608 awards), although doctors, management, fundraisers and PAMs were also supported.

Major grants – £155,000

Projects supported from the Ellerman Awards included: new or extended service, such as lymphoedema services, a pre-breavement visiting service and an interpretation service; research projects such those into 'the user voice' and enhancing in-patients' quality of life; provision of equipment or renovation such as providing a dedicated children's room and renovating a viewing room.

Direct hospice funding – £262,00

This was an increase from the £168,000 given in the previous year as the charity was chosen as the beneficiary of the BAE Systems Charity Challenge.

Millennium awards – 200 totalling £276,000

This fund, which expired in June 2002, was principally funded by the Millennium Commission and funded projects carried out by hospice volunteers, such as patient self-help groups, therapeutic activities and a Reminiscence Project to help patients produce booklets looking back at their lives.

Applications Generally on a form available from Karl Benn, Grants Officer, from whom further information is also available. For major grant programmes, potential applicants should request details first as policies change. The trust's website contains detailed information of the grant-making policy and should be viewed before an application is considered. For emergency grants, applicants should write directly to the chief executive.

The Christina Mary Hendrie Trust for Scottish & Canadian Charities

Youth, people who are elderly, general

£81,000 (1999)

Beneficial area Scotland and Canada.

48 Castle Street, Edinburgh EH2 3LX

Tel. 0131 220 2345

Correspondent George R Russell

Trustees *Mrs A D H Irwin; C R B Cox; J K Scott Moncrieff; Miss C Irwin; Maj. Gen. A S H Irwin; R N Cox; A G Cox.*

CC Number SC014514

Information available Information was supplied by the trust.

General The trust was established in 1975 following the death in Scotland of Christina Mary Hendrie. The funds constituting the trust originated in Canada. Grants are distributed to charities throughout Scotland and Canada, although the majority is now given in Scotland. There is a preference for charities connected with young or older people, although other groups to receive grants include cancer charities.

Grants in 1999 totalled £81,000. Grants normally range from £1,000 to £5,000. Unfortunately there was no information available on the beneficiaries supported.

Exclusions Grants are not given to individuals.

Applications In writing to the correspondent. The trustees meet twice a year to consider grants, usually in March and November.

The Bernhard Heuberger Charitable Trust

Jewish

£39,000 (2000/01)

Beneficial area Worldwide.

12 Sherwood Road, London NW4 1AD

Correspondent H Heuberger, Secretary

Trustees *D H Heuberger; S N Heuberger.*

CC Number 294378

Information available Accounts were on file at the Charity Commission, but without a narrative report.

General This trust was established in 1986. In 2000/01 it had assets of £2.8 million and an income of £728,000 including £622,000 profit on disposal of fixed assets. Grants totalled £39,000 down from £80,000 in 1999/2000.

The accounts listed the largest 12 grants made, where were for £1,000 or more. Beneficiaries included Beis Brucha (£5,300), BH Gur, Bridge Lane Beth Hamerdrash and Jewish Free School (£5,000 each), United Jewish Israel Appeal (£2,000) and British Friends of Shalva, CST, Imrey Chaim Synagogue and World Emunah (£1,000 each).

Small unlisted donations totalled £5,600.

Applications In writing to the correspondent.

Highmoor Hall Charitable Trust

Christian mission societies and agencies

£230,000 (2001/02)

Beneficial area UK and overseas.

Highmoor Hall, Highmoor, Henley-on-Thames, Oxfordshire RG9 5DH

Correspondent P D Persson, Trustee

Trustees *P D Persson; Mrs A D Persson; J P G Persson; A S J Persson.*

CC Number 289027

Information available Basic accounts were on file at the Charity Commission.

General This trust makes grants to Christian mission societies and agencies.

In 2001/02 it had an income of £156,000 and a total expenditure of £239,000. In the previous year charitable expenditure was divided into three categories: home missions, overseas missions and 'other charities'.

About two thirds of its charitable expenditure has previously gone to 'other charities'; during this year that percentage was around £159,000.

No further information was available on the size or number of beneficiaries.

Exclusions No grants to non-registered charities.

Applications The trust states that it does not respond to unsolicited applications. Telephone calls are not welcome. The correspondent has now moved from the above address, although mail will be forwarded.

The Hilden Charitable Fund

Minorities, overseas, penal, homelessness, general

£538,000 (2000/01)
Beneficial area UK, overseas.

34 North End Road, London W14 0SH
Tel. 020 7603 1525 **Fax** 020 7603 1525
Email hildencharity@hotmail.com
Website www.hildencharitablefund.org.uk
Correspondent Rodney Hedley, Secretary
Trustees *Mrs A M A Rampton; Prof. D S Rampton; Mrs G J S Rampton; J R A Rampton; A J M Rampton; C S L R Rampton; Dr M B H Rampton; Prof. C H Rodeck; Mrs E K Rodeck; C H Younger; Ms M E Baxter.*
CC Number 232591
Information available Guidelines. 'Summary of funding request' form. Report and accounts with full grants list and considerable narrative analysis of grants.

General In 2000/01 the trust had assets of £13 million generating an income of £440,000. The trust received 1,167 enquiries about grant aid, and considered 561 applications, 125 (22%) of which received grants, totalling £538,000. Other expenditure included £64,000 for 'support costs', £23,000 for

administration and £40,000 for 'investment related expenditure'.

Grants were listed under the categories of overseas development, minorities and race relations, penal affairs and homelessness. Community organisations in Scotland were also supported through a grant made to the Scottish Community Foundation.

Grants are rarely given to well-established UK charities or to individuals. Fund policy is directed largely at supporting work at a community level within the categories of interest stated above.

Priorities given to different types of work within the main categories may change from time to time, as dictated by circumstances. It should not be assumed, therefore, that an application, even though it may generally qualify, will necessarily be considered. Grants, capital or revenue, rarely exceed £5,000 and are not often made for salaries.

Overseas development (£187,000 in 33 grants – 35%)
Grants ranged from £2,000 to £20,000, although most were for £5,000. Beneficiaries included: Care UK for its work following an earthquake in Gujrat (£20,000); Tanzania Development Trust to refurbish schools (£14,000 in total); Zenzele in Cape Town to provide skills training for employment (£12,000 in total); Coda International to help farmers affected by Hurricane Mitch (£10,000 in total); Baynard's Zambia Trust to develop the Chibanga School and CAFOD Mozambique (£10,000 each); Dhaka Ahsania Mission in Bangladesh for a loan scheme and International Childcare Trust – Sri Lanka (£6,000 each); Ashram International – Bombay, Fairtrade Foundation – Belize to develop a cocoa farmers collective, NICRO for a diversion from crime scheme and University College London Benfield Greig Hazard Research Centre for training for Asian 'hazard teams' in effective disaster management (£5,000 each); International Care and Relief (£4,000); Friends of Kaur – Gambia to develop a village food cooperative scheme (£3,000); The Wulugu Trust – Ghana to help with girls education (£2,000).

Overseas applications – the types of applications sought by trustees:

1. In supporting overseas development, trustees wish to hear from projects which focus on community development, education and health.
2. Funds are available for capital and revenue funding. The funding programme is designed to help small and medium-size initiatives.

3. Trustees will consider applications from countries within the developing world. At present, applications from Ghana, Ethiopia, Tanzania, South Africa and Bangladesh are particularly welcome.
4. In supporting community development, education and health initiatives, trustees will particularly welcome projects that address the needs and potential of girls and women.
5. Where possible, trustees would like to fund a number of projects in one geographical area. In funding projects, trustees will be interested in projects that develop the capacity of local people.
6. Trustees will be pleased to hear from UK NGOs and hope that UK NGOs will encourage their local partners, if appropriate, to apply directly to Hilden for grant aid.

The trustees are keen on matching funding, and feel that being aware of who else is funding a project is very important.

Minorities and Race Relations (£149,000 in 33 grants – 28%)
Grants were aimed at addressing the needs of asylum-seekers and refugees by funding the general running costs of beneficiaries. Grants were also made to a number of well-established agencies working on minority issues. They ranged from £1,000 to £10,000. Beneficiaries included: the Joint Council for the Welfare of Immigrants (£10,000); Royal Holloway College – University of London (£8,000); Detentions Advice Service (£7,500); Changing Faces for its schools programme (£6,000); Asian Resource Centre and Asian Women's Resource Centre, British Agencies for Adoption and Fostering, Baytree Centre Brixton - Dawliffe Hall Education Foundation, Finsbury Park Homeless Families Refugee Programme and Southall Black Sisters (£5,000 each); Migrant Resource Centre (£4,500); Bishop Ho Centre – Soho and Operation Black Vote (£3,000 each); Bail for Immigration Detainees (£2,000); Colombian Football Association Welfare Group (£1,000).

Penal Affairs (£74,000 in 18 grants – 14%)
Grants were made to organisations for pre-release training and resettlement of offenders, ranging from £1,000 to £6,000. Beneficiaries were: Stepping Stones – London, and the Sobriety Project working in Askham Grange women's prison in Humberside (£6,000 each); Shropshire Help & Advice for Relatives and Friends of Prisoners (£5,500 in total); Consultancy, Counselling, Training and Leadership – Ipswich for work with young

ex-offenders upon their release, Dance United Holloway, Female Prisoners Welfare Project for their work in women's prisons in London and the South East, Kestrel Theatre Company for their work in Grendon Prison, Mount Prison Visitors Centre Association, New Bridge for 'understanding fatherhood' courses at Feltham Young Offenders Institution, Women in Special Hospitals for running costs, Women's Link and Youth at Risk for its pre-release scheme at Moorland Young Offenders Institution (£5,000 each); Friends of Feltham for running costs for its Feltham FM radio project (£3,500); Housing Advice for Black & Asian Prisoners (£3,000); Irene Taylor Music in Prisons Trust at Mount Prison (£2,500); HM Lancaster Farms Young Offenders Institution (£1,200); Emile Littler Foundation to refurbish a chapel with a study space at Wandsworth Prison (£1,000).

Homelessness (£59,000 in 16 grants – 11% of total)

Grants under this category were mostly made to projects for the provision of services in hostels and day centres, and also for advice and support projects particluarly aimed at young people at risk of being homeless. Grants ranged from £1,000 to £6,000. Beneficiaries were Kaleidoscope – Kingston upon Thames (£6,000); St Petroc's Society – Cornwall (£5,500); Bondway Housing Association's soup run in London, Finsbury Park Street Drinkers Project, Kirby Youth Housing Trust and St Paul's Community Trust – Margate (£5,000 each); York Night Stop (£4,000); Padstone's – High Wycombe and Coventry Day Centre (£3,500 each); Dacorum Emergency Night Shelter, Deptford Churches Crypt Club and The Porch – Oxford (£3,000 each); Lamp – Leicester (£2,500); Droitwich Single Homeless Project and Furniture Station – Stockport (£2,000); and Spear – Richmond upon Thames (£1,200).

Grant aid in Scotland (£29,000 in 2 grants – 5%)

A grant of £26,000 was given to the Scottish Community Foundation, to support a grants programme for community groups and small voluntary organisations, which in turn made 26 grants, most notably to local self-help groups for women. Guidelines and application forms are available from: Scottish Community Foundation, 3rd Floor, 27 Palmerston Place, Edinburgh EH12 5AP – tel: 0131 225 9804. One other grant of £3,000 was given to the Scottish Council for Minority Rights.

Other grants (£27,500 in 3 grants - 5%)

Beneficiaries were: Mutual Aid Centre/ Institute of Community Studies, which received a grant of £20,000 to establish the Grandparents Plus research agency; Rhodes House Library received £5,000; South African musicians coming to London for a music festival received £2,500.

Playschemes (£12,000 in 20 grants – 2%)

Grants were of £1,500 or less. Applications from organisations working with refugee and immigrant communities were given priority. Most of the projects supported were in Greater London.

The trust also noted that just one grant was made in Wales, to Cardiff Gypsy Site, which received £5,000. During the year only a few applications were received from Wales and Northern Ireland.

Exclusions No grants to or on behalf of individuals and no circular appeals.

Applications All applicants are required to complete a very brief summary form outlining their request before they are considered. Otherwise all applications will be regarded as enquiries. Potential applicants should contact the office for guidelines and forms.

Applications should include:

- most recent financially inspected accounts
- most recent annual report
- projected income and expenditure for the current financial year
- explanation of how your reserves stand
- particular features of your costs, such as high transport costs in rural areas
- details of other funders approached
- any significant achievements and/or problems or difficulties
- how you approach equal opportunities
- any 'matching grant' arrangements.

Please be clear in your application about when the proposed work is to commence, and give the relevant timetable.

For projects overseas applicants should provide:

- Evidence of commitment among local people and communities to the proposed work programme.
- A coherent plan of how the work is going to be carried out with relevant budgets. Budgets should be presented in the context of the overall budget of the applicant NGO.
- A plan of how the work is going to be maintained and developed in the future by involving relevant agencies and attracting money and resources.
- An explanation of why the local project seeks the help of a UK aid agency.
- Details of local costs (e.g. salaries of state-employed teachers and medical personnel; cost of vehicles, petrol, etc.), and notes of any problems over exchange rates or inflation.
- An account of the political, economic, religious and cultural situation in the country/area.
- A comment on the extent to which the project can rely on government and local state funding in the country concerned.
- Details of monitoring and evaluation.

Trustees meet approximately every three months.

The Charles Littlewood Hill Trust

Health, disability, service, children (including schools)

£132,000 (2000)

Beneficial area UK, with a preference for Nottinghamshire and Norfolk.

Eversheds, 1 Royal Standard Place, Nottingham NG1 6FZ

Tel. 0115 950 7000 **Fax** 0115 950 7111

Correspondent W F Whysall, Trustee

Trustees *C W L Barratt; W F Whysall; T H Farr; N R Savory.*

CC Number 286350

Information available Full accounts were on file at the Charity Commission.

General The trust supports schools, disability, health, service and children's organisations. It gives UK-wide, although particular preference is given to applications from Norfolk and Nottinghamshire.

In 2000 the trust had assets of £3.5 million, which generated an income of £129,000 from property and investments. The accounts stated that £24,000 was paid towards administration and legal charges concerning a lease and £5,800 for stockbrokers fees and commission to companies that have a trustee as a partner – hopefully as these companies could provide the most competitive service to the trust rather than the most convenient. Grants to 52 organisations totalled £132,000, broken down as follows:

Norfolk

13 grants of £1,000 to £13,000 totalling £54,000.

The largest grants went to Norwich Cathedral Choir Endowment (£13,000), The Great Hospital (£10,000), Norwich Cathedral (£5,800) and Norfolk Churches Trust and Norwich & Norfolk Far East POWs (£5,000 each). Other beneficiaries included SSAFA (£3,000), We Care 2000 Appeal (£2,500) and Fire Services Benevolent Fund and How Hill Trust Appeal (£1,000 each).

Nottinghamshire

18 grants of £1,000 to £10,000 totalling £48,000.

The largest grants were £10,000 to Nottingham City Hospital for the breast unit fund, £5,000 to St Peter's Church and £4,000 to Nottinghamshire Hospice. Other recipients included St John Ambulance (£3,500), Macmillan Cancer Relief and Royal British Legion – Nottinghamshire and Derbyshire (£3,000 each) and Downing Street Church and Nottingham Care Watch Project (£1,000 each).

Elsewhere

19 grants of £1,000 to £5,000 totalling £26,000.

Great Ormond Street Hospital received £5,000 while Royal Star and Garter Home received £2,000. All the other grants were for £1,000 each and beneficiaries included ASBAH, Canine Partners for Independence, Ex-Service Mental Welfare Society, National Missing Persons Helpline and National Association of Swimming Clubs for the Handicapped.

Exclusions Applications from individuals are not considered. Grants are seldom made for repairs of parish churches outside Nottinghamshire.

Applications In writing to the correspondent including the latest set of audited accounts. Unsuccessful applications will not be acknowledged. Trustees meet in March, July and November.

The Holly Hill Charitable Trust

Environmental education, conservation and wildlife

£134,000 (2001/02)
Beneficial area UK.

Flat 5, 89 Onslow Square, London SW7 3LT
Tel. 020 7589 2651

Correspondent M D Stanley, Trustee
Trustees *M D Stanley; A Lewis.*
CC Number 1044510
Information available Full accounts were on file at the Charity Commission.

General This trust was established in 1995 to support environmental education, conservation and wildlife organisations.

In 2001/02 the trust had assets of £1.3 million and an income of £43,000. Grants totalling £134,000 were made to eight organisations. (In 1998/99 grants totalled £416,000).

The main beneficiaries were Kasanka Trust (£40,000), which manages the Kasanka National Park in Zambia, Rainforest Concern (£35,000) and Wildlife Conservation Research Unit (WildCRU £25,000.)

The other beneficiaries were Sussex Wildlife Trust (£13,000), Soil Association (£9,000), Oxford University (£6,000), Berkshire, Buckinghamshire and Oxfordshire Wildlife Trust (£4,000) and Plymouth University (£2,000).

Exclusions No grants to individuals.

Applications In writing to the correspondent. Applications need to be received in April and September, and trustees meet in June and November.

R G Hills Charitable Trust

General

£215,000 (1999/2000)
Beneficial area UK and overseas.

Furley Page, 39 St Margaret's Street, Canterbury, Kent CT1 2TX
Tel. 01227 763939
Correspondent Mr Barton
Trustees *D J Pentin; V E Barton.*
CC Number 1008914
Information available Full accounts are on file at the Charity Commission.

General This trust was dormant until Mrs E M Hill's death in March 1996, when she left three quarters of the residue of her estate to the trust. The balance was received in June 1999.

The 1999/2000 report says 'various donations have been made, or are currently being considered, by the

trustees for both national and local charities, some of which are engaged in overseas charitable work'.

During the year the trust had an income of £136,000, assets of £3.2 million and gave grants totalling £215,000, which after other expenditure left a deficit of £111,000 at the year end. They were 11 beneficiaries, only one recipient of which had received a donation the previous year. There were five donations of £25,000, to Barnardos, British Executive Service Overseas (BESO), Injured Jockeys Fund, RNIB and St John Ambulance. Other donations included £20,000 to National Society for Epilepsy, four grants of £15,000 each to Canterbury Oast Trust, Cruse Bereavement Trust, Federation for Artistic & Creative Therapy and WaterAid, and £10,000 to Kent Music School.

Applications In writing to the correspondent.

Hinchley Charitable Trust

Mainly evangelical Christian

£99,000 (2001)
Beneficial area UK and overseas.

Watersmeet, 56 Barton Road, Haslingfield, Cambridge CB3 7LL
Tel. 01223 741120
Email bs217@cam.ac.uk
Correspondent Dr Brian Stanley, Trustee
Trustees *Dr B Stanley; J D Levick; B Levick; S P Dengate.*
CC Number 281178
Information available Accounts were on file at the Charity Commission, but without a full narrative report.

General In 2001 the trust's assets totalled £1.9 million following substantial income of £1.4 million during the year. Grants were made totalling £99,000.

Larger grants were: £12,000 to Tearfund for Christian relief and development work; £11,000 each to Associated Bus Ministries for evangelistic work and Mildmay Hospital for general expenses; £10,000 to Crusader's Union for Christian youth work; £5,000 each to Epsom and Ewell Boys' Club for youth work and Spurgeon's College for theological training; £2,500 to Arbury Road Baptist Church, Cambridge for church work; and

£1,500 to Church Pastoral Aid Society for church work.

Applications The trust states that it does not respond to unsolicited applications. Replies will rarely, if ever, be made to applications for grants by post or on the telephone, as existing funds are all fully committed to charities which are regularly supported.

Lady Hind Trust

General
£309,000 (2001)
Beneficial area England and Wales only, with a preference for Nottinghamshire and Norfolk.

c/o Eversheds, 1 Royal Standard Place, Nottingham NG1 6FZ

Tel. 0115 950 7000

Correspondent W F Whysall, Trustee

Trustees *C W L Barratt; W F Whysall; T H Farr; N R Savory.*

CC Number 208877

Information available Full accounts were on file at the Charity Commission.

General This trust makes mainly one-off grants for general charitable purposes, with some preference for supporting health and disability-related charities. It has similar criteria to, and the same trustees as, Charles Littlewood Hill Trust.

In 2001 the trust had an income of £338,000. Management and administration expenses included £39,000 paid to two companies that had a trustee as a partner. Grants were given to 89 organisations and totalled £309,000, broken down as follows:

Nottinghamshire
38 grants of £1,000 to £20,000 totalling £134,000.
The largest grants went to Macmillan Cancer Relief for its Nottinghamshire Appeal (£20,000), Nottingham City Hospital for the breast unit fund (£15,000), St John Ambulance (£14,000), St Peter's Church for the Nottingham Tower Appeal (£13,000) and Nottingham Dyslexia Association (£7,500). Recipients of £5,000 or less included Elizabeth Fry Family Centre, Mencap Nottinghamshire, Ollerton Youth Project, Organisation for Sickle Cell Anaemia Research and Venue 3:16.

Norfolk
27 grants of £1,000 to £10,000 totalling £80,000.

The largest grants went to 2nd Reedham Scout Group (£10,000), Norfolk and Norwich Association for the Blind (£9,000), Heydon Church – Norfolk (£7,000) and St Martin's Housing Trust (£5,500). Beneficiaries receiving £5,000 or less included East Anglian Air Ambulance, The Papworth Trust, Playground 2000, The Stable – Norfolk and Victim Support North Norfolk.

UK
37 grants ranging from £1,000 to £10,000 totalling £63,000.
Cancer Care Society received £10,000. Other beneficiaries included Countryside Foundation for Education, Oakfield Donations Trust and WellBeing.

Exclusions Grants are seldom made for parish church appeals unless they are within Nottinghamshire. Applications from individuals are not considered.

Applications Applications, in writing and with accounts, must be submitted one month in advance of meetings in March, July and November. Unsuccessful applicants are not notified.

Stuart Hine Trust

Evangelical Christianity
£101,000 (1999/2000)
Beneficial area UK and overseas.

'Cherith', 23 Derwent Close, Hailsham, East Sussex BN27 3DA

Tel. 01323 843948

Correspondent Raymond Bodkin, Trustee

Trustees *Raymond Bodkin; Nigel Coltman; Amelia Gardner; Philip Johnson.*

CC Number 326941

Information available Information was supplied by the trust.

General The trust gives grants to evangelical Christian organisations that have been supported by the trustees or by the settlor during his lifetime and that are known to the trustees. In 1999/2000 the trust had an income of £146,000 and gave grants totalling £101,000.

The most recent grants list on file at the Charity Commission was for 1995/96, when grants were made to 11 evangelical Christian organisations totalling £51,000. The bulk of the grant total in that year was given to Wycliff Bible Translators

(£40,000). Other grants included £1,500 each to The Retired Missionary Aid Fund and Bible Text Publicity Mission and £1,000 each to Manchester City Mission, The Open Air Mission, FEBA Radio and Kingsway Trust.

Applications In writing to the correspondent, although please note, the trust states that 'unsolicited requests for funds will not be considered'. Funds are basically distributed in accordance with the wishes of the settlor.

Hobson Charity Ltd

Social welfare, education
£1.5 million (2000/01)
Beneficial area UK.

21 Bryanston Street, Marble Arch, London W1H 7PR

Tel. 020 7495 5599

Correspondent Mrs Deborah Clarke, Trustee & Secretary

Trustees *R F Hobson; Mrs P M Hobson; Sir Donald Gosling; Mrs Deborah Clarke.*

CC Number 326839

Information available Full accounts are on file at the Charity Commission.

General In 2000/01 this trust had an income of £135,000. Grants totalled £1.5 million and were made from both income and capital funds; assets were down to £2 million from £3.4 million in 1999/2000.

A total of 53 grants in the range of £500 to £253,000 were made in the year. There were seven of £100,000 or more: beneficiaries were John Grooms Association for the Disabled (£253,000), Westminster Council Christmas Appeal Building Trust (£225,000), Samuel Johnson Prize (£135,000), CSV People for People (£132,000) and Churchill College Archives Fund, Health Foundation and Prince's Trust (£100,000 each).

Other beneficiaries of larger donations included Oriel College (£50,000), White Ensign Association (£40,000), British School of Osteopathy (£25,000), Neil and Anne Benson Charity, British Sports Trust and Keeper of the Green (£10,000 each).

Other grants included those to Terrence Higgins Trust, Hilda Laing Care Centre, Royal Albert Hall Trust, Royal Ballet,

David Shepherd Foundation and Wooden Spoon Society.

Applications In writing to the correspondent.

The Hockerill Educational Foundation

Education, especially Christian education

£131,000 to organisations (2000/01)

Beneficial area UK, with a preference for the dioceses of Chelmsford and St Albans.

16 Hagsdell Road, Hertford, Hertfordshire SG13 8AG

Tel. 01992 303053 **Fax** 01992 425950

Correspondent C R Broomfield, Secretary

Trustees *Dr S Hunter, Chair; Rt Revd Lord Bishop of Chelmsford; Rt Revd Lord Bishop of St Albans; Rt Revd Bishop of Bedford; Rt Revd Bishop of Bradwell; Ven. T P Jones; Ven. P Taylor; Prof. B J Aylett; Revd P Hartley; Mrs M L Helmore; H Marsh; Mrs H Potter; J O Reynolds; R Woods.*

CC Number 311018

Information available Full accounts, guidelines and an information leaflet were provided by the trust.

General The foundation was established in 1978 following the closure of Hockerill College, which was established in 1852 to train women teachers who 'would go to schools in the service of humanity'. When the Secretary of State for Education and Science decided in 1976 to wind down Hockerill College, the proceeds of the sale of its assets where given to this foundation to use for the purposes for which the college was created. The foundation's priorities are:

- education and training of teachers and others involved in education (particularly religious education)
- research and development of religious education
- support for students in further and higher education (normally only to first degree level)
- those involved in non-statutory education, including adult and Christian education.

These grants are made to individuals wishing to train as teachers and to existing teachers who wish to improve their qualifications, particularly with regards to education. For further information, please see *The Educational Grants Directory* (published by DSC).

Grants are also made to organisations for projects and research likely to enhance the Church of England's contribution to higher and further education or religious education in schools. The trust's Guidance for Applicants states:

'The trustees will normally consider applications from corporate bodies or institutions associated with education on Christian principles. There is a religious dimension to all education, but the trustees would expect any activity, course, project or research supported to be likely to be of real benefit to religious education and/or the church's educational work. They will give priority to imaginative new projects which will enhance the Church of England's contribution to higher and further education and/or promote aspects of religious education in schools.

'Recurrent grants may be made, normally for up to three years and for a maximum of five years. Grants for the funding of research or appointment of individuals will be paid termly or quarterly and subject to funds being available. The trustees will wish to make suitable arrangements to monitor research or the progress of a project, and will ask for a report on the progress of any course or project they are funding. They shall also be entitled to ask for a line of credit in the final line of a research project.'

The foundation also arranges the annual Hockerill Lecture, which was given in 2001 by the Rt Revd. Alan Chesters, Chair of the Church of England Board of Education, on the subject 'Distinctive or Divisive? The Role of Church Schools'.

In 2000/01 the trust had assets of £6 million. Total income was £207,000, mostly derived from investments. There was £6,100 spent on the Hockerill Lecture, with £72 generated in lecture notes. Management, administration and staff costs totalled £34,000. Grants were made to eight organisations totalling £131,000, with 40 students receiving £33,000 in total.

Chelmsford Diocesan Board of Finance received the most support during the year: six grants totalling £60,000. These were £20,000 for the salary of a children's officer and related costs (fifth of five grants), £15,000 towards the salary costs of staff at St Mark's College (first of three grants), £11,000 towards the employment

and travel costs of the FE officer (first of five grants), £6,000 towards the expenses of the children's work advisor (first of five grants) and the costs of the Diocesan early years advisor (third of four grants) and £2,000 towards resources for school visits.

St Albans Diocesan Board of Education also received multiple grants, totalling £49,000. These were £27,000 towards the salary of the youth outreach worker (the third and part of the fourth of four grants), £16,000 towards the salary of an RE support teacher (first of three grants), £5,000 towards resources for the Diocesan RE Centre in Welwyn Garden City, £1,000 towards a children's spirituality project and £550 towards a children's IT project.

Other grants went to Faculty of Initial Education at St Andrew's Paraguay for student bursaries (£5,000 – first of five grants), Luton Grassroots Programme to promote interfaith dialogue (£4,500 – third of three grants), Bedford Chaplaincy Committee to support the Ecumenical Chaplaincy at de Montfort (Bedford) University (£4,000 – first two of three grants), Luton Churches Educational Trust for training of workers (£3,000 – second of two grants), St Albans Cathedral Music Trust to help develop the boys' and girls' choirs (£3,000 – second of three grants) and Chelmsford Cathedral for resources for school visits (£2,000 – third of three grants).

Exclusions Grants are not given for general appeals for funds, 'bricks and mortar' building projects or purposes that are the clear responsibility of another body.

With regard to individuals, grants will not normally be considered from:

- teachers who intend to move out of the profession
- those in training for ordination or for other kinds of mission
- clergy who wish to improve their own qualifications, unless they are already engaged in teaching in schools and/or intend to teach in the future
- students of counselling, therapy or social work
- undergraduates or people training for other professions, such as accountancy, business, law or medicine
- people doing courses or visits abroad, including 'gap' year courses (except as an integral part of a course, or a necessary part of research)
- children at primary or secondary school.

Applications On a form available from the correspondent and submitted by 1 March each year. Results of applications will be communicated in early April. Receipt of applications are not acknowledged. Applications which do not fit the criteria would not normally receive a reply. Further information on the grants to individuals can be found in The Educational Grants Directory published by DSC.

The J G Hogg Charitable Trust

Welfare, animal welfare, general

£101,000 (2000/01)
Beneficial area Worldwide.

Chantrey Vellacott DFK, Russell Square House, 10–12 Russell Square, London WC1B 5LF
Tel. 020 7509 9000
Correspondent C M Jones, Trustees' Accountant
Trustees *Sarah Jane Houldsworth; Joanna Wynfreda Hogg.*
CC Number 299042
Information available Accounts were provided by the trust.

General The trust states that it has no set policy on the type of charity supported, but would give favourable consideration to those based primarily in the UK that support the relief of human and animal suffering.

In 2000/01 the trust had assets of £657,000 and an income of £203,000, including a donation of £120,000 from J G Hogg Children's Settlement, plus the income tax recoverable. A donation from this settlement is the trust's main annual source of income. Grants to 23 organisations totalled £101,000.

Over half the grants were for £5,000 the only two higher were £6,600 to Tree Aid and £6,000 to Oxfam. Other beneficiaries appeared to cover a range of well and less well known charities as well as both UK and local organisations. Examples include Brecon & District Disabled Club, Carleton Hedgehog Hospital, Cruse Bereavement Care, Hackney Empire Appeal, Landmark Trust, Relate and Spadework.

Exclusions No grants to individuals. Registered charities only are supported.

Applications In writing to the correspondent.

The Holst Foundation

Arts

£317,000 (2000/01)
Beneficial area UK.

c/o Finers Stephens Innocent, 179 Great Portland Street, London W1W 5LS
Tel. 020 7323 4000
Email pcarter@fsilaw.co.uk
Correspondent Peter Carter, Secretary
Trustees *Rosamund Strode, Chair; Noel Periton; Prof. Arnold Whittall; Peter Carter; Andrew Clements; Julian Anderson.*
CC Number 283668
Information available Accounts were on file at the Charity Commission but without a list of grants.

General The trust has two objects: firstly, to promote public appreciation of the musical works of Gustav and Imogen Holst; and secondly, to encourage the study and practice of the arts.

In practice the trust tends to be proactive. Funds are available almost exclusively for the performance of music by living composers. An annual awards scheme is offered to performing groups who wish to commission new work. The trust has historical links with Aldeburgh in Suffolk and is a major funder of new music at the annual Aldeburgh Festival. It also promotes the recording of new music by means of substantial funding to the recording label NMC, which the foundation also provided the funds to set up.

In 2000/01 the trust had assets of almost £2 million and an income of £288,000 including £206,000 from G & I Holst Ltd, a trading subsidiary. It made grants totalling £317,000 including £144,000 to NMC. There were 42 grants of £1,000 or more and 53 under £1,000. Unfortunately there were no further details on grants made in this year.

In previous years beneficiaries have included Birmingham Contemporary Music Festival, Cheltenham International Festival, Gogmagogs, Opera North, Piano Circus, Purcell School, Roehampton Institute, Schubert Ensemble, SPNM, University of York and Western Sinfonia.

Exclusions No support for the recordings or works of Holst that are already well supported. No grants to individuals for educational purposes.

Applications In writing to: The Grants Administrator, 43 Alderbrook Road, London SW12 8AD. Trustees meet four times a year. There is no application form. Seven copies of the application should be sent. Applications should contain full financial details and be as concise as possible. Funding is not given retrospectively.

P H Holt Charitable Trust

General

£277,000 (2000/01)
Beneficial area UK, with a preference for Merseyside.

India Buildings, Liverpool L2 0RB
Tel. 0151 473 4693
Correspondent Roger Morris, Secretary
Trustees *K Wright, Chair; John Utley; John Allan; D Morris; Tilly Boyce; Christopher Stephens.*
CC Number 217332
Information available Full accounts were provided by the trust.

General The trust makes a large number of mostly small grants, about three quarters of them in Merseyside. This trust is a welcome and exceptional example of Liverpool shipping money staying in and around the city. It continues to organise its giving in three established grant programmes concerned with Merseyside, 'Holt tradition' and elsewhere.

In 2000/01 the trust had an income of £398,000 and a total expenditure of £400,000. Grants were made totalling £277,000.

The trust summarised its activities and the categories supported in 2000/01 as shown in the tables. A full list of grants was provided by the trust, with brief descriptions of the purpose of the larger grants made.

Payments in 2000/01 were categorised as shown in the table below.

Merseyside one-off grants
By far the largest grant made during the year was £80,000 to the Bluecoat Arts Centre. £75,000 was to support the c ntre's major project to restore its histo ic buildings and construct a new building to extend and improve its facilities, he other £5,000 was to support the centre's art and education programmes. Other larger grants included those to

111

P H HOLT CHARITABLE TRUST – PAYMENTS IN 2000/01

Category £	Total	Merseyside	'Holt tradition'	Elsewhere
Community	60,000	48,000	4,700	7,100
Welfare	46,000	38,000	4,400	3,400
Education	56,000	43,000	13,000	0
Arts	94,000	93,000	1,500	0
Heritage	7,500	4,000	3,500	0
Environment	12,000	5,800	6,300	0
Medicine	2,500	1,500	0	1,000
Total	278,000	233,000	33,000	12,000

Activity 2000/01	Merseyside	'Holt tradition'	Elsewhere
No. of applications received	285	24	279
No. of grants made	93	34	11
of which			
recipients previously supported	60	29	5
recipients supported for the first time	28	5	6
consortium projects	5	0	0
total value of grants	£233,000	£34,000	£12,000

University of Liverpool (£15,000 to assist with three separate projects), St Cyprian's Church Kensington (£6,000 to help with development of a new community facility), LIPA (£5,600 to help with a number of outreach projects) and Landlife (£5,000 towards costs of the educational programme).

Recipients of £1,000 to £4,000 included Big Issue in the North Trust, Chara Trust, Merseyside Dance Initiative, Open Eye, Toxteth Health & Community Care Forum and Tranmere Alliance. Smaller grants ranged all the way down to £100, with the average being about £2,500. The trust states that other grants, made in response to specific appeals, are normally for projects or equipment which significantly assist the development of the recipient's work, but occasionally, in the case of established organisations, help with continuing activities that have encountered funding difficulties.

Merseyside ongoing grants
About 30 organisations receive routine grants each year. The largest grants were £10,000 to PSS, £7,500 to Liverpool Council of Social Service, £5,000 to Local Solutions and £2,500 to Merseyside Youth Association. Smaller grants included those to Birkenhead School, Bluecoat Arts Centre, Liverpool One Parent Families, Liverpool Parish Church and Merseyside Buildings Preservation Trust.

The 'Holt Tradition'
One-off grants were given to 11 organisations, the largest of £7,500 went to the Society of Nautical Research. Other grants included National Museums and Galleries on Merseyside and Kirkby

Lonsdale Brow Heritage Group (£5,000 each) and Lake District Art Gallery and Museum Trust (£2,500). The regular annual subscriptions are small and declining in number, often going to bodies with which the Holt families or businesses had a connection. They included Liverpool Domestic Mission Society, Mersey Mission to Seamen, Merseyside & Deeside Outward Bound, Merseyside International Network, Royal Liverpool Seamen's Orphans Insititution, RNLI – Port of Liverpool Branch and Sail Training Association – Merseyside.

Elsewhere
Grants to 13 organisations totalled £17,000. The largest was £5,000 to Business in the Community, an organisation regularly supported by the trust. Other beneficiaries included Outward Bound Trust (£4,000), Berkshire Community Council and Dukes Barn (£2,000 each), CRISIS and FPWP Hibiscus (£1,000 each), Hypatia Trust and Imperial Cancer Research Fund (£500 each) with £200 each to Across, Age Concern Bracknell, ANWAB, St Francis Hospice and Streatham Youth Centre.

Exclusions No grants to individuals. Grants are not usually given to organisations outside Merseyside (see above for exceptions to this).

Applications In writing to the correspondent at any time.

The Homelands Charitable Trust

The New Church, health, social welfare
£242,000 (2001/02)
Beneficial area UK.

c/o Alliotts, Ingersoll House, 5th Floor, 9 Kingsway, London WC2B 6XF
Tel. 020 7240 9971
Correspondent N J Armstrong, Trustee
Trustees *D G W Ballard; N J Armstrong; Revd C Curry.*
CC Number 214322
Information available Information was provided by the trust.

General This trust was established in 1962, the settlors were four members of the Curry family and the original endowment was in the form of shares in the Curry company.

In 2001/02 the trust had assets of £5.7 million and a total income of £266,000. Grants were made totalling £242,000. Management and administration charges remained low at £10,000, including payments of £7,500 to a firm which had a trustee amongst its partners. Whilst wholly legal, these editors always regret such payments unless, in the words of the Charity Commission, 'there is no realistic alternative'.

No grants information was included in the accounts, although the following was included under the heading 'Future plans and commitments':

'The trustees intend to continue supporting registered charities with a bais towards:

1) General Conference of the New Church
2) medical research
3) care and protection of children
4) hospices.

'The trustees are aware of the proposed extension and refurbishment of the New Church Residential Centre in the Midlands at an estimated cost of £1.5 million and are considering a substantial donation towards this project.'

Exclusions No grants to individuals.

Applications In writing to the correspondent.

Sir Harold Hood's Charitable Trust

Roman Catholic

£431,000 (2000/01)

Beneficial area Worldwide.

31 Avenue Road, St John's Wood, London NW8 6DS

Tel. 020 7722 9088

Correspondent Sir Harold Hood, Trustee

Trustees *Sir Harold J Hood; Lady Ferelith R Hood; Kevin P Ney; Mrs Margaret Gresslin; Nicholas E True; Mrs A M True; James Hood.*

CC Number 225870

Information available Full accounts were on file at the Charity Commission.

General The trust supports Roman Catholic causes. In 2000/01 it had assets with a market value of £8.5 million and an income of £1.6 million including £1.4 million from additional shares and funds settled. Grants totalled £431,000, of which £269,000 was from the income fund and £162,000 from the capital fund. Management and administration costs were low at £5,500.

From the income funds, 40 grants were made, of which 26 were recurrent from the previous year. Grants ranged from £3,000 to £20,000. The largest included those to Hospital of St John & St Elizabeth (£20,000), Diocese of Kingstown – West Indies and Sisters of La Retraite – Clifton (£16,000 each) and Margaret Beaufort Institute of Theology, Hope Residential & Nursing Care – Cambridge and Housetop Centre, St Francis' Leprosy Guild (£10,000 each).

Smaller grants included those to Archdiocese of Birmingham, Cardinal Hulme Centre, Catholic Housing Aid Society, Little Sisters of the Poor – Dundee, Marriage Care and Sacred Heart Church – Frinton-on-Sea.

From the capital fund, 13 grants were given, all of which were recurrent. Grants ranged from £4,000 to £33,000. The largest went to Bourne Trust (£33,000), Craig Lodge – Argyll (£24,000), Downside Settlement and Duchess of Leeds Foundation (£20,000 each), Diocese of Brentwood (£17,000) and Coming Home Appeal – Clapham (£12,000).

Other grants went to Diocese of Aberdeen, Langsyde Schoool – South

Africa, Providence Row St Gregory's Charitable Trust and Westminster Cathedral.

Exclusions No grants for individuals.

Applications In writing to the correspondent. Applications are considered in late November and need to be received by October.

The Hope Trust

Temperance, reformed protestant churches

£119,000 (2000)

Beneficial area Worldwide, with a preference for Scotland.

Drummond Miller, 32 Moray Place, Edinburgh EH3 6BZ

Tel. 0131 226 5151

Correspondent Robert P Miller, Secretary

Trustees *Revd Prof. D W D Shaw; Prof. G M Newlands; Prof. D A S Ferguson; Revd G R Barr; Revd Dr Lylal; Carole Hope.*

CC Number SC000987

Information available Information was provided by the trust.

General This trust was established to promote the ideals of temperance in the areas of drink and drugs, and protestant church reform through education and the distribution of literature. In 2000 its income was £174,000. Grants towards temperance causes totalled £15,000, and other grants to causes related to the protestant reformed tradition in Scotland and worldwide totalled £104,000. PhD students of theology studying at Scottish universities were also supported.

Larger grants included those to Church of Scotland Priority Areas Fund (£11,000), World Alliance of Reformed Churches (£10,000), National Bible Society for Scotland (£4,000) and Feed the Minds and Waldensian Mission Aid (£3,000 each).

Exclusions No grants to gap year students, scholarship schemes or to any individuals, with the sole exception of PhD students of theology studying at Scottish universities. No grants for the refurbishment of property.

Applications In writing to the correspondent. The trustees meet to consider applications in June and

December each year. Applications should be submitted by mid-May or mid-November each year.

Hospital Saturday Fund Charitable Trust

Medical, health

£120,000 to organisations (2000/01)

Beneficial area UK, the Republic of Ireland and overseas.

24 Upper Ground, London SE1 9PD

Tel. 020 7928 6662 **Fax** 020 7928 0446

Email trust@hsf.co.uk

Correspondent K R Bradley, Administrator

Trustees *K R Bradley, Chair; D C Barnes; L I Fellman; P P Groat; Miss I Racher; A F Tierney; Mrs L M C Warner.*

CC Number 327693

Information available Full accounts were on file at the Charity Commission.

General The Hospital Saturday Fund is a healthcare cash plan organisation, which was founded in 1873. In 1987 it established a charitable trust to support a wide range of hospitals, hospices and medical charities for care and research, as well as welfare organisations providing similar services. The trustees are now trying to provide more support to smaller, lesser-known charities connected with diseases and disabilities about which there is little public awareness. Individuals can also be supported by the trust, usually for special equipment to relieve their condition or in cases where their health has contributed to their financial hardship, although sponsorship can be given to people studying for a medically-related career.

In 2000/01 the trust had assets of £147,000 and an income of £139,000, including a donation of £128,000 for the Hospital Saturday Fund. Grants totalled £131,000 and were broken down as follows:

Category	No. of grants	Total
Charities, hospitals and hospices	225	£120,000
Sponsorship	12	£1,800
Individuals 9	0	£8,900

Apart from the £1,000 given to Glasgow Royal Infirmary, all grants to organisations were of £650 in the Republic of Ireland and £500 elsewhere. They were broken down as follows:

UK: 76 charities were supported.
Beneficiaries included Child Poverty Action Group, Dermatrust, IMPACT Foundation, Manningford Trust and Women's Royal Voluntary Service.

South east England and London: 21 hospitals and 19 charities.
Recipients included Action for Independence in Merton, Greenwich and Bexley Cottage Hospice, Link Centre for Deafened People – Eastbourne, Peace Hospice – Watford, Sight Centre – London and Spadework – Kent.

Wales and south west England: 8 hospitals and 9 charities.
These included Broadway Trust – Weston-super-Mare, Friends of Medilinc – Redruth, Leukaemia Lifeline – Bristol and Ty Hafan Children's Hospice – Cardiff.

Midlands and north of England: 9 hospitals and 9 charities.
Recipients included Byker Bridge Housing Association, East Anglia Children's Hospices, Movement Foundation – Oswestry and Royal Schools for the Deaf – Manchester.

Scotland: 12 hospitals and 20 charities.
As well as Glasgow Royal Infirmary, other beneficiaries included Crossroads – Glasgow, Hansel Foundation – Ayrshire, Milestone House – Edinburgh and Scottish Council on Alcohol.

Northern Ireland and Isle of Man: 2 hospitals and 4 charities.
These included Blind Centre for Northern Ireland, Northern Ireland Association for Mental Health, St Bridget's Hospice – Douglas and Sargent Cancer Care for Children.

Republic of Ireland: 8 hospitals and 27 charities
Recipients included Brothers of Charity – Galway, Carlour Kilkenny Homecare Unit, Donegal Hospice, Disabled People of Clare, Dublin Simon Community and L'Arche Dublin.

Overseas: 3 charities
Beneficiaries were Komso Children's Hospital – Russia, Medical Missionary Association and Relief Fund for Romania.

Exclusions Unless there are exceptional circumstances, organisations are not supported in successive years.

Applications Hospitals, hospices and medically-related charities are invited to write detailed letters or to send a brochure with an accompanying letter. There is a form for individuals to complete available from the personal assistant to the trust administrator.

The Hudson Foundation

Older people, general
£240,000 (1999/2000)
Beneficial area UK, with a preference for the Wisbech area.

12–13 The Crescent, Wisbech, Cambridge PE13 1EP
Tel. 01945 584113
Correspondent A D Salmon, Trustee
Trustees *P A Turner, Chair; M A Bunting; H A Godfrey; A D Salmon.*
CC Number 280332
Information available Full accounts were on file at the Charity Commission.

General The trust makes grants for general charitable purposes, although in practice groups caring for people who are elderly or infirm are more favoured. Grants are given mostly to organisations in the Wisbech area.

In 1999/2000 it had assets of £1.8 million and an income of £132,000 over half of which came from the activities of trading subsidiaries. In the year 12 grants were made totalling £240,000.

By far the largest grant was £157,000 to Ely Diocesan School Fund; this donation was made from designated funds. All other grants were made from the general fund and included those to: Wisbech Grammar School (£35,000), Alexandra House (£15,000), Methodist Homes for the Aged (£8,600), Wisbech Swimming Club (£8,000), Wisbech St Mary PCC (£5,200), Royal Naval Football Association (£1,500) and Wisbech and Fenland Museum (£300).

Applications In writing to the correspondent. Applications are considered throughout the year.

The Huggard Charitable Trust

General
£97,000 (2000/01)
Beneficial area UK, with a preference for south Wales.

Blacklands Farm, Five Mile Lane, Bonvilston, Cardiff CF5 6TQ
Correspondent S J Thomas, Trustee
Trustees *Mrs E M Huggard; T R W Davies; S J Thomas.*
CC Number 327501
Information available Accounts were on file at the Charity Commission.

General In 2000/01 the trust had asset of £1.7 million and an income of £93,000. Grants to organisations totalled £97,000 (£209,000 in 1997/98).

The main beneficiary during the year was Amelia Methodist Trust in Llancarfan, which received £63,000. Just two other beneficiaries were listed in the accounts; Holme Tower Marie Curie Cancer Centre in Penarth and Ty Olwen Hospice in Morristown, both of which received £2,000. Grants under £2,000 totalled £30,000 and were not listed.

The trust has previously stated that it has supported a wide variety of organisations, including some major projects in south Wales which have received substantial funding. These have included the Amelia Trust Farm in the Vale of Glamorgan, Penrhys Community Partnership in the Rhondda Valley and Cardiff Action for the Single Homeless. For the future the trustees wish to concentrate on a specific list of organisations (about 80) whom they will support, and therefore do not seek applications from others.

Applications The trustees are not inviting applications for funds.

Miss Agnes H Hunter's Trust

Social welfare
£254,000 (1999/2000)
Beneficial area UK, with a preference for Scotland.

Robson McLean WS, 28 Abercromby Place, Edinburgh EH3 6QF
Tel. 0131 556 0556

Correspondent Mrs Jane Paterson, Grants Administrator

CC Number SC004843

Information available Information, but with no grants list, was supplied by the trust. An explanatory leaflet is also available from the correspondent.

General The trust was established in 1954. Its main aims are to support:

- charities for people who are blind in Scotland
- people who are disabled
- training and education for people who are disadvantaged
- research on the cause, relief or cure of cancer, tuberculosis or rheumatism.

These aims are currently being pursued in the following areas: children and family support, youth development, older people, homelessness, physical and mental illness.

The trustees are highly selective and priority is given to Scottish projects. The trustees review their policies periodically and areas of interest may change.

Grants range from £500 to £8,000, although they are usually not higher than £5,000. In 1999/2000 the trust gave 67 grants totalling £254,000. Further information was not available for this year.

Its capital assets in property and investments were valued at £3.4 million in 1997/98. In that year 55 grants totalling £224,000 were approved. A grants list was not provided.

Exclusions No grants to individuals, or to organisations under the control of the UK government.

Applications Applicants should write, in the first instance, to request the trust's guidance notes. The closing dates for final applications are 15 January and 1 September every year.

Hurdale Charity Limited

Jewish

£388,000 (1999/2000)

Beneficial area Worldwide.

54–56 Euston Street, London NW1 2ES

Tel. 020 7387 0155 **Fax** 020 7388 4758

Correspondent The Trustees

Trustees M Oestreicher; Mrs E Oestreicher.

CC Number 276997

Information available Accounts were on file at the Charity Commission, but without a grants list.

General In 1999/2000 the trust had assets of £1.2 million, an income of £1.4 million, mainly from donations, and a total expenditure of £459,000. Grants totalled £388,000.

No grants information was included in the accounts, but the report stated it had 'continued its philanthropic activities in support of religious, educational and other charitable institutions'. The trust supports Jewish organisations that are seen to uphold the Jewish way of life, both in the UK and overseas.

In 1994/95, the last year when a grants list was available, grants totalled £197,000; most were for £2,000 or more. The largest went to Imrei Chaim College (£28,000), Gemilas Chesed & Endowment of Bride Bridal Society (£21,000) and Mesifta Talmudical College (£17,000).

Applications In writing to the trustees.

The Hyde Charitable Trust

Disadvantaged children and young people

£71,000 (2001/02)

Beneficial area UK, with a preference for the south of England including Greater London.

Youth Plus London Regional Office, Hollingsworth House, 181 Lewisham High Street, London SE13 6AA

Tel. 020 8297 7575 **Fax** 020 8297 7565

Email Scott.mckinven@hyde-housing.co.uk

Website www.hyde-housing.co.uk

Correspondent Scott McKinven

Trustees D Small, Chair; B Bishop; P Breathwick; R Finlinson; J Fitzmaurice; V Stead; R Collins.

CC Number 289888

Information available Information was provided by the trust.

General This trust works closely with organisations addressing the needs of children and young people who are disadvantaged in the areas in which the Hyde Group operates. One-off grants will be considered for core, capital and project

costs; funding is available for three years or more.

In 2001/02 the trust had assets of £686,000 and an income of £82,000. Grants were made totalling £71,000.

The following projects were supported: Deptford Youth Project (£28,000), Respond (£15,000), NACRO (£11,000), Islington Women's Aid (£10,000) and Learning to be Local (£4,000).

Exclusions No grants to individuals, medical research, hospices, residential homes for older people, and any other projects the trustees decide fall outside the main criteria.

Applications In writing to the correspondent.

The Idlewild Trust

Performing arts, culture, restoration & conservation, occasional arts education

£136,000 (2001)

Beneficial area UK.

54–56 Knatchbull Road, London SE5 9QY

Tel. 020 7274 2266 **Fax** 020 7274 5222

Email idlewildtrust@lineone.net

Correspondent Mrs Angela Freestone, Administrator

Trustees *Lady Judith Goodison, Chair; Mrs A S Bucks; M H Davenport; J C Gale; Mrs A C Grellier; A Ford; M Wilson.*

CC Number 268124

Information available Full accounts and annual report were provided by the trust.

General The trust was founded in 1974 by Peter Brissault Minet, who had previously set up the Peter Minet Trust (see separate entry). Its policy is to support charities concerned with the encouragement of performing and fine arts and preservation for the benefit of the public of lands, buildings and other objects of beauty or historic interest. Occasionally support is given to bodies for educational bursaries in these fields or for conservation of the natural environment. The trust prefers to support UK-charities and it is unlikely to support a project of local interest only.

In 2001 the trust had assets of £3.7 million and an income of £156,000; 58 grants were made totalling £136,000 and ranged from £500 to £5,000.

Grants were categorised in the trust's annual report as follows:

Category	No. grants	Total £
Education in the arts	11	23,000
Performing arts	11	25,000
Museum and galleries	11	28,000
Preservation and restoration	15	36,000
Fine art	5	13,000
Nature/conservation	51	2,000

The largest grants were £5,000 each to St Mary's Church – Banbury and Moggerhanger House Preservation Trust. Natural History Museum received to grants totalling £6,000. Other grants included: £4,000 each to Council for Music in Hospitals, Courtauld Institute of Art, Great Hospital – Norwich, Reading University Library and Verulanium Museums Trust; £3,000 each to Dorset Opera, National Trust, Norfolk Wildlife Trust, Sinfonietta Productions Limited, Wey & Arun Canal Trust and Youth Brass 2000; £2,000 to Royal Academy of Arts, University of Bristol and Whitby Literary Society; £1,500 to Kala Chethena Kathakali Theatre Co.; £1,000 to Cotswold Canals Trust and Uppingham PCC; and £500 to All Saints – Highfield.

Exclusions Grants to registered charities only. No grants are made to individuals. The trust will not give to:

- repetitive UK-wide appeals by large charities
- appeals where all, or most, of the beneficiaries live outside the UK
- local appeals unless the artistic significance of the project is of more than local importance
- appeals whose sole or main purpose is to make grants from the funds collected
- endowment or deficit funding.

Applications On a form available from the correspondent, which can be sent via post or e-mailed as a Microsoft Word file. Applications should include the following information:

- budget breakdown (one page)
- most recent audited accounts
- a list of other sponsors, including those applied to
- other relevant information.

Potential applicants are welcome to telephone the trust on Tuesdays or Wednesdays between 10am and 4pm to discuss their application and check eligibility. Trustees meet twice a year in March and November.

All eligible applications, which are put forward to the trustees, are acknowledged; other applications will not be acknowledged unless an sae is enclosed. Applications from organisations within 18 months of a previous grant will not be considered.

The Iliffe Family Charitable Trust

Medical, disability, heritage, education

£196,000 (2000/01)

Beneficial area UK.

Barn Close, Yattendon, Berkshire RG18 0UY

Correspondent Miss Julia Peel, Secretary to the Trustees

Trustees *N G E Petter; G A Bremner; Lord Iliffe; The Hon. Edward Iliffe.*

CC Number 273437

Information available Full accounts were on file at the Charity Commission.

General The trust gives grants towards groups concerned with medical causes, disability, heritage and education. The bulk of the grants made are to charities already known to the trustees, to which funds are committed from year to year. Other donations are made for a wide range of charitable purposes in which the trust has a special interest.

In 2000/01 the trust had assets of £1.6 million and an income of £125,000. Grants totalled £196,000, and ranged from £100 to £25,000.

The largest grants were £25,000 to Sherborne School Foundation, £15,000 to Arthur Rank Centre General Fund, £10,000 each to National and Cornwall Maritime Museum Trust, Royal Naval Museum – Portsmouth, The Jim and Olga Lloyd Trust, Game Conservancy Trust, Coventry Cathedral Development Trust and the University of Reading, £8,800 to Berkshire Community Foundation and £6,000 to Heartlands Cystic Fibrosis Centre Appeal.

Other beneficiaries include Bradfield College G C Fund (£5,000), Berkshire Community Foundation (£3,800), Social Affairs Unit (£2,500), Yattendon and Frilsham Christian Stewardship, Park House Sports College and CPU Press Training (£1,500 each), Farm Africa and Rhino Rescue (£1,000 each), British Heart Foundation (£500) and Cancer Research Campaign (£250).

Exclusions No grants to individuals and rarely to non-registered charities.

Applications In writing to the correspondent. Only successful applications will be acknowleged. Grants are considered at ad hoc meetings of the trustees, held throughout the year.

The Inland Waterways Association

Inland waterways

£110,000 (2001)

Beneficial area UK and Ireland.

c/o IWA Head Office, P O Box 114, Rickmansworth WD3 1ZY

Tel. 01923 711114 **Fax** 01923 897000

Email iwa@waterways.org.uk

Website www.waterways.org.uk

Correspondent The Chairman of the IWA Restoration Committee

Trustees *The Council of the Association.*

CC Number 212342

Information available Accounts were on file at the Charity Commission.

General The trust supports organisations promoting the restoration of inland waterways (i.e. canal and river navigations).

It makes grants for:

(a) construction, especially works relating to the restoration of navigation such as locks, bridges, aquaducts, culverts, weirs, pumps, excavation, dredging, lining and so on

(b) administration – support for a particular purpose, such as a project officer, a funding appeal or for promotional literature or events

(c) professional services, such as funding of feasibility studies or detailed work on engineering, economic or environmental issues

(d) land purchase

(e) research on matters affecting waterway restoration, including original research, reviews of research undertaken by others and literature reviews

(f) education, such as providing information to local authorities or agencies to promote the nature and benefits of waterway restoration.

Grants of up to £20,000 are made from the Restoration Grants Fund. In exceptional cases, larger grants can be made.

In 2001 the association had assets of £1.6 million and an income of £1 million. Grants were made totalling £110,000.

In the previous year, when grants totalled £33,000, offers of grants included: £20,000 to Wey & Arun Canal Trust towards the rebuilding of Drungewick Lane Canal Bridge; £4,500 to Lancaster Canal Northern Reaches Group for repairs to bridges near Holme and dredging at Millness; £3,000 to North Cornwall District Council towards essential repairs to the sea lock at Bude; and £1,000 each to a study into the impacts of user disturbance on wildlife led by British Waterways and to Worcester & Birmingham Canal Society. Grants were made to Lichfield & Hatherton Canals Restoration Trust and Wiltshire & Berkshire Canal Amenity Group for replacement and repair of working party machinery.

Exclusions No grants to individuals. No retrospective grants for projects where expenditure has already been incurred or committed.

Applications In writing to the correspondent. Applications should comply with the 'Guidelines for Applicants', also available from the correspondent. Each applicant should provide a full description of its proposal, show that the organisation can maintain a satisfactory financial position and demonstrate that it is capable of undertaking the proposed project.

Applications for up to £2,000 are assessed under a simplified procedure – each application should demonstrate that the grant would be used to initiate or sustain a restoration scheme or significantly benefit a specific small project.

Applications for over £2,000 should demonstrate that the grant would be applied to one of the types of projects (a–f). Applicants should also demonstrate the extent to which the project satisfies one or more of the following conditions:

- the grant would unlock (lever) a grant several times larger from another body
- the grant would not replace grants available from other sources
- the project does not qualify for grants from major funding sources
- the grant would enable a key project to be undertaken which would have a significant effect on the prospect of advancing the restoration and gaining funds from other sources for further restoration projects

- the result of the project would have a major influence over the progress of a number of other restoration projects
- The Inland Waterways Association Restoration Committee would have a major influence in the management of the project, including monitoring of expenditure.

The Inlight Trust

Religion
£127,000 (2000/01)
Beneficial area UK.

P O Box 2, Liss, Hampshire GU33 6YP
Correspondent Mrs Judy Hayward
Trustees *Sir Thomas Lucas; Michael Collishaw; Michael Meakin; Stuart Neil; Richard Wolfe; Wendy Collett.*
CC Number 236782
Information available Full accounts were provided by the trust.

General The trust makes grants for the advancement of religion only. It states that its funding priorities are: 'To make donations on an undenominational basis to charities providing valuable contributions to spiritual development and charities concerned with spiritual healing and spiritual growth through religious retreats.'

Grants are usually one-off for a specific project or part of a project. Bursary schemes may also be supported.

In 2000/01 the trust's assets totalled £3.8 million, it had an income of £131,000 and gave seven grants totalling £127,000. Grants were: £67,000 to White Eagle Lodge; £40,000 to Holy Island Project – Dumfriesshire; £5,000 each to Emmaus House, Great Ocean Dharma Refuge and Vairochara Buddhist Centre; £3,000 to International Interfaith Centre – Oxford; and £2,000 to Jamyang Buddhist Centre – London.

Exclusions Core funding or salaries are rarely considered. Non-registered charities are not supported. No grants are made to individuals, including students, or to general appeals from large UK organisations. Grants for church buildings are seldom made.

Applications In writing to the correspondent including details of the need the intended project is designed to meet plus an outline budget and the most recent available annual accounts of the charity. Only applications from eligible

bodies are acknowledged. Applications must be accompanied by a copy of your trust deed or of your entry in the Charity Commission register. Only successful applicants are informed.

Grants are considered at trustees' meetings four times a year in March, June, September and December and applications should be submitted two months before those meetings.

The Inman Charity

Social welfare, disability, older people, hospices
£252,000 (2000)
Beneficial area UK.

Payne Hicks Beech, 10 New Square, Lincoln's Inn, London WC2A 3QG
Correspondent The Trustees
Trustees *A L Walker; Miss B M A Strother; M R Matthews; Prof. J D Langdon.*
CC Number 261366
Information available Full accounts were on file at the Charity Commission.

General The trust states: 'The trust maintains a list of charitable organisations which it regularly supports and the list is reviewed half-yearly at the meeting of the directors. Surplus income funds are distributed to other charitable organisations during the year'. The trust aims to disburse £250,000 a year, including an annual bursary to Uppingham School (£14,000). This grant stands outside its main areas for support – disability, medical, research, older people and hospices.

In 2000 it had assets of £5.3 million generating an income of £228,000. Grants to 63 organisations totalled £252,000. After the grant of £14,000 to Uppingham School – Victor Inman Bursary Fund, remaining grants were in the range of £1,000 to £7,500. Beneficiaries of larger grants Deafblind UK (£11,000) and Counsel and Care for the Elderly, Gurkha Welfare Trust, National Benevolent Fund for the Aged, Queen Elizabeth's Foundation for the Disabled, Samaritans and Winged Fellowship (£7,500 each).

Most other grants were for £3,000 or less. Beneficiaries included Cancer Resource Centre, Guideposts Trust, New Bridge, Reach, Reading YMCA, Iain Rennie Hospice at Home, Women's Link,

Shaftesbury Society, Thrift Urban Housing and REMAP.

Exclusions No grants to individuals.

Applications In writing only to the correspondent, including up-to-date reports and accounts. Trustees meet half-yearly usually in March and September.

The Worshipful Company of Innholders General Charity Fund

General
£132,000 (1999/2000)
Beneficial area UK.

30 College Street, Dowgate Hall, London EC4R 2RH

Tel. 020 7236 6703 **Fax** 020 7236 0059

Email mail@innholders.co.uk

Correspondent The Clerk

Trustees *J R Edwardes Jones; Brian W Hall; Anthony C Lorkin; Sir Malcolm Chaplin.*

CC Number 270948

Information available Full accounts were on file at the Charity Commission.

General This trust supports children and young people, older people and education and training, particularly regarding the hotel industry.

In 1999/2000 the trust had assets of £489,000. Total income was £119,000, including £100,000 in donations received. Grants were made totalling £132,000, of which £110,000 was given in educational and research awards and £22,000 to other charities.

The largest grants were £45,000 to Research into Ageing and £32,000 to City of London Schools Scholarships.

Other beneficiaries included Tommy's Campaign (£12,000), Community Health South London NHS Trust (£6,000), Master Innholder Scholarships (£5,700), Treloar Trust (£5,000), Sail Training Association (£4,000), Master Innholders Charitable Trust (£3,000), Corporation of the Sons of the Clergy (£2,000) and Falklands Islands Memorial Chapel and Sports Aid (£1,000 each).

Exclusions No grants to individuals.

Applications In writing to the correspondent, including the reason for applying and current financial statements, etc.

The Inverforth Charitable Trust

General
£86,000 (2001)
Beneficial area UK (as a whole).

The Farm, Northington, Alresford, Hampshire SO24 9TH

Correspondent E A M Lee, Secretary and Treasurer

Trustees *Elizabeth Lady Inverforth; Lord Inverforth; Hon. Mrs Jonathan Kane; Michael Gee.*

CC Number 274132

Information available Full accounts were provided by the trust.

General The trust supports national charities only, especially 'small nationals'. A wide variety of causes are supported, including music, the arts, religion, heritage, health, youth, older people, education and disability. It has a core list of 50 organisations that receive grants each year. The trust usually supports around 75 other applicants annually. Since a recent change of policy, the trust now only provides £500 to be spent generally, including on covering core costs, rather than for projects or specific items, with the number of beneficiaries being reduced.

The 2001 trustees' report stated: 'By spreading its donations, the ICT avoids becoming too significant a funder of any charity, and does not require allocation of its funds to a new project, especially where the recipient's main activity is going well. In these times, when charities

are often a necessary filler of gaps in charitable activity, we support the creation of non-project orientated grant-making trusts such as ours, and feel their contribution to "trading" charities is valuable as well as appreciated.'

In 2001 the trust had assets of £3.3 million, which generated an income of £63,000. Management and administration costs were high at £25,000, including £23,000 in secretarial expenses despite the trust employing no staff. Grants were made to 131 organisations totalling £86,000, creating a deficit for the year of £110,000. This was much less than in the previous year when the trust had a similar income but spent £209,000 on grants, giving a deficit of £236,000. The accounts acknowledged this overspend and stated that they would take a more conservative approach to grantmaking in the next few years, as the changes mentioned above indicate.

Despite the large difference in grant totals in recent years, the percentage of grants by category appears to remain stable, as the breakdown in the table below shows.

Grants during 2001 ranged from £500 to £2,000. For example, beneficiaries listed under 'C' were Cancer Bacup, The Cassel Hospital, Cathedral Camps, CentrePoint, The Chantry Trust, ChildLine, Clonter Farm Music Trust, Crimestoppers Trust, Crisis, Crossroads – Caring for Carers and Cystic Fibrosis Trust; and those under 'R' were RAF Association, Rehearsal Orchestra, Relate – National Marriage Guidance Council, Remap, Remedi, Richard House Children's Hospice, Royal Hospital for Neuro-disability, Royal National Lifeboat Institution, Royal National Theatre, Royal Star and Garter Home and RPS Rainer.

Exclusions No grants are made to:

- local churches, village halls, schools and so on unless connected to the trust
- animal charities
- branches, affiliates or subsidiary charities
- individuals

THE INVERFORTH CHARITABLE TRUST				
	2001		2000	
category	total	%	total	%
music and the arts	£16,000	19%	£37,000	18%
churches, heritage etc.	£3,000	4%	£10,000	5%
health and mental health	£27,000	32%	£74,000	35%
hospices	£3,300	4%	£10,000	5%
youth and education	£3,300	4%	£4,500	2%
handicapped and aged	£15,000	17%	£33,000	16%
sundry (including international)	£14,000	16%	£34,000	16%

- advertisers or fundraising events
- organisations that have been supported in the last 12 months
- charities which are not registered in the UK
- charities with the word 'community' or a relevant place name in their title (which are unlikely to be considered by the trust as a national charity).

Applications In writing to the correspondent at least one month before meetings. No special forms are necessary, although accounts are desirable. A summary is prepared for the trustees, who meet quarterly in March, June, September and early December. Replies are normally sent to all applicants; allow up to four months for an answer or grant. Over 1,000 applications are received each year, producing a high failure rate for new applicants. The trust has stated that nearly half of all applicants are ineligible for support, so potential applicants should read 'exclusions' above carefully. Telephone calls are discouraged, particularly from ineligible applicants or people enquiring to see if they are eligible.

The Ireland Fund of Great Britain

Welfare, community, education, peace and reconciliation, the arts

£442,000 (2000)

Beneficial area Ireland and Great Britain.

158 Regent Street, London W1B 5SW

Tel. 020 7439 4299 **Fax** 020 7439 4298

Email irelandfundgb@btclick.com

Correspondent Aileen Ross, Director

Trustees Bryan Hayes, Chair; Josephine Hart; Hon. Kevin Pakenham; Dr Anthony O'Reilly; John Riordan; Gavin O'Reilly; Stanley Watson.

CC Number 327889

Information available Full accounts and other information was provided by the fund.

General The trust's grant application leaflet states: 'The Ireland Funds are a confederation of concern, connecting people around the world with Ireland, north and south. Through the generosity of those linked to Ireland in interest, ancestry and compassion, the organisation assists groups in Ireland whose initiatives serve the people of the island directly. The Ireland Funds are non-political and non-sectarian.

'Each year, The Ireland Fund supports hundreds of projects, north and south, which promote peace and reconciliation, arts and culture, community development and education. Grants range from a few hundred pounds to several thousand. For many projects, a seed grant from the funds provides the leverage necessary to qualify for additional monies from government agencies and other organisations.

'Founded in 1976 by Sir Anthony O'Reilly and a number of key American businessmen. The Ireland Funds now operate in 11 countries, i.e. Australia, Canada, France, Germany, Great Britain, Ireland, Japan, Mexico, Monaco, New Zealand and the United States.

'All of the funds' monies are secured from private sources, either by donors making contributions directly to the funds or by attending its many events. In 2001, for instance, the funds held approximately 65 events in 11 countries involving 25,000 people. The funds are growing rapidly as they translate the real affection and concern for Ireland worldwide into practical help and support.'

The following eligibility criteria for each programme is taken from the trust's website:

Arts and culture
'The funds wish to support excellence and innovation in arts activities within communities across the island and especially projects which make the arts more accessible to the wider community. In particular, The Ireland Funds will focus on the following:

- arts applied in settings of socio-economic disadvantage
- arts applied in educational or health settings
- arts promoting tolerance and reconciliation.

Community development
'Ireland is undergoing tremendous economic, social and cultural changes. The Ireland Funds are seeking ways to promote an inclusive and integrated society and to ensure the regeneration of marginalised urban and rural communities. The Funds see the following areas as priorities:

- increasing the capacity of the social economy
- support of rural development initiatives

- promotion of social inclusion
- promotion of tolerance and diversity.

Education
'Investment in education is investment in Ireland's future. Economic and social development depends on a well educated population. For this reason, The Ireland Funds will focus on programmes promoting and supporting:

- access and progression from second level to third level
- lifelong learning
- tolerance through education.

Peace and reconciliation
'The Ireland Funds are seeking to support communities in Northern Ireland working together and towards a shared future. The skills and culture of negotiation and compromise need to be honed politically and organisationally within and between communities. To this end, programmes supporting the following areas have been prioritised for assistance:

- citizenship and participation
- a greater understanding of cultural identity within and between communities
- social inclusion
- support for those affected by the troubles.

What The Ireland Funds are looking for:
'When assessing the merits of each application, The Ireland Funds' Advisory Committee shall be looking for the following:

- Is the application form fully completed? Is it clear what the group is proposing?
- Does the proposal address a particular problem? Has it been well researched and planned?
- What impact will the proposal have?
- Is the proposal creative and innovative?
- Is the project sustainable?
- Are the financial figures provided accurate? Is the proposal offering good value for money?
- What benefits does the organisation bring to the community? Is the Community involved in the planning and implementation stages of the proposal?
- Does the organisation have a good track record?'

In 2001 there were 26 beneficiaries in Britain. Beneficiaries included Comhaltas Ceoltoiri Eireann, Conference of Irish Historians in Britain, Cot Death Society, Cricklewood Homeless Concern, Irish Community Care – Manchester, Irish World Heritage Centre, Kilburn Irish Pensioners, London Irish Women's Centre, National Museums and Galleries on Merseyside and Triskellion Irish Theatre Company.

In 2000 the fund had assets of £156,000. Total income was £728,000, including £438,000 from functions and £282,000 in donations received. Grants were made to organisations totalling £442,000, broken down as follows:

Art – 6 grants totalling £13,000

Beneficiaries were Irish Women's Theatre (£3,500), Hammersmith Irish Centre and London Irish Centre (£3,000 each), Triskellion Theatre Company (£1,500) and Celtic Connections and Irish in Greenwich (£1,000 each).

Education – 11 grants totalling £115,000

Large grants were £50,000 to Newman Institute and £38,000 to All Hallows College. Other recipients included Culra na nog (£6,000), City Motor Sports (£4,000), Cairde na nGael (£3,000), Irish Support and Advice Service (£2,500), Shannon College of Hotel Management (£2,200), Clongowes Wood College (£1,500) and Ealing Irish Autism Support Group for Children (£1,000).

Alleviation of poverty/community care – 38 grants totalling £192,000

The largest grants were £42,000 to Tyrrell Trust and £30,000 to CORE.

Exclusions Grants are generally not given for: general appeals; purchase of buildings or land; major construction or repairs to buildings; other grant-making trusts; individuals; purchase of vehicles; debt repayment; tuition or student expenses; travel or transport costs; commercial trading businesses; replacement of statutory funding; medical research; or general administration.

Applications On a form available from the correspondent. In Ireland, applications are welcome between 1 October and 31 January, with successful applicants notified in early June. In Great Britain, the deadline for receipt of applications is 15 August with grants distributed in December/January.

'Notification of outcome will be by letter. In the meantime we would ask you not to contact the office, due to our small staff number. Lobbying will disqualify.'

There is a stringent application of the guidelines and exclusions criteria. Applicants must submit copies of their constitution and audited accounts before receiving funding. Projects supported must make regular reports of progress and monitoring as well as providing promotional material and publicity.

The Irish Youth Foundation (UK) Ltd

Irish young people

£184,000 (2000/01)

Beneficial area UK.

The Irish Centre, Blacks Road, Hammersmith, London W6 9DT

Tel. 020 8748 9640 **Fax** 020 8748 7386

Email info@iyf.org.uk

Website www.iyf.org.uk

Correspondent Linda Tanner, Administrator

Trustees J O'Hara, Chair; Mary Clancy; F Hucker; P Kelly; D Murray; John O'Neill; Nessa O'Neill; John Power; Colin McNicholas; Sean O'Neill.

CC Number 328265

Information available Full accounts, guidelines and other information was provided by the trust.

General This trust supports organisations anywhere in the UK working with young Irish people aged up to 25 who are socially or culturally disadvantaged. The foundation gets its annual income from fundraising events it stages, including golf days, ladies' lunches, musical events and an annual ball.

Funding is available for a wide range of projects, including training, counselling, drug rehabilitation, advice, advocacy, youth work, homelessness, education, cultural and social activities, disability and travellers. The trust will support projects or capacity building, recognising that improving resources and personnel is often the best way for projects to develop.

For applicants in England, Scotland and Wales, there are three categories of grant given. Small grants are of £2,000 or less and medium grants are for larger amounts which are less than £10,000; applications forms A or B should be used respectively. Large grants range from £10,000 to £25,000 and can be recurrent; they should be applied for using form C, which requests detailed information on the organisation, project, breakdown of beneficiaries, monitoring, budget and coordination with other services.

There is a separate programme for organisations based in Northern Ireland to those based on the British mainland. Grants are one-off of up to £5,000 each and can be used to extend an existing activity, to employ additional staff, to purchase equipment, undertake an evaluation, publish a report, improve organisational capacity or try something new and different.

In 2000/01 the trust gave grants totalling £184,000, of which £35,000 was given in total in eight grants in Northern Ireland and £149,000 in 38 grants elsewhere.

The largest grants in Northern Ireland were £5,000 each to Ardoyne Youth Club for a development sport programme for 10–12 year olds, Make Your Mark for an art therapy pilot project for young adults in the north west who are traumatised and Public Achievement for a one-year training and learning programme for volunteer coaches in civic youth work and community relations. Other grants were: £4,600 to Northern Ireland Children's Holiday Scheme for a young leaders training programme; £4,000 each to Children's Express for a report by young members for distribution to Belfast secondary schools and youth clubs, Drake Music Project Northern Ireland towards providing music technology workshops and performances to children and young people with physical disabilities and REACH Across for the spring induction programme which provided cross-community contact such as residential weekends for personal development training, group activities and international exchanges; and £3,500 to Newry Women's Aid towards developing the childcare programme.

Large grants given in England, Scotland and Wales were £20,000 to Irish Community Care – Manchester for the salary of a youth development coordinator, £13,000 to Irish Community Centre – Merseyside for a full-time worker's salary and £10,000 to London Irish Centre for the youth resettlement project.

Solas Anois – London received two grants during the year: £8,500 towards a children's playscheme and annual holiday and £8,100 for a part-time children's worker's salary. Other medium-sized grants included those to Irish Commission for Prisoners Overseas for the salary of an administration assistant (£9,000), Bristol Playbus for a junior youth community development worker's salary (£8,000), Immigrant Counselling and Psychotherapy for weekly counselling sessions (£5,000), Irish Charitable Trust towards the drug and alcohol rehabilitation and counselling programme (£4,000) and West Midlands School GAA for the Gaelic Games Primary Schools Initiative (£3,000).

Beneficiaries of small grants included Northampton Irish Support Group towards establishing an advice, information and advocacy service for the Irish community in Northampton (£2,000), The Maya Centre towards counselling and mothering support for young Irish women (£1,500), Celtic Connections in Wales for an Irish/Welsh exchange project including music, art and dance workshops (£1,000), Great Famine Commemoration Committee towards producing colour posters and information leaflets for schools on Merseyside (£750), St Benedict's Harp GAA – Leeds towards equipment replacement, trophies and injury scheme insurance (£500).

In the previous year, the foundation had assets of £57,000. Total income was £196,000, of which £191,00 came from donations received. Grants were made totalling £204,000.

Exclusions The foundation generally does not support: projects which cater for people over 25 years of age; individuals; general appeals; work in the arts, museums, or of an environmental nature; grants for academic research; educational bursaries; to substitute state support; alleviation of deficits already incurred; services run by statutory/public authorities; and major capital appeals.

Applications In writing to the correspondent, requesting an application form. The application period is short, with forms being available at the end of August to be returned by the third week of September. Applicants should photocopy and send six copies of the completed form if they are in Northern Ireland and eight copies if they work elsewhere. Applications are considered in November and all applicants notified in January. Applications are assessed on the following requirements: need; continuity; track record/evaluation; disadvantaged young people; innovativeness; funding sources; and budgetary control. Faxed applications are not considered.

The Ironmongers' Quincentenary Charitable Fund

General

£73,000 (2000/01)

Beneficial area UK.

Ironmongers' Hall, Barbican, London EC2Y 8AA

Tel. 020 7776 2311

Website www.ironhall.co.uk

Correspondent Ms H Sant, Charities Administrator

Trustees *Worshipful Ironmongers' Company.*

CC Number 238256

Information available Full accounts were on file at the Charity Commission.

General Set up under trust deed in 1964, the fund's assets stood at £1.9 million in 2000/01. Its income for the year was £177,000 and grants totalled £73,000. The accounts listed beneficiaries in receipt of awards over £1,000 each, divided as follows:

Crafts £9,400
The major beneficiary was Surrey Institute of Art and Design, which received funding towards travel bursaries (£2,200), equipment (£2,500) and an artist in residence (£2,500).

Universities and industry £13,000
Four universities were supported, each receiving £2,700. A grant of £1,800 was also made towards the Foundry Industry Jubilee Award.

National Trust and other restoration £32,000
The National Trust received a grant of £19,000. Grants for other restoration totalled £14,000 and included those to St John's School – Leatherhead (£5,000), Goose Green Centre (£2,000), Thornhill Primary School (£1,500) and St Christopher's Hospice (£1,300).

Other organisations £18,000
Beneficiaries included Lord Mayor's Appeal (£5,000), Arkwright Scholarship (£3,800), Guildhall School of Music and Drama (£2,100) and Army Cadets (£1,100).

Applications Applicants should send a brief outline of their work, including an sae. The trust will send an application

form to those which fit its criteria. The committee meets twice a year in March and October; applications should be received before the end of January and the end of August.

The J R S S T Charitable Trust

Democracy and social justice

£447,000 (2001)

Beneficial area UK.

The Garden House, Water End, York YO30 6WQ

Tel. 01904 625744

Website www.jrrt.org.uk

Correspondent Tina Walker

Trustees *Archibald J Kirkwood, Chair; Trevor A Smith (Lord Smith of Clifton); David A Currie (Lord Currie of Marylebone); Christine J Day; Christopher J Greenfield; Diana E Scott; Pam Giddy.*

CC Number 247498

Information available Full accounts were on file at the Charity Commission.

General The trust was originally endowed by the non-charitable Joseph Rowntree Reform Trust Ltd. It will consider and sometimes instigate charitable projects which relate specifically to the work of The Joseph Rowntree Reform Trust Ltd in supporting the development of an increasingly democratic and socially-just society in Great Britain.

In 2001 the trust had assets of £3.1 million and an income of £182,000. Grants totalled £467,000.

Grants included £354,000 to Institute for Citizenship – Democracy through Citizenship Project, £38,000 to Investigation in Private Finance Initiative, £34,000 to Future of Philanthropy Project and £25,000 to UK Noise Association.

Exclusions No student grants are funded.

Applications The trustees meet quarterly. They do not invite applications.

The Dorothy Jacobs Charity

Jewish care, medical

£62,000 (2001)

Beneficial area UK.

Heywards, St George's House, 15 Hanover Square, London W1R 0HE

Tel. 020 7629 7826

Correspondent R H Moss, Trustee

Trustees *R H Moss; A M Alexander.*

CC Number 328430

Information available Accounts were on file at the Charity Commission, but without a grants list or a narrative report.

General The trust was established in 1989 to provide 'relief of sickness by provision of medical aid and undertaking of medical research, advancement of education and relief of the elderly and infirm'.

The trust only supports the 15 nominated charities which are listed in the trust deed – three hospitals, four Jewish charities, three cancer-related charities, and five others: Arthritis and Rheumatism Council, BBC Children in Need, British Red Cross, Oxfam and Scope. Other charities are rarely supported, as there appears to be very little scope or money for this.

In 2001 the trust had assets of £592,000 generating an income of £20,000. Grants totalled £23,000.

Applications The trust states that it cannot accept unsolicited applications.

The J P Jacobs Charitable Trust

Art, community, health, religion, youth

£178,000 (2000/01)

Beneficial area UK, with a preference for Merseyside, and overseas.

9 Southwood Park, Southwood Lawn Road, London N6 5SG

Tel. 020 8348 4287 **Fax** 020 8348 4287

Correspondent G Young

Trustees *David Swift; Paula Swift.*

CC Number 263161

Information available Full accounts were on file at the Charity Commission.

General This trust principally supports organisations working in the fields of art, religion, community, health research and youth. There is a preference for supporting causes on Merseyside, although less emphasis has been placed upon this in recent years.

Grants range from £50 to £7,500, although they are usually of £1,000 or less. The 2000/01 annual report stated: 'Some income is accumulated with the intent of making larger specific donations. None of the charity's funds are restricted or designated.'

In 2000/01 the trust had assets of £1.7 million, which generated an income of £108,000. Grants were made to 78 organisations totalling £178,000.

Actors Professional Centre Ltd received a large grant of £110,000 and a smaller grant of £10,000. The accounts stated that the larger grant 'was a specific donation, for a particular purpose, paid out of reserves' in line with the policy stated above of accumulated funds for this reason.

Other large grants were to Lake District Art Gallery (£7,500 each), Liverpool Jewish Youth Centre and New Israel Fund of Great Britain (£5,000 each), Cumbria Rivers Foundation (£3,000) and Cambridge Foundation and Handel House Trust (£2,500 each).

Recipients of £1,000 each were Arthritis Care, British Red Cross, Marie Curie Cancer Care, Eden Project, Terrence Higgins Trust, Howard League for Penal Reform, Iris Trust, Helena Kennedy Bursary, Macmillan Cancer Relief, Mencap, Mind, Motability, One World Action, Oxfam, The Passage Day Centre, Royal Academy, Royal National Institute for the Deaf, Shelter, Stonewall Lobby Group and YMCA. All other grants were for £50 to £500 each.

Exclusions No support for individuals.

Applications The trust stated that funds are fully committed and new applications cannot be considered.

The James Pantyfedwen Foundation

Religion, education, general, in Wales

£166,000 to organisations (2001/02)

Beneficial area Wales.

Pantyfedwen, 9 Market Street, Aberystwyth SY23 1DL

Tel. 01970 612806 **Fax** 01970 612806

Email pantyfedwen@btinternet.com

Correspondent Richard H Morgan, Executive Secretary

Trustees *There are 24 trustees in all. A full list is available in the annual report. It includes Emrys Wynn Jones, Chair.*

CC Number 1069598

Information available Accounts and separate annual report with most grants listed and some narrative analysis.

General The foundation resulted from a merger of the John and Rhys Thomas James Foundation and the Catherine and Lady Grace James Foundation in April 1998. The original foundations were set-up by Sir D J James who established the first 'super' cinema in London (the Palladium in Palmers Green) and owned 13 other pre-war cinemas.

The foundation states that 'priority is given to "local" charities. UK-wide charities can apply but the project for which money is being sought must be of benefit to the people of Wales'.

Applications are considered from (a) students following approved courses mainly of a postgraduate nature, (b) churches for the repair of the fabric, and (c) registered charities for capital expenditure only. Salaries and general revenue costs are not considered. Grants are one-off for capital expenditure such as building improvements, items of office furniture and play equipment. Grants ranged between £30 and £8,000 and were given to church buildings, Eisteddfodau (Welsh arts festivals), students and general charities in Wales.

In 2001/02 the foundation had assets of £9.5 million and an income of £425,000. Grants were paid totalling £273,000, with £166,000 given to organisations.

Grants were allocated as follows:

Educational purposes	£106,000
Religious buildings	£58,000
Religious purposes	£47,000
(ministerial students, religious charities, denominational stipend and pension funds, Sunday schools)	
Eisteddfodau	£41,000
Registered charities	£20,000
Books	£1,000

Religious buildings

The largest grants went to Woodville Baptist Church – Cardiff and Eaton Road Methodist Church – Swansea (£5,000 each). Other beneficiaries included St Mary the Virgin – Troedrhiwgarth, St Michael – Maesteg, Capel Coffa Henry Rees Presbyterian Church – Llansannan and Peniel Evangelical Church – Maesteg (£3,000 each), St John the Evangelist – Cilybebyll, St John the Baptist – Cardiff, Seion Baptist Church – Maerdy and Saron Congregational Church – Aberdare (£2,000 each), and St Issell – Haroldston, Bethel Baptist Church – Tumble, Caeronnen Unitarian Church – Aberdare (£1,000 each).

Registered charities

The largest grants went to Urdd Gobaith Cymru (£4,000), Unitarian Churches Ministerial Training Fund (£3,000), Neuadd Ddyfi (£2,000), and Centre for Advanced Welsh and Celtic Studies, The Harriet Davies Trust, The Mansel Thomas Trust, Wales Videon Gallery and Llandudoch Memorial Hall (£1,000 each). Grants of £500 or less included those to The Albert Hall – Llandrindod Wells, Welsh Kite Trust – Llandrindod Wells, Pantyfedwen Village Hall and Beacon of Hope – Aberystwyth.

The foundation made grants to 29 students who are undertaking research work or postgraduate study, thirteen of whom received bursaries of £6,000 each. Grants to denominational stipend and pension funds totalled £34,500. A total of 50 grants were paid to Eisteddfodau, the largest being to the National Eisteddfod in Denbigh (£8,000), and 20 to Sunday schools, mostly for £500 or less.

Applications Applications should be made on a form available from the correspondent. Applications from churches and registered charities can be submitted at any time (trustees meet about five times a year in March, May, July, September and December); student applications should be submitted before 31 July in the academic year for which the application is being made. All unsuccessful applicants receive a reply.

The John Jarrold Trust

Arts, churches, environment/ conservation, third world, social welfare, medical research

£173,000 (2001/02)

Beneficial area UK and overseas, but mostly Norfolk.

Messrs Jarrold & Sons, Whitefriars, Norwich NR3 1SH

Tel. 01603 660211

Correspondent Brian Thompson, Secretary

Trustees A C Jarrold, Chair; R E Jarrold; P J Jarrold; Mrs D J Jarrold; Mrs J Jarrold; Mrs A G Jarrold; Mrs W A L Jarrold.

CC Number 242029

Information available Full accounts were on file at the Charity Commission.

General The trust supports a wide range of organisations including churches, medical, arts, environment/conservation, welfare and overseas aid. It prefers to support specific projects, rather than contribute to general funding. In practice, most of the funds are given in Norfolk.

In 2001/02 the trust had assets of £1.5 million, which generated an income of £107,000. Grants were made to 274 organisations totalling £173,000, broken down as follows:

The arts – 37 grants totalling £43,000
The largest grants were £11,000 to Northern Ballet Theatre, £10,000 to Broadland Music Festival and £5,000 to Christopher Hepworth Organs Trust. Other grants included £2,000 to Theatre Royal Norfolk Schools Project, £1,000 to Norwich Arts Centre, £500 each to History of Advertising Trust and Pilgrim Players, £250 each to Folk Norfolk, Musical Keys and Norwich School of Art and Design, £150 to Frontier Publishing and £100 each to Rig-a-jig-jig and National Youth Music Theatre.

Schools/education – 29 grants totalling £6,500
These included 17 school prizes of £25 each. Other grants included those to UEA School of English and American Studies (£2,000), Thorpe St Andrew School (£1,000), Arkwright Scholarship Trust (£750), Harford Manor School (£250), Oriel High School (£100) and Cawston VC Primary School.

Social welfare and community – 92 grants totalling £48,000
Beneficiaries included UEA Sports Park (£8,000), The Hamlet Centre (£3,000), Norwich Mark Place Ideas Competition (£2,500), Prince's Trust (£2,000), Salvation Army and Tapping House Hospice (£1,000 each), Cathedral Camps, Escape Artists, Families House and RSPCA (£500 each), Army Benevolent Fund, ChildLine and Mid Norfolk Railway Preservation Trust (£250 each), Buckingham Emergency Food Appeal (£200), Royal British Legion and Norfolk Junior Chess (£100 each) and Norwich Sea Cadets (£57).

Medical – 27 grants totalling £27,000
These included £5,000 to East Anglian Air Ambulance, £2,000 each to Cancer Care Society, National Asthma Campaign and Wheelchair Children Association, £1,000 each to Alzheimer's Society, Break, National Autistic Society and Royal College of Surgeons, £500 each to Orchid Cancer Appeal and Starlight Children's Trust and £250 to Access Partnership.

Developing Countries – 27 grants totalling £10,000
Farm Africa and Leprosy Mission both received two grants, one of £1,000 and one of £500. Other grants included £1,000 each to Concern, Feed the Minds and Sight Savers International and £100 to Otjiwaranjo Veterinary Clinic.

Ecclesiastical – 29 grants totalling £28,000
By far the largest grant was £12,000 to Norwich Cathedral Trust. Other beneficiaries included St Peter's Church – Cringleford (£2,000), Octagon Organ Appeal (£1,500), Chelmsford Cathedral and Peterborough Cathedral Trust (£1,000 each), Diss Methodist Church and Holy Innocents Church – Foulsham (£500 each) and RC Diocese of East Anglia (£100).

Environment – 9 grants totalling £9,500
Norfolk Wildlife Trust received three grants totalling £6,300. Other recipients included National Trust for the Neptune coastline and Plantation Garden Preservation Trust (£1,000 each), The Green Quay and Plantlife (£500 each) and ACF Wilderness Expedition – South Africa and Benjamin Britten High School (£100 each).

Exclusions Educational purposes that should be supported by the state will not be helped by the trust. Local groups outside of Norfolk are very unlikely to be supported unless there is a personal connection to the trust.

Applications Applications should be in writing and reach the correspondent before the trustees' meetings in January and July. Grants of up to £250 can be made between meetings.

Rees Jeffreys Road Fund

Road and transport research and education

£360,000 (2001)

Beneficial area UK.

13 The Avenue, Chichester, West Sussex PO19 4PX

Tel. 01243 787013 **Fax** 01243 790622

Email fieldhouse@reesjeffreys.co.uk

Correspondent B Fieldhouse, Secretary

Trustees *P W Bryant, Chair; D Bayliss; Prof. S Glaister; M N T Cottell; Mrs June Bridgeman; Sir James Duncan; M J Kendrick; Prof. J Wootton.*

CC Number 217771

Information available Report and accounts with full grants list, explanation of grants, and descriptions of the trust's history and objects.

General This trust was established in 1950 by the sole settlor, the late William Rees Jeffreys. Mr Rees Jeffreys was a 'road enthusiast' and was described by Lloyd George as 'the greatest authority on roads in the United Kingdom and one the of the greatest in the world'. The fund is just one legacy of a life time dedicated to the improvement of roads; Rees Jeffreys was the author of an historical and autobiographical record of sixty years of road improvement (The King's Highway, published 1949) which is introduced by the words 'I early knew my mission in life'. Ironically, given the conquering of the roads by the petrol engine and cycling's shift off-road, he was also a very keen cyclist.

The fund 'gives financial support for research to improve the quality and efficiency of roads and their use by vehicles, cyclists, pedestrians and public transport'.

The trust's priorities are:

• Education of transport professionals, largely through financial support for teaching staff and bursaries for postgraduate studies. The trust is concerned about the supply of trained professionals and has launched a study of future requirements.

• Stimulating research into all aspects of roads, road usage and road traffic – this commands a large share of the trust's budget. The trust develops its own research programmes as well as responding to proposals from recognised agencies and researchers. Proposals are assessed against prevailing transport issues, such as environmental questions, congestion, modal choice and resource development.

• Roadside environment. Applications for the provision of roadside rests are welcome, while support for the work of country wildlife trusts for improving land adjoining main roads is also maintained. The trust is not normally able to buy land or to fund improvements to roads, footpaths or cycle tracks.

The trust will support projects and pump-priming for longer-term ventures for up to a maximum of five years. Operational or administrative staff costs are rarely supported. In almost all cases applicants are expected to provide or arrange match funding.

In 2001 the fund had assets of £6.8 million and an income of £248,000. Grants in the range of £450 to £30,000 totalled £360,000, divided as follows:

Research and general	£162,000
Education	£123,000
Physical projects	£75,000

Research and other projects

Grants were given to 15 organisations, ranging from £2,500 to £30,000. Two grants of £30,000 each went to Independent Transport Commission for research on transport pricing, taxation and investment and to Leeds University towards an international knowledge-base of Urban Transport Instruments. Other grants included: £25,000 to Transport Research laboratory towards a study into demand for public transport; £15,000 to Nottingham University for research into the design and maintenance of lightly trafficked roads; £10,000 to National Children's Bureau towards IT programmes and training for developing and linking school to 'Young Transnet'; £5,000 to the Bicycle Helmet Trust towards promotional material; £4,800 to Environmental Transport Planning towards the costs of printing a report on decisive factors in the success of light rail; and £250 to Cycle West to help with research and production of a cycle-friendly employer guide.

Education

This category included £99,000 for academic posts and studentships; and £23,000 in support of PhD research.

Physical projects

Grants to 11 organisations ranged from £800 to £30,000. The largest grant went to National Urban Forestry Unit to extend the Road Corridor Greening Programme. Others grants included: £10,000 each to the Greensand Trust for facilities at layby A6 south of Bedford, and Highways Agency for a picnic site at Haggerston Castle – Northumberland; £4,800 to Transport Planning Skills for a brochure on transport postgraduate courses; and £800 to West Lothian Council for Newton layby. Six wildlife trusts also received grants of between £3,000 and £5,000 for specific areas.

Exclusions Operational and administrative staff costs are rarely considered. Grants are not given to environmental projects not related to highways, individual works for cycle tracks or works of only local application.

Applications There is no set form of application for grants. Brief details should be submitted initially. Replies are sent to all applicants. A preliminary telephone call is helpful but not essential. The trustees meet five times in the year, usually in January, April, July, September and November.

The Jenour Foundation

General

£97,000 (2000/01)

Beneficial area UK, with a special interest in Wales.

Deloitte & Touche, Blenhein House, Fitzalan Court, Newport Road, Cardiff CF24 0TS

Tel. 029 2048 1111

Correspondent Sir Peter Phillips, Trustee

Trustees *Sir P J Phillips; G R Camfield; D M Jones.*

CC Number 256637

Information available Full accounts were on file at the Charity Commission.

General This foundation has general charitable purposes, with a preference for Welsh causes.

In 2000/01 it had assets of £2.4 million, which generated an income of £100,000. Grants totalling £97,000 were made to 35 organisations, only 3 of which were not also supported in the previous year.

Welsh beneficiaries were Atlantic College and Wales National Opera (£6,000 each), Children's Hospital for Wales (£5,000), Princess of Wales Macmillan Cancer Care Centre (£4,000), NSPCC Cardiff Central Committee and Wales Council for the Blind (£3,500 each), Provincial Grand Lodge of Monmouth (£3,000), Representative Body of the Church of Wales and RNLI – Welsh District (£2,000 each), Bridgend YMCA Gymnastics Club (£1,500), with £1,000 each to Help the Aged for the Cardiff safety handy van, Maes Y Dyfan, Parish of Llanishen and Lisvane Church and Welsh St Donats Arts.

Beneficiaries elsewhere included Red Cross International (£8,000), British Heart Foundation and Cancer Research Campaign (£5,000 each), Save the Children (£4,000), Bath Institute of Medical Engineering and SCOPE (£3,000 each), Army Benevolent Fund (£2,500), British Deaf Society and Samaritans (£2,000 each), Multiple Sclerosis Society and Physiotherapy Training Fund (£1,000 each) and Society for the Welfare of Horses and Ponies (£500).

Exclusions No support for individuals.

Applications Applications should be in writing and reach the correspondent by February for the trustees meeting in March.

The Jephcott Charitable Trust

Alleviation of poverty in developing countries, general

£97,000 (2000/01)

Beneficial area UK, developing countries overseas.

Cotley, Streatham Rise, Exeter EX4 4PE

Correspondent Mrs Meg Harris, Secretary

Trustees *Mrs M Jephcott, Chair; Dr P Davis; Judge A North; H Wolley; K Morgan; J Bunnell; Mrs C Thomas.*

CC Number 240915

Information available Accounts were provided by the trust.

General In the trust's 2000/01 annual report it states that it is particularly interested in giving grants for start-up costs.

Previously it has stated that its priorities are population control, education, health and the environment. Grants are usually for a specific project or part of a project. Core funding and/or salaries are rarely considered. 'Pump-priming' donations are offered – usually grants to new organisations and areas of work. As well as being reactive (responding to applications) the trust is becoming increasingly proactive.

The trustees are flexible in their approach, but take the following into account when considering a project:

- the ability to evaluate a project. With overseas projects local involvement is thought to be essential for on-going success
- the involvement of a third party e.g. ODA, NGOs, National Heritage
- financial: level of administration costs, reserves held within the group, etc.
- whether the project is basic or palliative
- whether it is one-off or on-going
- to what extent the organisation helped themselves.

In 2000/01 the trust's assets stood at £4.6 million giving an income of £198,000. A total of £97,000 was given in 18 grants, ranging from £640 to £16,000.

By far the largest grant was £16,000 to Dorothea School in South Africa. Other grants included £9,400 to Bazaruto Archipelago – Mozambique, £7,800 to Get It While You Can, £6,600 to Speakeasy Advice Centre, £6,500 to Inroads, £6,300 to HOESO – Uganda, £6,000 to Kindu Trust and St Lukes' Khayelitsha Day Hospice – South Africa, £5,500 to Friends of Swanirvar, £5,000 to St Michaels Church, £3,400 to Computers for Africa, £2,500 to Faculty of Classics – Cambridge University, £1,800 to Springtime Crisis Pregnancy Centre – South Africa and £1,000 to Coventry Sea Scouts Group.

Exclusions No grants to individuals, including students, or for medical research. No response to general appeals from large, UK organisations nor from organisations concerned with poverty and education in the UK. Core funding and/or salaries are rarely considered.

Applications Guidelines and application forms are available on request and receipt of an sae. Applications can be made in writing at any time to the correspondent. Trustees meet twice a year (in April and October) and must have

detailed financial information about each project before they will make a decision. Only applications from eligible bodies are acknowledged, when further information about the project may be requested. Monitoring of grant expenditure is usually required.

Jewish Child's Day

Jewish children in need or with special needs

£355,000 (2000/01)

Beneficial area Worldwide.

5th Floor, 707 High Road, North Finchley, London N12 0BT

Tel. 020 8446 8804 **Fax** 020 8446 7370

Email info@jewishchildsday.co.uk

Website www.jewishchildsday.co.uk

Correspondent P Shaw, Executive Director

Trustees *The National Council.*

CC Number 209266

Information available Full accounts were on file at the Charity Commission.

General The trust was established in 1947 to encourage Jewish children in the UK to help less fortunate Jewish children who were survivors of the Nazi holocaust. Now it supports projects benefiting Jewish children in the UK or overseas. It disburses funds raised itself through appeals.

In 2000/01 it had assets of £725,000 and an income of £587,000. Grants totalled £355,000. The largest were £102,000 to Hamifal Educational Children's Home and £66,000 to Shalva.

Other beneficiaries included Eden Foundation (£18,000), Eliya (£8,300), Youth Aliya (£6,700), Micha Society for the Deaf – Tel Aviv (£6,600), Manchester Jewish Federation (£5,700), Gimmel Foundation (£5,100), Israel Crisis Management Centre and Mercaz Harmony (£5,000 each), Israel Sports Centre for the Disabled (£4,900), Chernobyl Children's Lifeline (£4,400), Association for Research into Stammering in Childhood and Crosgrove Care (£3,500 each), Binoch of London (£2,500), Beit University (£2,000), Camp Aguda (£1,000) and Bikur Cholim Hospital (£400).

Exclusions Individuals are not supported. Grants are not given towards general services, building or maintenance of property or staff salaries. No grants are made in response to general appeals from large UK organisations or to smaller bodies working in fields other than those set out above.

Applications There is an application form which needs to be submitted together with a copy of the latest annual report and accounts and any supporting information. The trustees meet to consider applications twice a year, usually in March and September/October, applications should be submitted two months earlier.

The trust states 'if you require any advice as to the eligibility of your application or assistance in preparing it please do not hesitate to contact us and we shall be happy to help.'

The Jewish Youth Fund

Jewish youth work

£72,000 (2000/01)

Beneficial area UK.

5th Floor, 707 High Road, North Finchley, London N12 0BT

Tel. 020 8445 1670 **Fax** 020 8446 7370

Email jyf@anjy.org

Correspondent Peter Shaw, Secretary

Trustees *Jonathan Gestetner; Richard McGratty; Lady Morris of Kenwood; Miss Wendy F Pollecoff.*

CC Number 251902

Information available Full accounts were on file at the Charity Commission.

General The fund's objectives are to promote and protect religious, moral, educational, physical and social interests of young members of the Jewish community in the UK.

In 2000/01 the trust had assets of £2 million, including properties in Kent and Lancashire, which generated an income of £114,000. Grants totalling £72,000 went to 18 organisations, 8 of which were also supported in the previous year.

The largest grants were £10,000 to Liverpool Jewish Youth and Community Centre, £7,500 to Habonim Dror, £5,400 to Redbridge Jewish Youth and Community Centre and £5,000 each to

Friends of Bnei Akiva, Jewish Lads and Girls Brigade, Noam Masorti Youth, SPEC Jewish Youth and Community Centre, and Union of Maccabi Associations.

Other beneficiaries were Kenton Maccabi Jewish Youth Club and North Manchester Jewish Youth Project (£4,000 each), Jewish Scouts Advisory Council (£3,000), Get Set Girls and Lubavitch Foundation (£2,500 each), Bushey Youth Scence and Southend Jewish Youth Centre (£2,000 each) with £1,500 each to B'Nei B'rith Youth Organisation, Friends of Jewish Servicemen and Golders Green Synagogue.

Exclusions Grants are not made in response to general appeals. Formal education is not supported.

Applications On an application form available from the correspondent, enclosing a copy of the latest accounts and an annual report.

The Joanna Herbert-Stepney Charitable Settlement (also known as The Paget Charitable Trust)

General, see below

£253,000 (2000/01)

Beneficial area Worldwide, with an interest in Loughborough.

Old Village Stores, Dippenhall Street, Crondall, Farnham, Surrey GU10 5NZ

Tel. 01252 850253

Correspondent Joanna Herbert-Stepney, Trustee

Trustees *Joanna Herbert-Stepney; Lesley Mary Blood; Mrs Joy Pollard.*

CC Number 327402

Information available Information was provided by the trust.

General The trust supports both UK and local charities for general charitable purposes. Priorities include international aid and development,

children who are disadvantaged, older people, animal welfare and environmental projects. The trust states that there is a preference for the 'unglamorous' and 'projects where a little money goes a long way'. In many cases ongoing support is given to organisations.

In 2000/01 the trust had assets of £3.7 million and an income of £183,000. After high administration and management costs of £51,000, the trust gave grants to 167 organisations totalling £253,000 – both the income and some of the capital funds were distributed.

Beneficiaries included Oxfam (£7,000), Peper Harrow Foundation and Manacare Foundation (£5,000 each), Royal Agricultural Benevolent Institute (£4,000), Help the Aged, Ockenden International, Soil Association and Tree Aid (£3,000 each), Dian Fossey Gorilla Fund, Children's Aid Direct, Alzheimer's Disease Society, ApTibeT, Eastern European Development Association, Health Unlimited and Clinical Service Foundation (£2,000 each).

Other beneficiaries included CHICKS, Childhope UK, Dodford Children's Holiday Farm, World Society for the Protection of Animals, Friends of the Earth Trust, Derbyshire Association for the Blind, Shelter and Crossroads (£1,000 each), Global Cancer Concern and Greenpeace Environmental Trust (£750 each) and St Andrew's Evangelical Mission (£500).

Exclusions The trust states that 'sheer need is paramount, in practice, nothing else is considered'. Grants are only given to registered UK charities. Overseas projects can only be funded via UK charities; no money can be sent overseas. The trust does not support individuals (including students), projects for people with mental disabilities, medical research or AIDS/HIV projects.

Applications In writing to the correspondent, there is no application form. The trustees meet in spring and autumn. The trust regrets that it cannot respond to all applications.

The Lillie Johnson Charitable Trust

Children, young people who are blind or deaf, medical

£230,000 (1998/99)

Beneficial area UK, with a preference for the west midlands.

Heathcote House, 136 Hagley Road, Edgbaston, Birmingham B16 9PN

Tel. 0121 454 4141

Correspondent Victor M C Lyttle, Trustee

Trustees *Victor Lyttle; Peter Adams.*

CC Number 326761

Information available Full accounts were on file at the Charity Commission.

General In 1988/89 the trust received £1.6 million from the estate of Miss L C Johnson. It mainly supports charities concerned with children or young people and medical causes.

In 1998/99 the trust had assets of £4.4 million generating an income of £183,000. Grants totalled £230,000.

The largest grants went to Birmingham Heartlands Hospital for their vascular disease project (£40,000), University of Birmingham for tinnitus research (£29,000) and Webb Care Services (£22,000). Other recipients included Primrose Hospice (£8,500), Edwards Trust (£7,000), BMOS Youth Theatre (£6,700), Scouts Association (£6,000), Queen Alexander College (£5,000), Pulse (£3,500), Birmingham Dogs Home and Warwickshire Junior Tennis Foundation (£2,000 each), Island Trust (£1,300) and £1,000 each to Acorn Hospital, Birmingham & District Theatre Guild, European Aid Trust, Mary Stevens Hospice, RSPCA Walsall and Shirley Round Table.

Exclusions No support for individuals.

Applications Applications are only considered from charities which are traditionally supported by the trust.

The H F Johnson Trust

Christian education

£68,000 (1999)

Beneficial area Worldwide, but mainly the UK.

PO Box 300, Kingstown Broadway, Carlisle, Cumbria CA3 0QS

Correspondent Miss Janet Busk

Trustees *Denis Colby; Miss Nancy B Johnson.*

CC Number 1050966

Information available Full accounts were on file at the Charity Commission.

General Established by trust deed in 1962, the trust's main object is the advancement of the Christain faith.

In 1999 the trust had assets of £984,000 and an income of £132,000, this came mainly from rental income from properties owned by the trust. Grants totalled £68,000.

Most of the trust's grant fund each year gives towards distributing Bibles and Christian books to state schools where teachers or heads are concerned with the promotion of good educational reading materials. In 1999 there were 159 schools supported at the cost of £46,000. There were also over 45 volunteers who visited schools to conduct assembly.

The trust listed nine other organisations which received grants in the year, four of which had been supported in the previous year. The largest grant was £5,000 to Tearfund. Two grants of £2,000 each went to Scripture Union and Manna Trust and £1,500 each went to Crusade for World Revival and St Paul's Church Kingston Hill. Grants of £1,000 went to Elim Pentecostal Church, CRIBS Trust, London Emmanuel Choir and Saltmine Trust.

An undisclosed number of smaller grants under £500 were made. Those going to Christian institutions totalled £5,200 and those to Christian evangelists totalled £1,600.

Applications The trust stated that it only supports organisations and individuals which are personally known to the trustees and requests that you do not write in.

The J E Joseph Charitable Fund

Jewish

£93,000 (2000/01)

Beneficial area UK, with a preference for London, the Far East, Israel and Palestine.

6 Lyon Meade, Stanmore, Middlesex HA7 1JA

Fax 020 7289 8780

Correspondent Roger J Leon, Secretary

Trustees *F D A Mocatta, Chair; D Silas; J H Corre; P S Gourgey; J S Horesh; S Frosh.*

CC Number 209058

Information available Full accounts were available at the Charity Commission.

General The trust was established for the benefit of Jewish communities; the relief of poverty; relief of suffering of poor Jews; advancement of education and the Jewish religion; and other purposes beneficial to Jewish communities. Grants are only given to or through Jewish organisations. In 1995/96 the trust decided to regularise its grantmaking in the following proportions:

Home organisations	55%
Israeli charities	35%
Eastern charities	5%
Sundry requests	5%

In 2000/01 the trust had assets of £3.7 million and an income of £112,000. Grants totalled £93,000 and were broken down by the trust as shown below:

Home – general	£33,000	(8 grants)
Home – schools	£24,000	(3)
Eastern	£5,000	(1)
Israeli	£31,000	(9)

'The trustees believe it inappropriate to disclose the names of grantees, being other charities and individuals.'

Exclusions Grants to individuals in exceptional cases only and are usually made to assist towards education and in particular further and higher education. No application from an organisation will be considered without a copy of its most recent set of accounts. Only Jewish individuals or organisations need apply.

Applications In writing to the correspondent. The trustees respond to all applications which are first vetted by the secretary.

The trust stated that many applications are unsuccessful as the number of application exceeds the amount available from limited income.

The Jungels-Winkler Charitable Foundation

Visually impaired – generally and in the arts

£512,000 (2000)

Beneficial area UK.

Herbert Smith, Exchange House, Primrose Street, London EC2A 2HS

Tel. 020 7374 8000 **Fax** 020 7374 0888

Correspondent Nicole Aubin-Parvu

Trustees *Gabrielle Jungels-Winkler; Jonathan Wood; Alexandra Jungels-Winkler; Christophe Jungels-Winkler.*

CC Number 1073523

Information available Information was provided by the trust.

General Grants are towards projects or charities for the benefit of people who are visually impaired, with some preference for those charities which are arts-related. The trustees are proactive in deciding which organisations benefit.

In 2000 the trust had an income of £1.3 million, nearly all of which can in donations received from the founder, who is one of the trustees. Grants were made to three organisations totalling £512,000. Assets at the year end stood at £784,000.

By far the largest grant was £500,000 to Royal Academy Trust. Courtauld Institute of Art at University of London received £9,700, after having received three grants totalling £125,000 in the previous year. The other grant was £2,000 to Committee of Hackney Carriage Drivers Charitable Trust, which was also supported in the previous year.

Applications In writing to the correspondent.

The Anton Jurgens Charitable Trust

Welfare, general

£309,000 (1999/2000)

Beneficial area UK, mainly the south east England.

Saffrey Champness, Lion House, 72–75 Red Lion Street, London WC1R 4GB

Tel. 020 7841 4000 **Fax** 020 7841 4100

Correspondent Michael J Jurgens, Trustee

Trustees *C V M Jurgens, Chair; J Jurgens; B W M Jurgens; E Deckers; M J Jurgens; F A V Jurgens.*

CC Number 259885

Information available Full accounts were on file at the Charity Commission.

General This trust has general charitable purposes, although welfare and children's groups feature prominently in the grants, as do organisations based in the south east of England.

In 1999/2000 the trust had assets of £8 million which generated an income of £406,000. Grants were made to 104 organisations totalling £309,000.

The largest grants were £12,000 to Tommy's Campaign at St Thomas Hospital, £10,000 each to Combat Stress, Fairbridge Mission, Gabbijas Truman and Tring Educational Trust, Hyperbaric Oxygen Trust and International Social Service of UK, £7,500 to Treloar Trust and £7,000 to Downside Clubs for Young People.

Beneficiaries in the south east of England included Alone in London (£5,000), 1st St Alban's Scout Group and Project Christchurch (£4,500 each), Winchester Crown Court Witness Service (£4,000), Essex Association of Boys Clubs (£3,500), Hertfordshire Community Foundation and West Berkshire Hospitals Charity (£3,000 each), Reading Dyslexia Association (£2,000) and Ashford Sea Cadets and Greenwich Toy and Library Association (£1,000 each).

Recipients elsewhere included International Social Service of the UK (£5,000), Interact, Northern Pinetree Trust and Yoga for Health Foundation (£3,000 each), Common Ground Sign Dance Theatre and Friends of Russian Children (£2,500), Open Door Foundation and Phab (£2,000), Gwent Mobility and Teesside Lions (£1,500

each), Royal British Legion (£1,000), Institute of Cultural Affairs (£1,000) and St Columbia's House (£500).

Applications In writing to the correspondent. The trustees meet twice a year in the spring and the autumn. It is recommended that applications be submitted by 31 March for consideration at the spring meeting and by 31 August for the autumn meeting. The trustees do not enter into correspondence concerning grant applications beyond notifying successful applicants.

The Bernard Kahn Charitable Trust

Jewish

£236,000 (1998/99)

Beneficial area UK and Israel.

18 Gresham Gardens, London NW11 8PD

Correspondent The Trustees

Trustees *Mrs C B Kahn; S Fuehrer.*

CC Number 249130

Information available Accounts were on file at the Charity Commission.

General In 1998/99 the trust had assets of £2.3 million and an income of £229,000, including £39,000 in donations from the Kahn family. Grants to 63 organisations totalled £236,000. Over half of the grants were of under £1,000.

The largest grants were £60,000 to Yeshivat Margenita d'avrohom, £25,000 each to Ohr Somayach College and Orthodox Council of Jerusalem and £20,000 each to Gevurath Ari Academy and Tels Academy. Other grants included £7,000 to Gateshead Jewish High School, £5,000 to Friends of Religious Settlement, £1,750 to Hasmonean High School, £800 to Woodstock Sinclair Trust, £250 to Enuno EC and £75 each to Finchley Road Synagogue and Marbeh Torah Trust.

Applications In writing to the correspondent.

The Stanley Kalms Foundation

Jewish charities, general

£314,000 (2000/01)
Beneficial area UK and overseas.

Dixons Group plc, 29 Farm Street, London W1J 5RL
Tel. 020 7499 3494
Correspondent Mrs Jane Hunt-Cooke
Trustees *Sir Stanley Kalms; Pamela Kalms; Stephen Kalms.*
CC Number 328368
Information available Accounts were on file at the Charity Commission.

General Established in 1989 by Sir Stanley Kalms, the president of Dixons Group plc, this charity states its objectives as the encouragement of Jewish education in the UK and Israel. Other activities include support for the arts and media and other programmes, both secular and religious.

In 2000/01 the foundation had assets of £1.4 million and an income of £46,000. Grants were made to 55 organisations and 3 individuals totalling £314,000.

Grants were mainly to Jewish organisations (social and educational) with grants also going to the arts, education and health. Donations over £1,000 each were listed in the accounts and went 29 organisations. The largest included those to Shalom Hartman Institute (£75,000), Jewish Educational Development Trust (£34,000), Royal Opera House Trust (£32,000), Pluto Productions (£28,000), Group Relations Education Trust (£25,000) and Institute for Policy Research (£20,000).

Other grants included £15,000 to Community Security Trust, £10,000 to Oxford Centre for Jewish and Hebrew Studies, £7,200 to Norwood Ltd, £5,000 to Israel Philharmonic Orchestra Foundation, £2,200 to NSPCC, £2,000 to Memorial Gates Fund and £1,000 each to British Technion Society and Jewish Marriage Council.

Unlisted donations under £1,000 each totalled £8,800.

Applications In writing to the correspondent, but note that most of the trust's funds are committed to projects supported for a number of years.

The Kasner Charitable Trust

Jewish

£227,000 (2000/01)
Beneficial area UK and Israel.

Kimberley House, 172 Billet Road, London E17 5DT
Tel. 020 8342 0211
Correspondent Josef Kasner, Trustee
Trustees *Mrs Elfreda Erlich; Baruch Erlich; Josef Kasner.*
CC Number 267510
Information available Full accounts were on file at the Charity Commission.

General In 2000/01 this trust's assets totalled £936,000 and it had an income of £825,000. Over 250 donations were made totalling £227,000, most of which were for £200 or less.

Grants included those to Gevurath Ari Academy Trust (£51,000), Telz Academy Trust (£35,000), Beis Eliyahu and Law of Trust Talmudical College (£20,000 each) and Torath Moshe Moshe Educational and Charitable Trust (£10,000), Gateshead Talmudical College (£5,500) and Menovah Grammar School and North London Communal Mikveh (£5,000 each).

Applications In writing to the correspondent.

The Michael & Ilse Katz Foundation

Jewish, music, medical, general

£175,000 (2000/01)
Beneficial area Worldwide.

The Counting House, Trelill, Bodmin, Cornwall PL30 3HZ
Tel. 01208 851814 **Fax** 01208 851813
Email osman.azis@virgin.net
Correspondent Osman Azis, Trustee
Trustees *Norris Gilbert; Osman Azis.*
CC Number 263726
Information available Full accounts were on file at the Charity Commission.

General Established in 1971, this foundation supports many Jewish organisations, although musical and medical charities also received funds.

In 2000/01 the assets totalled £1.7 million and generated an income of £28,000. Grants were made totalling £175,000.

Management and administration expenses were very high at £19,000, and included £9,300 in trustee's professional expenses, comprised of £5,800 in general fees (consistant with in recent years) and £3,700 'for work carried out over a period of more than a year which was of considerable financial benefit to the foundation'. Whilst wholly legal, these editors always regret such payments unless, in the words of the Charity Commission, 'there is no realistic alternative'.

Bournemouth organisations received the two largest grants, £56,000 to Royal Bournemouth Hospital and £21,000 to Bournemouth Orchestral Society. The only other grant of over £1,000 in this area was to Poole Hospital for the Ladybird appeal (£4,800).

Most of the other beneficiaries listed in the accounts had a Jewish connection. They included Jewish Care (£16,000), Norwood and UK Friends of the Well Being of Israel's Soldiers (£10,000 each), Federation of Jewish Relief Organisations and Hillel Foundation (£5,000), Holocaust Educational Trust (£3,000), Nightingale House (£1,500) and British ORT and Hannah Levy House Trust (£1,000 each).

Applications In writing to the correspondent.

The Mathilda and Terence Kennedy Charitable Trust

General

£61,000 (1999/2000)
Beneficial area UK.

H W Fisher & Co., Acre House, 11–15 William Road, London NW1 3ER
Tel. 020 7388 7000
Correspondent The Trustees
Trustees *Hon. Amanda Sieff; John O'Neill; Mrs L Sieff; J Henderson.*

CC Number 206330

Information available Accounts were on file at the Charity Commission.

General The trust makes grants to a range of organisations. In 1999/2000 its assets totalled £723,000 and its income was £47,000. Grants totalled £61,000 and ranged from £1,000 to £20,000.

The largest grant was £20,000 to Royal Ballet School. Other large grants were £7,500 to Royal National Theatre, £5,000 each to Mathilda Marks Kennedy School and Young Vic, £4,500 to Mathilda & Terence Kennedy Institute of Rheumatology, £3,000 each to Stonewall Irish Trust and University College of London, £2,500 each to Alternative Theatre Company Limited (Bush Theatre) and Arc Dance Company, £2,000 each to Albert Kennedy Trust, Terrence Higgins Trust and Weizmann Institute Foundation and £1,500 to CRUSAID.

Applications Grants are mainly made to charities known personally to the trustees, rather than as a result of unsolicited applications. Unsuccessful applications will not receive a reply.

The Kennel Club Charitable Trust

Dogs

£308,000 (June 1999 to December 2000)

Beneficial area UK.

1–5 Clarges Street, Piccadilly, London W1J 8AB

Tel. 020 7518 1029 **Fax** 020 7518 1050

Email mwetherell@the-kennel-club.org.uk

Website www.the-kennel-club.org.uk

Correspondent Mrs Mary Wetherell, Secretary

Trustees Brig. R J Clifford; W R Irving; M Townsend.

CC Number 327802

Information available Full accounts were on file at the Charity Commission.

General The trust describes its objects as 'science, sentiment and support'. It supports the furthering of research into canine diseases and hereditary disorders of dogs and also organisations concerned with the welfare of dogs in need and those which aim to improve the quality of life of

humans by promoting dogs as practical or therapeutic aids. The trust gives both ongoing and one-off grants.

At December 2001 the trust had assets of £838,000 of which £651,000 was unrestricted. In the 18 months to December 2001 income amounted to £617,000, of which £592,000 was from donations. Grants totalled £308,000 and were divided into 'research project support' which received £248,000 and 'donations' totalling £60,000.

Animal Health Trust received a total of £217,000 (£135,000 to support the work of the KC Genetics Coordinator, £50,000 for epidemiology and £32,000 towards the cost of setting up a canine tumour registry). Other larger grants were made to the Universities of Bristol (£14,000 for canine gastro-enterology research) and Glasgow (£13,000 for a molecular genetic study of canine cancer).

The largest non-research grant was £10,000 to Greyhound Rescue. Other larger donations included £7,000 each to Blue Cross, Canine Partners for Independence and Royal College of Veterinary Surgeons and £5,000 each to NCDL and Support Dogs. There were a further 11 smaller donations.

Exclusions The trust does not give grants directly to individuals, veterinary nurses can apply to the Royal College of Veterinary Surgeons where bursaries are available, see above. The trustees tend not to favour funding the costs of building work.

Applications In writing to the correspondent, including latest accounts as well as the rationale for the request for a grant. The trustees meet three times a year.

E & E Kernkraut Charities Limited

General, education, Jewish

£175,000 (2001/02)

Beneficial area UK.

The Knoll, Fountayne Road, London N16 7EA

Tel. 020 8806 7947

Correspondent E Kernkraut, Chair

Trustees E Kernkraut, Chair; Mrs E Kernkraut; Joseph Kernkraut; Jacob Kernkraut.

CC Number 275636

Information available Accounts were on file at the Charity Commission, but without a list of grants.

General The trust states that it makes grants for educational, Jewish and other charitable purposes. It did not provide a list of grants with its accounts or further detail of its grant-making criteria, so we were unable to tell what type of educational charity is likely to be supported by this trust.

In 2001/02 the trust's assets totalled £111,000 and it received an income of £145,000, mainly from doantions. Grants exceeded the income at £174,000.

Applications In writing to the correspondent.

The Graham Kirkham Foundation

General

£105,000 (2000/01)

Beneficial area UK and Ireland.

Bentley Moor Lane, Adwick-le-Street, Doncaster, South Yorkshire DN6 7BD

Tel. 01302 330365

Correspondent Barry Todhunter

Trustees Lord G Kirkham; Lady P Kirkham; M Kirkham.

CC Number 1002390

Information available Full accounts were provided by the trust.

General The objectives of the foundation are:

- promotion or development of the study and/or appreciation of literature, art, music or science
- advancement of education of people of any age
- advancement of physical education among young people at school or university
- relief of poverty or hardship by providing financial assistance and accommodation for people who are disadvantaged
- relief of illness and disease through provision of treatment, financial assistance or accommodation

- support of research into treatment and prevention of illness
- relief of suffering of animals and birds through support or rescue homes, hospitals, sanctuaries and so on
- relief of poverty, hardship and distress amongst members of the armed services, and their dependants
- provision of support on protection for people with drugs, or in danger of becoming dependent on drugs
- provision of facilities for public recreation
- protection and preservation of buildings of architectural interest or sites of historical interest or natural beauty.

In 2000/01 the foundation had assets of £41,000 and an income of £123,000, almost all of which came from donations received from one of the trustees. Grants were made to six organisations totalling £105,000, the largest of which was £50,000 to The Presidents Award. Other beneficiaries were NSPCC (£20,000), Charlotte Beadle Italia Conti School (£15,000), Martin House Children's Hospice (£10,000) and Cancer Bacup and London Immunotherapy Cancer Trust (£5,000 each).

Applications In writing to the correspondent.

Kirschel Foundation

Jewish, medical
£61,000 (1999/2000)
Beneficial area UK.

171 Wardour Street, London W1V 3TA
Tel. 020 7437 4372
Correspondent John Hoare, Trustee
Trustees *Laurence Grant Kirschel; John Hoare*
CC Number 1067672
Information available Accounts were on file at the Charity Commission.

General This trust states its aims and objectives are 'to provide benefits to underprivileged persons, who may be either handicapped or lacking resources'. In practice this includes many Jewish organisations.

In 1999/2000 the trust received an income, comprised of donations, totalling £61,000. All of this was given in grants. The main beneficiaries during the year

were Jewish Educational Trust (£25,000), Friends of Ohr Somayach (£19,000) and Lubavitch Foundation of Scotland (£11,000). Other grants were £2,500 to Variety Club of Great Britain and ten others of less than £1,000. Beneficiaries included Jewish Blind and Disabled, Leukaemia Research Fund, Lolev Charitable Trust and Sense.

The trust stated that its income has since grown to around £80,000 a year.

Applications In writing to the correspondent.

The Kobler Trust

Arts, Jewish, medical
£333,000 (1998/99)
Beneficial area UK.

Lewis Silkin, 12 Gough Square, London EC4A 3DN
Correspondent Ms J L Evans, Trustee
Trustees *A Xuereb; A H Stone; Ms J L Evans; J W Israelsohn.*
CC Number 275237
Information available Full accounts were on file at the Charity Commision.

General In 1998/99 the trust had assets of £4.5 million and an income of £217,000. After administration and management costs of £23,000, grants totalling £333,000 were given to 56 organisations, 16 of which were supported in the previous year.

The largest grant was £60,000 to Friends of Amutat Avi (Beit Issie Shapiro). Other sizeable grants included £25,000 to Crusiad, £20,000 each to Chicken Shed Theatre, Covent Garden Festival, Jewish Care and Royal Academy of Music and £15,000 to BACUP.

Other grants ranged from £200 to £13,000. Art organisations supported included Tricycle Theatre Company Limited (£13,000), Pavilion Opera Education Trust (£12,000), Magic Mirror Theatre Company Limited (£5,000) and British Youth Theatre (£1,000). Jewish beneficiaries included £2,000 each to Jewish Blind and Disabled and Norwood Ravenswood. Medical grants included Express Link Up (£10,000), FACTS (£4,000) and Jewish Aids Trust (£2,000).

Exclusions Grant are only given to individuals in exceptional circumstances.

Applications In writing to the correspondent.

The Kohn Foundation

Scientific and medical projects, the arts – particularly music, education, Jewish charities
£78,000 (2000)
Beneficial area UK.

100 Fetter Lane, London EC4A 1BN
Correspondent Dr R Kohn, Chair to the Trustees
Trustees *Dr Ralph Kohn, Chair; Zahava Kohn; Anthony A Forwood.*
CC Number 1003951
Information available Full accounts were on file at the Charity Commission.

General The foundation supports advancement of scientific and medical research, promotion of the arts – particularly music, general educational projects and Jewish charities.

In 2000 the foundation had assets of £3.4 million, which generated an income of £78,000. Grants were made totalling £78,000, including £500 to individuals. Other expenses totalled £1,800, of which £880 was given to an accountancy firm in which one of the trustees is a partner. Whilst wholly legal, these editors always regret such payments unless, in the words of the Charity Commission, 'there is no realistic alternative'.

By far the largest grant was £145,000 to Monteverdi Choir and Orchestra Ltd. Other large grants were £50,000 to Royal Society and £25,000 to Wigmore Hall International Song Contest.

Other grants listed in the accounts were £10,000 each to National Osteoporosis Society and Vega Science Trust, £6,000 to Hasmonean High School, £5,000 each to Jewish Music Institute and Liver Research Trust, £2,000 to Rudolf Kempe Society, £1,300 to United Jewish Israel Appeal and £1,000 each to Collel Chibath Yerushalayim and North West London Jewish Day School. Smaller grants totalled £8,400.

Applications In writing to the correspondent.

Krattiger Rennison Charitable Trust

AIDS, education

£102,000 (2000/01)

Beneficial area Devon and the UK.

35 Sherbrooke Road, London SW6 7QJ

Correspondent Professor Robert J Pratt, Trustee

Trustees *A L Banes; Ruth M Blaug; Prof. Robert J Pratt.*

CC Number 1015838

Information available Accounts were on file at the Charity Commission.

General This trust works in two main areas, these being the advancement of education specifically relating to artistic subjects, and work with AIDS including research into the disease, assistance to those suffering from AIDS and the promotion of information relating to AIDS.

In 2000/01 the trust had assets of around £300,000 and an income of £25,000. Grants were made to six beneficiaries, each supported in the previous year, totalling £102,000.

Beneficiaries were Crusaid (£27,000), British Youth Opera (£20,500), London East Aids Network (£20,000), Grandma's (£17,500), Bristol Old Vic Theatre School (£15,000) and National HIV Nurses Association (£2,200).

Applications In writing to the correspondent.

This entry was not confirmed by the trust, but is correct according to information on file at the Charity Commission.

The Neil Kreitman Foundation

Culture, education, health, welfare

£277,000 (2000/01)

Beneficial area UK and Israel.

Citroen Wells (Chartered Accountants), Devonshire House, 1 Devonshire Street, London W1W 5DR

Tel. 020 7304 2000

Correspondent Eric Charles, Trustee

Trustees *N R Kreitman; Mrs S I Kreitman; Eric Charles.*

CC Number 267171

Information available Full accounts were on file at the Charity Commission.

General The foundation supports cultural, educational, health and welfare organisations.

In 2000/01 it had assets of £5.8 million, which generated an income of £278,000. Grants were made to 23 organisations totalling £277,000. Management and administration expenses were high at £45,000, including £12,000 to a firm one of the trustees is a consultant for. Whilst wholly legal, these editors always regret such payments unless, in the words of the Charity Commission, 'there is no realistic alternative'.

The largest grant was £137,000 to Ashmolean Museum at Oxford University, which was promised in December 1998 eight annual grants of £100,000 each.

Other large grants were £30,000 to British Library, £15,000 to Ancient India and Iran Trust, £14,000 to Corpus Inscriptionium Iranicarum and £10,000 each to British Museum, Onaway Trust, Release Legal Emergency and Drugs Service, SE Cross College Development Fund and Victoria and Albert Museum.

Other beneficiaries included Hindu Kush Conservation Association and International PEN Foundation (£5,000 each), Royal Numismatic Society (£4,000), British Heart Foundation, NSPCC and Save the Children Fund (£2,000 each) and ApTibeT and Henry Spink Foundation (£1,000 each).

The only three beneficiaries not also supported in the previous received the smallest grants. They were Anti-Slavery International and Royal National College for the Blind (£1,000 each) and School of Oriental and African Studies (£500).

Exclusions No grants to individuals.

Applications In writing to the correspondent.

The Kyte Charitable Trust

Medical, disadvantaged and socially isolated people

£99,000 (2000/01)

Beneficial area UK.

Business Design Centre, 52 Upper Street, London N1 0QH

Tel. 020 7390 7777

Correspondent The Trustees

Trustees *D M Kyte; T M Kyte; A H Kyte.*

CC Number 1035886

Information available Accounts were on file at the Charity Commission, but without a list of grants or a narrative report.

General The trust supports organisations benefiting medical professionals and research workers. Support may go to organisations working with at risk groups, and people who are disadvantaged by poverty or socially isolated.

In 2000/01 the trust had an income of £61,000, including £60,000 in donations received, mostly from a company in which one of the trustees is a director. Grants were made totalling £99,000, leaving assets of £120. No further information was available in the accounts.

Applications In writing to the correspondent.

The Christopher Laing Foundation

Social welfare, environment, culture, health and medicine throughout the UK; general in Hertfordshire

£234,000 (2001/02)

Beneficial area UK, with an interest in Hertfordshire.

c/o Ernst & Young, 400 Capability Green, Luton LU1 3LU

Tel. 01582 643128

Correspondent Mrs Margaret R White, Senior Trust Consultant

CC Number 278460

Information available Full accounts were provided by the trust, at the cost of £10.

General In 2001/02 the trust had assets of £4.6 million, which generated an income of £171,000. Management, administration and investment manager's charges totalled £23,000. Grants were made totalling £234,000. Of this, £40,000 was given to Charities Aid Foundation for disbursement amongst smaller charities. Other grants were broken down as follows:

Animal welfare – one grant of £3,000
This went to Royal Veterinary College Animal Care Trust.

Child & youth – six grants totalling £57,000
The Lords Taverners and NPFA both received £25,000. Other beneficiaries were Youth Centre (£3,500), Stevenage Sea Cadets (£2,000), Make a Wish Foundation (£1,000) and Award Events Ltd (£880).

Cultural & environmental – three grants totalling £6,500
These went to Bunbury ESCA Festival (£5,000), Hertfordshire Gardens Trust (£1,200) and Fund for the Future (£250).

Health and medicine – seven grants totalling £109,000
The largest grant during the year was £102,000 to Tyingham Foundation, which also received a loan of £300,000. Other grants went to Marie Curie Cancer Care (£2,500), St John Ambulance (£2,000), GUTS and Rowan Breast Cancer Unit (£1,000 each), Diabetes UK (£250) and ICRF Trading Ltd (£150).

Social welfare – 13 grants totalling £19,000
High Sheriff's Fund received £10,000. Other grants were £2,500 to Hertfordshire Action on Disability, £2,000 to Army Benevolent Fund, £1,500 to Garden House Hospice, £500 to Luton Women's Aid and £250 each to nine organisations including Hertfordshire Hearing Advisory Service, Isabel Hospice, Relate, Stevenage Community Trust and Watford New Hope Trust.

Exclusions Donations are only made to registered charities.

Applications In writing to the correspondent.

The David Laing Foundation

Youth, disability, mental health, the arts, general
£79,000 (2000/01)
Beneficial area Worldwide.

The Studio, Mackerye End, Harpenden, Hertfordshire AL5 5DR

Tel. 01582 461606 **Fax** 01582 461232

Correspondent David E Laing, Trustee

CC Number 278462

Information available Information was provided by the trust.

General This trust has general charitable purposes, with emphasis on youth, disability, mental health and the arts. It makes large grants to a wide and varied number of organisations as well as donating smaller grants through Charities Aid Foundation.

In 2000/01 the foundation had assets of £5 million and a total income of £126,000. Grants to organisation totalled £79,000, including £55,000 in smaller grants given through CAF. Administration charges for the year were high at £48,000.

Grants made directly by the foundation were £8,700 to Emmanus St Albans, £5,000 each to DEMAND, Harpenden Music Foundation and London Pro Arte Orchestra and £500 to RLEK.

Exclusions No grants to individuals.

Applications In writing to the correspondent. Trustees meet in March, June, October and December, although applications are reviewed weekly. Due to the large number of applications received, and the relatively small number of grants made, the trust is not able to respond to all requests.

The Martin Laing Foundation

General
£93,000 (2001/02)
Beneficial area UK and worldwide.

c/o Ernst & Young, 400 Capability Green, Luton LU1 3LU

Tel. 01582 643128 **Fax** 01582 643006

Correspondent Mrs Margaret R White, Senior Trust Consultant

CC Number 278461

Information available Full accounts were provided by the foundation, at the cost of £10.

General This trust makes a large number of small grants, given through the Charities Aid Foundation. Most of the support is given to organisations and projects with which the trustees have a personal connection. A small number of larger grants are also made.

In 2001/02 the foundation had assets of £4.3 million, which generated an income of £195,000. Management and administration charges totalled £17,000, while the investment manager's charges totalled £9,100. Grants were made to 69 organisations totalling £93,000.

£30,000 was distributed through CAF to 62 organisations, which received between £75 and £10,000 each. Two organisations of which Sir Martin Laing is a vice president were among the recipients of the seven grants made directly by the trust, which were broken down as follows:

- Cultural and environmental – Ponds Conservation Trust received £13,000.
- Education and training – Princess Helena College received £10,000.
- Health and medicine – Three grants were made; £10,000 to Action for ME, £5,500 to Westminster Pastoral Foundation and £5,000 to Macmillan Cancer Relief.
- Overseas aid – £10,000 to British Executive Service Overseas.
- Social welfare – £10,000 to Business in the Community.

Applications The trust states: 'The trustees receive an enormous and increasing number of requests for help. Unfortunately the trustees are only able to help a small proportion of the requests and consequently they limit their support to those charities where they have a personal connection or interest in their activities.'

The Lambert Charitable Trust

Health, welfare, Jewish, arts

£110,000 (2000/01)

Beneficial area UK and Israel.

Messrs Mercer & Hole, 76 Shoe Lane, London EC4A 3JB

Fax 020 7353 1748

Correspondent M Lambert, Trustee

Trustees *M Lambert; Prof. H P Lambert; H Alexander-Passe; Jane Lambert.*

CC Number 257803

Information available Full accounts were on file at the Charity Commission.

General This trust usually uses half of its funds supporting Jewish and Israeli causes and half for medical, welfare and arts causes.

In 2000/01 it had assets of £2.5 million, which generated an income of £107,000. Grants totalling £110,000 went to 124 organisations, broken down as follows:

Charitable purposes in Israel – £17,000 in 19 grants

Beneficiaries included British Friends of the Rambah Medical Centre (£1,800), Friends of Magen David Adom (£1,500), CBF World Jewish Relief and Operation Wheelchairs Committee (£1,000 each), Boys Town Jerusalem and Weizmann Institute (£750) and JNF Israel (£500).

Jewish faith in the UK – £27,000 in 19 grants

The largest grant made was £12,000 to Jewish Care. Other recipients included Jewish Museum (£2,000), Norwood (£1,500), Nightingale House (£1,200), Foodline and Kisharon Day School (£1,000 each), Jewish Marriage Guidance and Women's Campaign for Soviet Jewry (£750) and Camp Aguda and Jewish Child's Day (£500 each).

Other charitable purposes – £66,000 in 86 grants

The largest were £3,200 to Royal Opera House Trust, £2,500 to THET, £1,500 each to CFS Research Foundation and Facing the Future Together. Other grants included £1,000 each to Action for Addiction, Brick by Brick, Help the Aged, Listening Books and Quaker Social Action, £750 each to Child Poverty Action Group, Defeating Deafness, NSPCC and Royal Air Forces Association, £500 each to Maternity Alliance, Pace Centre, Riverpoint and Young Vic Theatre

Company and £250 each to British Stammering Association and St Giles Trust.

Applications In writing to the correspondent before July for payment by 1 September.

The Langdale Trust

Social welfare, Christian, medical, general

£96,000 (2000/01)

Beneficial area Worldwide, but with a special interest in Birmingham.

c/o Lee Crowder, 39 Newhall Street, Birmingham B3 3DY

Tel. 0121 236 4477

Correspondent M J Woodward, Trustee

Trustees *T R Wilson; Mrs T Whiting; M J Woodward.*

CC Number 215317

Information available Accounts were on file at the Charity Commission.

General The trust was established in 1960 by the late Antony Langdale Wilson. There is a preference for local charities in the Birmingham area and those in the fields of social welfare and health, especially with a Christian context.

In 2000/01 the trust had assets of £3.3 million, which generated an income of £118,000. Management and administration charges were £6,200, including £5,300 to a firm of solicitors of which one of the trustees is a partner for 'professional services on a commercial basis'. Grants totalling £96,000 were made to 37 organisations, of which 24 were also supported in the previous year.

The largest grants were £5,000 to British & Foreign Bible Society and £4,000 each to The Leprosy Mission and United Christian Broadcasters Ltd. Other grants included £3,000 each to Addaction, Mental Health Foundation, National Trust, Oxfam, Sargent Cancer Care for Children, YMCA Birmingham and Y Care International, £2,000 each to Apex Trust, Downside Up Limited, Mercy Ships, Prisoners Abroad, Salvation Army, St Martin's in the Bull Ring and Survival International.

Applications In writing to the correspondent. The trustees meet in September/October.

The R J Larg Family Charitable Trust

Education, health, medical research, arts – particularly music

About £100,000 (1999/2000)

Beneficial area UK but generally Scotland, particularly Tayside.

Messrs Thorntons WS, 50 Castle Street, Dundee DD1 3RU

Correspondent N Barclay

Trustees *R W Gibson; D A Brand; Mrs S A Stewart.*

CC Number SC004946

Information available Information was provided by the trust.

General The trust has an annual income of approximately £127,000. Grants, which totalled about £100,000 in 1999/2000, ranged between £250 and £6,000 and were given to a variety of organisations.

These include organisations concerned with cancer research and other medical charities, youth organisations, university students' associations and amateur musical groups.

Beneficiaries of larger grants included: High School, Dundee (£6,000 for the cadet force and £5,000 for the Larg Scholarship Fund); Whitehall Theatre Trust (£4,000); Macmillan Cancer Relief – Dundee and Sense Scotland Children's Hospice (£2,500 each); and £2,000 to Rachel House.

Exclusions Grants are not available for individuals.

Applications In writing to the correspondent. Trustees meet to consider grants in February and August.

Largsmount Ltd

Jewish

£237,000 (2000/01)

Beneficial area UK and overseas.

Cohen Arnold & Co Accountants, 13–17 New Burlington Place, Regent Street, London W1S 2HL

Correspondent Mrs I R Kaufman, Trustee

Trustees *Z M Kaufman; Mrs I R Kaufman; S Kaufman.*

CC Number 280509

Information available Accounts were on file at the Charity Commission.

General This trust supports orthodox Jewish charities. In 2000/01 it had assets of £2.4 million and had an income of £409,000. Out of a total expenditure of £294,000, grants to 40 organisations were made totalling £237,000.

The largest donations were £95,000 to Yetev Lev Jerusalem and £45,000 to Shaarei Zion Turda. A further 14 grants were made for £1,000 or more including those to A & H Pillar Charitable Trust (£27,000), Dushinsky Trust (£25,000), Gateshead Foundation for Torah (£14,000), Tomechi Torah Family Relief (£4,100), Gateshead Jewish High School (£1,800), UTA (£1,400) and Bobov Charities and Kimche de Pische (£1,000 each).

Applications In writing to the correspondent.

Rachel & Jack Lass Charities Ltd

Jewish, children, education, medical research

£171,000 (2000/01)

Beneficial area England, Scotland and Wales.

43 Linden Lea, London N2 0RF

Correspondent Mrs R Lass, Governor

Trustees *Leonard Lass; Rachelle Lass; Sally Lass.*

CC Number 256514

Information available Full accounts were on file at the Charity Commission.

General The trust gives primarily to Jewish charities, preferring those involved with children, education and medical research.

In 2000/01 it had an income of £82,000, mostly in donations received from four investment companies one of the trustees is the director of. Grants were made totalling £171,000. At the year end, assets totalled £167,000.

The largest grants were £36,000 to Yeshiva Horomo Talmudical College, £20,000 each to Friends of Ilan and Ravenswood Foundation, £15,000 to Tevini Ltd and £10,000 each to Gevurath Ari Torah Academy Trust and Yesodey Hatdlah

Other beneficiaries listed in the accounts were Beth Hamedrash Ponovez, Minister Centre and Yad Eliezer (£5,000 each), United Synagogue (£2,700), Mogen David Adom (£2,000), World Jewish Relief (£1,200) and Jewish Care (£600). A total of £19,000 was given in smaller grants.

Exclusions No grants to individuals or for educational purposes. Only registered charities are considered.

Applications In writing to the correspondent. Grants are paid annually during July/August/September.

The Lauffer Family Charitable Foundation

Jewish, general

£172,000 (2000/01)

Beneficial area Commonwealth countries, Israel and USA.

18 Norrice Lea, London N2 0RE

Email bethlauffer@lineone.net

Correspondent J S Lauffer, Trustee

Trustees *Mrs R R Lauffer; J S Lauffer; G L Lauffer; R M Lauffer.*

CC Number 251115

Information available Full accounts were on file at the Charity Commission.

General This trust has general charitable purposes, supporting Jewish causes in the Commonwealth, Israel and USA.

In 2000/01 it had assets of £2.9 million, which generated an income of £151,000. Grants were made to 176 organisations and totalled £172,000.

The largest grants were £15,000 each to British Friends of Ariel and Spiro Ark, £13,000 to British Friends of Ohr Somayach, £12,000 to United Jewish Israel Appeal and £10,000 to British Friends of Sarah Herzog Memorial Hospital.

Other beneficiaries included Jewish Learning Experience (£7,000), Menorah Foundation School (£5,900), B'nai B'rith Hillel Foundation and Jerusalem Foundation (£5,000 each), Od Yosef Chai (£4,800), Maccabi Union (£6,300), Holocaust Educational Trust (£3,000) and World Jewish Relief (£2,000). A total of £49,000 was given in smaller grants.

Exclusions No support for individuals.

Applications In writing to the correspondent, applications are considered once a year.

The Mrs F B Laurence Charitable Trust

Social welfare, medical, disability, environment

£88,000 (2001/02)

Beneficial area Worldwide.

PO Box 28927, London SW14 7WL

Correspondent The Trustees

Trustees *M Tooth; G S Brown; D A G Sarre.*

CC Number 296548

Information available Information was provided by the trust.

General The trust produces guidelines which state: 'Our priority is for the care and/or improvement of conditions of the disadvantaged members of society within the United Kingdom or those overseas to whom the United Kingdom owes a duty of care.

'Whilst we support charities that are known to the trustees or are established in their field and have a good track record, we are constantly looking for new small, innovative charities with a hands-on approach and notwithstanding that their work may be primarily devoted to a particular locality, or if they are likely to provide a model for wider application.'

This trust gives for general charitable purposes, including many service, medical and welfare charities as well as hospices and environmental groups.

In 2001/02 the trust had assets of £2.3 million, which generated an income of £87,000. Grants were made totalling £91,000. Management and administration expenses were high at £17,000, including a payment of £12,600 to a firm in which one of the trustees is a partner. Whilst wholly legal, these editors always regret such payments unless, in the words of the Charity Commission, 'there is no realistic alternative'.

The largest grants were: £2,000 each to Marie Curie Cancer Care, RNID, WWF–UK, SSAFA, Médecins Sans Frontières (UK); £1,500 each to Dreams Come True, Ghurka Welfare Trust, Fairtrade Foundation.

All other grants were for £1,000 or less and totalled £74,750.

Exclusions No support for individuals. The following applications are unlikely to be considered:

- appeals for endowment or sponsorship
- overseas projects, unless overseen by the charity's own fieldworkers
- maintenance of buildings or landscape
- provision of work or materials that are the responsibility of the state
- where administration expenses, in all their guises, are considered by the trustees to be excessive
- where the fundraising costs in the preceding year have not resulted in an increase in the succeeding year's donations in excess of these costs.

Applications The guidelines state: 'Write to us on not more than two sides of A4 paper with the following information:

- who you are
- what you do
- what distinguishes your work from others in your field
- where applicable describe the project that the money you are asking for is going towards and include a business plan/budget
- what funds have already been raised and how
- how much are you seeking from us
- how do you intend to measure the potential benefits of your project or work as a whole.

'Trustees usually meet in April and November. Please submit your application by 1 February for the April meeting and by 1 September for the November meeting.

'To save on our administration costs, we will only notify the successful applicants.'

The Kathleen Laurence Trust

General

£87,000 (1998/99)
Beneficial area UK.

Trustee Department, Coutts & Co, 440 Strand, London WC2R OQS

Tel. 020 7753 1000 **Fax** 020 7663 6794

Correspondent David Breach, Assistant Trust Manager

Trustees *Coutts & Co.*

CC Number 296461

Information available Full accounts were on file at the Charity Commission up to 1998/99.

General In 1998/99 the assets stood at about £3.2 million with an income of £100,000, all from investments and interest receivable. Grants, ranging from £500 to £4,000, were given to 55 organisations totalling £86,500. The trust incurred large administration costs totalling £61,000, including £58,000 in fees to Coutts & Co.

The trust states that 'donations are given to a wide range of institutions, particularly favouring smaller organisations and those with specific requirements such as for the purchase of land, the restoration of cathedrals, churches or other buildings of beauty or interest to which the public can have access or for the specific raising of funds for an anniversary year'. Grants are also given towards organisations concerned with people who are ill or mentally or physically disabled.

The largest grants were to British Kidney Patient Association and IVCS (£4,000 each). Dreams Come True and Rinoht Special Trustees both received £3,000.

There were 24 grants of £2,000; 1 of £1,500; 18 of £1,000 and 7 of £500. The larger grants included £2,000 each to Hope House, Imperial Cancer Research, National Asthma Campaign, Papworth Trust, Princes Trust, Rainbow Trust and Wildside Trust and £1,000 each to Evelina Children's Hospital, Society at Work, SPADEWORK and Stroke Association. Organisations receiving smaller grants included ACTIVE, King Edward Grammar School and Ron Pickering Memorial Fund. A number of grants were recurrent from the previous year.

Exclusions No donations are made for running costs, management expenses or to individuals.

Applications In writing to the correspondent. Trustees meet quarterly, usually in February, May, August and November.

The Law Society Charity

Law and justice, worldwide

£338,000 to unconnected charities (2001/02)
Beneficial area Worldwide

113 Chancery Lane, London WC2A 1PL

Tel. 020 7320 5899

Correspondent The Trustees

Trustees *The Law Society Trustees Ltd.*

CC Number 268736

Information available Full accounts were on file at the Charity Commission.

General As the name suggests, this trust is concerned with causes connected to the legal profession, particularly in advancing legal education and access to legal knowledge. Organisations protecting people's legal rights and lawyers' welfare are also supported, as are law-related projects from charities without an identifiable legal connection.

In 2001/02 the trust had assets of £1.1 million and an income of £2.5 million, including a donation of £2.4 million from The Law Society of England and Wales. Most of these funds were returned to The Law Society, in a grant of £1.6 million for educational purposes. Donations were also made to 22 unconnected organisations, totalling £338,000.

The Citizenship Foundation, LawCare Limited and Solicitors Benevolent Fund all received £75,000 each. The next largest grants were £15,000 to Common Purpose, £12,000 to Trainee Solicitors' Group and £10,000 each to Galleries of Justice and Speakeasy Advice Service.

Smaller grants included those to Accis (£8,000), National Centre for Volunteering (£7,500), Fair Trials Abroad (£6,000), Book Aid International (£5,100), Law Centres Federation (£5,000), Minority Lawyers Conference (£3,600), The Howard League (£3,000), People in Need (£2,500) and Disability Law Service and VSO (£1,000 each).

Applications In writing to the correspondent. Applications are considered at quarterly trustees' meetings, usually held in April, July, September and December.

The Edgar E Lawley Foundation

Older people, disability, children, medical research

£154,000 (2000/01)

Beneficial area UK, with a preference for the West Midlands.

Hollyoak, 1 White House Drive, Barnt Green, Birmingham B45 8HF

Tel. 0121 445 3536 **Fax** 0121 445 3536

Email philipjcooke@aol.com

Correspondent Philip J Cooke, Trustee

Trustees *Mrs M D Heath, Chair; J H Cooke; Mrs G V H Hilton; P J Cooke; F S Jackson; Mrs E E Sutcliffe.*

CC Number 201589

Information available Full accounts were on file at the Charity Commission.

General The trust's primary objects are 'the making of grants to charitable bodies for provision of medical care and services to children and the aged, the advancement of medicine and for educational purposes'. There is a preference for the West Midlands.

In 2000/01 the trust had assets of £3.5 million and an income of £161,000. Grants totalling £154,000 were made to 66 organisations.

Three substantial grants over £20,000 were made in the year, to Imperial College School of Medicine – also a major beneficiary in previous years – towards equipment costs (£30,000), St Mary's Hospital, Paddington (£29,000) and the King's Fund (£23,000). Walsall Society for the Blind received £5,000, with all other grants ranging from £500 to £1,500.

Recipients included Acorns Children's Hospice Trust, Birmingham Settlement, Cystic Fibrosis Trust, Dorset Scope, Merseyside CVS, Cot Death Society and Rainbow Centre, Bristol.

Many grants were repeated from the previous year. A mix of local and UK organisations were supported.

Exclusions No grants to individuals.

Applications In writing to the correspondent in April.

The Lawlor Foundation

Social welfare, education, general

£101,000 to organisations (2000/01)

Beneficial area Principally Northern Ireland, also Republic of Ireland, London and the home counties.

Traceys Farm, Stanford Rivers, Ongar, Essex CM5 9QD

Tel. 01277 364805 **Fax** 01277 364805

Correspondent Virginia Lawlor, Chairman

Trustees *Virginia Lawlor; Kelly Lawlor; Martin Spiro; Frank Baker; K R P Marshall; Blanca Fernadez Drayton.*

CC Number 297219

Information available A comprehensive annual report and accounts was provided by the foundation.

General The following is taken from the 2000/01 annual report:

'There are four principal objectives: support for organisations working with troubled adolescents (these organisations having an identifiable Irish component); the relief of poverty and the advancement of education in Northern Ireland and the Republic of Ireland; educational grants for individual students with an Irish background; projects underpinning the peace process in Ireland.

'The foundation is permitted to support "general charitable purposes" and a number of donations reflect the trustees' personal interests.

'From the foundation's earliest days, the trustees have had a particular interest in adolescent problems and in promoting cooperation and mutual understanding between the peoples of Ireland, North and South. Currently the emphasis is on education and the principal beneficiaries include a number of Northern Irish schools and individual students, British-based projects supporting Irish immigrants, and vulnerable young people.

'Grants are made on a one-off or recurring basis and can include core funding and salaries. A substantial

proportion of the foundation's income is committed on a long-term basis, which restricts the funds available for new applicants.'

Grants range between £250 and £10,000 and can be given for a maximum of three years, although beneficiaries may reapply at the end of the grant.

The trust aims to be even-handed in its grantmaking across the communal divide in Belfast. Since 1996 the foundation has run the Shankill Education Project to allow children from disadvantaged families in the Greater Shankill area of West Belfast to attend grammar schools, which they would not otherwise be able to afford. 2001 saw the pupils from the first year of funding sit their GCSEs, gaining an average of 11 GCSEs at C or above and with no failures. This project has received funds from other trusts, companies and individual donations. However, due to lack of demand from schools no new students are starting this scheme. Those already on it are being supported through to the completion of their fifth year.

In 2000/01 the foundation had assets of £2.3 million. Total income was £150,000, including £21,000 in donations received. Grants totalling £101,000 were made to 17 organisations, of which 11 worked in Northern Ireland, 5 in London and the home counties and 1 in the Republic of Ireland. All but two of these grants were recurrent. A further £12,000 was given in total to 24 individual students. Grants were broken down as follows:

Education
Grants were made to 12 organisations totalling £79,000. The £12,000 given to students was also included under this category (see *The Educational Grants Directory*, also published by DSC, for further information). The largest grant made by the foundation during the year was £21,000 to Shankill Educational Project to support 53 children. Most of the other grants in this category were to help young people in Northern Ireland who are disadvantaged attend university, as bursaries and sometimes also for school projects; these grants included £10,000 to St Louise's College – Belfast, £7,200 to Jesus College – Cambridge, £6,000 each to La Salle Boy's Secondary School – Belfast, St Cecilia's College – Derry, St Mary's Christian Brothers' Boys' Grammar School – Belfast and St Mary's College – Derry and £5,000 to Irish Studies Centre at the University of London. The only grant made in the Republic of Ireland during the year was £5,000 to Tullow Community School – County Carlow, an annual grant to enable people to attend university and to support school projects.

Other grants were £5,000 to Belfast Royal Academy for sports equipment, music lessons, Duke of Edinburgh Award projects and bursaries and a one-off grant of £2,000 to Integrated Education Fund – Northern Ireland to provide free school meals, which now receives statutory funding.

Social welfare

Three grants were made during the year. Brent Adolescent Centre received £10,000 as a recurrent grant towards core costs for its mental health service for vulnerable young people aged 14 to 21 London-wide. New Horizon Youth Centre was given £5,000 to increase the number of drug advice sessions provided to groups and on a one-to-one basis at the centre in King's Cross in London and to introduce a drugs education service to schools and youth clubs in the city. Brandon Centre, also in London, received £3,000 as a one-off payment towards core costs at the centre, which provides specialist support to young people aged 12 to 25 whose mental or physical health is at risk.

Peace and reconciliation

One grant of £1,300 was made to Lifeline – Belfast as part of ongoing commitment towards the running costs of the befriending scheme providing respite for the victims of paramilitary violence, including their families, throughout Northern Ireland.

Women's interests

Creggan Pre-school and Training Association in Derry City received £2,000 as the first of three grants towards the salary of an education liaison officer to work with parents under the age of 24 in a disadvantaged area, addressing issues such as childcare, health, housing, benefits, career guidance and education. The other grant was £1,000 to Belfast Women's Training Services for childcare for women in the Greater Shankill area who were experiencing stress and being rehoused due to loyalist feuding and who wished to undertake courses to improve their quality of life and employment prospects.

Exclusions No grants are made in response to general appeals from large organisations or from organisations outside the geographical areas of Ireland, London and the Home Counties. Grants are not normally made to the arts, medicine, the environment, building projects, expeditions, children's projects or national causes.

Applications By letter to the correspondent at any time, with a description of the project and a copy of the latest accounts. Preliminary telephone enquiries are welcomed. Applications will only be acknowledged if they relate to the trust's general interests. The trustees normally meet in January, April, July and October.

Please note that the trust has many ongoing commitments, which restrict the funds available for new applicants.

The Carole & Geoffrey Lawson Foundation

Jewish, child welfare, poverty, arts, education

£310,000 (2000/01)

Beneficial area UK.

Stilemans, Munstead, Godalming, Surrey GU8 4AB

Tel. 01483 420757

Correspondent Geoffrey Lawson, Trustee

Trustees *Geoffrey C H Lawson; Hon. Carole Lawson; Harold I Connick; E C S Lawson.*

CC Number 801751

Information available Full accounts were on file at the Charity Commission.

General This trust has general charitable purposes, particularly supporting Jewish organisations. Beneficiaries require a good track record and should be concerned with child welfare, relief of poverty and advancement of education and the arts. It particularly supports rebuilding work at Covent Garden.

In 2000/01 the trust had assets of £628,000. Total income was £347,000, much higher than in recent years due to the receipt of £323,000 worth of shares from one of the trustees. After low management and administration charges of £2,100, grants were made to 14 organisations totalling £310,000.

By far the largest grant was £135,000 to World ORT Trust. Other large donations went to Royal Opera House (£57,000) and Central Synagogue (£40,000).

Other grants were £18,000 to London Symphony Orchestra, £10,000 each to British Council of Shaare Zedek, Central Cecil Housing Trust, Community Security Trust and Jewish Care, £5,000 each to Abracadabra Appeal, British ORT, London Marriage Guidance Council and UJIA and £500 to Friends of Biale.

Exclusions No grants to local charities or individuals.

Applications In writing to the correspondent.

The Raymond & Blanche Lawson Charitable Trust

General

£77,000 (2000/01)

Beneficial area UK, with an interest in West Kent and East Sussex.

28 Barden Road, Tonbridge, Kent TN9 1TX

Tel. 01732 352183 **Fax** 01732 352621

Correspondent Mrs P E V Banks, Trustee

Trustees *John V Banks; John A Bertram; Mrs P E V Banks; Mrs Sarah Hill.*

CC Number 281269

Information available Information was provided by the trust.

General The trust has a preference for local organisations and generally supports charities within the following categories:

- scouts, guides, brownies, cubs, etc.
- preservation of buildings
- hospices
- care in the community
- assistance for people who are blind
- armed forces benevolent funds.

In 2000/01 the trust had assets of £1.3 million and an income of £94,000 from investments, rents and donations. Grants amounting to £77,000 were awarded to 64 organisations.

The largest grant was £10,000 to Age Concern Tonbridge, also a major beneficiary in previous years. Grants in the range of £1,000 to £5,000 were made to 41 organisations, with the others ranging between £100 and £750.

Beneficiaries included Maidstone Trust and Hospice in the Weald (£5,000 each), Kent Music School (£4,000), Royal British Legion Poppy Appeal (£3,000), Cancer Research, Heart of Kent Appeal and Royal Society for the Blind (£2,000 each), 3H Fund, Compaid, Dyslexia Institute, Peper Harow Foundation, National Trust,

Sargent Cancer Care for Children and Spadework (£1,000 each).

Organisations receiving less than £1,000 each included Mencap (£750), Battle of Britain Memorial Trust, Disability Aid Foundation, Kenward Trust and Samaritans – Maidstone (£500 each), Royal Association for the Deaf (£250) and Fun in Action for Children (£100).

Exclusions No support for churches or individuals.

Applications In writing to the correspondent.

The Lawson-Beckman Charitable Trust

Jewish, welfare, education, arts
£78,000 (2000/01)
Beneficial area UK.

A Beckman plc, P O Box 1ED, London W1A 1ED

Tel. 020 7637 8412 **Fax** 020 7436 8599

Correspondent Maurice Lawson

Trustees M A Lawson; J N Beckman.

CC Number 261378

Information available Full accounts were on file at the Charity Commission.

General The report states that the trust gives grants for the 'relief of poverty, support of the arts and general charitable purposes'. Grants are allocated two years in advance.

In 2000/01 the trust had assets of £1.8 million and an income of £127,000. A total of £78,000 was distributed in 39 grants, they were broken down by the trust as follows:

General	£3,000	(6 grants)
Education and training	£13,000	(6)
Medical, health and sickness	£26,000	(15)
Disability	£2,700	(2)
Overseas aid	£1,000	(1)
Accommodation and housing	£26,000	(3)
Religious activities	£4,000	(4)
Art and culture	£1,700	(2)

The trust mainly supports Jewish causes, with the largest grants being £23,000 to Jewish Care. A further 16 grants were made of £1,000 or more. Other

beneficiaries included British ORT and Nightingale House (£8,000 each), Norwood Ltd (£6,800), Centrepoint (£3,000), Community Security Trust (£2,500), Cystic Fibrosis Holiday Fund (£2,200), Friends of Hebrew University and Who Cares Trust (£2,000 each) and British Red Cross, London Philharmonic Orchestra and World Jewish Relief (£1,000).

Smaller grants included those to British WIZO, Friends of Covent Garden, Noah's Ark, United Jewish Israel Appeal and Women Fighting Breast Cancer.

Exclusions No grants to individuals.

Applications In writing to the correspondent, but please note that grants are allocated two years in advance.

The Leach Fourteenth Trust

Disability, general
£97,000 (2000/01)
Beneficial area UK, with some preference for south west England and the home counties, and overseas.

Nettleton Mill, Castle Combe, Nr Chippenham, Wiltshire SN14 7NJ

Correspondent Roger Murray-Leach, Trustee

Trustees W J Henderson; M A Hayes; Mrs J M M Nash; Roger Murray-Leach.

CC Number 204844

Information available Accounts were on file at the Charity Commission.

General Although the trust's objectives are general, the trustees support mainly disability organisations. The trust has previously also had a preference for conservation (ecological) organisations. In practice there is a preference for south west England and the home counties. In 2000/01 the trust had assets of £2.4 million, an income of £100,000, and gave grants totalling £97,000.

A few charities receive regular donations. The trustees prefer to give single grants for specific projects rather than towards general funding, and also favour small organisations or projects. The trust informed us that, in recent years, it has supported a local swimming pool appeal for autistic children, and causes such as child bereavement care and cancer care. Grants ranged up to £15,000.

The trust made 32 grants over £1,000. The largest were £15,000 to Fosse Way School, £10,000 to Middlesex Hospital Special Trustees RYMD, £5,000 each to Deafblind UK, Isles of Scilly Environment Trust, Orbis and Royal College of Radiologists, £3,500 each to Mobility Trust and Countryside Restoration Fund, £3,000 to RUH Forever Friends Appeal and £2,250 to Lymphoma Association.

Other beneficiaries included The Burned Children's Trust, Cancer BACUP, Changing Faces, The Drama Practice, Durrell Wildlife Conservation Trust, St Michael's Hospice, Salvation Army, Wiltshire Air Ambulance and Winston's Wish.

Exclusions Only registered charities based in the UK are supported (the trust only gives overseas via a UK-based charity). No grants to: individuals, including for gap years or trips abroad; private schools, unless for people with disabilities or learning difficulties; or for pets.

Applications In writing to the correspondent. Applications for a specific item or purpose are favoured. Only successful appeals can expect a reply. A representative of the trust occasionally visits potential beneficiaries. There is an annual meeting of trustees in the autumn, but not necessarily to consider grants. Grants tend to be distributed twice a year.

The Leche Trust

Georgian art, music and architecture
£172,000 to organisations (2000/01)
Beneficial area UK.

84 Cicada Road, London SW18 2NZ

Tel. 020 8870 6233 **Fax** 020 8870 6233

Correspondent Mrs Louisa Lawson, Secretary

Trustees Mrs Primrose Arnander, Chair; Simon Jervis; John Porteous; Dr Ian Bristow; Sir John Riddell; Mrs Felicity Guinness; Simon Wethered.

CC Number 225659

Information available Full accounts and list of grants were on file at the Charity Commission.

General The trust was founded and endowed by the late Mr Angus Acworth in 1950. Grants are normally made in the following categories:

- the promotion of amity and good relations between Britain and developing world or former 'Iron Curtain' countries by financing visits to such countries by teachers or other appropriate persons
- preservation of buildings and their contents, primarily of the Georgian period
- repair and conservation of church furniture, including such items as bells or monuments, but not for structural repairs to the fabric – preference is given to objects of the Georgian period
- assistance to conservation, including museums
- assistance to academic, educational or other organisations concerned with music, drama, dance and the arts
- assistance to students from overseas during the last six months of their postgraduate doctorate study in the UK
- support with the charitable activities associated with the preservation of rural England.

In 2000/01 the trust had assets of £6.3 million and an income of £252,000. After management and administration costs of £25,000, it approved 57 grants to organisations totalling £172,000 (a further £89,000 went on grants to individuals). Grants ranged from £500 to £16,000. They can be broken down as follows:

Arts – 26 grants totalling £63,000
Benficiaries included the Parkhouse Award for the sponsorship of a concert (£6,000), Artangel and Opera Circus to produce performances (£5,000 each), St Albans International Organ Festival (£3,000), Dartington International Summer School (£2,000) and International Cello Festival, Manchester (£1,500). The trust also sponsored several commissions of new musical works by groups such as the Birmingham Contemporary Music Group (£1,000), Okeanos (£600) and the Gough Duo (£500).

Church furniture and monuments – 13 grants totalling £30,000
Grants included £10,000 towards the restoration of a monument to Lady Alice Duchess Dudley in Stoneleigh, Warwickshire, £5,000 towards the restoration of books in Boston Parish Church Library, Lincolnshire, £4,000 towards restoration of the table tombs in the churchyard of St John's Church, Kingscote, Gloucestershire, and £600 towards restoration of a mid-18th century rococo clock at St Leonard's Church, Shoreditch, London.

Education, institutions and museums – 9 grants totalling £46,000
Among those receiving grants were the Royal Academy towards regilding in the Council Room (£16,000), British School in Athens to conserve rare books and documents (£5,000 over two years), and Northampton Museums and Art Gallery for a restoration project on The Boot and Shoe Collection (£5,000).

Historic buildings – 9 grants totalling £33,000
Beneficiaries included The Landmark Trust for the restoration of the doors and windows at The Ruin, Hackfall in Yorkshire (£5,500), Mihai Emineso Trust to enable a conservator to travel to Romania to teach local people how to restore buildings in local villages (£5,000) and Buxton Opera House (£3,500). Five other beneficiaries received between £2,500 and £3,000.

Grants to individuals – totalling £63,000
Beneficiaries receiving grants on behalf of individuals included Textile Conservation Centre to help with fees for two students on the MA Conservation course (£40,000 over four years), and Foundation for Young Musicians (£9,000 over three years).

Grants totalling £26,000 were also made to overseas students.

Exclusions No grants are made for: religious bodies; overseas missions; schools and school buildings; social welfare; animals; medicine; expeditions; British students other than music students.

Applications In writing to the secretary. Trustees meet three times a year, in February, June and October and applications need to be received the month before.

The Arnold Lee Charitable Trust

Jewish, educational, health
£85,000 (2001/02)
Beneficial area UK.

47 Orchard Court, Portman Square, London W1H 9PD

Correspondent A Lee, Trustee

Trustees *Arnold Lee; Helen Lee; Alan Lee.*
CC Number 264437
Information available Full accounts were on file at the Charity Commission, but without an up-to-date grants list.

General The policy of the trustees is to distribute income to 'established charities of high repute' for any charitable purpose or object. The trust supports a large number of Jewish organisations.

In 2001/02 the trust had assets of £1.4 million and an income of £98,000. There were 48 grants made, totalling £85,000. Further information was not available.

The largest grants list filed at the Charity Commission was from 1997/98 when 63 grants were made totalling £89,000. The largest grant went to Joint Jewish Charitable Trust (£34,000). Other recipients of substantial grants included Project SEED (£7,500), Jewish Care (£6,500), Lubavich Foundations (£5,000), The Home of Aged Jews (£2,500) and Yesodey Hatorah School and Friends of Akim (£2,400 each).

Virtually all remaining grants were to Jewish charities and most were for around £500 or less. Recipients included The President's Club (£600), Gesher (£500), British Technion Society and Institute of Higher Rabbinical Studies (£250 each), Bolton Village Appeal Fund (£100) and Society of Friends of the Torah (£50).

Exclusions Grants are rarely made to individuals.

Applications In writing to the correspondent.

This entry was not confirmed by the trust, but the address was correct according to the Charity Commission database.

Morris Leigh Foundation

Jewish, general
£98,000 (2000/01)
Beneficial area Worldwide.

Berwin Leighton Paisner, Bouverie House, 154 Fleet Street, London EC4A 2JD

Tel. 020 7353 0299

Correspondent M D Paisner, Trustee

Trustees *Mrs Manja T Leigh; Martin D Paisner; Howard D Leigh.*

CC Number 280695

Information available Full accounts were on file at the Charity Commission.

General This foundation has general charitable purposes, mostly supporting Jewish, welfare and arts organisations.

In 2000/01 it had assets of £1.7 million, which generated an income of £80,000. Grants were made to 40 organisations totalling £98,000.

The largest grants were £15,000 to Jewish Policy Research, £6,000 to Rycotwood College, £5,200 each to Community Security Trust and Royal Opera House and £5,000 each to Board of Deputies, Jerusalem Academy of Music and Dance, London Business School and St Mary's Hospital Special Trustees.

Among other Jewish/Israeli beneficiaries were Israel Philharmonic Orchestra (£4,000), World Jewish Relief (£1,500), UJIA (£1,300), Magen David Adom UK (£1,000), British ORT (£800), Friends of Hebrew University (£500), Weizmann Institute (£300) and Tel Aviv University Trust (£100).

Other recipients included Pavilion Opera Educational Trust (£3,000), London Philharmonic Orchestra (£2,500), Royal Albert Hall (£1,900), NCH Action for Children (£630), Racing Welfare Charities (£600) and Chiltern Open Air Museum (£200).

Applications In writing to the correspondent.

The Leverhulme Trade Charities Trust

Charities benefiting commercial travellers, grocers or chemists

£612,000 to organisations and individuals (2001)
Beneficial area UK.

1 Pemberton Row, London EC4A 3BG
Tel. 020 7822 6915
Correspondent The Secretary
Trustees *Sir Michael Angus, Chair; Sir Michael Perry; N W A Fitzgerald; Dr J I W Anderson; A S Ganguly.*
CC Number 288404
Information available Report and accounts available.

General Grants are made only to:

- trade benevolent institutions supporting commercial travellers, grocers or chemists
- schools or universities providing education for them or their children.

The Leverhulme Trade Charities Trust derives from the will of the First Viscount Leverhulme, who died in 1925. He left a proportion of his shares in Lever Brothers Ltd upon trust and specified the income beneficiaries to included certain trade charities. In 1983, the Leverhulme Trade Charities Trust itself was established, with its own shareholding in Unilever, and with grantmaking to be restricted to charities connected with commercial travellers, grocers or chemists, their wives, widows or children. The trust has no full-time employees, but the day-to-day administration is carried out by the director of finance of the Leverhulme Trust.

In 2001 the trust's assets stood at £31 million and income was £987,000. Grants to organisations and individuals totalled £612,000. Grants to organisations included those to Commercial Travellers' Benevolent Institution (£160,000), The Girls' Public Day School Trust (£94,000), Royal Pinner School Foundation (£80,000), UCTA Samaritan Fund (£45,000), Royal Pharmaceutical Society (£30,000), Provision Trade Benevolent Institution (£17,000) and United Reformed Church Schools (£10,000). A number of these organisations are supported on an ongoing basis.

Over £160,000 was disbursed in undergraduate bursaries.

Exclusions No capital grants. No response is given to general appeals.

Applications By letter to the correspondent. All correspondence is acknowledged. The trustees meet in February and applications need to be received by the preceding October.

Undergraduate bursary applications should be directed to the relevant institution.

The Ralph Levy Charitable Company Ltd

Educational, medical, general

£133,000 (1999/2000)
Beneficial area UK, occasionally overseas.

14 Chesterfield Street, London W1J 5JN
Tel. 020 7408 9333 **Fax** 020 7408 9346
Correspondent Christopher Andrews, Trustee
Trustees *S M Levy; D S Levy; C J F Andrews.*
CC Number 200009
Information available Accounts were on file at the Charity Commission, but without a grants list.

General This trust has general charitable purposes, with a preference for educational and medical organisations. In 1999/2000 the trust had assets of £1 million, which generated an income of £56,000. Grants were made to 51 UK organisations and an Israeli educational project totalling £133,000, including a grant of £81,000 from the large accumulated surplus.

The trust provided a guaranteed rental commitment to a charity of £138,000 over five years. No further information on the beneficiaries and the size and type of grants made was included in the accounts.

Exclusions No educational grants to individuals.

Applications In writing to the correspondent. Written applications must be received three clear months before the commencement of the proposed project.

Lewis Family Charitable Trust

Medical research, health, education, Jewish charities

£399,000 (1998/99)
Beneficial area UK and overseas.

Chelsea House, West Gate, London W5 1DR
Correspondent David Lewis, Trustee

141

Trustees *David Lewis; Bernard Lewis.*

CC Number 259892

Information available Accounts were on file at the Charity Commission.

General Grants are made, in particular, to charities involved in the promotion of medical research. In addition, Jewish charities have in the past accounted for a large part of the trust's grant expenditure, but the proportion appears to be decreasing.

In 2000/01 this trust had an income of £168,000 and a total expenditure of £418,000. Unfortunately no further details were available for this year. In 1998/99 net assets were £3.3 million but a £500,000 donation saw the trust's income rise to £679,000, up from £206,000 the year before.

Out of 12 organisations receiving grants of over £10,000 (accounting for over three quarters of the total), 10 had been supported in the previous year. Most were medical research organisations receiving repeat awards, many with a long-standing relationship with the trust, including:

- King's College Hospital, £58,500 (£25,500 in 1997/98)
- Birth Defects Foundation, £57,000 (£59,000)
- Association for the Advancement of Cancer Therapy, £42,000 (£25,000)
- University of Nottingham, £19,000 (£25,000)
- Queen Mary and Westfield College Hospital, £19,000 (also funded in 1996/97)
- Imperial Cancer Research, £17,000 (£55,000)

In addition, the British Council received £40,000 for the Lewis Fellowship Fund, while the largest grant to a Jewish organisation was for £21,000 to UJIA/ Joint Jewish Charitable Trust, both long-term beneficiaries.

The only apparently new beneficiary receiving a large grant was the Bedford Square Charitable Trust (£30,000).

A further 15 recipients received grants ranging from £1,000 to £3,000. Only Norwood Ravenswood and CACDP had been supported in the previous year, receiving £2,000 and £1,750 respectively.

Others included Chernobyl Children's Lifeline (£3,000); the Multiple Sclerosis Society (£2,000); West London Synagogue (£1,000); Teenage Cancer Trust (£1,000), and the Council for Christians and Jews (£1,000). Another £15,000 was spent on grants under £1,000.

Exclusions No grants to individuals.

Applications To the correspondent in writing. Grants are normally made only once a year. The trust states: 'grants are not made on the basis of applications received'.

The Sir Edward Lewis Foundation

General

£114,000 (2000/01)

Beneficial area UK and overseas, with a preference for Surrey.

Messrs Rawlinson & Hunter, Eagle House, 110 Jermyn Street, London SW1Y 6RH

Tel. 020 7451 9000

Correspondent The Trustees

Trustees *R A Lewis; K W Dent; Christine Lewis; Sarah Dorin.*

CC Number 264475

Information available Full accounts were on file at the Charity Commission.

General The trust was established in 1972 by Sir Edward Roberts Lewis. By 2000/01 it had assets of £8.1 million producing an income of £190,000. After expenses of £12,000, grants were made totalling £114,000.

The trust has revised its policy and now plans to make one substantial donation every two or three years to an appropriate cause as well as smaller donations on an annual basis. Therefore it will not distribute all its income every year. The trustees prefer to support charities known personally to them and those favoured by the settlor.

Of the 80 grants made in the year, many had been supported previously. By far the largest distributions were £25,000 to Gurkha Welfare Trust and £10,000 to Accord International.

Other donations included those to British Wheelchair Sports Foundation, Chudley Blind Centre, CRISIS, Institute of Economic Affairs, Iris Fund, MIND, Music Trade Benevolent Society, National Asthma Campaign, Pain Relief Foundation, Rainbow Trust, Royal Society of Medicine, Salvation Army, See Ability, Sports Aid London and Treloar Trust.

Exclusions Grants are only given to charities, projects or people known to the trustees. No grants are given to individuals.

Applications In writing to the correspondent. The trustees meet every six months.

Limoges Charitable Trust

Animals, services, general

£83,000 (2000/01)

Beneficial area UK, with a preference for Birmingham.

Tyndall Woods Solicitors, 5 Greenfield Crescent, Edgbaston, Birmingham B15 3BE

Tel. 0121 243 3025

Correspondent Ms J A Dyke, Trustee

Trustees *Catherine Harriet Mary Bligh St George; Albert Kenneth Dyer; Judy Ann Dyke; Andrew Miller.*

CC Number 1016178

Information available Full accounts were on file at the Charity Commission.

General This trust has general charitable purposes, although there are preferences for animal and service organisations. Many of the beneficiaries are based in Birmingham.

In 2000/01 the trust had assets of £915,000 and an income of £21,000. Administration expenses and investment managers fees were very high, totalling £390 more than the year's income. Grants were made to 61 organisations totalling £83,000, and to 11 individuals totalling £11,000.

Symphony Hall (Birmingham) Ltd received two grants totalling £20,000, including £15,000 for the organ appeal. Many of the other larger grants were also given to Birmingham organisations, including Blue Coat School for the piano appeal (£15,000), University of Birmingham (£5,000), Birmingham Parish Church (St Martin's) Renewal Campaign (£3,000) and Birmingham Early Music Fund (£2,000).

Smaller Birmingham grants included those to Birmingham and Midland Limbless Ex-Servicemen's Association (£1,400), Royal Marine Association (£1,000), MSA for Midlands People with Cerebral Palsy and Wythall Village Hall (£500 each), Birmingham Dogs Home and West Birmingham Scout Association (£250 each), Edgbaston Rotary Club (£150) and Edgewood Court Day Centre (£50).

Grants made elsewhere included £2,700 to Elizabeth Svendsen Trust, £2,000 each to KGFS and Web Care Services, £1,200 to Edwards Trust, £1,000 each to Arthritis Research Campaign, Dogs for the Disabled, Gloucester Three Choirs Appeal, Hope and Homes for Children and Live Music Now!, £600 to Royal British Legion for the Poppy appeal, £500 each to Caring for Victims of Torture and When You Wish Upon a Star, £400 to RSPCA, £350 to Canine Partners for Independence, £250 to Rehab UK, £200 to Children Nationwide and £140 to Alexander MacMillan Trust.

Applications In writing to the correspondent.

Lindale Educational Foundation

Roman Catholic
£200,000 (2001/02)
Beneficial area UK and overseas.

1 Leopold Road, London W5 3PB
Correspondent J Valero
Trustees *Netherhall Educational Association; Dawliffe Hall Educational Foundation; Greygarth Association.*
CC Number 282758

General This foundation supports the Roman Catholic religion and the advancement of education. Its aims are to:

- train priests
- establish, extend, improve and maintain churches, chapels, oratories and other places of worship
- establish, extend, improve and maintain university halls and halls of residence for students of all nationalities
- arrange and conduct courses, camps, study centres, meetings, conferences and seminars
- provide financial support for education or research by individuals or groups of students
- provide financial support for other individuals or institutions which meet the trust's criteria, including the corporate trustees.

In 2001/02 the foundation had an income of £180,000, of which £175,000 came from donations received. Assets totalled £6,400. Grants were made totalling £200,000, whilst other expenditure amounted to just £20.

The main emphasis was on the training of priests, with grants being made to Collegio Romano della Santa Croce (four grants totalling £60,000), Fondation Belmont (two grants totalling £55,000) and Collegio Mayor de Humanidades (£2,000 to support seminarians).

The accounts stated: 'LEF was able to help projects run by its charitable trustees, with £12,000 going to the Brixton Baytree Centre, part of Dawliffe Hall Educational Foundation, which itself received a grant of £12,000 for general educational purposes. Wickenden Manor, the Natherhall Educational Association Centre for Retreats and Study Activites received six grants totalling £41,000 and Thornycroft Hall, a centre for similar activities and which is part of the Charity Siddington Trust Limited, received five grants totalling £6,100.'

Other grants were £10,000 to Fundacion para el desarrollo integral (FUDI) for a humanitarian/educational project in Guatemala and £1,000 to a school project in Ghana.

Exclusions No grants to individuals.

Applications In writing to the correspondent, but note that most funds are already committed.

The Linden Charitable Trust

General
£123,000 (2000/01)
Beneficial area UK, with a preference for West Yorkshire.

Addleshaw Booth & Co., Sovereign House, PO Box 8, Sovereign Street, Leeds LS1 1HQ
Tel. 0113 209 2000
Correspondent The Trustees
Trustees *G L Holbrook; M H Pearson; J F H Swales.*
CC Number 326788
Information available Full accounts were on file at the Charity Commission.

General This trust supports a wide range of organisations including medical and

healthcare charities and those related to the arts. In 2000/01 it had assets of £2.5 million and an income of £960,000. Grants totalled £123,000.

A total of 57 grants were made in the year the largest of which were £15,000 to Leeds International Pianoforte Competition and £10,000 each to Elizabeth Foundation and Leeds University School of Medicine.

Other donations were in the range of £500 and £5,000 and included those to: Caring for Life, Guide Dogs for the Blind Association, Help the Aged, Leeds Grammar School, Little Sisters of the Poor, Macmillan Cancer Relief, Mission to Seafarers, Opera North Foundation, SENSE and Yorkshire Dales Millennium Trust.

Exclusions No grants to individuals.

Applications In writing to the correspondent.

The Linmardon Trust

General
About £80,000 (1999/2000)
Beneficial area UK, with a preference for the Nottingham area.

HSBC Trust Company Limited, Norwich House, Nelson Gate, Commercial Road, Southampton SO15 1GX
Tel. 023 8072 2244
Correspondent Barry Sims, Trust Manager
Trustees *HSBC Trust Company Limited.*
CC Number 275307
Information available Full accounts were on file at the Charity Commisssion.

General The trust supports charities in the UK with a preference for those in the Nottingham area. In 1999/2000 it had an income of £74,000 and an expenditure of £87,000. Further information was not available.

In 1997/98 the trust had assets of £854,000 and an income of £31,000. Grants totalling £36,000 were given to 122 organisations. The grants were all less than £1,800.

Exclusions Grants are made to registered charities only. No support to individuals.

143

Applications In writing to the correspondent. The trustees meet quarterly, in February, May, August and November.

The Lister Charitable Trust

Water-based activities for young people who are disadvantaged

£264,000 (2002)

Beneficial area UK.

Windyridge, The Close, Totteridge, London N20 8PT

Fax 020 8445 3156

Correspondent Mrs S J Sharkey

Trustees *Noel A V Lister; Benjamin Piers Cussons; Stephen John Chipperfield; D A Collingwood; David J Lister.*

CC Number 288730

Information available Information was provided by the trust.

General This trust aims to help disadvantaged young people through sailing and other water-based activities. Grants are usually one-off for a specific project or part of a project. Core funding and/or salaries are rarely considered. Funding may be given for up to one year.

In 2002 the trust had assets of £9.5 million and income of £264,000. Grants totalling £264,000 were made to four organisations: Miami Project (£125,000), Bobath Centre (£100,000), UK Sailing Academy (£38,000) and Treasury Cay Community Centre (£1,500).

Exclusions Applications from individuals, including students, are ineligible. No grants are made in response to general appeals from large, UK organisations or to smaller bodies working in areas outside its criteria.

Applications In writing to the correspondent. Applications should include clear details of the need the intended project is designed to meet, plus an outline budget. Only applications from eligible bodies are acknowledged, when further information may be requested.

Frank Litchfield Charitable Trust

Medical, agriculturists

£80,000 (2002)

Beneficial area Mostly in and around Cambridge.

Taylor Vinters, Merlin Place, Milton Road, Cambridge CB4 0DP

Tel. 01223 423444

Correspondent M T Womack, Trustee

Trustees *M T Womack; D M Chater; P Gooderham.*

CC Number 1038943

Information available Full accounts were provided by the trust.

General The trust supports medical services in and around the Cambridge area as well as relieving poverty amongst those involved in agriculture.

In 2000/01 the trust had assets of £975,000. Total income was £151,000, including £104,000 in donations received from the settlor. After low management and administration expenses of £1,300, grants were made to four organisations and totalled £50,000. They were £25,000 to University of Cambridge, £10,000 each to Royal Agricultural Benevolent Fund and Royal Star and Garter Home and £5,000 to Camsight.

The trust has received a large donation since its 2000/01 accounting period and stated it now has assets of around £2 million and expects to make grants of around £80,000 a year.

Applications In writing to the correspondent.

The Second Joseph Aaron Littman Foundation

General

£180,000 (2001)

Beneficial area UK.

190 Strand, London WC2R 1JN

Tel. 020 7379 0000 **Fax** 020 7379 6854

Correspondent Barry Lock

Trustees *Mrs C C Littman; R J Littman.*

CC Number 201892

General This trust has general charitable purposes with special preference for academic and medical research. In 2001 it had an income of £180,000 all of which was given in grants. No further information was available.

Exclusions Applications from individuals are not considered.

Applications The trust's funds are fully committed and no new applications are considered.

Harry Livingstone Charitable Trust

Jewish, general

£63,000 (2000/01)

Beneficial area UK.

Westholme, The Springs, Park Road, Bowdon, Altrincham, Cheshire WA14 3JH

Tel. 0161 928 3232

Correspondent Jack Livingstone, Trustee

Trustees *J Livingstone; Mrs H Bloom.*

CC Number 263471

Information available Information was provided by the trust.

General This trust makes grants to Jewish organisations and also for general charitable purposes, particularly in Manchester. In 2000/01 its assets totalled £1.2 million, it had an income of £80,000 and made grants totalling £63,000. In the year a major grant was made to UJIA as well a number of smaller grants to other organisations.

Previous beneficaries have included Alone in London, Altrincham and District Spastics Association, Heathlands, Manchester Jewish Federation – Sale, One to One Charity, Southport Jewish Convalescent and Southport New Synagogue.

Applications The trust does not respond to unsolicited applications.

Jack Livingstone Charitable Trust

Jewish, general

£53,000 (2000/01)

Beneficial area UK and worldwide, with a preference for Manchester.

Westholme, The Springs, Park Road, Bowdon, Altrincham, Cheshire WA14 3JH

Tel. 0161 928 3232 **Fax** 0161 928 3232

Correspondent Mrs Janice Livingstone, Trustee

Trustees *Mrs J V Livingstone; Brian White.*

CC Number 263473

Information available Full accounts were on file at the Charity Commission.

General In 2000/01 the trust had assets of £1.4 million and an income of £89,000. After management and administration costs of £6,400, grants were made totalling £53,000.

Grants were given to large Jewish organisations and local groups in Manchester and the north west of England for various purposes including arts and welfare. Grants of £1,000 or more were listed in the accounts, beneficiaries included Christie's Against Cancer (£11,000), UJIA (£10,000), Royal Exchange Theatre Appeal Fund (£7,500), Jerusalem Foundation (£5,000), Community Security Trust (£3,500), National Councl of YMCAs (£2,500), Heathlands Village (£2,300), Manchester Balfour Trust, (£1,500) and Ashten Trust, Brookvale Royal Schools for the Deaf and Manchester Jewish Federation (£1,000 each).

Unlisted grants totalled £5,800.

Applications The trust does not respond to unsolicited applications.

The Locker Foundation

Jewish

£76,000 (1998/99)

Beneficial area UK and overseas.

28 High Road, East Finchley, London N2 9PJ

Tel. 020 8455 9280

Correspondent The Trustees

Trustees *I Carter; M Carter; Miss S Carter.*

CC Number 264180

Information available Full accounts were on file at the Charity Commission.

General This trust mainly supports Jewish organisations. In 1998/99 it had assets of £1.5 million and an income of £276,000 (£146,000 in 1997/98). It made nine grants totalling £76,000 (£58,000 in 1997/98). Management and administration totalled £14,000 with £2,500 going on trustees' fees. There was a surplus of £184,000 in the year.

The largest grant was £33,000 to Jewish National Fund. Grants of £15,000 each went to Society of Friends of Torah and Kahal Cassidim Bobov, both of which had been major recipients in the previous year.

Other grants went to Jewish Care (£6,000), British Friends of Boys Town Jerusalem (£3,500), Yad Sarah (£3,000), BUGS and Craven Walk Charities Trust (£150 each) and Teenage Cancer Trust (£100).

Applications In writing to the correspondent.

The Loftus Charitable Trust

Jewish

£140,000 (2000/01)

Beneficial area UK and overseas.

48 George Street, London W1U 7DY

Tel. 020 7486 2969

Correspondent A Loftus, Trustee

Trustees *R I Loftus; A L Loftus; A D Loftus.*

CC Number 297664

Information available Accounts were on file at the Charity Commission.

General The trust was established in 1987 by Richard Ian Loftus. Its objects are the:

* advancement of the Jewish religion
* advancement of Jewish education and the education of Jewish people
* relief of the Jewish poor.

In 2000/01 the trust had assets of £716,000. Total income was £226,000, including £184,000 in donations received from trustees and connected people. After low management and administration

expenses of £780, grants were made totalling £140,000.

The largest grants were £28,000 to Jewish Care and £26,000 to Lubavitch Foundation. Other large grants went to Chief Rabbinate Trust and Community Security Trust (£10,000 each), Habad Orphan Aid (£6,500), Chief Rabbinate Council (£6,000), British ORT (£5,000) and United Jewish Israel Appeal (£4,000).

Other beneficiaries included United Synagogue (£3,700), Norwood (£3,200), Camp Simeya and Holocaust Educational Trust (£2,500 each), Nightingale House (£2,000), Jewish Association for the Mentally Ill (£1,700), Craven Walk Charity Trust (£1,200), with £1,000 each to Jerusalem Educational Trust, Jewish Museum, Saatchi Synagogue, Yad Benjamin and Yesoden Hatoch.

Applications The trustees state that all funds are committed and unsolicited applications are not welcome.

London Law Trust

Health and personal development of children and young people

£207,000 (2000/01)

Beneficial area UK.

Messrs Hunters, 9 New Square, Lincoln's Inn, London WC2A 3QN

Tel. 020 7412 0050

Correspondent G D Ogilvie, Secretary

Trustees *Prof. Anthony R Mellows; R A Pellant; Sir Michael Hobbs; Sir Ian Gainsford.*

CC Number 255924

Information available Full accounts were provided by the trust.

General The trust's aims are to:

* prevent and cure illness and disability in children and young people
* alleviate or reduce the causes or likelihood of illness and disability in children and young people
* encourage and develop, in young people, the qualities of leadership and services to the community.

Within these guidelines, the trust favours seedcorn grants, small research projects and new ventures.

In 2000/01 the trust had assets of £4.1 million, which generated an income of £146,000. There was £41,000 spent on management and general expenses and £4,900 on audit, accountancy and taxation fees; these included £15,000 to a firm in which the secretary of this trust is a partner, and fees paid to two trustees of £3,500 and £2,500. Grants to 72 organisations totalled £207,000 and were broken down as follows:

Charities which prevent and cure illness and disability in children and young people – 12 grants totalling £49,000

Grants of £5,000 each were made to Christie's Hospital Manchester, Early Bird Diabetes Trust, Nottingham Trent University, Royal College of Paediatrics and Child Health, University of Southampton and Visceral Research into Irritable Bowel Disease. Other beneficiaries included Addenbrookes Hospital (£4,900), Royal Brompton and Harefield Hospital (£4,700), The Little Foundation (£2,500), and Brooklands (£1,000).

Charities which alleviate or reduce the causes or likelihood of illness and disability in children and young people – 32 grants totalling £87,000

Grants of £5,000 each went to Association of Children's Hospitals, CRY, Dame Hannah Rogers School, Downs Syndrome Association and Mind with £4,500 to NICOD. Other beneficiaries included Soundabout (£3,000), ChildLine and Multiple Births Foundation (£2,500 each), Epilepsy Association of Scotland and Fosse Way School (£2,000 each) and Newlife Foundation and Tofaen Opportunity Group (£1,000 each).

Charities which encourage and develop in young people the qualities of leadership and services to the community – 18 grants totalling £72,000

The largest grant made by the trust was £10,000 to Outward Bound. Grants of £5,000 each went to Adventure Unlimited, Focus, Fulcrum, The Island Trust Sailing Activities, Raleigh International, Tullochan Trust, Weston Spirit and Youth Net UK. Other beneficiaries included Dorset Fire Cadets (£4,500), British Youth Band Association (£2,500), Mountbatten Community Trust (£1,500) and Cathedral Camps (£1,000).

Exclusions Applications from individuals, including students, are ineligible. No grants made in response to local appeals from branches of UK organisations.

Applications In writing to the correspondent. The trustees employ a grant advisor whose job is to evaluate applications. Grant applicants are requested to supply detailed information in support of their applications. The grant advisor makes on-site visits to almost all applicants.

The trustees meet twice a year to consider the grant advisor's reports. Most grants are awarded in the autumn.

The William & Katherine Longman Trust

General

£240,000 (2000/01)

Beneficial area UK.

Charles Russell, 8–10 New Fetter Lane, London EC4A 1RS

Tel. 020 7203 5000 **Fax** 020 75203 5301

Email grainnef@cr-law.co.uk

Correspondent W P Harriman, Trustee

Trustees *W P Harriman; J B Talbot; A C O Bell.*

CC Number 800785

Information available Accounts were provided by the trust.

General The trust supports a wide range of organisations with grants of £2,000 upwards, about half of which receive regular support.

In 2000/01 the assets of the trust totalled £4.4 million generating an income of £126,000. Grants for the year totalled £240,0000 using funds from the capital account. The management and administration costs came to over £26,000, including £18,000 to Charles Russell, a firm in which the correspondent trustee is a partner.

Three grants of £20,000 made up a quarter of the total amount given. These went to Care (£15,000 the previous year), Sargent Cancer Care for Children (£10,000 the previous year) and World Vision UK. Tearfund received £15,000 (£15,000 in 1999/2000) and there were two grants for £10,000 both to organisations not supported the previous year: Action for ME and St George's Cathedral. Just over half of the remaining 41 grants, which ranged from £2,000 to £9,000, were recurrent from 1999/2000.

The only grant smaller than this was £500 to Chelsea Old Church.

Other beneficiaries included Age Concern (Kensington & Chelsea), Chelsea Festival, Fairbridge Drake Society, Horse Rangers Association, MENCAP, Prison Reform Trust, Streatham Youth Centre, Woodland Trust and Youth Sport Trust. Virtually all the recipients appear to be UK charities, with only a couple of local organisations in London.

Exclusions Grants are only made to registered charities.

Applications The trustees believe in taking a proactive approach in deciding which charities to support and it is their policy not to respond to unsolicited appeals.

Lotus Foundation

Children and families, women, animal protection, addiction recovery, education, general

£290,000 (1999)

Beneficial area UK and overseas.

Startling Music Limited, 90 Jermyn Street, London SW1Y 6JD

Tel. 020 7930 5133

Correspondent Mrs B Starkey, Trustee

Trustees *Mrs B Starkey; R Starkey.*

CC Number 1070111

Information available Accounts were on file at the Charity Commission.

General This trust was established in 1998 and aims to make grants to other established and newly-formed charities. The primary objectives of the trust are 'to offer financial aid and assistance to facilitate family and child welfare, women's issues, animal protection, addiction recovery and education'.

In 2001 it had an income of £281,000 and a total expenditure of £200,000. This information was taken from the Charity Commission database; unfortunately further information for this year was not available.

In 1999 the trust's income, comprised mainly of donations received, totalled £332,000. The trust's assets at the year end totalled £43,000. Grants totalled £290,000, including those to Variety Club of Great Britain Children's Charity, Kids Company (London), UCLA Intervention Programme (Los Angeles) and British Red Cross for the Kosovo appeal.

Applications In writing to the correspondent. This trust is proactive in examining requests that meet with its criteria: in 1999 the trustees visited various organisations requiring funding, seeing first hand the type of assistance required and where the trust could best help.

This entry was not confirmed by the trust, but the address was correct according to the Charity Commission database.

The C L Loyd Charitable Trust

General
£106,000 (2000/01)
Beneficial area UK, with a preference for Berkshire and Oxfordshire.

Lockinge, Wantage, Oxfordshire OX12 8QL
Tel. 01235 833265
Correspondent C L Loyd, Trustee
Trustees *C L Loyd; T C Loyd.*
CC Number 265076
Information available Full accounts were on file at the Charity Commission.

General The trust supports UK charities and local charities (in Berkshire and Oxfordshire) involved in welfare, animals, churches, medical/disability, children/youth and education.

In 2000/01 the trust had assets of £2.4 million and an income of £95,000. After management and administration fees of £23,000, 155 grants were made totalling £106,000, half of which was given to local charities.

The largest single grant made was £25,000 to Coldstream Regimental Charity, although Countryside Buildings Protection Trust received three grants totalling £29,000.

All other grants were for £5,000 for less. These included £5,000 each to West Hendred Playground and Management Group, Injured Jockey's Fund, Holy Trinity – West Hendred, £3,000 to King Alfred's Educational Charity, £2,600 (in three grants) to Ardington and Lockinge

PCC, £2,500 each to Helen House Charity and Royal Agricultural Benevolent Institution and £1,000 each to Jockey Club Charitable Trust, National Trust, Ukraine Christian Ministries and Wantage Counselling Service.

Smaller grants included those to Oxfordshire Council of Voluntary Action (£500), Oxford Radcliffe Hospitals Charitable Fund (£250), Oxfordshire Woodland Group (£200), St John Ambulance – Berkshire (£100), Berkshire Macmillan Nurse Appeal (£50), Reading YMCA (£20) and Newbury Hospital Helpers' League (£10).

Exclusions No support for individuals or medical research.

Applications In writing to the correspondent. Grants are made several times each month.

The Luck-Hille Foundation

Education, health, welfare
£50,000 (2000/01)
Beneficial area UK.

c/o Citroen Wells, Devonshire House, 1 Devonshire Street, London W1N 2DR
Tel. 020 7304 2000
Correspondent J W Prevezer, Trustee
Trustees *Mrs Jill Luck-Hille; P M Luck-Hille; J W Prevezer.*
CC Number 269046
Information available Full accounts were on file at the Charity Commission.

General This trust was established in 1975 as The Jill Kreitman Charitable Trust, daughter of the founders of the much larger trust The Kreitman Foundation. Grants are made to registered and exempt charities in the UK working concerned with education, health and welfare.

In 2000/01 the foundation had assets of £4.4 million which generated an income of £202,000. Grants were made to seven organisations totalling £50,000.

The largest grant was £37,000 to Middlesex University. Due to an agreement in 1998 to construct and refit a real tennis court on the campus of Middlesex University to a maximum of £1.5 million, the institution actually received £175,000 from the foundation

during the year, most of which was accounted for in previous financial years.

King Alfred School Appeal was given £8,500 whilst Norwood received £3,600. Other grants went to Project Trust (£500), The National Hospital and Raleigh International (£250 each) and Children with Aids Charity (£200).

Exclusions No grants to individuals.

Applications To the correspondent in writing. The trustees seem to have a list of regular beneficiaries and it may be unlikely that any new applications will be successful.

Robert Luff Foundation Ltd

Medical research
£762,000 (2000/01)
Beneficial area UK

294 Earls Court Road, Kensington, London SW5 9BB
Tel. 020 7373 7003 **Fax** 020 7373 8634
Correspondent Ms R Jessop, Secretary
Trustees *Sir Robert Johnson; Lady Johnson; R P J Price; Gynia Favot; Mrs J Tomlinson.*
CC Number 273810
Information available Full accounts were on file at the Charity Commission.

General The foundation supports medical research, through their own knowledge rather than by responding to applications.

In 2000/01 the trust had an income of £551,000, of which £24,000 was the net profit of a trading subsidiary (Futurist Light and Sound Ltd) and £527,000 was generated by the assets of £19 million. Management and administration fees were very high at £143,000, although the accounts stated that during the year the construction of a new building was completed (which will be rented to the subsidiary company for £37,000 a year) whilst it appears that some of the subsidiary's expenditure (such as the director's salary) was listed as expenditure of the foundation.

Grants were made to 10 organisations totalling £762,000. This was much larger than in previous years due to a payment of £530,000 to Cystic Fibrosis Trust for a five year research project into finding a cure for the condition.

147

Other large grants, which are more typical of the larger payments in previous years, were £50,000 to Harpur Trust, £45,000 to National Heart and Lung Institute, £30,000 to St John Ambulance and £27,000 to British Lung Foundation.

The only beneficiary which has not been supported in previous years was St Briavels Centre, which received £20,000. The remaining beneficiaries were Sheffield Health Authority Trust Fund and University College London Medical School (£16,000 each), National Asthma Campaign (£15,000) and British Scoiosis Research Foundation (£13,000).

Applications The foundation makes its own decisions about what causes to support. It has stated that 'outside applications are not considered, or replied to'.

The Lyndhurst Settlement

Social problems, civil liberties, environment, conservation

£175,000 (2001/02)

Beneficial area Usually UK, but overseas applications are considered if there is a strong civil liberty component.

The Lyndhurst Settlement, 2nd Floor, 15–19 Cavendish Place, London W1G 0DD

Correspondent Michael Isaacs, Administrative Trustee

Trustees *Michael Isaacs; Anthony Skyrme; Kenneth Plummer.*

CC Number 256063

Information available Full accounts were provided by the trust.

General The policy of the trust is to encourage research into social problems with a specific emphasis on safeguarding civil liberties, maintaining the rights of minorities and protecting the environment which the trustees regard as an important civil liberty. The trustees prefer to support charities (both innovatory and long-established) that seek to prevent, as well as relieve, hardship.

Beneficiaries include not only civil liberties, immigration and penal reform organisations, but a number of birth

control advisory centres, environmental and conservation groups, AIDS groups and homeless organisations.

In 2001/02 the settlement had assets of £633,000, down from over £804,000 in the previous year. It had an income of £46,000 and grants totalled £175,000.

A total of 62 grants were made in the year. They were categorised by the trust as follows, shown here with examples of grants:

Asylum and refugees (21%)
Among the 13 beneficiaries were: London Detainees Support Group and Sheffield Vietnamese Community Association (£4,000 each); Tibet Information Network (£3,500); Bromley Refugee Network, Student Action for Refugees and Western Kurdistan Association (£3,000 each); Community Development and Advocacy Centre (£2,000); and AIRE Centre (£1,500).

Community care (20%)
12 grants were made in this category, including those to Release (£6,000), Quaker Social Action (£4,000), Crossroads and Telephone Helplines Association (£3,000 each) and Bedford Advocacy for Older People, Care Share and Summerfield Care and Repair (£2,000 each).

Environment and heritage (18%)
Among the 14 beneficiaries were Common Ground and Sustrans (£4,000 each), NSCA and Waste Watch (£3,000 each), Cambridge Museum of Technology, Cycle West and Wheatley Windmill Restoration Society (£2,000 each), Centre for Sustainable Energy (£1,000) and Stepping Stones Farm (£500).

HIV/AIDS (15%)
The 10 grants made included those to Food Chain, Terrence Higgins Trust, NAZ Project London, Student Partnerships Worldwide and Waverley Care (£3,000 each), Wear Body Positive (£2,500) and Tyddyn Bach Trust (£2,000).

Prisoners (12%)
Seven grants were made, including those to Prison Reform Trust (£5,000), Prisoners Abroad (£4,500), New Bridge (£3,000) and Fine Cell Work (£1,000).

Family planning (8%)
Beneficiaries were Education for Choice (£9,000), Family Planning Association (£3,000) and Salford Brook Advisory Centre (£2,000).

Civil liberties (4%)
The two donations in this category went to Civil Liberties Trust (£4,000) and Stonewall Iris Trust (£2,500).

Racial harassment (2%)
One grant was made of £3,000 to the Monitoring Group.

Exclusions No grants to non-registered charities or individuals. Medical or religious charities are not normally supported.

Applications Requests for grants should include a brief description of the aims and objects of the charity and must be in writing and not by telephone. Unsuccessful applications will not be acknowledged unless an sae is enclosed. Applications are considered throughout the year.

Note: It is the trustees' policy to maintain a level of distribution in excess of income. With this in mind, they stated the following: 'The trustees anticipate that the work of the Settlement will be concluded soon after 31/12/2004.

'It is not anticipated that there will be any further distributions after that date.'

The Lyndhurst Trust

Christian

£98,000 (2000/01)

Beneficial area UK and overseas, with preferences for north east England and the developing world.

66 High Street, Swainby, Northallerton, North Yorkshire DL6 3DG

Correspondent W P Hinton, Trustee

Trustees *W P Hinton; J A L Hinton; Dr W J Hinton.*

CC Number 235252

Information available Full accounts were on file at the Charity Commission.

General This trust supports:

- organisations concerned with the propagation of the gospel or the promotion of the Christian religion
- the distribution of Bibles and other Christian religious works
- the establishment, maintenance or support of Christian missions in the UK and overseas

- the provision of clergy or the augmentation of stipends of the clergy of any Christian denomination
- the provision or maintenance of churches or chapels of any Christian denomination or of similar buildings.

The 2000/01 accounts stated: 'The trustees have sought opportunities for the promotion and advancement of the Christian religion in any part of the world, in accordance with the trust's deed. The trustees have continued to support opportunities to promote and advance the spreading of the Christian religion in any part of the world. The policy has continued to be to regularly support charities that are promoting the awareness of the Christian gospel, in those areas of the world where people are prevented from hearing it through normal channels of communication. Agencies operating in difficult circumstances are given special consideration.

'The needs of the disadvantaged in the United Kingdom and Europe have been given special attention, particularly those charities involved in meeting the needs of those with drug and alcohol problems through Christian rehabilitation programmes.'

In 2000/01 it had assets of £1.5 million generating an income of £59,000. Grants totalled £98,000, broken down as follows:

	%	No. grants	Total
North east England	42%	25	£41,000
Third world countries	30%	22	£29,000
UK – general	19%	20	£19,000
Europe and the rest of the world	9%	8	£9,000

One donation of £100,000 was made to Teen Challenge (UK) for the Women's Detoxification Centre. This is not included in these figures. All other grants were between £800 and £10,000.

Beneficiaries in the north east of England included North East Youth for Christ (£10,000), Crusaders Union (£8,000), Christian Institute, Emmanuel Prison Ministry, St George's Youth Worker and South Bank Baptist Church Community Worker (£1,500 each), Church of Nazarene, Lightfoot Grove Church and New Life Pentecostal Church (£1,300 each), and Gideon's International – Darlington, Lakeshore Christian Ministries and Redcar Baptist Church (£1,000 each). Grants of £800 and under included those to All Saints Church Eaglescliffe, Clarence Trust, Marton Christian Fellowship, Scripture Union In Schools and South Bank Mission.

Other beneficiaries in the UK included Betel International and Yeldall Christian Centres (£1,500 each), Teen Challenge UK – Men's Rehabilitation and Teen Challenge UK – Women's Rehabilitation (£1,300 each), and Care Trust, Evangelical Alliance and Prison Christian Fellowship (£1,000 each).

Grants to the developing world included those to OMS International – South Africa (£2,000), Middle East Christian Outreach – Kurdistan and Overseas Missionary Fellowship – China (£1,700 each), St Andrew's Evangelical Mission – Peru (£1,500), Christian Fellowship Ministry – Kenya and UFM Worldwide – Sierra Leone (£1,300 each), Church Missionary Society – Sudan, International Connections – Guyana and Operation Mobilisation – Bangladesh (£1,000 each).

Beneficiaries in Europe and the rest of the world include European Christian Mission in Romania, Albania and Kosovo (£1,000 each), Haggai Institute – Middle East (£1,000), Albania Evangelical Society, Bible Society – Europe, International Bible Society – Europe, Operation Mobilisation – Spain, Pocket Testament League – Spain and Youth with a Mission – Hungary (£800 each).

Exclusions No support for individuals or buildings.

Applications In writing to the correspondent, enclosing an sae if a reply is required. Requests are considered quarterly.

The Lynn Foundation

General
£92,000 (1999/2000)
Beneficial area UK and overseas.

Blackfriars, 17 Lewes Road, Haywards Heath, West Sussex RH17 7SP
Tel. 01444 454773 **Fax** 01444 456192
Correspondent Guy Parsons, Trustee
Trustees *Guy Parsons, Chair; J F Emmott; Dr P E Andry; P R Parsons; Ian Fair.*
CC Number 326944
Information available The information for this entry was provided by the trust.

General The trust has previously stated that it supports a very wide range of organisations, including those in the areas

of music, the arts, Masonic charities, disability, older people and children.

In 1999/2000 the the trust had assets of £4.9 million and received an income of £355,000 including £240,000 from share dividends and £91,000 from the estate of S S Lynn, the trust's deceased founder. Grants totalled £92,000, but no grants list was available for the year.

Applications In writing to the correspondent.

The Lyons Charitable Trust

Health, medical research, children
£70,000 (1999/2000)
Beneficial area UK.

Field Fisher Waterhouse, 35 Vine Street, London EC3N 2AA
Correspondent Mrs H Fuff
Trustees *M S Gibbon; Nick Noble.*
CC Number 1045650
Information available Accounts were on file at the Charity Commission, but without a recent grants list.

General The trust in particular makes grants in the fields of health, medical research and children in need.

In 1999/2000 it had assets of £1.5 million and an income of £87,000. Administration and accountancy charges for the year were high at £8,000. Grants were made to six organisations totalling £70,000.

As in recent years, there was no grants list included in the 1999/2000 accounts. The most recent available grants information refers to 1994/95, when five grants of £12,000 and one grant of £5,000 were made; the beneficiaries were Great Ormond Street Hospital for Sick Children, Terrence Higgins Trust, Florence Nightingale Fund, Printers Charitable Corporation and WWF.

Applications In writing to the correspondent.

The Sir Jack Lyons Charitable Trust

Jewish, arts, education

£58,000 (2000/01)

Beneficial area UK and overseas.

Sagars, 3rd Floor, Elizabeth House, Queen Street, Leeds LS1 2TW

Tel. 0113 297 6789

Correspondent M J Friedman, Trustee

Trustees *Sir Jack Lyons; Lady Roslyn Marion Lyons; M J Friedman; J E Lyons; D S Lyons.*

CC Number 212148

Information available Full accounts were on file at the Charity Commission.

General This trust shows a particular interest in Jewish charities and also a consistent interest in the arts, particularly music. In 2000/01 the trust had assets of £2.3 million and an income of £138,000. After management and administration costs of £17,000, grants were made to 19 organisations totalling £58,000 (£106,000 in 1998/99). Grants ranged from £40 to £10,000.

The largest went to Jewish Music Institute at SOAS and University of York (£10,000 each). Other beneficiaries included Jewish Community Foundation (£6,000), Community Security Trust (£5,500), UJIA and Joint Jewish Charitable Trust (£5,000 each), York Early Music Festival (£3,500), City University London, Royal Academy of Arts and The Jewish Museum (£2,500 each) and Amnesty International and London String Quartet Foundation (£1,500 each).

Smaller grants went to Friends of Magen David Adom in Great Britain and Royal Free Hospital Trust (£1,000 each), Western Marble Arch Synagogue (£700), St Paul's School (£200), Get Kids Going (£100), Balfour Diamond Jubilee Trust (£50) and Lennox Children's Cancer Fund (£40).

Exclusions No grants to individuals.

Applications In writing to the correspondent. In the past the trust has stated: 'In the light of increased pressure for funds, unsolicited appeals are less welcome and would waste much time and money for applicants who were looking for funds which were not available.'

Malcolm Lyons Foundation

Jewish

£131,000 (2000/01)

Beneficial area UK.

BDO Stoy Hayward, 8 Baker Street, London W1U 3LL

Tel. 020 7893 2318

Correspondent J S Newman, Trustee

Trustees *M S Lyons; Mrs J Lyons; D Mendoza; J S Newman.*

CC Number 1050689

Information available Full accounts were on file at the Charity Commission.

General This trust supports Jewish and Israeli organisations. In 2000/01 it had assets of £24,000. Total income was £92,000, including £90,000 in donations received. Grants totalled £131,000.

The largest grants were £75,000 to Friends of Horim Establishments, £37,000 to Mesorah Heritage Foundation and £10,000 to Jewish Care. Other beneficiaries included Jewish Learning Council (£2,100), Mesoral Publications Limited (£1,200), United Synagogue (£1,100), Friends of Adereth Yaakov (£1,000), Finchley Synagogue (£640), United Jewish Appeal (£500), Friends of Bnei Akiva (£380) and Kisharon (£200).

Applications The trust states that it will not consider unsolicited applications.

The M B Foundation

General

Around £250,000

Beneficial area Some preference for Greater Manchester.

Clark & Terry, Newhaven Business Park, Barton Lane, Eccles, Manchester M30 0HH

Correspondent S B Bamberger, Trustee

Trustees *Rabbi W Kaufman; Rabbi M Bamberger; S B Bamberger.*

CC Number 222104

Information available Accounts were on file at the Charity Commission, but only up to 1997/98 and only in the public files up to 1983.

General In 1997/98 the trust had an income and an expenditure of £250,000. We have not been able to obtain any further information on this trust other than that it supports general and educational causes

Applications In writing to the correspondent, although the trust states that its funds are already committed.

The M & C Trust

Jewish, social welfare

£188,000 (2000/01)

Beneficial area UK.

c/o Chantrey Vellacott DFK, Russell Square House, 10–12 Russell Square, London WC1B 5LF

Tel. 020 7509 9000 **Fax** 020 7509 9219

Correspondent A C Langridge, Trustee

Trustees *A Bernstein; Mrs J B Kemble; A C Langridge; Elizabeth J Marks; Rachel J Lebus.*

CC Number 265391

Information available Full accounts were provided by the trust.

General Since 1999 the trust's primary charitable objects have been Jewish causes and social welfare.

In 2000/01 the trust had assets of £5.4 million and an income of £150,000. Grants totalling £188,000 were awarded to 21 charities, most of these were Jewish.

By far the largest grant of £35,000 went to Jerusalem Foundation. Grants of £10,000 each went to 10 organisations: Action for Kids, Connect, CSV, Friends of Israel Education Trust, Helen House, Jewish Children's Holiday Fund, Jewish Women's Aid, Nightingale House, Tree House and World Jewish Relief.

Other grants were either for £2,500, £5,000 or £7,500 and included those to Bradians Trust, Centre for Jewish–Christian Relations, Deafblind UK, Jewish Marriage Council and Spiro Institute.

The trust is connected with Quercus Trust, being under the same administration and having similar objectives.

Exclusions No grants to individuals.

Applications In writing to the correspondent, but the trust states that funds are currently earmarked for existing projects. In order to keep administration costs to a minimum, they are unable to reply to any unsuccessful applications.

The M D & S Charitable Trust

Jewish

£146,000 (2000/01)
Beneficial area UK and Israel.

22 Overlea Road, London E5 9BG
Tel. 020 7272 2255
Correspondent Martin D Cymerman, Trustee
Trustees *M D Cymerman; Mrs S Cymerman.*
CC Number 273992
Information available Full accounts were on file at the Charity Commission.

General This trust supports Jewish organisations in the UK and has general charitable purposes in Israel.

In 2000/01 the trust had assets of £645,000. Total income was £233,000, including £135,000 surplus on sale of property. A total of £146,000 was given in 57 grants.

The largest grants were £13,000 to Ichud Mosdos Gur, £11,000 each to Yeshivat Dromah and Yeshivat Gaon Yaakov, £9,800 to Mosdos Kaliv, £8,000 to Yeshivat Magen Aurohom, £7,000 to Yeshivat Kolel Zecher Yaakov, £6,100 to Yeshivat Ponevez, £5,500 to Yeshivat Nechomos Isa Yisroel and £5,000 each to Telz Academy Trust and Yeshivat Tomchey Temimen.

Other beneficiaries included Seminar Ateres Malkah (£4,000), Yeshivat Sheais Yossef (£2,500), Ponevez Aid and Benevolence Fund (£2,300), Kiryat Banot Girls' Town (£1,500) and Yeshivat Nachalat Shay (£1,000).

Applications In writing to the correspondent.

M N R Charitable Trust

General

£159,000 (2001)
Beneficial area UK, overseas.

Mazars, 24 Bevis Marks, London EC3A 7NR
Tel. 020 7220 3462 **Fax** 020 7377 9975
Email peter.hyatt@mazars.co.uk

Correspondent Bryan K H Rogers
Trustees *Peter R Hyatt, Chair; John S Mellows; David E Ryan.*
CC Number 287735
Information available Full accounts were provided by the trust.

General This trust acts as a conduit for the charitable giving of the Mazars firm of chartered accountants (formerly Mazars Neville Russell). Up to 10% of the funds raised from each of the regional branches can be given to local organisations at the discretion of the managing partner, the rest of the funds are given by the trustees for general charitable causes to charities which must be known personally to a trustee or staff member.

Grants are made towards particular projects such as capital expenditure, research or an event rather than core costs unless the applicant is financially sound and launching a strategic initiative. The trustees like to give grants which will make a significant impact on the recipient organisation and as such rarely support the largest organisations, while the availability of funding from the local partners make the trustees wary of supporting causes specific to a particular locality. 30% of total funds is directed towards community projects.

In 2001 the trust received Gift Aid contributions totalling £152,000, which contributed to the total income of £154,000. Grants to 59 organisations ranged from £25 to £15,000 and totalled £159,000. Assets at the year end totalled £25,000.

The 27 grants of £2,000 or more were listed in the accounts. The largest were £15,000 each to Indian Earthquake Appeal (via Christian Aid) and London City Mission and £10,000 each to Bonny Downs Community Association, Primary Immunodeficiency Association, Saltmine, and Scriptural Knowledge Institution (regarding Mercy Ships).

Other grants included £7,000 to Sight Savers International, £5,000 each to ACCORD, Catholic Children's Rescue Society, Communities United Project and Operation Mobilisation – India, £4,000 to Carousel, £3,000 each to Friends of Foreland School and Redcliffe College, £2,500 to Leeds Faith in Schools and £2,000 each to Barnardos, Lambeth Partnership, Lightforce International, Royal Zoological Society of Scotland and Walk Thru the Bible Ministries.

Exclusions Support is not given to an organisation within three years of an early grant, and as such recurrent grants are not made. No grants are made to individuals.

Applications Unsolicited applications will rarely be considered or acknowledged. Applications will generally only be considered from charities with which the partners or staff of Mazars already have an active relationship.

The Madeline Mabey Trust

Medical research, children's welfare

£242,000 (2000/01)
Beneficial area UK, and UK-registered international charities.

Mabey House, Floral Mile, Twyford, Reading RG10 9SQ
Correspondent Joanna Singeisen, Trustee
Trustees *Alan G Daliday; Bridget A Nelson; Joanna L Singeisen.*
CC Number 326450
Information available Accounts were on file at the Charity Commission, but without a list of grants, or a full narrative report.

General The sparse 2000/01 trustees report and accounts provided little detail of the nature of this trust, containing no grants list or narrative report. In previous years the trust has stated that it principally, but not exclusively, supports medical research and children's welfare charities.

In 2000/01 the trust had assets of £168,000. Total income was £297,000, most of which came from donations received. After auditors' fees of just £100, grants were made to 147 organisations totalling £242,000. No further information was available.

Applications In writing to the correspondent. Please note, unsuccessful applications are not acknowledged.

The Robert McAlpine Foundation

Children with disabilities, older people, medical research, welfare

£250,000 (1999/2000)

Beneficial area UK.

Eaton Court, Maylands Avenue, Hemel Hempstead, Hertfordshire HP2 7TR

Tel. 01442 233444

Correspondent Graham Prain

Trustees *Hon. David McAlpine; M H D McAlpine; Kenneth McAlpine; Cullum McAlpine; Adrian N R McAlpine.*

CC Number 226646

Information available Full accounts were on file at the Charity Commission.

General This foundation generally supports causes concerned with children with disabilities, older people, medical research and social welfare. A small number of other charities are also supported, through a long-term connection with the foundation and therefore no new beneficiaries are considered from outside the usual areas.

In 1999/2000 it had assets of £6.3 million and an income of £266,000, including the usual donation of £35,000 from Sir Robert MacAlpine Limited. Grants totalled £250,000. Ewing Foundation received £40,000 while £35,000 was donated to Fairbridge.

Other grants included £17,000 to Stoke Mandeville Burns and Reconstruction Surgery, £10,000 each to Devas Club and H & F Skills Centre, £7,500 to Brittle Bone Society, £5,000 each to Age Concern, Beamsley Project, Glasgow Old People's Welfare Association, St Briavels Centre for Child Development, Somers Workshop and Thrift Urban Housing, £4,500 to Defeating Deafness, £4,000 to Child & Sound, £3,000 to Side by Side, £2,500 each to Age Concern Wirral, League of Venturers Search and Rescue, Mountsandel Christian Fellowship and Ro-Ro Sailing Project and £1,000 to New Horizons.

Exclusions The trust does not like to fund overheads. No grants to individuals.

Applications In writing to the correspondent at any time. Considered annually, normally in November.

Macdonald-Buchanan Charitable Trust

General

£106,000 (2001)

Beneficial area UK, with a slight preference for Northamptonshire.

Rathbone Trust Ltd, 159 New Bond Street, London W1S 2UD

Tel. 020 7399 0820

Correspondent Miss Linda Cousins

Trustees *Capt. John Macdonald-Buchanan; A J Macdonald-Buchanan; A R Macdonald-Buchanan; H J Macdonald-Buchanan; Mrs M C A Philipson.*

CC Number 209994

Information available Full accounts were on file at the Charity Commission.

General The Hon. Catherine Macdonald-Buchanan set up this trust in 1952 for general charitable purposes and endowed it with 40,000 shares in the then Distillers Company.

In 2001 the trust had assets of £2.9 million which generated an income of £123,000. After high management and administration costs of £31,000, grants were made to 127 organisations.

Two substantial grants were made during the year: £30,000 to Carrie Jo Charitable Trust and £23,000 to Orrin Charitable Trust. The only other grant of over £1,000 went to Queen Margaret's School (£1,500).

A number of organisations in Northamptonshire were supported. Northamptonshire Association of Youth Clubs received £500 while Clubs for Young People Northamptonshire and YMCA Northamptonshire each received two grants totalling £400. Grants of £250 each went to Northampton and District Mind, Northamptonshire Council for Disabled People and Northamptonshire Association for the Blind.

Other grants included £500 each to British Red Cross, Cot Death Society, East Anglia Children's Hospice, Imperial Cancer Research Fund, National Asthma Association, Anthony Nolan Bone Marrow Trust, Oxfam and Spinal Injuries Association, £200 each to Age Concern, Battersea Central Mission, Canine Partners for the Independence, Ex-Service Mental Welfare Society and Gurkha Welfare Trust, £150 each to Game

Conservancy Trust and £25 to Philharmonic Choir.

Exclusions No grants to individuals.

Applications In writing to the correspondent, for consideration once a year. Appeals will not be acknowledged.

D D McPhail Charitable Settlement

Medical research, disability, older people

£177,000 (1999/2000)

Beneficial area UK.

PO Box 285, Pinner, Middlesex HA5 3FB

Correspondent Mrs Sheila Watson, Administrator

Trustees *I McPhail; P Cruddas; J K Noble.*

CC Number 267588

Information available Accounts were on file at the Charity Commission.

General This trust has been growing in size since 1997, when it began to receive sums from the Estate of the late Mr D D McPhail. Assets at the end of 1995/96 totalled £223,000 and grants were made in that year of £17,000. By 1999/2000 the assets had risen to £10 million and it made grants totalling £177,000. In that year the trust had an income of £873,000, comprised in the main of a legacy (£518,000) and investment income (£343,000).

In 1999/2000 a grant of £150,000 was made to a local hospice. Similar large donations were committed to this recipient for the following two years, subject to satisfactory reports being produced.

This large grant dwarfed the remaining 20 donations, which were mostly of £1,000 or £2,000. The trust prefers to support:

- the furtherance of medical research
- the care of people who are disabled, particularly disabled children
- the care of people who are elderly and infirm.

Other beneficiaries in 1999/2000 included Condover Hall School for the Blind, Harrow Blind Social Club, The Barbara Bus Fund, International League for the Protection of Horses, Invalid Children's Aid Association, National Society for

Epilepsy, RADAR, Cancer Relief Macmillan Fund and The National Meningitis Trust.

Applications In writing to the correspondent.

This entry was not confirmed by the trust, but is correct according to information on file at the Charity Commission.

The Magen Charitable Trust

Education, Jewish

£116,000 (1999/2000)

Beneficial area UK.

Lopian Gross Barnett & Co., Harvester House, 37 Peter Street, Manchester M2 5QD

Tel. 0161 832 8721

Correspondent The Trustees

Trustees *Jacob Halpern; Mrs Rose Halpern.*

CC Number 326535

Information available Accounts were on file at the Charity Commission, but without a narrative report or list of grants.

General In the accounts the trust's aims were stated as making donations to charitable and educational institutions. In 1999/2000 the trust had assets of £562,000 and an income of £153,000 derived mainly from rent and donations. Grants totalled £116,000, but unfortunately there was no grants list available.

In 1995/96 the last year for which information was available, the trust had assets totalling £206,000, its income was £50,000 and it made grants totalling £43,000. The largest grants were £12,000 to Manchester Yeshiva Kollel, £6,000 to Talmud Educational Trust, £5,000 to Bnos Yisroel School and £4,000 to Mesifta Tiferes Yisroel. A further 40 grants were made, including four of over £1,000. All the beneficiaries were Jewish organisations.

Applications In writing to the correspondent.

Mageni Trust

Arts

£62,000 (1998/99)

Beneficial area UK.

17 Hawthorne Road, Bromley, Kent BR1 2HN

Correspondent G L Collins, Trustee

Trustees *G L Collins; Mrs G L Collins; S J Hoare.*

CC Number 1070732

Information available Accounts were on file at the Charity Commission.

General This recently registered trust received an income in 1998/99 of £646,000. After distributing grants totalling £62,000 the balance was tranferred to the trust's capital account. Three of the four grants were to arts organisations, the fourth and largest grant was donated to CAF, probably to distribute to other charities.

Grants were: £50,000 to CAF as a Gift Aid donation; £10,000 to National Youth Orchestra; £1,000 to National Theatre; and £500 to London Philharmonic Orchestra School Appeal.

Applications In writing to the correspondent.

Maranatha Christian Trust

Christian

£368,000 (1997/98)

Beneficial area UK and worldwide.

208 Cooden Drive, Bexhill-on-Sea, East Sussex TN39 3AH

Fax 01424 844741

Correspondent G P Ridsdale

Trustees *A C Bell; Revd L Bowring; Rt Hon. Viscount Brentford.*

CC Number 265323

Information available Accounts were on file at the Charity Commission but without a list of grants.

General The trust makes grants towards the advancement of the Christian gospel in the UK and overseas.

In 1997/98 the trust's assets totalled £2 million, it had an income of £65,000 and grants were made totalling £368,000.

In 1996/97 grants totalled £215,000 including £27,000 to individuals. The largest grant was £30,000 to CARE Trust, and it also received a further grant of £5,000 towards its intern programme. Other larger grants included £10,000 each to Stewards Trust and Riding Lights and £7,500 to Portman House Trust.

Other grants mostly ranged from £1,000 to £5,000 and included £5,000 to Oasis Media, £4,000 to Clasp, £1,500 to Women in Mission and £1,000 each to Christians in Entertainment, Rewick Park Initiative – Rwanda, Southeast Asian Outreach – Rajana Craft Project Cambodia and Stepping Stones.

Applications In writing to the correspondent, but please note, the trust does not consider unsolicited applications.

Marbeh Torah Trust

Jewish

£208,000 (2000/01)

Beneficial area UK and Israel.

116 Castlewood Road, London N15 6BE

Correspondent M C Elzas, Trustee

Trustees *Moishe Chaim Elzas; Jacob Naftoli Elzas; Simone Elzas.*

CC Number 292491

Information available Accounts were on file at the Charity Commission, but without a list of grants for 2000/01.

General The trust objects are to further and support Jewish education and religion as well as the relief of poverty.

In 2000/01 the trust had an income of £214,000, almost entirely comprised of donations received. Grants were made totalling £208,000, leaving assets of £20,000. No further information was available for this year.

In 1999/2000, grants were made to 18 organisations totalling £239,000. The largest were £70,000 to Yeshiva Marbeh Torah, £36,000 to Sharei Shimon Aryeh, £25,000 to Yeshiva Beis Meir, £15,000 to Mishkenos Yakov, £13,000 each to Ezer Mitzion and Nachalat Avrohom and £10,000 each to Knesess Hatorah and Nechomas Isser Yisoroel. The remaining nine grants ranged from £2,800 to £7,500 and included those to Beis Hillel, Kollel Beth Hamedrash and Yeshiva Beis Hillel.

Applications In writing to the correspondent.

Marchig Animal Welfare Trust

Animal welfare

£120,000 (2001)
Beneficial area Worlwide.

10 Queensferry Street, Edinburgh EH2 4PG
Tel. 0131 225 6039 **Fax** 0131 220 6377
Email marchigtrust@marchigawt.org
Website www.marchigawt.org
Correspondent The Administrator
Trustees *Madame Jeanne Marchig; Trevor Scott; Les Ward, Bill Jordan; Jenny Palmer.*
CC Number 802133
Information available Full accounts and an information leaflet were provided by the trust.

General The objects of the trust are to protect animals and to promote and encourage practical work in preventing cruelty. There are no restrictions on the geographical area of work, types of grants or potential applicants, but all applications must be related to animal welfare and of direct benefit to animals. Projects supported by the trust have included mobile spay/neuter clinics, alternatives to the use of animals in research, poster campaigns, anti-poaching programmes, establishment of animal sanctuaries as well as smaller groups committed to animal welfare and special projects in sanctuaries and refuges.

As well as giving grants, the trust also makes two Marchig Animal Welfare Awards, one of which is for the development of alternative methods to the use of animals in experimental work and their practical implementation in scientific and manufacturing procedures (worth 40,000 Swiss Francs) and the other for practical work in the field of animal welfare by a society or individual anywhere in the world (20,000 Swiss Francs).

In 2001 the trust had assets of £2.4 million and an income of £244,000, including £102,000 in donations received. Grants were made to 56 organisations totalling £120,000.

The largest grants were US$25,000 each to Cat Welfare Society of Israel and CHAI – Israel and £10,000 each to Blue Cross of India and Compassion Unlimited Plus Action – India.

Grants in the UK were made to 30 organisations and 2 individuals and totalled £30,000. Beneficiaries included Puss in Boots (£4,500), Advocates for Animals (£4,000), Assisi Sanctuary (£2,000), Farm Animal Welfare Society and Society for the Protection of Animals Abroad (£1,000 each), Easterleigh Animal Sanctuary (£750), Cats Protection League branches in Huddersfield & Halifax and Pembrokeshire (£500 each), Hessilhead Wildlife Rescue Trust and Wildlife in Need (£250 each) and Barn Owl Trust and Isle of Wight Bat Hospital (£200 each).

Beneficiaries overseas included Foundation for the Protection of Community Dogs – Romania and Society for the Protection of Stray Animals – Turkey (£5,000), Brooke Hospital for Animals – Delhi, India (£3,500), International Aid for Korean Animals (US$5,100), Animals Asia Foundation – Hong Kong and Domestic Animal Rescue Group – South Africa (£2,000), Help in Suffering – India (£1,500), White Cross AP Society – Hungary (£1,300), Parque Animal PR International – Spain (£1,000), Animals Angels – Germany (£500) and Safe Havens for Donkeys in the Holy Land – Israel (£250).

Applications In writing to the correspondent.

The Linda Marcus Charitable Trust

General

£188,000 (1999/2000)
Beneficial area Worldwide.

Seymour Pierce Advisory Limited, 79 Mount Street, London W1Y 5HJ
Tel. 020 7616 4700
Correspondent Mrs Sarah Hunt
Trustees *Dame Shirley Porter; Mrs Linda Streit; Peter Green; Steven Nigel Porter.*
CC Number 267173
Information available Information was provided by the trust.

General In 1999/2000 grants totalled £188,000. A total of 30 grants were given, with a total of £60,000 in four grants going to Tel Aviv University – Porter Super Centre. other larger grants were £32,000 to Arava Institute – New Israel Fund, £20,000 to Israel Family Therapy Advancement Fund and £16,000 to British Friends of Israel Philharmonic Orchestra. Other grants ranged from £250 upwards with most to Jewish causes, although arts organisations such as Open Air Theatre (£5,000) and Royal National Theatre (£1,000) also benefited. The only other recipients were Children's Leukaemia Trust (£1,000) and Teenage Cancer Trust (£250).

Applications In writing to the correspondent.

The Stella and Alexander Margulies Charitable Trust

Jewish, general

£132,000 (2000/01)
Beneficial area UK.

23 Grosvenor Street, London W1K 4QL
Tel. 020 7416 4160
Correspondent M J Margulies, Trustee
Trustees *Marcus J Margulies; Martin D Paisner; Sir Stuart Lipton.*
CC Number 220441
Information available Accounts were on file at the Charity Commission.

General This trust has general charitable purposes, with a preference for Jewish organisations.

In 2000/01 it had assets of £6.3 million, which generating an income of £333,000. Grants were made to 23 organisations totalling £132,000.

The largest grant was £90,000 to UJIA for Alma and other projects. Royal Opera House Trust received £20,000 for the development appeal.

Other grants ranged from £100 to £3,100. Jewish organisations to benefit included Central Synagogue (£3,100), Community Security Trust and Nightingale House (£2,000 each), Friends of Bnei Akiva and British Technion Society (£500 each) and Leeds Jewish Welfare Board (£200).

Other beneficiaries included British Red Cross (£2,500), Heal the World Foundation (£1,800), Prince's Trust

(£1,500), Royal Academy Trust and Royal Albert Hall Trust (£1,000 each), Great Ormond Street Hospital Children's Charity (£500), Barnardos and NSPCC (£200 each) and Children's Heart Unit Fund (£100).

Applications In writing to the correspondent.

Michael Marks Charitable Trust

Arts, environment
£371,000 (2000/01)
Beneficial area UK and overseas.

5 Elm Tree Road, London NW8 9JY
Tel. 020 7286 4633 **Fax** 020 7289 2173
Correspondent The Secretary
Trustees *Martina, Lady Marks; Prof. Sir Christopher White; Dr D MacDiarmid.*
CC Number 248136
Information available Full accounts were on file at the Charity Commission.

General The trust supports the arts (including galleries and museums), and environmental groups, with grants generally ranging from £150 to £25,000, although larger grants have been given.

In 2000/01 it had assets of £3.5 million, which generated an income of £177,000. Grants totalling £371,000 were made to 32 organisations, a quarter of which were also supported in the previous year.

The largest grants were £50,000 to Walton-on-Thames Community Arts Trust, £36,000 to British Museum, £27,000 to Christchurch College – Oxford, £25,000 each to Arc Dance Company, and Victoria and Albert Museum, £20,000 each to British Institute of Florence, British School at Rome, Mauritshuis and Vivat Trust, £15,000 each to Early English Organ Project, National Library of Scotland and Wordsworth Trust, £13,000 to Woodland Trust and £12,000 each to Burlington Magazine and Hellenic Centre.

Other grants ranged from £150 to £5,300, with beneficiaries including English Chamber Choir Society (£5,300), BT Scottish Ensemble and Polish Knights of Malta (£5,000 each), St Pancras Community Centre (£4,800), Patriarchate of Constantinople (£3,000), International Centre for Missing and Exploited Children (£2,000), Anglo Israel Association (£1,000), Ionian Society (£310), Lifeline Humanitarian Organisation (£250) and Lykion ton Hellinidon (150).

Exclusions Grants are given to registered charities only. No grant to individuals or profit organisations.

Applications In writing to the correspondent before July. Applications should include audited accounts, information on other bodies approached and details of funding obtained. Requests will not receive a response unless they have been successful.

The Hilda & Samuel Marks Foundation

Jewish, general
£172,000 (2000/01)
Beneficial area UK and Israel.

1 Ambassador Place, Stockport Road, Altrincham, Cheshire WA15 8DB
Tel. 0161 941 3183 **Fax** 0161 927 7437
Email davidmarks@mutleyproperties.co.uk
Correspondent D L Marks, Trustee
Trustees *S Marks; Mrs H Marks; D L Marks; Mrs R D Selby.*
CC Number 245208
Information available Accounts were provided by the trust.

General This trust mainly gives support to UK charities and to charities based in Israel.

In 2000/01 the assets of the trust stood at £2.6 million with an income of £383,000 including £227,000 from donations). Grants, which totalled £172,000, were categorised as follows:

	£	%
Community	12,000	7
Religious activity	5,700	3.3
Education	37,000	21.6
Health	39,000	22.5
Welfare 7	9,000	45.7

UK charities received £88,000 of the total, with £78,000 to charities in Israel and a small amount given to projects in other countries. The largest grant was to Child Resettlement Fund for £30,000, towards support of their homes in Israel. Capital funding has been given to these homes in the past, and the trustees anticipate continuing their support in the foreseeable future. The trust has also committed to give £100,000 over the next two years for a new home for disruptive children in Even Shmuel, Israel. Other large grants included those to Alyn Hospital (£25,000), Manchester Talmud Torah (£15,000) and Manchester Jewish Federation (£20,000). Support has been given to all these organisations for a number of years.

18 other organisations received grants of £1,000 to £10,000 including Heathlands – Manchester (£10,000), Norwood (£6,000), NSPCC and Bournemouth Jewish Day School Charitable Trust (both £5,000) and Lubavitch Foundation (£2,500). Smaller grants went to a similar organisations, with a few very small grants to well-known health-related charities.

Exclusions No grants to individuals.

Applications In writing to the correspondent. However, the trust primarily supports projects known to the trustees and its funds are fully committed.

The Erich Markus Charitable Foundation

Welfare, hospices, medical, general
£138,000 (2001)
Beneficial area UK.

10 New Square, Lincoln's Inn, London WC2A 3QG
Correspondent Payne Hicks Beach
Trustees *Erich Markus Charity Trustees Ltd.*
CC Number 283128
Information available Full accounts were provided by the trust.

General Erich Markus died in 1979, leaving half of his residual estate to the trust. The original capital was made up of 355,000 ordinary 25p shares in Office & Electronic Machines Ltd. In 2001 assets stood at £3.2 million.

In 2001 the foundation had an income of £100,000 and made 61 grants totalling £138,000. Management and administration costs totalled £23,000.

The largest grants went to Magen David Adom (£15,000), St Francis Hospice and World Jewish Relief (£5,000 each) and St Christopher's Hospice (£4,500). All other grants were of £4,000 or less.

Grants of £4,000 were given to Chai Lifeline Cancer Care, In Kind Direct, Jewish Blind & Disabled, Jewish Care, Kisharon, Lady Hoare Trust, Nightingale House, Norwood, RABI, Samaritans, Spanish & Portuguese Jews' Home for the Aged and Trinity Hospice.

The remaining grants were for either £1,000 or £2,000. Beneficiaries included Action on Elder Abuse, British Blind Sport, Charing Cross Hospital Dialysis Trust, Children with Aids Charity, Headway, Motability, Royal School for the Blind, Weston Spirit and Umbrella.

Exclusions No grants to individuals.

Applications In writing to the correspondent. Applications will only be considered if accompanied by a copy of the latest report and accounts. Trustees meet twice a year, usually in April and October. No telephone enquiries please.

The Marsh Christian Trust

General

£123,000 (2000/01)
Beneficial area UK.

Granville House, 132–135 Sloane Street, London SW1X 9AX
Tel. 020 7730 2626 **Fax** 020 7823 5225
Correspondent Lorraine McMorrow, Administrator
Trustees *B P Marsh; R J C Marsh; N C S Marsh.*
CC Number 284470
Information available Full accounts and a copy of their triennial review were provided by the trust.

General The trust was established in 1981 and has increased steadily in size with each year. In 2000/01 it had an income of £168,000 and assets of £4.3 million. It made 251 grants totalling £123,000, 130 of which went to organisations supported in the previous year. The financial report showed high administration costs of £80,000, but this can be accounted for by the proactive nature of the charity and the large number of small grants made.

Based on the report for 1997–2000 report during which time £336,000 was distributed (£491,000 between 1994–1997), causes were supported in the following areas (percentage of grant fund allocation is shown in brackets):

Social welfare (20%)
Small donations went to charities helping people with physical and mental disabilities. Charities working amongst the young, the aged, the homeless, alcoholics and drug abusers were all supported as far as is possible, especially those displaying a Christian emphasis in their work. The largest grant given in this area was £1,600.

Environmental causes/animal welfare (15%)
The trust has been a supporter of various organisations devoted to nature conservation and the well being of wildlife, both within Britain and overseas. A particular project, Wildlife Information Network, which was previously an initiative of the Marsh Christian Trust, has now become fully independent and established itself within the Royal Veterinary College. The largest grant was £2,000.

Healthcare and medical research (22.5%)
Much of the money distributed under this category went to hospices and other organisations working with the terminally ill. (The trustees try to avoid giving funds to hospitals in the belief that it is the responsibility of the local and national community to maintain these.) The largest grant was £3,000.

Education and training (9%)
Funding and training for children and adults with disabilities is a part of the trust's programme. The trust regularly makes grants to the Royal College of Music, English Speaking Union, Young Enterprise and Oxford Evangelical Research Trust among others. (The trustees try to avoid giving funds to ordinary schools, colleges or universities in the belief that it is the responsibility of the local and national community to maintain these.) The largest grant was £3,000.

Literature, arts and heritage (22.5%)
The trust gives support to a number of museums and galleries, including the National Portrait Gallery, the V&A Museum and the British Museum.

(The trustees try wherever possible to avoid making donations to appeals for individual church buildings or cathedrals, believing that it is the responsibility of individual congregations and the church to maintain these). The largest grant was £3,000.

Overseas appeals (8.5%)
Examples of causes supported during the year include Voluntary Service Overseas, ActionAid and Sight Savers International. The largest grant was £2,000.

Miscellaneous (2.5%)
The Highgate Cemetery, Prisoners Abroad and Population Concern are examples of causes supporting during the period. The largest grant was £1,250.

The Marsh Awards Scheme
Educational, literary, social and animal welfare awards ranging between £600 and £3,500 were also made by the trust; 14 were given out during the period.

The trustees will normally only make grants to registered charities experienced within their chosen field of work. Long-term core funding of appropriate work is the trust's normal approach, taking the form of money given on a recurring annual basis subject to yearly resubmission and review.

The size of donations normally ranges from £250 to £4,000 but can be as low as £10 and as high as £6,000. In 2000/01, 13 grants of £1,000 or over were awarded, the largest going to English Speaking Union (£6,000). Other recipients of larger grants were The Arts Club (£4,700), Wildlife Information Network (£4,000) and Radiological Research Trust (£2,000).

Grants under £1,000 included Sight Savers International (£900), Rare Breeds Survival Trust (£850), The Grubb Institute (£800), Mayday Trust and Crusaid (£750 each), The Aidis Trust (£650), Acorn Christian Foundation (£600), Action Centres UK (£500), Campaign for Learning (£400), Young People's Trust for the Environment (£350), Youth Inclusive (£300), Special Toys Educational Postal Service (£250), Health Unlimited (£200), Rainer Foundation (£150), Nevis Historical and Conservation Society (£100), Small Woods Association (£80), Society of Authors (£75), Society of Friends of the National Army (£50) and Friends of National Maritime Museum (£35).

The trust also offers advice on fundraising and other organisational issues to its active 'customer charities'.

Exclusions No grants can be made to individuals or for sponsorships. No start-up grants. No support for building funds, ordinary schools, colleges, universities or hospitals, or research.

Applications In writing to the correspondent, including a copy of the most recent accounts. The trustees currently receive about 8,000 applications every year, of which 7,800 are new. Decisions are made at monthly trustee meetings.

The trustees attempt to visit each long-term recipient at least once every three years to review the work done, to learn of future plans and renew acquaintance with those responsible for the charity. Advice on fundraising and other organisational problems is also offered free of charge by the trust.

The Charlotte Marshall Charitable Trust

Roman Catholic, general
£141,000 (2000/01)
Beneficial area UK.

c/o C & C Marshall Limited, 55–65 Castleham Road, Castleham Industrial Estate, Hastings, East Sussex TN38 9NU

Tel. 01424 856020

Correspondent S Roy

Trustees *Miss C C Cirket; T P Cirkett; K B Page; J M Russell.*

CC Number 211941

Information available Full accounts were on file at the Charity Commission.

General The trust has general charitable purposes in the UK, mainly supporting educational, religious and other charitable purposes for Roman Catholics.

In 2000/01 the trust had assets of £751,000 and a total income of £164,000. Grants were given to 47 organisations totalling £141,000, of which £93,000 went to Roman Catholic causes.

The largest grants were £15,000 to St Mary Magdalenes Church, £11,000 to St Michael's Hospice, £10,000 to Cardinal Hume Centre and £9,000 each to St Augustine of Canterbury Roman Catholic School, and St Gregory Youth Project.

Other Catholic beneficiaries included St Mary Star of the Sea (£5,600), Apostleship of the Sea, Festival of Hope 2001 and St Patricks Missionary Society (£5,000 each) and Pilgrimage Trust (£1,500).

Other organisations supported included Depaul Trust (£6,500), Brighton and Hove Parents Children's Group (£1,800), Rescue Foundation (£1,300), Rotary Club of Hastings, Scottish Marriage Care and Shelter (£1,000 each), British Dyslexics (£750) and Action Support (£500).

Exclusions No grants are given to individuals.

Applications On a form available from the correspondent. Completed forms must be returned by 31 December for consideration in March.

The Jim Marshall Charitable Trust

General
£285,000 to individuals and organisations (2000)
Beneficial area UK.

Simpson Wreford and Co, 62 Beresford Street, London SE18 6BG

Tel. 020 8854 9552

Correspondent Mr Graham

Trustees *J Marshall; K W J Saunders; B Charlton; S B Marshall; L Hack.*

CC Number 328118

Information available Accounts were on file at the Charity Commission, but without a list of grants.

General Established in 1989 by the founder of Marshall Amplification plc, this trust supports organisations concerned with children, young people, families and people who are sick or have disabilities. Grants are also made directly to individuals. The trust deed lists Buckinghamshire Association of Boys' Clubs, London Federation of Boy's Clubs, Macintyre Homes, Variety Club Children's Charity and Wavedon All Music Plan as specific, but not exclusive, beneficiaries.

In 2000 it had assets of £115,000 and an income of £228,000, including £226,000 in donations received. After low management and administration expenses of just £100, around 100 grants were made totalling £285,000. No details of the beneficiaries or size of grants was included in the accounts.

Applications In writing to the correspondent at any time.

Sir George Martin Trust

General
£258,000 (2001/02)
Beneficial area Largely north and west Yorkshire and occasionally in Cumbria.

Netherwood House, Ilkley, West Yorkshire LS29 9RP

Tel. 01943 831019 **Fax** 01943 831570

Email sirgeorgemartintrust@care4free.net

Correspondent Peter Marshall, Secretary

Trustees *T D Coates, Chair; M Bethel; R F D Marshall; P D Taylor; Miss Janet Martin.*

CC Number 223554

Information available Report and accounts with full grants list and excellent narrative analysis; guidelines.

General The trust was formed from endowments from Sir George Martin. It 'prefers to make grants available for capital rather than revenue projects and is reluctant to give grants for general running costs or areas previously supported by state funds.'

'The trust does not normally repeat grants to any charity in any one year and the maximum number of consecutive grants is usually three. The trust prefers to adopt a one-off policy in terms of its giving'.

In future the trust will concentrate on a smaller number of large grants to a more limited number of applicants.

The Beneficial area is described as: largely north and west Yorkshire and occasionally Cumbria. The trust is now unable to support applications in South Yorkshire, the old Yorkshire coalfield area, Sheffield or Humberside.

Guidelines for giving in various areas:

- Church appeals: The trust will in future only normally give money to church appeals that have a definite outreach factor. Requests for restoration schemes of roofs, spires, etc., will not be supported.
- Music and the arts: The trust is getting so many requests in this area that it has decided to restrict the giving to areas which are known to have been of definite interest to Sir George Martin in his lifetime. These include Leeds Pianoforte Competition, Bradford Subscription Concerts, Harrogate Festival, Harrogate Choral Society, Leeds Philharmonic Society and Wharfedale Festival. Only on rare

occasions will the trust give to other charities outside those listed.

The trust will consider appeals for the capital needs of theatres in the geographical areas of interest. The trust does not support individuals, sponsorship of productions, touring companies, etc.

- Social welfare: The trust will support registered charities, which come under the general description of 'social welfare'. This might include visits and holidays for children, playgrounds, help for winter aid for older people, holidays and visits for people who are disabled and charities which fall in this general area.
- Old age: The trust prefers local projects and will support projects concerning holidays for old people, winter aid, Christmas parties, etc.
- Schools, education, universities: The trust will not support education in areas funded by the state. The trust will occasionally fund outreach projects from schools that do not concern the school itself.
- Children: The trust supports children's charities and activities.
- Medical: The trust is no longer able to fund medical appeals of a capital or revenue nature. Medical research projects are also no longer supported.
- Hospices: The trust will take a special interest in the work of hospices in its geographical area preferring one-off grants of a capital nature rather than for revenue purposes.
- Museums: The trustees have, in the past, supported important museums in the Beneficial area, such as Eureka Children's Museum in Halifax, Captain Cook Memorial Museum and Yorkshire Dales Museum. They will continue to look at the capital needs of museums in their geographical area of giving.
- The countryside in crisis, the countryside, environment, green issues: The trust is taking an increasing interest in the charitable needs of organisations in rural areas.

In 2001/02 it had assets of £5.4 million and an income of £171,000. About 500 applications were received, from which 117 grants were made totalling £258,000. They were broken down as follows:

Arts	15.2%
Church outreach	2.8%
Community outreach	27.8%
Education	15.5%
Environment	0.2%
International	1.1%
Medical	24%
Medical research	1.2%
Old age	3.4%

Playschemes and holiday schemes	1%
Youth	7.8%

The largest grants were £28,000 to St Gemma's Hospice – Leeds towards a refurbishment scheme, £25,000 to Woodhouse Grove School for capital developments and £20,000 to RABI to assist farmers in severe distress in the Yorkshire area.

Other beneficiaries of over £1,000 each included Leeds Grammar School (£13,000), Square Chapel Appeal – Halifax (£10,000), Captain Cook Museum – Whitby (£7,500), Roses Charitable Trust (£5,000), Harrogate Festival (£4,500), National Gardens Scheme and Yorkshire Association for the Disabled (£3,000 each), Ripon Cathedral Trust (£2,500), Dewsbury Health Centre (£2,000) and Grassington Festival, Holyrood House, Manningford Parish Church, Salvation Army and Sea Cadet Corps – Filey (£1,000 each).

Smaller grants of under £1,000 each were made to 53 organisations. Beneficiaries included Addington Gala, Bradford Toy Library, Buttershaw Advice and Social Centre, Cancer Research, Hebden Bridge Arts Festival, Andrew Hepper Memorial Fund, Ilkley Community Fund, Leeds Festival Chorus, Project Trust, Riding for the Disabled, Seacroft Parish and York Student Community Action.

Exclusions See the exclusions under the various programmes described in the guidelines detailed in the General section.

Applications The trust meets in March, July and December each year to consider applications. These should be made in writing to the secretary in good time for the meetings, which take place in the middle of the month. Applications that are not within the guidelines cannot be answered due to substantial increase in costs. Applications that are relevant will be acknowledged and, following meetings, successful applicants will be told of the grants they are to receive. Unsuccessful applicants will not be informed.

The trust is unable to consider applications from organisations without charitable status. Telephone calls are not encouraged as the office is not always staffed – it is better to write or fax.

The Mason Porter Charitable Trust

Christian
£140,000 (2000/01)
Beneficial area UK.

Liverpool Council of Social Service (Inc.), 14 Castle Street, Liverpool L2 0NJ
Tel. 0151 236 7728
Correspondent The Secretary
Trustees *Liverpool Council of Social Services (Inc.).*
CC Number 255545
Information available Accounts were provided by the trust, without a full grants list.

General In 2000/01 the trust's assets totalled £1.8 million generating an income of £101,000. Grants were made totalling £140,000 and appear to have been given mostly to Christian causes. In the past some beneficiaries have received grants in more than one year.

Grants over £1,000 were made to 15 beneficiaries. The largest was given to PSS (Personal Service Society), which received £66,000. The other main beneficiaries were Abernethy Trust (£14,000), Cliff College (£13,000), New Creations (£11,000), Just Care (£6,000), Worldwide Christian Outreach (£4,000), Philo Trust (£2,500), International Youth Exchange of Methodist Church, Life Changing Ministries, Liverpool Hope University, St Luke's Methodist Church in Hoylake and the University of Lincolnshire and Humberside (£1,500 each), Crusade for World Revival, Elim International Missions and The Messengers (£1,000 each).

Other smaller grants totalled just over £13,000.

Applications The trust states that it only makes grants to charities known to the settlor and unsolicited applications are not considered.

Masonic Trust for Girls and Boys

Children, young people

£352,000 to non-Masonic charities (2000)

Beneficial area UK.

31 Great Queen Street, London WC2B 5AG

Tel. 020 7405 2644 **Fax** 020 7831 4094

Website www.mtgb.org

Correspondent Lt Col J C Chambers, Secretary

Trustees Col G S H Dicker; Rt Hon. the Lord Swansea; M B Jones; P A Marsh.

CC Number 285836

Information available Information was provided by the trust.

General This trust was established in 1982; it predominantly makes grants to individual children of Freemasons who are in need; grants are also made to UK non-Masonic organisations working with children and young people. The trust also supports bursaries at 21 cathedrals and collegiate chapels.

In 2000 the trust had assets of over £153 million and an income of £8.5 million. Out of a total charitable expenditure of £7.6 million, grants to other charities totalled £352,000. Beneficiaries of grants of over £10,000 each were Caldecott Foundation (£100,000), Fountaindale Trust Communication Project (£25,000), Dame Hannah Rogers School (£23,000), Royal Wolverhampton School (£20,000) and Gordon's School (£10,000). Recipients of smaller grants in the range of £50 to £7,500 include The Blue Cross, Brainwave, Nigel Clare Network Trust, Girls Guild of Good Life, Ormskirk Grammar School (school prize), Winston's Wish and Wolverhampton Grammar School (school prize).

Choral bursaries were made from the 'general fund' totalling £113,000 and from the 'boys' fund' totalling £23,000.

The trust marked the millennium with 'Lifelites' a special commitment of £7.5 million for children's hospices throughout England and Wales. Half of this was to pay for IT equipment, the other half was set aside to fund future upgrading of the systems.

Applications In writing to the correspondent.

Matliwala Family Charitable Trust

Islam, general

£114,000 (2001/02)

Beneficial area UK and overseas, especially Bharuch – India.

9 Brookview, Fulwood, Preston PR2 8FG

Tel. 01772 706501

Correspondent A V Bux, Trustee

Trustees Ayub Vali Bux; Usman Salya; Abdul Aziz Vali Patel; Yousuf Bux; Ibrahim Vali Patel.

CC Number 1012756

Information available Full accounts were on file at the Charity Commission.

General The trust's areas of giving are:

- the advancement of education for pupils at Matliwala School Of Bharuch in Gujerat – India, and other schools, including assisting with the provision of equipment and facilities
- the advancement of the Islamic religion
- the relief of sickness and poverty
- the advancement of education.

In 2001/02 the trust had assets totalling £1.7 million. Total income was £279,000, including £147,000 in donations received and £123,000 in rents received from a property in Skegness. Management and administration costs for the year were low at £2,700.

Grants were made totalling £114,000. Of this, £70,000 was given to various causes in Bharuch, including hospital care, improvements to water supply, food, oil and housing construction for people who are disadvantaged. Other grants were £14,000 to Jamia Faizanul Quran, £5,000 each to Bharuch Muslim Medical and Welfare Trust and Munshi (Manubarwaia) Educational Trust, £3,400 to Dar-ul-aloom Jamia Habibia and £2,500 each to Islamic Research Institute of Great Britain and Preston Muslim Girl's School.

The accounts also stated that 48 non-material grants were made during the year, totalling £12,000.

Applications In writing to the correspondent.

The Maxwell Family Foundation

Disability/medical, welfare, conservation, education and animals

£46,000 (2000/01)

Beneficial area UK.

181 Whiteladies Road, Clifton, Bristol BS8 2RY

Correspondent E M Maxwell, Trustee

Trustees E M Maxwell; P M Maxwell; R P Spicer.

CC Number 291124

Information available Full accounts were on file at the Charity Commission.

General This trust was established in 1984, by Eric McLean Maxwell and as well as having general charitable purposes, its objects are the promotion of health, medical research, and the relief of people who are elderly, disabled or sick. Support for these objects is pursued on a national basis and in the main, from an established list with which the foundation has been involved for some years.

In 2000/01 the assets stood at £2.2 million and the income was £126,000. Management and administration costs were £8,400, this included £3,000 to Mr P M Maxwell for administration services and £4,000 to Mr E M Maxwell for management charges. A total of 26 grants were made totalling £46,000 (£143,000 in 1999/2000).

Grants over £1,000 each were made to ten organisations and included those to: Home Farm Trust (£22,000), Royal International Air Tatoo Flying Scholarships for the Disabled (£7,800), Deafblind UK (£3,500), Newcastle Society for Blind People (£1,500) and Mental Health Foundation, MRI Scanner Appeal – Southmead Hospital and Multiple Sclerosis Nerve Centre Appeal (£1,000 each).

Beneficiaries of smaller grants included Admiral Ramsay Appeal, Army Benevolent Fund, Broadway Trust, Extra Care Charitable Trust, Northern Pinetree Trust and Samaritans.

Exclusions The trust states explicitly that there is no support for unsolicited applications. It clearly abides by this policy and we would urge readers who do not know the trustees personally not to write to the trust.

Applications Applications are neither sought nor acknowledged. There appears little purpose in applying to this trust as no application will be supported unless accompanied by a personal request from someone known by the trustees.

The Mayfield Valley Arts Trust

Arts, especially chamber music

£115,000 (2000/01)

Beneficial area Unrestricted, but with a special interest in Sheffield and South Yorkshire.

Irwin Mitchell, St Peter's House, Hartshead, Sheffield S1 2EL

Tel. 0870 1500 100 **Fax** 0114 275 3306

Correspondent J M Jelly, Administrator

Trustees *A Thornton; J R Thornton; P M Thornton; D Whelton; D Brown; J R Rider.*

CC Number 327665

Information available Full accounts were on file at the Charity Commission.

General Established in 1987, the objects of this trust are the advancement of education by the encouragement of art and artistic activities of a charitable nature, especially music and the promotion and preservation of concerts and other musical events and activities. In recent years, particular favour has been given towards chamber music.

In 2000/01 the trust had assets of £2.3 million, which generated an income of £119,000. After management and administration costs of £7,680, grants totalled £115,000.

Sheffield Chamber Music in the Round received a total of £42,000 in six grants, for the May 2000 festival (second instalment), a student subsidy, the autumn/spring series, the international series, the May 2001 festival (first instalment) and a May 2001 guarantee.

York Early Music Foundation received £28,000 in total, for the 2000 festival and as a foundation grant for 1999/2000. Wigmore Hall was given £25,000 towards its 2000/01 season and its spring 2001 Young Masters Festival. Live Music Now! received a total of £18,000 in three grants.

Exclusions No grants to students.

Applications The trust states that no unsolicited applications are considered.

The Anthony and Elizabeth Mellows Charitable Settlement

Arts, national heritage, Church of England churches, hospitals, hospices, training and development of children and young people

£62,000 (2001/02)

Beneficial area UK.

22 Devereux Court, Temple Bar, London WC2R 3JR

Tel. 020 7353 6221

Correspondent Prof. A R Mellows, Trustee

Trustees *Prof. Anthony R Mellows; Mrs Elizabeth Mellows.*

CC Number 281229

Information available Full accounts were on file at the Charity Commission.

General This trust gives grants towards arts and national heritage to national institutions and to churches on recommendation from Council for Care of Churches.

In 2001/02 it had assets of £547,000 and an income of £46,000, including £25,000 in donations received. Grants totalled £62,000.

The largest grants went to two regular beneficiaries, Order of St John (£24,000) and Royal Opera House (£14,000).

Other grants included those to St John Ambulance (£1,500), National Art Collections Fund (£1,400), Arc Dance Company (£1,100), Great Hospital – Norwich, National History Museum and The Sixteen (£1,000 each), Matlock PCC for the preservation of 18th century crances (£800), King Edward VII Hospital for Officers (£500) and St John of Jerusalem Eye Hospital (£400).

Exclusions Applications from individuals, including students, are ineligible.

Applications Applications are considered when received, but only from UK institutions. No application forms are used. Grants will be made three times a year when the trustees meet to consider applications.

Melodor Ltd

Jewish, general

£82,000 (1999/2000)

Beneficial area UK and overseas.

148 Bury Old Road, Manchester M7 4SE

Correspondent The Trustees

Trustees *B Weiss; M Weiss; P Weiss; S Weiss; J L Weiss; H Weiss; R Sofer; F Neuman; H Neuman; M Neuman; E Neuman; M Friedlander; P Neumann; J Bleier; E Henry; R De Lange.*

CC Number 260972

Information available Full accounts were on file at the Charity Commission.

General This trust supports religious, educational and similar causes, with most grants going to Jewish organisations.

In 1999/2000 it had assets of £764,000 and an income of £149,000. Grants to 89 organisations totalled £82,000.

The largest grants were £15,000 to Chasdei Yoel; £10,000 to Beis Michas Yitchok and £7,900 each to Yeshivas Ohel Shimon and Yeshiva of Nitra.

Smaller grants included those to Shaarei Torah (£4,600), Belz – Manchester (£3,200), Beth Yaakov Seminary – Manchester (£3,000), Jewish High School for Girls (£2,500), Manchester Charitable Trust (£1,500), Rabbinical Research College (£1,300), Try (£500), Broughton Jewish Primary School (£330), Gateshead Talmudical College (£240), Ponevez Yeshua (£130) and British Friends of Laniado Hospital (£100).

Applications In writing to the correspondent.

This entry was not confirmed by the trust, but the address was correct according to the Charity Commission database.

Melow Charitable Trust

Jewish

£324,000 (2000/01)
Beneficial area UK and overseas.

21 Warwick Grove, London E5 9HX
Tel. 020 8806 1549
Correspondent J Low
Trustees *M Spitz; E Weiser.*
CC Number 275454

Information available Accounts were on file at the Charity Commission, but with only a brief narrative report.

General This trust makes grants to Jewish charities both in the UK and overseas. In 2000/01 its assets totalled £1 million and it had an income of £530,000 comprised mainly of donations received (£275,000) and rents (£234,000). Grants to 32 organisations totalled £324,000. Of the organisations supported, 18 had received a grant in the previous year.

Of grants made, 13 were for £10,000 or more. The largest grants were £33,000 to Shalom Torah Centre – USA, £30,000 each to Nextgrant and United Talmudical Associates – USA and £28,000 to Congregation Yeter Lev – USA. Other larger grants included those to Yesodey Hatorah School (£17,000), Beis Rochel D'Satmar Girls School (£15,000), Belz Institutions (£12,000) and Friends of Horim (£10,000).

Beneficiaries of smaller grants included British Jewish Heritage Society, Chasdei Yoel, Craven Walk Charitable Trust, Rehabilitation Trust, Yeshiva Horomoh Talmudical College and Yeter Lev Youth Club.

Applications In writing to the correspondent.

Mental Health Foundation

Mental health & learning disability research

About £500,000 annually
Beneficial area UK.

83 Victoria Street, London SW1H 0HW
Tel. 020 7802 0300 **Fax** 020 7802 0301
Email mhf@mhf.org.uk

Website www.mentalhealth.org.uk
Correspondent Helen Gravatt, Financial Controller
Trustees *Christopher S Martin, Chair; Jane Carter; Clare Euston; Abel Hadden; Prof. Rachel Jenkins; Dr Zenobia Nadirshaw; Giles Ridley; Philippa Russell; David Sachon; Daphne Statham; Lady Weston.*

CC Number 801130

Information available Accounts, but without a list of grants, were provided by the foundation.

General The mission of the foundation is to generate new understandings, knowledge, support and services which are exemplary and replicable. These should promote emotional wellbeing and improve the lives of people with mental health problems and/or with learning disabilities. The foundation's objectives are to:

- increase knowledge and understanding about mental health across society
- combat the stigma associated with mental distress
- improve policy and practice in the field of mental health and learning disabilities
- empower users and carers
- build the confidence and competence of people working in the mental health/learning difficult field
- influence governments on issues relating to mental health/learning disability policies, practices and services.

Much of this work is carried out by the foundation itself. However, the 2001/02 accounts stated the following, under the heading 'Grant making policy': 'The foundation has an internal process for identifying areas of work where it can make a useful contribution. For some projects this will involve the funding of other organisations through a grants programme. The foundation identifies such organisations through a tendering process. Organisations awarded a grant work to an agreed contact, which specifies the conditions. The monitoring of satisfactory delivery of the contract is in the first instance the responsibility of the project/programme manager.'

In 2001/02 the foundation had assets of £950,000. Total income was £4 million, mostly comprised of donations, gifts, legacies, charitable trading, fundraising events and grants from statutory sources and Community Fund. Total expenditure also totalled £4 million, included £1 million in grants, although details of these were not included in the accounts.

Exclusions No grants for:

- individual hardship, education and training
- travel
- attendance at conferences
- capital
- expenses such as vehicles or property
- general appeals
- general running costs
- overseas events.

Applications Please contact the foundation offices for current grant priorities, guidelines and closing dates.

Menuchar Ltd

Jewish

£301,000 (2000/01)
Beneficial area UK.

Equity House, 128–136 High Street, Edgware HA8 7EL
Correspondent The Trustees
Trustees *N Bude; G Bude.*
CC Number 262782

Information available Accounts were on file at the Charity Commission, but without a list of grants.

General The main objects of the trust are the advancement of religion in accordance with the orthodox Jewish faith and the relief of people in need.

In 2000/01 the trust had assets of £370,000. Total income was £232,000, including £200,000 in donations received. After low management and administration charges of £1,300, grants were made to 34 organisations totalling £301,000. No further information was available.

Exclusions No grants to non-registered charities or to individuals.

Applications In writing to the correspondent.

Mercury Phoenix Trust

AIDS, HIV
£601,000 (1998/99)
Beneficial area Worldwide.

The Mill, Mill Lane, Cookham, Berkshire SL6 9QT

Tel. 01628 527874

Correspondent Peter Chant

Trustees M Austin; Jim Beach; B H May; R M Taylor.

CC Number 1013768

Information available Accounts were on file at the Charity Commission, but without a list of grants. An information leaflet describing its work and listing some of the beneficiaries of grants was provided by the trust.

General The trust was set up in memory of Freddie Mercury by the remaining members of the rock group, Queen, and their manager. It makes grants to 'help relieve the poverty, sickness and distress of people with AIDS and HIV and to stimulate awareness and education in connection with the disease throughout the world'. The trust stated in November 2000 that the trust is 'only funding projects in developing countries during 2000 and, unless the policy changes, this will also be the case for 2001.'

Starting with the Freddie Mercury Tribute Concert for AIDS Awareness, the trust's fundraising activities have been spectacular. Income has been raised from, for example, a fan-initiated annual national street collection, a Queen album and from a ballet which was inspired by the music of Queen and Mozart.

The trust's information leaflet states 'Applications for grants have come in from many counties around the world and collaboration has been realised with groups as far removed as the World Health Organisation, to grass-root organisations run partly by voluntary workers in Uganda, Kenya, South Africa, Zambia, Nepal and India. The trust is following the latest developments in drug therapies and adapting funding policy to the changing needs of those affected by HIV/AIDS in the UK and elsewhere'.

In 1998/99 the trust's assets totalled £1.4 million and it had an income of £259,000, including £143,000 from Gift Aid and other donations. Grants were made totalling £601,000, resulting in a large deficit for the year.

Further information was not available in the accounts about the beneficiaries or size of grants. However, the trust's information leaflet includes a list of over 200 previous beneficiaries. The following are examples: AIDS Fondet Denmark, All Hallows Hospital, Barnardos Broad Street Project, Bihar State Dalit Women's Organisation, Blackpool and Preston Body Positive, Buddies, Children with AIDS Charity, Fondation d'Aide Direct, HARASS – Hastings and Rother, Life AIDS Project, National AIDS Manual, Open Road, Rajasthan Mahila Kalyan Mandal, Rural Heal Mission, TASO – Uganda, World Medical Fund and Zambia Charitable Trust.

Applications In writing to the correspondent.

The Miller Foundation

General, animal welfare
£161,000 (1999)
Beneficial area UK, with a preference for Scotland, especially the West of Scotland.

c/o Maclay Murray & Spens, 151 St Vincent Street, Glasgow G2 5NJ

Tel. 0141 248 5011 **Fax** 0141 248 5819

Correspondent A Biggart, Secretary to the Foundation

Trustees C Fleming-Brown; G R G Graham; J Simpson; G F R Fleming-Brown.

CC Number SC008798

Information available Information was provided by the trust.

General The trust supports the following:

- charities in Scotland, especially in the west of Scotland
- UK, animal welfare charities.

It will support a wide range of charities in Scotland. In 1999 grants totalled £161,000 and ranged from £1,000 to £2,000. Several grants were recurrent. Examples of beneficiaries were not available.

Exclusions No grants to individuals.

Applications On a form available from the secretary. Trustees meet once a year to consider grants in April. Applications should be received by the end of March.

The Millfield Trust

Christian
£67,000 to organisations (2000/01)
Beneficial area UK and worldwide.

Millfield House, Bell Lane, Liddington, Swindon, Wiltshire SN4 0HE

Tel. 01793 790181

Correspondent D Bunce, Trustee

Trustees D Bunce; Mrs R Bunce; P W Bunce; S D Bunce; A C Bunce.

CC Number 262406

Information available Full accounts were on file at the Charity Commission.

General This trust was set-up to provide grants to Christian organisations, and have supported a number of missionary societies for the last 50 years. Grants are given solely to organisations known to the trust and new applications are not considered.

In 2000/01 the trust had assets of £142,000 and an income of £79,000 comprised of including over £57,000 in Gift Aid donations from two of its trustees. Grants to organisations totalled £67,000. A further £8,000 was given in grants to individual missionaries and evangelists and £350 to older people.

There were 16 grants made over £1,000 each and these were listed in the accounts. The largest grants were £15,000 to Gideons International and £10,000 to Mission to Europe. Other beneficiaries included Mark Gillingham Charitable Trust (£6,000), Tear Fund (£3,300), Ashbury Evangelical Free Church (£3,200), Overseas Council (£2,000), Scripture Union (£1,800) and British Red Cross, Leoprosy Mission, Prospect Hospice and Schools Outreach (£1,000 each).

Remaining grants were mainly for £500 each and included those to Abacus Trust, Action Partners, London City Mission, NSPCC, Revival, Salvation Army, Swindon Churches Together, UFM Worldwide and Willows Counselling Service.

Applications No replies to unsolicited applications.

The Millhouses Charitable Trust

Christian, overseas aid, general

£78,000 (1997/98)

Beneficial area UK and overseas.

Medicos House, 79 Beverly Road, Hull HU3 1XR

Correspondent Dr A W Harcus, Trustee

Trustees *Revd J S Harcus; Dr A W Harcus.*

CC Number 327773

Information available Accounts were on file at the Charity Commission, but without a narrative report or grants list.

General This trust mostly gives recurrent grants, only adding new beneficiaries that are already known to the trustees. In 2001/02 the trust had an income of £49,000 and a total expenditure of £44,000. Unfortunately, further information for this year was not available.

The most recent grants information we have comes from 1996/97, when 40 grants totalled £55,000. The largest were £10,000 to Batah Foundation and £5,000 to six organisations including Amnesty International UK, Baptist Missionary Society, Christian Aid and NSPCC. Five organisations received £1,000 each, including Bible Society, Child Hope UK and Children of the Andes. A grant of £750 was given to Ethiopiaid and other grants were all for £250.

Exclusions Grants are made to registered charities only, no grants to individuals.

Applications In writing to the correspondent, but note that most of the grants given by this trust are recurrent. If new grants are made, they are usually to organisations known to the trustees.

The Millichope Foundation

General

£186,000 (1998/99)

Beneficial area UK, especially the West Midlands and Shropshire.

Millichope Park, Munslow, Craven Arms, Shropshire SY7 9HA

Tel. 01584 841234 **Fax** 01584 841445

Correspondent Mrs S A Bury, Trustee

Trustees *L C N Bury; Mrs S A Bury; Mrs B Marshall.*

CC Number 282357

Information available Full accounts were on file at the Charity Commission.

General The trust makes donations to a wide range of different organisations including:

- UK charities
- local charities serving Birmingham and Shropshire
- conservation charities.

In 1998/99 the assets stood at £4.2 million, the income was £253,000, £52,000 of which came from donations. The 139 donations made totalled £186,000. Grants were in the range of £50 to £13,000, 85 of these were for £1,000 or more. A number of recipients had received grants in the previous year.

The largest grant of the year went to the Fauna & Flora Preservation Society. This organisation received two grants totalling £13,000 and has been the major beneficiary in previous years. The trust made six grants of £5,000; beneficiaries included Midlands Centre for Spinal Injuries Appeal, Oxfam Hurricane Appeal, National Trust and Save the Children Fund.

Other larger grants included: £3,500 to Royal Opera House Covent Garden; £2,500 to St Basil's Centre and National Institute of Conductive Education; and £1,000 each to Royal Academy of Music Education, Relate, Castle Vale Homestart, Barnardos, Centre of Earth and English Bridge.

Grants given locally to the Birmingham and Shropshire areas included: Birmingham City Mission (£1,000); £500 each to Midland Youth Orchestra, Age Concern, Shropshire Family Mediation, Shropshire Youth Adventure Trust; and Shropshire Helping Hand (£50).

Exclusions No grants to individuals or non-registered charities.

Applications In writing to the correspondent

The Peter Minet Trust

General

£121,000 (2001)

Beneficial area Mainly south east London boroughs, particularly Lambeth and Southwark.

54–56 Knatchbull Road, London SE5 9QY

Tel. 020 7274 2266 **Fax** 020 7274 5222

Email peterminet@lineone.net

Correspondent Angela Freestone, Administrator

Trustees *J C B South, Chair; N McGregor-Wood; Mrs R L C Rowan; Ms P C Jones; R Luff; Revd Bruce Stokes.*

CC Number 259963

Information available Accounts were provided by the trust.

General In the mid-sixties, the Minet family sold much of their property to local councils. Part of the proceeds were used by Peter Brissault Minet to set up the trust in 1969. Peter Minet died in 1988.

The trust gives priority to registered charities working with people in the boroughs of Lambeth and Southwark, particularly those working in the areas of social welfare, health and the community, and with people who are young, sick, disabled, disadvantaged or elderly.

The trust's assets totalled £3.2 million in 2000/01 producing an income of £155,000. A total of £121,000 was distributed in 82 grants after administrative expenses of £37,000 had been paid.

Grants were distributed in the following categories:

- children and youth £43,000 (43 grants) – for playschemes, holidays, youth clubs, after-school projects, adoption agencies and sports programmes
- health and disability £33,000 (16) – for counselling projects, holidays for people with disabilities, medical education and information, and access projects
- community projects £39,000 (21) – for projects providing information, advice and support to various groups including ex-offenders, homeless people, single parents and unemployed people
- general and cultural £6,300 (2).

Grants were in the range of £350 to £5,000, but most were for amounts of £2,000 or less. Beneficiaries of larger amounts included India Earthquake

163

Appeal and Southwark Bereavement Care (£5,000 each), Springfield Community Flat (£4,000), Southwark Churches Care (£3,500), Cancer Resource Centre, Frankie Miller Songwriting Project and Riverpoint (£3,000 each) and 198 Gallery and Pegasus Opera Company (£2,500 each).

Other beneficiaries included Adfam National, Brixton Society, Charterhouse in Southwark, Child and Sound, Groundwork Southwark, Kennington Park Community Centre, Lambeth Summer Projects Trust, Nehemiah Project, Pembroke College Mission, Rockingham Estate Play Association, Single Homeless Project, Southwark Arts Forum, Southwark Irish Pensioners Project, Toucan Employment, Trinity Hospice, Waterloo Action Centre and Vauxhall Community Children's Projects.

Exclusions Grants to registered charities only. No grants are made to individuals. The trust will not give to: repetitive nationwide appeals by large charities for large sums of money; overseas appeals; parochial organisations outside Lambeth and Southwark; grant-making charities; or within 18 months of a previous grant.

Applications A form is available from the correspondent with a leaflet giving guidelines for applicants, either by post or via e-mail as a Microsoft Word file. The form should be submitted including audited accounts, details of the project (no more than two sides of A4), a budget breakdown, money raised so far, and a list of other bodies to whom you have applied for funding. Meetings are usually held in January, June and October. Unsuccessful applicants will not be acknowledged unless an sae is enclosed.

The Laurence Misener Charitable Trust

Jewish, general
£108,000 (2000/01)
Beneficial area UK.

Messrs Bourner Bullock, Sovereign House, 212–224 Shaftesbury Avenue, London WC2H 8HQ
Correspondent C A Letts
Trustees J E Cama; P M Tarsh; Mrs J M Cama.
CC Number 283460

Information available Accounts were on file at the Charity Commission.

General In 2000/01 this trust had assets of £2.9 million and an income of £96,000. In the year 30 grants were awarded totalling £108,000, all of these were recurrent and appear to be ongoing commitments.

The largest donation was to Richard Dimbleby Cancer Fund for £10,000. Other grants for £5,000 or more went to Home for Aged Jews, Jewish Association for Physically Handicapped and Jewish Care (£7,500 each), Robert Owen Foundation (£6,000) and Royal College of Surgeons of England (£5,000).

Remaining grants ranged from £1,400 to £4,400. Beneficiaries included Age Concern, Blond McIndoe Centre, Jews' Temporary Shelter, Royal College of Surgeons, Sussex Stroke and Circulation Fund and SGHMS Haematology Research Fund.

Applications In writing to the correspondent.

The Victor Mishcon Charitable Trust

Jewish, social welfare
£106,000 (2000/01)
Beneficial area UK.

Summit House, 12 Red Lion Square, London WC1R 4QD
Tel. 020 7440 7000
Correspondent Miss M Grant
Trustees Lord Mishcon; P A Cohen; P Mishcon; R Mishcon; J Landau.
CC Number 213165

Information available Full accounts were on file at the Charity Commission.

General The trust supports mainly Jewish charities, but also gives grants to general social welfare and medical/disability causes, especially children's charities.

In 2000/01 the trust had assets of £1.6 million, which generated an income of £90,000. After very low management and administration charges of £900, grants were made to 170 organisations totalling £106,000.

The largest grants were £35,000 to British Council of Shaare Zedak, £14,000 to UJIA and £13,000 to Joint Jewish Charitable Trust.

Many of the other grants were also made to Jewish organisations. Larger grants included those to Friends of Alyn (£4,600), United Synagogue (£2,600), Nightingale House (£1,500), Central Synagogue (£1,400), Maccabi Union and West London Synagogue (£1,000 each). Smaller grants included £400 to Chevras Ezras Nitzrochem, £250 each to Community Security Trust and Jewish Chaplaincy, £200 to Jewish Child's Day, £160 to Beth Shalom Reform Synagogue, £100 each to Cambridge University Jewish Society, Friends of Yad Idud, Jewish Marriage Council and ZSV Trust and £50 to Institute of Jewish Affairs.

Grants for other charitable purposes included £1,000 to Life Neurological Research Trust, £500 to UNICEF, £450 to European Children's Trust, £250 each to Central and Cecil Housing Trust, Craniofacial Support Group, Mind, River Point and University of Warwick Students Union, £100 each to Bognor Funbas Co., Donkey Sanctuary, Kindness to Kids, Midland Narrow Boat Project, NSPCC and Pearson's Holiday Fund, £50 to Gingerbread and £5 to Royal Free Hospital Breast Cancer Trust.

Applications In writing to the correspondent.

The Mizpah Trust

General
£60,000 to organisations (2000/01)
Beneficial area UK.

Foresters House, Humbly Grove, South Warnborough, Hook, Hampshire RG29 1RY
Correspondent A C O Bell, Trustee
Trustees A C O Bell; J E Bell.
CC Number 287231

Information available Full accounts were on file at the Charity Commission.

General The trust is proactive and makes grants to a wide range of organisations. In 2000/01 it had assets totalling £84,000 and its income was £129,000 mainly from gifts of shares. Grants to 12 organisations totalled

£60,000 with £18,000 going to individuals.

The three largest grants to organisations were £10,000 each to CARE, H & B Alpha Partners and Relationships Foundation. Other grants included those to Downe House 21st Century Appeal (£7,500), Stewards Trust (£6,000), Action for ME (£5,000), Cloud Trust (£1,800), Love for the Family (£1,000) and Harvester Trust and Timothy Trust (£500 each).

Applications The trust has stated that 'no applications will be considered'.

This entry was not confirmed by the trust but the information was correct according to the Charity Commission.

The Mole Charitable Trust

Jewish, general

£468,000 (2001/02)

Beneficial area UK, with a preference for Manchester.

2 Okeover Road, Salford M7 4JX

Tel. 0161 832 8721

Correspondent Martin Gross

Trustees M Gross; Mrs L P Gross.

CC Number 281452

Information available Accounts were on file at the Charity Commission.

General In 2001/02 this trust had assets amounting to £2.1 million. Its income was low at just £42,000. In recent years its income has been much higher; in 2000/01 it received an income tax repayment of £600,000 and in 1999/2000 Gift Aid donations of £462,000 were recieved.

Grants to 35 organisations totalled £468,000. Beneficiaries of the largest donations were Shaarei Torah Buildings Ltd (£200,000), Manchester Jewish Grammar School (£55,000), Bar Yochai Charitable Trust and Broom Foundation (£50,000 each), Binoh of Manchester (£25,000), Shaarei Chested Trust (£15,000) and Manchester Charitable Trust (£11,000).

Remaining grants were all for £5,000 or less and included those to Community Security Trust, Kisharon, Kollel Rabbi Yechiel, Lubaritch Manchester, Sayser Charity and United Jewish Israel Appeal.

Applications In writing to the correspondent.

George A Moore Foundation

General

£105,000 (2001/02)

Beneficial area Principally Yorkshire and the Isle of Man but also some major UK appeals.

Mitre House, North Park Road, Harrogate, North Yorkshire HG1 5RX

Correspondent Miss L P Oldham

Trustees George A Moore; Mrs E Moore; J R Moore; Mrs A L James.

CC Number 262107

Information available Information and grants list provided by the trust.

General In previous years the trustees of the foundation have selected causes and projects from applications received during the year, as well as using independent research to identify specific objectives where they wish to direct assistance. However, in its 2001/02 report it stated that it plans to follow a more definite policy where particular areas will be targeted and ongoing relationships formed. As a result, fewer funds will become available for unsolicited requests. These changes have resulted in donations for 2001/02 being lower than in previous years.

In 2001/02 the trust had assets of £7.5 million and an income of £475,000. A total of £105,000 was given in 50 grants, over half of which were for £500 or less.

The largest grants over £5,000 each were: £22,000 to HMS Illustrious Central Fund; £10,000 each to Duke of Edinburgh Award, Marie Curie Cancer Care and RNLI; and £5,000 to Second World War Experience Centre.

Other smaller grants included £3,000 to Dyslexia Institute Bursary Fund, £2,800 to Outward Bound Trust, £2,600 to British Red Cross, £2,000 each to Bradford Bears Wheelchair Sports Club, Haig Homes, St John Ambulance and Tockwith Show; £1,500 to Childline Yorkshire & North East, and £1,000 each to Craven Trust Dales Recovery Appeal, Encephalitis Support Group, Motability, Salvation Army, Suzy Lamplugh Trust and York Foundation for Conservation and Craftsmanship.

Exclusions No assistance will be given to individuals, courses of study, expeditions, overseas travel, holidays, or for purposes outside the UK. Local appeals for UK charities will only be considered if in the area of interest. Because of present long-term commitments, the foundation is not prepared to consider appeals for religious property or institutions, or for educational purposes.

Applications In writing to the correspondent. No guidelines or application forms are issued. The trustees meet approximately four times a year, on variable dates, and an appropriate response is sent out after the relevant meeting.

The Nigel Moores Family Charitable Trust

Arts

£498,000 committed (2000/01)

Beneficial area UK, but mostly Wales and Liverpool.

c/o Macfarlane & Co., 2nd Floor, Cunard Building, Water Street, Liverpool L3 1DS

Tel. 0151 236 6161 **Fax** 0151 236 1095

Correspondent P Kurthausen, Accountant

Trustees J C S Moores; Mrs L M White; Mrs P M Kennaway.

CC Number 1002366

Information available Full accounts were on file at the Charity Commission.

General The main focus of this trust is promoting the arts, particularly among the wider community. Outside of this, grants are available towards education, the environment, recreational and leisure-time facilities and the advancement of religion. The grants list indicates most of the beneficiaries are Welsh, although arts organisations in Liverpool often receive large grants, probably due to the Moores family connections.

In 2000/01 the trust had assets of £2.4 million. Total income was £1.6 million, including donations of £1.5 million. Professional fees for the year were very low at just £940. Grants were awarded to nine organisations totalling £498,000.

The A Foundation, a connected charity, received a grant totalling £486,000, of which £94,000 was paid during the year and £392,000 committed in future years. The foundation was established in 1998 by James Moores to support the development and exhibition of

165

contemporary art in Liverpool and shares trustees with this trust.

Other grants were £3,600 to Bellan House School Parents Association, £2,300 to Llantysilio School Fund, £2,000 to Pentrdwr Community Association, £1,000 each to Llangollen Pre School Playgroup, Nightingale Appeal and Wrexham Maelor Hospital for its cancer and maternity wards, £500 each to the Llangollen and Glenafron branches of Cylch Meithrin Llangollen and Glenrafon and £250 to Millennium Seedbank Appeal.

Applications In writing to the correspondent.

Morgan Williams Charitable Trust

Christian

£238,000 (1999/2000)
Beneficial area UK.

2 Finsbury Avenue, London EC2M 2PP
Tel. 020 7568 2569 **Fax** 020 7568 0912
Email sally.baker@ubsw.com
Correspondent K J Costa, Trustee
Trustees *K J Costa; Mrs A F Costa.*
CC Number 221604
Information available Full accounts were on file at the Charity Commission.

General In 1999/2000 the trust had assets of £2,900. The total income was £137,000, mostly from donations. Grants were made totalling £238,000 and there were three payments for consultancy fees totalling £75,000, producing a deficit of £176,000.

The largest grant was £180,000 to Holy Trinity Church, a regular beneficiary; there was no indication in the accounts why this grant was larger than the year's income.

Other grants of £1,000 or over went to Oasis Trust (£5,800), Chasah Trust, New Life Outreach and Philo Trust (£5,000 each), Fusion (£3,000), Youth for Christ (£2,200), St Eterburgha's Centre and Salvation Army (£2,000 each), Lambeth Partnership and A Rocha Trust (£1,500 each) with £1,000 each to Besom Foundation, JC2000 and Joshua Generation. Smaller grants totalled £4,400.

Applications The trust states that only charities personally connected with the trustees are supported and absolutely no applications are either solicited or acknowledged.

The Oliver Morland Charitable Trust

Quakers, general

£95,000 (2000/01)
Beneficial area UK.

Thomas's House, Stower Row, Shaftesbury, Dorset SP7 0QW
Tel. 01747 853524
Correspondent J M Rutter, Trustee
Trustees *Priscilla Khan; Stephen Rutter; Joseph Rutter; Jennifer Pittard; Kate Lovell; Charlotte Jones.*
CC Number 1076213
Information available Accounts were on file at the Charity Commission.

General The trustees state that the majority of funds are given to Quaker projects or Quaker-related projects, which are usually choosen through the personal knowledge of the trustees. In 2000/01 the trust had an income of £112,000 and made grants totalling £95,000.

Grants were divided into the following categories:

Quaker projects and schools £58,000
Grants included those to Quaker Peace and Service (£22,000), Quaker Home Service - Children and Young People (£6,500), Woodbrooke (£4,500), Quaker Council for European Affairs (£2,500), Sibford School (£2,000), Capetown Quaker Peace Centre (£1,500), Uganda Peace Education (£1,000) and Dabane Water Workshops (£500).

Health and social care £16,000
Beneficiaries included Positive Ethos (£1,600), Sightsavers International (£1,500), NSPCC (£1,000), Kids Active (£600), National Deaf Children's Society (£500) and Bishop Creighton House (£250).

International and environment £8,000
Grants included those to Pakistan Environmental Protection Foundation (£2,500), Oxfam and Jangessah Girls

School (£1,000 each), SOS Sahel International (£800), Tools for Self Reliance (£300) and Stoneham Housing Association Yeovil (£200).

Animals and nature £4,500
Dorset Wildlife Trust, Somerset Wildlife Trust, Woodland Trust and National Trust (£1,000 each), PDSA and Blue Cross Animal Hospital (£250 each).

Meeting house appeals £1,500
Wokingham, South Belfast and Newcastle meeting houses (£500 each).

Sundry £7,000
Beneficiaries included Dabane Support Fund Appeal (£2,500), Reading Meeting for East Timor (£2,000), Ockenden International Appeal (£1,000), Compton Dundon Parent and Toddler Group (£200).

Exclusions No grants to individuals.

Applications The trustees meet twice a year, probably in May and November. The trust tends to support the same charities each year and only limited funds are available for unsolicited applications.

The Morris Charitable Trust

Relief of need, education, community support and development

£144,000 (2000/01)
Beneficial area UK and overseas, with a preference for Islington.

Management Office, Business Design Centre, 52 Upper Street, Islington Green, London N1 0QH
Tel. 020 7359 3535
Correspondent Julie Davies, Chairman's PA
Trustees *Mrs G Morris; J A Morris; P B Morris; A R Stenning.*
CC Number 802290
Information available An information leaflet was provided by the trust. Full accounts were on file at the Charity Commission.

General This trust was established in 1989 by the Morris family, owners of a number of businesses in Islington, including The Business Design Centre, venue of DSC's annual Charityfair. A proportion of the profits of these businesses, together with investment income, makes up the funds available for grants each year.

The trust has general charitable purposes, placing particular emphasis on alleviating social hardship and deprivation, supporting national, international and local charities. There is a preference for supporting causes within Islington.

In 2000/01 the trust had assets of £89,000. Total income was £83,000, including £80,000 in donations received. Grants were made to 310 organisations totalling £144,000.

The largest grants made during the year were £15,000 to Harborough School, £13,000 to Holloway School, £6,000 to Pavilion Opera Trust, £5,000 each to Anne Frank Trust and Hackney Empire, £3,800 to Youth Aliyah Child Rescue and £2,500 to Finsbury Park Action Group.

The trust produces an information leaflet, which lists many organisations that have been supported in the past. Beneficiaries in Islington include Angel Association, Archway Festival, Bumpers After School Workshop, ChildLine, Copenhagen Youth Trust, Finsbury Park Action Group, Freightliners City Farm, Highbury Roundhouse, Islington Boat Club, Islington Green School, Leap Theatre Group, Manors Garden Centre, Mayville Community Centre, Safer Islington Trust, Shape, South Sudanese Community Association, Thirty Sunnyside Road and Whittington Festival.

Recipients elsewhere included Age Concern, British Heart Foundation, Children with Leukaemia, Diabetes Foundation, Jewish Care, National Children's Bureau, Norwood, Quidenham Children's Hospice, RNLI, Romanian Orphanage Trust, Shelter and War on Want.

Exclusions No grants for individuals.

Applications By application form available from the trust.

Morris Family Israel Trust

Jewish
£93,000 (2000/01)
Beneficial area UK and Israel.

Flat 90, North Gate, Prince Albert Road, London NW8 7EJ
Correspondent Conrad J Morris, Trustee

Trustees *Conrad Morris; Ruth Morris; Sara Jo Ben Zvi; Elisabeth Pushett; David Morris.*

CC Number 1004976

Information available Accounts were provided by the trust.

General In 2000/01 the trust had assets of £17,500 and an income of £73,000 from donations. Grants were made to 63 beneficiaries totalling £93,000. Grants ranged from £23 to £25,000, although most were for under £500.

The largest grants were to Karliver Rebbe (£25,000) and Bet Haggi (£23,000). Other beneficiaries included Keren Le Pituach (£14,000), Elad and Jewish Community of Hebron (£5,000 each), Palestine Media Watch (£3,000), Mosdot Neu Zvia (£2,800) and Keren Miarachit Ie Israel (£1,800).

Beneficiaries receiving grants of under £500 included Beer Avrahom, Bet Yisrael, Galrinai, Keren Klita and Ohr Semeach.

Applications In writing to the correspondent.

Ruth and Conrad Morris Charitable Trust

Jewish, general
£302,000 (2000/01)
Beneficial area UK and Israel.

c/o Paul Maurice, MRI Moores Rowland, 3 Sheldon Square, Paddington, London W2 6PS
Tel. 020 7470 0000
Correspondent Conrad Morris, Trustee
Trustees *R S Morris; C J Morris.*
CC Number 276864

Information available Full accounts were on file at the Charity Commission.

General This trust has Jewish charitable purposes. In 2000/01 it had an income of £273,000, almost all of which came from donations received. Assets were listed in the accounts as minus £201,000, due to a total of £228,000 being owed to creditors, although these creditors were presumably charities promised recurrent grants since the assets generated £3,600. After low management and administration expenses of £2,500, grants were made totalling £302,000.

The largest grants were £46,000 to Morris Family Israel Trust, £37,000 to Lubavitch, £25,000 to Hertsmere and £22,000 to Friends of Bar Ilan.

Other beneficiaries included Aish Hatorah Jerusalem Fellowship (£12,000), Sage and UJIA (£10,000 each), SAJFID (£7,500), Remembering the Future (£7,000), Immanuel College (£6,000), School J-Link (£5,000), Menorah Grammar School (£4,500), Community Security Trust (£2,700), Beir Yehudit (£2,000), Boys Town (£800) and Naima JPS (£600).

Applications In writing to the correspondent.

The Willie & Mabel Morris Charitable Trust

Medical, general
£108,000 (1999/2000)
Beneficial area UK.

Bramfield Place, Church Road, Sutton, Sandy, Bedfordshire SG19 2NB
Correspondent Angela Tether
Trustees *Michael Macfadyen; Joyce Tether; Peter Tether; Andrew Tether; Angela Tether; Suzanne Marriott.*
CC Number 280554

Information available Full accounts were on file at the Charity Commission.

General The trust was established in 1980 by Mr and Mrs Morris. It was constituted for general charitable purposes and specifically to relieve physical ill-health, particularly cancer, heart trouble, cerebral palsy, arthritis and rheumatism. Grants are usually only given to registered charities.

In 1999/2000 the trust had assets of £3.5 million and an income of £116,000. Grants were made totalling £108,000.

A total of 28 grants were made in the year, donations were in the range of £250 to £4,000. Beneficiaries of larger grants included Association for International Cancer Research and British Lung Foundation (£4,000 each), Arthritis Research Campaign and British Heart Foundation (£2,500), Back Care, Bedford Hospital NHS Trust, Brain Research trust, Changing Faces, DEBRA, High Blood Pressure Foundation and David Tolkien Trust for Stoke Mandeville (£2,000 each).

There were 12 grants of £1,000 or less, including those to Barnet Cancer Care, British Diabetic Association, Childline, Hearing Dogs for Deaf People, Invalids at Home and Sports Association.

Exclusions No grants for individuals or non-registered charities.

Applications The trustees 'formulate an independent grants policy at regular meetings so that funds are already committed'.

G M Morrison Charitable Trust

Medical, education, welfare

£145,000 (2001/02)

Beneficial area UK and worldwide charities registered in the UK.

Currey & Co, 21 Buckingham Gate, London SW1E 6LS

Correspondent A E Cornick, Trustee

Trustees G M Morrison; N W Smith; A E Cornick.

CC Number 261380

Information available Full accounts were provided by the trust.

General Grants are given to a wide variety of activities in the social welfare, medical and education/training fields. The trust maintains a list of beneficiaries that it has regularly supported.

In 2001/02 the trust had assets of £5.7 million and a total income of £230,000. Grants to 263 organisations were made totalling £145,000. They were in the range of £250 and £10,000, but were mainly for amounts under £1,000; the average grant was £550. The trust produced a comprehensive summary of the grants made which is shown in the adjacent table.

The largest grants were £10,000 to University of Aberdeen Development Trust and £6,000 to Wolfson College – Wolfson Course (Police). A further 27 grants were made, of over £1,000 each; beneficiaries included Royal College of Surgeons (£2,200), Royal Society of Arts Endowment Fund (£2,000), Royal College of Paediatrics and Child Health (£2,000), Help the Aged (£1,300), Ninewells Hospital Cancer Campaign – Dundee (£1,200) and Echo International Health Services Ltd, Northwick Park Institute of

Medical Research, Royal Academy of Music, SSAFA, St Luke's Hospital for Clergy, Understanding Industry and YMCA England (£1,000 each).

The remaining grants were in the range of £250 to £900 and included those to: Alzheimer's Research Trust, Arthritis Research Campaign, Anti-Bullying Campaign, Bibles for Children, British Geriatrics Society, Canine Partners for Independence, Carr Gomm Society, Children Nationwide, Christian Aid, Cord Blood Charity, East Grinstead Medical Research Trust, Friends of King Edward VII Hospital, Institute of Child Health, Intermediate Technology, Liverpool School of Tropical Medicine, McCabe Educational Trust, Population Concern, Princess Royal Trust for Carers, Raleigh International, Royal Society of Edinburgh, RNLI, RSPB, Samaritans, Schools Outreach, Shaftesbury Society, South Downs Planetarium Trust, Weston Spirit, Woodland Trust and Young Enterprise.

Exclusions No support for individuals, non-registered charities, schemes or activities which are generally regarded as the responsibility of statutory authorities, short-term projects or one-off capital grants.

Applications In writing to the correspondent. However, grants are normally selected on the basis of trustees' personal knowledge and recommendation. As the trust's grantmaking is of a long-term recurring nature and is restricted by available income, very few new grant applications can be accepted each year. Applications are not acknowledged. Grants are distributed once a year in January. Please note, telephone applications are not considered.

Monitoring is undertaken by assessment of annual reports and accounts which are required from all beneficiaries, and by occasional trustee visits.

G M MORRISON CHARITABLE TRUST
Grants in 2001/02

Category	No.	Total £	Average £
Medical and health			
Medical research and support	71	36,800	518
Disabled (mental and physical)	35	12,600	360
Professional bodies (medical)	6	6,400	1,067
Hospitals/hospices	9	5,000	556
Respite care	4	2,100	525
Social welfare			
Benevolent associations	14	5,300	378
Residential and nursing homes	4	1,650	413
Elderly support	9	4,450	494
Young people (homes and support)	21	10,400	495
Homeless	8	3,600	450
Drugs and alcohol	2	500	250
Prisoners	3	1,050	350
Refugees and immigrants	1	250	250
Counselling and advice (social)	4	1,700	425
Crime prevention/victim support	2	550	275
Holidays	4	1,850	463
Housing trusts	3	1,100	366
Families	2	850	425
Welfare general	1	250	250
Education and training			
Universities, colleges and adult education	8	20,500	2,563
Schools	6	4,700	783
Music and arts	5	4,400	880
Spiritual and religious education	5	1,450	290
Others			
Overseas aid	15	6,800	453
Churches	9	4,550	505
Conservation, nature	7	2,350	47
Research general	3	2,850	950
Sports and recreation	1	600	600
Environment/transport	1	250	250

Vyoel Moshe Charitable Trust

Education, relief of poverty

About £400,000 (2001/02)
Beneficial area UK and overseas.

2–4 Chardmore Road, London N16 6HX
Tel. 020 8806 2598
Correspondent J Weinberger, Secretary
Trustees *Rabbi M Teitelbaum; Rabbi J Meisels; Y Frankel; B Berger; S Seidenfeld.*
CC Number 327054
Information available Accounts were on file at the Charity Commission , but without a list of grants or a narrative report.

General In 2001/02 the trust's assets totalled only about £35,000 and it had an income from donations of £430,000. Grants were made totalling around £400,000. About two thirds to three quarters of donations are made to UK charities.

No further information was available.

Applications In writing to the correspondent.

The Moss Charitable Trust

Christian, education, poverty, health

£189,000 to organisations (2000/01)
Beneficial area Worldwide, with an interest in Dorset, Hampshire and Sussex.

7 Church Road, Parkstone, Poole, Dorset BH14 8UF
Tel. 01202 730002
Correspondent P D Malpas
Trustees *J H Simmons; A F Simmons; P L Simmons; D S Olby.*
CC Number 258031
Information available Full accounts were on file at the Charity Commission.

General The objects of the trust are to benefit the community in the county borough of Bournemouth and the counties of Hampshire, Dorset and Sussex, and also the advancement of

religion in the UK and overseas, the advancement of education and the relief of poverty, disease and sickness. It achieves this by providing facilities for contributors to give under Gift Aid or direct giving and redistributes them according to their recommendations. The trustees also make smaller grants from the general income of the trust.

In 2000/01 the trust had assets of £823,000 and an income of £399,000. Grants to organisations totalled £189,000, including £135,000 in 32 grants of £1,000 or more, 16 of which went to organisations also supported in the previous year. Grants to individuals totalled £32,000, including one grant of £15,000.

The largest grants to organisations were £10,000 each to Life for the World Trust and Slavic Gospel Association Limited. Other grants included £8,000 to Tearfund, £6,500 to CCC Ltd, £5,300 to Christ Church – Westbourne, £5,000 each to Carrot Tops, NCCB Missions Account, Outreach to Kenya and Youth for Christ and £4,300 to Scripture Union.

Applications No funds are available by direct application. Because of the way in which this trust operates it is not open to external applications for grants.

The Moulton Charitable Trust

Asthma

£205,000 (2000/01)
Beneficial area UK, with a preference for Kent.

The Mount, Church Street, Shoreham, Sevenoaks, Kent TN14 7SD
Tel. 01959 524008
Correspondent J P Moulton, Trustee
Trustees *J P Moulton; P M Moulton.*
CC Number 1033119
Information available Accounts were on file at the Charity Commission, but without a list of grants.

General The trust supports established organisations benefiting people with asthma. In 2000/01 the trust had assets of £347,000 and an income of £69,000. Grants totalled £205,000. A list of beneficiaries was not available.

Previous research has shown that one-off grants of £5,000 or more are made,

towards buildings, capital, core costs, project, research, recurring costs and running costs.

Exclusions No grants for individuals, students or animal charities.

Applications In writing to the correspondent.

Mountbatten Festival of Music

Royal Marines and Royal Navy charities

£88,000 (2000/01)
Beneficial area UK.

HMS Excellent, Whale Island, Portsmouth PO2 8ER
Correspondent Lt. Col. A J F Noyes, Corps Secretary
Trustees *Commandant General Royal Marines; Chief of Staff; Chief Staff Officer Personnel.*
CC Number 1016088
Information available Full accounts were on file at the Charity Commission.

General The trust was set up in 1993 and is administered by the Royal Marines. It raises funds from band concerts, festivals of music and beating retreat. Unsurprisingly, the main beneficiaries are service charities connected with the Royal Marines and Royal Navy. The only other beneficiaries are those hospitals or rehabilitation centres etc which have recently directly aided a Royal Marine in some way and Sargent Cancer Care for Children. Both one-off and recurrent grants are made.

In 2000/01 the trust had assets totalling £103,000 and an income of £213,000 mainly from fundraising. It made donations totalling £88,000 and spent £130,000 on fundraising expenses. The trust has two major fundraising events which raise the bulk of the trust's annual income: a concert in Royal Albert Hall in mid-February each year (at a cost of £106,000 in 2000/01), and the Beat Retreat Ceremony on Horse Guards Parade ,which is held every three to five years.

Grants, ranging from £500 to £17,000, were made to 25 organisations, most of which were supported in the previous year. The largest grants were made to Malcolm Sargent Cancer Fund (£17,000) and The 1939 War Fund (£16,000).

Other larger grants included those to RN Benevolent Trust (£9,000), RM Museum (£8,000), St Loye's Foundation and RM/RN Children's Home (£4,000 each), St Dunstan's Home and The Mountbatten Trust (£3,000 each), Metropolitan Police Benevolent Fund (£2,500), St John Ambulance, Erskine Hospital and Royal British Legion (£1,000 each).

Grants of £500 each included those to 3 Cdo Bde Memorial Fund and Pembroke House.

Exclusions Charities/organisations unknown to the trustees.

Applications Unsolicited applications are not considered as the trust's income is dependent upon the running and success of various musical events. Any money raised by this means is then disbursed to a set of regular beneficiaries.

The Edwina Mountbatten Trust

Medical

£227,000 (2000)

Beneficial area UK and overseas.

Estate Office, Broadlands, Romsey, Hampshire SO51 9ZE

Tel. 01794 518885

Correspondent John Moss, Secretary

Trustees *Countess Mountbatten of Burma, Chair; Noel Cunningham-Reid; Lord Faringdon; Lord Romsey; Peter H T Mimpriss; Mrs Mary Fagan.*

CC Number 228166

Information available Full accounts were on file at the Charity Commission.

General This trust was established in 1960 to honour the causes Edwina, Countess Mountbatten of Burma was involved with during her lifetime. Each year support is given to St John Ambulance (of which she was superintendent-in-chief) for work in the UK and its Commonwealth, and Save the Children (of which she was president) for the relief of children who are sick, distressed or otherwise in need. Nursing organisations are also supported, as she was the patron or vice-president of a

number of nursing organisations. Grants, even to the core beneficiaries, are only given towards specific projects rather than core costs.

In 2000 the trust had assets of £3.1 million and an income of £91,000, including £3,500 in donations received. Grants were made to 12 organisations totalling £227,000. Other expenditure was just £2,700.

A special one-off grant of £100,000 was made to the 40th Anniversary grant of St John Ophthalmic Hospital for a capital project. St John Ambulance and Save the Children each received £35,000. Other grants were £10,000 each to Countess Brecknock Hospice, Demelza Hospice, Edwina Mountbatten House and Pilgrims House, £5,000 each to Changing Faces, Sargent Cancer Care and Soma Project and £2,000 to Ashram Project.

Exclusions No grants for research or to individual nurses working in the UK for further professional training.

Applications In writing to the correspondent. The trustees meet once a year, generally in September/October.

The Edith Murphy Foundation

General

£247,000 (1998/99)

Beneficial area UK.

c/o Crane & Walton, 113–117 London Road, Leicester LE2 0RG

Correspondent D L Tams, Solicitor

Trustees *Edith A Murphy; David L Tams; Pamela M Breakwell; Freda Kesterton; Jack Kesterton.*

CC Number 1026062

Information available Accounts were on file at the Charity Commission.

General This trust was established in 1993 it supports organisations helping medical causes and people who are poor or in need. There is a strong preference for animal charities.

In 2001/02 this trust had an income of £1.3 million and a total expenditure of £422,000. Unfortunately no further details were available for this year.

In 1998/99 the income was £55,000 (£1.7 million in 1997/98, £1.6 million of which

came from donations and gifts). The assets at the year end stood at £749,000. Grants to 10 organisations totalled £247,000, exceeding the foundation's income by £193,000 and deducted from the accumulated fund.

The largest grant went to Leicester Animal Aid Association for £110,000. Two other substantial grants went to the Winged Fellowship Trust (£54,000) and National Kidney Research Fund (£50,000).

Other grants included £10,000 each to Leicester Children's Holiday Centre, Lord Mayor Scanner Appeal and Mainline Steam Trust. Smaller grants included those to Burleigh Houses for the Elderly (£1,500), Glenfield Hospital Breast Care Appeal (£500), Aylestone Park Youth Football Club (£300) and Dr Hadwen's Trust (£250).

Applications In writing to the correspondent.

The Mushroom Fund

General

£62,000 (2000/01)

Beneficial area UK and overseas, with a preference for St Helens.

Liverpool Council of Social Services (Inc.), 14 Castle Street, Liverpool L2 0NJ

Tel. 0151 236 7728

Correspondent Marjorie Staunton

Trustees *Liverpool Council of Social Services (Inc.); D F Pilkington; Lady K Pilkington; Mrs R Christian; Mrs J Wailing.*

CC Number 259954

Information available Information was provided by the trust.

General The trust has general charitable purposes, usually supporting causes known to the trustees. In 2000/01 the trust had assets of £975,000 generating an income of £26,000. Grants totalled £62,000.

Grants of £1,000 or more were listed in the annual report. The largest grants were £10,000 each to Cambridge University and St Helens Housing – Retirement Village Project. Refraid and Roy Castle Lung Cancer Foundation each received £5,000.

Beneficiaries receiving £1,000 each were Children's Trust, Médecins Sans Frontières, Drugs Initiative Group, Halo

Trust, Macmillan Cancer Relief, Marie Curie Cancer Care, Merseyside Police and High Sheriff's Charitable Trust, Middlefield Community School – Gainsborough, Sherbourne School, National Trust – Foot and Mouth Crisis Appeal, Urolink and Walesby Village Hall.

Grants under £1,000 totalled £20,000.

Exclusions No grants to individuals or to organisations which are not registered charities.

Applications In writing to the correspondent. Please note, the trust does not respond to unsolicited applications.

The Music Sound Foundation

Music education
£500,000 (2001)
Beneficial area UK.

4 Tenterden Street, Hanover Square, London W1A 2AY
Tel. 020 7355 4848 **Fax** 020 7495 1424
Email orrj@emigroup.com
Website www.emigroup.com/msf
Correspondent Ms Janie Orr, Administrator
Trustees *Sir Colin Southgate, Chair; Jim Beach; Jason Berman; John Deacon; Leslie Hill; David Hughes; Steve O'Rourke; Rupert Perry; Richard Holland; John Hutchinson.*
CC Number 1055434
Information available Information was provided by the trust.

General Established in 1997 by EMI Records, this foundation is an independent charity dedicated to the improvement of music education. Grants are given to individuals and schools for the purchase of instruments and equipment and for music courses for teachers. Assistance with sponsorship for art college status can be provided, although this is co-ordinated through the Technology Colleges Trust.

The foundation has agreed to sponsor a minimum of 15 schools over five years to become art colleges, totalling £1.5 million. Six colleges have also recieved funds from the foundation for bursaries to music students.

In 2001 the foundation had assets totalling £6.3 million and an income of £468,000. Grants totalled £500,000. Grants average £750 but can be up to £5,000 for schools, individuals and music teachers. For bursaries, each college receives a £5,000 annual donation for distribution.

The six colleges receiving funds for bursaries were Royal Scottish Academy of Music & Drama – Glasgow, Royal Welsh College of Music & Drama - Cardiff, Royal Academy – London, Institute of Popular Music – University of Liverpool, Birmingham Conservatoire and Drumtech drum and percussion school – London.

Further information on beneficiaries during the year was not available. Previous beneficiaries have included North Leamington School, Churchfield School, Brentwood Ursulie Convent, Egglescliffe School, Guthlaxton College, Focus Events for the String of Pearls Millennium Festival, King William's College, Young Persons Concert Foundation and Music Wheel.

Exclusions Community projects, student fees/living expenses and music therapy are not funded.

Applications On a form available from the correspondent. Application for Music Sound Foundation funds from students are considered by the colleges themselves. Applicants must come from within the UK and be able to show evidence of severe financial hardship.

MYA Charitable Trust

Jewish
£147,000 (1999/2000)
Beneficial area Worldwide.

4 Amhurst Parade, Amhurst Park, London N16 5AA
Tel. 020 8800 3582
Correspondent M Rothfield, Trustee
Trustees *M Rothfeld; Mrs E Rothfeld; Mrs H Schraiber.*
CC Number 299642
Information available Accounts were on file at the Charity Commission.

General In 1999/2000 this trust had assets of £540,000 and an income of £272,000. Grants totalled £147,000. There

were 22 grants listed in the accounts. Beneficiaries included Torah Ve-emuno (£20,000), Beis Avrohom Trust, Society of Friends of the Torah and Torah Vachesed Leezrah Vesaad (£10,000 each), Friends of Nachalas Osher and Yad Eliezer (£7,000 each), Friends of Ponevezh (£6,100), Beis Ruzin Trust (£6,000), Beis Yaakov Institution and Dushinsky Trust (£5,000 each), Keren Association (£1,000) and CM Trust (£500).

Applications In writing to the address below.

The Willie Nagel Charitable Trust

Jewish, general
£71,000 (2000/01)
Beneficial area UK.

Lubbock Fine, Russell Bedford House, City Forum, 250 City Road, London EC1V 2QQ
Tel. 020 7490 7766
Correspondent A L Sober, Trustee
Trustees *W Nagel; A L Sober.*
CC Number 275938
Information available Accounts were available at the Charity Commission, but without a full narrative report or a grants list.

General The trust makes grants to registered charities, committing its income before the funds have been generated.

In 2000/01 it had assets of £15,000. Total income was £65,000, mostly from donations received. Grants were made totalling £71,000. No further information on the size or type of grants, or any details of the beneficiaries, was available.

The most recent grants information available was for 1989/90, when grants generally ranged from £20 to £2,000, but were mostly for £100 or less. There were five larger grants made, one of which was for £20,000, the others for £5,000 or less. These went to Board of Deputies Charitable Trust, Friends of Wiznitz, Israel Music Foundation, National Children's Home and Victoria and Albert Museum.

Applications In writing to the correspondent, but note that the trust stated in its report that 'all income is fully spoken for.'

The Naggar Charitable Trust

Jewish, general

£228,000 (2000/01)

Beneficial area Worldwide.

15 Grosvenor Gardens, London
SW1W OBD

Tel. 020 7834 8060

Correspondent Mr & Mrs Naggar, Trustees

Trustees *Guy Naggar; Hon. Marion Naggar.*

CC Number 265409

Information available Accounts were on file at the Charity Commission but with only a limited narrative report.

General The trust mainly supports Jewish organisations and a few medical charities. Arts organisations also receive some support.

In 2000/01 the trust had assets of £79,000 and an income of £169,000. Grants totalling £228,000 were made to 42 organisations.

The trust made 10 grants of £1,000 or more each. By far the largest donation was £99,000 to Jerusalem Foundation. Other beneficiaries of larger grants included Society of the Friends of Torah (£60,000), BFAMI (£38,000), Community Security Trust (£10,000), British Friends of Hebrew University (£3,300), Israel Philharmonic Orchestra Fund (£2,500), British Aid Committee (£2,000), Tate Gallery Foundation (£1,000).

Other smaller grants included those to Cancer Research Campaign, Donmar Warehouse, Jewish Policy Research, Norwood Ltd, Project Seed, Whitechapel Art Gallery, WIZO Charitable Foundation and Youth Aliyah.

Applications In writing to the correspondent.

The Janet Nash Charitable Trust

Medical, general

£110,000 to organisations (2000/01)

Beneficial area UK.

Ron Gulliver and Co. Ltd, The Old Chapel, New Mill, Eversley, Hampshire RG27 0RA

Tel. 0118 973 0300 **Fax** 0118 973 0022

Correspondent R Gulliver, Trustee

Trustees *Ronald Gulliver; M S Jacobs.*

CC Number 326880

Information available Full accounts were on file at the Charity Commission.

General In 2000/01 the trust had an income of £327,000, almost all of which came in donations from an electrical firm. It had assets of £118,000 and made grants to organisations totalling £110,000. 32 individuals received a total of £246,000, of which £234,000 was given for medical needs and £12,000 as hardship relief.

Grants of £1,000 or more were £33,000 to Vail Valley Foundation, £19,000 to Croix-Rouge Monegasque, £17,000 to Northwestern University Medical School, £15,000 to Duke of Edinburgh's Award International Foundation, £10,000 to Acorn's Children's Hospice Trust, £5,000 to Ovingdean Hall School, £4,000 to Dyslexia Institute, £3,800 to Child Advocacy International and £1,000 to Headway Coventry and Warwickshire. A further £1,100 was given in smaller grants to organisations.

Applications In writing to the correspondent. The trustees meet monthly.

The National Catholic Fund

Catholic welfare

£166,000 (2001)

Beneficial area England and Wales.

39 Eccleston Square, London SW1V 1BX

Tel. 020 7901 4810 **Fax** 020 7901 4819

Correspondent Monsignor Andrew Summersgill

Trustees *Archbishops Cormac Murphy O'Connor, Michael Bowen, Vincent Nicholls; Robin Smith; Mrs Elspeth Orchard; Monsignor Michael McKenna; John Gibbs.*

CC Number 257239

Information available Information was provided by the trust.

General The fund, formerly New Pentecost Fund, was established in 1968 and is concerned with 'the advancement of the Roman Catholic religion in England & Wales'. The trust achieves its objectives through the work of 23 Committees of the Bishops' conference and various agencies such as the Catholic Communications Service. Each committee is concerned with a different area of work of the Church. Grants are only given to organisations which benefit England and Wales as a whole, rather than local projects.

In 2001 the trust had assets of £1.8 million and an income of £1.6 million, £950,000 of which was from diocesan assessments. The majority of its income was spent on running the General Secretariat and the Catholic Communications Service but £166,000 was also spent on Christian organisations (£185,000 in 2000). A total of 29 grants were awarded ranging from £200 to £30,000. These grants were broken down as follows:

Grants to organisations

19 grants totalling £166,000 ranging from £200 to £30,000. Recipients of larger grants included: Young Christian Workers (£30,000), National Board of Catholic Women (£18,000), Diocesan Vocational Service and Movement of Christian Workers (£16,000 each), National Conference of Priests (£11,000) and Linacre Centre (£10,000). Other beneficiaries included Catholic Housing Aid Society and Catholic Student Council.

National expenses

10 grants totalling £33,000 ranging from £100 to £14,000. Recipients included Churches Commission on Mission (£14,000), Universities (£6,500), CTBI Interfaith (£4,700) and CCEE (£4,100).

Exclusions No grants to individuals, local projects or projects not immediately advancing the Roman Catholic religion in England and Wales.

Applications In writing to the correspondent before June.

National Committee of The Women's World Day of Prayer for England, Wales, and Northern Ireland

Christian education and literature

£130,000 (2001)

Beneficial area UK and worldwide.

Commercial Road, Tunbridge Wells, Kent TN1 2RR

Tel. 01892 541411 **Fax** 01892 541745

Email office@wwdp-natcomm.org

Correspondent Mrs Lynda Lynam

Trustees *The Officers of the National Committee.*

CC Number 233242

Information available Annual report was provided by the trust.

General The trust makes grants to charitable Christian educational projects and Christian organisations publishing literature and audio-visual material designed to advance the Christian faith.

The main object of the trust is to unite Christians in prayer, focused in particular on a day of prayer in March each year. The trust's income is mainly from donations collected at this event. After the trust's expenses, including the costs of running the day of prayer, the income can be used for grantmaking.

Future themes for the Day of Prayer are:

Year	Country	Theme
2003	Lebanon	Holy Spirit, Fill Us
2004	Panama	In Faith, Women Shape The Future
2005	Poland	Let Our Light Shine
2006	South Africa	Signs Of The Times
2007	Paraguay	United Under God's Tent

In 2001 the organisation had an income of £293,000. Grants and 'international donations' totalled £130,000.

Ongoing grants were made to 16 organisations. The beneficiaries were Bible Society, Feed the Minds and United Society for Christian Literature (£20,000 each), Scripture Gift Mission (£10,000), Bible Reading Fellowship, International Bible Reading Association and Society for Promoting Christian Knowledge (£7,500 each), Scripture Union and The Salvation Army – Missionary Literature Fund (£3,000 each), Royal National Institute for the Blind, St John's Guild for the Blind, The Leprosy Mission and Cafod (£2,000 each), Northern Ireland Bible Society (£1,500), Royal National Mission to Deep Sea Fishermen – Scriptures for Deep Sea Fishermen Scheme and United Christian Broadcasters (£1,000 each).

Three 'International donations' were made to World Day of Prayer International Committee – Annual (£10,000), World Day of Prayer National Committee – Samoa (£4,000) and World Day of Prayer European Committee (£200).

Nine grants were made by the Committee for Welsh Speaking Churches for £800 or less, all made to Welsh branches. These were to Sunday School Council (£800), Christian Aid, Fellowship of Reconciliation and Christians Against Torture (£500 each), Alcohol and Drug Council and Society for the Blind in Wales (£400 each), Cytun (£300), Cafod (£200) and Bible Society (£100).

Two one-off grants were made of £1,000 each to OMS International and Release International.

Exclusions No grants to individuals.

Applications In writing to the correspondent, before the end of June. Grants are made in November.

The National Manuscripts Conservation Trust

Conserving manuscripts

£76,000 (2001)

Beneficial area UK.

The British Library, Co-operation and Partnership Programme, 96 Euston Road, London NW1 2DB

Tel. 020 7412 7052 **Fax** 020 7412 7155

Email nmct@bl.uk

Website

www.bl.uk/concord/nmct-about.html

Correspondent The Secretary

Trustees *Lord Egremont; B Naylor; C Sebag-Montefiore.*

CC Number 802796

Information available Annual report and accounts were provided by the trust.

General The object of the trust is to make grants towards the costs of conserving manuscripts and archives that are of historic or educational value, and of national importance.

Grants are available to record offices, libraries and other similar publicly funded institutions including local authority, university and specialist record repositories, as well as to owners of manuscript material which is conditionally exempt from capital taxation or owned by a charitable trust. Grants are made towards the cost of repair, binding and other preservation measures, including reprography and may cover the cost of contract preservation and conservation or the salaries and related expenses of staff specially employed for the project, as well as expendable materials required for the project.

In 2001 the trust had assets of £1.7 million and an income of £107,000 (£79,000 from investment income and £28,000 from donations). Management and administration of the trust totalled £3,000. Grants totalling £76,000 were made to nine organisations in the year. Donations to the trust have fallen significantly since the previous year (£28,600 in 2001, compared to £225,000 in 2000), meaning income has dropped by almost a third for the year, from £315,000 in 2000, to just £107,000 in 2001. However, the trust has maintained its levels of grantmaking (£79,000 in 2000).

The largest grant was £21,000 to Berkeley Castle to complete the conservation and microfilming of the Berkeley Castle muniments. The remaining grants were as follows: £12,500 to University of Nottingham Library towards the conservation of the Wollaton Antiphonal, a service book from the fifteenth century; £11,000 to Staffordshire and Stoke-on-Trent Archive Service towards a project to conserve the Staffordshire Tithe maps; £9,000 to London Metropolitan Archives towards the conservation of architectural plans of three London theatres: the Theatre Royal at Drury Lane, the Savoy and the Gaiety; £9,000 to The Royal Institute of British Architects Architectural Library towards the Architects' Papers Conservation Project; £5,500 to York City Archives towards the repair and rebinding of volume A/Y, which contains material from the fourteenth to the sixteenth centuries on the life and customs of York; £4,000 to the University of Surrey Library towards the conservation of the manuscript letters of E H Shepard; £2,500 to D'Oyly Carte Opera Company to conserve their archives; and £2,000 to Glasgow University Archive Services towards the conservation of the Blackhouse charters.

The trust is administered by the Co-operation and Partnership Programme at the British Library, which also lends its support, along with The Royal Commission on Historical Manuscripts.

Exclusions The following are not eligible: public records within the meaning of the Public Records Act; official archives of the institution or authority applying except in the case of some older records; loan collections unless exempt from capital taxation or owned by a charitable trust; and photographic, audio-visual or printed materials.

Applications Applications must be submitted on a form in the Guide to Applicants, which is available from the trust. Deadlines are 1 April and 1 October each year. The trustees are prepared to be flexible and each application is considered on its own merits; the trust encourages potential applicants to contact the secretary for further advice and an informal discussion about eligibility.

Newby Trust Limited

Medical welfare, education and training, and the relief of poverty

£160,000 to institutions (2000/01)

Beneficial area UK.

Hill Farm, Froxfield, Petersfield, Hampshire GU32 1BQ

Tel. 01730 827557 **Fax** 01730 827938

Website www.newbytrust.org.uk

Correspondent Miss W Gillam, Secretary

Trustees Mrs S A Charlton; Mrs J M Gooder; Dr R D Gooder; Mrs A S Reed; R B Gooder; Mrs A L Foxell.

CC Number 227151

Information available Full accounts and report were provided by the trust.

General The trust works throughout the UK to promote, in particular, medical welfare, training and education and the relief of poverty. The directors have a policy of selecting one category for special support each year. In 2002/03 the trust's focus is on supporting families with healthcare problems and in 2003/04 on people who are homeless. Recent causes have included children under the age of 11 with particular educational needs (2000/01) and regeneration of the urban community (2001/02, as outlined below). Grants can be given to either organisations or individuals.

In 2001/02 the trust had assets of £8.8 million, which generated an income of £350,000. Grants were made totalling £332,000, broken down as follows:

Medical welfare – £34,000 in 31 grants to organisations and 72 grants to individuals

The largest grants were £5,000 each to Camphill Village Trust and Medical Foundational for the Care of Victims of Torture, £2,000 to Hope in the Valley Riding Group and £1,000 to Sheffield Children's Hospital.

Training and education – £213,000 in 51 grants to organisations and 145 grants to individuals

The largest grants were £25,000 to Hampshire Rose Bowl Appeal and £10,000 each to Academy of Ancient Music Trust, Hanley Crouch Community Association, Sheffield Cathedral Development Project, St Cuthbert Copnor Regeneration Project, and Voluntary Action Leicester. Other large grants were £5,000 each to Amber Foundation, Bedales Grants Trust Fund, Friends of Fitzwilliam Museum, National Gallery and University of Cambridge, £2,000 each to Berkshire PHAB, Crimestoppers Trust, Ebbisham Association, Hub Hazelwell, L'Arche – Liverpool, Museum of Garden History, Reading University and £1,000 to The Courtyard – Petersfield.

Relief of poverty – £86,000 in 20 organisations and 481 individuals

Grants were made to institutions for equipment, mini-buses, fixtures and fittings and ongoing costs, with the largest grant £1,000 to The Salvation Army.

Sundry – £1,600 in 3 grants to organisations

The largest of these was £1,000 to LIFT (London International Festival of Theatre).

Exclusions Funding is not provided for the following:

- CPE Law Exam
- BSc intercalated with a medical degree
- postgraduate medical/veterinary degrees in the first or second years
- courses which are outside of the UK
- adventure or volunteer courses, including gap-year projects.

In addition, first degrees are generally excluded.

For medical welfare and relief of poverty, grant applications from individuals are not considered (see Applications).

Applications The secretary takes principal responsibility for most of the smaller grants for relief of poverty and medical welfare, the directors being responsible for the remaining grants, either at the twice-yearly meetings in November and March or in response to specific applications, especially educational grants.

Relief of poverty and medical welfare: applications on behalf of individuals are only acceptable if they are made by the social services or other similar bodies on an individual's behalf. Grants are restricted to a maximum of two per household.

Special category: applications are invited from registered charities by way of two A4 pages giving full particulars of the project, supported by annual report and/or budget together with any photographs if relevant. The directors will award grants at their meetings in November and March each year.

Education: The trust's general policy is to make grants available to those taking second degrees, to mature students, and to students from abroad whose circumstances have been affected by adverse events beyond their control (but not including students whose funds have been cut off by their own government).

Individuals (students) should submit the following paperwork, in duplicate and by post: a full cv, statement of financial situation, two letters of reference (preferably academic), and an sae. No reply is made without an sae.

Awards usually range from £150 to £1,000 (maximum). Cheques are made out to the educational institution and not to the individual student.

It is recommended that applications intended for the start of a new academic year should be submitted at least four months in advance, preferably earlier.

Newpier Charity Ltd

Jewish, general
£129,000 (1998/99)
Beneficial area UK.

Wilder Coe, Auditors, 233–237 Old Marylebone Road, London NW1 5QT

Correspondent Charles Margulies, Trustee & Secretary

Trustees C Margulies; H Knopfler; R Margulies; S Margulies; M Margulies.

CC Number 293686

Information available Accounts were on file at the Charity Commission, but without a list of grants.

General The main objectives of the charity are the advancement of the orthodox Jewish faith and the relief of poverty. In 2000/01 the trust had an income of £526,000 and a total expenditure of £431,000. Unfortunately no further details were available for this year. In 1998/99 it had an income of £412,000 including donations totalling £271,000 and rent received totalling £124,000. Grants totalled £129,000.

No grants list was included in the 1998/99 accounts. The last available list was from 1997/98 when grants were made to 23 organisations totalling £80,000. All the beneficiaries were Jewish organisations and nine had also received a grant the year before. The largest donation was to SOFT for redistribution to other charities (£23,000 was given in 1996/97).

Other larger grants were £17,000 to KID (£14,000 in 1996/997), £7,000 to Mesdos Wiznitz, £6,100 to BML Benityashvut, £5,000 to Friends of Biala (£1,500 in 1996/97) and £3,000 to Gateshead Yeshiva.

Applications In writing to the correspondent. The address given is effectively a PO Box, from where letters are passed on to the trustees and telephone calls are not invited.

The Chevras Ezras Nitzrochim Trust

Jewish
About £190,000 (2001)
Beneficial area UK, with a preference for London.

53 Heathland Road, London N16 5PQ

Correspondent H Kahan, Trustee

Trustees H Kahan; J Stern.

CC Number 275352

Information available Accounts were on file at the Charity Commission, but without a grants list.

General 'The objects of the charity are the relief of the poor, needy and sick and the advancement of Jewish religious education.'

There is a preference for Greater London, but help is also given further afield. Grants can also be made to individuals.

In 2001 the trust had an income £197,000, which was raised by the trustees and voluntary helpers. The previous year assets stood at just £4,700. Total expenditure was £195,000, most of which would have been given in grants. Further information was unavailable about the beneficiaries and size of grants.

Applications In writing to the correspondent.

The Noel Buxton Trust

Child and family welfare, penal matters, Africa
£82,000 (2001)
Beneficial area UK, eastern and southern Africa.

PO Box 393, Farnham, Surrey GU9 8WZ

Correspondent Ray Waters, Secretary

Trustees Richenda Wallace, Chair; Joyce Morton; Simon Buxton; Paul Buxton; David Birmingham; Angelica Mitchell; Jon Snow; Jo Tunnard, Vice Chair; John Littlewood; Brendan Gormley.

CC Number 220881

Information available Full accounts and guidelines for applicants were provided by the trust.

General Grants are made for the following:

- The welfare of children in disadvantaged families and of children in care. This will normally cover families with children of primary school age and younger, although work with children in care will be considered up to the age at which they leave care. (Grants are NOT given for anything connected with physical or mental disability or any medical condition.)
- The prevention of crime, especially work with young people at risk of offending; the welfare of prisoners' families and the rehabilitation of prisoners (housing of any kind is excluded).
- Education and development in eastern and southern Africa.

The trust seldom gives grants of more than £2,000 and often considerably less. Applications for recurrent funding over several years and for core running costs are considered. Due to the size of grants, contributions are not normally made towards salary costs. The trust does not respond to appeals from large, well-supported UK charities, but welcomes appeals from small local groups throughout England, Scotland and Wales. Preference is given to areas outside London and south east England.

In 2001 the trust had assets of £2.1 million and an income of £119,000. Donations were made to 89 organisations totalling £82,000, broken down as follows:

Education and development in eastern and southern Africa – 25 grants totalling £29,000 (35% of fund)
APT Enterprise Development – Zimbabwe (£4,000), WaterAid – Tanzania (£3,300), Harvest Help – Zambia (£2,500), Farm Africa – Tanzania and Intermediate Technology Development Group (£2,000 each), Book Aid International (£1,500). Beneficiaries receiving £1,000 each included African Initiatives – Tanzania, Books Abroad – Zimbabwe, Busoga Trust – Uganda, Lewa Water Conservancy – Kenya, Tools for Self Reliance – Africa.

Penal matters – 27 grants totalling £27,000 (33% of fund)
Howard League for Penal Reform (£3,000), Centre for Crime and Justice Studies and Prisoners Abroad (£2,500 each), Consett Churches Detached Youth Project, New Bridge and Prisoners' Advice Service (£2,000). Grants of £1,000

each went to Inside Out Trust, Prisoners' Education Trust, Waterville Projects for Children & Young People and Wood End and Bell Green Truancy & Exclusion Group.

Welfare of disadvantaged children (UK) – 37 grants totalling £26,000 (32% of fund)

Family Rights Group (£4,000) and Asylum Aid (£2,000). Grants of £1,000 each went to bfriends, Birmingham Settlement, Family Meditation Scotland, Family Welfare Association, National Family Meditation, Playbus Scotland, Respect, Space for Parents and Children to Enjoy, Thamesmead Family Service Unit and Think Children. Smaller grants included those to Central Community Group – Crewe, Hansworth Community Nursery, Home-Start Telford & Wrekin and Quaker Social Action.

The trust was able to give grants to about 16% of applicants. Four organisations were offered the possibility of repeat grants during the year but did not reply to the offer.

Exclusions The trust does not give to: academic research; advice centres; animals; the arts of any kind; buildings; conferences; counselling; development education; drug and alcohol work; the elderly; the environment; expeditions, exchanges, study tours, visits, etc. or anything else involving fares; housing and homelessness; human rights; anything medical or connected with illness or mental or physical disability; anywhere overseas except eastern and southern Africa; peace and disarmament; race relations; youth (except for the prevention of offending); and unemployment. Grants are not made to individuals for any purpose.

Applications There is no application form and applications may be submitted at any time. They should include the organisation's charity registration number and the name of the organisation to which grants should be paid if different from that at the head of the appeal letter. The following should be included with applications: budget for current and following year; details of funding already received, promised, or applied for from other sources and the last available annual report/accounts in their shortest available form.

In order to reduce administration costs the trust does not acknowledge receipt of applications or reply to unsuccessful appeals. Every effort is made to communicate a decision on successful appeals as soon as possible (normally within six months).

The Norman Family Charitable Trust

General

£250,000 (2000/01)

Beneficial area Primarily south west England.

14 Fore Street, Budleigh Salterton, Devon EX9 6NG

Tel. 01395 446699 **Fax** 01395 446698

Email enquiries@nfct.org

Website www.nfct.org

Correspondent R J Dawe, Chairman of the Trustee

Trustees *R J Dawe, Chairman; Mrs M H Evans; M B Saunders; Mrs M J Webb; Mrs C E Houghton.*

CC Number 277616

Information available Full accounts were provided by the trust.

General This trust has general charitable purposes, with a preference for organisations in the south west of England.

In 2000/01 the trust had assets of £5.1 million. The total income was £473,000, of which £318,000 came from investments and the rest from legacies and donations received. The trust distributed toys to charities worth £12,000. Financial grants totalled £238,000 and were broken down as follows:

Animal welfare – 20 grants totalling £11,000

Devon Horse and Pony Society received £2,000 with £1,000 each to Cinnamon Trust and National Animal Rescue.

Blind welfare – 14 grants totalling £33,000

£25,000 was given to West of England School for Children with Little or No Sight. Other grants included £2,000 to Devon County Association for the Blind and £1,000 to Action for Blind People.

Children's welfare – 27 grants totalling £21,000

These included £5,000 to Bristol Royal Hospital for Sick Children, £2,500 each to Children's Hospice Care – South West, Great Ormond Street Hospital Children's Charity and REACT and £1,000 to Children's World.

Teenagers and youths – 36 grants totalling £12,000

Recipients included Axminster Task Centre (£2,500) and British Schools Exploring Society (£1,000).

Mental disability – 14 grants totalling £18,000

The Doyle Centre received £10,000. Devon and Exeter Spastics Society received £2,500 while £1,000 each went to Brain Injured Children, Brainwave, Down Syndrome Association and Manic Depression Fellowship.

Physical disability – 28 grants totalling £17,000

Grants included £2,500 each to Disabled Young Adults Centre and St Loyes Foundation and £1,000 each to Motability, Multiple Sclerosis Therapy Centre, Northam Lodge and Staffordshire University Robotic Aid.

Medical other – 29 grants totalling £39,000

The largest grants were £10,000 to Exeter Leukaemia Fund, £5,000 each to Exeter and District Hospital Endowment Fund and National Asthma Campaign and £2,500 each to CLIC and Devon Air Ambulance. Beneficiaries of £1,000 each included Alzheimer's Society, Bath Cancer Research, Exmouth Hospital League of Friends, Motor Neurone Disease Association, Parkinson's Disease Society, St Luke's Hospice – Plymouth, David Tolkien Trust and West Country Ambulance Service.

Senior citizens – 8 grants totalling £23,000

Resthaven Residential Home and Shandford Fundraising Account each received £10,000. Abbeyfield BS was given £2,000.

Research – 2 grants totalling £26,000

Fountain Foundation received £25,000.

Homeless – 5 grants totalling £1,500

The largest grant was £1,000 to St Petrock's Church.

Miscellaneous – 65 grants totalling £35,000

Exeter University received £9,500. Exmouth Furniture Project received £2,500 while £1,000 each went to Crimestoppers Trust, Depression and Anxiety Support Services, East and Mid Devon Victim Support, Exmouth Beach Rescue, Exmouth Ring and Ride, Historic Chapels Trust and The Samaritans.

Social services – 34 grants totalling £2,400

Alcohol services – 1 grant of £100

Exclusions No support will be given to projects involving experiments on live animals or the maintenance of churches, ancient monuments and so on, or to overseas projects. No grants to individuals.

Applications In writing to the correspondent. The trustees meet regularly to agree the distribution of grants.

The Duncan Norman Trust Fund

General

£69,000 (2000/01)

Beneficial area UK, with a preference for Merseyside.

Liverpool Council of Social Service (Inc.), 14 Castle Street, Liverpool L2 0NJ

Tel. 0151 236 7728

Correspondent The Trustees

Trustees J A H Norman; R K Asser; Mrs V S Hilton; Mrs C E Lazar.

CC Number 250434

Information available Accounts were provided by the trust, without a full grants list.

General This trust has general charitable purposes, particularly supporting Merseyside organisations.

In 2000/01 it had assets of £2.1 million, generating an income of £63,000. Grants totalled £69,000.

The fund made 18 grants of £1,000 or more. These were to Petrus (£10,000), St Judes-on-the-Hill Parish Church Organ Appeal, The Children's Society and The Royal Agricultural Benevolent Institution (£5,000 each), Christ Church Youth and Community Centre (£3,800), Personal Service Society (£2,500), Hereford College and Oundle School Foundation (£2,000 each), Merseyside Drugs Council (£1,500), All Saints PCC Special Projects, Banbury District Housing Connection, Imagine, Marie Curie Cancer Care, Motor Neurone Disease Association, PCC of St Paul's Banbury, Sahir House, St Nicholas Church PCC and The Spring Centre (£1,000 each).

Other smaller grants totalled £23,000.

Exclusions No grants to individuals.

Applications The trust states that it only makes grants to charities known to the settlor and unsolicited applications are not considered.

The Normanby Charitable Trust

Social welfare, disability, general

£197,000 (2000/01)

Beneficial area UK, with a special interest in north east England.

Morgan Intakes, Great Fryup Dale, Lealholm, Whitby, North Yorkshire YO21 2AT

Correspondent Lady Henrietta Burridge

Trustees *The 5th Marquis of Normanby; The Dowager Marchioness of Normanby; Lady Lepel Kornicka; Lady Evelyn Buchan; Lady Peronel Phipps de Cruz; Lady Henrietta Burridge.*

CC Number 252102

Information available Full accounts were on file at the Charity Commission.

General The trust supports social welfare, disability and the arts, with a special interest in north east England. The trust will occasionally consider giving grants for the preservation of religious and secular buildings of historical or architectural interest in the north east of England.

In 2000/01 the trust had assets of £8.5 million, which generated an income of £313,000. Grants were made to 56 organisations totalling £197,000.

The largest grants were £10,000 each to Lythe Village Hall Committee, Northumberland Aged Mineworkers' Home Association, Rainbow Trust, Redcar Literacy Institute, Royal Free Hospital and University College Medical School, St Mary's Church – Clymping, and Teesside Hospital Care Foundation.

Fryup Village Hall received £6,500 while grants of £5,000 each went to 15 organisations including Albion Trust, Crisis, Fairbridge Teesside, Help the Aged, Lythe School, Multiple Sclerosis Society, Newby Hall Appeal, RNLI Crew Training Centre, SSAFA and Springhead School.

The grants list suggested there is a preference for Whitby, with grants including £2,000 to Whitby and District Young Musicians, £850 to Whitby Music

Port, £500 each to Whitby 2000 Christmas Light Appeal, Whitby Community College and Whitby Pre-school Learning and £25 to Whitby Trust for the Blind.

Other beneficiaries included Bicton College of Agriculture (£4,000), Cleveland Ironstone Mining Museum (£3,000), Helix Arts (£2,500), City of York Council (£1,500), Thirsk and District Community Care Association (£1,000), Scope on Teesside (£500), St John Ambulance (£20) and Runswick Bay Methodist Church (£10).

Also listed in the accounts were future commitments totalling £170,000. These were to Whitby Literacy and Philosophical Society (£100,000), Cook Museum Trust (£50,000) and Northumberland Aged Miners' Association (£20,000).

Exclusions No grants to individuals, or to non-UK charities.

Applications In writing to the correspondent. Only successful applications will be acknowledged. Telephone calls are not encouraged. There are no regular dates for trustees' meetings.

Norwood & Newton Settlement

Christian

£240,000 (2001/02)

Beneficial area England and Wales.

126 Beauly Way, Romford, Essex RM1 4XL

Tel. 01708 723670

Correspondent David M Holland, Trustee

Trustees *P Clarke; D M Holland; W W Leyland.*

CC Number 234964

Information available Full accounts were on file at the Charity Commission.

General The trust supports Methodist and other mainline Free Churches and some other smaller UK charities in which the founders had a particular interest. As a general rule, grants are for capital building projects which aim to improve the worship, outreach and mission of the church.

Where churches are concerned, the trustees take particular note of the contribution and promised contributions towards the project by members of the church in question.

In 2001/02 the trust had assets of £6.6 million and an income of £285,000. Grants totalling £240,000 were given in 53 grants ranging from £1,500 to £10,000. Over 70% of grants (38) were to Methodist churches engaged in the building of new premises, or in making improvements to their existing premises. Other grants were made to various other churches. Grants were given throughout the UK in areas ranging from Isle of Man to Essex and Middlesbrough to Wiltshire.

Exclusions Projects will not be considered where an application for National Lottery funding has been made or is contemplated. No grants to individuals, rarely to large UK charities and not for staff/running costs, equipment, repairs or general maintenance.

Applications In writing to the correspondent. In normal circumstances, the trustees' decision is communicated to the applicant within seven days (if a refusal), and if successful, immediately after the trustees' quarterly meetings.

The Oakdale Trust

Social work, medical, general

£161,000 (2001/02)
Beneficial area Worldwide, especially Wales.

Tansor House, Tansor, Oundle, Peterborough PE8 5HS
Email oakdale@tanh.demon.co.uk
Correspondent Rupert Cadbury
Trustees *B Cadbury; Mrs F F Cadbury; R A Cadbury; F B Cadbury; Mrs O Tatton-Brown; Dr R C Cadbury.*
CC Number 218827
Information available Full accounts were provided by the trust.

General This trust's main areas of interest include:

- Welsh-based social and community projects
- medical – support groups operating in Wales and UK-based research projects

- UK-based charities working in the third world
- environmental conservation in the UK and overseas
- penal reform.

Some support is also given to the arts, particularly where there is a Welsh connection.

In 2001/02 the trust had an income of £188,000 and made 180 grants totalling £161,000. The average grant was around £750.

The largest grants were £10,000 each to The Brandon Centre and Concern Universal. Other large donations over £1,000 each included: £5,000 each to The Bracken Trust, CARAD and Howard League for Penal Reform; £4,000 to Youth Hostel Association; £3,000 to Survivors Fund; £2,000 each to Cambridge Female Education Trust and WaterAid; and £1,000 each to Action Research, Camarthen Youth Project, International Refugee Trust, Marie Stopes International, Mid Wales Opera, Prisoners of Conscience Fund, Simon Community, Stroke Association and Weston Spirit.

Grants under £1,000 each included those to AIDS Trust Cymru, Arts Care Ltd, Brainwave, Bristol Drugs Project, Canine Partners for Independence, Cardiff School for Biosciences, Harvest Trust, Independent Adoption Service, Llandelio Summer Play Scheme, National Back Pain Association, Save the Family, Soil Association, St Vincent de Paul Society, Staffordshire Wildlife Trust and Vision Support.

Exclusions No grants to individuals, holiday schemes, sport activities or expeditions.

Applications An application form is available from the trust; however, applicants are free to submit requests in any format, providing they are clear and concise, covering aims, achievements, plans and needs, and supported by a budget. Applications for grants in excess of £1,000 are asked to submit a copy of a recent set of audited accounts (these can be returned on request).

The trustees meet twice a year in April and October to consider applications, the deadline for these meetings is 1 March and 1 September respectively; no grants are awarded between meetings. Unsuccessful applicants are not normally notified and similarly applications are not acknowledged even when accompanied by an sae.

The Odin Charitable Trust

General

£135,000 (2001/02)
Beneficial area UK.

PO Box 1898, Bradford on Avon, Wiltshire BA15 1YS
Correspondent Mrs M Mowinckel, Trustee
Trustees *Mrs S G P Scotford; Mrs A H Palmer; Mrs M Mowinckel.*
CC Number 1027521
Information available Annual report and accounts were provided by the trust.

General In 2000/01 the trust had assets of £4.2 million and an income of £123,000. Grants were made to 40 organisations, some of whom have been awarded recurrent grants up to 2004. A total of £135,000 was given during the year, with a further £100,000 to be distributed between six of the beneficiaries up to 2004.

Although the objects of the charity are wide, the trust has a preference for making grants towards: furthering the arts; providing care for people who are disabled and disadvantaged; supporting hospices, the homeless, prisoners' families, refugees, gypsies and 'tribal groups'; and furthering research into false memories and dyslexia.

The trustees are more likely to support small organisations and those, that by the nature of their work, find it difficult to attract funding.

Beneficiaries receiving recurrent grants were British False Memory Society, which will receive £35,000 each year up to 2004, Crisis Fairshare (£9,000 in total to 2003), Dorothy House (£15,000 in total to 2004), Helen Arkell Dyslexia Centre (£17,000 in total to 2004), Mustard Tree (£9,000 in total to 2003) and New Bridge (£15,000 in total to 2003).

Other beneficiaries included Crisis, Detection Advice Centre, Karten CTEC Centre and Naomi House (£5,000 each), Finsbury Park Street Drinkers Initiative (£4,000), Bath Recital Artists' Trust and Crossroads – Caring for Carers (£3,000 each), Edinburgh Young Carers Project (£2,000), Harvest Trust, Pearson's Holiday Fund and Primrose Cancer Help Centre (£1,500 each), Bag Books, Geese Theatre Company and Jessie's Fund (£1,000 each), Neighbourly Care Southall and Southwark Children's Foundation (£500).

Exclusions Applications from individuals are not considered.

Applications In writing to the correspondent.

The Ofenheim & Cinderford Charitable Trusts

Health and welfare, arts, environment

£348,000 (2000/01)
Beneficial area UK.

Baker Tilly, 1st Floor, 46 Clarendon Road, Watford, Hertfordshire WD17 1HE
Tel. 01923 657700
Correspondent G Wright
Trustees *R J Clark; R McLeod.*
Information available Information was provided by the trust.

General These trusts operate in conjunction and have the same founder and trustees. It has been the practice for the two trusts to make their donations jointly, in proportion to funds available. The Cinderford Charitable Trust also makes some additional grants.

The trusts made donations to a variety of mainly UK, high-profile organisations in the fields of health, welfare, arts and the environment. The additional grants made by The Cinderford Trust also gave grants within these areas. Many of the same organisations are supported each year.

In 2000/01 The Cinderford Charitable Trust had assets of £8.2 million and an income of £282,000. Grants totalled £278,000. The Ofenheim Trust had assets of £1.5 million and an income of £51,000. Grants totalled £70,000.

The grants list which appears in the accounts for both trusts is identical, containing 53 grants, with additional donations by The Cinderford Charitable Trust.

Eight organisations received donations of £12,000 each; these were St Wilfred's Hospice Eastbourne, Save The Children Fund, Musician's Benevolent Fund, Dr Barnardos Home, World Wildlife Fund, Salvation Army, NSPCC and Scope. Fifteen organisations received £7,500 each, including British Stroke

Association, Royal Surgical Aid Society, National Youth Orchestra of Great Britain, National Trust, Glyndebourne Arts Trust, Elizabeth Finn Trust and Marie Curie Memorial Foundation.

Nine organisations received £4,500 each, including Game Conservancy Trust, Alzheimers Disease Society, Motor Neurone Disease Association, Toynbee Hall, Trinity Hospice and Greater London Fund for the Blind. Eleven organisations received £3,000, including House of St Barnabas in Soho, Centrepoint in Soho, Ability Net, Hospice Care Kenya, Sisters of the Sacred Heart of Jesus and Mary, St Luke's Hospital for the clergy and Universal Beneficient Association. Moray Concert Brass received £2,000, with a further eight beneficiaries receiving £1,750 each; these were Enham Trust, Wildfowl & Wetlands Trust, Chaseley Trust, Friends of Eastbourne Hospitals, Rainbow Children's Holidays, Royal Academy of Music, Barn Owl Trust and Home Start UK. One organisation, DisCASS, received a grant of £1,500.

The Cinderford Charitable Trust also made five additional grants to PCC All Saints Margaret Street (£37,000), Trinity College of Music (£9,000), Fettes College (£1,500), The Greenwich, Deptford & Rotherhithe Sea Cadet Unit (£1,000) and The Guildhall School of Music and Drama (£750).

Applications In writing to the correspondent. Unsuccessful applications will not be acknowledged. Trustees meet in March and applications need to be received by February.

The Ogle Christian Trust

Evangelical Christianity

£146,000 (2001)
Beneficial area Worldwide.

2 Park Farm Stables, Stopham Rd, Pulborough, West Sussex RH20 1DR
Tel. 01798 874692
Email oglectrust@aol.com
Correspondent Chris Fischbacher, Secretary
Trustees *D J Harris, Chair; S Procter; Mrs F J Putley; C A Fischbacher; Mrs L M Quanrud.*
CC Number 1061458

Information available Accounts were on file at the Charity Commission but without a list of grants.

General This trust mainly directs funds to new initiatives in evangelism worldwide, support of missionary enterprises, publication of Scriptures and Christian literature and famine and other relief work.

In 2001 it had assets amounting to £2.4 million and an income of £162,000. Grants to 81 beneficiaries totalled £146,000. No further information was available.

This trust receives approximately 400 to 500 applications per year of which around 75% are rejected.

Exclusions Applications from individuals are discouraged; those granted require accreditation by a sponsoring organisation. No grants are made for building projects. Grants will not be offered in response to general appeals from large national organisations.

Applications In writing to the correspondent, accompanied by documentary support and an sae. Trustees meet in May and November, but applications can be made at any time.

The Oizer Charitable Trust

Welfare, education

£169,000 (1999/2000)
Beneficial area Preference for Greater Manchester.

35 Waterpark Road, Salford M7 0FT
Correspondent Joshua Halpern, Trustee
Trustees *J Halpern; Mrs C Halpern.*
CC Number 1014399
Information available Accounts were on file at the Charity Commission, but without a list of grants.

General The trust supports welfare and education purposes. In 1999/2000 it had assets of £23,000 and an income of £125,000, entirely from donations. Grants totalled £169,000. Further information for this year was not available.

Applications In writing to the correspondent.

Old Possum's Practical Trust

General

£146,000 to organisations

(2000/01)

Beneficial area UK and overseas.

Baker Tilly, 5th Floor, Exchange House, 446 Midsummer Boulevard, Milton Keynes MK9 2EA

Tel. 01908 687800 **Fax** 01908 687801

Correspondent Judith Hooper, Trustee

Trustees *Mrs Esme Eliot; Judith Hooper; Brian Stevens.*

CC Number 328558

Information available Full accounts were on file at the Charity Commission.

General The trust supports a wide range of causes, with an interest in literacy and the arts. Children's, educational, animal, welfare and medical research charities are also supported.

In 2000/01 the trust had assets of £2.8 million, which generated an income of £327,000. It also received a capital endowment of £2.7 million. After management and administration fees of just £1,000, grants totalled £161,000, including £15,000 given in total to four individuals. Grants were broken down as follows:

Medical research – 3 grants totalling £8,000

These went to RNIB (£5,000), The Inspire Foundation (£3,000) and Great Ormond Street Hospital (£30).

Support for disabled people – 12 grants totalling £49,000

Parkinson's Disease Society received £10,000 while £5,000 each was given to Guide Dogs for the Blind, Handel House Trust and Hearing Dogs for Deaf People. The other eight grants were for £3,000 each.

Animal welfare – 2 grants totalling £8,000

£5,000 went to People's Dispensary for Sick Animals and £3,000 was given to The Wildlife Trusts.

Literacy – 4 grants totalling £15,000

These were £10,000 to Poetry Book Society, £10 to Friends of the National Library and £5,200 in two grants to individuals.

The arts – 3 grants totalling £26,000

Beneficiaries were The Arvon Foundation (£11,000), Victoria and Albert Museum (£10,000) and Golgonooze Prom (£5,000).

Children's welfare – 10 grants totalling £32,000

The largest grants were £5,000 to the Vale of Elham Trust and £3,000 each to Derian House Children's Hospice, Dreams Come True Charity, The Movement Foundation, The Rainbow Centre, Rainbow Family Trust and St Piers National Centre for Young People with Epilepsy. There was also a grant of £5,000 to an individual.

Education overseas – 1 grant of £3,000

This went to Books Abroad.

Historical Conservation – 3 grants totalling £18,000.

These went to St Stephens Organ Appeal (£10,000), Anglican Centre – Rome (£5,000) and Cathedral Camps (£3,000).

Further education of individuals – 1 grant of £2,000

This went to South Devon Healthcare.

Exclusions No grants towards sports or to students for academic studies or overseas trips, unless special circumstances apply.

Applications In writing to the correspondent. The 2000/01 annual report stated: 'The trustees wish to continue the policy of using the trust's income to support a few carefully chosen cases, generally located in the UK, rather than make a large number of small grants. The emphasis will be on continued support of those institutions and individuals who have received support in the past. Unfortunately we have to disappoint the great majority of applicants who nevertheless continue to send appeal letters. The trustees do not welcome telephone calls from applicants soliciting funds.'

The John Oldacre Foundation

Research and education in agricultural sciences

£90,000 (2000/01)

Beneficial area UK.

Hazleton House, Hazleton, Cheltenham, Gloucestershire GL54 4EB

Tel. 01453 835486

Correspondent Henry Shouler, Trustee

Trustees *H B Shouler; S J Charnock; D G Stevens.*

CC Number 284960

Information available Full accounts were on file at the Charity Commission.

General Grants are made to universities and agricultural colleges towards the advancement and promotion, for public benefit, of research and education in agricultural sciences and the publication of useful results.

In 2000/01 the trust's assets totalled £3.1 million and it had an income of £93,000. Grants to nine organisations were given totalling £90,000.

The main beneficiary, which appears to receive support on an ongoing basis, was the Royal Agricultural College, with a grant of £35,000 this year. Other grants included Arable Research Centre and University of Bristol (£12,000 each), Nuffield Farming Scholarship Trust (£7,500), Wye College (£6,000), Writtle College (£3,000), Cranfield University (£2,700) and Paignton Zoo (£2,500).

Exclusions No grants towards tuition fees.

Applications In writing to the correspondent.

Onaway Trust

General

£199,000 (2001)

Beneficial area UK, USA and worldwide.

275 Main Street, Shadwell, Leeds LS17 8LH

Tel. 0113 265 9611

Email david@onaway.org

Website www.onaway.org

Correspondent David Watters, Trust Administrator

Trustees *J Morris; Ms B J Pilkinton; A Breslin; Annie Smith; Elaine Fearnside; C Howles; D Watters.*

CC Number 268448

Information available Full accounts, with a detailed narrative report, were on file at the Charity Commission.

General This trust's objects are stated in its 1996/97 annual report as follows:

'To relieve poverty and suffering amongst indigenous peoples by providing seed grants for (small) self-help, self-sufficiency and environmentally sustainable projects.

'… These projects aim to make significant differences to the lives of the world's traditional/indigenous peoples who continue to struggle for both spiritual and physical survival in their own lands.

'… These (grants) empower the recipients to flourish and affirm the quality of their lives within traditional communities; thereby preserving invaluable knowledge, which might otherwise be lost to future generations.'

Additional, secondary objects are to make grants for the benefit of the 'world environment and animal welfare'.

In 2001 the trust's assets totalled £5.3 million and its income was £206,000. Grants totalling £199,000 were given to 39 new and ongoing projects (15 of the beneficiaries had been supported in the previous year). Grants were divided in the annual report between those given in the UK (£107,000) and those given in the USA (£92,000). A further £54,000 was spent in management and administration costs.

The largest grants were £19,000 to PISIL – Honduras, £10,000 to Rainy Mountain Society for Indigenous Peoples, £8,700 to Compassion in World Farming, £8,500 to Forest Peoples Programme – Africa, £8,200 to Simon Community and £8,000 each to British Red Cross, Academy for Development Science – India and Jeel Al Amal – Middle East.

Other grants were mainly between £1,000 and £7,000 and included £6,600 to the Society for the Welfare of Horses and Ponies, £5,000 each to Care International – Central America and Friends of Conservation, £4,000 Drukpa Kargyud Trust – India.

Exclusions No grants for administration costs, travel expenses, projects considered unethical or detrimental to the struggle of indigenous people.

Applications In writing to the correspondent, enclosing an sae.

Oppenheim Foundation

General
£108,000 (2000/01)
Beneficial area UK.

39 King Street, London EC2V 2DQ
Tel. 020 7623 9021
Correspondent Peter Smith, Trustee
Trustees *J N Oppenheim; T S Oppenheim; P A Smith.*
CC Number 279246
Information available Accounts were on file at the Charity Commission, but without a description of its grant-making practice.

General In 2000/01 the foundation had assets of £268,000 and an income of £9,100, including £3,000 in donations received. Grants were made totalling £108,000. As in previous years, no information was available on the beneficiaries or the size and type of grants made. The only information that has been available is that Glyndbourne Productions Limited has been regularly supported.

Applications The trust stated that it does not welcome applications.

The Raymond Oppenheimer Foundation

General
£87,000 (2000/01)
Beneficial area UK and worldwide.

40 Holborn Viaduct, London EC1N 2PB
Tel. 020 7404 0069
Correspondent D Murphy, Trustee
Trustees *Alec G Berber; David Murphy; Clifford T Elphick.*
CC Number 326551
Information available Accounts were on file at the Charity Commission, but without a full narrative report.

General In 2000/01 the foundation had assets of £734,000 and an income of £28,000. Grants to four organisations totalled £87,000.

The largest grant was US$100,000 (£64,000) to Stichting Mario Montessori 75 Fund, which has received similar amounts in previous years. African Medical & Research Foundation received US$25,000 (£17,000). Other beneficiaries were York Minster Fund (£5,000) and Imperial Cancer Research Fund (£500).

Applications In writing to the correspondent.

The Ouseley Trust

Choral services of the Church of England, Church in Wales and Church of Ireland, choir schools
£66,000 (2001)
Beneficial area England, Wales and Ireland.

127 Coleherne Court, London SW5 0EB
Tel. 020 7373 1950 **Fax** 020 7341 0043
Email clerk@ouseleytrust.org.uk
Website www.ouseleytrust.org.uk
Correspondent Martin Williams, Clerk
Trustees *Dr Christopher Robinson, Chair; Dr J A Birch; Rev Canon Mark Boyling; Dr R J Shephard; N E Walker; Revd A F Walters; Mrs Gillian Perkins; Sir David Willcocks; N A Ridley; Dr S M Darlington; Dr J Rutter.*
CC Number 527519
Information available Accounts were on file at the Charity Commission.

General The trust administers funds made available from trusts of the former St Michael's College, Tenbury. Its object is 'projects which promote and maintain to a high standard the choral services of the Church of England, the Church in Wales and the Church of Ireland', including contributions to endowment funds, courses, fees and the promotion of religious, musical and secular education for pupils connected to the churches and observing choral liturgy.

In 2001 the trust had assets of £2.9 million and an income of £121,000. Eighteen grants were made totalling £66,000 (£152,000 in 1999).

Grants awarded fell into five categories. During the year, grants were broken down as follows:

Endowments – eight grants totalling £49,000

St Michael & All Angels - Croydon, Norwich Cathedral Choir Endowment Fund and Bangor Cathedral (£10,000 each), Worcester Cathedral (£7,000), St Bartholomew the Great - Smithfield and St Patrick's Cathedral - Armagh (£5,000 each) and Holy Trinity - Stroud (£2,000 in total). Grants awarded will usually be paid in one sum to provide an immediate contribution to an endowment fund.

Fees for individuals – four grants totalling £9,000

Salisbury Cathedral School (2 grants totalling £6,000) and Wells Cathedral School (2 grants totalling £3,000). Applications must be submitted by an institution. Grants awarded will be paid in one sum as an immediate contribution. The trustees may require an assurance that the sum offered will achieve the purpose for which help has been requested.

Courses – two grants totalling £2,000

Grants were made to two choirs for training. Grants will be awarded only where there is a clear indication that an already acceptable standard of choral service will be raised. Under certain circumstances grants may be awarded for organ tuition.

Music – three grants totalling £1,500

Grants were made to three choral foundations. Grants will be awarded only where the replacement of old, or the purchase of new music will render specific assistance to the promotion or maintenance of high choral standards.

Other – one grant of £5,000

Royal School of Church Music received the grant for bursaries for the Millennium Youth Choir.

Each application will be considered on its merits, keeping in mind the specific terms of the trust deed. Unique, imaginative ventures will receive careful consideration.

The trust does not normally award further grants to successful applicants within a two-year period. The trustees' policy is to continue making grants to cathedrals, choral foundations and parish churches throughout England, Wales and Ireland.

Exclusions Grants will not be awarded to help with the cost of fees for ex-choristers, for chant books, hymnals or psalters. Grants will not be made for the purchase of new instruments nor for the installation of an instrument from another place of worship where this involves extensive reconstruction. Under normal circumstances, grants will not be awarded for buildings, cassettes, commissions, compact discs, furniture, pianos, robes, tours or visits.

Applications Applicants are strongly advised to obtain a copy of the trust's guidelines (either from the correspondent or their website, currently under construction at the time of writing) before drafting an application. Applications must be submitted by an institution on a form available from the correspondent. Closing dates for applications are 31 January for the March meeting and 30 June for the October meeting.

The Gerald Palmer Trust

Education, medical, religion, general

£148,000 (2000/01)
Beneficial area UK, especially Berkshire.

Eling Estate Office, Hermitage, Thatcham, Berkshire RG18 9UF
Tel. 01635 200268 **Fax** 01635 201077
Correspondent The Clerk
Trustees J M Clutterbuck; D R W Harrison; J N Abell; R Broadhurst.
CC Number 271327
Information available Accounts were on file at the Charity Commission.

General The trust's main activity is the management of its Eling Estate, but it also gives grants to organisations. In 2000/01 it had assets of over £16 million and an income of £712,000 comprised mainly of income from the estate and woodland. Expenditure on the estate and woodlands totalled £472,000 and £148,000 was given in grants.

The trust tends to support mainly UK education, medical and health-related charities together with a range of local charities in Berkshire.

In 2000/01 grants were given to 59 orgnaisations ranging from £50 to £10,000. The two largest donations were £10,000 each to GAP and Ripon College – Cuddesdon. Other larger grants included those to Abbeyfield House Appeal, Advance Housing and Support Ltd, Enham Trust, Guideposts Trust, Heritage Education Trust, Hermitage Primary School, Iris Fund, National Star Centre, Newbury and District Agricultural Society, Newbury Spring Festival, Riding for the Disabled Association, St John Ambulance, Sobell House Hospice Charity, Thames Valley Jubilee Sailing Trust, Toynbee Hall and West Berkshire Mencap.

Exclusions No grants to individuals or to local charities geographically remote from Berkshire.

Applications In writing to the correspondent.

Panahpur Charitable Trust

Missionaries, general

£139,000 (2000/01)
Beneficial area UK, overseas (see below).

Jacob Cavenagh and Skeet, 6–8 Tudor Court, Brighton Road, Sutton, Surrey SM2 5AE
Tel. 020 8643 1166
Correspondent The Trust Department
Trustees P East; Miss D Haile; Mrs E R M Myers; A E Perry; R Moffett.
CC Number 214299
Information available Accounts were on file at the Charity Commission.

General The trust's 2000/01 accounts stated: 'The trust was established for the distribution of funds to Christian charities and other Christian organisations and individuals, both in the UK and overseas. In particular, the trust has sought to support a wide range of Christian missionary organisations.'

In 2000/01 it had assets of £4.8 million, which generated an income of £188,000. Grants totalling £139,000 were made to 77 organisations, of which 47 were also supported in the previous year. Grants were broken down as follows:

Geographic area	2000/01	1999/2000
Africa	£12,000	£18,000
Britain	£79,000	£76,000
Eastern Europe	£150	£100
Far East	£1,100	£5,200
India	£31,000	£45,000
Israel	–	£50
Middle East	–	£4,500
Nepal	£1,500	–
Spain	£1,200	£1,200
South America	£10,000	–

Category	2000/01	1999/2000
Scripture distribution/ reading encouragement	–	£12,000
Relief work	£85	£3,200
Missionary work (UK)	£76,000	£32,000
Missionary work (overseas)	£48,000	£84,000
Missionary welfare	–	£830
Work amongst students	–	£200
Direct preaching of the gospel	£2,800	£3,000
Educational	–	£5,500
Sundries	–	£120
Christian retreats	–	£9,500
Others	£10,000	–

The largest grants were £11,000 to Interserve, £10,000 each to Himlit and Word for Life Trust, £9,600 to Relationships Foundation, £8,000 to Penhurst Retreat Centre, £6,000 to EHA UK, £5,400 to Outlook Trust and £5,000 to Christian Outreach.

Other grants of over £1,000 each included those to SIM International (£4,100), Evangelical Missionary Alliance (£4,000), London Bible College (£3,500), SIM UK (£3,000), North Kasai Mission (£2,400), COST and London Institute of Contemporary Christianity (£2,000 each) and Nepal Leprosy Trust and Sugandh (£1,500 each).

Smaller grants included those to RSCPA and San Martin Bible Institute (£750), Church Ministry amongst Jews (£500), Language Recordings International (£450), London City Mission and Stroud Christian Centre (£400 each), Langham Trust (£250), LSE Library and United Christian Broadcasters (£200 each), Clarion Ministries (£100), Age Concern (£60), Rowan Tree Centre (£50) and Amnesty International (£15).

Applications In writing to the correspondent, although the trust informed us that applicants will not be successful unless they are already known to the trust.

The Samuel & Freda Parkinson Charitable Trust

General
£110,000 (2000/01)
Beneficial area UK.

Pattinson & Scott, Trustees' Solicitors, Stonecliffe, Lake Road, Windermere, Cumbria LA23 3AR

Tel. 01539 442233 **Fax** 01539 488810

Correspondent J R M Crompton, Solicitor

Trustees D E G Roberts; Miss J A Todd; J F Waring.

CC Number 327749

Information available Information was provided by the trust.

General This trust was established in 1987 with £100. The fund stayed at this level until 1994/95 when £2.1 million worth of assets were placed in the trust on the death of the settlor.

In 2000/01 the trust had assets amounting to £2.6 million and its income was £71,000. Grants were made totalling £110,000. Other expenditure totalled £46,000, higher than usual due to the trustees' decision to dispose of freehold properties held locally.

'Annual distributions' were given as follows: £25,000 to Leonard Cheshire Foundation; £23,000 each to Salvation Army and Church Army; £10,000 each to RNLI and RSPCA; and £5,000 each to Animal Rescue and Animal Concern. A 'special distribution' of £10,000 was paid to RSPCA – Foot and Mouth Appeal. All of the organisations had been supported in previous years.

Applications The founder of this charity restricted the list of potential beneficiaries to named charities of his choice and accordingly the trustees do not have discretion to include further beneficiaries, although they do have complete discretion within the stated beneficiary list.

The Patrick Charitable Trust

General
£650,000 (2001/02)
Beneficial area UK, with a special interest in the Midlands.

The Lakeside Centre, 180 Lifford Lane, Kings Norton, Birmingham B30 3NU

Correspondent J A Patrick, Chair

Trustees J A Patrick, Chair; M V Patrick; Mrs H P Cole; W Bond-Williams; N Duckitt; G Wem.

CC Number 213849

Information available Information was provided by the trust.

General Joseph Patrick lived in Worcestershire when he established the trust in 1962 for general charitable purposes. Grants can be one-off or ongoing.

In 2001/02 the trust had assets of £6.1 million and an income of £1.5 million, of which £369,000 came from gifts and donations. Grants totalled £650,000.

Major grants went to Muscular Dystrophy Campaign (£500,000 designated loan), Sir Josiah Mason Trust (£100,000), Martha Trust – Hereford and Symphony Hall Organ Appeal (£10,000 each), Peckwood Centre (£6,000), Black Country Museum (£4,800), Make A Wish Foundation (£4,000) and Muscular Dystrophy Campaign (£3,000). Other sundry donations totalled £13,000.

The trust has also made future commitments to Black Country Museum totalling £1 million.

Exclusions No grants to individuals.

Applications In writing to the correspondent at any time.

The Late Barbara May Paul Charitable Trust

Older people, young people, medical care and research, preservation of buildings

£62,000 (2000/01)

Beneficial area East Anglia and UK-wide.

Lloyds TSB Private Banking Ltd, UK Trust Centre, The Clock House, 22–26 Ock Street, Abingdon, Oxfordshire OX14 5SW

Tel. 01235 232731

Correspondent Chris Shambrook, Trust Manager

Trustees *Lloyds TSB Bank plc.*

CC Number 256420

Information available Accounts were on file at the Charity Commission, but without a list of grants.

General Lloyds TSB Bank plc is the sole trustee for this and two other trusts, each founded by a different sister from the Paul family. This trust is the largest and makes larger grants but they all appear to have very similar grant-making policies. There is a preference throughout the trusts for Suffolk and some organisations have been supported by all three trusts.

This trust has stated in recent years that it is increasingly focusing its grant-making on local organisations in East Anglia, and East Anglian branches of UK charities. UK-wide organisations can, and do, receive funding, although local groups outside of East Anglia are not.

In 2000/01 the trust had assets of £14,000, and an income of £20,000. Grants were made totalling £62,000. Further information for this year was not available.

In 1998/99 grants were made to 55 organisations totalling £74,000. Donations were in the range of £500 and £5,000 but most were for £1,000. Many of the organisations supported had received grants in the previous year. The largest grant of £5,000 went to Whizz-Kidz, while two organisations received £3,000 each, Suffolk Preservation Society and Norfolk Millennium Trust for Carers. 10 grants of £2,000 each included those to Essex County Youth Service, Bus Project, Shelter, One-to-One, East Suffolk Mines, Essex Voluntary Association for the Blind, Cancer Research Campaign and Norfolk & Norwich Scope.

Six grants of £1,500 and over thirty of £1,000 were made, recipients included Queen Elizabeth's Foundation for Disabled People, FNA, RNIB, British Red Cross, Tannington Church, Salvation Army, Macmillan Cancer Relief, Age Concern, Malcolm Sargent Cancer Fund, Suffolk Association for Youth and Ipswich Scouts & Guides Council. Grants under £1,000 went to Rotary Club of Ipswich and Ipswich Disabled Advice (£750 each).

Exclusions No grants to overseas charities.

Applications In writing to the correspondent at any time.

Penny in the Pound Fund Charitable Trust

Hospitals, health-related charities

£106,000 (2002)

Beneficial area Northern England, southern Scotland, Wales and Northern Ireland, but mostly around the Merseyside area.

Medicash Health Benefits Limited, Merchants Court, 2–12 Lord Street, Liverpool L2 1TS

Tel. 0151 702 0202 **Fax** 0151 702 0250

Email karnold@medicash.org

Website www.medicash.org

Correspondent K Arnold, Finance Officer

Trustees *P B Teare; K W Monti; K Arnold; W Gaywood; J E Brown.*

CC Number 257637

Information available Full accounts were on file at the Charity Commission.

General This trust was established in 1968 by a health benefits insurance company, from which the trust continues to receive donations each year. The objects of the trust are to provide amenities to patients in hospital or under the care of health-related charities by reimbursing them with the cost of facilities purchased to make their patients stays more comfortable and enjoyable. Grants are given in Wales, Northern Ireland, southern Scotland and the north of England, although they are centred around the north west of England, especially Merseyside.

In 2001 the trust had assets of £106,000. Total income was £86,000, of which £71,000 came from donations received. Grants were made to 45 organisations and totalled £83,000.

The 2001 accounts included details of the grant allocations for 2002, broken down as follows:

Health authorities – 35 grants totalling £81,000

The largest grants were given on Merseyside, with £15,000 each to Aintree Hospitals NHS Trust and Royal Liverpool and Broadgreen University Hospitals NHS Trust, £10,000 to Wirral Hospitals NHS Trust and £5,200 to St Helens and Knowsley NHS Hospitals Trust. Other beneficiaries included Countess of Cheshire Hospital NHS Trust (£3,900), Morecambe Bay Hospitals NHS Trust (£1,800), Chorley and South Ribble NHS Trust (£1,400), Conwy and Denbighshire NHS Trust (£990), South Tyneside Health Care Trust (£800), North East Wales NHS Trust (£770), Argylle and Clyde Acute Hospitals NHS Trust and Ulster Community and Hospitals Trust (£750 each), Blackpool Victoria Hospital NHS Trust (£730), Ayrshire and Arran Acute Hospitals NHS Trust (£700) and Chester and Halton Community NHS Trust (£620).

Charities – 26 grants totalling £25,000

The largest went to Wrexham Hospital (£4,000), Children's Heart Foundation (£3,000), Abbeyfield North Mersey Society Ltd (£2,900), Brook (£2,600), Royal School for the Blind (£1,500) and Abbeyfield Furness Extra Care Society (£1,100). Other beneficiaries included PSS (£990), Arch Initiatives (£960), St Joseph's Hospice Association – Thornton (£800), Bradford Toy Library (£700), Motor Neurone Disease Association (£610), Cheshire Residential Homes Trust (£500), Listening Ear (£490), Cystic Fibrosis Trust (£400), Ty Hafan – The Children's Hospice in Wales (£300), Erskine Hospital (£260) and Children's Transplant Foundation Ltd (£200).

Exclusions No grants towards medical equipment.

Applications In writing to the correspondent. Applications need to be received in July and trustees meet in October.

The Pet Plan Charitable Trust

Dogs, cats and horses

£563,000 (2000/01)
Beneficial area UK.

Great West Road, Brentford, Middlesex
TW8 9EG

Tel. 020 8580 8013 **Fax** 020 8580 8186
Email
roz-hb-petplanct@allianzcornhill.co.uk
Correspondent Roz Hayward-Butt,
Administrator
Trustees *David Simpson, Chair; Clarissa
Baldwin; Patsy Bloom; John Bower; Dave
Bishop; Nicholas Mills; George Stratford;
Michael Tucker.*
CC Number 1032907
Information available Information was
provided by the trust.

General This trust was established by a
pet insurance company by adding an
optional £1 a year to the premiums paid
by its members. The trust provides grants
towards the welfare of dogs, cats and
horses by funding clinical veterinary
investigation, education and welfare
projects. Funding is sometimes given for
capital projects. Educational grants are
given to fund projects aimed at both the
general public and the welfare industry.

In 2000/01 the trust had assets of
£850,000. Its income was £488,000 and
administration costs were high at £69,000.
Grants were made totalling £563,000.

Beneficiaries included Animal Health
Trust for research into the cause of cancer
in dogs (£39,000), University of
Cambridge Veterinary School to
investigate joint disease in horses
(£21,000), Royal Veterinary College for a
study investigating insulin resistance in
diabetic cats (£20,000), Paws for Kids for
its pet fostering service (£12,000) and Ada
Cole Rescue Stables for a replacement van
and Ty-Agored Animal Sanctuary for
neutering and veterinary assistance
(£8,000 each).

Exclusions No grants to individuals or
non-registered charities. The trust does
not support or condone invasive
procedures, vivisection or
experimentation of any kind.

Applications In writing, or by telephone
or e-mail, to the correspondent. Closing
dates for scientific and welfare
applications vary so please check first.
Grants are generally announced at the end
of the year.

The Philanthropic Trust

Homelessness, developing world, welfare (human and animal), environment, human rights

£200,000 (2000/01)
Beneficial area UK, Africa, Asia.

Trustee Management Limited,
19 Cookridge Street, Leeds LS2 3AG
Correspondent The Trust Administrator
Trustees *Paul H Burton; Jeremy J Burton;
Amanda C Burton.*
CC Number 1045263
Information available Full accounts
were provided by the trust.

General Although the trust has general
charitable purposes, special consideration
is given to institutions relating to
homelessness, the developing world,
human and animal welfare, the
environment and human rights.

In 2000/01 the trust had assets of £2.4
million. The total income was £175,000,
including £98,000 in Gift Aid donations.
Grants were made to 167 organisations
totalling £200,000.

The largest grants were £20,000 to Crisis,
£10,000 each to Medical Foundation for
the Care of Victims of Torture and The
Samaritans and £5,000 to National Centre
for Conductive Education.

St Basil's and St Mungo's received £3,000
each while £2,500 went to Shelter. The
other grants were spread evenly across
£500, £1,000 and £2,000 each, with a few
smaller donations also made. They were
given to local, national and international
organisations across all the geographic
and priority areas mentioned above.

Beneficiaries in the UK included
Aberdeen Foyer, Addaction, The Ark, Big
Issue Foundation, Caring for Life, Cot
Death Society, Find Your Feet, Habitat for
Humanity – Northern Ireland, Liverpool
Student Community Action, Macmillan
Cancer Relief, Norwood, NSPCC,
Scottish Society for Autism and Victim
Support – London.

Beneficiaries working overseas included
African Orphans Aid Appeal, African
People's Link, Farm Africa, India
Development Group, Kenya Acorn
Project, Mines Advisory Group, Rwanda

Development Trust, UNICEF, World
Medical Fund and Y Care International.

Exclusions No grants for the arts,
education, religious organisations,
expeditions or individuals. Grants are
given to UK registered charities only.

Applications In writing to the
correspondent. Unsuccessful appeals will
not necessarily be acknowledged.

The Ruth & Michael Phillips Charitable Trust

General, Jewish

£135,000 (2000/01)
Beneficial area UK.

Berkeley Square House, Berkeley Square,
London W1J 6BY
Tel. 020 7491 3763 **Fax** 020 7491 0818
Correspondent M L Phillips, Trustee
Trustees *M L Phillips; Mrs R Phillips; M D
Paisner.*
CC Number 260378
Information available Full accounts
were on file at the Charity Commission.

General The trust supports a wide range
of causes, including medical research,
education, disability, old age, poverty,
sheltered accommodation and the arts. In
practice, almost all the grants are made to
Jewish/Israeli organisations.

In 2000/01 the trust had assets of £1
million. Total income was £201,000,
including £140,000 donated by J B
Rubens Charitable Foundation which is,
alongside The Phillips Family Charitable
Trust, connected to this trust through a
common trustee. Administration charges
were high at £40,000, including £19,000 in
rent and £3,000 in salaries to J B Rubens
Charitable Foundation.

Grants were made totalling £135,000, the
largest of which were £36,000 to Jewish
Care and £25,000 to Community Security
Trust. Other beneficiaries listed in the
accounts included London School of
Jewish Studies (£10,000), Marble Arch
Synagogue (£6,400), Norwood (£6,000),
Royal Opera House Benevolent Fund
(£5,200), British ORT and Naima Jewish
Prep School (£5,000 each), Variety Club
Children's Charity Ltd (£2,900),
Holocaust Educational Trust (£2,500),
Welfare Works Charitable Trust (£2,000),

B'nai B'rith Hillel Foundation (£1,500) and Wizo Charitable Foundation (£1,300). Smaller grants totalled £9,000.

Exclusions No grants are made to individuals.

Applications In writing to the correspondent at any time.

A M Pilkington's Charitable Trust

General

£130,000 (1999/2000)

Beneficial area UK, with a preference for Scotland.

Carters, Chartered Accountants, Pentland House, Saltire Centre, Glenrothes, Fife KY6 2AH

Tel. 01592 630055 **Fax** 01592 630555

Email cartersca@sol.co.uk

Correspondent The Trustees

CC Number SC000282

Information available Information was provided by the trust.

General The trust supports a wide variety of causes in the UK, with few causes excluded (see below). In practice there is a preference for Scotland – probably half the grants are given in Scotland. In 1999/2000 the trust had assets of £3.1 million and an income of £172,000. It gave grants to 146 charities totalling £130,000. There is a preference for giving recurring grants. Grants normally range from £500 to £1,500. Details on the beneficiaries were not available.

Exclusions Grants are not given to overseas projects or political appeals.

Applications The trustees state that, regrettably, they are unable to make grants to new applicants since they already have more than enough causes to support. Trustees meet in June and December, applications should be received by April and October.

The Cecil Pilkington Charitable Trust

Conservation, medical research, general on Merseyside

£177,000 (1999/2000)

Beneficial area UK, particularly Sunningwell in Oxfordshire and St Helens.

PO Box 8162, London W2 1JG

Correspondent A P Pilkington, Trustee

Trustees *A P Pilkington; R F Carter Jones.*

CC Number 249997

Information available Full accounts were on file at the Charity Commission.

General This trust supports conservation and medical research causes across the UK, supporting both national and local organisations. It also has general charitable purposes in Sunningwell in Oxfordshire and St Helens.

In 1999/2000 the trust had assets of £6.9 million, which generated an income of £179,000. Grants to 60 organisations totalled £177,000.

St Helens beneficiaries included Willowbreak Hospice (£10,000), Citadel Arts Centre (£5,000), St Helens District CVS (£2,000), Crossroads Carers and Groundwork Trust (£1,000 each), St Helens Deaf Society (£500) and St Helens Bereavement Service (£300). Other Merseyside recipients included Liverpool School of Medicine (£10,000), Royal School for the Blind (£5,000) and PSS (£4,000).

Recipients in Sunningwell included Sunningwell Church Appeal (£10,000), Sunningwell School of Art (£2,000) and Sunningwell Pre-School (£1,000). Other Oxfordshire beneficiaries included Victoria History of Oxfordshire Trust (£2,000), University of Oxford's Department of Plant Sciences (£1,600), Oxfordshire Woodland Project (£1,000) and University of Oxford's Wildlife Conservation and Research Unit (£900).

Medical research grants outside these counties included £8,000 to Exeter University Postgraduate School of Medicine and £5,000 each to Alzheimer's Research Trust, Bristol Cancer Help Centre and Covent Gardens Cancer Research Trust.

Environmental beneficiaries included British Trust for Ornithology and Soil Association (£5,000 each), BCTV and Rare Breeds Survival Trust (£3,000), Green Alliance and RSPB (£2,000 each), Barn Owl Trust and Countryside Foundation for Education (£1,000 each) and Agroforestry Research Trust (£500).

Exclusions No grants to individuals or non-registered charities.

Applications In writing to the correspondent.

The Elsie Pilkington Charitable Trust

Equine animals, welfare

£350,000 (2000/01)

Beneficial area UK.

Taylor Johnson Garrett, Carmelite, 50 Victoria Embankment, London EC4Y 0DX

Correspondent Lord Brentford

Trustees *Mrs Caroline Doulton; Mrs Tara Economakis; Richard Scott.*

CC Number 278332

Information available Accounts were on file at the Charity Commission, but without a list of grants.

General The trust's objects are shown below with the total given in grants for 2000/01 (1999/2000 in brackets):

- to prevent cruelty to equine animals – £145,000 (£65,000)
- to relieve suffering and distress amongst such equine animals and to care for and protect such equines in need of care and protection – £105,000 (£100,000)
- to provide social services and help for the relief of older people, and people who are infirm and poor – £100,000 (£160,000).

A grants list was not available for the year. Nineteen grants were made under the final object heading above, with the remaining ten grants made in the other two categories.

In 2000/01 the trust's assets totalled £3.3 million (£4.9 million in 1999/2000) and its income was £112,000 (£96,000). This income was far exceeded by expenditure.

The Sir Harry Pilkington Trust

General

£144,000 (2000/01)

Beneficial area UK and worldwide, with a preference for the St Helens area.

Liverpool Council of Social Service (Inc.), 14 Castle Street, Liverpool, Merseyside L2 0NJ

Tel. 0151 236 7728 **Fax** 0151 258 1153

Correspondent The Trustees

Trustees *Liverpool Council of Social Service (Inc.).*

CC Number 206740

Information available Full accounts were provided by the trust.

General This trust has general charitable purposes, giving most of its grants in and around St Helens.

In 2000/01 it had assets of £5.1 million, which generated an income of £147,000. Grants totalled £144,000.

By far the largest grant was £80,000 to Liverpool Council for Social Service. Other large grants went to Colden Children's Club (£15,000), Roy Castle Foundation and Guy Pilkington Benefit Fund (£10,000 each) and United Reformed Church – St Helens (£9,200).

Other beneficiaries included Southport Flower Show and Willow Brook Hospice (£5,000 each), Weston Spirit (£4,000), St Helens and District Crossroads (£2,000), PSS for St Helens Young Carers (£1,500) and Mencap – St Helens and The Roc Centre (£1,000 each).

Applications In writing to the correspondent.

Before this entry (top of first column):

Applications In writing to the correspondent.

This entry was not confirmed by the trust, but the address was correct according to the Charity Commission database.

The Platinum Trust

Disability

£622,000 (1999/2000)

Beneficial area UK.

19 Victoria Street, St Albans, Hertfordshire AL1 3JJ

Correspondent The Secretary

Trustees *G K Panayiotou; A D Russell; C D Organ.*

CC Number 328570

Information available Accounts were on file at the Charity Commission, but without a list of grants.

General This trust gives grants in the UK for the relief of children with special needs and adults with mental or physical disabilities 'requiring special attention'.

In 1999/2000 the trust had assets of £86,000. Total income was £605,000, including a donation of £600,000 from one of the trustees who usually gives £100,000 a year. This increase was used to fund a donation of £500,000 to Kosovo Appeal to aid children and families affected by the troubles in the region.

Grants to eight other organisations £122,000. Beneficiaries were BCODP (£39,000), Alliance for Inclusive Education and Parents for Inclusion (£20,000 each), CSIE (£18,000), DPPI (£11,000) with £5,000 each to Disability Equality in Education, Regard and Muscle Power.

Exclusions No grants for services run by statutory or public bodies, or from mental health organisations. No grants for: medical research/treatment or equipment; mobility aids/wheelchairs; community transport/disabled transport schemes; holidays/exchanges/holiday playschemes; special needs playgroups; toy and leisure libraries; special Olympic and Paralympics groups; sports and recreation clubs for people with disabilities; residential care/sheltered housing/respite care; carers; conservation schemes/city farms/horticultural therapy; sheltered or supported employment/community business/social firms; purchase/construction/repair of buildings; and conductive education/other special educational programmes.

Applications The trust does not accept unsolicited applications; all future grants will be allocated by the trustees to groups they have already made links with.

Polden-Puckham Charitable Foundation

Peace and security, ecological issues, social change

£348,000 (2001/02)

Beneficial area UK and overseas.

BM PPCF, London WC1N 3XX

Website www.polden-puckham.org.uk

Correspondent The Secretary

Trustees *Carol Freeman; David Gillett; Harriet Gillett; Jenepher Gordon; Heather Swailes; Anthony Wilson.*

CC Number 1003024

Information available Full accounts and information for applicants were provided by the trust.

General This foundation supports 'projects that change values and attitudes, that promote equity and social justice, and that develop radical alternatives to current economic and social structures', giving towards:

Peace – development of ways of resolving international and internal conflicts peacefully, and of removing the causes of conflict

Ecological issues – work which tackles the underlying pressures and conditions leading towards global environmental breakdown, particularly initiatives which promote sustainable living

Other areas – human rights work, in particular where it is related to peace, ecological and women's issues; there is also a long-standing link with the Society of Friends.

It prefers to make grants available to small, pioneering organisations which find it difficult to attract funds from other sources. Due to this emphasis, grants are often for long periods and may be given towards core costs. The average grant size for new applicants is £2,500.

In 2001/02 the trust had assets of £9.9 million. Total income was £299,000, included £28,000 in grants refunded. Grants were made totalling £348,000, broken down as follows:

category	grants	total
Peace and security issues	23	£144,000
Ecological issues	15	£82,000
Other	26	£123,000

Quaker Peace and Service received £20,000 as a core grant and £5,000 for the Quaker UN Office in Geneva. Other beneficiaries linked to the Society of Friends included Quaker Peace Studies Trust (£5,000), Quaker Social Action (£4,000) and Leaveners (£1,000).

Other large grants were £20,000 to Responding to Conflict, £15,000 each to New Economics Foundation, Oxford Research Group and Saferworld, £13,000 to Sustain and £10,000 each to Food Ethics Council, Transport 2000 Trust, World Development Movement Trust – Corporate Europe Observatory and World Information Service on Energy.

Recipients of smaller grants included Lansbury House Trust Fund for disbursement to Peaceworkers UK (£7,500), Trust for Research and Education on the Arms Trade and Food Commission (£6,000 each), World Court Project (£5,300), Womankind Worldwide for Transforming Violence (£5,100), Climate Action Network UK, Environmental Research Association for the Schumacher Society, Pesticides Action Network UK – Genewatch and People and Planet (£5,000 each), Environmental Law Foundation (£4,000), Scottish Centre for Nonviolence (£3,000), Friends of the Earth Scotland (£2,500), Railway Development Society (£2,100) and Millennium Environment Debate for Corporate Watch (£2,000).

Exclusions The trust does not support: individuals; travel bursaries (including overseas placements and expeditions); study; academic research; capital projects (e.g. building projects or purchase of nature reserves); community or local projects (except innovative prototypes for widespread application); general appeals; or organisations based overseas.

Applications The trustees meet twice a year in spring and autumn; applications should be submitted by 15 February and 15 September respectively. Decisions can occasionally be made on smaller grants between these meetings. The foundation will not send replies to applications outside its area of interest. Up-to-date guidelines will be sent on receipt of an sae.

Applications should be no longer than two pages and should include the following:

- a short outline of the project, its aims and methods to be used
- the amount requested (normally between £500 and £5,000 over one to three years), the names of other funders and possible funders, and expected sources of funding after termination of PPCF funding

- information on how the project is to be monitored, evaluated, and publicised
- background details of the key persons in the organisation.

Please also supply:

- latest set of audited accounts
- a detailed budget of the project
- list of trustees or board of management
- names of two referees
- charity registration number
- annual report.

The foundation strongly recommends that potential applicants should view their website. Applications outside of the trust's criteria will not receive a reply.

The George & Esme Pollitzer Charitable Settlement

Jewish, health, social welfare, general
£123,000 (1999/2000)
Beneficial area UK.

Saffery Champness, Courtyard House, Oakfield Grove, Clifton, Bristol BS8 2AE
Tel. 0117 915 1617
Correspondent J Barnes, Trustee
Trustees *J Barnes; B G Levy; R F C Pollitzer.*
CC Number 212631
Information available Full accounts were on file at the Charity Commission.

General This trust has general charitable purposes with no exclusions. Most funds are given to Jewish causes.

In 1999/2000 it had assets of £2.4 million, which generated an income of £112,000. Grants were made to 59 organisations totalling £123,000.

The largest grants were £10,000 each to Big Issue Foundation, Jewish Museum, Nightingale House and Prince's Youth Business Trust, £5,000 to Breast Cancer Care and £2,000 each to Alexandra Rose Day, AFASIC, Barnardos, BHHI, Crisis, Design Trust, Jewish Lads and Girls Brigade, NSPCC, Peper Harow Foundation, Royal Free and University College Medical School, Scope, United World College of the Atlantic and VSO.

Aside from the £500 each to Children's Leukaemia Trust and Cord Blood

Charity, all other grants were for £1,000 each. Beneficiaries included Aidis Trust, Bliss, Deafblind UK, Delamere Forest School, Family Holiday Association, Gingerbread, Listening Books, Motability, RNIB, Royal Star and Garter Home, Trinity Hospice, Winged Fellowship and Young Vic.

Applications In writing to the correspondent.

Edith & Ferdinand Porjes Charitable Trust

Jewish, general
£204,000 (2000/01)
Beneficial area UK and overseas.

Berwin Leighton Paisner, Bouverie House, 154 Fleet Street, London EC4A 2JD
Tel. 020 7353 0299 **Fax** 020 7583 8621
Correspondent M D Paisner, Trustee
Trustees *M D Paisner; A H Freeman; A S Rosenfelder.*
CC Number 274012
Information available Full accounts were on file at the Charity Commission.

General Although the trust has general charitable purposes, the trust is inclined to support applications from the Jewish community in the UK and overseas. It has a British Friends of the Art Museums of Israel Endowment Fund and in 2000 provisionally designated a fund for London School of Jewish Studies out of proceeds from the sale of manuscripts which had been on loan to the school.

In 2000/01 the trust had assets of £2 million which generated an income of £89,000. A total of £204,000 was given in 18 grants. In the previous year, £613,000 was given in a similar number of grants due to an extra income of £174,000 from chattels.

The management and administration costs were accounted as a gain of £4,400 due to the inclusion of £19,000 in exchange gains. Among the outgoing costs of £15,000 was a payment of £7,300 to a firm in which one of the trustees is a partner. Even though wholly legal, these editors always regret such payments unless, to use the words of the Charity

Commission, 'there is no realistic alternative'.

Four large grants were made to Jerusalem Foundation, regarding other organisations. These were £52,000 regarding Bikar Cholim, £28,000 regarding Haninar, £18,000 regarding YMCA and £11,000 regarding Beit David.

Other grants ranged from £1,500 (to St John's Hospice) to £12,000 (to both Jewish Care and Oxford Centre for Hebrew and Jewish Studies). Jewish Book Council received two separate grants totalling £14,000, including £4,000 for translation prizes. Other recipients included Royal Academy Trust (£10,000), British Friends of Rabbi Steinsaltz (£6,000), Centre for Jewish-Christian Relations (£5,000) and Ben Uri Gallery and Yesadey Hatorah Grammar School (£2,500 each).

Applications In writing to the correspondent.

The John Porter Charitable Trust

Jewish, education, general

£63,000 to institutions (1998/99)
Beneficial area Worldwide, but mainly UK and Israel.

79 Mount Street, London W1Y 5HJ
Correspondent The Trustees

Trustees *Sir Leslie Porter; John Porter; Steven Porter; Peter Green.*

CC Number 267170

Information available Full accounts were on file at the Charity Commission.

General This trust makes grants to projects in the fields of education, culture, environment, health and welfare 'which encourage excellence, efficiency and innovation, and enhance the quality of people's lives'. It makes grants to registered charities and exempt charities.

Up until 1992/93 this trust had a regular surplus of income over expenditure enabling a solid asset base to be established. By 1998/99 the assets stood at £5.8 million generating an income of £172,000. Five grants to institutions were made totalling £63,000.

Several beneficiaries have received ongoing support over a number of years including the trust's major project for the

year, Tel Aviv University Trust – Porter Super-Centre for Environmental and Ecological Studies which received £40,000. JPAIME – Daniel Amichai Education Centre also received further support, of £7,000.

The other three grants went to Institute for Jewish Policy Research (£10,000) and Israel Music Foundation and Wiener Library (£3,000 each).

One grant of £25,000 was given to an individual although the trust's policy normally excludes individuals.

Exclusions No grants to individuals.

Applications In writing to the correspondent.

This entry was not confirmed by the trust, but is correct according to information on file at the Charity Commission.

The J E Posnansky Charitable Trust

Jewish charities, health, welfare

£398,000 (2000/01)
Beneficial area UK and overseas.

c/o Baker Tilly, 2 Bloomsbury Street, London WC1B 3ST
Tel. 020 7413 5100 **Fax** 020 7413 5101

Correspondent The Trustees

Trustees *Lord Mishcon; Philip A Cohen; Gillian Raffles; Anthony Victor Posnansky; P A Mishcon; E J Feather; N S Ponansky.*

CC Number 210416

Information available Accounts were on file at the Charity Commission.

General The trust gives mainly to Jewish charities, although grants are also made to social welfare and health charities.

In 2000/01 the trust had an income of £242,000 generated from assets of £5.6 million. Grants totalling £398,000 were given to 109 organisations. Grants ranged from £300 to £29,000, along with one large grant of £110,000 being given to WaterAid.

Six other grants of £10,000 or over were given to UK Friends of Magen David Adom (£29,000), JPAIME (£25,000), British Wizo (£15,000), Friends of the Hebrew University of Jerusalem

(£13,000), Oxfam and Norwood Ravenswood (£10,000 each).

Other beneficiaries included Médecins Sans Frontières (£5,000), The Sue Ryder Foundation, Leukaemia Research Fund and The Jewish Aid Committee (£2,500 each), B'nai B'rith Hillel Foundation and National Head Injuries Association (£2,000 each), PHAB and St Martin In The Fields Christmas Appeal Fund (£1,000 each), Action for Kids, Age Concern, Eaves Housing for Women, Greater London Fund for the Blind, Jewish Bereavement Counselling Service, Riding for the Disabled Association, The Samaritans and Toynbee Hall (£500 each).

Exclusions No grants to individuals.

Applications In writing to the correspondent. The trustees meetings are held in May.

Premierquote Ltd

Jewish, general

£236,000 (1997/98)
Beneficial area Worldwide.

Harford House, 101–103 Great Portland Street, London W1N 6BH

Tel. 020 8203 0665

Correspondent D Last, Trustee

Trustees *D Last; Mrs L Last; H Last; M Weisenfeld.*

CC Number 801957

Information available Accounts were on file at the Charity Commission, but without a list of grants.

General The trust was established in 1985 for the benefit of Jewish organisations, the relief of poverty and general purposes. In 2000/01 it had an income of £774,000 and a total expenditure of £678,000. Unfortunately no further details were available for this year.

In 1997/98 it had assets of £3.5 million and an income of £439,000 from investments. Grants totalled £236,000, but no information was available on the beneficiaries. The trustees stated in their report that they have a large, continually growing demand from institutions for grants and donations.

Applications In writing to the correspondent.

The Nyda and Oliver Prenn Foundation

Arts, education, health

£192,000 (2000/01)

Beneficial area UK, with a preference for London.

Moore Stephens, Chartered Accountants, 1 Snow Hill, London EC1A 2EN

Correspondent T Cripps

Trustees O S Prenn; Mrs N M McDonald Prenn; S Lee; Mrs C P Cavanagh; A D S Prenn; N C N Prenn.

CC Number 274726

Information available Accounts were provided by the trust, but without a full narrative report.

General This trust supports arts, education and health organisations, usually based in London, which have been identified by the trustees through their own research.

In 2000/01 the foundation had assets of £624,000. Total income was £245,000, including £100,000 in Gift Aid and £123,000 in reclaimed tax from Gift Aid for the previous year. After low administration costs of £2,300, grants totalling £192,000 were made to 31 organisations, of which 20 were also supported in the previous year.

Tate Gallery Foundation received £100,000. The next largest grants were £30,000 to UCL Development Fund and £10,000 each to Rambert Dance Company and Union Dance Trust.

Other larger grants included those to SOS Poland (£3,200), Amadeus Scholarship Fund and Contemporary Arts Society (£3,000 each), Hearing Dogs for the Deaf and KIDS (£2,500 each), Age Concern and Notting Hill Housing Trust (£2,000 each), Royal National Theatre (£1,800) and British Heart Foundation and University of Warwick (£1,000 each).

Smaller grants included those to The Serpentine Trust (£650), National Asthma Campaign and Streatham Youth Centre (£500 each), Almeida Theatre (£300) and Ronald Raven Cancer Research Trust and The Sick Children's Trust (£250 each).

Exclusions Local projects outside London are unlikely to be considered.

Applications Unsolicited applications are not acknowledged.

The Primrose Trust

General

£112,000 (2000/01)

Beneficial area UK.

5 South View, Horton, Wiltshire SN10 3NA

Correspondent M Clark, Trustee

Trustees M G Clark; Susan Boyes-Korkis.

CC Number 800049

Information available Full accounts were on file at the Charity Commission.

General The trust was established in 1986 with general charitable purposes. In 2000/01 it had assets of £3.2 million and an income of £147,000. Grants to 12 organisations were made totalling £112,000.

The largest grants, of £20,000 each, went to Bluebell Charitable Trust and Langford Trust. Other beneficiaries included National Federation of Badger Groups (£15,000), Fovant Youth Club, Gloucestershire Wildlife Rescue and Raptor Rescue (£10,000 each), Clwyd Special Riding Centre, Sail Training Centre Association and Splitz (£5,000 each) and Children's Transplant Centre (£2,000).

Exclusions Grants are given to registered charities only.

Applications In writing to the correspondent, including a copy of the most recent accounts. The trust does not wish to receive telephone calls.

The Prince of Wales's Charitable Foundation

See below

£387,000 (1998/99)

Beneficial area UK.

The Prince of Wales Office, St James's Palace, London SW1A 1BS

Tel. 020 7930 4832 **Fax** 020 7930 0119

Correspondent Angela Wise

Trustees Rt Hon. Earl Peel; Sir Michael Peat; Stephen Lamport; Mrs Fiona Shackleton.

CC Number 277540

Information available Accounts were provided by the trust, only the four largest grants were listed.

General The trust principally continues to support charitable bodies and purposes in which The Prince of Wales has a particular interest.

In 2000/01 the trust had an income of £1.4 million and a total expenditure of £1.3 million. Unfortunately no further information was available for this year. During 1998/99 the total income of the trust was £972,000 including £525,000 net income from subsidiary companies, £255,000 from donations received and an investment income of £192,000. The foundation has two wholly owned subsidiaries, Duchy Originals Ltd and A G Carrick Ltd, from which most of its income is derived. To ensure an even flow of income for the foundation, £150,000 was transferred to the designated fund (part of the capital) during the year. The assets totalled £3.8 million.

The restricted fund is held by the foundation for the purpose of enabling United World Colleges (International) Ltd to provide scholarships to students to attend at the ten United World Colleges located around the world.

Other grants were broken down into the following classifications:

Category	1999	1998
Animals	£11,000	£1,500
Armed services	£16,000	£1,000
Children and youth	£6,300	£1,300
Culture	£85,000	£49,000
Education	£57,000	£65,000
Environment	£52,000	£59,000
Hospices and hospitals	£56,000	£73,000
Medical welfare	£28,000	£100
Overseas aid	£18,000	£14,000
Restoration of churches and cathedrals	£23,000	£25,000
Social welfare	£36,000	£11,300

Only those grants of over £10,000 were listed in the accounts. They were to United World Colleges (£55,000), SANE Helpline (£20,000) and Soil Association and Temenos Academy (£15,000 each). Three of these had been supported at a similar level in the previous year.

Exclusions No grants to individuals.

Applications In writing to the correspondent, with full details of the project including financial data.

Princess Anne's Charities

Children, medical, welfare, general

£169,000 (2000/01)
Beneficial area UK.

Buckingham Palace, London SW1A 1AA
Correspondent Capt. N Wright
Trustees *Hon. M T Bridges; Commodore T J H Laurence; B Hammond.*
CC Number 277814
Information available Accounts were on file at the Charity Commission, but without a list of grants.

General This trust has general charitable purposes, with a preference for charities or organisations in which The Princess Royal has a particular interest.

In 2000/01 the trust had assets of £4.2 million, which generated an income of £114,000. After high management and administration costs of £14,000, grants were made totalling £169,000.

No information was contained in the accounts as to which organisations were supported, although they were broken down as follows (1999/2000 figures in brackets):

Children and youth	£54,000	(£35,000)
Environment	£5,000	(£11,000)
Medical	£23,000	(£25,000)
Social welfare	£48,000	(£48,000)
Education	£23,000	(nil)
Animals	£7,000	(£550)
Armed forces	£6,500	(nil)
General	(£2,000)	(£2,000)

Exclusions No grants to individuals.

Applications Trustees meet to consider applications in January, and applications need to be received by November. 'The trustees are not anxious to receive unsolicited general applications as these are unlikely to be successful and only increase the cost of administration of the charity.'

The Priory Foundation

Health and social welfare, especially children

£198,000 (1998)
Beneficial area UK.

20 Thayer Street, London W10 2DD
Correspondent The Trustees
Trustees *N W Wray; L E Wray; M Kelly; T W Bunyard.*
CC Number 295919
Information available Accounts were on file at the Charity Commission.

General The trust was established in 1987 to make donations to charities and appeals that directly benefit children.

In 2001 this trust had an income of £209,000 and a total expenditure of £340,000. Unfortunately no further details were available for this year. In 1998 it had assets of £4.5 million, having increased from £2.1 million in 1995 following realised and unrealised gains on investments. Over 600 grants were given, totalling £198,000.

The largest grants were to the London Borough of Barnet for social needs cases (over £30,000), and over £5,000 each to ABCD, Birthright and MEP.

Most of the remaining grants were under £1,000 with beneficiaries including Action for Sick Children, ChildLine, Disability Aid Fund, East Belfast Mission, Sandy Gall's Afghanistan Appeal, Teenage Trust Cancer Appeal and Training Ship Broadsword. Most grants were one-off and given to UK organisations.

Applications In writing to the correspondent.

Prison Service Charity Fund

General

About £70,000 (2001)
Beneficial area UK.

68 Hornby Road, Walton, Liverpool L9 3DF
Tel. 0151 524 0537
Correspondent The Trustees

Trustees *A N Joseph, Chair; D Magill; C F Smith; Revd P Beaman; P McFall; R Howard.*
CC Number 801678
Information available Accounts were on file at the Charity Commission.

General The trust's accounts included the following narrative, describing how the trust was started: 'Having started a cash collection to assist in the treatment of a very sick local child, Liverpool's [prison] staff were obliged to seek help from other prisons nationwide, in order to achieve their financial goal. This resulted in us receiving considerably more money than we needed for our appeal and we used the spare cash to launch the Prison Service Charity Fund.' The charity is now an established fundraiser and grant-making trust.

In 2001 the fund had assets totalling around £430,000, an income of £116,000 and a total expenditure of £83,000. Most of the fund's income is raised through various fundraising efforts by prison staff. Grants totalled around £70,000.

The trust stated that the fund is 'for the staff, run by the staff'; the staff comprises 5–6,000 members of the Prison Service. The trust does not accept outside applications, and the person making the application has got to be a member of staff.

During the previous financial year, grants were made to almost 100 organisations, mostly local charities nationwide. Grants were mainly for less than £1,000 each.

Previous beneficiaries include: Donna Rose Appeal – Frankland, Jim McDermott Heart Foundation – Wetherby, ACROSS Trust – Frankland, Prison Service Special Games – Grendon, Joshua Walter Trust – Nottinghamshire, Spirit of Freedom – Lindholm, Dr Naquis Heart Fund Appeal – Manchester, Leeds Prison Service, Leicester Oncology Cancer Unit and Susan White Appeal – Dartmoor.

Applications The trust does not accept outside applications – the person making the application has got to be a member of staff.

The Privy Purse Charitable Trust

General

£293,000 (2000/01)

Beneficial area UK.

Buckingham Palace, London SW1A 1AA

Tel. 020 7930 4832

Email privypurse@royal.gov.uk

Correspondent Ian McGregor, Trustee

Trustees Sir M C Peat; G N Kennedy; I McGregor.

CC Number 296079

Information available Accounts were on file at the Charity Commission, but with only a brief narrative report and without a full grants list.

General This trust supports a wide range of causes, giving grants to UK-wide and local charities.

In 2000/01 the trust had assets of £2.4 million and an income of £338,000, including £272,000 in donations received. Grants to organisations totalled £293,000, broken down as follows (1999/2000 grant total in brackets):

Aged	£7,300	(£5,800)
Animals	£3,800	(£5,200)
Armed services	£7,400	(£5,900)
Blind	£2,400	(£2,400)
Children and youth	£13,000	(£11,000)
Cultural	£2,800	(£2,400)
Deaf	£570	(£600)
Disabled	£3,900	(£2,900)
Ecclesiastical	£122,000	(£107,000)
Education	£83,000	(£62,000)
Environment	£5,100	(£900)
Ethnic and foreign	£550	(£50)
Family welfare	£830	(£800)
Hospices and hospitals	£5,300	(£4,700)
Medical research	£2,000	(£2,000)
Medical welfare	£3,700	(£3,900)
Mental handicap and illness	£1,400	(£1,600)
Overseas aid	£510	(£500)
Restoration of cathedrals and churches	£3,900	(£7,100)
Royal almonry	£5,000	(£3,800)
Social welfare	£6,800	(£5,900)
Sport	£3,200	(£3,100)
Trades and professions	£7,600	(£7,500)
Voluntary services	£1,400	(£1,600)

The only grants listed in the accounts were those of over £10,000, given to five organisations who were also supported in the previous year. Under the heading Education, Choristers' School received £72,000 towards fees (£51,000 in the previous year) and The Queen's Chorister received £11,000 towards scholarships (£10,000 in 1999/2000). Three grants were listed as ecclesiastical grants, to the Chapel Royals at Hampton Court Place (£38,000) and St James's Place (£35,000) and to Sandringham Group of Parishes (£21,000).

Applications The trust makes donations to a wide variety of charities, but does not respond to applications.

The Puebla Charitable Trust

Community development work, relief of poverty

£90,000 (2000/01)

Beneficial area Worldwide.

Ensors, Cardinal House, 46 St Nicholas Street, Ipswich IP1 1TT

Correspondent The Clerk

Trustees J Phipps; M A Strutt.

CC Number 290055

Information available Accounts were on file at the Charity Commission.

General The trust has stated that: 'At present, the council limits its support to charities which assist the poorest sections of the population and community development work – either of these may be in urban or rural areas, both in the UK and overseas.'

Grants are normally in the region of £5,000 to £20,000, with support given over a number of years where possible. Most of the trust's income is therefore already committed, and the trust rarely supports new organisations.

In 2000/01 the trust's assets were £2.4 million. The income was £108,000 and the administration expenses were low at £1,800. Grants were made to seven organisations totalling £90,000. Beneficiaries were Wandsworth and Merton Law Centre (£20,000), Child Poverty Action Group and Shelter (£15,000 each), Action on Development, Cambodian Trust, Immigrants Aid and Medical Foundation for the Victims of Torture (£10,000 each).

Exclusions No grants for capital projects, religious institutions, research or institutions for people who are disabled. Individuals are not supported and no scholarships are given.

Applications In writing to the correspondent. The trustees meet in July. The trust is unable to acknowledge applications.

Quercus Trust

Arts, general

£192,000 (2000/01)

Beneficial area UK.

Chantrey Vellacott, Russell Square House, 10–12 Russell Square, London WC1B 5LF

Tel. 020 7509 9000

Correspondent A C Langridge, Trustee

Trustees Lord Bernstein of Craigwell; A C Langridge; Kate E Bernstein; Lady Bernstein.

CC Number 1039205

Information available Full accounts were on file at the Charity Commission.

General In February 1999 the trustees declared by deed that distributions would in future be directed principally (but not exclusively) to the arts and any other objects and purposes which seek to further public knowledge, understanding and appreciation of any matters of artistic, aesthetic, scientific or historical interest.

In 2000/01 the trust had assets of £6.1 million and an income of £158,000. Grants were made to 16 organisations totalling £192,000.

The largest grant of £100,000 was made to Old Vic Theatre Trust (£29,000 in 1999/2000). Other larger beneficiaries were Tate Gallery Foundation (£31,000), Gate Theatre (£15,000), Royal Court Theatre (£12,500) and Young Vic Theatre Company (£10,500).

Other beneficiaries were Royal Opera House Trust (£7,000), Royal National Theatre (£4,500), Guggenheim Foundation and Jazz Xchange Music & Dance Company (£2,500 each), British Friends of the Art Museums of Israel (£2,000), National Gallery Trust (£1,500), Royal Academy of Art and Donmar Warehouse Projects Ltd (£1,000 each), Resources for Autism (£500), Artangel and Kirov Opera and Ballet (£375 each).

Exclusions No grants to individuals.

Applications In writing to the correspondent, but please note, the trust states: 'All of the trust's funds are currently earmarked for existing projects. The trust has a policy of not making donations to individuals and the trustees regret that, in order to keep administrative costs to a minimum, they are unable to reply to any unsuccessful applicants'.

R S Charitable Trust

Jewish, welfare

£159,000 (2000/01)
Beneficial area UK.

138 Stamford Hill, London N16 6QT

Correspondent Max Freudenberger, Trustee

Trustees *M Freudenberger; Mrs M Freudenberger; H C Freudenberger; S N Freudenberger; C Margulies.*

CC Number 1053660

Information available Accounts were on file at the Charity Commission, but without a list of grants.

General Established in 1996, this trust states that it supports Jewish organisations and other bodies working towards the relief of poverty.

In 2000/01 the trust had assets of £3.8 million. Total income was £517,000, including £395,000 in property income and £221,000 in donations received. Management and administration expenses were very high at £187,000. The accounts stated grants totalled £159,000, including £137,000 in material grants. There was no explanation of what these non-material grants consisted of.

No grants list has ever appeared in the accounts of this trust. The 2000/01 set stated: 'The trustees consider that disclosure of the recipients' names may prejudice the furtherance of the purposes of the recipient institutions.' No further information was available.

Applications In writing to the correspondent.

The R V W Trust

Music education and appreciation, relief of need for musicians

£387,000 (2001)
Beneficial area UK.

16 Ogle Street, London W1W 6JA

Tel. 020 7255 2590 **Fax** 020 7255 2591

Correspondent Helen Faulkner, Secretary/Administrator

Trustees *Michael Kennedy, Chair; Lord Armstrong of Ilminster; Sir John Manduell; Mrs Ralph Vaughan Williams; Hugh Cobbe*

CC Number 1066977

Information available Accounts were provided by the trust.

General The trust's current grant-making policies are as follows:

- to give assistance to British composers who have not yet achieved a national reputation
- to give assistance towards the performance and recording of music by neglected or currently unfashionable 20th century British composers, including performances by societies and at festivals which include works by such composers in their programmes
- to assist UK organisations that promote public knowledge and appreciation of 20th and 21st century British music
- to assist education projects in the field of music.

In 2001 the trust had assets of £1.4 million and an income of £332,000, mainly from royalties from the musical works of Ralph Vaughan Williams paid through the Performing Rights Society. Grants were paid to 106 beneficiaries and totalled £387,000. They were broken down in the following categories:

	no. of grants	total
Public performance	63	£127,000
Music festivals	15	£49,000
Public education	13	£161,000
Education grants	15	£50,000

The largest grants were given to British Music Information Centre (£87,500), Society for the Promotion of New Music (£60,000), BBC Philharmonic Orchestra (£22,000), Huddersfield Contemporary Music Festival (£20,000), Royal Philharmonic Society (£18,000) and Sinfonia 21 (£15,000).

Grants ranging from £1,250 to £8,000 were given to beneficiaries including Oxford Bach Choir, Classico Records,

Almeida Theatre, Between the Notes, London Guildhall University, Lichfield Cathedral Special Choir, Brighton Festival, Bournemouth Symphony Orchestra, Dartington International Summer School, Hampstead and Highgate Festival, Hereford Choral Society, York Late Music Festival, Birmingham Ensemble and Contemporary Music Making for Amateurs.

Smaller grants below £1,000 totalled £41,000.

Exclusions No grants for local authority or other government-funded bodies, nor degree courses, except first Masters degrees in musical composition. No support for dance or drama courses. No grants for workshops without public performance, private vocal or instrumental tuition or the purchase or repair of musical instruments.

Applications In writing to the correspondent, giving project details, at least two months before the trustees meet. Trustees' meetings are held in February, June and October. Masters in Music Composition applicants will only be considered at the June meeting; applications must be received by the end of April. Further details are available from the trust.

The Radcliffe Trust

Music, crafts, conservation

£355,000 (1999/2000)
Beneficial area UK.

5 Lincoln's Inn Fields, London WC2A 3BT

Tel. 020 7405 1234

Correspondent John Burden, Secretary to the Trustees

Trustees *Lord Cottesloe, Chair; Lord Quinton; Lord Balfour of Burleigh; Christopher J Butcher; Dr Ivor F Guest.*

CC Number 209212

Information available Full accounts were provided by the trust.

General The 2000 annual report stated: 'The Radcliffe Trust was founded in 1714 by the will of Dr John Radcliffe, the most prominent physician of his day, who left his residuary estate for the income to be applied for general charitable purposes.

'The trustees' present grant-making policy is concentrated in two main areas – music and the crafts – but they may consider applications which do not fall within those two categories provided that they do not come with the exclusions listed below.

'In the area of music they operate a scheme under which the Allegri Quartet make regular visits to a selected number of universities and other centres, master-classes and teaching sessions. As a further development of this scheme the trustees have appointed John Cooney as composer-in-association with the Allegri Quartet. The trustees have also initiated a highly successful series of specialist seminars in double-reed playing and on the technology of pianos. In addition the trustees make grants for classical music education, but they do not accept applications from individuals ....

'In the area of crafts, the main thrust is the support of craft training among young people both at the level of apprenticeships (mostly, but not exclusively, in cathedral workshops) and also at the postgraduate and post-experience levels. This can be by way of direct grants to employers, contributions to bursaries or other awards on offer to students or interns at appropriate training establishments, or support for the setting up of relevant new posts or courses at such institutions. For other grants, the trustees' main concern is to achieve a standard of excellence in crafts related particularly to conservation. The trustees monitor the progress of projects for which grants are made, particularly those which are spread over a period of more than one year, in which cases satisfactory progress reports are required as a condition of later instalments being paid ...

'The trustees make small grants for the repair and conservation of church furniture, including bells and monuments. Such grants are made in England through the Council for the Care of Churches and in Scotland through the Scottish Churches Architectural Heritage Trust; direct applications are not accepted. Grants are not made for structural repairs to church buildings, nor for organs.

'Miscellaneous applications which do not fall within the above categories may be considered subject to availability of surplus income, but the following categories are excluded:

- construction, conversion, repair or maintenance of buildings
- grants directly to individuals for education fees or maintenance

- sponsoring of musical and theatrical performances
- medical research
- social welfare
- support of excellence.

'The trustees are only empowered to make grants to bodies with charitable status, and do not make grants to clear or reduce past deficits.'

In 1999/2000 the trust had assets of £11 million and an income of £327,000. Grants totalled £355,000, broken down as follows:

Crafts – 33 grants totalling £213,000
The largest grants were £26,000 to West Dean College, £11,000 each to Iona Cathedral Trust and Meridian Trust Association and £10,000 each to Green Wood Trust and Stained Glass Museum. Other beneficiaries included Tate Gallery – London (£9,500), National Gallery (£8,000), Council for the Care of Churches (£7,500), Scottish Churches Architectural Heritage Trust (£6,000), Woodchester Mansion Trust (£5,300), Devon Guild of Craftsmen (£4,000), Institute of Paper Conservation (£2,500) and Salisbury Cathedral (£1,200).

Music – 27 grants totalling £117,000
The largest grants were £18,000 each to Allegri String Quartet and Birmingham Conservatoire and £13,000 to University of Cambridge for the Faculty of Music. Other beneficiaries included City of Birmingham Symphony Orchestra and Live Music Now! (£5,000 each), Jessie's Fund (£4,000), Cambridge Opera Group and Mid Wales Opera (£3,000 each), Sounds New (£2,500), Amadeus Scholarships and Isle of Wight International Oboe Competition (£2,000 each), Music for Youth (£1,000) and Skye and Localsh Young Music Makers (£750).

Miscellaneous – 9 grants totalling £25,000
The largest were £10,000 to Dance Research Committee, £5,500 to Spanish Dance Society, £3,800 to Clifton Handbell Ringers and £3,000 to RNIB. Other beneficiaries were Oxford University for a science lab (£1,500), St Bartholomew's Hospital (£600), Dolmetsch Historical Dance Society (£430), St Mary's and St Giles PCC (£25) and Radcliffe School Welfare Fund (£15).

Exclusions No grants to individual applicants. No grants to non-registered charities, or to clear or reduce past debts.

Applications 'Applications for music grants are short-listed for consideration by a panel of musicians who make recommendations, where appropriate;

recommended applications are then placed before the trustees for decision. The music panel usually meets in March and October in advance of the trustees' meetings in June and December, and applications should be submitted by the end of January and the end of August respectively to allow time for any further particulars (if so required) to be furnished.'

'Applications for music grants are short-listed for consideration by a panel of musicians who make recommendations, where appropriate; recommended applications are then placed before the trustees for decision. The music panel usually meets in March and October in advance of the trustees' meetings in June and December, and applications should be submitted by the end of January and the end of August respectively to allow time for any further particulars (if so required) to be furnished.'

Applications for miscellaneous grants should be in writing and received by the end of April for consideration at the June meeting, or by October for consideration at the December meeting.

The Ragdoll Foundation

Children and the arts
£155,000 (November 1999–March 2001)

Beneficial area UK and worldwide.

Russell House, Ely Street, Stratford upon Avon CV37 6LW

Tel. 01789 773059 **Fax** 01789 773059

Email info@ragdollfoundation.org.uk

Website www.ragdollfoundation.org.uk

Correspondent Lydia Thomas, Director

Trustees *Anne Wood; Mark Hollingsworth; Katherine Wood; Ann Burdus.*

CC Number 1078998

Information available Information was provided by the foundation.

General Formed in November 1999 and formally registered as a charity in January 2000, the foundation's primary focus is to make grants for charitable purposes around the world with particular focus on giving to projects, activities or events which promote the education and development of young children through the arts. Preference is given to original projects which are in the spirit of the Ragdoll Foundation, being imaginative, creative and innovative. It seeks to fund those projects which show an understanding of how to listen to children and allow the 'voices' of the children themselves to be heard. The foundation sees this as a most important distinction. It is keen to support strategic initiatives which deal with the causes of problems and projects which may influence thinking and good practice elsewhere.

The focus is on children aged up to eight years old, but appropriate projects for older children will not be dismissed without consideration. The foundation will also consider support for individual children up to the age of 18 where it can add to their developing potential, progress and wellbeing.

In the period between November 1999 and March 2001 the foundation had an income of £614,000, mainly from donations from Ragdoll Limited television production company, gifts and legacies. Grants were made to nine organisations directly by the foundation, with a further three organisations being funded by the foundation through the Ragdoll Charities Committee. Grants totalled £155,000.

The largest project supported was Coram Family London's Listening to Young Children Project, which received £105,000. The project explores ways of listening and responding to children under the age of eight, with particular emphasis on the use of the arts as a medium of communication.

Other beneficiaries were Hope and Homes for Children (£16,000), towards the renovation of the arts centre in Sarajevo Children's Home; Sibford School, Oxfordshire (£10,000), for their Arts Development Project; The Drama Practice, Edinburgh, to support Clowndoctors' visits to children in hospitals and hospices, and Gellideg Infants School, Merthyr Tydfil, to fund a nursery garden creative play area (£5,000 each); Unicef Colour for Kosovo Project (£2,500), towards Unicef in Kosovo children's colouring book project; Tibet Relief Fund of the UK (£1,500), for stage costumes and musical instruments for the Tibetan Homes Foundation School in Mussorie, India; Parenting, Education and Support Forum, Romania (£950), to enable two arts and health delegates to attend international Parent/Child Conference in London; National Youth Theatre (£600), for Summer School 2000.

The Ragdoll Charities Committee awarded a total of £8,200 to Hope and Homes for Children, for Romania

Children's Home, Royal School for the Blind and Children in Crisis.

The foundation also administers The Jean Russell Gift, an annual gift of books to children with special needs.

Exclusions Grants are not given for:

- work that has already started or will have been completed while the application is being considered
- promotion of religion
- animal welfare charities
- vehicles
- emergency relief work
- general fundraising or marketing appeals
- open-ended funding arrangements
- loans or business finance
- retrospective grants
- replacement of statutory funding
- charities which are in serious deficit
- holidays of any sort
- any large capital, endowment or widely distributed appeal.

Applications A leaflet detailing guidelines and the application process is available in standard and large-scale print, and on audio cassette.

Applications should be in writing and should include: the precise purpose for the grant and how it will make a difference; full budget details (including how the budget has been determined); total grant required; information about potential partners from whom other sources of income are being sought, where relevant, including any firm commitments of support; full information about the aims and purposes of your organisation or project including your legal status and registered charity number; latest annual report and audited accounts; and a clear indication of how the project will be monitored and evaluated.

The trustees meet in April and October to review applications: applications should be submitted by 1 March for a decision by 1 July, and by 1 September for a decision by 1 December. The trust aims to issue a letter of acknowledgement within 14 days of receipt of an application.

The trust states: 'Please note that our initial work on a grant application may involve discussion and consultation, further development or modification and, where possible, an on-site visit or meetings. We prefer to progress matters steadily to give time for full and thorough consideration of each proposal.'

The Rainford Trust

Social welfare, general

£105,000 (2000/01)

Beneficial area Worldwide, with a preference for areas in which Pilkington plc have works and offices, especially St Helens and Merseyside.

c/o Pilkington plc, Prescot Road, St Helens, Merseyside WA10 3TT

Tel. 01744 20574 **Fax** 01744 20574

Correspondent W H Simm, Secretary

Trustees Mrs J Graham; A L Hopkins; Mrs A J Moseley; H Pilkington; Lady Pilkington; R E Pilkington; R G Pilkington; Mrs I Ratiu.

CC Number 266157

Information available Full accounts were provided by the trust.

General The trust confirmed that its current policy is as follows:

'To consider applications from organisations that aim to enhance the quality of community life. To help initiate and promote special projects by charitable organisations which seek to provide new kinds of employment. To assist programmes whose objects are the provision of medical care, including holistic medicine, the advancement of education and the arts, and the improvement of the environment. Applications from religious bodies and individuals will be considered if they fall within the scope of these aims.

'Although the trust will continue to give preference to applications from St Helens (as stated in the trust deed), and from other main Pilkington UK areas, this does not prejudice the trustees' discretion to help charities that operate outside these areas.'

In 2000/01 the trust had assets of £5.5 million and an income of £223,000. Grants were given to 120 of the 856 applicants and totalled £105,000. An additional £10,000 was given as continued funding to the Citadel Arts Centre. Most grants were for £1,000 or less. Grants were broken down geographically as follows:

St Helens	£40,000
Merseyside	£12,000
Rest of UK (regionally and nationally)	£49,000
Overseas	£14,000

These were further broken down as follows:

	St Helens	Rest of UK	National	Overseas
Medical	nil	£2,250	£14,000	nil
Welfare				
General	£2,500	£7,300	£13,000	£5,500
Old	£4,250	£2,750	nil	nil
Young	£5,000	£8,250	£4,500	£8,000
Education	£16,000	£1,250	£1,600	£750
Humanities	£12,000	£500	nil	nil
Religion	£500	£250	£1,000	nil
Environmental	nil	nil	£4,250	nil

The largest grants went to Clonter Opera for All, which received £13,000 in total (£8,000 plus £5,000 for a project which provides opera workshops and performances to schools), and Citadel Arts Centre, which received £10,000 for revenue spending. Other grants over £1,000 were given to Bristol Cancer Help Centre (£3,000), towards funding of therapy programmes, patients' bursaries, telephone counselling and other services, Ratiu Foundation Romanian Leukaemia Aid and Voluntary Service Overseas (£2,500 each), Age Concern St Helens, BASIC and Marine Conservation Society (£2,000 each) and Merseyside Police and High Sheriff's Charitable Trust (£1,500).

Beneficiaries receiving £1,000 each included Cathedral Camps, North West Rhinos Wheelchair Rugby Club, Eccleston Mere Primary School, Relate Cheshire and Merseyside – St Helens Branch, Merseyside Guide Association – Woodbank Activity Centre in Prescot, ChildLine North West and St Helens Choral Society.

Other smaller beneficiaries included Apostleship of the Sea, Eyeless Trust, Fairtrade Foundation, Knowsley Pensioners Advocacy and Information Service, Listening Books, Liverpool Cancer Information Centre, Neuro Muscular Centre, Northern Friends of ARMS and Thrift Charitable Trust.

Exclusions Funding for the arts is restricted to St Helens only. Applications from individuals for grants for educational purposes will be considered only from applicants who are normally resident in St Helens.

Applications On a form available from the correspondent. Applications should be accompanied by latest accounts and cost data on projects for which funding is sought. Applicants may apply at any time. Only successful applications will be acknowledged.

The Peggy Ramsay Foundation

Writers and writing for the stage

£116,000 to organisations (2001)
Beneficial area British Isles.

Harbottle & Lewis Solicitors, Hanover House, 14 Hanover Square, London W1S 1HP

Tel. 020 7667 5000 **Fax** 020 7667 5100

Email laurence.harbottle@harbottle.com

Website
www.peggyramsayfoundation.org

Correspondent G Laurence Harbottle, Trustee

Trustees *Laurence Harbottle; Simon Callow; John Welch; Michael Codron; Sir David Hare; John Tydeman; Baroness McIntosh of Hudnall; Harriet Walker.*

CC Number 1015427

Information available Full accounts were provided by the trust.

General This trust exists to help writers and writing for the stage. It was established from Peggy Ramsay's personal estate in accordance with her will. The objectives of the foundation are:

- the advancement of education by the encouragement of the art of writing
- the relief of poverty among those practising the arts, together with their dependants and relatives, with special reference to writers
- any charitable purpose which may, in the opinion of the trustees, achieve, assist in, or contribute to, the achievement of these objectives.

In 2001 the trust had assets totalling £5 million and an income of £357,000. Grants were made to 54 beneficiaries, divided equally between organisations (27) and individuals (27), totalling £202,000. Grants to organisations amounted to £116,000, while individuals received £86,000. Management and administration costs totalled £57,000.

Grants made to organisations were mainly for initiatives to help individual writers to create new work. The foundation continues to support certain prizes such as the Alfred Fagon Award, the George Devine Award and the Society of Authors. There is a preference for concentrating more on encouraging new writing than rewarding success. All grants to individuals are made in cases of need to established writers of stage plays.

During the year the foundation created a new award to replace the Peggy Ramsay Play Award. While the Play Award supported new work, this was not an essential factor in its production, and so the new award requires managers to submit a project that they consider would encourage creative writing for the theatre. This was won by Paines Plough, which became entitled to £50,000 and received the first instalment of £10,000 in 2001. (In 2002 this award was given to Bush Theatre and amounted to £30,000.)

Apart from the Project Award, the largest grant was £20,000 to Theatre Centre Limited. Other beneficiaries included Contact Theatre (£6,500), Eastern Angles Theatre Company Limited (£6,000), Warehouse Theatre Company Limited (£6,000 in total), UK Arts Explore/Festcep, TAPS and The George Devine Memorial Fund (£5,000 each), The Ashton Group Contemporary Theatre Limited and Magnetic North Theatre Productions Limited (£4,000 each), Wilson Wilson Company and Production Line (£3,000), Artists in Exile – Gog Theatre, New Perspectives Theatre Company, PMA Award, Stellar Quines, Theatre & Beyond and Union Theatre (£2,000 each).

Exclusions No grants are made for productions or writing not for the theatre. Commissioning costs are often considered as part of production costs. Course fees are not considered. Aspiring writers without some production record are not usually considered.

Applications Applications should be made by writing a short letter, when there is a promising purpose not otherwise likely to be funded and which will help writers or writing for the stage. Grants are considered at four or five meetings during the year, although urgent appeals can be considered at other times. All appeals are usually acknowledged.

The Joseph & Lena Randall Charitable Trust

General

£129,000 (2001/02)

Beneficial area Worldwide.

Europa Residence, Place des Moulins, Monte-Carlo, 98000 Monaco

Tel. 00 377 93 50 03 82

Fax 00 377 93 25 82 85

Correspondent D A Randall, Trustee

Trustees *D A Randall; B Y Randall.*

CC Number 255035

Information available Information was provided by the trust.

General It is the policy of this trust to provide regular support to a selection of charities.

In 2001/02 the trust's assets totalled £1.7 million, it had an income of £105,000 and 38 grants were made totalling £129,000. Beneficiaries included Aldenham School 400 Development Appeal, Diabetes UK, Glyndebourne Festival Opera, Imperial Cancer Research Campaign, London School of Economics and Political Science, and Royal Opera House Development Fund.

Exclusions No grants to individuals.

Applications In writing to the correspondent. The trust stated in in 2001/02 report that funds were fully committed, and that it was 'unable to respond to the many worthy appeals'.

Ranworth Trust

General

£118,000 (1999/2000)

Beneficial area UK and developing countries, with a preference for Norfolk.

The Old House, Ranworth, Norwich NR13 6HS

Tel. 01603 270300

Correspondent Hon. Mrs J Cator, Trustee

Trustees *Hon. Mrs J Cator; F Cator; Mrs E A Thistlewayte; C F Cator.*

CC Number 292633

Information available Full accounts were on file at the Charity Commission.

General The trust underwent tremendous growth in 1999/2000, due to the receipt of a donation of £2.9 million from one of the trustees in the form of 155,000 shares in Portsmouth & Sunderland Newspapers plc. In 1999/2000, however, the trust made a substantial one-off donation of over £1.2 million to Jubilee Sailing Trust from the sales proceeds of these shares. Other income in 1999/2000 totalled £121,000, derived from investments. Other grants were made to 35 charities and totalled £118,000 and administration costs were only £2,400. Assets at the year end totalled £4.5 million (£1.8 million the year before).

The trustees' report for 1999/2000 stated: 'The scope of charitable causes benefiting from the trust was varied and covered such areas as medical research, local community, health and welfare and social charities in the Norfolk area, and national and international charities'.

Of the 35 organisations receiving smaller grants, 15 had also been supported in the previous year. Grants included £10,000 to Ranworth PCC, £5,000 each to Children's Hospice for the Eastern Region and Norfolk Wildlife Trust, £2,000 each to East Anglian Arts Foundation, Norfolk & Norwich Families House and Norfolk Youth Projects and £1,000 to South Walsham Millennium Group.

The remaining grants were mostly of either £1,000 or £2,000.

Applications In writing to the correspondent.

The Ratcliff Foundation

General

£181,000 (2001/02)

Beneficial area UK, with a preference for local charities in the Midlands, north Wales and Gloucestershire.

Felton & Co, 36 Great Charles Street, Birmingham B3 3RQ

Tel. 0121 236 8181 **Fax** 0121 200 1614

Email chris.gupwell@feltonandco.co.uk

Correspondent C J Gupwell, Secretary

Trustees *Miss C M Ratcliff; E H Ratcliff; D M Ratcliff; J M G Fea; Mrs G M Thorpe; C J Gupwell.*

CC Number 222441

Information available Full accounts were on file at the Charity Commission.

General The trust was established in 1961, by Martin Rawlinson Ratcliffe. In 2001/02 it had assets of £3 million, with an income of £212,000 from investments and an additional £69,000 from the F R Ratcliff Charitable Settlement. Management and administration costs were high at £33,000, over 10% of the income.

A total of £181,000 was given in 73 grants in the range of £1,000 to £23,000. Major grants included £23,000 to Holy Trinity Belfry Appeal – Conway, £11,000 to CRAB Appeal for Cancer Research – Birmingham and £10,000 to Birmingham Parish Church Renewal Campaign.

Other larger grants included £6,300 to Acorn Children's Hospice Trust,

£5,000 each to Cancer Research Campaign – Kemerton and St Nicholas Church – Kemerton, £4,000 to YMCA Birmingham, £3,500 to British Blind Sport, £3,300 to Birmingham Federation of Clubs for Young People and £3,000 each to Extra Care, Hearing Dogs for Deaf People, Myton Hamlet Hospice, Soil Association, Tewkesbury Welfare & Volunteer Centre and Warwickshire Wildlife Trust.

The accounts show the grants grouped under the name of each individual trustee. This may be due to the trustees preferring particular causes and living in different areas. Grants have shown an interest in health/disability, social welfare, children/youth, wildlife/conservation/ environment and education causes. The trustees have a preference for Worcester/ Gloucester, Birmingham/Midlands, Warwickshire and Wales.

Organisations to benefit include Avoncroft Museum of Historic Buildings, British Blind Sport, CBSO Society Ltd, Devon Wildlife Trust, Dogs for the Disabled, Elgar School of Music, Motability, Pershore Theatre Arts Association, Roundabout, St David's Hospice, Tewkesbury Hospital League of Friends, Well Trust and YMCA Birmingham.

Exclusions No grants to individuals.

Applications In writing to the correspondent, by 30 November for consideration by trustees in following January. Grants made once a year only, by 31 March.

The Eleanor Rathbone Charitable Trust

Merseyside, women, unpopular causes

£233,000 (1999/2000)

Beneficial area UK, with the major allocation for Merseyside; also women-focused international projects.

3 Sidney Avenue, Wallasey, Merseyside CH45 9JL

Email eleanor.rathbone.trust@tinyworld.co.uk

Website www.eleanorrathbonetrust.org

Correspondent Lindsay Keenan

Trustees *W Rathbone; Ms Jenny Rathbone; P W Rathbone; Lady Morgan.*

CC Number 233241

Information available Full information was provided by the trust.

General The trust concentrates its support largely on the following:

- charities and charitable projects focused on Merseyside (63% of beneficiaries in 2000/01)
- charities benefiting women and unpopular and neglected causes but avoiding those with a sectarian interest
- special consideration is given to charities with which any of the trustees have a particular knowledge or association or in which it is thought Eleanor Rathbone or her father William Rathbone VI would have had a special interest.

Most grants are made on a one-off basis, although requests for commitments over two or more years are considered.

In 2000/01 the trust had assets of £6.3 million, producing an income of only £262,000. Grants to 129 organisations totalled £228,000. The accounts listed the 60 largest grants made over £2,000; they were broken down as follows with specific beneficiaries shown beneath each category:

Merseyside charities – 81 grants

The Merseyside Appeal – Liverpool Cardiothoracic Centre (£10,000); Liverpool CSS (£8,100 paid in four quarterly payments); NMGM Development Trust (£5,000); YMCA of Great Britain – Kirkby (£3,000); Merseyside Holiday Service and Merseyside Police and High Sheriff's Trust (£2,500 each); and Fairbridge in Merseyside, Liverpool Hope University College, Liverpool Somali Women's Group, Liverpool University – Vice Chancellor's Discretionary Fund, Toxteth CAB, Tranmere Alliance and Wirral Disabled Motorists Club (£2,000 each).

International charities – 21 grants

Canon Collins Educational Trust for South Africa (£5,000); Relief Fund for Romania (£2,200); and Afghanaid, Africa Now, Farm Africa, International Care and Relief and Tree Aid (£2,000 each).

Other UK/regional charities – 27 grants

I Can (£4,000); Halton Crossroads Caring for Carers and Refuge (£2,500 each); and Barnardos, Charterhouse in Southwark, Christians Against Poverty, Hope and Homes for Children, Motor Neurone Disease Association, North West Disability Arts Forum, Peace Brigades International and Research into Ageing (£2,000 each).

Exclusions Grants are not made in support of:

- any activity which relieves a statutory authority of its obligations
- individuals, unless (and only exceptionally), it is made through a charity and it also fulfils at least one of the other positive objects mentioned above.

The trust does not generally favour grants for running costs, but prefers to support specific projects, services or to contribute to specific developments.

Applications No application form. The trust asks for a brief proposal for funding including costings, accompanied by the latest available accounts and any relevant supporting material. It is useful to know who else is supporting the project.

To keep administration costs to a minimum, receipt of applications is not usually acknowledged. Applicants requiring acknowledgement should enclose an sae.

Trustees currently meet three times a year, dates vary.

The Roger Raymond Charitable Trust

Older people, education, medical

£205,000 (2001/02)

Beneficial area UK (and very occasionally large, well-known overseas organisations).

Suttondene, 17 South Border, Purley, Surrey CR8 3LL

Tel. 020 8660 9133

Email russell@pullen.cix.co.uk

Correspondent R W Pullen, Trustee

Trustees *R W Pullen; P F Raymond; M G Raymond.*

CC Number 262217

Information available Information was provided by the trust.

General In 2001/02 the trust had assets of £7 million and an income of £231,000. After management and administration costs of £25,000, grants were made to about 50 organisations totalling £205,000.

The principal beneficiary during the year, as in previous years, was Bloxham School, which received a donation of £126,000. Other grants ranged up to £5,000, although most were for £1,000 or less. Many beneficiaries are regularly supported.

Beneficiaries during the year included King Edward VII Hospital and Macmillan Cancer Relief (£5,000 each), National Trust and Royal Commonwealth Society for the Blind (£3,000 each), Putney Animal Hospital and Salvation Army (£2,000 each), Huntington's Disease Society, Defeating Deafness and Children with Leukaemia (£1,000 each).

Previous beneficiaries include Leonard Cheshire Foundation, Barnardos, British Heart Foundation, British Wheelchair Sports Foundation, ChildLine, Handy 1 Robotic Appeal, Isle of Purbeck Club, MIND, National Asthma Campaign, NSPCC, RNLI, Save the Children Fund, WaterAid, Woodlands Trust, WWF, Girl Guides Association, Scout Association and College of Law.

Exclusions Grants are rarely given to individuals.

Applications The trust stated that applications are considered throughout the year, although funds are not always available.

The Rayne Trust

Jewish, general

£167,000 (2000/01)
Beneficial area UK.

33 Robert Adam Street, London
W1U 3HR
Tel. 020 7935 3555
Correspondent Robert Dufton, Director
Trustees *Lord Rayne, Chair; Lady Rayne; Hon. R A Rayne.*
CC Number 207392
Information available Full accounts were provided by the trust.

General This trust supports the welfare of young and older people. Nearly all of the grants are made to Jewish organisations. There are connections between this trust and the much larger Rayne Foundation.

In 2000/01 the trust had assets of £2.2 million. Income was £234,000, including £125,000 in donations received, the same level of donations as in the previous year. Management and administration costs were very low at just £3,300. Grants totalled £167,000. Of the 29 organisations receiving £1,000 or more, 13 were also supported in the previous year.

The largest grants were £25,000 to Home for Aged Jews, £20,000 to Yehudi Menuhin School, £15,000 to Centre for Jewish–Christian Relations and £10,000 each to Community Security Trust, Jewish Care and Royal Academy of Dramatic Art.

Other beneficiaries included Royal Opera House and West London Synagogue (£6,000 each), Jewish Association for the Mentally Ill (£5,600), Finchley Reform Synagogue (£5,200), Arnott Cato Foundation and Edinburgh House (£5,000 each), Otto Schiff Housing Association (£2,500), Leo Baeck Institute and British Red Cross (£2,000 each), Jewish Museum London (£1,500), British Friends of the Art Museums of Israel (£1,300), with £1,000 each to British Friends of the Israel Philharmonic Orchestra Foundation, The Holocaust Centre, Institute for Jewish Policy Research, Emile Littler Foundation, The Reform Foundation Trust and Wizo Charitable Foundation.

Exclusions No grants to individuals or non-registered charities.

Applications In writing to the correspondent at any time, enclosing annual report and accounts.

The Albert Reckitt Charitable Trust

General

£67,000 (2001/02)
Beneficial area UK.

Southwark Towers, 32 London Bridge Street, London SE1 9SY
Correspondent J Barrett, Secretary
Trustees *Mrs S C Bradley, Chair; Sir Michael Colman; Mrs G M Atherton; D F Reckitt; J Hughes-Reckitt; P C Knee; Dr A Joy.*
CC Number 209974
Information available Accounts were on file at the Charity Commission, but without a list of grants.

General The trust's 2001/02 accounts stated its objects are 'to make grants to a wide variety of registered charities, including non-political charities connected with the Society of Friends'.

In 2001/02 it had assets of £2 million, which generated an income of £67,000. Grants totalled £67,000, given as £45,000 in subscriptions (annual grants), the rest in donations (one-off grants).

No further information for the year was available. However, in previous years the trust has tended to supported UK organisations rather than local groups, giving grants of £250 to £750 each.

Exclusions No grants for political or sectarian charities, except for Quaker organisations. No support to individuals.

Applications In writing to the correspondent. Trustees meet in June/July and applications need to be received by March.

This entry was not confirmed by the trust, but the address was correct according to the Charity Commission database.

The C A Redfern Charitable Foundation

General

£199,000 (1998/99)
Beneficial area UK.

PricewaterhouseCoopers, 9 Greyfriars Road, Reading, Berkshire RG1 1JG
Tel. 0118 959 7111
Correspondent The Trustees
Trustees *C A G Redfern; T P Thornton; S R Ward; Sir R A Clark; D S Redfern.*
CC Number 299918
Information available Full accounts were on file at the Charity Commission.

General This trust supports a wide range of organisations with some preference for those concerned with health and welfare.

In 1998/99 the assets of this trust stood at £4.7 million. The total income for the year was £231,000 and 61 grants were made totalling £199,000 (£250,000 in 1997/98). Over two-thirds of the organisations supported had received a grant in the previous year.

The largest grant was for £30,000 and went to South Buckinghamshire Riding for the Disabled. Other large grants went to Saints and Sinners Club (£25,000) and Motor and Allied Trades Benevolent Fund (£10,000).

Awards included: 14 grants of £5,000, 9 of £3,000 and 14 of £1,000. Grants included £5,000 each to Cancer Support Centre Wandsworth, Canine Partners for Independence, Seven Springs Play and Support Centre and Farms for City Children; £3,000 each to Campus Children's Holidays, CRUSE, RNIB and The De Paul Trust; and £1,000 each to British Red Cross, Help the Aged, Northwick Park Institute for Medical Research and NSPCC – Berkshire.

The remainder of grants were mainly for £250 or £500. Recipients included Fight for Sight, London Lighthouse, New Heart Start Appeal, RNLI, Save the Children Fund, Shelter and YMCA.

Exclusions No grants for building works or individuals.

Applications The trust does not accept unsolicited applications.

The Christopher H R Reeves Charitable Trust

Food allergies, disability

£158,000 (2001)

Beneficial area UK.

Hinwick Lodge, Nr Wellingborough, Northamptonshire NN29 7JQ

Tel. 01234 781090 **Fax** 01234 781090

Correspondent E M Reeves, Trustee

Trustees *E M Reeves; V Reeves; M Kennedy.*

CC Number 266877

Information available Full accounts were on file at the Charity Commission.

General The trust states that it is 'holding about 75% of its income and capital for application in the limited area of food allergy and related matters. Nearly all the income in this section has already been committed to Allergy Research and Environmental Health at King's College, London and to the production and distribution of a database of research references under the title of Allergy and Environmental Medicine Database'.

'New appeals related to food allergy and intolerance are invited and a response will be made to applicants.'

'The remaining 25% of the trust's income and capital will be held for general donations. The main area of interest is in disability. Donations will largely be made to charities already associated with the trust. Only successful applicants will receive a response.'

In 2001 the trust had assets of £4 million and an income of £156,000. Grants were made to 25 beneficiaries totalling £158,000. 'Professional fees' paid by the trust totalled £40,000.

Two large grants were made during the year to University College London (£65,000) and King's College (£50,000). Other larger grants went to Uppingham School (£10,000), Western Australia Cancer Foundation, SeeAbility and RASE (£5,000 each).

A grant of £2,000 was made to Solicitors Benevolent Fund. A further 14 grants of £1,000 each were made to Centre Point, Clergy Orphan Corporation, Countryside Foundation for Education, East of England Agricultural Society, London Youth Clubs, Malcolm Sargent Children Cancer Fund, NSPCC, Papworth Trust, Project Trust, Red Poll Cattle Society,

Salvation Army, Schizophrenia Society of Great Britain, SSAFA and Uppingham Church Refurbishment.

Four small grants were also made to Befordshire Housing Association, Farming and Wildlife Advisory Group, Northamptonshire Society for Autism (£500 each) and Podington School (£300).

Exclusions No grants for individuals, overseas travel and expeditions, animal charities, church/community hall/school appeals outside the north Bedfordshire area, overseas aid, children's charities, drugs/alcohol charities, mental health charities, or education.

Applications In writing to the correspondent. Trustees meet five times a year in March, May, July, September and November.

The Max Reinhardt Charitable Trust

Medical schools and research

£62,000 (2000/01)

Beneficial area UK.

Flat 2, 43 Onslow Square, London SW7 3LR

Correspondent The Secretary

Trustees *Joan Reinhardt; Alexandra Reinhardt; Veronica Reinhardt; Belinda McGill.*

CC Number 264741

Information available Accounts were on file at the Charity Commission.

General The trust supports organisations benefiting musicians and people who are deaf.

In 2000/01 the trust's assets totalled £529,000 and its income was £75,000. It made 21 donations totalling £62,000.

The largest donation by far was £58,000 to St George's Medical School, also a major beneficiary in the previous year. Other grants were £1,000 to DBA Support Group, £750 to Delta, £500 each to Mencap and National Trust and £250 to Motability. Over half of grants were for £100 each, including those to Brain Research Trust, Onslow Neighbourhood Association, Paintings in Hospital, Sound

Seekers, Thames Salmon Trust and Volunteer Reading Help.

Applications In writing to the correspondent.

REMEDI

Research into disability

£227,000 (2001/02)

Beneficial area UK.

The Old Rectory, Stanton Prior, Bath BA2 9HT

Tel. 01761 472662 **Fax** 01761 470662

Email director.remedi@btinternet.com

Website www.remedi.org.uk

Correspondent Lt Col Patrick Mesquita, Director

Trustees *Brian Winterflood, President; Dr A K Clarke, Chair; Alan Line; Dr A H M Heagerty; Dr A St J Dixon; Dr I T Stuttaford; David Hume; Rosie Wait; Michael Hines.*

CC Number 1063359

Information available Full information was provided by the trust.

General REMEDI supports pioneering research into all aspects of disability in the widest sense of the word, with special emphasis on the way in which disability limits the activities and lifestyle of all ages.

The trust receives most of its income from companies and other trusts, which is then given towards research projects carrying out innovative and original work which struggle to achieve funding themselves. Grants are generally for one year, although funding for the second year is considered sympathetically and for a third year exceptionally. There is a preference for awarding a few sizeable grants rather than many smaller grants. The priority funding area for 2003 is research into stroke.

In 2001/02 the trust had assets of £338,000. Total income was £310,000, including donations from 28 charitable trusts and 41 companies. Grants were made to 11 research projects totalling £227,000.

The largest grants were £54,000 to the research project 'Can functional magnetic resonance imaging (MRI) studies help to develop effective therapy interventions for stroke patients?' at King's College, London; £49,000 for research into the underlying cause of autism at the Newcomen Centre at Guy's Hospital; and

£40,000 towards research into prostate cancer at St Mary's Hospital, London.

Other large grants included £38,000 towards early intensive home-based intervention for the treatment of autism and the analysis of tutor performance at the University of Southampton; £32,000 towards further development of intensive single-case methods for investigation of recovery after stroke at the University of Nottingham; £26,000 towards the clinical trial of ossointegrated prostheses for Transfemoral amputees at Queen Mary's Hospital, Roehampton; and £25,000 towards reseach in the control of prosthetic wrist rotation from residual rotation of the amputated forearm at the University of Salford.

Smaller grants included those towards research into caregiver strain in spouses of stroke patients at University of Nottingham (£10,000); an anal sphincter rupture repair study at North Staffordshire Hospital and Keele University (£9,000); and courses for carers at The Research Institute for the Care of the Elderly, Bath (£3,800).

Exclusions Cancer and cancer-related diseases are not normally supported.

Applications By e-mail to the correspondent. Applications are received throughout the year. They should initially include a summary of the project on one side of A4 with costings. The chair normally examines applications on the third Tuesday of each month with a view to inviting applicants to complete an application form by e-mail.

The Rhodes Trust Public Purposes Fund

Oxford University, overseas, general

£2.7 million (1998/99)

Beneficial area UK and overseas.

Rhodes House, Oxford OX1 3RG

Tel. 01865 270902**Fax** 01865 270914

Email admin@rhodeshouse.ox.ac.uk

Website www.rhodeshouse.ox.ac.uk

Correspondent Dr John Rowett

Trustees *Rt Hon. William Waldegrave of North Hill; Sir John Kerr; Sir Colin Lucas; Rt Hon Lord Fellowes; Lord Butler of Brockwell; J Ogilvie Thompson; Prof. J I Bell; Dame Ruth Deech; Miss R Hedley-Miller.*

CC Number 232492

Information available Full accounts were provided by the trust.

General The primary purpose for which the trust was established, and for which it continues to be used and managed, is to provide scholarships to be allocated each year to enable students from selected countries of the Commonwealth, the USA and the Federal Republic of Germany to spend two or three years on an undergraduate or postgraduate course of study at Oxford University.

The Public Purposes Fund, from which the trustees can appropriate property to the scholarship fund, can make grants for educational and other charitable purposes, in any part of the Commonwealth or the USA. The policy has been to restrict its use to educational purposes in Oxford University and Commonwealth countries in Africa and the Caribbean.

In 2000/01 the trust had an income of £2.1 million and a total expenditure of £5.2 million. This information was taken from the Charity Commission database, no further details were available for this year. In 1998/99 the income was £6 million. The cost of maintaining the scholarship programme was £3.9 million and charitable donations from the Public Purposes Fund amounted to £2.7 million. In addition, £75,000 was granted from the Scholarship Capital Reserve Fund and £44,000 from the South Africa Fund. At the year-end, the assets stood at about £197 million.

The grants from the Public Purposes Fund were broken down as follows:

	1998	1997
Oxford University	£1.3 million	£920,000
African and Commonwealth	£1.3 million	£588,000
Other	£41,000	£20,000

Oxford University grants

Nine grants were made to £862,000 to Rothermere America Institute, £250,000 to Oxford University Scholarships for overseas students, £90,000 to Oxford University Sports Committee and £50,000 to Erasmus Exchange Scheme.

African and Commonwealth

A total of 22 grants were given, with 3 for £100,000 or more, these were University of Witwatersan Foundation (£517,000), Rhodes University – Eden Grove Centre (£274,000) and University of Cape Town (£100,000). Other grants ranged from £5,000 to £61,000 and included Liverpool University's Diabetes Education (£61,000), Valley Trust (£51,000), World University Service UK – Campus Scheme (£7,000) and African Book Collection Trust (£5,000).

Other

Four grants were made: £25,000 to British School in Rome, £10,000 to British Academy, £5,000 to Churches Commission on Overseas Student Hardship and £1,000 to the Round Table.

Exclusions Grants to institutions only. No grants to individuals.

Applications To the correspondent in writing. Trustees meet in June and November.

Daisy Rich Trust

General

£95,000 (2000/01)

Beneficial area UK, with a priority for the Isle of Wight.

The Cranbourn Suite, 61 Upper James Street, Newport, Isle of Wight PO30 1LQ

Tel. 01983 521236

Correspondent Mrs J Williams, Secretary

CC Number 236706

Information available Basic details were provided by the trust, without a list of beneficiaries.

General In 2001/02 the trust had assets totalling £2.3 million and an income of £84,000. It made grants totalling £82,000. A list of beneficiaries was not available. There is a priority for supporting organisations and individuals on the Isle of Wight, with any available surplus given in the UK or elsewhere.

No further information was available for this trust

Applications In writing to the correspondent.

Cliff Richard Charitable Trust

Spiritual and social welfare

£192,000 (2000/01)

Beneficial area UK.

Harley House, 94 Hare Lane, Claygate, Esher, Surrey KT10 0RB

Tel. 01372 467752 **Fax** 01372 462352

Correspondent Bill Latham, Trustee

Trustees *William Latham; Malcolm Smith.*

CC Number 259056

Information available Accounts were on file at the Charity Commission, but without a detailed breakdown of all donations, or a full narrative report.

General This trust has general charitable purposes, with a preference for causes seeking to improve spiritual and social welfare.

In 2000/01 the trust had assets of £1 million and a total income of £464,000, of which £408,000 came fron donations received. Administration expenses were very low at £810. Grants totalled £192,000, of which £81,000 was given in sundry donations not listed in the accounts.

Grants of £50,000 each to British Lung Foundation and Cliff Richard Tennis Development Trust. The other two donations listed were £6,500 to Genesis Art Trust and £5,000 to Arts Centre Group.

Exclusions Capital building projects, church repairs and renovations are all excluded. No support for individuals.

Applications Applications should be from registered charities only, in writing, and for one-off needs. All applications are acknowledged. Grants are made quarterly in January, April, July and October.

The Clive Richards Charity Ltd

Disability, poverty

£218,000 (2000/01)

Beneficial area Preference for Herefordshire.

40 Great James Street, London WC1N 3HB

Tel. 020 7831 3310

Correspondent John Manby

Trustees *W S C Richards; Mrs S A Richards.*

CC Number 327155

Information available Full accounts were on file at the Charity Commission.

General The area of this trust's interest is people with disabilities and those disadvantaged by poverty. Priority has been given to education, arts and sport.

In 2000/01 the trust had assets of £470,000, an income of £34,000 and it gave grants totalling £218,000.

The accounts listed 26 grants made over £1,000 each. The largest was for £94,000 to Catholic Church. Other beneficiaries of larger grants included SAS Jubilee Fund (£27,000), Premanda Orphange Centre (21,000), Bishop Vessey's Grammar School (£15,000) and Royal Opera House Trust (£5,800).

Remaining listed grants were for £5,000 or less. Beneficiaries included Barnardos, Cancer Research Campaign, Christ College – Brecon, Grassington Opera, Hereford Cathedral School, Royal National College for the Blind, Save the Children, St Michael's Hospice and Shaw Trust.

Exclusions No grants for political causes.

Applications In writing to the correspondent. However, the trust states that 'due to the generally low interest rates that have been available over the last few months, the charity's resources are fully committed and thus it is extremely selective in accepting any requests for funding'.

The Violet M Richards Charity

Older people, sickness, medical research and education

£88,000 (2000/01)

Beneficial area UK, with a preference for East and West Sussex and Kent.

c/o Wedlake Bell (ref CAH), 16 Bedford Street, London WC2E 9HF

Tel. 020 7395 3000 **Fax** 020 7395 3118

Correspondent Charles Hicks

Trustees *Mrs E H Hill; G R Andersen; C A Hicks; Miss M Davies.*

CC Number 273928

Information available Full accounts were provided by the trust.

General The trust's objects are relief of age and sickness, through advancement of medical research (particularly into geriatric problems), medical education, homes and other facilities for people who are elderly or sick. The trustees are happy to commit themselves to funding a research project over a number of years, including 'seedcorn' projects. Applications from Kent and East or West Sussex are especially favoured by the trustees.

In 2000/01 (a 16-month accounting period), the charity had assets of £2.2 million, which generated an income of £83,000. Management and administration expenses were high at £12,000, including £7,300 to a firm of solicitors in which one of the trustees is a partner. Whilst wholly legal, these editors always regret such payments unless, in the words of the Charity Commission, 'there is no realistic alternative'. Grants were made to 13 organisations totalling £88,000.

The largest grants were £25,000 to University of Cambridge for the Huntington's Disease Promoter Project and £10,000 to Imperial College of Science, Technology and Medicine.

Aside from the £3,000 to British Heart Foundation, all other donations were of £5,000 each. Recipients were Alzheimer's Society, Children with Leukaemia, Demelza House Children's Hospice, Housing Research Trust, Little Foundation, Multiple Sclerosis Society, Anthony Nolan Bone Marrow Trust, Queen's Nursing Institute, Royal College of Radiologists and Royal Surgical Aid Society.

Exclusions No support for individuals.

Applications In writing to the correspondent. There is no set format for applying. The trustees generally meet to consider grants approximately twice a year. Only successful applications are acknowledged.

The Muriel Edith Rickman Trust

Medical research, education

£127,000 (2000/01)
Beneficial area UK.

12 Fitzroy Court, 57–59 Shepherds Hill, London N6 5RD
Correspondent H P Rickman, Trustee
Trustees *H P Rickman, Chair; M D Gottlieb; Raymond Tallis.*
CC Number 326143
Information available Full accounts were on file at the Charity Commission.

General The trust makes grants to medical research organisations towards equipment. The trust prefers to support physical disabilities rather than mental illnesses.

In 2000/01 the trust had assets of £41,000 and an income of £45,000, mostly from donations. Grants to 13 organisations totalled £127,000.

The largest were £24,000 to King's College London, £18,000 to Elimination of Leukaemia Fund, £15,000 each to Cardiothoracic Centre NHS Trust and Spencer Dayman Meningitis Laboratories, £14,000 to Muscular Dystrophy Campaign and £13,000 to Colon Cancer Concern.

Other grants went to Christie Hospital NHS Trust (£7,900), Myasthenia Gravis Association (£7,000), Salford Royal Hospitals NHS Trust (£5,700), Motor Neurone Disease Association (£3,500), Girls' Aid School Trust (£2,100), Juvenile Diabetes Foundation (£2,000) and Guide Dogs for the Blind (£250).

Exclusions The trustees will not respond to individual students, clubs, community projects or expeditions.

Applications There are no guidelines for applications and the trust only replies if it is interested at first glance; it will then ask for further details. Trustees meet as required.

The Ripple Effect Foundation

General

£61,000 (2000/01)
Beneficial area UK.

Marlborough Investment Consultants Ltd, Wessex House, Oxford Road, Newbury, Berkshire RG14 1PA
Tel. 01635 814470
Correspondent Miss Caroline D Marks, Trustee
Trustees *Miss Caroline D Marks; I R Marks; I S Wesley.*
CC Number 802327
Information available Full accounts were on file at the Charity Commission.

General The 2000/01 accounts stated: 'The objectives of the trustees are to support a range of charitable causes over a few years that meet their funding criteria. They proactively seek out projects that meet their criteria and do not respond to unsolicited applications. The Ripple Effect continued its policy of making donations towards effective charities working in the broad fields of environmental work, third world development and empowering young people in the UK. However, it is now beginning to focus on local community projects based in the south west of England.'

In 2000/01 the trust had assets of £1.5 million, which generated a low income of £30,000. Three payments were made (£50,000 to Network Foundation, £12,000 to Devon Community and £250 to Breakthrough), mostly to be passed on to smaller organisations.

Network Foundation received £50,000, which was passed on to other charities. Funding for environmental projects centred around growing issues in the UK, particularly genetically modified food. Soil Association received £1,000 through Network Foundation, while Global Commons Institute was also supported. Third world work supported included Oxford Research Group's work towards developing peaceful resolutions between warring factions.

Numerous young people's organisations were also supported from the funds given to Network Foundation. The foundation also worked with Devon Community Foundation to identify youth homeless projects and problems in rural areas.

£5,000 went to a small community project improving social, sport and leisure facilities for young people, while £6,600 went towards the community foundation's core costs. An emerging Exeter group was also identified as a potential beneficiary once the organisation is fully established.

Applications The trust states that it does not respond to unsolicited applications.

The Rivendell Trust

Sickness, disability, family problems, education, music

£66,000 to individuals and organisations (2000/01)
Beneficial area UK only.

PO Box 19375, London W4 2GH
Email jayne@rivendelltrust.freeserve.co.uk
Correspondent Jayne Buchanan
Trustees *Mrs S D Caird; Miss M J Verney; E R Verney; A W Layton; Dr I Laing; S P Weil; G Caird.*
CC Number 271375
Information available Accounts were on file at the Charity Commission, but without a list of grants.

General The trust aims to 'enable those with disadvantages to receive benefits which would not usually come their way'. It achieves this by providing grants for groups working with people of any age who are sick, disabled or have special learning difficulties, as well as schoolchildren and students with personal or family difficulties. Musically and artistically gifted people who are unable to fulfil their potential can be directly supported (for further information, please see *The Educational Grants Directory*, also published by DSC).

In 2000/01 the trust had assets of £1.3 million, which generated an income of £38,000. Grants were made totalling £66,000, broken down as follows:

Groups and organisations – £23,000
There were two subdivisions in this category: organisations helping adults, which included social clubs, mental health and rehabilitation, retraining for work, prison reform, respite holidays, single parent organisations, daycentres

and disability groups; and organisations helping children, which included nurseries, playschemes, providers of specialist equipment, youth groups, after-school clubs, toy libraries, holidays and special activities such as sport and music.

Individuals – £14,000

Grants were made to: adult students with disabilities or serious personal difficulties, mostly towards special equipment or items for study; children with disabilities or serious personal difficulties for fees and equipment; adults with disabilities for equipment, holidays and living expenses; music students for fees and instruments, including £500 each to two students at Birmingham Conservatoire as The Rivendell Trust Award; and single parents towards childcare, fees and items for study.

Endowment for Neo-natal research – £31,000

A research project into the relief of pain in neo-natal infants at University of Edinburgh Simpson Memorial Hospital was promised £92,000, paid in quarterly instalments over three years, in 2000. At the end of the financial year seven instalments were remaining.

Prisoners and reform – £5,000

Under a new area of award, Forum for Prison Education received £5,000 as the first of three equal grants, subject to satisfactory progress reports.

Exclusions Applications for the construction, restoration or purchase of buildings are not normally considered. Grants to individuals are limited to those in the above categories, and children and bona fide students within the UK in connection with education in music. Further grants to charities or individuals will normally be considered once every three years.

Applications Charities should send comprehensive details including a statement of the previous two years' accounts. Individuals apply in writing with an sae to the correspondent for an application form. Because of the number of grants received, failure to supply an sae could result in an application failing. Trustees meet three times a year (usually March, July and November) to consider applications. The list of applications is closed six weeks before the date of each meeting, and any applications received after the closing date are carried forward.

The River Trust

Christian

£127,000 (2000/01)

Beneficial area UK, with a preference for Sussex.

c/o Kleinwort Benson Trustees Ltd, PO Box 191, 10 Fenchurch Street, London EC3M 3LB

Tel. 020 7475 5093

Correspondent Chris Gilbert, Secretary

Trustees *Kleinwort Benson Trustees Ltd.*

CC Number 275843

Information available Accounts were on file at the Charity Commission.

General Gillian Warren formed the trust in 1977 with an endowment mainly of shares in the merchant bank Kleinwort Benson. It is one of the many Kleinwort trusts. The River Trust is one of the smaller of the family trusts. It supports Christian causes.

In 2000/01 the trust had assets of £493,000 and an income of £191,000. Grants were made totalling £127,000. A number of the 50 organisations supported had received help in the previous year, grants ranged from £400 to £16,000.

Grants were broken down into the following categories:

Advancement of the Christian faith – 21 grants totalling £50,000

Grants included those to Youth with a Mission (£16,000), Timothy Trust (£12,000), Tear Fund and Ashburnham Christian Trust (£3,000 each), Prison Fellowship and Relationship Foundation (£2,000 each), Bourne Trust and Release International (£1,000 each), Beauty from Ashes (£750) and Interhealth (£500).

Religious education – 13 grants totalling £40,000

Beneficiaries included London Bible College (£10,000), Genesis Arts Trust and Care Trust (£8,000 each), Scripture Union and Chasah Trust (£4,000 each), Bible Society (£1,500), Arts Group Centre (£1,000) and Bibles for Children (£500).

Church funds – 7 grants totalling £25,000

Beneficiaries were Barcombe Parochial Church Council (£9,000), St Luke's Prestonville Church (£6,000), St Peter & James Hospice (£5,000), All Souls Church Eastbourne (£2,500), St Barnabus Church (£750) and St Margaret's PCC (£400).

Missionary work – 7 grants totalling £7,500

Beneficiaries were On the Move and St Stephen's Society (£1,500 each), ICCOWE (£1,200), Indian Christian Mission Centre – Tamilnadu (£1,000), African Enterprise, Arab Vision Trust Fund and Olive Tree Chritian Fellowship (£750 each).

Religious welfare work – 2 grants totalling £6,000

These went to Care for the Family (£5,000) and Mercy Ships UK (£1,000).

Exclusions Only appeals for Christian causes will be considered. No grants to individuals. The trust does not support 'repairs of the fabric of the church' nor does it give grants for capital expenditure.

Applications In writing to the correspondent. Unsolicited appeals are considered as well as causes which have already been supported and are still regarded as commitments of the trust. Only successful applicants are notified of the trustees' decision. Some charities are supported for more than one year, although no commitment is usually given to the recipients.

Riverside Charitable Trust Limited

Health, welfare, older people, education, general

£202,000 (2000/01)

Beneficial area Mainly Lancashire.

c/o E Suttons & Sons, Riverside, New Church Ward, Bacup, Lancashire OL13 0DT

Tel. 01706 874961

Correspondent Jackie Davidson, Trustee

Trustees *B J Lynch; I B Dearing; J A Davidson; F Drew; H Francis; A Higginson; G Maden.*

CC Number 264015

Information available Accounts were on file at the Charity Commission.

General The trust's objects are to support the following: poor, sick and older people; education; healthcare; the relief of poverty of people employed or formerly employed in the shoe trade; and other charitable purposes.

In 2000/01 the trust had assets of £2.3 million and an income of £125,000. A total of £202,000 was distributed in 156 grants which were mostly recurrent.

Of grants made, 53 were for £1,000 or more. The largest donations went to two branches of Macmillan Cancer Relief, in Burnley and London. Other beneficiaries of larger grants included Rossendale Valley Mencap and St Mary's Hospice (£6,000 each), Rossendale Society for the Blind (£5,000), British Heart Foundation and Royal Northern College of Music (£3,000 each), Derian Hose Hospice – Bolton and Furness Lions' Club (£2,500 each), Barrow and District Society for the Blind and Cumbria Deaf Association (£2,000 each), Samaritans (£1,500) and Age Concern, Dalton Sports Hall and Duddan Inshore Rescue Lifeboat (£1,000 each).

Beneficiaries of smaller grants under £1,000 each included Bacup Credit Union, Footwear Benevolent Society, Help the Aged, Lancashire Partnership Against Crime, Pendle Ski Club, Rossendale Talking Newspaper Association, Save the Children and Williams Syndrome Foundation.

Exclusions No grants for political causes.

Applications In writing to the correspondent.

Richard Rogers Charitable Settlement

Housing, homelessness
£165,000 (1999/2000)
Beneficial area UK

Lee Associates, 5 Southampton Place, London WC1A 2DA
Tel. 020 7831 3609
Correspondent K A Hawkins
Trustees *Lord R G Rogers; P Rogers; G H Camamile.*
CC Number 283252
Information available Accounts were on file at the Charity Commission, but without a grants list or a description of the trust's grant-making policy.

General In 1999/2000 the trust's assets totalled £401,000 and it received an income of £21,000 (£293,000 in the

previous year). Grants totalled £165,000 (£113,000 in 1998/99) and only £270 was spent on management and administration costs. A grant of £100,000 was made to National Tenants Resource Centre. Further information on beneficiaries was not available.

The low income in this year can be explained since the donations that would normally have been received from Richard Rogers Architects Limited on 30 June 1999 were received on 31 March 1999, still within the 1998/99 financial year.

Applications In writing to the correspondent.

Rokach Family Charitable Trust

Jewish, general
£103,000 (2000/01)
Beneficial area UK.

20 Middleton Road, London NW11 7NS
Tel. 020 8455 6359
Correspondent Norman Rokach, Trustee
Trustees *N Rokach; Mrs H Rokach; Mrs E Hoffman; Mrs M Feingold; Mrs A Gefilhaus; Mrs N Brenig.*
CC Number 284007
Information available Full accounts were on file at the Charity Commission.

General This trust supports Jewish and general causes in the UK. In 2000/01 its assets totalled £1.3 million and it had an income of £155,000, mainly from rent on its properties. Grants totalled £103,000.

The accounts listed 51 grants made over £100 each. The beneficiary of the largest grant was Finchley Road Synagogue (£33,000). Seven further grants of over £1,000 were made, to Beth Hamedrash Ponovez (£21,000), Adath Israel Synagogue and Woodstock Sinclair Trust (£10,000 each), Cosmon Belz Ltd (£7,600), Moreshet Hatorah Ltd (£2,400), Jewish Education Trust (£2,000) and Institute of Rabbinical Studies D'Chasidei Belz London (£1,500).

Other smaller donations included those to Before Trust, Beis Yaakov Primary School, CMZ Trust, British Friends of Laniado Hospital, CMZ Trust, Friends of Mir, Gertner Trust and Pardes House School.

Unlisted smaller grants under £100 each totalled £3,100.

Applications In writing to the correspondent.

The Sir James Roll Charitable Trust

General
£149,000 (2000/01)
Beneficial area UK.

5 New Road Avenue, Chatham, Kent ME4 6AR
Tel. 01634 830111 **Fax** 01634 408891
Correspondent N T Wharton, Trustee
Trustees *N T Wharton; B W Elvy; J M Liddiard.*
CC Number 1064963
Information available Full accounts were on file at the Charity Commission.

General The trust's main objects are the:

* promotion of mutual tolerance, commonality and cordiality in major world religions
* furtherance of access to computer technology as a teaching medium at primary school levels
* promotion of improved access to computer technology in community based projects other than political parties or local government
* funding of projects aimed at early identification of specific learning disorders.

In 2000/01 the trust had assets totalling £3.8 million and an income of £179,000. Grants were made to 117 beneficiaries totalling £149,000. Grants ranged from £500 to £15,000, although over half were for £500.

Beneficiaries included: DEC India Earthquake Appeal (£15,000), CRISIS at Christmas (£10,000), Howard League for Penal Reform and Prison Reform Trust (£6,000 each), The Community Self Build Agency and Frontline Community Project (£5,000 each), National Missing Persons Helpline and Mission in Houndslow (£3,000 each), The National Autistic Society and The Dyslexia Institute (£2,000 each).

Grants of £1,000 included those to Alzheimers Disease Society, Battersea Dogs Home, Children's Aid Foundation and Great Ormond Street Hospital. Beneficiaries receiving £500 each included ACE Centre Advisory Trust, Africa NOW, Barnados, British Red Cross, Combat Stress, Dermatrust, Five Ways School, MIND, NatureWatch, Vision Aid and YMCA Swansea.

Applications In writing to the correspondent.

The Helen Roll Charitable Trust

General

£98,000 (2001/02)
Beneficial area UK.

Manches, 3 Worcester Street, Oxford OX1 2PZ
Correspondent F R Williamson, Trustee
Trustees *Jennifer Williamson; Dick Williamson; Paul Strang; Christine Chapman; Terry Jones; Christine Reid.*
CC Number 299108
Information available Full accounts were provided by the trust.

General 'One of the trustees' aims is to support work for charities which find it difficult or impossible to obtain funds from other sources. Some projects are supported on a start-up basis, others involve funding over a longer term.'

The charities supported are mainly those whose work is already known to the trustees and who report on both their needs and achievements. Each year a handful of new causes are supported. However the trust states that 'the chances of success for a new application are about 100-1'.

In 2001/02 the assets of the trust were £1.7 million and the income was £51,000. Grants totalled £98,000 and administration expenses £15,000.

Of the 25 organisations that received grants, 19 had also benefited in the previous year. The largest grants went to Trinity College of Music (£10,000), Pembroke College Oxford (£9,000), Friends of Home Farm Trust (£8,000), Oxford University Bodleian Library, Purcell School and Sick Children's Trust Cambridge (£6,000 each).

A wide range of causes received support, with recipients of other grants including Canine Partners for Independence, Michael Sobell House, Peterborough

Cancer Treatment Appeal and Notting Hill Housing Trust (£4,000 each), Berkshire, Buckinghamshire and Oxfordshire Wildlife Trust (£3,000), Children's Society (£2,000), Compassionate Friends (£1,000), Disability Aid Fund and Gerald Moore Award (£500 each).

Exclusions No support for individuals or non–registered charities.

Applications In writing to the correspondent during the first fortnight in February. Applications should be kept short, ideally on one sheet of A4. Further material will then be asked of those who are short-listed. The trustees normally make their distribution in March.

The M K Rose Charitable Trust

Jewish, general

£1.3 million (2000 – an exceptional year)
Beneficial area UK, mostly West Midlands, and Israel.

20 Coppice Close, Dovehouse Lane, Solihull, West Midlands B91 2ED
Tel. 0121 706 6558
Correspondent M K Rose, Trustee
Trustees *M K Rose; Mrs I W Rose; H Aron; S Gould.*
CC Number 1039857
Information available Information was provided by the trust.

General This trust has general charitable purposes, with most grants given to Israel/Jewish and West Midlands organisations.

In 2000 the trust gave 80 grants totalling £1.3 million. In previous years the trust has had both an income and a total expenditure of around £70,000 to £80,000. The 2000 trustees' report stated: 'During the year the settlor introduced a further £100,000 into the trust. Following this a decision was taken to realise all the investments and distribute the majority of the proceeds, mainly to charities that have been supported over the years. (In the light of the decline in stock market prices over recent months this has proved to be a very wise move.) The trust continues, but at a substantially reduced size, now having assets of approximately £265,000.'

Substantial grants were £330,000 to Friends of Nahariya Hospital, £101,000 each to Diana Princess of Wales Children's Hospital – Birmingham and United Jewish Israel Appeal and £100,000 each to ALDEMI, Jerusalem Foundation and United Jewish Israel Appeal.

Othr large grants went to Solihull and District Hebrew Congregation (£80,000), Jewish National Fund and World Jewish Relief (£50,000), Beth Shalom Holocaust Memorial Centre and B'nai B'rith Hillel Foundation (£21,000) and Birmingham Royal Ballet Trust, CBSO Endowment Fund and Symphony Hall Organ Appeal (£20,000).

Other Jewish/Israeli charities included Birmingham Hebrew Congregation (£12,000), Holocaust Educational Trust (£11,000), Friends of Hebrew University – Jerusalem and Friends of Israel Education Trust (£10,000 each), Jewish Child's Day and Joint Jewish Charitable Trust (£5,000 each), Habakkuk Trust, Jewish Children's Holiday Fund and Magen David Adom Appeal (£2,000 each), Association of Jewish Refugees in Great Britain (£1,000), World Jewish Relief (£500) and New Israel Fund (£200).

Beneficiaries in the West Midlands included The MAC Centre and Trinity Housing Resource Centre (£10,000 each), Birmingham Institute for the Deaf and Institute for Conductive Education (£5,000 each), Mary Stevens Hospice (£2,200), MSA for Midland People with Celebral Palsy and South Birmingham Club for People with Disabilities (£2,000 each), Edgbaston Women Zionists (£1,000) and Ovingdean Hall School (£200).

Among the other beneficiaries were Marie Curie Cancer Care and The Refugee Council (£10,000 each), Macmillan Cancer Relief (£5,000), Fund for Needy Immigrants and London 35's (£2,000 each), Variety Club of Great Britain (£200).

Applications In writing to the correspondent.

The Cecil Rosen Foundation

Welfare, especially older people, infirm, people who are mentally or physically disabled

£216,000 (2000/01)
Beneficial area UK.

118 Seymour Place, London W1H INP
Tel. 020 7262 2003
Correspondent M J Ozin, Trustee
Trustees *Mrs L F Voice; M J Ozin; J A Hart.*
CC Number 247425
Information available Accounts were on file at the Charity Commission, but without a list of grants and only a limited review of activities.

General Established in 1966, the charity's main object is the assistance and relief of the poor, especially older people, the infirm or people who are disabled.

The correspondent has previously stated that almost all the trust's funds are (and will always continue to be) allocated between five projects. The surplus is then distributed in small donations between an unchanging list of around 200 organisations. 'Rarely are any organisations added to or taken off the list.'

In 2000/01 the trust had assets of £2.9 million and an income of £304,000. Grants were made totalling £216,000. As in recent years, no grants list was included in the accounts. However, the accounts stated that payments were given to two charities connected to this foundation by common trustees and a common address; these were £80,000 to Jewish Blind and Disabled and £50,000 to The Cecil Rosen Charitable Trust.

Exclusions No grants to individuals.

Applications The correspondent stated that 'no new applications can be considered'. Unsuccessful applications are not acknowledged.

The Roughley Charitable Trust

General in the West Midlands

£202,000 (2000/01)
Beneficial area Mainly Birmingham and surrounding area.

90 Somerset Road, Edgbaston, Birmingham B15 2PP
Correspondent J R L Smith, Correspondent
Trustees *Mrs M K Smith; Mrs D M Newton; M C G Smith; J R L Smith.*
CC Number 264037
Information available Accounts were on file at the Charity Commission, but without a full narrative report.

General In 2000/01 the trust had assets of £3.2 million. The settlor and her family provided an additional £975,000 in funds during the year, most of which was transferred to assets. After low administration costs of £6,600, grants totalled £202,000, broken down as follows:

Annual grants
There were 17 grants made, ranging from £30 to £3,000 and totalling £13,000. The largest was £3,000 to St James Church. Other beneficiaries included Medical Foundation for the Care of Victims of Torture (£2,000), Relate (£1,500), Amnesty International UK Section Charitable Trust (£1,000), Dodford Children's Holiday Farm (£500), BVSC (£450), Birmingham Rathbone Society (£300), YMCA (£200), Leonard Cheshire Services in Birmingham (£50) and West Midlands Charitable Trust Group (£30). Grants in this category for the same amount to the same organisations of the same amount each year.

Specific
Grants totalling £191,000 were made to 19 organisations. By far the largest was £145,000 to Birmingham Settlement towards their centenary appeal, funded from the additional income provided by the settlor. Other grants to organisations in the Birmingham area were £12,000 to MAC (Midlands Arts Centre), £1,000 each to Birmingham CAB and Shard End Youth Centre and £500 to Birmingham Centre for Arts Therapies. Other beneficiaries included Rehabilitation for Addicted Prisoners (£12,000), Emmaus UK (£10,000), St Paul's Church Appeal (£3,000), Hamlin Churchill Childbirth

Injuries Fund and Open Door Youth Counselling Service (£1,000 each), Buxton Opera House and Ladywood Furniture Project (£500 each) and Norman Laud Association (£200).

Exclusions No support for animal charities.

Applications This trust states that it does not normally respond to unsolicited applications. The annual meeting is held in September.

Rowanville Ltd

Orthodox Jewish

£428,000 (1999/2000)
Beneficial area UK and Israel.

8 Highfield Gardens, London NW11 9HB
Tel. 020 8458 9266
Correspondent J Pearlman, Governor
Trustees *J Pearlman; Mrs R Pearlman; M Neuberger; M D Frankel.*
CC Number 267278
Information available Full accounts were on file at the Charity Commission.

General The objectives of the trust are 'to advance religion in accordance with the orthodox Jewish faith' and to support 'philanthropic religious and educational activities'. Only 'established institutions' are supported.

In 1999/2000 the trust carried assets of £1.7 million and had an income of £506,000, a large proportion of this came from Gift Aid and other donations. Grants totalled £428,000, (£355,000 in 1998/99). The trust tends make a large number of recurrent grants each year, giving all of its support to Jewish organisations.

By far the largest grant was £109,000 to Lerose Charitable Trust. Other large grants went to Yesodey Hatorah Grammar School (£48,000), Menorah Grammar School (£35,000), KKL Executor and Trustee Company (£27,000), Achisomoch Aid Company and Notza Cheshed (£20,000).

Educational organisations to benefit included Yeshivas Shaarei Torah (£15,000), Centre for Advanced Rabbinics (£13,000), Torah Vechased Le'ezra Vesed (£12,000), Telz Talmudical Academy and Talmud Torah Trust (£11,000), Gateshead Jewish Academy for Girls (£5,000), Talmud Torah Education (£2,000), Pinto Talmudical College

(£1,800), Beth Jacob Grammar School for Girls Ltd (£1,800), Emuna Educational Centre and Gateshead Jewish Boarding School (£250 each) and Manchester Collel (£100).

Other beneficiaries included British Friends of Ohr Somajach (£5,000), Friends of Mir (£1,200), Finchley Road Synagogue (£1,000), United Synagogue (£840) and Jewish Care (£200).

Applications The trust states that applications are unlikely to be successful unless one of the trustees has prior personal knowledge of the cause, as this charity's funds are already very heavily committed.

Joshua and Michelle Rowe Charitable Trust

Jewish
£247,000 (2000/01)
Beneficial area UK and worldwide.

84 Upper Park Road, Salford M7 0JA
Correspondent J Rowe, Trustee
Trustees *J Rowe; Mrs M B Rowe.*
CC Number 288336
Information available Accounts were on file at the Charity Commission.

General In 2000/01 the trust had assets of just £124,000 and an income of £232,000 mainly from donations and gifts. After management and administration charges of £180, grants totalled £247,000.

The largest grants over £10,000 each were £29,000 to King David School, £17,000 to Chief Rabbi Charitable Trust, £15,000 to Manchester Great and New Synagogue, £12,000 to Aish Hatorah and £10,000 to Friends of Yeshivat Kerem B'yavneh.

Other beneficiaries included Midreshet Lindenbaum (£9,000), Manchester Jewish Grammar School (£8,200), Sharei Torah Yeshiva (£7,000), Manchester Talmudical College (£3,000), Community Security Trust (£2,100), Manchester Charitable Trust (£1,000), Broome Foundation (£500), Jerusalem Great Synagogue (£100) and Friends of Beth Jacob (£25).

Applications In writing to the correspondent.

The J B Rubens Charitable Foundation

Mainly Jewish causes
£175,000 (2000/01)
Beneficial area UK, Israel, USA, India, Sri Lanka, Pakistan, South Africa, New Zealand, Australia, Canada

Berkeley Square House, Berkeley Square, London W1J 6BY
Tel. 020 7491 3763 **Fax** 020 7491 0818
Correspondent Michael Phillips, Trustee
Trustees *Michael Phillips; J B Rubens Charity Trustees Limited.*
CC Number 218366
Information available Full accounts were on file at the Charity Commission.

General The 2000/01 accounts stated: 'The trustees receive applications from a wide variety of charitable institutions, including those engaged in medical and ancillary services (including medical research), education, helping the disabled and old aged, relieving poverty, providing sheltered accommodation, developing the arts, etc. The trustees consider all requests which they receive and make donations as they feel appropriate.'

The foundation is connected to two other charities, Ruth and Michael Phillips Charitable Trust and The Phillips Family Charitable Trust, sharing a common address and some of the trustees.

In 2000/01 the foundation had assets of £8.7 million, which generated an income of £371,000. Grants were made to five organisations totalling £175,000. Administration costs for the year were very high at £121,000.

The largest grants was £140,000 to Ruth and Michael Phillips Charitable Trust, a connected charity. Other beneficiaries were Simon Weisenthal Centre (£17,000), Charities Aid Foundation (£10,000), Jerusalem Foundation (£7,700) and Jewish Blind and Physically Handicapped Society (£500).

Exclusions No grants are made to individuals.

Applications In writing to the correspondent, at any time.

The Russell Trust

General
£232,000 (2000/01)
Beneficial area UK, especially Scotland.

Markinch, Glenrothes, Fife KY7 6PB
Tel. 01592 753311
Correspondent Mrs Cecilia Croal, Secretary
Trustees *Mrs Cecilia Croal; Fred Bowden; Duncan Ingram; David Erdal; Mrs Margaret Russell Granelli.*
CC Number SC004424
Information available Limited information was provided by the trust, without a recent grants list.

General In 2000/01 the trust had assets of £5.1 million and an income of £287,000. Grants totalled £232,000. Grants are usually in the range of £250 to £2,000, but can be up to £10,000. Three or four large grants of up to £20,000 may also be awarded each year.

The trust has several categories of grantmaking, including health and welfare, education, youth work, archaeology, the arts, preservation and conservation, churches and museums. A recent grants list was not available.

In 1998/99 recipients of £10,000 were Edinburgh Green Belt Trust for an educational initiative, National Galleries of Scotland to set up a 'friends' scheme, National Trust for Scotland for Hew Lorimer project at Kellie Castle, Royal Society of Edinburgh, and St Andrews University for PhD awards. Other grants included £6,000 to Liberating Scots Trust for a military museum to commemorate Scots in the Second World War and £5,000 went to Clovenstone Primary School for a new playground and Craighead Institute.

Exclusions Only registered charities are supported.

Applications On a form available from the correspondent.

The Audrey Sacher Charitable Trust

Arts, medical, care
£198,000 (2000/01)
Beneficial area UK.

c/o H W Fisher & Co, Acre House, London NW1 3ER
Correspondent The Trustees
Trustees *Mrs Nicola Shelley Sacher; Michael Harry Sacher.*
CC Number 288973
Information available Accounts were on file at the Charity Commission, without a full list of grants.

General The trust states its main areas of work as the arts, medical and care. Grants are only made to charities known personally to the trustees.

In 2000/01 the trust had assets of £2.3 million and an income of £65,000. After management and administration costs of £9,600, grants were made totalling £198,000. The accounts listed the two largest grants which were made to Royal Opera House (£123,000) and National Gallery (£25,000).

The trust gifted £513,000 to Michael Sacher Charitabale Trust during 2000/01, bringing its total expenditure to over £722,000.

Exclusions No grants to individuals or organisations which are not registered charities.

Applications In writing to the correspondent.

The Michael Sacher Charitable Trust

Jewish
£161,000 (2000/01)
Beneficial area UK and Israel.

16 Clifton Villas, London W9 2PH
Tel. 020 7289 5873
Correspondent Mrs Irene Wiggins, Secretary

Trustees *Simon John Sacher; Jeremy Michael Sacher; Hon. Mrs Rosalind E C Sacher; Mrs Elisabeth J Sacher.*
CC Number 206321
Information available Accounts were on file at the Charity Commission, but without a list of grants in recent years.

General This trust supports a wide range of Jewish/Israeli causes. In 2000/01 it had assets of £5.1 million, which generated a healthy income of £647,000. Grants were made totalling £161,000. No further information was available for the year.

The most recent grants list available at the Charity Commission was that for 1997/98 when 22 organisations received £127,000 in total. The largest grants were £40,000 to Israel Disapora Trust, £33,000 to British Friends of the Art Museums of Israel and £30,000 to J'Paime.

Other grants ranged from £200 (to Redbridge Jewish Youth and Community Centre) to £7,500 (to Community Security Trust). Beneficiaries included Friends of the Hebrew University of Jerusalem (£4,500), Jewish Care (£2,500), New Israel Fund (£2,000), CBF World Jewish Relief (£1,000), West London Synagogue (£890), Nightingale House (£700), Oxford Centre for Hebrew and Jewish Studies (£500) and Jewish Film Foundation and Maccabi Union (£250 each).

Applications In writing to the correspondent at any time.

Dr Mortimer and Theresa Sackler Foundation

Arts, hospitals
£421,000 (2000)
Beneficial area UK.

15 North Audley Street, London W1K 6WZ
Tel. 020 7493 3842
Correspondent Christopher B Mitchell, Trustee
Trustees *Mortimer Sackler; Theresa Sackler; Christopher Mitchell; Robin Stormonth-Darling; Raymond Smith.*
CC Number 327863

Information available Accounts were on file at the Charity Commission.

General The foundation was set up in 1985 by Mortimer Sackler of Rooksnest, Berkshire for general charitable purposes and 'the advancement of the public in the UK and elsewhere in the fields of art, science and medical research generally'.

The assets of the foundation stood at £3.9 million in December 2000 and its income of £215,000 came entirely from bank deposit interest. Grants were made totalling £421,000. Grants made over £8,000 each were made to 11 organisation and were listed in the accounts. Beneficiaries were Dulwich Picture Gallery (£105,000), Kings College London and London University – Courtauld Institute (£50,000 each), Tate Modern (£46,000), University Of Reading (£30,000), National Maritime Museum and Royal National Theatre Board (£25,000 each), St Thomas' Schools Foundation (£15,000) and Stoke Mandeville Hospital and Serpentine Trust (£10,000 each).

Unlisted grants made under £10,000 each totalled £57,000.

Applications To the correspondent in writing.

The Ruzin Sadagora Trust

Jewish
£290,000 (2000/01)
Beneficial area UK, Israel.

269 Golders Green Road, London NW11 9JJ
Correspondent I M Friedman, Trustee
Trustees *Israel Friedman; Sara Friedman.*
CC Number 285475
Information available Limited accounts were on file at the Charity Commission without a grants list since 1993/94.

General In 2000/01 the trust had an income of £345,000, of which £103,000 came from donations. Grants totalled £290,000 for the year.

In its annual report the trustees stated that they continued to:

a. fund the cost, upkeep and activities of the Ruzin Sadagora Synagogue in London (£28,000)
b. fund and support the parent and other associated and affiliated Sadagora

209

institutions and other religious causes and charities (£262,000).

No further details were available about the size or number of the beneficiaries in 1997/98. The last grants list on file at the Charity Commission from 1993/94 saw the trust giving only to Jewish organisations.

Applications In writing to the correspondent.

This entry was not confirmed by the trust, but is correct according to information on file at the Charity Commission.

The Saddlers' Company Charitable Fund

General

£301,000 (2001/02)

Beneficial area UK, but mainly England in practice.

Saddlers' Hall, 40 Gutter Lane, London EC2V 6BR

Tel. 020 7726 8661 **Fax** 020 7600 0386

Email clerk@saddlersco.co.uk

Website www.saddlersco.co.uk

Correspondent W S Brereton-Martin

Trustees *The Saddlers' Company. The company is directed by the Court of Assistants consisting of the Master, three Wardens, a number of Past Masters and up to four junior assistants. There shall be a minimum of 12 and a maximum of 24.*

CC Number 261962

Information available Annual report and financial statements were provided by the trust.

General In 2001/02 the charity had an income of £321,000 and assets of £7.9 million. It made grants totalling £301,000 in support of the City of London, the saddlery trade, the equestrian world, education and general charitable activities.

In order to structure the charity's grant-making policy the trustees have, for the past six years, focused on aiding smaller charities assisting people with disabilities. This policy is being continued. To meet the trust's policy, members of the livery are asked to visit a charity local to them and report on the charity's suitability to receive a grant. This is then considered by

a grant committee whose recommendations are passed on to the trustees.

Significant grants over £10,000 went to Alleyn's School (£130,000), Riding for the Disabled (£28,000) and British Horse Society (£24,000). The trust supports many of the same charities each year such as Alleyn's School and Riding for the Disabled. After making these allocations, about one quarter of the remaining money is allocated to major UK charities working in all charitable sectors, and about three quarters for responding to specific charitable appeals in support of people with disabilities, which are received throughout the year.

Grants made in the City of London included £5,000 to the Lord Mayor's Appeal for the Square Smile and £1,000 each to City of London Police Widow's and Orphan's Fund and St Paul's Cathedral. Other grants given in Greater London include the £130,000 to Alleyn's School, £2,000 each to London Ambulance Services Benevolent Fund, London Area Sea Cadets and London Youth.

Other beneficiaries included Leather Conservation Centre (£3,000), Army Benevolent Fund, Middlesex & NW ACF and Combined Services Equitation Association (£2,000 each), Berkshire MS Therapy Centre, Exeter House Special School, Royal British Legion and UMBRELLA (£1,800 each) and Derbyshire Coalition for Inclusive Living (£1,300) and Research into Ageing and Walsall Leather Museum (£1,000 each).

The trustees' report points out that grants given in one year do not necessarily serve as a precedent for giving in subsequent years. The following is a breakdown of grants by category made in 2001/2002:

City of London	£8,000
The equestrian world	£30,000
Education	£148,000
Disability	£82,000
Saddlery trade	£7,000

General charitable activities £25,000

Exclusions Appeals by individuals for educational grants cannot be considered.

Applications By letter, with supporting background information. Grants are made in January and July, following trustees' meetings. Charities are asked to submit reports at the end of the following year on their continuing activities and the use of any grant received.

The Jean Sainsbury Animal Welfare Trust

Animal welfare

£218,000 (2001)

Beneficial area Mainly the UK, but overseas charities are considered.

PO Box 469, London W14 8PJ

Fax 020 7371 4918

Correspondent Miss Ann Dietrich, Administrator

Trustees *Jean Sainsbury; Cyril Sainsbury; Colin Russell; Gillian Tarlington; James Keliher; Mark Spurdens; Jane Winship; Audrey Lowrie.*

CC Number 326358

Information available Financial statements along with a grants list were provided by the trust.

General The trust was established in 1982 with the objective of benefiting and protecting animals from suffering. Around £3 million had been donated by 2001. The policy of the trustees is to support smaller charities concerned with animal welfare and wildlife. Some organisations receive regular donations. Seven overseas organisations were supported during the year.

In 2001 the trust had assets of £7.3 million, generating an income of £262,000. A total of 141 grants were made to animal welfare organisations, some of which received more than one grant during the year. Grants totalled £218,000, and ranged from £200 to £10,000.

Grants of £10,000 each went to Celia Hammond Animal Rescue, The Blue Cross and North Clwyd Animal Rescue. Other grants of £5,000 or more went to Donkey Sanctuary and Royal Veterinary College Small Animals Hospital, Beaumont (£7,500 each), Three Owls Bird Sanctuary & Rescue (£7,000), Remus Memorial Horse Sanctuary (£7,000 in total), Worcestershire Animal Rescue Shelter and Brent Lodge Bird & Wildlife Trust (£6,000 each), Hull & East Riding Boxer Rescue, Society for the Welfare of Horses & Ponies and Vidanimal Colombia (£5,000 each).

Other beneficiaries included Skye View Animal Home in Gairloch and Suffolk Animal Rescue (£4,500 each), Millhouse Animal Rescue (£4,000), Celia Cross

Greyhound Trust in Guildford, Easterleigh Animal Sanctuary in St Annes and Knoxwood Bird Sanctuary & Wildlife Rescue Centre (£3,500 each), Warnham Animal Sanctuary, Sussex Pet Rescue and Horses & Ponies Protection Association (£3,000 each), Greyhounds in Need and Redgate Farm Animal Sanctuary (£2,000 each), and The Working Horse Trust in Tunbridge Wells, Animals in Need in Melling, Liverpool, Animals in Distress in Manchester, Worcestershire Animal Rescue Shelter and Capricorn Animal Rescue in Buckley (£1,000 each).

Beneficiaries receiving less than £1,000 each included Pets Need People in Clifton, Phillips Cat Sanctuary in Leeds, Compassion in World Farming, Care for the Wild International, Japan Animal Welfare Society, Pet Care Network in Edinburgh, Newmarket Cats, Wellingborough Dog Welfare and Brooke Hospital for Animals.

During the year the trust supported 21 charities who suffered financially as a result of the foot-and-mouth crisis. The sum of £10,000 was set aside for this purpose.

Regular contact is maintained with beneficiaries, and wherever possible the trust tries to visit charities who are new to it. 19 newly supported charities were visited during the year. The trust states that 95% of applicants are successful in obtaining a donation.

Exclusions No grants are made to individuals or non-registered charities and no loans can be given.

Applications In writing to the correspondent, including a copy of accounts. There are three trustees meetings every year, usually in March, July and November.

St Gabriel's Trust

Higher and further religious education

£129,000 to organisations (2001)
Beneficial area Mainly in the UK, with an interest in the diocese of Southwark.

Ladykirk, 32 The Ridgeway, Enfield, Middlesex EN2 8QH

Tel. 020 8363 6474

Correspondent Peter Duffell, Clerk

Trustees *General Secretary of the National Society; nine co-optative trustees and two nominated trustees.*

CC Number 312933

Information available Reports and financial statement were provided by the trust.

General The trust is concerned with the the advancement of higher and further education in one or more of the following ways:

- promotion of the education and training of people who are, or intend to become, engaged as teachers or otherwise in work connected with religious education
- promotion of research in, and development of, religious education
- promotion of religious education by the provision of instruction, classes, lectures, books, libraries and reading rooms
- granting of financial assistance to institutions of higher or further education established for charitable purposes only.

In 2001 the trust had assets of £5.4 million and an income of £221,000. Grants totalling £141,000 were made comprising £37,000 in corporate awards, £92,000 to the St Gabriel's Programme (see below) and £12,000 to 18 individuals.

A total of nine corporate grants were made in the year, the largest was for £10,000 and went to the National Society towards its website. Other grants included £7,300 to Millennium Development Programme and College Centenary, £7,100 to University of Exeter, £6,600 to Lambeth Palace Symposium, £2,000 to Churches' Action for Racial Equality, £1,800 to St Pierre International Youth Trust, £840 to Ignite Anglican Church and £500 to Goldsmiths' College.

The trustees have committed funds for several corporate projects including:

(i) an initiative to recruit RE teachers, in conjunction with other trusts

(ii) the St Gabriel's Programme, an ongoing venture which has been run jointly with Culham College Institute, 'to develop thought and action in support of RE teachers'.

Awards to individuals are given towards course fees and expenses for teachers taking part-time RE courses whilst continuing their teaching jobs. Occasional grants have been given to those undertaking specialist research that will clearly benefit the religious education world.

Exclusions Grants are not normally available for: any project for which local authority money is available, or which ought primarily to be funded by the church – theological study, parish or missionary work – unless school RE is involved; and research projects where it will be a long time before any benefit can filter down into RE teaching. No grants are made to schools as such; higher and further education must be involved.

Applications In writing to the correspondent with an sae. Applicants are asked to describe their religious allegiance and to provide a reference from their minister of religion. Applications need to be received by the beginning of January, April or September as trustees meet in February, May and October.

St James' Trust Settlement

General

£325,000 (2001/02)
Beneficial area Worldwide.

44a New Cavendish Street, London W1G 8TR

Tel. 020 7486 4663

Correspondent Edwin Green, Secretary

Trustees *Jane Wells; Cathy Ingram; Simon Taffler.*

CC Number 280455

Information available Full accounts were on file at the Charity Commission.

General The trust's main aims are to make grants to charitable organisations that respond to areas of concern which the trustees are involved or interested in. In the UK, the main concerns are in areas of social justice; in the USA the main areas are in education, especially to the children of very disadvantaged families, and in community arts projects.

Grants are made by the trustees through their involvement with the project. Projects are also monitored and evaluated by the trustees.

In 2001/02 the trust had assets of £3.9 million and an income of £118,000. After management and administration costs of £25,000, grants were paid totalling £325,000. Grants were made to 31 organisations the UK totalling £221,000 and 13 in the USA totalling £104,000. A further £129,000 was committed for future projects.

In the UK the largest single grant was £25,000 to Elizabeth House; Yakar Educational Foundation received the same amount in two grants of £15,000 and £10,000. Other larger grants over £10,000 each included Lord Ashdown Charitable Settlement (£15,000) and Children of Chernobyl, Community Security Trust, In Kind Direct, Marchant-Holliday School, Matthew Trust and Norwood Ltd (£10,000 each).

Smaller UK grants included those to Family Welfare Association (£7,500), Action for Kids Charitable Trust and UK Jewish Aid (£5,000 each), Children's Music Club (£2,000) and Butterflies (£500).

In the USA, grants included those to Trevor Day School (£36,000), Theatre for a New Audience (£29,000), Teleosis Foundation (£7,000), Big Apple Circus (£6,900) and Achilles Track Club (£5,200).

Exclusions No grants to individuals.

Applications 'The trust does not seek unsolicited applications to grants, the trustees do not feel justified in allocating administrative costs to responding to applications. If you do send an application you must send a stamped addressed envelope.'

St James's Place Foundation

Children and young people who are disabled
£676,000 to organisations (2001)
Beneficial area UK.

St James's Place House, Dollar Street, Cirencester, Gloucestershire GL7 2AQ
Tel. 01285 640302 **Fax** 01285 640436
Correspondent Gail Mitchell-Briggs, Secretary
Trustees M Cooper-Smith; J Newman; Sir Mark Weinberg; M Wilson; D Bellamy.
CC Number 1031456
Information available An annual report, comprehensive grants list and full application details were provided by the foundation.

General Established in 1992 to provide employees at the parent company with a motivation to undertake fundraising activities, this foundation was supported entirely from donations from members of the company for the first seven years of its life. The company views the efforts of its employees as important in terms of both raising funds for a much needed cause and improving the community spirit in the workplace. The foundation's management committee is comprised of one member of each of its branches and one member of head office, to keep the sense of community spirit within the workplace. Employees have jumped out of planes, run and cycled through deserts and climbed mountains, while in 2001 the foundation enjoyed its first national fundraising event, the Three Peaks Challenge. Since 1999, the funds raised through these activities have been matched pound-for-pound by the company as corporate donations.

The foundation selects one theme that it will support. The current theme has been 'Cherishing the Children', which supports young people who are aged 25 or under who have a physical or mental disability or who have a life-threatening or degenerative illness. Organisations must have at least 75% of its users meet this criteria to be considered. Beneficiaries must be registered/recognised charities or special needs schools. When this category was first selected for the theme (1996–1998), it was aimed at pre-teen children, with the age range first extended to 17 years old in 1999, and then to 25 from January 2003.

The following criteria are stated to be true of any theme the trust runs:

- 'Applicants should be well-established registered charities with a proven track record, which have worthwhile objectives and are run efficiently and economically. Applications from individuals will not be considered.
- 'Applications should be in respect of tangible projects or equipment with visible end results.
- 'The project should help as many people as possible or, where this is not applicable, have a major impact on the lives of those helped.
- 'UK only.'

In addition to this, grants can be made by the local branches of the parent company, to a maximum of £1,000 each, for general charitable purposes. A small number of grants are also made outside the current theme, although these are usually as recurrent grants applicable to the theme at the time and matching the money raised by employees of the parent company undertaking a major fundraising activity.

In 2001 the foundation had assets of £876,000. The total income was £1.1 million, including £528,000 from corporate donations and £193,000 from fundraising. After additional expenditure of just £11,000, grants were made to 121 organisations and six individuals totalling £678,000.

By far the largest grant made during the year was £318,000 to Hope and Homes for Children. This included £125,000 as part of a two-year commitment in 2000 to support the purchase of additional homes, in the Ukraine in 2000 and in Belarus in 2001, a commitment which has since been extended for a further two years. Three further donations to the charity, totalling £186,000, were made following specific donations from individuals, which were then matched as a corporate donation. Two other smaller payments were made as a result of activity sponsorship. These grants paid for the purchase of other homes in Eastern Europe.

Hope and Homes for Children received support outside of the 'Cherishing the Children' theme. In total, there were five grants from outside the main programme totalling £343,000. The Variety Club Children's Charity received £15,000 to sponsor the first of 21 Sunshine coaches that have been committed to, which will total a further £300,000 over several years. Other beneficiaries were National Deaf Children's Society to match the funds raised by an individual's China Trex (£4,900), Greater London Fund for the Blind (£3,900) and Foxwood Association through sponsorship of a parachute jump (£1,100).

Under the theme 'Cherishing the Children' grants were made to 95 organisations, totalling £322,000. The largest grants were: £6,500 to Rainbow Children's Hospice for a two-day mobility training and assessment project in Truro for nine children who use electric wheelchairs, £6,200 to The Scottish Council of The Scout Association for a sailing dinghy designed for people who are disabled: and £6,000 each to The Archie Foundation towards an enhanced room in the surgical ward of New Royal Aberdeen Children's Hospital, Manchester Appeals Committee for NCH for three computers with specialist software, printers and workstations for people who are disabled, and Manchester YMCA Mavericks for five sports wheelchairs for the wheelchair basketball club.

Other beneficiaries included Hospice of the Valleys to provide pre- and post-bereavement support to children under 17 for one year (£5,500), Wessex Autistic Society towards equipping a multi-sensory room (£5,000), Cumbria Deaf

Association to increase its communication support for families with children who are deaf (£4,700), The Donna Louise Trust for a specialist cot (£3,200), Derian House Children's Hospice for a heated trolley and replacement furniture and flooring (£3,000), Ty Hafan for a massage chair (£2,300), Friends for Young Deaf People for an Animation Day in the Midlands for 40 people who are aged between 10 and 17 and have hearing difficulties or who are deaf (£2,200), Hadleigh Community Primary School towards the match funding required to purchase a lift (£500) and Pathfinders – Swindon for protective helmets (£300).

The regional branches of the parent company supported 22 organisations (totalling £11,000) and six individuals (totalling £2,200) during the year. These grants are given for general charitable purposes. The maximum grant of £1,000 was given to five organisations, Muriel Bol Mission to Romania, CINS, Reed School, Richard House Children's Hospice and SKCV. Other beneficiaries included Comic Relief (£910), Chernobyl Children's Lifeline and Gullemont Junior School (£500 each), World Vision (£360), Woodlands Primary School (£330), BT Swimathon Charity and London Air Ambulance Service (£250 each), National Society for Deaf Children (£130) and Estuary League of Friends (£100).

Exclusions The foundation will not consider applications in relation to respite care or holidays. It has a policy of not considering an application from any charity within two years of receiving a previous application, regardless of the outcome of that appeal.

The trust does not provide support for:

- political, sectarian, religious and cultural organisations
- research projects
- sponsorship or advertising
- building projects, running costs, administration or salaries.

Applications All applications must be submitted on a fully completed application form and be accompanied by the latest audited report and accounts, together with any supporting explanatory documents as appropriate. The trustees meet quarterly.

The Late St Patrick White Charitable Trust

General

£104,000 (1999/2000)

Beneficial area UK, with a possible preference for Hampshire.

HSBC Trusts, Cumberland House, 15–17 Cumberland Place, Southampton SO15 2UY

Tel. 023 8053 1378

Correspondent Barry Stubbs, Trust Manager

Trustees *HSBC Trusts Co. (UK) Ltd.*

CC Number 1056520

Information available Accounts were on file at the Charity Commission.

General This trust has general charitable purposes, with most grants going to health, medical and welfare charities.

In 1999/2000 the trust had assets of £2.6 million. The total income was £96,000, including £22,000 in donations received. Grants were made to 82 organisations totalling £104,000.

The largest grants were £9,800 to Age Concern, £8,800 to Arthritis Research Campaign, £8,200 each to Guide Dogs for the Blind Association and Salvation Army, £6,200 to Barnardos and £6,000 to National Eye Research Centre.

Other grants were £4,100 to 2Care, £4,000 to Institute of Cancer Research, £2,600 to Extra Care Charitable Trust, £2,200 to Pramacare, £1,600 each to Action for Blind People, Deafblind UK, Guide Dogs School, RNIB and Royal School for the Blind, with £1,000 each to 18 organisations including Action for Kids Trust, Cancer Bacup, Roy Castle Lung Cancer, Hartlepool and District Hospice, Rainbow Centre for Children, Sussex Autistic Society, Wessex Children's Hospital Trust, Whizz-Kidz and Winchester and Central Hampshire Intestinal Cancer Trust.

Applications In writing to the correspondent. Applications are considered in February, May, August and November.

Saint Sarkis Charity Trust

Armenian churches and welfare, disability, general

£346,000 (2000/01)

Beneficial area UK and overseas.

c/o Economic & General Secretariat Ltd, 98 Portland Place, London W1N 4ET

Tel. 020 7636 5313

Correspondent Mrs Christine Lewis, Secretary

Trustees *Mikhael Essayan; Boghos Parsegh Gulbenkian; Paul Curno.*

CC Number 215352

Information available Full accounts were on file at the Charity Commission.

General 'The principal objectives of the trust are the support of the Armenian Church of St Sarkis in London and Gulbenkian Library at the Armenian Patriarchate in Jerusalem. In addition, the trustees support other charities concerned with the Armenian Community in the UK and abroad, and to the extent that funds are available, grants are also made to small registered charities concerned with social welfare and disability.'

In 2000/01 the trust had assets of £6.9 million, and a total income of £297,000. Grants totalled £346,000.

The largest grants were £139,000 to Armenian Church of St Sarkis, £111,000 to Surp Pirgic Hospital in Turkey and £70,000 to University of Cambridge.

The other grants listed in the accounts were £5,500 to Trama After Care, £3,400 to Armenian General Benevolent Fund, £3,000 to Christian Solidarity Worldwide, £2,800 to Armenian 17th Century Concert, £2,000 each to Noah's Ark Community Venture, and People First (Self Advocacy) and £1,500 to Wavendon All Music Plan. A total of £26,000 was given in smaller grants.

Exclusions No grants to individuals.

Applications In writing to the correspondent. Trustees meet monthly.

The Saintbury Trust

General

£210,000 (2000)

Beneficial area Gloucestershire, West Midlands and Worcestershire; UK in exceptional circumstances.

Hawnby House, Hawnby, Nr Helmsley, York YO62 5QS

Correspondent Mrs V K Houghton, Trustee

Trustees *Victoria K Houghton; Anne R Thomas; Jane P Lewis; Amanda E Atkinson-Willes; Harry O Forrester.*

CC Number 326790

Information available Accounts were on file at the Charity Commission.

General The trust gives grants for general charitable purposes, although the trust deed states that no grants can be given to animal charities. Grants are made to organisations in Gloucester, West Midlands and Worcestershire. They are only made in other parts of the UK in exceptional circumstances.

In 2000 the trust had assets of £3.7 million and an income of £164,000. Grants to 43 organisations totalled £210,000. The largest grants, over £10,000 each, included those to Fortune Riding Centre (£30,000), University of Birmingham (£25,000), Emmaus – Gloucester (£20,000), RAPt (£15,000), St Paul's Church – Birmingham and Avoncroft Museum (£10,000).

Other smaller grants included those to Agape, CAB – Cirencester, Open Door – Cheltenham, Home for Life Appeal, Home Start UK, Lucy Fund, Queen Alexandra College and Sue Ryder Care.

Exclusions No grants to individuals or to animal charities. The trust stated that they do not respond to 'cold-calling' from organisations outside its main Beneficial area , and groups from other parts of the UK are only considered if personally known to one of the trustees.

Applications In writing to the correspondent. Applications are considered in April and November and should be received one month earlier.

The Saints & Sinners Trust

Welfare, medical

£92,000 (2000/01)

Beneficial area Mostly UK.

Lewis Golden & Co., 40 Queen Anne Street, London W1G 9EL

Tel. 020 7580 7313

Correspondent N W Benson, Trustee

Trustees *N W Benson; Sir Donald Gosling; P Moloney; N C Royds; I A N Irvine.*

CC Number 200536

Information available Full accounts were on file at the Charity Commission.

General This trust supports welfare and medical causes through the proceeds of its fundraising efforts.

In 2000/01 the trust had assets of £199,000. Total income was £92,000, including £57,000 from a golf tournament and £27,000 in donations received. Grants were made to 34 organisations totalling £92,000.

The largest grants were £10,000 to Outward Bound Trust, £7,000 to University of Sheffield and £5,000 each to Help the Aged – Royal Buckinghamshire, Riding for the Disabled – South Buckinghamshire group and White Ensign Association Ltd.

Aside from the £500 to Pattaya Orphanage, all other grants were for £1,000 to £3,000. Recipients included Dance Teachers Benevolent Fund, Demelza House Children's Hospice, Bud Flanagan Leukaemia Fund, Friends of St Mary's Hospital, Kent Air Ambulance, Manor House Trust, Nuffield Orthopaedic Centre Appeal, Mary Peter's South Africa Fund, Royal National Institute for Deaf People, Sight Savers International, Unicorn Theatre for Children and Winged Fellowship Trust.

Exclusions No grants to individuals or non-registered charities.

Applications Applications are not considered unless nominated by members of the club.

The Salamander Charitable Trust

Christian, general

£74,000 (2000/01)

Beneficial area Worldwide.

Threave, 2 Brudenell Avenue, Canford Cliffs, Poole, Dorset BH13 7NW

Correspondent John R T Douglas, Trustee

Trustees *J R T Douglas; Mrs Sheila M Douglas.*

CC Number 273657

Information available Full accounts were on file at the Charity Commission.

General Founded in 1977, the principal objects of the trust are the:

- relief and assistance of people who are poor or in need, irrespective of class, colour, race or creed
- advancement of education and religion
- relief of sickness and other exclusively charitable purposes beneficial to the community.

In 2000/01 the trust had assets of £2.3 million and an income of £69,000. After management and administration expenses of £2,500, grants were made to 246 organisations totalling £74,000.

There were 12 grants of £1,000 or more, all to organisations which received £1,000 in the previous year. The largest grant was £1,500 to SAT-7 Trust. All other grants listed were for £1,000 each and went to Birmingham Bible Institute, Christian Aid, Churches Committee on Overseas Students, FEBA Radio, International Christian College, London Bible College, Maltersey Hall Bible School, Moorlands College, Saint James' PCC – Poole, SAMS and Trinity College.

Exclusions No grants to individuals. Only registered charities are supported.

Applications The trust's income is fully allocated each year, mainly to regular beneficiaries. The trustees do not wish to receive any further new requests.

Salters' Charities

General

£154,000 (1999/2000)

Beneficial area Greater London or UK.

The Salters' Company, Salters' Hall, 4 Fore Street, London EC2Y 5DE

Tel. 020 7588 5216 **Fax** 020 7638 3679

Email diane@salters.co.uk

Correspondent The Charities Administrator

Trustees *The Salters' Company: Master, Upper Warden and Clerk.*

CC Number 328258

Information available Full accounts were filed at the Charity Commission.

General The trust supports UK-wide charities concerned with children and young people, health, Christian aid, the developing world, the environment and members of the armed forces. Grants are also available to local charities connected with the City of London. As a livery company, the trust pays particular interest to charities a liveryman is involved with. In previous years, grants of around £2,000 have been given to around 80 charities each year, although the trust is now considering making slightly larger grants to a smaller number of charities, placing less emphasis on giving small grants to large organisations.

In 1999/2000 the trust had an income of £150,000 and grants were made totalling £154,000. Most grants were for £2,000, though three were for considerably more and some for less. The trust broke down its giving as follows.

- Children and youth – £40,000. This included one of three exceptionally large grants, £18,000 to Christ's Hospital. Other beneficiaries included Home-Start UK, Kings Corner Project and Foundation for the Study of Infant Deaths. All the organisations in this category received grants the previous year.
- Medical – £41,000 in 32 donations, only one of which was to a charity not supported the previous year. Recipients included Business Against Drugs, British Digestive Foundation, Fight for Sight, Home Farm Trust and Westminster Pastoral Foundation.
- Christian aid – £8,000 in eight donations, to charities such as CARE, Church Urban Fund, Prison Fellowship and Stepping Stones Trust.
- Environment/Third World – £9,000 in two donations to World Conservation Monitoring Centre (£7,000) and TearFund (£2,000).
- City – £10,000 in four grants to Lord Mayor's Appeal, Lord Mayor Treloar Trust, St John Ambulance – city branch and Guildhall School of Music Drama.
- Armed forces – £5,000 in four recurrent donations with recipients including District 5 Central London Sea Cadet Corps and SW London Army Cadet Force.
- Other donations – £13,000 in 14 grants, over half of which were for under £1,000. These included Bryson House, Family Welfare Association and Oxfordshire Community Foundation.

Many beneficiaries receive grants over a number of years.

Exclusions Grants are not normally made to charities working with people who are homeless unless there is some connection with a liveryman of the company or with the Salters' City Foyer and the charities therein involved.

Applications In writing to the correspondent.

Basil Samuel Charitable Trust

General

£372,000 (2001/02)

Beneficial area UK and overseas.

c/o Great Portland Estates Plc, Knighton House, 56 Mortimer Street, London W1N 8BD

Tel. 020 7580 3040

Correspondent Mrs Coral Samuel

Trustees *Coral Samuel; Richard Peskin.*

CC Number 206579

Information available Accounts were provided by the trust.

General The trust describes its policy as making 'a limited number of grants of £45,000 or more to medical, socially supportive, educational and cultural charities plus a number of smaller donations to other charities'. The larger awards are often part of ongoing support, while the remainder are more typically one-off awards for between £5,000 and £10,000.

The income in 2001/02 was £466,000, with £372,000 given in grants. The largest were £50,000 each to GRET, Old Vic Theatre – London, Royal Academy of Arts, Royal Horticultural Society and St Paul's School. Frances Mary Buss Foundation, Coram Foundation, Macmillan Cancer Relief, Prince's Trust and Royal Geographical Society received between £25,000 and £30,000 each.

Grants of between £10,000 and £15,000 went to five organisations, of which three were Jewish, including UJIA. Smaller grants were mostly for £5,000 and went to 11 organisations, including National Meningitis Trust and Police Foundation.

Exclusions Grants are given to registered charities only.

Applications In writing to the correspondent. 'The trustees meet on a formal basis annually and regularly on an informal basis to discuss proposals for individual donations.'

Coral Samuel Charitable Trust

General, health, the arts

£122,000 (2000/01)

Beneficial area UK.

c/o Great Portland Estates plc, Knighton House, 56 Mortimer Street, London W1N 8BD

Tel. 020 7580 3040

Correspondent Mrs Coral Samuel, Trustee

Trustees *Coral Samuel; P Fineman.*

CC Number 239677

Information available Full accounts were provided by the trust.

General This trust was established in 1962 by Coral Samuel, the wife of Basil Samuel, who has a larger charitable trust in his name.

It makes grants of £10,000 or more to educational, cultural and social welfare charities plus a number of smaller donations to other charities.

In 2000/01 the trust's assets totalled £4.3 million. The income was £226,000 and grants to charities totalled £122,000.

In total grants were made to 23 organisations, 14 of which were supported in the previous year. The two largest grants of £25,000 each went to British Museum Development Trust and Natural History Museum Development

Trust. Other recipients of £10,000 or more included Royal Opera House Trust (£20,000) and Brighton Festival Society (£10,000).

The remaining, smaller grants ranged from £500 to £6,000. A wide variety of organisations were supported including Norwood Ltd (£6,000), Godolphin & Latymer School, Jackdaws Educational Trust, RNLI and Weizmann Institute Foundation (£5,000 each), Friends of the MDA (£1,300), the Costume Society, IM Prussia Cove, Nightingale House and Sick Children's Trust (£1,000 each) and Breakthrough Breast Cancer, New London Synagogue, Royal Free Hospital Breast Cancer Trust and St Mary Abbots Church (£500 each).

Exclusions Grants are only made to registered charities.

Applications In writing to the correspondent.

The Peter Samuel Charitable Trust

Health, welfare, conservation, Jewish care

£196,000 (2000/01)

Beneficial area UK, with a preference for local organisations in Berkshire.

Bridge Farm, Reading Road, Arborfield, Berkshire RG2 9HT

Tel. 0118 976 0412 **Fax** 0118 976 0147

Correspondent Keith Morris, Secretary

Trustees *Hon. Viscount Bearsted; Hon. Michael Samuel.*

CC Number 269065

Information available Accounts were on file at the Charity Commission, without a recent grants list.

General The trustees' report states: 'The trust seeks to perpetuate the family's interest in the medical sciences, the quality of life in the local areas, heritage and land/forestry restoration'.

In 2000/01 the trust had assets of £3.7 million and an income of £101,000. A total of £196,000 was given in grants during the year, although a grants list was not available.

In 1999/2000 the trust made 57 grants. The largest beneficiaries were Pippin

(£65,000), ULPS Lord Goodman Appeal (£20,000), The Game Conservancy Trust (£18,720), British Red Cross (£10,000), Jewish Care (£5,000), Child Bereavement Trust (£5,000), Barkingside Jewish Youth Centre (£3,000), Norwood (£3,000), World Jewish Relief (£3,000) and Chicken Shed Theatre Company (£2,500).

Exclusions No grants to local charities outside Berkshire or to individuals.

Applications In writing to the correspondent. Trustees meet twice-yearly.

The Sandra Charitable Trust

Health, social welfare, animal welfare

£325,000 to organisations (2000/01)

Beneficial area UK, with a preference for the south east of England.

Moore Stephens, St Paul's House, Warwick Lane, London EC4P 4BN

Tel. 020 7334 9191 **Fax** 020 7528 9934

Correspondent K Lawrence

Trustees *Richard Moore; M Macfayden.*

CC Number 327492

Information available Accounts were provided by the trust.

General In 2000/01 the trust had assets of £13 million and an income of £430,000. Grants for the year totalled £382,000 including £57,000 given in 92 grants to individuals. The donations to individuals comprise solely grants made to nurses. There were 51 grants to organisations listed in the accounts, totalling £282,000, with £43,000 given in smaller grants, making total donations to organisations £325,000.

The trust's review of activities states that 'beneficiaries included nurses, charities involved in animal welfare and research, environmental protection, relief of poverty and youth development'.

The largest grants went to VIRART (£42,000), Dorchester Abbey Preservation Trust (£25,000), Stoke Row Pavillion Fund (£19,000), Barnados (£16,000), Florence Nightingale Foundation (£15,000), Youth Sport Trust (£12,000), Junior League of Friends of the Royal Marsden Hospital and Museum of

London (£10,000 each), Cancer Research Campaign (£7,500) and Lloyds Officer Cadet Scholarship (£6,000).

The remainder of listed grants were in the range of £1,300 to £5,000. Recipients included BTCV, ChildLine, Development Trust, Friends of Felsted School, Grubb Institute of Behavioural Studies, Home Start, Pestalozzi Children's Village Trust, Save the Children, Starlight Foundation, The Candlelight Trust, Thoroughbred Rehabilitation Centre, Trinity Hospice, Whirlow Hall Farm Trust and Whizz Kidz. Many of these beneficiaries have been supported in previous years.

Exclusions No grants to individuals other than nurses.

Applications The trust states that 'unsolicited applications are not requested, as the trustees prefer to support charities whose work they have researched ... funds are largely committed.'

The Schapira Charitable Trust

Jewish

£121,000 (1999)

Beneficial area UK.

2 Dancastle Court, 14 Arcadia Avenue, Finchley, London N3 2JU

Correspondent The Trustees

Trustees *Issac Y Schapira; Michael Neuberger; Suzanne L Schapira.*

CC Number 328435

Information available Accounts were on file at the Charity Commission, but without a narrative report.

General This trust appears to make grants exclusively to Jewish charities. In 2001 it had an income of £411,000 and a total expenditure of £343,000. This information was taken from the Charity Commission database, unfortunately no further details were available for this year. In 1999 it received an income of £125,000 from Gift Aid donations. Grants totalled £121,000.

A total of 108 grants were made, although several organisations received more than one grant. The Society of Friends of the Torah, for example, received 13 grants amounting to £27,000. Other beneficaries included the Keren Association, which received £9,000 in three grants and the

Gur Trust, which received £6,000 in four grants. Smaller grants included those to New Rachmistrvke Synagogue (£3,800), Toldos Aharon (£2,000) and Gateshead Talmudical College (£1,000).

Applications In writing to the correspondent.

The Annie Schiff Charitable Trust

Orthodox Jewish education

£72,000 (2001/02)
Beneficial area UK, overseas.

8 Highfield Gardens, London NW11 9HB
Tel. 020 8458 9266
Correspondent J Pearlman, Trustee
Trustees *J Pearlman; Mrs R Pearlman.*
CC Number 265401
Information available Full accounts were on file at the Charity Commission.

General The trust's objectives are:

• relief of poverty, particular amongst the Jewish community
• advancement of education, particularly the study and instruction of Jewish religious literature
• advancement of religion, particularly Judaism.

In 2001/02 it had assets of £256,000 and an income of £62,000, which included £28,000 in donations received. Grants were made to 15 organisations totalling £72,000. Beneficiaries were

£11,000 to Beis Yaacov Primary School (£11,000), Be'er Avrohom (UK) Trust (£8,000), Friends of Nachalat Osher Charitable Trust (£7,500), Gevurath Ari Torah Academy Trust (£7,000), Telz Talmudical Academy and Talmud Torah Trust (£6,000), Torah Teminah Primary School (£5,500), Friends of Beis Yisroel Trust (£5,000), Friends of Ohel Moshe (£4,000), Choshen Mishpat Centre (£2,000), Yeshivo Horomo Talmudical College (£1,500) with £1,000 each to Gateshead Beis Hatalmud Scholarship Fund, Institute for Higher Rabbinical Studies, Mechinoh L'Yeshiva and Yesodey Hatorah Schools.

Exclusions No support for individuals and non-recognised institutions.

Applications In writing to the correspondent, but grants are generally made only to registered charities. The trust states that presently all funds are committed.

The Schmidt-Bodner Charitable Trust

Jewish, general

£73,000 (2000/01)
Beneficial area Worldwide.

3 Wyndham Place, London W1H 1AP
Tel. 020 7724 4044
Correspondent Harvey Rosenblatt
Trustees *Mrs E Schmidt-Bodner; Marion Diner; Linda Rosenblatt.*
CC Number 283014
Information available Full accounts were on file at the Charity Commission.

General This trust mainly supports Jewish organisations though it has also given a few small grants to medical and welfare charities. In 2000/01 it had assets of £803,000, an income of £41,000 and made 25 grants totalling £73,000.

Of grants made in the year, 17 were for £1,000 or more. By far the largest donation was £21,000 to United Synagogue. Other beneficiaries included Yesodey Hatorah Schools (£6,200), Norwood Ltd (£6,000), Institute of Cancer Research (£5,000), World Jewish Relief Fund (£4,000), Gateshead Talmudical College (£3,300), British Friends of Chadash and British Friends of Laniado Hopsital (£3,000 each), British Friends of Ahuut Ami (£1,500), Friends of Bobov (£1,000), Woodstock Sinclair Trust (£500) and Institute for Special Children (£100).

Applications In writing to the correspondent.

The Schreib Trust

Jewish, general

£2.1 million (1999/2000)
Beneficial area UK.

147 Stamford Haill, London N16 5LG
Correspondent Mrs R Niederman, Trustee
Trustees *Mrs I Schreiber; J Schreiber; A Green; Mrs R Niederman.*
CC Number 275240
Information available Accounts were on file at the Charity Commission, but without a list of grants or a full narrative report.

General It is difficult to glean an enormous amount of information about this trust's grant-giving policies as only brief accounts were on file at the Charity Commission. Although the trust's objects are general, it lists its particular priorities as relief of poverty and advancement of religious education. In practice, the trust may only support Jewish organisations.

The trust's assets totalled £2.8 million in 1999/2000 and income for the year was £900,000, including £318,000 from Gift Aid. The trust made grants totalling £2.1 million (£499,000 in 1998/99), although it is not known who received the money or what size the grants were.

Applications In writing to the correspondent.

The Schreiber Charitable Trust

Jewish

£97,000 (2000/01)
Beneficial area UK.

PO Box 35547, The Exchange, 4 Brent Cross Gardens, London NW4 3WH
Correspondent G S Morris, Trustee
Trustees *Graham S Morris; David A Schreiber; Mrs Sara Schreiber.*
CC Number 264735
Information available Full accounts were on file at the Charity Commission.

General In 2000/01 the trust had assets of £2.4 million, which generated an income of £141,000. Grants totalling

£97,000 were made to 15 organisations, of which 7 were also supported in the previous year.

The largest grant was £23,000 to Friends of Rabbinical College Kol Torah. Other large donations were £7,500 to Gateshead Talmudical College, £7,000 each to Aish Hatorah UK and Conference of European Rabbis, £6,100 to Friends of Ohr Somayach and £5,470 to Friends of Ohr Torah Limited. Smaller grants went to British Friends of Israel Museums (£3,700), British Friends of Gesher (£3,500), Finchley Road Synagogue (£2,700), Yesodeh Hatorah Grammar School (£1,700), Society of Friends of the Torah (£1,300) with £1,000 each to Beth Hayeled, Collel Chibath Yerushalayim and Friends of the Bikur Cholim Hospital.

Applications The trust states that all funds are currently committed. No applications are therefore considered or replied to.

The Scouloudi Foundation

General

£209,000 (2001/02)
Beneficial area UK charities working domestically or overseas.

c/o Haysmacintyre, Southampton House, 317 High Holborn, London WC1V 7NL

Tel. 020 7969 5500 **Fax** 020 7969 5529

Correspondent The Administrators

Trustees *Miss Sarah E Stowell, Chair; David J Marnham; James R Sewell.*

CC Number 205685

Information available Full accounts were provided by the trust.

General The foundation has three types of grants:

- Historical grants are made each year to the Institute of Historical Research at University of London for research and publications, to reflect the interests of the settlor, Irene Scouloudi, who was a historian
- Regular grants, generally of £1,000 each, are made to organisations on a five-year cycle
- Special grants are given towards capital projects and emergency relief as a one-off payment.

In 2001/02 the foundation had assets of £5.2 million, which generated an income of £226,000. Management and administration charges for the year were high at £22,000. Grants were made to 119 charities, totalling £209,000 and broken down as shown in the table below.

Institute of Historical Research at University of London, which received £68,000 as the historical award, also received a regular donation of £5,000. Aside from the £1,500 to British Museum, the other 92 regular donations were of £1,000 each. Recipients included Arthritis Research Campaign, Barnardo's, British and International Sailors' Society, British Records Association, Cathedral Camps, Centrepoint, Crossroads Caring for Carers, CORDA, Environment Council, Family Welfare Association, Habitat Scotland, Help the Hospices, Historical Association, London Topographical Society, Mental Health Foundation, National Art Collections Fund, NSPCC, Professional Classes Aid Council, Reed's School, Royal Commonwealth Society for the Blind, Samaritans and UK Youth.

Special, one-off grants went to 27 organisations. Merlin received £3,000 while Motability was given £1,000. All other grants were of £1,500 each, with beneficiaries including Bedfordshire and Northamptonshire Multiple Sclerosis Therapy Centre, Leukaemia Lifeline

Centre, National Centre for Young People with Epilepsy, Royal Surrey County Hospital, Shaftesbury Society, St Helena Hospice – Clacton and St Peter's Church – Powick.

Exclusions Donations are not made to individuals, and are not normally made for welfare activities of a purely local nature.

The trustees do not make loans or enter into deeds of covenant.

Applications Applications for special donations, giving full but concise details, should be sent to the administrators at the above address by 1 March for consideration in April.

Copies of the regulations and application forms for historical awards can be obtained from: The Secretary, The Scouloudi Foundation Historical Awards Committee, c/o Institute of Historical Research, University of London, Senate House, London WC1E 7HU.

Seamen's Hospital Society

Seafarers

£231,000 to organisations (2001)
Beneficial area UK.

29 King William Walk, Greenwich, London SE10 9HX

Tel. 020 8858 3696

Email shs@btconnect.com

Website www.seahospital.org.uk

Correspondent Peter Coulson, General Secretary

Trustees *Capt. S T Smith, Chair; A P J Lydekker; J C Jenkinson; J Allen; J D Guthrie; Capt. P M Hambling; P McEwan; Capt. G W S Miskin; A R Nairne; Capt. A G Russell; T Santamera; Capt. A J Speed; A F D Williams; Mr G P Ellis; Dr J F Leonard; Capt. A J R Tyrrell.*

CC Number 231724

Information available Accounts were on file at the Charity Commission.

General This trust makes grants to medical, care and welfare organisations working with seafarers and to individual seafarers and their dependants. In 2001 it had assets of £9 million and an income of £360,000. From direct charitable expenditure of £423,000, the sum of £231,000 was given to 10 organisations and £70,000 to 168 individuals.

THE SCOULOUDI FOUNDATION Grants in 2001/02					
Category	Historical	Regular	Special	Total	%
Aged	–	£7,000	–	£7,000	3
Children & youth	–	£9,000	£12,000	£21,000	10
Environment	–	£11,000	£4,500	£15,500	7
Famine relief & overseas aid	–	£5,000	£3,000	£8,000	4
Handicapped & disability	–	£17,000	£5,500	£22,500	11
Humanities	£68,000	£14,000	–	£81,000	39
Medicine & health	–	£19,000	£15,000	£34,000	16
Social welfare	–	£11,000	£3,000	£14,000	7
Welfare of armed forces & sailors	–	£6,000	–	£6,000	3
Total	£68,000	£99,000	£43,000	£209,000	100

Organisations to benefit included: Royal Alfred Seafarers' Society (£55,000); NUMAST Welfare Fund and Merchant Seamen's War Memorial Society (£25,000 each); Queen Victoria Seamen's Rest (£15,000); Royal National Mission to Deep Sea Fishermen (£12,000); International Seafarers' Centre at Great Yarmouth and Royal Merchant Navy School Foundation (£5,000 each); and Glasgow Veterans Seafarers' Association (£4,000).

The society also operates the Seafarers' Benefits Advice Line, the running costs of which came to £62,000 for the year, and makes a contribution – amounting to £17,000 for the year – to costs associated with the Dreadnought Facility at Guys & St Thomas' Hospital NHS Trust.

Applications On a form available from the correspondent.

The Searchlight Electric Charitable Trust

General

£75,000 (2000/01)

Beneficial area UK, with a preference for Manchester.

Searchlight Electric Ltd, 900 Oldham Road, Manchester M40 2BS

Tel. 0161 203 3300

Correspondent H E Hamburger, Trustee

Trustees *H E Hamburger; D M Hamburger; M E Hamburger; J S Fidler.*

CC Number 801644

Information available Full accounts were on file at the Charity Commission.

General This trust has general charitable purposes, although most grants are given to Jewish organisations. A large number of grants are made in the Manchester area.

In 2000/01 the trust had assets of £747,000, as well as holding a loan of £1.5 million from Searchlight Electric Ltd to be repaid on demand within a year. The total income for the year was £73,000, with management and administration expenses low at just £120. Grants were made totalling £75,000.

The largest grants were £30,000 to UJIA and £10,000 to OHR Yerusalem. Other large grants were £5,000 to British Friends

of Laniado Hospital, £4,900 to VHT, £2,500 each to King David Schools and Shaare Torah Yeshiva and £2,000 each to Bachad Fellowship, Lubavitch and Young Israel Synagogue – Netanya.

Beneficiaries in the Manchester area included Manchester Great and New Synagogue (£1,900), Manchester Jewish Federation (£1,000), The Hálle and Manchester Charitable Trust (£500 each) and Central Manchester Health Care (£250).

Other recipients included Cultural Centre (£1,000), Community Security Trust (£700), Guide Dogs for the Blind (£500) and Cafod and Langdon College (£250 each).

Exclusions No grants for individuals.

Applications In writing to the correspondent, but note that in the past the trustees have stated that it is their policy to only support charities already on their existing list of beneficiaries or those already known to them.

The Helene Sebba Charitable Trust

Disability, medical, Jewish

£91,000 (2000/01)

Beneficial area UK, Canada and Israel.

PO Box 326, Bedford MK40 3XU

Tel. 01234 266657

Correspondent David L Hull

Trustees *Mrs N C Klein; Mrs J C Sebba; L Sebba.*

CC Number 277245

Information available Full accounts were on file at the Charity Commission.

General The trust supports disability, medical and Jewish organisations and in the past has made grants to causes in the UK, Canada and Israel.

In 1999/2000 this trust experienced a huge increase in size when it received a legacy of over £2 million from the estate of the late Max Sebba, the founder of the trust. In 2000/01 it had assets of £2.8 million and an income of £44,000. Grants were made totalling £91,000 including the second of three grants of £43,000 to Norwood Ravenswood, towards a hydrotherapy pool.

Grants were: £15,000 each to Akim and the Ehlers-Danlos and Connective Tissue Disorders Fund; £5,000 each to the Bridge Project and Edward L Erdman Environmental Fund; £2,000 each to Sayser, Norwood Ltd and We Care 2000 – Norfolk Millennium Trust for Carers; £1,000 to AdFam – Suffolk; and £200 to Break.

Applications In writing to the correspondent.

The Seedfield Trust

Christian, relief of poverty

£103,000 (2000)

Beneficial area Worldwide.

Regent House, Heaton Lane, Stockport, Cheshire SK4 1BS

Tel. 0161 477 4750

Correspondent David Ryan, Trustee

Trustees *John Atkins; Keith Buckler; David Ryan; Revd Lionel Osborn; Janet Buckler; D Heap.*

CC Number 283463

Information available Accounts were on file at the Charity Commission.

General The trust's main objects are the furthering of Christian work and the relief of poverty.

In 2000 the trust had assets of £2.4 million and an income of £108,000. Grants totalling £103,000 were made in the year and administration costs of £17,000 were recorded.

During the year the trust made 34 grants. A number of the beneficiaries had been supported at the same or similar levels in the previous year, these included some of the recipients of the largest grants: European Christian Mission (£22,000), Dorothea Trust (£11,000) and Overseas Missionary Fellowship (£10,000). Others larger grants included those to Thana Trust (£10,000), Gideons International (£7,000), Muller Homes (£6,000), Pentecostal Child Care Association (£4,000), Operation Mobilisation (£3,000) and Cosmo Club (£2,500).

Recipients of grants of £500 or £1,000 included those to Crosslinks, Billy Graham Evangelical Association, Manchester Chinese Church, Manchester City Mission, Prison Fellowship and Wycliffe Bible Translators.

Exclusions No grants to individuals.

Applications In writing to the correspondent, for consideration by the trustees who meet twice each year. Please enclose an sae for acknowledgement.

Leslie Sell Charitable Trust

Uniformed youth groups

£148,000 (2001/02)
Beneficial area UK and worldwide.

Ground Floor Offices, 52/58 London Road, St Albans, Hertfordshire AL1 1NG
Tel. 01727 843603 **Fax** 01727 843663
Correspondent J Byrnes
Trustees *P S Sell, Chair; Mrs M R Wiltshire; A H Sell.*
CC Number 258699
Information available Accounts were provided by the trust.

General Established in 1969 by the late Leslie Baden Sell, the trust supports youth groups, mainly scouts and guides, but also community groups.

In 2001/02 the trust had an income of £178,000 and assets totalling £2.3 million. Grants were made totalling £148,000, which included modest donations to Ivinghoe Aston Village Hall, Chalton Barn and Cottesloe School, and £128,000 to scout and guide groups.

A total of 202 grants were made to scout and guide groups (including rangers, brownies and sea scouts groups) throughout the UK, with some grants to overseas guide associations. Grants to individual scout or guide groups were mostly for £500 or less, with some larger grants up to £4,000 also being given.

Applications In writing to the correspondent. Applications should include clear details of the project or purpose for which funds are required, together with an estimate of total costs and total funds raised by the group or individual for the project.

Sellata Ltd

Jewish, welfare

£75,000 (1999/2000)
Beneficial area UK.

29 Fontayne Road, London N16 7EA
Correspondent E S Benedikt, Trustee
Trustees *E S Benedikt; Mrs N Benedikt; P Benedikt.*
CC Number 285429
Information available Accounts were on file at the Charity Commission, but without a list of grants.

General The trust says it supports the advancement of religion and the relief of poverty.

In 1999/2000 the trust's assets totalled £532,000 and its income was £192,000 including £51,000 from donations received. Grants totalled £75,000.

Applications In writing to the correspondent.

This entry was not confirmed by the trust, but is correct according to information on file at the Charity Commission.

SEM Charitable Trust

Disability, general, Jewish

£110,000 (2000/01)
Beneficial area Mainly South Africa, Israel and UK.

Saffery Champness, Red Lion Street, London WC1R 4GB
Tel. 020 7841 4000
Correspondent M Cohen, Trustee
Trustees *Mrs Sarah E Radomir; Michael Cohen.*
CC Number 265831
Information available Infomation was provided by the trust.

General The trust makes grants mainly to disability-related organisations. In 2000/01 its assets totalled £776,000, it had an income of £73,000 and grants were made totalling £110,000. Grants included £17,000 to Together in Notre Dame, £10,000 each to Beth Shalon, CET, HAFAD, Kwa Zulu National Philharmonic Orchestra and £8,000 to Sea World.

Exclusions No grants to individuals.

Applications In writing to the correspondent.

This entry was not confirmed by the trust, but the information was correct according to the trust's file at the Charity Commission.

The Ayrton Senna Foundation

Children's health and education

£345,000 (1998)
Beneficial area Worldwide, with a preference for Brazil.

34–43 Russell Square, London WC2B 5HA
Correspondent Julian Jakobi, Trustee
Trustees *Viviane Lalli, President; Milton Guerado Theodoro da Silva; Neyde Joanna Senna da Silva; Leonardo Senna da Silva; Fabio da Silva Machado; Christopher Bliss; Julian Jakobi.*
CC Number 1041759
Information available Accounts were on file at the Charity Commission.

General The trust was established in 1994 by the father of the late Ayrton Senna, in memory of his son, the racing driver. The trust was given the whole issued share capital of Ayrton Senna Foundation Ltd, a company set up to license the continued use of the Senna trademark and copyrights.

In 2001 the trust had an income of £451,000 and a total expenditure of £292,000. Unfortunately no further details were available for this year. In 1998 it had a total income of £433,000, of which £321,000 came from copyrights. The annual report in that year noted that 'in particular, the objectives seek to provide education, healthcare and medical support for children'. To this end, nearly all the trust's giving has been directed towards the Instituto Ayrton Senna in Brazil, which received £993,000 in 1997 and £342,000 in 1998.

The only other beneficiaries in those years were the Grand Prix Mechanics Charitable Trust (£7,000 in 1997) and Cancer Bacup (£3,000 in 1998).

Exclusions No grants to individuals.

Applications In writing to the correspondent.

Servite Sisters' Charitable Trust Fund

Women, refugees

£224,000 (2001)

Beneficial area UK and Worldwide.

Parkside, Coldharbour Lane, Dorking, Surrey RH4 3BN

Tel. 01306 875756 **Fax** 01306 889339

Email m@servite.demon.co.uk

Correspondent Michael J W Ward, Secretary

Trustees *Sister Joyce Mary Fryer OSM; Sister Ruth Campbell OSM; Sister Eugenia Geraghty OSM; Sister Catherine Ryan OSM.*

CC Number 241434

Information available A grants list and information for applicants was provided by the trust.

General This trust is run by the English province of the international religious order of The Servants of Mary (known as Servites). The province has 63 members, most of whom have given their working lives to the charitable activities of the order. When any of the members carry out any work independently of the charity, any earnings are covenanted to the charity.

The trust was set up in 1993 and makes grants principally to support:

- activities intended primarily to help women who are marginalised physically, spiritually or morally
- activities intended to alleviate the distress of refugees and other disadvantaged migrants.

The funds may also be used to help:

- the Servite family in the developing world/Eastern Europe
- students and youth groups the Servites are associated with.

Grants are one-off and average £1,000. In 2000/01 grants totalled £224,000 of which £116,000 was given in the UK.

UK grants included £2,000 to a women's alcoholism self-help project, £1,800 for English classes for Sudanese immigrant students, £1,500 each for a drama project by young immigrants during National Refugee Week and for support for mothers whose children have been removed, and £1,000 for life skill courses for Asian women who have experienced domestic violence.

Overseas grants included £2,000 each towards an asylum seekers support worker at a Hamburg day centre and for women's literacy and numeracy work in Tanzania, £1,700 each towards baking and other income-generating equipment for women in South Africa and for a diocesan women's development programme in India, and £1,000 for a fishing boat engine for a women's income-generation group in Uganda.

Exclusions No grants to individuals. No grants towards building projects and no recurring grants.

Applications In writing to the correspondent with brief details of your organisation, project and needs.

The Seven Fifty Trust

Christian

£101,000 (2000/01)

Beneficial area UK and worldwide.

All Saints Vicarage, Chapel Green, Crowborough, East Sussex TN6 1ED

Tel. 01892 667384

Correspondent Revd Andrew C J Cornes, Trustee

Trustees *Revd Andrew C J Cornes; Katherine E Cornes; Peter N Collier; Susan M Collier.*

CC Number 298886

Information available Full accounts were on file at the Charity Commission.

General This trust is for the advancement of the Christian religion in the UK and throughout the world.

In 2000/01 the trust had assets of £1.4 million and an income of £65,000, including £41,000 in donations received from individuals. Grants were made totalling £101,000, mostly to organisations that were also supported in the previous year.

A large grant of £42,000 was given to the Faith in the Future fund of All Saints Church – Crowbridge, which received another grant of £7,600. The other sizeable grant given was £21,000 to Care for the Family.

Other beneficiaries included St Mathew's Fulham (£3,800), Universities and Colleges Christian Fellowship (£2,800), Coalition for Christian Outreach (£2,600), Langham Trust (£2,400), Tearfund (£2,200), International Fellowship of Evangelical Students (£2,000), Church Mission Society (£1,900), Evangelical Literature Trust (£1,500) and Christian Solidarity Worldwide (£500).

Exclusions No support for unsolicited requests.

Applications It should be noted that the trust's funds are fully committed and unsolicited requests are not entertained. No reply is sent unless an sae is included with the application, but even then the reply will only say that the trust does not respond to unsolicited applications.

The Severn Trent Water Charitable Trust

Relief of poverty, money advice, debt counselling

£320,000 designated to organisations (2001/02)

Beneficial area The area covered by the Severn Trent Water Ltd, which stretches from Wales to east Leicestershire and from the Humber estuary down to the Bristol Channel.

Emmanuel Court, 12–14 Mill Street, Sutton Coldfield, West Midlands B72 1TJ

Tel. 0121 355 7766 **Fax** 0121 354 8485

Email office@sttf.org.uk

Website www.sttf.org.uk

Correspondent S Braley, Director

Trustees *Dr Derek W Harris, Chair; John R A Crabtree; Mrs L Pusey; Mrs Edna Sadler; Roy Simpson; Mrs Mary Milton; Mrs Sheila Barrow; Andrew D Peet.*

CC Number 1064005

Information available Information was provided by the trust.

General The trust makes one-off grants to give immediate and direct help to individuals and grants to organisations to facilitate and develop money advice.

221

The trust was established by Severn Trent Water Ltd in 1997 with £2 million to help those in financial need or hardship meet the cost of water bills. It will also help with other household costs if it can be demonstrated that it will help towards future financial stability or make a significant improvement to the recipient's circumstances.

Grants are given to organisations in the area to improve or expand money advice/debt counselling to eligible people. The organisation must be able to demonstrate that a project is likely to benefit customers of Severn Trent Water Ltd.

Grants are available for both revenue and/or capital expenditure and can be for up to three years. Organisations seeking revenue funding of more than one year must be able to prove that the project will be able to continue to achieve its objectives and deliver a quality service with reduced funding. The continuation of funding beyond one year will always be subject to satisfactory project performance and availability of funding. Recipients will be required to report on the progress of the project. The funding will be made quarterly in advance. Capital purchases must normally be made within three months of the grant award.

All recipient organisations will be required to provide an end of year report detailing project achievements. The trust may require the provision of further information to help publicise the work of the trust.

In 2001/02 the trust had an income of £2.7 million and a total expenditure of £2.3 million, of which £1.9 million designated to individuals. A further £320,000 was designated to organisations for money advice/debt counselling services.

Applications for small capital grants e.g. training aids/computer equipment can be submitted up to a maximum of £1,500.

Exclusions People who do not have a liability to pay water charges to Severn Trent Water Ltd.

Applications On a form available from advice agencies or direct from the trust at a freepost address: Severn Trent Trust Fund, FREEPOST MID 16999, Sutton Coldfield B72 1BR. Further details can be found on the website.

The Shanti Charitable Trust

General, Christian, international development

£81,000 (2000/01)
Beneficial area UK, with preference for West Yorkshire and developing countries.

53 Kirkgate, Silsden, Keighley, West Yorkshire BD20 0AQ
Tel. 01535 653094
Correspondent J E Brown
Trustees *Miss J B Gill; T F X Parr; R K Hyett.*
CC Number 1064813
Information available Accounts were on file at the Charity Commission.

General This trust's main interest has previously been in supporting a certain charity working in Nepal, and this preference appeared to continue in 2000/01, with a grant of £50,000 to International Nepal Fellowship. The trust states that most of the beneficiaries are those which the trustees already have links with and this priority also influences them in giving to local branches of national organisations.

In 2000/01 the trust had assets of £213,000 and an income of £54,500, mainly from donations. Grants were made to ten organisations, including International Nepal Fellowship, totalling £80,500.

The other nine beneficiaries during the year were Sue Ryder Foundation, Tear Fund, All Nations Christian College and CBRS (£5,000 each), Marie Curie Cancer Care, The Corinthian Trust and St John's Church (£3,000 each), Foundation for Conductive Education (£1,000) and The Gate Christian Outreach (£500).

Exclusions No grants to gap year students, or political or animal welfare causes.

Applications In writing to the correspondent. Please note, most beneficiaries are those the trustees already has contact with.

The Linley Shaw Foundation

Conservation

£60,000 (2000)
Beneficial area UK.

National Westminster Bank plc, Natwest Private Banking, 153 Preston Road, Brighton BN1 6BD
Tel. 01273 545035 **Fax** 01273 545075
Correspondent The Trust Section
Trustees *National Westminster Bank plc.*
CC Number 1034051
Information available Non-financial information was provided by the trust.

General The trust supports charities working to conserve, preserve and restore the natural beauty of the UK countryside for the public benefit.

Generally the trust prefers to support a specific project, rather than give money for general use. In his will, Linley Shaw placed particular emphasis on those charities which organise voluntary workers to achieve the objects of the trust. This may be taken into account when considering applications. Grants can be given towards any aspect of a project. Previous examples include the cost of tools, management surveys and assistance with the cost of land purchase.

In 2000 it had an income of £97,000 and gave grants totalled £60,000. The largest grants were to British Trust for Conservation Volunteers (£6,600) and £5,000 each to Carfare Winnowed, Trees for Life, Wildfowl and Wetlands Trust, West Country Rivers and Worcestershire Wildlife Trust.

Exclusions No grants to non-charitable organisations, or to organisations whose aims or objects do not include conservation, preservation or restoration of the natural beauty of the UK countryside, even if the purpose of the grant would be eligible. No grants to individuals.

Applications In writing to the correspondent. All material will be photocopied by the trust so please avoid sending 'bound' copies of reports etc. Evidence of aims and objectives are needed, usually in the forms of accounts, annual reports or leaflets, which cannot be returned. Applications are considered in February/early March and should be received by December/early January.

The Patricia and Donald Shepherd Trust

General

£68,000 to organisations
(2000/01)

Beneficial area Worldwide, particularly the north of England.

PO Box 10, York YO1 1XU

Correspondent Mrs Patricia Shepherd, Trustee

Trustees *Mrs P Shepherd; Mrs J L Robertson; Patrick M Shepherd; D R Reaston; I O Robertson; Mrs C M Shepherd.*

CC Number 272948

Information available Full accounts were provided by the trust.

General The trust makes grants through charitable organisations to benefit people in need and society in general. There is a preference for supporting charities in the north of England and Scotland, or those connected with the trustees, particularly those involving young people.

In 2000/01 it had assets of £515,000 generating an income of £98,000. The trust made 211 grants during the year totalling £71,000, including £3,000 to individuals

Just seven organisations received £1,000 or over. These were St Leonard's Hospice, Macmillan Cancer Relief and Yorkshire Air Museum (£5,000 each), York Archaeological Trust (£2,800), St Gemma's Hospice (£2,000) and York Early Music Festival and NCH Action for Children (£1,000 each). All but two of the remaining grants were for £500 or less.

Other beneficiaries included Dial A Ride, Catholic Youth Services, Dermatrust, Caring for Life, Books Abroad, Swaledale Festival, The Ready Steady Groves Club, Filey Sea Cadets, National Playing Fields Association, Yorkshire Agoonoree, Camphill Village Trust, York Women's Aid, Durham Victim Support Scheme, York Scout Activity Centre, St Dunstan's, Stockton Speech After Stroke Support Group, Sheffield Association for People with Cerebral Palsy, Botton Village Appeal Fund and The Missing Persons Helpline.

Applications In writing to the correspondent.

The David Shepherd Wildlife Foundation

Conservation of endangered mammals

£358,000 (2000/01)

Beneficial area Africa and Asia.

61 Smithbrook Kilns, Cranleigh, Surrey GU8 6JJ

Tel. 01483 272323 **Fax** 01483 272427

Email dswf@davidshepherd.org

Website www.davidshepherd.org

Correspondent Ms Melanie Shepherd, Director

Trustees *Bruce Norris, Chair; Peter Giblin; David Gower; Avril Shepherd; Nigel Colne; Nigel Keen.*

CC Number 289646

Information available Information was available on the foundation's website.

General This foundation was established in 1984 by the internationally renowned wildlife artist to increase public awareness and funds for wildlife conservation both in this country and overseas. The objectives are the conservation and preservation for the public benefit of flora and fauna landscapes and other features of the environment in any part of the world of importance to the heritage of mankind, with current emphasis on the survival of tigers, elephants, rhinos and other endangered mammals in the wild.

The foundation's website states: 'DSWF is a UK-based organisation, benefiting from the active support of leading wildlife experts around the world and many celebrities. It publishes bi-annual editions of its magazine 'Wildlife Matters', and raises funds through countrywide 'David Shepherd' chat shows, exhibitions and other events, membership, appeals, corporate sponsorship, legacies, adoptions and the DSWF Trading Company which offers a wide variety of David Shepherd merchandise.'

In 2000/01 the foundation had an income of £733,000 and a total expenditure of £586,000. Grants were made to 23 projects totalling £358,000.

The largest grants were £31,000 to Save the Rhino – Namibia for field equipment for anti-poaching, monitoring and tracking rhinos and desert elephants, and

£30,000 each to The Prakratik Society, Ranthambhore – India to provide healthcare, education and alternative farming techniques.

A grant of £30,000 was made through the foundation by Maurice Laing Foundation to Wildlife Trust of India for life insurance for Indian forest staff.

Other large grants included £27,000 to Lusaka Agreement Task Force (LAFT) for vehicles, other equipment, undercover operations and training, £25,000 to Khao Yai Project and Border Patrol Training Programme – Thailand, for training, equipment and a community outreach project creating alternative income sources in the area around the park, £24,000 to Anti-poaching and Investigations – Zambia towards undercover operations, and work with regional enforcement agencies, in the fight against wildlife criminals, and £20,000 each to Asian Conservation Awareness Programme for a campaign to stop the trade in body parts of endangered animals and The Sunderbans Tiger Project – India to provide training and basic anti-poaching kits to the team of 400 forest rangers.

Smaller grants included those to Painted Dog Research Project – Zambia for an educational project (£15,000), Snow Leopard Project – Mongolia for research, monitoring and community development programmes in the remote Altai Mountains and the Gobi Desert (£11,000), Asian Elephant Conservation Project – India for undercover operations investigating the illegal ivory trade (£10,000) and Orag Wildlife Sanctuary – India for equipment and supplies (£8,400).

Exclusions Applications for grants must be related to the conservation of the world's major endangered mammals and to field projects.

Applications In writing to the correspondent.

The Bassil Shippam and Alsford Trust

Older people, health, education, Christian

£209,000 (1998/99)

Beneficial area UK with a preference for West Sussex; international.

Messrs Thomas Eggar, The Corn Exchange, Bassins Lane, Chichester, West Sussex PO19 1GE

Tel. 01243 786111 **Fax** 01243 775640

Correspondent C W Doman, Trustee Administrator

Trustees J H S Shippam; C W Doman; D S Olby; S W Young; Mrs M Hanwell; R Tayler; Mrs S Trayler.

CC Number 256996

Information available Full accounts were on file at the Charity Commission.

General This is basically a Christian trust and the trustees mainly support charities active in the fields of care for older people, health, education and religion. Many of the organisations supported are in West Sussex.

In 1998/99 the trust had assets of £4.2 million, and received investment income of £179,000, as well as donations totalling £76,000 from Mrs D L Alsford deceased (£2.6 million in 1997/98).

Grants totalled £209,000, of which £12,000 was paid to five regular beneficiaries which receive several payments over the year by standing order. These were Outset Youth Action South West Sussex (£5,000 in total), West Sussex County Council Voluntary Fund (£2,200), Chichester District Council for the Elderly (£1,800), Shippams Retirement Association (£1,200) and West Sussex Probation Service and Social Skills Fund (£1,500 each).

A further 175 grants were made, with at least 20 going to individuals. Most of the grants ranged from £100 to £500. By far the largest grant was £50,000 to Lodge Hill Residential Care. Other larger grants included £15,000 each to Christian Youth Enterprises Sailing Centre Ltd and British Luffce Parents and Friends Association and £10,000 to St Anthony's School.

Other grants were in the range of £50 to £5,000. A wide variety of organisations were supported, with recipients including St Wilfred's Hospice, Chichester Eventide Housing Association, West Sussex Association for the Blind, Distressed Gentlefolk's Association, Sussex Autistic Society, Church Pastoral Aid Society, Raleigh International and Streatham Youth Centre.

Applications In writing to the correspondent. Applications are considered in May and November.

The Shipwrights Company Charitable Fund

Maritime or waterborne connected charities

£105,000 to organisations (2001/02)

Beneficial area UK.

Worshipful Company of Shipwrights, Ironmongers' Hall, Barbican, London EC2Y 8AA

Tel. 020 7606 2376 **Fax** 020 7600 8117

Email clerk@shipwrights.co.uk

Website www.shipwrights.co.uk

Correspondent Capt. R F Channon

Trustees The Wardens of the Shipwrights' Company.

CC Number 262043

Information available Information for this entry was provided by the trust.

General The trust supports youth organisations, working mostly with the maritime industry. As part of the Worshipful Company of Shipwrights, it holds a particular interest in work around the City of London. Young people are also directly supported to attend sail training and outward activity courses which they would not otherwise be able to afford, on nomination of a member of the livery company.

In 2001/02 the fund had assets of £1.5 million. Total income was £161,000, including £94,000 from donations received. After high administration charges totalling 25% of the income (£41,000), grants totalling £132,000 were broken down as follows:

general charitable donations	£64,000
outdoor activity bursaries	£27,000
special donations	£41,000

Two major donations were made during the year, from income that had been left unspent in previous years. George Green's School received £28,000 towards a minibus with wheelchair hoisting and securing facilities while Jubilee Sailing Trust received £20,000 to employ a ships' carpenter on the Lord Nelson and Tenacious for one year.

Under the heading 'general charitable donations', 25 regular grants were made during the year, including 7 of less than £500. Beneficiaries included City of London Unit Sea Cadet Corps for HMS Belfast, Fairbridge West (Bristol) and Fairbridge West Midlands (Birmingham), Jubilee Sailing Trust, King George's Fund for Sailors, Missions to Seafarers, Ocean Youth Club Northern Ireland, Royal Alfred Seafarers Society, Royal National Mission to Deep Sea Fishermen, STA and St Paul's Cathedral for a refurbishment project.

Responsive grants were made to 41 organisations, including 6 grants of less than £500. Amongst those supported were 15 sea cadet units, including those in Arbroath for a minibus, Filey for an outboard engine, Folkestone for headquarters maintenance, Inverness for berths in TS Royalist, Lytham St Anne's for a topper boat, Portrush to repair damage caused by vandals, Scarborough for running costs and Sheffield for a canoe. Sea scout groups in Lochgoilhead, Reading, South Shields and Totnes were also supported for boats and dinghies. Other beneficiaries included Island Trust for sail training, Hertfordshire Scouts Canoeing Section, Meridian Trust – Portsmouth for a new yacht, National Association of Clubs for Young People for a 100-mile canoe test, Pendle Duke of Edinburgh's Award for a safety boat, Royal Albert Dock Trust for a rowing coach and the church of St Lawrence Jewry for a new organ.

The outdoor activity bursaries were made to 43 individuals.

Exclusions Any application without a clear maritime connection. Outdoor activities bursaries are awarded only to young people sponsored by liverymen in response to an annual invitation.

Applications In writing to the correspondent. Applications are considered in February, June and November.

The Charles Shorto Charitable Trust

General

£686,000 (2000/01)

Beneficial area UK.

Blackhams, King Edward House, 135a New Street, Birmingham B5 4HG

Tel. 0121 643 7070

Correspondent T J J Baxter

Trustees *Joseph A V Blackham; Brian M Dent.*

CC Number 1069995

Information available Full accounts were on file at the Charity Commission.

General This trust was established under the will of Edward Herbert Charles Shorto with general charitable purposes. Whilst welcoming applications, the trustees also like to identify causes that they know Charles Shorto had an interest in.

In 2000/01 the trust had assets of £4.1 million, which generated an income of £198,000. Grants were made to 16 organisations totalling £686,000. Management and administration expenses were very high at £71,000, including £50,000 in legal fees.

Rugby School Charitable Trust received £315,000 for a new organ at the school where Charles Shorto was a pupil.

Optimum received two large grants. The Wharf Project in Coventry received £270,000 to acquire premises on the canal system to allow access and work experience to people who are disadvantaged and their carers, while £7,000 was given towards fixtures and fittings at Conner Cottage – Sea Paling.

Other grants ranged from £1,000 to £33,000 and went to Cumnor PCC (£33,000), League of Friends – Budleigh Salterton (£15,000), Oxford Youth Works (£14,000), Usk House (£9,000), Balnain House and Catherdine PCC (£5,000), Age Concern – Budleigh Salterton (£4,600), Bicton Church (£2,000) with £1,000 each to Special Children of Gwyed and Ynys Mon, Ymdeth Megan and Trevor Griffiths Trust, Tralllong Church, Emmbrook Village Hall, Guide Dogs for the Blind and St Basils.

Applications In writing to the correspondent at any time.

L H Silver Charitable Trust

Jewish, general

£150,000 (2000/01)

Beneficial area UK, but mostly West Yorkshire

Wilson Braithwaite Scholey, 21–27 St Paul's Street, Leeds LS1 2ER

Tel. 0113 244 5451 **Fax** 0113 242 6308

Correspondent I J Fraser, Trustee

Trustees *Leslie H Silver; Mark S Silver; Ian J Fraser.*

CC Number 1007599

Information available Full accounts were provided by the trust.

General This trust principally supports Jewish-based charities and appeal funds launched in the West Yorkshire area.

The trustees' report for 2000/01 stated that major donations have been made to educational institutions and Jewish charities. Most of the smaller donations were made to charities and appeal funds operating in the Leeds area.

In 2000/01 the trust had assets of £763,000 generating an income of £49,000. After administrative costs of only £1,400, grants totalling £150,000 went to 20 organisations.

The largest grants were £50,000 to United Jewish Israel Appeal and £38,000 to Imperial Cancer Research, both of which were supported in the previous year. Other beneficiaries included Brodetsky Primary School and West Yorkshire Playhouse (£10,000 each), Beth Shalom and Yorkshire Women of the Century Project (£5,000 each), Leeds Judean Club for Boys and Girls (£4,000), Leeds Wizo Council (£3,000), Commmunity Security trust (£2,500), Emmaus and Leeds Education 2000 (£2,000 each), Variety Club Children's Charity Ltd (£1,500), Giggleswick School – Settle (£1,000) and Leeds Jewish Welfare Board (£600).

Exclusions No grants to individuals or students.

Applications The trustees state that 'the recipients of donations are restricted almost exclusively to the concerns in which the trustees take a personal interest and that unsolicited requests from other sources, although considered by the trustees, are rejected almost invariably'.

The Simpson Education & Conservation Trust

Environmental conservation, with a preference for the neotropics (South America).

£72,000 (2000/01)

Beneficial area UK and overseas, with a preference for the neotropics (South America)

Honeysuckle Cottage, Tidenham Chase, Chepstow, Gwent NP16 7JW

Tel. 01291 689423 **Fax** 01291 689803

Correspondent N Simpson, Acting Chair

Trustees *Dr R N F Simpson, Chair; Prof. D M Broom; Dr J M Lock; Prof. S Chang; Dr K A Simpson.*

CC Number 1069695

Information available Full and detailed accounts were on file at the Charity Commission.

General Established in 1998, the trust produced a detailed annual report for 1998/99 giving a full description of its activities. Its main objectives were listed as follows:

a) the advancement of education in the UK and overseas, including medical and scientific research

b) the conservation and protection of the natural environment and endangered species of plants and animals with special emphasis on the protection of forests and endangered avifauna in the neotropics (South America).

The trust receives its income from Gift Aid donations, which totalled £78,000 in 2001/02. Its priority for that year was to support the Jocotoco Conservation Foundation (JCF) in Equador. This charity is dedicated to the conservation of endangered special birds through the acquisition of forest habitat. The chair of this trust, an expert in ornithology and conservation, is also on the board of trustees for Jocotoco Conservation Foundation.

In 2001/02 JCF received a grant of $80,000 (about £56,000) from the trust. Other grants were: $10,000 (about £7,000) to Association Armonia for a conservation project in Bolivia; £3,000 each to World Lands Trust towards a training and education project to encourage sustainable use of tropical forests in Costa Rica and BirdLife International; and £1,000 each to Caius College Cambridge University, Sound Seekers – Royal Commonwealth Institute for the Deaf and Treloar Trust.

Exclusions No grants to individuals.

Applications In writing to the correspondent. The day-to-day activities of this trust are carried out by e-mail, telephone and circulation of documents, since the trustees do not all live in the UK.

Sinclair Charitable Trust

Jewish learning, welfare
£149,000 (2000)
Beneficial area UK.

Apect Gate, 166 College Road, London HA1 1BH

Correspondent Dr M J Sinclair, Trustee

Trustees *Dr M J Sinclair; Mrs P K Sinclair; E J Gold.*

CC Number 289433

Information available Accounts were on file at the Charity Commission, but without a list of grants.

General The objects of the trust are to support organisations concerned principally, although not necessarily exclusively, with Jewish learning and welfare. Most of the income derives from substantial donations received from a company controlled by two of the trustees.

In 2000 the trust had an income of £190,000, of which £760 was generated from the assets of £20,000. Grants were made totalling £149,000, although details of the beneficiaries and the types of size of grants made were not included in the accounts.

The management and administration charges were high at £37,000, the equivalent of nearly 20% of the total income for the year. These included wages of a paid member of staff, £1,900 for travel expenses (£12,000 in previous year) and £8,000 for advertising. Given a trustee is the correspondent, and the size of the trust, it was unclear from the accounts what benefits these payments bought.

Applications In writing to the correspondent.

The John Slater Foundation

Medical, animal welfare, general
£170,000 (1999/2000)
Beneficial area UK, with a preference for the north west of England especially West Lancashire.

HSBC Trust Services, Norwich House, Nelson Gate, Commercial Road, Southampton SO15 1GX

Tel. 023 8072 2230

Correspondent Colin Bould

Trustees *HSBC Trust Co. Ltd.*

CC Number 231145

Information available Full accounts were on file at the Charity Commission.

General The trust gives grants for £1,000 to £5,000 to a range of organisations, particularly those working in the fields of medicine or animal welfare.

In 1999/2000 grants totalled £170,000. Beneficiaries included Bispham Parish Church, Blackpool and Fylde Society for the Blind, Blue Cross Hospital, Duchess of York Hospital for Babies and Wildlife Hospital Trust, Guide Dogs for the Blind, Liverpool School of Tropical Medicine, RNLI and Samaritans.

Exclusions No grants to individuals.

Applications Applications are considered twice a year on 1 May and 1 November.

Rita and David Slowe Charitable Trust

General
£74,000 (2000/01)
Beneficial area UK and overseas.

32 Hampstead High Street, London NW3 1JQ

Correspondent R L Slowe, Trustee

Trustees *R L Slowe; Ms E H Slowe; J L Slowe; G Weinberg.*

CC Number 1048209

Information available Accounts were on file at the Charity Commission, but

without a full description of the trust's grant-making policy.

General The trust makes grants to a range of registered charities. In 2000/01 its assets totalled £364,000 and its income was £78,000. Grants totalling £74,000, included £20,000 to Motivation Charitable Trust, £5,000 to Africa Equipment for Schools and £3,000 to Books Abroad.

Applications In writing to the correspondent.

The SMB Trust

Christian, general
£176,000 (2001/02)
Beneficial area UK and overseas.

15 Wilman Rd, Tunbridge Wells, Kent TN4 9AJ

Tel. 01892 537301

Correspondent Mrs B M O'Driscoll, Trustee

Trustees *Miss K Wood; E D Anstead; P J Stanford; Mrs B O'Driscoll; J A Anstead.*

CC Number 263814

Information available Full accounts were on file at the Charity Commission.

General In 2001/02 the trust had assets of £5.1 million and an income of £227,000. The chairman's report for this trust states: 'The trustees have continued to give regular support to a number of core charities covering a wide spectrum of needs'. One-off appeals are also considered.

During the year the trust gave 154 grants totalling £176,000, of which 53 were recurrent. Grants ranged from £250 to £4,000, but were mainly of £1,000. The London City Mission, as it appears to do every year, received one of the largest grants (£4,000). Other larger grants were to Pilgrims Homes (£4,000) and Salvation Army (£3,000).

Grants also went to Christian causes and to health and social welfare organisations, recipients of £1,000 or more included British Red Cross, Christian Aid, Church Army, Dentaid, Gideons International, Leprosy Mission, MENCAP and Oasis Trust.

Some local organisations also received grants, for example Liverpool City Mission, Notting Hill Housing Trust, Salvation Army – Swansea and Tonbridge Wells Mental Health Resource Ltd.

Exclusions Grants to individuals are not normally considered.

Applications In writing to the correspondent. Trustees meet quarterly.

SMILES (Slimmers Making it a Little Easier for Someone)

Children, young people

£126,000 (2000/01)

Beneficial area UK.

c/o Slimming World, Clover Nook Industrial Estate, Clover Nook Road, Derbyshire DE55 4RF

Correspondent D Rathbone, Trustee

Trustees *Margaret Whittaker; Ronald Whittaker; David Rathbone.*

CC Number 1061429

Information available Accounts were on file at the Charity Commission.

General This trust was established in March 1997. In 2000/01 it had assets of £86,000 and an income of £72,000 mostly from donations. Grants were made to two organisations totalling £126,000. Beneficiaries were: RSPCA (£106,000); and Barnardos (£20,000).

Applications In writing to the correspondent.

The Albert & Florence Smith Memorial Trust

Social welfare

£286,000 (2000/01)

Beneficial area UK, with a strong emphasis on Essex.

Messrs Tolhurst Fisher, Marlborough House, Victoria Road South, Chelmsford, Essex CM1 1LN

Tel. 01245 216123

Correspondent Mrs A Mason, Secretary

Trustees *W J Tolhurst, Chair; P J Tolhurst; E C Watson.*

CC Number 259917

Information available Accounts were provided by the trust.

General The trust supports nominated charities on an annual basis, with the balance given to local charities in Essex. It has now been decided to concentrate its giving as follows:

- charities nominated by the original benefactors
- overseas projects jointly with CAFOD and Raleigh International
- Essex-based (only) church projects
- other Essex-related projects.

There is a fundamental criterion that any funding made must be matched by other funding or contributions.

In 2000/01 the trust had assets of £4.3 million. The income was £352,000 and grants totalled £286,000, up from £123,000 in the previous year.

Grants of £1,000 or more went to 40 organisations and these were listed in the accounts. Of these, 16 had received a grant in the previous year. By far the largest was £100,000 to the Farleigh Hospice. Other larger grants were £25,000 to Raleigh International and £11,000 to Langham Support.

The remaining listed grants were for £5,000 or less and included those to Alpha Community, Brentwood United Reformed Church, Chelmsford Cathedral, Essex Association of Boys Clubs, Maldon United Reformed Church, NSPCC, Royal British Legion, RNIB, RNLI, Salvation Army and Scope.

Exclusions No grants to individuals.

Applications In writing to the correspondent.

The Leslie Smith Foundation

General

£154,000 (2000/01)

Beneficial area UK.

The Old Coach House, Sunnyside, Bergh Apton, Norwich NR15 1DD

Correspondent M D Willcox, Trustee

Trustees *M D Willcox; E A Rose; H L Young Jones.*

CC Number 250030

Information available Full accounts were provided by the trust.

General In 2000/01 the trust had assets of £3.4 million and an unusually high income of £867,000, largely due to the receipt of an exceptional dividend on its holding in an unlisted company. Grants totalled £154,000.

The foundation, which regularly reviews its grant–making policy, is currently focusing on:

- children's hospices and bereavement counselling for children
- education
- matrimonial counselling
- children with disabilities
- welfare of retired clergy.

The foundation receives over 1,000 applications each year. A total of 21 grants were made, 14 of which were supported in the previous year.

By far the largest grants were £25,000 to Music for Living, £20,000 to Greenford Willow Tree Lions Club and £10,000 each to Gaddum Centre, Kings College Chapel Foundation, Paul Strickland Scanner Centre Appeal, Joseph Weld Hospice, Wessex Children's Hospice Trust and Wiltshire Community Foundation.

Other beneficiaries of smaller grants included Relate (£6,000), Cystic Fibrosis Holiday Fund for Children, Royal British Legion and Theatre Royal Training School (£5,000 each), Norfolk Accident Rescue Service and Imperial Cancer Research Fund (£1,000 each) and Pettaugh PCC (£500).

Exclusions Grants are given to registered charities only; no grants are available to individuals.

Applications In writing to the correspondent. Only successful applications are acknowledged.

The N Smith Charitable Trust

General

£96,000 (2000/01)

Beneficial area Worldwide.

Bullock Worthington & Jackson, 1 Booth Street, Manchester M2 2HA

Tel. 0161 833 9771 **Fax** 0161 832 0489

Email bulworjac@compuserve.com

Website www.bulworjac.co.uk

Correspondent Anne E Merricks

Trustees *T R Kendal; P R Green; J H Williams-Rigby; G Wardle.*

CC Number 276660

Information available Accounts were on file at the Charity Commission, but without a narrative description of its grantmaking policy.

General In 2000/01 the trust had assets of £3.7 million. The income was £123,000, with management and administration costs totalling £23,000. Grants were made to 157 organisations totalling £96,000, as follows:

Health and medical research charities – 41 grants totalling £26,000
There were 10 grants of £1,000 each and 31 grants of £500 each. Beneficiaries included Action Research, British Neurological Research Trust, Dermatrust, Headfirst, The Migration Trust, Prostate Cancer Appeal and WellBeing.

Poverty and social work – 60 grants totalling £32,000
These were for £500 or £750 each. Recipients included The Aidis Trust, Children 1st, Deaf Education Through Listening and Hearing, Hospital Radio Bedside, Salford Methodist Centre, Strathfoyle Women's Activity Group and Victim Support – London.

Environmental work and animals – 10 grants totalling £5,000
All these grants were for £500 each and included those to Born Free Foundation, Forest UCHAF Horse and Pony Rehabilitation, Tusk Trust, WaterAid and Wirral Urban Farm Association.

Arts – 7 grants totalling £4,500
Artline and Huntingdon Hall received £1,000 each. Five grants of £300 each were given, including those to The Art House, Opera North and Scottish Book Centre.

Overseas aid – 24 grants totalling £21,000
Grants ranged from £900 to £1,000. Recipients included Action Water, Children in Crisis, Computer Aid International, European Children's Trust, Find Your Feet, Mercy Ships, Father O'Mahony Memorial Trust, Relief Fund for Romania and Tools for Self Reliance.

Miscellaneous – 15 grants totalling £9,000
Grants ranging from £500 to £750 included those to Campus Connect, Castlegate Quay Trust, Manchester Grammar School, Norbrook Boys and Girls Club and Royal Botanic Gardens.

Exclusions Grants are only made to registered charities and not to individuals.

Applications In writing to the correspondent. The trustees met in October and March.

Philip Smith's Charitable Trust

Older people, children, welfare

£74,000 (2001)

Beneficial area UK, with a preference for Gloucestershire.

50 Broadway, Westminster, London SW1H 0BL

Tel. 020 7227 7039 **Fax** 020 7222 3480

Correspondent M Wood

Trustees *Hon. P R Smith; Mrs M Smith.*

CC Number 1003751

Information available Full accounts were on file at the Charity Commission.

General The trust makes grants to Gloucestershire-based organisations and to UK-wide charities in the fields of welfare, older people and children.

In 2001 the trust had an income of £31,000 from assets of £782,000. Grants totalled £74,000. The largest included £11,000 to North Foreland Lodge Ltd, £10,000 to Chelthenham and Gloucester College of Further Education and £5,000 to Chipping Campden School.

Applications In writing to the correspondent. The trustees meet regularly to consider grants. A lack of response can be taken to indicate that the trust does not wish to contribute to an appeal.

The Stanley Smith UK Horticultural Trust

Horticulture
£84,000 to organisations
(1998/99)

Beneficial area UK and, so far as it is charitable, outside the UK.

Cory Lodge, PO Box 365, Cambridge CB2 1HR

Tel. 01223 336299 **Fax** 01223 336278

Correspondent James Cullen, Director

Trustees *John Norton; Christopher Brickell; John Dilger; Lady Renfrew; J B E Simmons.*

CC Number 261925

Information available Full report and financial statements provided by the trustees along with a copy of Guidelines to Applicants, April 2000.

General Established by deed in 1970, the trust's objects are the advancement of horticulture. In particular the trustees have power to make grants for the following purposes:

- horticultural research
- the creation, development, preservation and maintenance of public gardens
- the promotion of the cultivation and wide distribution of plants of horticultural value/other value to mankind
- the promotion of the cultivation of new plants
- publishing books and work related to horticultural sciences.

In 1998/99 the trust's assets totalled £3.2 million and it had an income of £143,000. The director considered over 180 applications and 32 grants totalling £84,000 were made to organisations. Five scholarships totalling £39,000 were also awarded.

A full grants list was provided in the trust's annual report. Out of the general fund the largest grant of £10,000 went to the Conifer Conservation Programme operated from the Royal Botanic Garden, Edinburgh. Recipients of smaller grants included Curators of the University Parks – Oxford (£5,000), Flora for Fauna (£3,500), The Pukeiti Rhododendron Trust – New Zealand (£3,000), The Association of Garden Trusts (£2,000), The Marcher Apple Network (£1,200) and The Landscape Design Trust (£1,000).

Six grants totalling £20,000 were given out from the approved grants fund. Beneficiaries included University of York (£5,700), Chelsea Physic Garden (£4,500) and University of Bangalore – India (£2,000). All of these grants were awarded over three years.

The director continues to provide advice to actual and potential applicants, and to established projects which have already received grants. Any grant provided by the trust bears the condition that the recipient should provide within six months, or some other agreed period, a report on the use of the grant.

Exclusions Grants are not made for projects in commercial horticulture (crop production) or agriculture, nor are they made to support students taking academic or diploma courses of any kind, although educational institutions are supported.

Applications In writing to the correspondent. Detailed *Guidelines for Applicants* are available from the trust. The director is willing to give advice on how applications should be presented.

Grants are awarded twice a year, in spring and autumn. To be considered in the spring allocation, applications should reach the director before 15 February of each year; for the autumn allocation the equivalent date is 15 August. Potential recipients are advised to get their applications in early.

Solev Co Ltd

Jewish charities

£313,000 (1996/97)

Beneficial area UK

Romeo House, 160 Bridport Road, London N18 1SY

Correspondent O Tager, Trustee

Trustees *M Grosskopf; A E Perelman; R Tager.*

CC Number 254623

Information available Accounts were on file at the Charity Commission, but without a grants list.

General In 2000/01 the trust had an income of £345,000 and an expenditure of £524,000. Unfortunately further information for this year was not available.

In 1996/97 the trust had assets of £1.6 million, which generated an income of

£489,000. Grant giving was £313,000 and management and administrative costs were £10,000.

Only two donations are mentioned in the annual report: '£100,000 to the Dina Perelmam Trust Ltd, a charitable company of which Mr Perelman and Mr Grosskopf are governors; and £40,000 to Songdale Ltd, a charity of which Mr M Grosskopf is an governor.'

No grants list has been included in the accounts since 1972/73, when £14,000 was given to 52 Jewish charities. Examples then included Society of Friends of the Torah (£3,900); Finchley Road Synagogue (£2,300); NW London Talmudical College (£1,500); Yesodey Hatorah School (£700); and Gateshead Talmudical College (£400).

Applications In writing to the correspondent.

The Solo Charitable Settlement

Jewish, general

£76,000 (1998/99)

Beneficial area UK and Israel.

Rawlinson & Hunter, Eagle House, 110 Jermym Street, London SW1Y 6RH

Correspondent The Trustees

Trustees *P D Goldstein; Edna Goldstein; R S Goldstein; H Goldstein.*

CC Number 326444

Information available Accounts were on file at the Charity Commission up to 1998/99.

General The trust was established in 1983, by Peter David Goldstein. The trustees can hold the capital and income for 21 years to increase the trust's assets.

In 1998/99, the year for which most recent accounts were available, the trust had assets of £5.2 million and an income of just £103,000. Grants were made to 33 organisations totalling £76,000. Grants ranged from £50 to £18,000, although most were for £500 or under. Some organisations have previously been supported.

Beneficiaries receiving over £1,000 were Ashten Trust (£18,000), Joint Jewish Charitable Trust (£17,000), Jewish Care (£15,000), United Jewish Israel Appeal (£12,000), Children with Leukaemia and

Norwood Ravenswood (£2,500 each), Spiro Institute, Spanish and Portuguese Congregation and Sutton Synagogue (£1,000 each).

Beneficiaries receiving £500 or under included Alyn Hospital, Breakthrough Breast Cancer, Dream Come True, Group House, Leukaemia Research, Royal Academy of Arts, St Nicholas Church, WIZO and World Jewish Relief.

Applications In writing to the correspondent.

Songdale Ltd

Jewish

£163,000 (2000/01)

Beneficial area UK and Israel

6 Spring Hill, London E5 9BE

Correspondent M Grosskopf, Governor

Trustees *M Grosskopf; Mrs M Grosskopf; Y Grosskopf.*

CC Number 286075

Information available Accounts were on file at the Charity Commission.

General In 2000/01 the trust had assets of £1.5 million and an income of £242,000. Grants were made to 92 organisations totalling £163,000. Grants ranged from £20 to £44,500, although most were for under £500.

Beneficiaries receiving £1,000 or more were Cosmon Belz Limited (£44,500), Kedushas Zion and Nevey Eretz (£25,000 each), Toldos Avraham Bet Sh. (£10,500), Bnos Yroshalayim, B'H Govoha Lakewood and Yad Romoh (£7,000 each), Yeshiva Belz, Jerusalem (£6,000), C W C T and Tora Vemuma (£4,000 each), Ezras Yitchock Yisoe (£3,500), N W L Talmundical College and Yad Eliezer (£3,000 each), Ponovez Rabbi Pinter Memorial (£1,500) and New Rachmestriuke Trust (£1,000).

Grants of under £500 included those to Alexandra Institution, Belz Synagogue, Collel Yirey Hashem, Ezer Mitzion, Friends of Yeshivas Chevron, Glasgow Kollel, Keshev for Deaf, Miepi Ollelim, Mondos Shaarei, Noam Shabbos, Rambam Foundation and Yeshivas Midrash Shmuel.

Applications In writing to the correspondent.

This entry was not confirmed by the trust, but is correct according to information on file at the Charity Commission.

The South Square Trust

General

£239,000 (2000/01)
Beneficial area UK.

PO Box 67, Heathfield, East Sussex
TN21 9ZR
Tel. 01435 830778 **Fax** 01435 830778
Correspondent Mrs Nicola Chrimes,
Clerk to the Trustees
Trustees *C R Ponter; A E Woodall; W P Harriman; C P Grimwade; D B Inglis.*
CC Number 278960
Information available Accounts were provided by the trust.

General The trust was established in 1979 with shares in Christie's International. The trust now has a wide range of investments and in 2000/01 its assets totalled £3.8 million, generating an income of £188,000. After high administration costs of £46,000, grants totalled £239,000.

General donations are made to registered charities working in the fields of the arts, culture and recreation, health, social welfare, medical, disability and conservation and environment. Community facilities and services will also be considered.

The trust also gives grants to students for full-time postgraduate or undergraduate courses within the UK connected with the fine and applied arts, including drama, dance, music, but particularly related to gold and silver work. Students should be over 18 years old. Courses have to be of a practical nature. Help is given to various colleges in the form of bursary awards. A full list is available from the correspondent.

Grants are categorised by the trust as follows:

Annual donations to charities	£26,000
General donations to charities	£69,000
Students and single payment grants	£53,000
Bursaries and scholarships to schools/colleges	£91,000
Total	£239,000

Exclusions No grants given to individuals under 18 or those seeking funding for expeditions, travel, courses outside UK, short courses or courses not connected with fine and applied arts.

Applications

Registered charities
In writing to the correspondent with details about your charity, the reason for requesting funding, and enclosing a copy of your accounts. Applications are considered three times a year, in spring, summer and winter. It is advisable to telephone the correspondent for up-to-date information about the criteria for funding.

Individuals
Standard application forms are available from the correspondent. Forms are sent out between January and April only, to be returned by the end of April for consideration for the following academic year.

The W F Southall Trust

Quaker, general

£397,000 (2000/01)
Beneficial area UK and overseas, with an interest in Birmingham.

c/o Rutters Solicitors, 2 Bimport,
Shaftesbury, Dorset SP7 8AY
Tel. 01747 852377 **Fax** 01747 851989
Email southall@rutterslaw.co.uk
Correspondent Stephen T Rutter,
Secretary
Trustees *Donald Southall, Chair; Joanna Engelkamp; Claire Greaves; Mark Holtom; Daphne Maw; Christopher Southall; Annette Wallis.*
CC Number 218371
Information available Information was provided by the trust.

General This trust has general charitable purposes, with specific categories for causes in the Birmingham area and for Quaker charities. The trustees prefer to support smaller charities where the grant will make a more significant difference. Environmental and human right organisations feature strongly amongst the grants list.

In 2000/01 the trust had assets of £6.1 million and an income of £592,000. Grants were made to 80 organisations totalling £397,000, broken down as follows:

Central Committee of Society of Friends – 3 grants totalling £59,000
A substantial grant of £45,000 went to Britain Yearly Meeting. Friends World Committee for Consultant received £7,500 while Q S R & E Joint Bursaries Scheme was given £6,000.

Birmingham district – 9 grants totalling £11,000
The largest grants were £2,500 to Birmingham Rathbone, £2,000 each to City of Birmingham YMCA and Shelter for the West Midlands Centre, £1,500 to Birmingham Settlement and £1,000 to St Mary's Hospice. Other beneficiaries included Warwickshire Association of Boys Clubs (£750) and West Midlands Charitable Trusts Groups, which received three grants ranging from £20 to £25 each.

Meeting House appeals – 10 grants totalling £17,000
Beneficiaries included Derby P M Friends Meeting House (£3,000), Dabane Support Fund (£2,000), Heswell Preparative Meeting (£1,500) and Northern Friends Peace Board (£1,000).

Other Quaker charities – 16 grants totalling £91,000
This category included the largest grant during the year, £50,000 to Sibford School Appeal. Other beneficiaries included Woodbrooke (£7,500 in two grants), Quaker Social Action and South Belfast Friends Meeting (£5,000 each), Carlton Hill Leeds Friends Trust Fund (£2,500), QCEA British Committee (£2,000) and Westmorland General Meeting (£1,000).

Other charities – 45 grants (to 40 charities) totalling £51,000
Three charities were given more than one grant in this category: Leap Confronting Conflict received two grants totalling £6,500, Responding to Conflict received two grants totalling £5,500 whilst BCTV was given £4,400 in four grants. Other large grants were £10,000 to IVS, £6,500 to Oxfam, £5,000 to Medical Foundation, £4,000 to the Oxford branch of Relate (with a further £750 to the Worcestershire branch) and £3,000 each to Cornwall Scrap Store, John Muir Trust, Wildfowl and Wetlands Trust and Worcestershire Wildlife Trust. Smaller grants included £2,500 each to Inside Out Trust and Lisburn Methodist Church Youth Council, £2,000 each to Computeraid, Money for Madagascar and Tools for Self Reliance, £1,500 each to Alone in London, Balkans Community Initiatives and Fairtrade Foundation, £1,200 to Open Door, £1,000 each to Bristol Stepping Stone and Devon Wildlife Trust, £800 to International Community Assistance,

£750 each to Amnesty International UK Charitable Trust and Scottish Conservation Projects, £500 to Network of Christian Peace Organisations and £15 to WMCT Group.

Exclusions No grants to individuals.

Applications In writing to the correspondent. Applications are considered in February/March and November. Applications received between meetings are considered at the next meeting.

The Sovereign Health Care Charitable Trust (formerly known as The Charities Fund)

Health, disability
£310,000 (2000)
Beneficial area UK.

Royal Standard House, 26 Manningham Lane, Bradford, West Yorkshire BD1 3DN
Tel. 01274 729472 **Fax** 01274 722252
Email postroom@sovereignhealth.co.uk
Correspondent The Secretary
Trustees *G McGowan; S Benson; J Hellawell; M Austin; D Child; D J Lewis; M Bower; M Hudson; S W Johnson.*
CC Number 1079024
Information available Full accounts were on file at the Charity Commission.

General This trust is funded by donations received under the Gift Aid scheme from the investment income of The Hospital Fund of Bradford. Its objects are to provide amenities for hospital patients and to make grants to charities 'for the relief and assistance of needy sick and elderly people'.

In 2000 it had assets of £112,000 and an income of £423,000, mostly from donations. Grants totalled £310,000 and were broken down as follows:

grants to hospitals	£46,000
grants to associations and institutions	£236,000
nurses' training grant	£27,000

In the previous year, when grants totalled £315,000, the largest grants were £58,000 to Marie Curie Cancer Care for new premises, £13,000 to Cancer Support Centre for administration, £12,000 each to Sue Ryder Foundation for running costs and War on Cancer for research, £10,000 to Lord Mayor's Appeal, £8,000 to Bradford Bulls Study Centre for children's drug awareness and healthy lifestyle, £7,000 to Samaritans for premises, £6,000 each to Champion House for administration and York Conductive Education for various purposes and £5,000 to Bradford Sport & Recreation Association for People with Disabilities for administration and formation of new groups.

Exclusions No grants to individuals.

Applications In writing to the correspondent.

Sparquote Limited

Jewish charities
£134,000 (1999/2000)
Beneficial area A preference for north and west London, including Edgware in Middlesex.

Grosvenor House, 1 High Street, Edgware, Middlesex HA8 7TA
Correspondent Mrs A M Reichmann, Secretary
Trustees *David Reichmann; Dov Reichmann; Mrs A M Reichmann.*
CC Number 286232
Information available Accounts were on file at the Charity Commission.

General This trust makes grants to Jewish charities for educational and welfare purposes. In 1999/2000 it had assets amounting to £723,000 and an income of £260,000, which came mostly from rent. After low management and administration costs of £4,000 a total of £134,000 was distributed in grants (£100,000 in 1998/99).

Grants of over £500 were made to 25 beneficiaries, the largest of which were £15,000 each to Beth Jacob Youth Movement, Woodstock Sinclair Trust and Yeshiva Arteret Yisrael – Rabbinical College. Other grants included Sharei Ezrah Institute (£10,000), Shatnez Centre Trust (£6,000), Friends of Wiznitz Ltd (£3,000), Edgware Foundation (£2,300),

Union of Orthodox Hebrew Congregations (£1,000) and Commetville Ltd (£600). Other donations of £500 or under totalled £4,900.

Applications In writing to the correspondent.

The Spear Charitable Trust

General
£147,000 to organisations (2001)
Beneficial area UK.

Roughground House, Old Hall Green, Ware, Hertfordshire SG11 1HB
Email franzel@farmersweekly.net
Correspondent Hazel E Spear, Secretary
Trustees *P N Harris; K B Stuart Crowhurst; F A Spear; H E Spear; N Gooch.*
CC Number 1041568
Information available Full accounts were provided by the trust.

General Established in 1994 with general charitable purposes, this trust has particular interest in helping employees and former employees of J W Spear and Sons plc and their families and dependants.

In 2001 the assets totalled £4.4 million and generated an income of £175,000. Management and administration costs were very high at £49,000. Grants were made to 54 organisations totalling £147,000, whilst ex-employees received £50,000 in total.

The largest grants were £10,000 each to Enfield Baptist Church, Yehudi Menuhin School and Purcell School, £6,000 to RSPCA Enfield and £5,000 each to Botton Village, Guyana Diocesan Association, Music for Living, Pesticide Action Network, Royal Agricultural Benevolent Institution, Sargent Cancer Care for Children, David Tolkien Trust for Stoke Mandeville and Tree Aid.

Other beneficiaries included Cot Death Society (£4,000), Young Minds (£2,400), International Glaucoma Association and Marine Conservation Society (£2,500), Winged Fellowship (£2,400), Pathway (£2,000), Ballet West (£1,200), G T L N Wang Trust Fund (£1,100), and £1,000 each to Action for Blind People, Crosslands Centre – Liverpool, Get Set Girls, Live Music Now!, North Middlesex Oncology Ward Trust Fund, Sense, Spadework, Stroke Association and

Summer Adventure for Inner Londoners and £500 to National Canine Defence League.

Applications In writing to the correspondent.

Roama Spears Charitable Settlement

Welfare causes

£68,000 (1998/99)
Beneficial area Worldwide.

Silver Altman, Chartered Accountants, 8 Baltic Street East, London EC1Y 0UP

Tel. 020 7251 2200

Correspondent Robert Ward

Trustees Mrs R L Spears; P B Mendel.

CC Number 225491

Information available Full accounts were on file at the Charity Commission.

General This trust states that it makes grants to organisations towards the relief of poverty worldwide. In practice it appears to support a range of organisations including a number of museums and arts organisations. It has some preference for Jewish causes.

In 1998/99 the trust's assets totalled £2.2 million, generating an income of £127,000. After making grants totalling £68,000, and management and administration costs of £22,000, the trust had a surplus for the year of £37,000.

Donations of over £1,000 were as follows: £24,000 to Macmillan Cancer Relief; £14,000 to Royal Academy; £9,300 to Brooklyn Friends; £5,000 to Wellbeing; £3,800 to Haven Trust; £2,000 to Variety Israel; and £1,000 to British Museum.

Applications In writing to the correspondent.

The Jessie Spencer Trust

General

£158,000 to organisations

(2000/01)

Beneficial area UK, with a preference for Nottinghamshire.

1 Royal Standard Place, Nottingham NG1 6FZ

Tel. 0115 950 7000

Correspondent The Trustees

Trustees V W Semmens; Mrs E K M Brackenbury; R S Hursthouse; Mrs Jennifer Galloway.

CC Number 219289

Information available Full accounts were on file at the Charity Commission.

General In 2000/01 the trust had assets of £3.1 million, which generated an income of £136,000. Management and administration charges were high at £15,000, and included payments of £2,500 and £10,000 to companies which have a trustee as a partner. There were 61 grants totalling £159,000, broken down as follows:

Accomodation – 3 grants totalling £102,000
By far the largest grant made by the trust was £100,000 to Mansfield Road (Nottingham) Baptist Housing Association Limited. The other grants were £1,000 to Haven Housing Trust and £500 to St Mungo's.

Arts – 1 grant of £1,000
This went to Musica Donum Dei.

Churches – 9 grants totalling £11,000
The largest grants went to Nottinghamshire Historic Churches Trust (£3,800) and St Edmund's Church and St Peter's Church – Nottingham Tower Appeal (£2,000 each). Other beneficiaries included St Peter's Church (£500), Downing Street Church (£300) and Linby & Papplewick Parish Church (£100).

Environment – 1 grant of £500
This went to Wildfowl and Wetlands Trust.

Groups/clubs – 5 grants totalling £6,000
Concert 2000 received £4,500. Other recipients were Cathedral Camps and Oliver Hind Club (£500 each), Cyclops Productions (£300) and Zone Youth Project (£200).

Individuals – 4 grants totalling £1,500

Medical/disabled – 19 grants totalling £25,000
The largest grants were £5,000 to Nottingham City Hospital for the Breast Unit Fund, £3,800 each to Autonomic Disorders Association - Sarah Matheson Trust, Rainbows Children's Hospice and Winged Fellowship Trust and Nottingham Regional Society. Grants of £500 each included those to British Blind Sport, Deafblind UK, Dystonia Society, Headway, Eyeless Trust, Iris Fund, Nottingham Multiple Sclerosis Therapy Centre Limited and Nottingham Dyslexia Association, while North Nottinghamshire Arthritis Self Help Group received £250.

Other – 2 grants totalling £1,300
These were £1,000 to Women's Therapy Centre and £250 to Sneinton Festival Committee.

Welfare – 17 grants totalling £11,400
Nottinghamshire Hospice received £2,500 while £1,000 each went to Lenton Parish Children's Work, Macedon & NHHA and Wollaton Centre Project. Other grants included £750 to Prison Reform Trust, £500 each to Alone in London, Apex Trust, ChildLine Midlands, Methodist Homes for the Aged, West Area Project and National Association of Child Contract Centres and £300 to Lenton Community Association.

Exclusions Grants are rarely made for the repair of parish churches outside Nottinghamshire.

Applications In writing to the correspondent including the latest set of audited accounts. Unsuccessful applications will not be acknowledged.

W W Spooner Charitable Trust

General

£89,000 (2000/01)

Beneficial area UK, with a preference for Yorkshire especially West Yorkshire.

Addleshaw Booth & Co., PO Box 8, Sovereign House, Sovereign Street, Leeds LS1 1HQ

Tel. 0113 209 2000

Correspondent M H Broughton, Trustee

Trustees *M H Broughton, Chair; Sir James F Hill; R Ibbotson; T J P Ramsden; Mrs J M McKiddie; J H Wright.*

CC Number 313653

Information available Accounts were on file at the Charity Commission.

General The trust will support charities working in the following areas:

- Youth – for example, welfare, sport and education including school appeals and initiatives, clubs, scouting, guiding, adventure training, individual voluntary service overseas and approved expeditions
- Community – including churches, associations, welfare and support groups
- Healing – including care of people who are sick, disabled or underprivileged, welfare organisations, victim support, hospitals, hospices and selected medical charities and research
- The countryside – causes such as the protection and preservation of the environment including rescue and similar services and preservation and maintenance of historic buildings
- The arts – including museums, teaching, performing, musical and literary festivals and selective support for the purchase of works for art for public benefit.

It has a list of regular beneficiaries which receive grants each year and also supports around 40 to 50 one-off applications. Grants can range from £200 to £2,000, although they are usually for £250 to £350.

In 2000/01 the trust had assets of £1.8 million and an income of £78,000. Grants were given to 107 regular beneficiaries and 48 one-off applications and totalled £89,000.

The largest grants went to Wordsworth Trust – Grasmere (£5,000), Parish of Tong and Holme Wood (£2,500), Guide Dogs for the Blind (£1,700), St Margaret's PCC – Ilkley (£1,500) with £1,000 each to Abbeyfield Society, All Saints Church – Ilkley, Ardenlea, Hawksworth Church of England School, Leith School of Art, Martin House Hospice, North of England Christian Healing Trust, St Gemma's Hospice, St George's Crypt, Wheatfield House and Yorkshire Ballet Seminar.

Exclusions 'No grants for high-profile appeals seeking large sums.' Most donations are for less than £500.

Applications In writing to the correspondent.

Rosalyn and Nicholas Springer Charitable Trust

Welfare, Jewish, education, general

£118,000 to individuals and organisations (2000/01)

Beneficial area UK.

Flat 27, Berkeley House, 15 Hay Hill, London W1J 8NS

Tel. 020 7493 1904

Correspondent Nicholas Springer, Trustee

Trustees *Mrs R Springer; N S Springer; J Joseph.*

CC Number 1062239

Information available Full accounts were on file at the Charity Commission.

General In 2000/01 the trust had assets of £36,000. The income was £147,000, almost all of which came from donations received. Grants to 59 organisations and 3 individuals totalled £118,000.

The largest grants were £33,000 to UJIA and £16,000 to King Alfred School. Jewish Care received two grants totalling £17,000.

Other beneficiaries included Shaare Zedek (£6,000), Almeida Theatre (£5,100), Chicken Shed Theatre Co. (£3,700), Royal Opera House (£3,000), World Jewish Relief (£2,200), Holocaust Education Trust and Jewish Association for the Mentally Ill (£500 each), Pauline Foundation and Tower Hamlets Old Peoples Association (£200 each) and MS Society (£100).

Applications The trust states that it only supports organisations it is already in contact with. 99% of unsolicited applications are unsuccessful and because of the volume it receives, the trust is unable to reply to such letters. It would therefore not seem appropriate to apply to this trust.

The Stanley Charitable Trust

Jewish

About £100,000 (1998/99)

Beneficial area UK, with a preference for Greater Manchester.

32 Waterpark Road, Salford M7 4ET

Tel. 0161 708 8090

Correspondent David Adler

Trustees *A M Adler; I Adler; J Adler.*

CC Number 326220

Information available Brief accounts for 1990/91 were in the public files at the Charity Commission.

General The trust supports Jewish religious charities, with a preference for those in Greater Manchester and for projects and people known to the trustees.

In 1998/99 the trust had an income of £90,000 and an expenditure of £110,000. Further information for this year was not available.

In 1990/91 it owned 30% of Nailsea Estate Co. and also had £204,000 in property. Its income of £113,000 included £36,000 from rent, £33,000 loan interest and £41,000 share of surplus joint venture. Expenditure totalled £39,000, including £31,000 on a bank overdraft. This left a net income of £74,000 out of which £65,000 was given in unspecified donations.

Exclusions Only registered charities are supported.

Applications The trust has said that it gives regular donations and does not consider new applications.

The Stanley Foundation Ltd

Older people, medical, education, social welfare

£110,000 (1996/97)

Beneficial area UK.

Flat 3, 19 Holland Park, London W11 3TD

Correspondent The Secretary

Trustees *Nicholas Stanley, Chair; D J Aries; S R Stanley; Albert Rose; Mrs E Stanley; C Shale.*

233

CC Number 206866

Information available Full accounts were on file at the Charity Commission.

General In 2001/02 the trust had an income of £93,000 and an expenditure of £186,000. This information was taken from the Charity Commission database. Unfortunately no further information was available for this year.

For many years, the trust has been supporting charities helping older people and medical, educational and social welfare charities. According to the correspondent, the trust may now change its areas of giving every one or two years.

Grants totalled £110,000 in 1996/97, but no further details were available for this year.

In 1994/95 the trust had an income of £148,000 from assets of £3.1 million. 62 grants were made totalling £170,000. The trust also made a commitment for a large grant (£500,000) to King's College, Cambridge which it was to be paid in autumn 1995. During the year, the larger grants were £30,000 to St Mary's Hampstead Appeal, £15,000 each to King's College Cambridge and Wynn Institute and £11,000 to NSPCC and Discovery Factory. £5,000 each went to Cancer Research, Cheek by Jowl, Crisis at Christmas and MacIntyre Charitable Trust.

The other grants were all for £250 to £4,000. Most were to medical causes, but other organisations to benefit included BTCV, Pavilion Opera, Percy Thrower Gardening Club and Young Champions Tennis Trust.

Exclusions No grants to individuals.

Applications In writing to the correspondent.

The Cyril & Betty Stein Charitable Trust

Jewish causes

£153,000 (1999/2000)

Beneficial area UK and Israel.

c/o Clayton Stark & Co., 5th Floor, Charles House, 108-110 Finchley Road, London NW3 5JJ

Correspondent The Trustees

Trustees *Cyril Stein; Betty Stein; David Clayton.*

CC Number 292235

Information available Accounts were on file at the Charity Commission.

General The trust makes a small number of substantial grants each year, primarily for the advancement of the Jewish religion and the welfare of Jewish people.

In 2000/01 the trust had an income of £174,000 and a total expenditure of £165,000. Unfortunately, no further information was available for this year.

In 1999/2000 the trust's income was £143,000, mainly from donations. Assets for the year stood at £325,000. Grants were made to 41 organisations totalling £153,000.

The trust's accounts listed the top 11 beneficiaries, which were: The Institute for the Advancement of Education in Jaffa (£36,000), Friends of Yeshivat Kerem B' Yavneh (£20,000), Project Seed (£15,000), Friends of Bnei David and Friends of Bar Ilan University (£12,500 each), Carmel College (£8,000), L'Chaim Independent Charitable Trust (£7,500), Friends of Mifal Hatorah (£6,500), The Hope Charity and Lubavitch Foundation (£5,000 each) and Friends of the Hebrew University of Jerusalem (£2,000).

The remaining 30 grants not listed totalled £23,000.

Applications In writing to the correspondent.

The Steinberg Family Charitable Trust

Jewish, health

£116,000 (1997)

Beneficial area UK, with a preference for north west England.

Stanley House, 151 Dale Street, Liverpool L2 2JW

Correspondent L Steinberg, Trustee

Trustees *Ms B Steinberg; L Steinberg; J Steinberg; Ms L R Ferster; D K Johnston.*

CC Number 1045231

Information available Accounts were on file at the Charity Commission.

General This trust has general charitable purposes, with a preference for Jewish or

health organisations in the north west of England. In 2000/01 it had an income of £146,000 and a total expenditure of £226,000. Unfortunately no further details were available for this year.

In 1997 the trust had assets of £2.9 million and an income of £288,000. Grants totalled £116,000. Beneficiaries included Alder Hey Children's Hospital (£25,000), Manchester Jewish Federation and North West Cancer Research Fund (£10,000 each) and North Cheshire Jewish Primary School (£7,500).

Applications In writing to the correspondent.

The Sir Sigmund Sternberg Charitable Foundation

Jewish, inter-faith causes, general

£306,000 (2000/01)

Beneficial area Worldwide.

Star House, Grafton Road, London NW5 4BD

Tel. 020 7485 2538

Correspondent Sir S Sternberg, Trustee

Trustees *Sir S Sternberg; V M Sternberg; Lady Sternberg.*

CC Number 257950

Information available Full accounts were on file at the Charity Commission.

General This trust supports Jewish and Israeli charities, with a preference for organisations that address inter-faith issues and cooperation. It makes a small number of large grants, generally of £10,000 to £50,000 each, and a large number of smaller grants.

In 2000/01 the foundation had assets of £3.1 million, which generated an income of £256,000. Grants were made totalling £306,000. Management and administration costs appear high at £190,000, but this includes charitable activities carried out by the trust, particularly concerning the promotion of education between the Christian, Islamic and Jewish faiths.

The largest grants were £47,000 to Reform Foundation Trust, £45,000 to Manor

House Trust and £33,000 to Friends of the Hebrew University of Jerusalem.

Other beneficiaries listed in the accounts were International Council for Christians and Jews (£20,000), Institute of Business Ethics (£16,000), Institute of Jewish Policy Research (£14,000), Interreligious Coordinating Council in Israel (£12,000), Millennium World Peace Summit (£11,000), Institute of Archaeo-Metallurgical Studies (£10,000) and Board of Deputies Charitable Foundation (£4,100).

Exclusions No grants to individuals.

Applications The foundation has stated in the past that its funds are fully committed.

Stervon Ltd

Jewish

£209,000 (1998)
Beneficial area UK.

c/o Stervon House, 1 Seaford Road, Salford, Greater Manchester M6 6AS
Tel. 0161 737 5000
Correspondent A Reich, Secretary
Trustees *A Reich; G Rothbart.*
CC Number 280958
Information available Full accounts were on file at the Charity Commission.

General 'The principal objective of the company is the distribution of funds to Jewish, religious, educational and similar charities.'

In 2001 this trust had an income of £132,000 and a total expenditure of £153,000. Unfortunately no further information was available for this year.

In 1998 the trust had assets of £146,000 and an income of £237,000, £158,000 of which came from donations. Grants totalled £209,000, the accounts listed 36 of over £500. They went to both previously supported and new organisations. Other donations totalled £15,000.

The largest grants over £10,000 went to Chasdei Yoel (£45,000), Bnos Yisorel (£32,000) and UTA (£12,000).

Other grants went to Machzikei Hadrass (£9,700), Shaarei Torah (£6,100), Friends of Masse Tsedoko (£5,500), Kesser Charities (£5,000), Jewish High School (£4,800), Agudas Yisroel Housing

Association (£2,500), Beis Aharon Trust (£1,200), Friends of Mir (£750) and Manchester Yeshiva (£600).

Applications In writing to the correspondent.

The Stewards' Charitable Trust

Rowing

£90,000 (2001)
Beneficial area Principally the UK.

Regatta Headquarters, Henley-on-Thames, Oxfordshire RG9 2LY
Correspondent R S Goddard, Secretary
Trustees *M A Sweeney; C G V Davidge; C L Baillieu; R C Lester.*
CC Number 299597
Information available Full accounts were on file at the Charity Commission.

General The trust makes grants to organisations and clubs benefiting boys and girls involved in the sport of rowing. It supports rowing at all levels, from grassroots upwards; beneficiaries should be in full-time education or training. Support is also given to related medical and educational research projects. Grants range from £1,000 to £60,000. They are preferably one-off and are especially made where matched funds are raised elsewhere.

In 2001 the trust's assets totalled £2.3 million and it had an income of £391,000 of which £302,000 came from donations. Grants totalled £90,000 and included: £40,000 to Amateur Rowing Association – Project Oarsome; £25,000 to Biodynamics Project; and £7,500 to Rowing Foundation.

Exclusions No grants to individuals or for building or capital costs.

Applications In writing to the correspondent. Applications are usually first vetted by Amateur Rowing Association.

The Stoller Charitable Trust

Medical, children, general

£390,000 (2000/01)
Beneficial area UK, with a preference for the Greater Manchester area.

c/o SSL International plc, Tubiton House, Oldham OL1 3HS
Tel. 0161 621 2003 **Fax** 0161 627 0932
Correspondent Alison Ford
Trustees *Norman Stoller; Roger Gould; Jan Fidler.*
CC Number 285415
Information available Accounts were on file at the Charity Commission.

General The trust supports a wide variety of charitable causes, but with particular emphasis on those which are local, medically-related or supportive of children. There is a bias towards charities in Greater Manchester where the trust is based. It also endeavours to maintain a balance between regular and occasional donations and between the few large and many smaller ones.

In 2000/01 the trust had an income of £254,000. Around 250 grants were made totalling £390,000. Most were for under £1,000, but donations of £10,000 or over went to Cancer Research Campaign, Emmaus – Greater Manchester, Hulme Grammar School, Make a Difference Appeal, Manchester High School, Manchester Grammar School, The Message and New Heart New Start.

Exclusions No grants to individuals.

Applications In writing to the correspondent. Applications need to be received by February, May, August or November and the trustees meet in March, June, September and December.

The Stone Foundation

Research into addiction, medical research, welfare

£111,000 (1999/2000)
Beneficial area UK.

24 Wilton Row, London SW1X 7NS
Tel. 020 7235 4871

Correspondent Lady Gosling, Chair of the Trustees

Trustees *Lady Shauna Gosling; M J Kirkwood; Adam Gosling.*

CC Number 1084454

Information available Full accounts were on file at the Charity Commission.

General The foundation continues to fund the field of addiction, directing resources to the area of research, education and treatment of addiction to alcohol and drugs as well as focusing on the alleviation of other compulsive disorders.

In 1999/2000 the foundation had an income of £119,000 and gave grants to 10 organisations totalling £111,000. The trust transferred its assets, worth £4.2 million, to The Stone Foundation Charity.

The largest grants were £35,000 to Camden and Islington CHS to develop a dual diagnoses programme, £25,000 to Chemical Dependency Centre for a quality assurance programme in line with EATA UK standards and £18,000 to Cancer Bacup for a nurse of the information service. All of these organisations also received the same amounts in the previous year.

Other beneficiaries were British Liver Trust for research into Hepatitis C (£10,000), NAADAC for development (£8,800); Glyndebourne (£5,100), Broadway Trust towards setting-up a fully endowed charity bed (£5,000), WRVS Contact Centres (£2,500) and The Passage Day Centre, and Royal Court (£1,000 each).

Applications In writing to the correspondent. Trustees meet in January, April, June, September and November.

The M J C Stone Charitable Trust

General

£164,000 (2000)
Beneficial area UK.

Estate Office, Ozleworth Park, Wotton-under-Edge, Gloucestershire GL12 7QA

Tel. 01453 845591

Correspondent M J C Stone, Trustee

Trustees *M J C Stone; Mrs L Stone; C R H Stone; A J Stone; N J Farquhar.*

CC Number 283920

Information available Full accounts were on file at the Charity Commission.

General While the trust has general charitable objects, giving to a range of causes, it stated that its main area of interest is the advancement of education.

In 2000 the trust had assets of £861,000 and an income of £594,000. Incoming resources have significantly increased this year due to shares with a value of £503,000 being gifted to the trust. Grants were made to 53 organisations totalling £164,000. Grants ranged from £100 to £25,000. Some beneficiaries were supported in the previous year.

The largest beneficiaries were Bradfield Foundation (£25,000), Blue Coat C of E School and Game Conservancy (£20,000 each). Other beneficiaries included United World College of the Atlantic (£13,500), National Hospital Development Trust and Countryside Foundation for Education (£12,000 each), University of Gloucestershire and Winnicott Foundation (£10,000 each), Macmillan Cancer Relief (£5,700), British Wheelchair Sports Foundation (£5,000) and NSPCC (£2,500).

Grants of £1,000 each included those to Arkholme Parish Hall & Institute, Cotswold Care Hospice, Gloucestershire Playing Fields Association, International Spinal Research Trust, Streatham Youth Centre, Tyndale Monument Appeal and Wildlife Trust Cumbria.

Beneficiaries receiving under £1,000 included Army Benevolent Fund, Christian Aid, Georgian Group, Hunt Servants, National Trust for Scotland, St John Ambulance, Tetbury Hospital Trust, Wester Ross Fisheries Trust and Whizzkidz.

Applications 'Unsolicited applications will not be replied to.'

The Samuel Storey Family Charitable Trust

General

£1.5 million (2000/01 – due to an exceptional payment)
Beneficial area Uk, with a preference for Yorkshire.

21 Buckingham Gate, London SW1E 6LS
Tel. 020 7802 2700 **Fax** 020 7828 5049

Correspondent Hon. Sir Richard Storey, Trustee

Trustees *Hon. Sir Richard Storey; Wren Hoskyns Abrahall; K Storey.*

CC Number 267684

Information available Full accounts were on file at the Charity Commission.

General This trust has general charitable purposes, supporting a wide range of causes, including the arts, gardens and churches. The grants list shows a large number of beneficiaries in Yorkshire.

In 2000/01 the trust had assets of £4.7 million, which generated an income of £244,000. A substantial payment of £1.5 million was made to Sir Harold Hillier Gardens and Arboretum. As the trust has often had a surplus in previous year, it appears that this grant was a one-off from accumulated funds although this was not confirmed in the accounts.

Smaller grants were made to 105 organisations and totalled £30,000. The largest were £5,000 each to Macmillan Cancer Relief, Florence Nightingale Aid in Sickness Trust and Paxton Trust, £2,000 each to JC2000 and Trinity Hospice and £1,000 each to Anglican Centre in Rome and Tukes.

Five of the grants were given to Settrington organisations, the PCC for the fabric fund (£210), Settrington School (£150), the village hall (£1,000), the under fives's group (£350) and the primary school (£25).

Other Yorkshire beneficiaries included York Scout Activity Centre (£500), Ryedale Festival (£320), Yorkshire Gardens Trust (£270), Coltman Area Community Association and Malton Hospital League of Friends (£250 each), Yorkshire Dales Millennium Trust (£200), Dales Care (£40) and York Mental Health Committee (£25).

Grants outside of Yorkshire included those to NSPCC (£400), Scottish Community Foundation and Tibet Foundation (£250 each), Anne Frank Educational Trust and National Asthma Campaign (£100 each), Royal Society of the Arts (£85), Woodland Trust (£75), SSAFA (£70), Sunderland Victim Support (£50), RSPB (£34), Great Ormond Street Hospital and VSO (£25 each), Kensington Society (£20) and ESSA (£2).

Exclusions The trust does not support non-registered charities or individuals.

Applications In writing to the correspondent.

Sueberry Ltd

Jewish, welfare
£61,000 (1999/2000)
Beneficial area UK and overseas.

11 Clapton Common, London E5 9AA
Correspondent Mrs M Davis, Trustee
Trustees *J Davis, Chair; Mrs M Davis; Mrs H Davis.*
CC Number 256566
Information available Accounts were on file at the Charity Commission but without a list of beneficiaries.

General The trust makes grants to Jewish organisations and also to other UK welfare and medical organisations benefiting children and young adults, at risk groups, people who are disadvantaged by poverty, or socially isolated people.

In 2000/01 the trust had an income of £120,000 and a total expenditure of £81,000. Further information for this year was not aviable.

In the previous year it had an income of £46,000, mostly from donations, and gave £61,000 in grants. It supported educational, religious and other charitable organisations but a list of beneficiaries was not available.

Applications In writing to the correspondent.

This entry was not confirmed by the trust but the information was correct according to the Charity Commission file.

The Alan Sugar Foundation

Jewish charities, general
£403,000 (2000/01)
Beneficial area UK.

Brentwood House, 169 Kings Road, Brentwood, Essex CM14 4EF
Tel. 01277 201333 **Fax** 01277 208006
Correspondent Colin Sandy
Trustees *Sir Alan Sugar; Colin Sandy; Simon Sugar; Daniel Sugar; Mrs Louise Baron.*
CC Number 294880
Information available Full accounts are on file at the Charity Commission with grants list but with no narrative report.

General This trust was established by the well-known ex-chair of Tottenham Hotspur FC, and gives a small number of substantial grants each year. Grants are made to registered charities that are of current and ongoing interest to the trustees.

In 2000/01 the trust's assets totalled £45,000. Its income of £425,000 was made up mostly of donations. Grants totalled £403,000. Beneficiaries were: Jewish Care (£125,000), Great Ormond Street Hospital and King Solomon School – Redbridge (£100,000 each), Jewish Blind and Disabled (£75,000) and Drugs Education in Schools (£3,000).

Exclusions No grants for individuals or to non-registered charities.

Applications This trust states that it does not respond to unsolicited applications. All projects are initiated by the trustees.

The Swan Trust

General, arts, culture
£122,000 (2001/02)
Beneficial area Overseas and the UK, with a preference for East Sussex, Kent, Surrey and West Sussex.

Pollen House, 10/12 Cork Street, London W1S 3LW
Tel. 020 7439 9061
Correspondent A J Winborn
Trustees *The Cowdray Trust Limited.*
CC Number 261442
Information available Information was provided by the trust.

General The trust makes grants to a range of organisations including a number that are arts and culture related. Priority is given to grants for one year or less; grants for up to two years are considered.

In 2001/02 its assets totalled £917,000, it had an income of £73,000 and 80 grants were made totalling £122,000. Grants were in the range of £20 and £60,000.

The largest grant was £60,000 to Magdelen College Development Trust. There were a further 16 grants of £1,000 or more including those to: Save the Children Fund (£20,000), British Museum Development Trust and Yehudi Menuhin School Ltd (£5,000 each), National Portrait Gallery and Sussex

Heritage Trust Ltd (£2,000 each), Friends of Covent Garden and Royal Academy Trust (£1,500 each), Lake District Art & Museum Trust (£1,200) and Broomhill Trust, Lewes Millennium Gallery Trust, Royal National Theatre, Sussex Housing & Care, Victoria and Albert Museum and Withyham Parochial Church Council (£1,000 each).

Beneficiaries of smaller grants included 999 Club Trust, British Agencies for Adoption & Fostering, Chelsea Old Church, English National Opera, Family Welfare Association, Handel House Trust, Hospice in the Weald, Live Music Now!, National Art Collections Fund, Shelter, Venice in Peril Fund and World Monuments Fund in Britain.

Exclusions No grants to individuals or non-registered charities.

Applications In writing to the correspondent. Acknowledgements will only be sent if a grant is being made.

The Swire Charitable Trust

General
£271,000 (2001)
Beneficial area Worldwide.

John Swire & Sons Ltd, Swire House, 59 Buckingham Gate, London SW1E 6AJ
Tel. 020 7834 7717
Correspondent B N Swire, Trustee
Trustees *Sir J Swire; Sir Adrian Swire; B N Swire; M J B Todhunter; E J R Scott.*
CC Number 270726
Information available Full accounts were on file at the Charity Commission.

General In 2001 the trust had assets of £192,000 and an income of £229,000 of which £225,000 came from donations from John Swire & Sons Ltd. Grants totalled £271,000.

There were 23 grants of £1,000 and more. The largest was £60,000 to Neak and Neck Cancer Research Trust. Other listed beneficiaries included Air League Educational Trust (£18,000), GAPAN (£13,000), University of Southampton – East Asia Centre (£10,000), VSO (£7,500), London School of Hygiene and Tropical Medicine (£3,500), Book Aid International (£2,500), KIDS (£1,500) and National Coastwatch Institution,

Police Foundation, Royal Air Force Museum and Westminster Volunteer Bureau (£1,000 each).

Applications In writing to the correspondent. Applications are considered throughout the year.

The John Swire (1989) Charitable Trust

General

£225,000 (2001)

Beneficial area UK.

John Swire & Sons Ltd, Swire House, 59 Buckingham Gate, London SW1E 6AJ

Tel. 020 7834 7717

Correspondent B N Swire, Trustee

Trustees *Sir John Swire; J S Swire; B N Swire; M C Robinson; Lady Swire.*

CC Number 802142

Information available Full accounts were on file at the Charity Commission.

General Established in 1989 by Sir John Swire of John Swire & Sons Ltd, merchants and ship owners, the trust supports a wide range of organisations including some in the area of arts, welfare, education, medicine and research.

In 2001 the trust had an income of £304,000 and assets totalling £7.4 million. Grants were made to 46 organisations totalling £225,000. They ranged from £1,000 to £25,000, although half were for £1,000.

The largest grants went to Caldecott Foundation, Demelza House Children's Hospice and Kent County Council for Selling C of E Primary School (£25,000 each).

Other beneficiaries included Durrell Institute for Conservation and Ecology (£12,500), Canterbury Open Centre (£10,000), Toynbee Hall (£6,000), Canterbury Festival and Helen House (£5,000 each), Leigh School PTA and Royal Caledonian Ball Trust (£2,500 each), Ataxia-Telangiectasia Society and Orchid Cancer Society (£1,500 each) and Selling Church Building Trust and Selling PCC (£1,250 each).

The trust made 23 grants of £1,000, including those to 999 Club, Age Concern, Alzheimer's Research Trust, British Heart Foundation, Finton House,

Kent Wildlife Trust, National Back Pain Association, NSPCC, Soil Association and UCL Development Fund.

A grant of £13,000 was also made to St Antony's College for a scholarship.

Applications In writing to the correspondent.

The Charles and Elsie Sykes Trust

General

£365,000 (2001)

Beneficial area UK and overseas. The trust stated that a preference is given towards applications 'from the northern part of the United Kingdom and in particular from Yorkshire'.

6 North Park Road, Harrogate, Yorkshire HG1 5PA

Correspondent David J Reah, Secretary

Trustees *John Ward, Chair; Mrs Anne E Brownlie; Martin P Coultas; Mrs G Mary Dance; John Horrocks; R Barry Kay; Dr Michael D Moore; Michael G H Garnett; Dr Michael W McEvoy.*

CC Number 206926

Information available Accounts were provided by the trust.

General The trust outlines its grant-making policy in its annual report. It has two main strands. Under the first it considers applications received. Preference is given to applications from Yorkshire, although many are received from outside the region that are unlikely to be successful, as are those which are received from individuals or without examined or audited accounts.

The trustees have previously stated that they welcome the availability to the public of information about charities and the mode of applications to them but nevertheless regret the receipt of so many unsuitable applications, which cause wasted time to all parties. (Less than 10% of applications to the trust are likely to be successful.)

Under a second strand, the trust makes annual donations to a number of registered charities (upon annual production of satisfactory accounts) where regular support is perceived to be desirable and proper. The trustees note with regret the failure of a number of those charities on the 'annual' list to

provide proper information about their accounts. In the year 2000, a staggering 22 recipients of grants were deleted because annual accounts were not supplied.

In 2001 it had assets of £9.7 million, an income of £459,000 and grants totalled £365,000. Although a wide range of causes are supported, the trustees have sub-committees to consider medical and non-medical grants respectively.

Annual grants in 2001 totalled £135,000 of which £36,000 had a medical aspect. Special (or one-off) grants totalled £229,000, of which £48,000 had a medical aspect. The trust provided the following breakdown of the categories supported, and number of grants made:

Social and moral welfare	£62,000	43
Medical research	£61,500	23
Mental health and mentally handicapped	£31,000	10
Children and youth	£25,000	15
Cultural and environmental heritage	£21,000	6
Medical welfare	£21,000	12
Old people's welfare	£14,500	6
Disabled and physically handicapped	£10,300	6
Blind and partially sighted	£7,500	5
Hospices and hospitals	£7,000	2
Trades and professions	£6,000	4
Animals and birds	£3,000	2
Deaf, hard of hearing and speech impaired	£1,700	2
Education	£1,000	1
Overseas aid	£1,000	1
Services and ex-services	£1,000	1

The four largest grants were detailed in the annual report. They were £26,000 to Age Concern – Knaresborough District towards a major building project; £25,000 to Royal Northern College of Music – Manchester (this grant was to mark, in a modest way, the new millennium: accordingly in 1998 it gave the college £25,000 to fund musical sponsorships. The intention is to make a further six grants, subject to annual review); £20,000 to Eureka Museum for Children – Halifax towards a new gallery covering the local and global environment; £19,500 to Disability Action Yorkshire for improved facilities and ancillary equipment.

The 50 largest grants were listed in the accounts, including 13 of £5,000 and 17 of £2,000. Recipients included Calderdale Mencap (Mayfield Resource Centre), Citizens Advice Bureau Harrogate, Craven Trust Dales Recovery Appeal, Leeds Women's Aid, Marrick Priory Richmond, Northdale Horticulture and Yorkshire Cancer Research.

Exclusions The following applicants are unlikely to be successful: individuals; local organisations not in the north of England; and recently-established charities. Non-registered charities are not considered.

Applications Applications from registered charities may be made with full details and an sae to the above address. Applications without up-to-date audited or examined accounts will not be considered. The trust regrets that it cannot conduct correspondence with applicants.

The Hugh & Ruby Sykes Charitable Trust

General, medical, education, employment

£144,000 (2000/01)
Beneficial area Principally South Yorkshire, also Derbyshire.

Bamford Hall Holdings Ltd, Bamford Hall, The Hollow, Bamford, Hope Valley S33 0AU
Tel. 01433 651190
Correspondent Sir Hugh Sykes, Trustee
Trustees *Sir Hugh Sykes; Lady Sykes.*
CC Number 327648
Information available Accounts were on file at the Charity Commission.

General This trust was set up in 1987 for general charitable purposes by Sir Hugh Sykes and his wife Lady Sykes. It supports local charities in South Yorkshire and Derbyshire, some major UK charities and a few medical charities.

In 2000/01 the trust had assets of £2.3 million. Total income was £163,000, including £59,000 generated by assets and £92,000 in rents. Sundry expenses and audit fees for the year were kept low at £1,600. Grants totalled £144,000.

No grants list was included in the accounts. However, the trust has previously stated that it had existing commitments until 2003, when the trustees plan to review their grant-making policy.

Exclusions No grants are made to individuals. Most grants are made to organisations which have a connection to one of the trustees.

Applications Applications can only be accepted from registered charities and should be in writing to the correspondent. In order to save administration costs, replies are not sent to unsuccessful applicants. If the trustees are able to consider a request for support, they aim to express interest within one month.

The Sylvanus Charitable Trust

Animal welfare, Roman Catholic

£90,000 in Europe and US$110,000 in North America (2000)

Beneficial area Europe and North America.

Vernor Miles & Noble, 5 Raymond Buildings, Gray's Inn, London WC1R 5DD
Tel. 020 7242 8688
Correspondent John C Vernor Miles, Trustee
Trustees *John C Vernor Miles; Alexander D Gemmill; Wilfred E Vernor Miles; Gloria Taviner*
CC Number 259520
Information available Full accounts were on file at the Charity Commission.

General This trust was established in 1968 by the Countess of Kinnoull, who spent the last 40 years of her life in California, and supports the animal welfare, prevention of animal cruelty and the teachings and practices of the Roman Catholic Church. Organisations in North America and Europe are supported, with the trust splitting its finances into two sections, the sterling section (Europe) and the Dollar section (North America) to avoid currency troubles.

In the Sterling section, it had assets of £2.2 million, which generated an income of £65,000. Grants were made to 13 organisations totalling £90,000. These were £30,000 to Fraternity of Saint Pius X – Switzerland, £15,000 to Mauritian Wildlife Trust, £7,500 to University College Oxford, £6,000 each to Frame, Oeuvre d'Assistance aux Bêtes d'Abattoirs and World Society for the Protection of Animals, £4,000 each to Environmental Investigation Agency and RSPCA, £3,000 each to Help in Suffering and Lynx Educational Trust, £2,500 to Ecole Biblique et Archéologique Française,

£2,000 to PDSA and £1,000 to Mare and Foal Sanctuary.

In the Dollar Section, it had assets of US$855,000, which generated an income of US$53,000. Grants were made to 12 organisations totalling US$110,000, the largest of which were US$25,000 each to Montery Institute of International Studies and SPCA Horse Power Project.

The management and administration charges included payments of £11,000 and US$11,000 to a firm in which one of the trustees is a partner. Whilst wholly legal, these editors always regret such payments unless, in the words of the Charity Commission, 'there is no realistic alternative'.

Exclusions No grants for expeditions, scholarships or individuals.

Applications In writing to the correspondent. The trustees meet once a year.

The Tajtelbaum Charitable Trust

Jewish, welfare

£313,000 (2000/01)
Beneficial area Generally UK and Israel.

17 Western Avenue, London NW11 9EH
Correspondent Mrs I Tajtelbaum, Trustee
Trustees *Mrs I Tajtelbaum; I Tajtelbaum; M Tajtelbaum; E Tajtelbaum; E Jaswon; H Frydenson.*
CC Number 273184
Information available Accounts were on file at the Charity Commission but without a list of grants.

General The trust makes grants to orthodox synagogues and Jewish educational establishments, and to homes for older people and hospitals, generally in the UK and Israel.

In 2000/01 the trust had an income of £399,000, mainly derived from rental income and Gift Aid donations. Grants totalled £313,000. Unfortunately no further information was available on the size or number of beneficiaries for this year.

Previous beneficiaries have included Friends of Arad, Friends of Horim, Gur Trust and Huntingdon Foundation.

Applications In writing to the correspondent.

This entry was not confirmed by the trust, but the information was correct according to the Charity Commission files.

Talteg Ltd

Jewish, welfare

£110,000 (2000)

Beneficial area UK, with a preference for Scotland.

90 Mitchell Street, Glasgow G1 3NA
Tel. 0141 221 3353
Correspondent F S Berkeley, Trustee
Trustees *F S Berkeley; M Berkeley; A Berkeley; A N Berkeley; M Berkeley; Miss D L Berkeley.*
CC Number 283253
Information available Accounts were on file at the Charity Commission, but without a grants list or a narrative report.

General In 2000 the trust had assets of £2.6 million, an income of £284,000 and an expenditure of £115,000. Grants totalled £110,000. Unfortunately, no grants list was included with the accounts.

No grants list has been available since 1993 when the trust had an income of £175,000 (£134,000 from donations) and gave £92,000 in grants. Of the 48 grants made in the year, 34, including the larger grants, were to Jewish organisations. British Friends of Laniado Hospital received £30,000 and £20,000 each was given to Centre for Jewish Studies and Society of Friends of the Torah. Other larger grants were to JPAIME (£6,000), Glasgow Jewish Community Trust (£5,000), National Trust for Scotland (£2,300) and Friends of Hebrew University of Jerusalem (£1,000).

The remaining grants were all for less than £1,000 with several to Scottish charities, including Ayrshire Hospice (£530), Earl Haig Fund – Scotland (£200) and RSSPCC (£150). Other small grants went to welfare organisations, with an unusual grant of £780 to Golf Fanatics International.

Applications In writing to the correspondent.

The David Tannen Charitable Trust

Jewish

£87,000 (1999/2000)

Beneficial area UK.

Sutherland House, 70–78 West Hendon Broadway, London NW9 7BT
Tel. 020 8202 1066
Correspondent J M Miller, Trustee
Trustees *J M Miller; S Jacobowitz.*
CC Number 280392
Information available Accounts were on file at the Charity Commission.

General The trust makes grants for the advancement of the Jewish religion. In 1999/2000 the trust's assets were £2.4 million and it received an income of £1.3 million. Total charitable expenditure was £92,000, of which £87,000 was given in grants.

There were nine grants made altogether which were £25,000 each to Huntington Foundation Limited and Northwest London Communal Mikveh, £20,000 to SOFT, £10,000 to Finchley Road Synagogue, £5,000 to Adath Yisroel Synagogue, £900 to Beth Hamedesh Hendon, £600 to Woodstock Sinclair Trust and £500 to Sparkle Children Charity.

Applications In writing to the correspondent.

The Tanner Trust

General

£203,000 (2000/01)

Beneficial area UK and overseas.

PO Box 4207, Worthing, West Sussex BN11 1PW
Tel. 01903 709229 **Fax** 01903 709229
Correspondent Mrs L Whitcomb, Trust Administrator
Trustees *Lucie Nottingham; Alice Williams; Peter Youatt.*
CC Number 1021175
Information available Full accounts were on file at the Charity Commission.

General This trust has general charitable purposes, supporting organisations worldwide. The grants list shows no cause or geographical regions favoured or missing, although there appears to be many organisations concerned with youth, welfare and relief work.

In 2000/01 the trust had assets of £4.9 million. Total income was £218,000, including £200,000 in donations received from Hedgerley Properties Ltd. Grants were made to 151 organisations totalling £203,000.

The largest grants were £7,000 to Royal Agricultural Benevolent Fund, £6,500 to Kings College Body and Soul, £5,000 each to British Retinitis Pigmentosa Society, DEC India Earthquake Appeal, Voices Foundation and Y Care International and £3,000 each to Miriam Dean Fund, Parkinson's Disease Society, Probus Gardens, Royal Scottish Agricultural Benevolent Fund and Sunrise Appeal.

Other grants in the UK included £2,000 each to Birkenhead Youth Club, Historic Chapels Trust and Truro County Junior Choir, £1,000 each to BTCV, Cornwall Community Carrier, Help the Aged, RNLI, Sea Cadets and Youth Clubs UK and £500 each to Barn Owl Trust, Cornwall Bat Group, Hedgerley PCC, Herefordshire Growing Project, Tommy's Campaign and Winged Fellowship.

Organisations receiving support for work outside of the UK included Premala De Mar – Colombo and Sister Agata Children's Home – India (£2,000 each), Help Tibet Trust and Nambiki (£1,500 each), Home and Homes for Children and Need in Nepal (£1,000 each) and Friends of Romanian Horses (£500).

Exclusions No grants to individuals.

Applications The trust states that unsolicited applications are, without exception, not considered. Support is only given to charities personally known to the trustees.

The Tay Charitable Trust

General

£189,000 (2001/02)

Beneficial area UK, with a preference for Scotland, particularly Dundee.

6 Douglas Terrace, Broughty Ferry, Dundee DD5 1EA
Correspondent Mrs Elizabeth A Mussen, Trustee

Trustees *Mrs E A Mussen; Mrs Z C Martin; G C Bonar.*

CC Number SC001004

Information available Accounts were provided by the trust.

General This trust has general charitable purposes and supports a wide range of causes. Grants are generally made to UK-wide charities or organisations benefiting Scotland or Dundee, although local groups elsewhere can also be supported.

In 2000/01 the trust had assets of £4.6 million, which generated an income of £199,000. Management and administration for the year was very low at just £1,300. Grants were made to 191 charities totalling £189,000, including 109 smaller grants of less than £1,000 totalling £52,000. Over half of the larger grants were made to organisations also supported in the previous year.

The largest grant was £11,000 to University of Dundee. Other beneficiaries in the city included Dundee Heritage Trust (£5,300), Dundee Congregational Church and Dundee Rep (£2,000 each) with £1,000 each to Dundee Choral Union, Dundee Cyrenians and the local branches of National Counselling Service and Victim Support.

Other grants made in Scotland included £10,000 to Maritime Volunteers – Scottish Headquarters, £5,000 to Gather in the Isles, £2,000 each to Perth Theatre and Scottish Seabirds, £1,500 to National Library of Scotland and £1,000 each to Children 1st, CSC Scotland, Prince's Scottish Youth Business Trust, Scottish Civic Trust, Scottish Forum on Prisons and Scottish Throughcare and Aftercare.

Grants given outside Scotland included £5,500 to RNLI, £5,000 each to Bliss and Link, £3,000 each to Imperial Cancer Research Trust and Mansfield Traquair Trust, £2,000 each to Little Sisters of the Poor, Youth at Risk and York Minster Fund, £1,800 to Project Trust, £1,300 to Erskine Hospital, £1,200 to East Grinstead Research and £1,000 each to Army Benevolent Fund, Breakthrough Breast Cancer, Cancer Research UK, Crossroads, Christian Aid, Hearts and Minds, Lincoln Cathedral, Macmillan Cancer Relief, Stepping Stones and Youth for Christ.

Exclusions Grants are only given to charities recognised by the Inland Revenue. No grants to individuals.

Applications No standard form; applications in writing to the correspondent, including a financial statement. An sae is appreciated.

C B & H H Taylor 1984 Trust

Quaker, general

£140,000 (2000/01)

Beneficial area West Midlands, Ireland and overseas.

c/o Home Farm, Abberton, Worcestershire WR10 2NR

Correspondent W J B Taylor, Trustee

Trustees *Mrs C H Norton; Mrs E J Birmingham; J A B Taylor; W J B Taylor; Mrs C M Penny; T W Penny; R J Birmingham.*

CC Number 291363

Information available Full accounts and guidelines were provided by the trust.

General The trust's geographical areas of benefit are:

- organisations serving Birmingham and the West Midlands
- organisations outside the West Midlands where the trust has well-established links
- organisations in Ireland
- UK-based charities working overseas.

The general areas of benefit are:
- the Religious Society of Friends (Quakers) and other religious denominations
- healthcare projects
- social welfare: community groups; children and young people; older people; disadvantaged people, disabled people; homeless people; housing initiatives; counselling and mediation agencies
- education: adult literacy schemes; employment training; youth work
- penal affairs: work with offenders and ex-offenders; police projects
- the environment and conservation work
- the arts: museums and art galleries; music and drama
- Ireland: cross-community health and social welfare projects
- UK charities working overseas on long-term development projects.

75% of grants are for the work and concerns of the Religious Society of Friends. The trust favours specific applications. It does not usually award grants on an annual basis for revenue costs. Applications are encouraged from minority groups and woman-led initiatives. Grants, which are made only to or through registered charities, range from £500 to £3,000. Larger grants are seldom awarded.

In 2000/01 the trust had assets of £5.8 million and an income of £174,000. Management and administration totalled only £850. Grants awarded in the year totalled £140,000, with by far the largest, as usual, going to Warwickshire Monthly Meeting, which received £31,000.

Over 90 other grants were made, with only two for over £3,000. International Integrated Health Association and Friends of Swanirvar both received £5,000. There were five grants of £3,000, to Birmingham Family Service Unit, Cape Town Quaker Peace Centre, Ironbridge Gorge Museum, Ockenden Venture Afghanistan and Responding to Conflict.

Over half the remaining grants were for £1,000 to £2,500 and covered the fields and geographical areas as outlined above. Examples of beneficiaries include Avoncroft Museum, Birmingham Settlement, Birmingham Young Volunteers, Campaign Against the Arms Trade, Canon Collins Educational Trust, Intermediate Technology, Money for Madagascar, St Mary's Hospice, Shelter West Midlands project and Worcestershire Wildlife Trust.

Exclusions The trust does not fund: individuals (whether for research, expeditions, educational purposes, etc.); local projects or groups outside the West Midlands; or projects concerned with travel or adventure.

Applications There is no formal application form. Applicants should write to the correspondent giving the charity's registration number, a brief description of the charity's activities, and details of the specific project for which the grant is being sought. Applicants should also include a budget of the proposed work, together with a copy of the charity's most recent accounts. Trustees will also wish to know what funds have already been raised for the project and how the shortfall will be met.

The trust states that it receives more applications than it can support. Therefore, even if work falls within its policy it may not be able to help, particularly if the project is outside the West Midlands.

Trustees meet twice-yearly in May and November.

Applications will be acknowledged if an sae is provided.

Tegham Limited

Orthodox Jewish faith, welfare

£127,000 (2000/01)
Beneficial area UK.

c/o Gerald Kreditor & Co., Tudor House, Llanvanor Road, London NW2 2AQ
Correspondent Mrs S Fluss, Trustee
Trustees *Mrs S Fluss; Miss N Fluss.*
CC Number 283066
Information available Accounts were on file at the Charity Commission but without a list of grants.

General This trust supports the promotion of the Jewish Orthodox faith and the relief of poverty.

In 2000/01 it had an assets of £1.4 million and an income of £188,000, including £10,000 in donations received. From a total expenditure of £139,000, grants were made totalling £127,000. No further information was available in the accounts.

Applications In writing to the correspondent, although the trust stated that it has enough causes to support and does not welcome other applications.

Thackray Medical Research Trust

History of medical products and of their supply trade

£150,000 available (2002/03)
Beneficial area Worldwide.

c/o Thackray Museum, Beckett Street, Leeds LS9 7LN
Website www.tmrt.org
Correspondent Martin Schweiger, Chair of the Trustees
Trustees *Martin Schweiger, Chair; Richard Keeler; Christin Thackray; Paul Thackray; Stanley Warren; Matthew Wrigley.*
CC Number 702896
Information available Full accounts were provided by the trust.

General This trust is concerned with two aspects of medical products: their history

with particular emphasis on the medical supplies trade; and their charitable supply and development for third world countries. The trust initiated and supported the establishment of the award-winning Thackray Museum in Leeds, one of the largest medical museums in the world, and continues to support the research resource there, to provide a unique information centre for the history of medical products and the medical supplies trade worldwide. Now that the museum is fully operational, the trust is looking to support its other areas of interest. Current programmes are:

Medical supply grants
Grants of up to £10,000 a year are available to charitable organisations specialising in the supply of medical equipment to charities working in developing countries, especially those which show the best 'value for money' (for instance, those interested in reusing equipment rather than buying new). Support is generally given towards pump-priming and start-up costs rather than for equipment purchases.

Conference organisers
Grants of up to £1,500 are available towards conferences, symposia and lecture series where the content relates in part to the history of medical products and supplies.

Research into the history of medicinal products and supplies
Support is given to researchers whose work is wholly or partly related to that aspect of medical history. Researchers or their supervisors must have demonstrated experience in this particular field. Grants of up to £2,000 are available for the reimbursement of expenses (excluding books) and subsistence grants for up to three years may be awarded with an upper limit of £20,000.

In November 2002 the trust had assets of £4.1 million. This was expected to generate £150,000 during the 2002/03 financial year, all of which was available for distribution.

Applications In writing to the correspondent, in duplicate. The trustees meet quarterly, in January, April, July and October; applications should be submitted no later than the start of the preceding month. Projects which are not supported cannot be resubmitted. All applications must include:

- names and addresses of applicant(s), with brief CVs
- a description of the activity to be supported

- a timetable against which progress can be measured
- a breakdown of the expected costs, with details of how any balance will be paid
- details of requests made to other sources of funding
- names and addresses of referees.

For medical supply grants, accounts for the last three years, a copy of the trust deed, and a summary of the operational policy must be provided.

For conference organisers grants, details must be provided of the applicant's experience in organising similar events and details of the intended speakers.

For research grants, a list of any previously published work, details of intended publication and/or dissemination of the results of the research and, where appropriate, a letter from a supervisor confirming the details of the application and their support for the research must be included.

The Thompson Family Charitable Trust

Medical, veterinary, education, general

£149,000 (2000/01)
Beneficial area UK.

Hillsdown Court, 15 Totteridge Common, London N20 8LR
Tel. 020 8445 4343
Correspondent Roy Copus
Trustees *D B Thompson; P Thompson; K P Thompson.*
CC Number 326801
Information available Accounts were on file at the Charity Commission.

General This trust has general charitable purposes. There appear to be preferences for educational, medical and veterinary organisations.

In 2000/01 the trust had assets of £31 million, which generated an income of £1.8 million. Grants were made to 26 organisations totalling £149,000. It regularly builds up its reserves to enable it to make large donations in the future, for example towards the construction of new medical or educational facilities.

By far the largest beneficiary was NSPCC, which received three grants totalling

£74,000. Other large grants were £12,000 to One to One Project and £10,000 each to Break Caring Homes for Special Children, Chicken Shed Theatre Company and Totteridge Manor Association

Other beneficiaries included North London Hospice (£6,200 in three grants), Colon Cancer Concern and Countryside Alliance (£5,000 each), Royal Opera House Trust (£3,200), British Horse Society (£1,800), British Heart Foundation (£1,600 in two grants), Cambridge Rowing Club and Papworth Trust (£1,000 each), Stable Lads Welfare Trust (£700 in two grants), Ely Diocesan Board and Norwood (£500 each), Racing Welfare Charities (£400) and MS Society (£200).

Exclusions No grants to individuals.

Applications In writing to the trustees.

The Thomson Corporation Charitable Trust

People who are physically, mentally and socially disadvantaged

£100,000 (2000)

Beneficial area UK with some preference for London and the home counties.

1st Floor, The Quadrangle, 180 Wardour Street, London W1A 4YG

Correspondent Sue Jenner

Trustees S J H Coles.

CC Number 1013317

Information available Accounts were on file at the Charity Commission.

General In 2000 the trust had assets of £100,000. Total income was £99,000, of which £96,000 was donated by the holiday company that founded the trust. Grants were made to 151 organisations totalling £100,000.

The largest grants were £2,000 each to Derwent House, Isabel Hospice and Portland College and £1,400 to Northgate School.

Grants of £1,000 each went to 43 organisations, including Age Concern, ASPIRE, British Wheelchair Sports Foundation, Roy Castle Lung Cancer

Foundation, Centrepoint, Colon Cancer Concern, History of Advertising Trust, Mencap, NCH Action for Children, Orbis Charitable Trust, The Pace Centre, Royal Marsden Hospital Charity, Sense and VSO.

Smaller grants included £500 each to Canine Partners for Independence, Gingerbread, Guideposts Trust, Heartline Association, Roy Kinnear Charitable Trust, Jubilee Sailing Trust, Merlin, Miracles, New Horizons Trust and Uphill Ski Club.

Exclusions No grants for advertisements in souvenir brochures, expeditions or to individuals.

Applications In writing to the correspondent; trustees meet on an ad hoc basis.

The Sue Thomson Foundation

Christ's Hospital School, education

£132,000 (2000/01)

Beneficial area UK.

Furners Keep, Furners Lane, Henfield, West Sussex BN5 9HS

Tel. 01273 493461 **Fax** 01273 495139

Correspondent Mrs S M Mitchell, Trustee

Trustees Mrs S M Mitchell; C L Corman; J Gillham.

CC Number 298808

Information available Full accounts were on file at the Charity Commission.

General In 2000/01 the foundation had assets totalling £2.4 million and an income of £57,000. Grants were made totalling £132,000, including £120,000 donated to Christ's Hospital, the foundation's main regular beneficiary.

Grants were also made to four former pupils of Christ's Hospital towards their further education expenses, totalling £3,000.

Other beneficiaries included Dechert Charitable Trust (£2,500), Publishing Training Centre and Bridewell Royal Hospital (£1,500 each). Other grants were for less than £500, including those to Sunfield & Community Arts Trust, Sequal

Trust, Royal National Theatre, Mathieson Music School, Friends of Crawley Hospital, Friends of Covent Garden, Friends for Young Deaf and Finnish Children's Songs. 'Miscellaneous grants' totalled £2,600.

Exclusions No grants to large charities or individuals, except as part of a specific scheme (see above).

Applications No guidelines. Applications are acknowledged only if an sae is enclosed.

The Thornton Foundation

General

£357,000 (2001/02)

Beneficial area UK.

Stephenson Harwood, 1 St Paul's Churchyard, London EC4M 8SH

Tel. 020 7329 4422

Correspondent Richard Thornton, Chair

Trustees R C Thornton, Chair; A H Isaacs; H D C Thornton; Mrs S J Thornton.

CC Number 326383

Information available Full accounts were provided by the trust.

General The object of the foundation are to make grants to charities selected by the trustees. The principal guideline of the trust is to use the funds to further charitable causes where their money will, as far as possible, act as 'high powered money', in other words be of significant use to the cause. Only causes that are known personally to the trustees and/or that they are able to investigate thoroughly are supported. The trust states it is proactive rather than reactive in seeking applicants.

In 2001/02 the trust had assets of £3.6 million, which generated an income of £159,000. Grants totalling £357,000 were made to 16 organisations, of which 10 were also supported in the previous year.

The largest grant of £110,000 was given to an exceptional project. Other large grants were £60,000 to Peper Harrow Foundation, £35,000 to St Christopher's Hospice, £30,000 each to 21st Learning Initiative and HMS Trincomlee Trust and £20,000 to Mary Rose Trust.

The other recipients were Stowe House Preservation Trust (£10,000), St Peter's Trust (£7,500), Helen House and Keble

243

College – Oxford (£5,000 each), Prisoners of Conscience (£2,000), Museum of London (£1,500), with £1,000 each to Break, Hope House and Scope. A further grant of £32,000 was also given to another capital project.

Applications The trust strongly emphasises that it does not accept unsolicited applications, and, as it states above, only organisations that are known to one of the trustees will be considered for support. Any unsolicited applications will not receive a reply.

The Thornton Trust

Evangelical Christianity, education, relief of sickness and poverty

£222,000 (2000/01)

Beneficial area UK and overseas.

Hunters Cottage, Hunters Yard, Debden Road, Saffron Walden, Essex CB11 4AA

Correspondent D H Thornton, Trustee

Trustees *D H Thornton; Mrs B Y Thornton; J D Thornton.*

CC Number 205357

Information available Full accounts were on file at the Charity Commission.

General This trust was created in 1962 for 'the promotion of and furthering of education and the Evangelical Christian faith, and assisting in the relief of sickness, suffering and poverty'.

In 2000/01 the trust had assets of £1.7 million and a total income of £92,000. Grants totalling £222,000 were made to 89 organisations, 57 of which were also supported in the previous year.

The largest grants were £46,000 to Saffron Walden Baptist Church, £30,000 to Redcliffe Missionary College and £24,000 to Africa Inland Mission.

Other grants included £5,000 each to Bible Society, Care Foundation, Carers Christian Fellowship, Eastbury Church – Northwood and Keswick Convention, £3,300 to Tearfund, £2,900 to Dugdale Trust, £2,500 to Scripture Union, £1,500 to Salisbury Baptist Church, £1,000 each to Crosslinks, City Church Cambridge, Christians in Sport and Send a Cow, £500 each to Cog Wheel Trust and RAF Benevolent Fund, £250 to Spring Harvest Trust, £100 to London Institute for

Contemporary Christianity, £70 to Hertford Baptist Church, £50 to Christians in Property and £25 to Chartered Institute of Building Benevolent Fund.

Exclusions No grants to general appeals or individuals.

Applications The trust states: 'Our funds are fully committed to charities which the trustees have supported for many years and we regret that we are unable to respond to the many calls for assistance we are now receiving.'

The Three Oaks Trust

Welfare

£217,000 to organisations

(2000/01)

Beneficial area Overseas, UK, with a preference for West Sussex.

The Three Oaks Family Trust Co. Ltd, PO Box 243, Crawley, West Sussex RH10 6YB

Website www.thethreeoakstrust.co.uk

Correspondent The Trustees

Trustees *The Three Oaks Family Trust Co. Ltd.*

CC Number 297079

Information available Full and detailed accounts were on file at the Charity Commission.

General The trust regularly supports the same welfare organisations in the UK and overseas each year. A small number of grants have also been made to individuals via statutory authorities or voluntary agencies, although this area of giving is being phased out and no further applications from individuals will be successful.

Grants were made totalling £253,000, of which £165,000 went to UK charities, £53,000 to overseas charities and £35,000 to individuals. Grants were given under the following programmes:

Projects that aid people with psychological or emotional difficulties
The largest grants were £10,000 each to Crawley Open House and Horsham Counselling Service for running costs. Other beneficiaries included Coventry Day Centre for Norton House, West Midlands Post Adoption Service for counselling for adults and YMCA – Hove

towards the training of professionals (£5,000 each) and Information for Young People (£3,000).

Welfare – Illness
Raynauds and Scleroderma Association received £15,000 towards the salary of a welfare support worker while Visceral received £5,000 as a research grant towards the study of gastro-intestinal disorders.

Support to individuals and families living in the community
A psychotherapeutic service for children was given £40,000 in a grant through West Sussex County Council. Grants totalling £35,000 were also given directly to individuals, through Surrey and West Sussex county councils.

Overseas aid
Beneficiaries included Kaloko Trust – Zambia to develop the livelihood of people who might otherwise be without work or food (£15,000), Ceco – Sri Lanka for computer equipment and student tuition to provide job opportunities for young people (£10,000) and Sight Savers International (£5,000).

The accounts also listed the following five future commitments: £60,000 to 2005 to Raynauds and Scleroderma Association; £15,000 to 2004 to Parkinson's Disease Society; £10,000 to 2002 each to Crawley Open House and Kaloko Trust; and £2,000 to 2002 to Anglican Church Argentina.

Applications The trust's 2000/01 annual report stated: 'The directors intend to continue supporting the organisations that they have supported in the past and are not planning to fund any new projects in the near future. To save administration costs, the directors do not respond to requests, unless they are considering making a donation.

'Requests from organisations for donations that exceed £2,000 are considered on a quarterly basis in meetings held in January, April, July and October.'

The Thriplow Charitable Trust

Higher education and research

£98,000 (2000/01)

Beneficial area Preference for British institutions.

PO Box 243, Cambridge CB3 9PQ

Correspondent Mrs E Mackintosh, Secretary

Trustees *Sir Peter Swinnerton-Dyer; Dr Harriet Crawford; Prof. Karen Sparck Jones; Prof. Christopher Bayly.*

CC Number 1025531

Information available Full accounts and guidance to applicants were provided by the trustees.

General The charity was established by a trust deed in 1983. Its main aims are the furtherance of higher and further education and research, with preference given to British institutions.

Projects that have generally been supported in the past include contributions to research study funds, research fellowships, academic training schemes, computer facilities and building projects. Specific projects are preferred rather than contributions to general running costs. The trust prefers to support smaller projects where grants can 'make a difference'.

In 2000/01 the trust had assets of £3.2 million and an income of £90,000. Grants totalling £98,000 were given to 21 organisations, ranging from £2,000 to £8,000.

The largest grants of £8,000 each went to Cambridge Foundation to purchase papers by Isaac Newton and Kew Foundation for plant research.

Other grants included £7,000 to the University of Bath for research; £5,500 each to the British Museum to buy trays for cuneiform tablets, and Quarriers for training costs; £5,000 each to

Chronic Fatigue Syndrome for research, Courtauld Institute of Art for scholarships, Early English Organ Project for research, University of Edinburgh biology department for microarray facilities, Girton College towards archive building costs, Pembroke College towards student hardship funds, Queen Alexandra College for accommodation for people who are blind and Stoke Manderville Hospital for research into spinal injuries.

Exclusions Grants can only be made to charitable bodies or component parts of charitable bodies. In no circumstances can grants be made to individuals.

Applications There is no application form. A letter of application should specify the purpose for which funds are sought and the costings of the project. It should be indicated whether other applications for funds are pending and, if the funds are to be channelled to an individual or a small group, what degree of supervision over the quality of the work would be exercised by the institution.

Trustee meetings are held twice a year – in spring and in autumn.

The Tolkien Trust

Christian – especially Catholic, welfare and general

£60,000 (1998/99)

Beneficial area UK, with a preference for Oxfordshire.

Manches Solicitors, 3 Worcester Street, Oxford OX1 2PZ

Tel. 01865 722106 **Fax** 01865 813687

Correspondent Mrs Cathleen Blackburn

Trustees *John Tolkien; Christopher Tolkien; Priscilla Tolkien.*

CC Number 273615

Information available Full accounts were on file at the Charity Commission.

General The trust's main assets are the copyright in certain works of J R R Tolkien. This provides the trust with its income, and although there is no permanent endowment, there should always be an income from book royalties during the period of copyright. There appears to be a preference for Christian organisations, especially Catholic, then welfare and organisations in Oxfordshire.

In 2000/01 the trust had an income of £212,000 and a total expenditure of £127,000. This information was taken from the Charity Commission database; unfortunately no further information was available for this year. In 1998/99 the income was £94,000, of which over £90,000 was from royalties. The trust gave 33 grants totalling £60,000.

Many of the beneficiaries, both UK and local had received grants in previous years. The largest were £13,000 to Find Your Feet Ltd, and £4,000 each to St Anthony's RC Church, Littlemore and Catholic Housing Aid Society.

Five grants of £3,000, two of £2,500, two of £2,000 and five of £1,000 were awarded. Recipients included Bodleian Library – Oxford, Centre of St Martin's-in-the-Field, CAFOD, North Staffordshire Marriage Care, Oxford Marriage Care, Samaritans, St Barnabas Society, Shelter, Tablet Trust and Wrexham Concern Trust.

The remainder of grants were in the range of £150 to £800, generally for smaller amounts, including those to Council for the Amnesty International (£700), Protection of Rural England (£500), Christian Psychotherapy Foundation (£350), Safer World (£400) and Inter Faith Network (£150).

Exclusions No support for non-registered charities.

Applications In writing to the correspondent.

Tomchei Torah Charitable Trust

Jewish educational institutions

£70,000 (1998/99)

Beneficial area UK.

Harold Everett Wreford, Second Floor, 32 Wigmore Street, London W1U 2RP

Tel. 020 7535 5900

Correspondent A Frei, Trustee

Trustees *I J Kohn; S M Kohn; A Frei.*

CC Number 802125

Information available Full accounts were on file at the Charity Commission.

General This trust supports Jewish educational institutions. Grants usually average about £5,000.

In 1998/99 the trust's assets were £58,000 and it had an income of £81,000 from Gift Aid donations. Grants totalled £70,000 and were made to 60 Jewish organisations, about two thirds of these were recurrent from the previous year.

By far the largest grant was £22,000 to Merkaz Hatorah. Other larger grants were £5,300 each to Chested Charity Trust and

Parsha Limited, £3,500 each to Woodstock Sinclair Trust and £2,500 to Notzer Chested.

Over 70% of grants were for amounts under £1,000, ranging from £40 to £900. Beneficiaries included Menorah Grammar School (£900), United Talmudical Academy (£430), Talmud Torah Education (£250), Friends of Bobov Foundation (£200), Jewish Learning Exchange (£150) and Holmleigh Trust (£40).

Applications In writing to the correspondent at any time.

The Tory Family Foundation

Education, Christian, medical

£74,000 (2000/01)
Beneficial area Worldwide, but principally Folkestone.

The Estate Office, Etchinghill Golf, Folkestone, Kent CT18 8FA
Tel. 01303 862280
Correspondent P N Tory, Trustee
Trustees *P N Tory; J N Tory; Mrs S A Rice.*
CC Number 326584
Information available Full accounts were on file at the Charity Commission.

General The trust's 2000/01 annual report stated: 'The charity was formed to provide financial help to a wide variety of charitable needs. It is currently supporting causes principally in the locality of Folkestone. These causes include education, religious, social and medical subjects, and the donees themselves are often registered charities.

'The charity does not normally aim to fund the whole of any given project, and thus applicants are expected to demonstrate a degree of existing and regular support.'

In 2000/01 assets totalled £2.4 million, which generated an income of £120,000. From an expenditure of £78,000, grants were made totalling £74,000, broken down as follows:

Churches – 7 grants totalling £7,800
These included £5,000 to St Mary's Church for maintenance, £1,000 to St Martin's Parish Church for the Seabrook Village Hall, £750 to St Rumwold's for

restoration and £230 to All Saints Church for Bibles.

Education – 15 grants totalling £17,000
Grants were made to 12 organisations and 3 individuals. Atlantic Education received £6,000 for an Atlantic partnership and £4,000 as an additional payment. Other beneficiaries included Elham Primary School for a book about Elham's history (£1,000), Cheriton Primary PTA for a new stage and Commonwork for a children's farm in Edenbridge (£250 each) and Aidis Trust for a Hopkinson PC (£220).

Local – 31 grants totalling £33,000
These went to 29 organisations and 2 individuals. They included Salvation Army for a worship and community centre (£7,000), Canterbury Festival to stage The Marriage of Figaro and Weald District Scouts for an activity centre (£2,000 each), Folkestone Rainbow Club for an anger management course and Samaritans for a charity auction (£1,000 each), Home Start (£500) and Kent Cricket Youth Teams for colts support (£250).

Health – 4 grants totalling £1,500
These were £500 each to Great Ormond Street Hospital for cochlear implants and St John Ambulance for defibrillators and £250 each to Macmillan Cancer Relief for the Cycle Mongolia project and Pilgrims Hospice for a holiday.

Overseas – 24 grants totalling £13,000
These went to 5 individuals and 19 organisations. Grants included £2,000 each to Apt Enterprise Development and Prisoners Abroad, £1,000 each to Population Concern, Raleigh International for a Mongolian airlift, Marie Stopes International for population health research and VSO for work in Tanzania, £712 to Institute Molecular Manufacturing, £250 to Sparrow Schools for a South African choir trip and £200 to Read E for Oakwood School – India.

Other – 3 grants totalling £1,600
YMCA received £1,000 for a saving scheme. Age Concern received two grants, £300 each for L Bulled-Everist Charitable Trust and an Easter fair.

Exclusions Grants are given to registered charities only. Applications outside Kent are unlikely to be considered. No grants are given for further education.

Applications In writing to the correspondent. Applications are considered throughout the year. To keep costs down, unsuccessful applicants will not be notified.

The Towry Law Charitable Trust

Education, medical research, welfare
£296,000 (2000/01)
Beneficial area UK, with a slight preference for the south of England.

Towry Law House, Western Road, Bracknell, Berkshire RG12 1TL
Tel. 01344 828009
Correspondent Mrs Merl Gurr
Trustees *Hon. C T H Law, Chair; K H Holmes; D G Ainslie.*
CC Number 278880
Information available Full accounts were on file at the Charity Commission.

General This trust supports two areas of work. Just over 50% of its funds each year is given towards medical research and the welfare of people who are elderly or have disabilities. The rest of the funds (just under 50%) are given towards work with children and young people, mostly for welfare or educational needs. The grants list showed grants were mostly given to organisations working UK-wide or in the south of England.

In 2000/01 the trust had assets of £2.3 million. The total income was £237,000, including £137,000 from school fees administration. Grants totalling £296,000 were made to 65 organisations, of which 56 were also supported in the previous year.

Imperial Cancer Research Campaign received two grants totalling £15,000, including £6,000 for the Everyman Appeal. Other large grants were £12,000 to Berkshire Community Trust, £10,000 each to RNIB Sunshine School for Blind Children, Sargent Cancer Care for Children and University of Exeter, £9,500 to Children's Hospital School and £9,000 to Break.

Other beneficiaries included Evelina Children's Hospital Appeal and King Edward VII's Hospital for Officers (£7,500 each), Macmillan Cancer Relief and Treloar Trust (£6,500 each), Camden Area Home Nursing Trust and Sue Ryder Foundation (£5,000), Parkinson's Disease Society (£4,500), Mencap (£4,000), Eton College for Bursaries (£3,800), Almshouse Association and Honeypot (£3,000 each), South Buckinghamshire Association for the Disabled and Thames Valley Family Mediation Service (£2,500), Jessie May Trust and Tokyo International Learning

Centre (£2,000 each) and With Jerusalem in Mind (£1,000).

Exclusions No grants to individuals, bodies which are not UK-registered charities, local branches or associates of UK charities.

Applications In writing to the correspondent. Unsolicited applications are not considered.

The Toy Trust

Children

£209,000 (2001)
Beneficial area UK.

British Toy & Hobby Association, 80 Camberwell Road, London SE5 0EG
Correspondent Ms Karen Baxter
Trustees *The British Toy and Hobby Association; T G Willis; A Munn; J D Hunter; B Ellis.*
CC Number 1001634
Information available Full accounts were on file at the Charity Commission.

General This trust was registered in 1991 to centralise the giving of the British Toy and Hobby Association. Prior to this, the association raised money from the toy industry, which it pledged to one charity on an annual basis. It was felt that the fundraising activities of the association were probably more than matched by its individual members, and that the charitable giving of the toy industry to children's charities was going unnoticed by the public. The trust still receives the majority of its income from fundraising activities, donating the proceeds to children's charities and charitable projects benefiting children.

In 2001 the trust had an income of £215,000, of which £211,000 came from donations received. Assets totalled £214,000 whilst administration costs were very low at £1,900. Grants were made to over 1000 charities totalling £209,000.

The largest grants were £10,000 each to DEBRA, NATLL, Toy Box Charity and Wexford Children Hospice. Other grants listed in the accounts were £9,000 to Kidscape, £7,800 to Diana Louise Trust, £5,000 each to Mildmay, Royal Liverpool Philharmonic Society, St Andrew's Hospice and Speech Language & Learn Centre, £4,000 each to Noah's Ark Trust (1998) Ltd and Mega Centre, £3,900 to Prison Fellowship, £3,800 to Brainwave,

£3,700 to Delta and £3,500 each to Kent Adventure Club for the Disabled and Woolsworthy Sports.

Applications In writing to the correspondent.

The Constance Travis Charitable Trust

General

£186,000 (2000/01)
Beneficial area UK (national charities only); Northamptonshire (all sectors).

Quinton Rising, Quinton, Northampton NN7 2EF
Correspondent A Travis
Trustees *Mrs C M Travis; E R A Travis.*
CC Number 294540
Information available Accounts were on file at the Charity Commission, but without a full list of grants.

General This trust has general charitable purposes, supporting local organisations in Northamptonshire as well as organisations working UK-wide.

In 2000/01 the trust had assets of £8.3 million, which generated an income of £215,000. After very low management and administration charges of £680, grants to organisations totalled £186,000.

The largest grants were £29,000 to NSPCC, £20,000 to Imperial Cancer Research Fund, £15,000 to Age Concern and £10,000 each to Macmillan Cancer Relief and The Stroke Association.

Quinton Village Hall Trust received £8,100 while £5,000 each was given to Colon Cancer Concern, Deafblind UK, Mental Health Foundation, NAYC, Northamptonshire Association for the Blind, Prince's Trust, Scope, Shaftesbury Hinwick Hall Appeal and The Spencer Contact. The other grants, totalling £49,000, were all for £4,000 or less and were not listed in the accounts.

Exclusions No grants to individuals or non-registered charities.

Applications In writing to the correspondent.

The Treeside Trust

General

£98,000 (2001/02)
Beneficial area UK, but mainly local.

4 The Park, Grasscroft, Oldham OL4 4ES
Tel. 01457 876422
Correspondent John Roger Beresford Gould, Trustee
Trustees *C C Gould; J R B Gould; J R W Gould; D M Ives; R J Ives; B Washbrook.*
CC Number 1061586
Information available Accounts were on file at the Charity Commission, but with only a brief narrative report and no list of grants.

General The trust supports mainly local charities, and a few UK charities which are supported on a regular basis. It states: 'In the main the trustees intend to make a limited number of substantial grants each year, rather than a larger number of smaller ones, in order to make significant contributions to some of the causes supported.'

In 2001/02 the trust had assets of £915,000 and an income of £47,000. Grants totalled £98,000. No further information was available.

Applications In writing to the correspondent, but unsolicited applications are unlikely to be supported.

Triodos Foundation

Overseas development, organics, community development

£120,000 (1999)
Beneficial area UK and developing countries.

Brunel House, 11 The Promenade, Clifton, Bristol BS8 3NN
Tel. 0117 973 9339
Correspondent The Trustees
Trustees *P Blom; M Robinson; M Bierman.*
CC Number 1052958
Information available Full accounts were on file at the Charity Commission.

General This trust, registered in 1996, makes grants both nationally and overseas, through its own networks. Wherever possible it prefers to act in partnership with existing charitable organisations to provide benefits.

The objectives of the foundation are to support charitable needs which have been identified through, but which are unable to be fully supported by, the work of Triodos Bank in the UK. It works closely with individuals, organisations and depositors of the bank to support projects that work in charitable areas.

Donations in 2002 included a grant to a leading micro-finance institution, K-Rep Bank in Kenya and support for the first organic research conference in the UK, in Aberystwyth.

In 1999, the trust had an income of £162,000, comprised mainly of donations. It made grants totalling £120,000 and, after further management and administration expenses of £2,000, transferred the surplus of £40,000 to the capital account, resulting in assets at the year end totalling £199,000.

Exclusions No grants to individuals or students.

Applications In writing to the correspondent. Initial telephone enquiries are welcome.

Truedene Co. Ltd

Jewish
£184,000 (1996/97)
Beneficial area UK and overseas.

Cohen Arnold & Co., 13–17 New Burlington Place, London W1X 2HL
Correspondent The Trustees
Trustees H Laufer; M Gross; S Berger; S Laufer; S Berger; Mrs Sarah Klein; Mrs Z Sternlicht.
CC Number 248268
Information available Accounts were on file at the Charity Commission up until 1996/97, but without a grants list.

General In 2000/01 this trust had an income of £138,000 and a total expenditure of £1.7 million. This information was taken from the Charity Commission database; unfortunately no further information was available for this year.

This trust's assets totalled £5 million in 1996/97. It had an income of £5,500, which was staggeringly different from the year before, when it was £425,000. Donations totalled £184,000 (£7.8 million in 1995/96). Unfortunately a grants list has not been included with the accounts at the Charity Commission since those for 1985/86, when grants were given to Jewish educational and religious organisations.

Applications In writing to the correspondent.

The Truemark Trust

General
£207,000 (2000/01)
Beneficial area UK only.

PO Box 2, Liss, Hampshire GU33 6YP
Correspondent Mrs Judy Hayward
Trustees Michael Collishaw; Michael Meakin; Richard Wolfe; Sir Thomas Lucas; Wendy Collett; Stuart Neil.
CC Number 265855
Information available Full accounts were on file at the Charity Commission.

General The trust favours small organisations with a preference for innovatory projects, particularly neighbourhood based community projects and less popular groups. Current main areas of interest are: disability, older people and people otherwise disadvantaged, including counselling and community support groups in areas of unrest or deprivation, alternative or complementary health projects. Charities with locations ranging from Cardiff to Sheffield and Yeovil to Glasgow received grants.

Grants are usually one-off for a specific project or part of a project. Core funding and/or salaries are rarely considered. The average size of grants is £1,000.

In 2000/01 the trust had assets of £5.3 million and an income of £217,000. Grants totalled £207,000. Of the 144 grants made, over 90% were for £1,000 or more. Beneficiaries of grants included: Bristol Cancer Help Centre, Foundation for Integrated Medicine and Prison Phoenix Trust – Oxford (£5,000 each), Bristol Stepping Stone (£3,500), Brainwave, Friends Fellowship of Healing, Hamlin Religious Trust and White Eagle Lodge (£3,000 each),

Citizen's Advice Bureau – Teignbridge (£2,500), Brighton & Hove Federation of Disabled People, Freshwinds Charitable Trust – Birmingham, Sport Forum for the Disabled and Step by Step Project (£2,000 each) and Breakout Children's Holidays – Middlesex, First Steps to Freedom – Warwickshire and Relate – Bournemouth (£1,500 each).

Among the 67 organisations receiving £1,000 each were: Amington Friendship Group – Tamworth, Camberley Care – Surrey, Community Care Association – North Yorkshire, Disability Access Charter – Birmingham, Newton-le-Willows Family & Community Association, Sailability and Victim Support – Southwark.

Exclusions No grants to individuals, for scientific or medical research or for church buildings. General appeals from large UK organisations are not supported.

Applications In writing to the correspondent, including the most recent set of accounts, clear details of the need the project is designed to meet and an outline budget. Trustees meet four times a year (in March, June, September and December). Only successful applicants receive a reply.

Trumros Limited

Jewish
£139,000 (2000)
Beneficial area UK.

182 Finchley Road, London NW3 7AD
Correspondent Mrs H Hofbauer, Trustee
Trustees R S Hofbauer; Mrs H Hofbauer.
CC Number 285533
Information available Full accounts were on file at the Charity Commission.

General This trust appears to support Jewish organisations only. In 2000 it had assets of £2.5 million and an income of £539,000, of which £446,000 came from rental income. A total of £139,000 was given in grants; unfortunately a list of donations was not included with the accounts that were on file at the Charity Commission.

In 1999 a total of £212,000 was distributed in 128 grants. Over 40% of donations were for £1,000 or more, with the remainder being mainly for £500 or less. The three largest grants were: £20,000 each to Menorah Primary School, Centre for Torah Education Zichron Yaacov and

Beis Yoseph Zvi Institutions. Other larger grants went to SOFOT (£11,000), General Cherra Kadish Jerusalem (£5,800), Oldos Aharon (£4,800), Jewish learning Exchange (£2,000) and Gateshead Jewish Academy for Girls (£1,000).

Smaller grants included: Beis Avrohom Synagogue (£600), London Jerusalem Academy, Friends of Ohr Someach and YMER (£500 each), Achiezer Assia (£200) and Israel Settlement Fund (£100).

Applications In writing to the correspondent, but note that the trust states it is already inundated with applications.

Trust Sixty Three

Disability, overseas aid, famine relief, general

£106,000 to organisations (2000/01)
Beneficial area UK and overseas, with a preference for Bedfordshire and Hertfordshire.

3 The Compasses, High Street, Clophill, Bedfordshire MK45 4AF
Tel. 01525 860777 **Fax** 01525 862246
Correspondent Mrs A F Tait, Trustee
Trustees *M W Tait; Mrs A F Tait; C G Nott; Mrs J Hobbs; Mrs D Staines.*
CC Number 1049136
Information available Accounts were on file at the Charity Commission.

General This trust has general charitable purposes, although in general grants are only made towards disability causes, overseas aid and famine relief.

In 2000/01 the trust had assets of £579,000, which generated an income of £22,000. Grants were made to 114 organisations totalling £106,000. Grants were also made to two individuals totalling £170. After management and administration costs of £6,000, there was a deficit for the year of £90,000. In the previous year, the deficit was £106,000.

The largest grants were £9,700 to North Hertfordshire Sanctuary, £7,000 to Christian Aid, £5,400 each to Bedfordshire Garden Carers and Rainbow School and £5,000 each to Pasque Hospital and Prebend Day Centre.

Other local beneficiaries included St Mary's Church (£4,300), Ridgeway School (£3,200), Richmond School (£2,500), Bedfordshire County Council

(£1,500) and Ridgeway Gardening Club (£90).

Overseas beneficiaries included DEC Indian Earthquake Appeal and El Salvador Earthquake (£2,500 each), Children of Bulgaria Appeal and Link Africa (£300 each).

Grants elsewhere included £2,500 to Scope, £2,000 each to Chicken Shed Theatre Company, Children Today and Farms for City Children, £1,300 to Make a Wish, £1,000 each to British Heart Foundation and VSO, £500 to Big Issue Foundation, £320 to Shelter, £300 to Mind, £200 to Dream Holidays, £30 to RNLI and £20 to Woodland Trust.

Exclusions No grants to individuals.

Applications In writing to the correspondent.

Tudor Rose Ltd

Jewish

£82,000 (2000/01)
Beneficial area UK.

Martin and Heller, Accountants, 5 North End Road, London NW11 7RJ
Tel. 020 8455 6789
Correspondent Samuel Taub, Secretary
Trustees *M Lehrfield; M Taub; A Taub; S Taub; S L Taub.*
CC Number 800576
Information available Full accounts were on file at the Charity Commission.

General This trust works for the promotion of the Orthodox Jewish faith and the relief of poverty.

In 2000/01 it had assets of £704,000. Total income was £254,000, including £8,300 from donations and £208,000 from property income. £110,000 was spent during the year on these properties and listed as expenditure. Grants were made totalling £82,000.

The eight grants of £1,000 or over were listed in the accounts. These were £29,000 to Ponovex, £18,000 to CWCT, £13,000 to Yetev Lev, £12,000 to Yad Eliezer, £4,100 to Torah Study Centre, £3,000 to Rihiliation Trust, £1,600 to NWL Synagogue and £1,000 to Gur Trust. Smaller grants totalled £1,100.

Applications In writing to the correspondent.

The Tufton Charitable Trust

Christian

£51,000 (2000)
Beneficial area UK.

Slater Maidment, 7 St James's Square, London SW1Y 4JU
Tel. 020 7930 7621
Correspondent C Sadlow
Trustees *Sir Christopher Wates; Lady Wates; J R F Lulham.*
CC Number 801479
Information available Full accounts were provided by the trust.

General This trust supports Christian organisations, by providing grants as well as allowing them to use premises leased by the trust for retreats.

In 2000 the trust had assets of £1.5 million. Total income was £1 million, including £885,000 from donations received, which were mostly transferred to assets. Direct charitable expenditure was £238,000, including grants totalling £51,000.

By far the largest grant was £22,000 to Church of England. Other recipients of over £1,000 were Dartmouth Prison Trust and Lambeth Partnership (£5,000 each), Prison Fellowship (£3,200), On the Move (£3,000), Institute of Contemporary Christianity (£2,500) and International Student Christian Service (£1,500). Smaller grants totalled £8,800.

Exclusions No grants for repair or maintenance of buildings.

Applications In writing to the correspondent, including an sae.

The Florence Turner Trust

General

£152,000 (2000/01)
Beneficial area UK, but with a strong preference for Leicestershire.

c/o Harvey Ingram Owston, 20 New Walk, Leicester LE1 6TX
Tel. 0116 254 5454 **Fax** 0116 255 3318
Correspondent The Trustees
Trustees *Roger Bowder; Allan A Veasey; Caroline A Macpherson.*

CC Number 502721

Information available Full accounts were provided by the trust.

General This trust has general charitable purposes, giving most of its support in Leicestershire. The grants list shows many grants to children's and welfare organisations.

In 2000/01 the trust had assets of £4.3 million and an income of £159,000. Grants were made to 147 organisations totalling £152,000. Management and administration costs were high at £32,000, including £13,000 in solicitors' charges as clerk to the trustees and £6,000 in trustees renumeration.

The largest grants were £23,000 to Leicester Grammar School for bursaries, library and prizes and £12,000 to Leicester Charity Organisation Society.

Other grants in Leicestershire included £5,000 to Barnardos – Leicestershire, £2,600 to Leicester and Leicestershire Historic Churches Preservation Trust, £2,200 each to Age Concern Leicester, Age Concern Leicestershire, Leicester YMCA, and Leicestershire Scout Council, £2,100 to Leicester Children's Holiday Centre, £1,800 to Leicester and District MS Society, £1,500 to Sir Jonathon North Community College, £1,300 to Salvation Army – Leicester and £1,000 each to Asfordby Captain's Close County Primary School, Harborough Anchor Staying Put, Leicestershire and Rutland Crimebeat, Newfoundpool Senior Citizen's Umbrella Group and Oadby Boys Club.

Beneficiaries elsewhere included EEIBA (£2,300), CARE Fund for the Mentally Handicapped (£2,000), Army Benevolent Fund, Marie Curie Cancer Care and PDSA (£1,800 each) and BREAK (£1,000).

Exclusions The trust does not support individuals for educational purposes.

Applications In writing to the correspondent. Trustees meet every eight or nine weeks.

The TUUT Charitable Trust

General, but with a bias towards trade union favoured causes

£87,000 (2000/01)

Beneficial area Worldwide.

Congress House, Great Russell Street, London WC1B 3LQ

Tel. 020 7637 7116 **Fax** 020 7637 7087

Email info@tufm.co.uk

Correspondent Ann Smith, Secretary

Trustees *Lord Christopher; J Monks; A Tuffin; M Walsh; M Bradley; E Chapman.*

CC Number 258665

Information available Accounts and a newsletter were provided by the trust.

General Established in 1969 by the trade union movement to ensure the profits of the company would go to good causes rather than individual schareholders. In previous years, the trust has had no particular areas of interest, with the trust deed requiring all trustees to be trade unionists so the giving of the funds represents the interests of the membership. Due to the large number of applications the trust is receiving but are unable to support, it has now decided to have specific areas of interest to enable it to make fewer, but more worthwhile, grants than it has been able to in recent years.

Preference is given to:

- charities established by the TUC or an affiliated trade union for the benefit of its members
- charities formally supported by the TUC or an individual trade union at national or branch level
- charities demonstrating a direct and active link with one or more unions (for instance, those that recognise an individual union for bargaining purposes)
- overseas applications accompanied by a letter of support on behalf of the ICFTU, CTUC, ETUC or a member organisation.

The trustees still also consider applications outside these categories from small to medium-sized non-religious charities in the UK that benefit a wide range of people, with reference to one of the following:

- medical research
- support for victims of war or natural disaster

- relief of poverty, age or mental or physical illness or disability
- influencing public policy on human rights, welfare or employment issues
- education
- promoting economic and social development in developing countries.

In 2000/01 the trust had assets of £1.9 million. The total income for the year was £100,000. Grants were made to over 60 causes totalling £87,000. A Fellowship Award was also made worth £5,000.

Beneficiaries included ASHRAM International for a milk chilling plant in a remote mountainous Nepalese tribal area, British Ex-Services Wheelchair Sports Association to send a team to the National Veterans' Wheelchair Games in Cleveland – Ohio, Claire House Children's Hospice – Wirral for electric fire doors, Dogs for the Disabled to buy puppies, Motor Neurone Disease Association for a Lightwriter electronic voice synthesiser, Re-solv for core costs, Survival International towards its report Disinherited – Indians in Brazil and Winged Fellowship to modernise one of its holiday centres.

Exclusions No grants to individuals.

Applications In writing to the correspondent. Applications should be submitted from a head office (where appropriate) and include latest accounts, purpose for donation and details of trade union links. Trustees meet three times a year.

Trustees of Tzedakah

Jewish, welfare

£833,000 (2000/01)

Beneficial area UK.

Brentmead House, Britannia Road, London N12 9RU

Tel. 020 8446 6767

Correspondent C Hollander

Trustees *Trustees of Tzedakah Ltd*

CC Number 251897

Information available Full accounts were on file at the Charity Commission.

General The objectives of this charity are:

- the relief of poverty
- advancement of education
- advancement of religion

- such other charitable purposes, causes or projects as the trustees see fit.

It makes a small number of large grants and a large number of small grants to meet these aims.

In 2000/01 the assets totalled £662,000. Income was £1 million, including £908,000 in legacies and donations received. Grants were made to 350 organisations, mostly for less than £500 each, and totalled £833,000.

Two substantial grants were made during the year: £225,000 to Gevuras Ari Torah Academy and £100,000 to Telz Institutions. The accounts contained no further information about these grants.

Other large grants were £26,000 each to Friends of Or Someach, Friends of Poneviez Yeshiva, Hasmonean Girls School and Woodstock Sinclair Trust, £22,000 to Torah Temimoh, £17,000 to Lubavitch Foundation, £16,000 to Hendon Adath Yisroel Synagogue, £14,000 to Menorah Foundation School, £12,000 to Beis Yisroel Trust Fund and £11,000 each to BSD Trust Fund and Mayim Rabim Schotz Yeshivas.

Other beneficiaries of £1,000 or more included Menorah Primary School (£9,700), CWCT Trust Fund (£7,800), Tzedoko Vocheseed Trust (£7,600), Federation of Synagogues (£6,800), Gateshead Talmudical College (£5,700), Ner Yisroel Educational Trust (£4,800), London Academy of Jewish Studies (£4,200), Emuna Child's Resettlement Society (£4,000), Beth Shalom Synagogue (£3,100), Bridge Lane Beth Hamedrash (£2,600), Agudas Yisroel Aid Society (£1,200) and City University Amenity Fund (£1,000).

Smaller grants included those to Marie Curie Cancer Care (£810), Acdut Aid Society (£510), Mind (£330), Project Seed Educational Trust (£260), Before Educational Trust (£230), UNICEF (£150), Wizo (£130), Mill Hill Synagogue (£84), Naima Primary School (£74), Crisis Helpline (£45) and Gibraltar Kollel (£35).

Exclusions Grants only to registered charities. No grants to individuals.

Applications This trust states that it does not respond to unsolicited applications.

The Ulverscroft Foundation

People who are sick and visually impaired, ophthalmic research

£312,000 (2000/01)

Beneficial area Worldwide.

1 The Green, Bradgate Road, Anstey, Leicester LE7 7FU

Tel. 0116 236 4325 **Fax** 0116 234 0205

Email foundation@ulverscroft.co.uk

Website www.ulverscroft.co.uk

Correspondent Joyce Sumner

Trustees *P H Carr; Allan Leach; Michael Down; A W Price; D Owen; R Crooks.*

CC Number 264873

Information available Report and accounts were provided by the trust.

General Formed in 1973, the foundation's aim is to help improve the quality of life for people who are blind and partially sighted (visually impaired). The foundation finances:

- eye clinics
- eye treatment departments in hospitals
- eye operating theatres
- ophthalmic diagnostic equipment
- research into eye diseases and their treatment
- library services for people who are visually impaired or housebound
- improvements in the quality of life for people who are visually impaired.

All financial help given by the foundation is made through channels such as NHS Trusts, hospitals, schools, libraries and groups for the visually impaired.

In 2000/01 the trust had assets of £7.4 million and an income and a total expenditure of £16 million, most of which was accounted for by the foundation's trading activities, including Ulverscroft Large Print Books. Income arising from investments totalled £93,000 while donations received totalled £124,000. Grants to organisations totalled £312,000.

The accounts listed the 20 largest grants over £1,000 each, by far the largest of which was £146,000 to Great Ormond Street Children's Ophthalmology Unit. Other larger grants included £57,000 to St Mary's Chair of Ophthalmology, £30,000 to Royal Australian College, £23,000 to Great Ormond Street Children's Hospital and £17,000 to National Library for the Blind.

Other beneficiaries included Action for Blind People, Cornwall County Council, Electronic Aids for the Blind, Gladhand Foundation, Royal London Society for the Blind, Stockport Libraries, Suffolk County Council, University of Edinburgh Development Trust and Vision Foundation.

Exclusions Applications from individuals are not encouraged. Generally, assistance towards salaries and general running costs are not given.

Applications In writing to the correspondent. Applicants are advised to make their proposal as detailed as possible, to include details of the current service to people who are visually impaired, if any, and how the proposed project will be integrated or enhanced. If possible the trust asks for an estimate of how many people who are visually impaired use/will use the service, the amount of funding obtained to date, if any, and the names of other organisations to whom they have applied.

The success of any appeal is dependent on the level of funding at the time of consideration.

The trustees meet four times a year to consider applications.

The Albert Van Den Bergh Charitable Trust

Medical/disability, welfare

£73,000 (1999/2000)

Beneficial area UK and overseas.

Triggs Wilkinson Mann, Broadoak House, Horsham Road, Cranleigh, Surrey GU6 8DJ

Tel. 01483 273515

Correspondent G R Oliver, Trustee

Trustees *P A Van Den Bergh; G R Oliver; Mrs J M Hartley.*

CC Number 296885

Information available Full accounts were on file at the Charity Commission.

General The trust was established in 1987. In 1999/2000, its assets were valued at £2.4 million, invested in property, a wide range of investments and cash at the bank. It had an income of £71,000 and after expenses of £17,000, the trust gave £73,000 in grants. Unfortunately there was no grants list on file at the Charity Commission for that year.

However in 1996/97, £38,000 was given in grants with the largest being: £5,000 to United Charities Fund – Liberal Jewish Synagogue, £2,100 to Care for the Elderly, £2,000 to Parentline Surrey, £1,200 to both Counsel & Care for the Elderly and Riding for the Disabled – Cranleigh and £1,000 to both Age Concern and St John Ambulance.

Smaller grants were generally of £500 and were given to charities such as: Bishop of Guildford's Charity, BLISS, British Heart Foundation, CSV, Leukaemia Research Trust, Multiple Sclerosis Society, National Osteoporosis Society, RNID and SSAFA.

Most grants went to national charities in the fields of health, welfare and disability. Some went to Jewish organisations and some to Surrey-based charities. A few grants went to local charities elsewhere, but mainly in the London area.

Applications In writing to the correspondent, including accounts and budgets.

Bernard Van Leer Foundation

Development of young children who are disadvantaged

£298,000 income (2000)

Beneficial area Worldwide.

The Royal Bank of Scotland plc, Private Trust and Taxation, 2 Festival Square, Edinburgh EH3 9SU

Tel. 0131 523 2657 **Fax** 0131 228 9889

Correspondent Mrs Claire Lundy, Senior Trust Administrator

Trustees *The Royal Bank of Scotland plc.*

CC Number 265186

Information available Information was provided by the trust. Accounts were on file at the Charity Commission.

General The objectives of the foundation are 'to enhance opportunities for children aged zero to seven years of age, growing up in circumstances of social and economic disadvantage to optimally develop their innate potential'. Support is generally given to projects lasting three years rather than general appeals, and is

concentrating on the 40 countries where the Van Leer Group is established.

The trust has undergone a period of change in recent years, with its grantmaking suspended during the late-1990's, with the trustees wishing to hold talks with the parent company, Van Leer (UK) Holdings, before applications could be considered. Applications are now being considered again, and since it had assets of £4.1 million generating an income of £298,000 in 2000, this is a very welcome development.

Exclusions Grants are not made to individuals, nor for the general support of organisations such as staffing/ administrative costs. The foundation does not provide study, research or travel grants. No grants are made in response to general appeals.

Applications On a form available from the correspondent, which requires a brief, 50-word description of the project. Applications are considered in March and September. Due to the large number of applications received, no acknowledgements are given and unsuccessful appeals will not receive a reply.

The Van Neste Foundation

Developing world, people who are older or disabled, religion, community and Christian family life, respect for the sanctity and dignity of life

£155,000 (2001/02)

Beneficial area UK, especially the Bristol area, and overseas.

15 Alexandra Road, Clifton, Bristol BS8 2DD

Tel. 0117 973 5167

Correspondent Fergus Lyons, Secretary

Trustees *M T M Appleby, Chair; F J F Lyons, Secretary; G J Walker.*

CC Number 201951

Information available Full accounts were on file at the Charity Commission.

General The trustees currently give priority to the following:

1. Third world

2. Disabled and older people
3. Advancement of religion
4. Community and Christian family life
5. Respect for the sanctity and dignity of life.

These objectives are reviewed by the trustees from time to time but applications falling outside them are unlikely to be considered.

In 2001/02 the trust had assets of £4.9 million and an income of £214,000. After administration expenses of £19,000 (of which £14,000 went towards secretary's fees), grants totalling £155,000 were given to 30 organisations.

The grants distributed can be broken down as follows:

Category	No.	£
Third world	3	3,300
Disabled and older	6	14,000
Advancement of religion	7	52,000
Community and Christian family life	12	33,000
Respect for the sanctity and dignity of life	2	53,000

The largest grants were £50,000 each to Clifton Diocese and Little Brother of Nazareth and £15,000 to Bristol Folk House.

The remainder were between £250 and £5,000. Beneficiaries included Bristol City Southmead Project, St Peters Hospice – Bristol and Seven Springs (£5,000 each), National Drug Prevention Alliance (£3,000), Bristol Children's Help Society, Lincoln College – Oxford and Whiteladies Health Project (£2,000 each) and CAFOD and Vassall Disabled Living Centre (£1,000 each).

Smaller grants under £1,000 each included those to Catholic Chaplaincy – Bath, Clifton Cathedral Parish, Clifton Diocesan Childrens Society, Jackdaws Educational Trust, Royal Free Hospital Kidney Patients Association, St Mary's Church – Cardiff and Salvation Army.

The foundation is connected with another charity, the Amazon Trust. While there are no financial relations between the charities, they share a majority of trustees.

Exclusions No grants to individuals or to large, well-known charities. Applications are only considered from registered charities.

Applications Applications should be in the form of a concise letter setting out the clear objectives to be obtained, which must be charitable. Information must be supplied concerning agreed funding from other sources together with a timetable for achieving the objectives of the appeal and a copy of the latest accounts.

The foundation does not normally make grants on a continuing basis. To keep overheads to a minimum, only successful applications are acknowledged. Even then it may be a matter of months before any decision can be expected, depending on the dates of trustees' meetings.

The Vandervell Foundation

General

£531,000 to individuals and organisations (2000)
Beneficial area UK.

Bridge House, 181 Queen Victoria Street, London EC4V 4DZ

Tel. 020 7248 9045

Correspondent Ms Sheila Lawler

Trustees *The Vandervell Foundation Limited Trustee Company.*

CC Number 255651

Information available Accounts were on file at the Charity Commission, but without a narrative report or grants list.

General This trust has general charitable purposes, supporting both individuals and organisations. A wide range of causes has been supported, included schools, educational establishments, hospices and other health organisations, with the trust stating there are no real preferences or exclusions. Grants generally range from £1,000 to £5,000 each.

In 2000 the trust had assets of £4.9 million. Total income was £826,000, including £676,000 received from G A Vandervell Deceased Will Trust. Management and administration totalled £75,000. Grants totalled £186,000 whilst donations totalled £345,000, although no explanation was given in the accounts explaining the difference between the two.

Applications In writing to the correspondent. Trustees meet every two months to consider major grant applications; smaller grants are considered more frequently.

Roger Vere Foundation

General

£551,000 to organisations and individuals (1999/2000)
Beneficial area UK and worldwide, with a special interest in High Wycombe.

19 Berwick Road, Marlow, Buckinghamshire SL7 3AR,

Tel. 01628 471702

Correspondent Peter Allen, Trustee

Trustees *Mrs Rosemary Vere, Chair; Mrs Marion Lyon; Peter Allen.*

CC Number 1077559

Information available Information was provided by the trust.

General This trust was established in September 1999 and it supports, worldwide:

- the relief of financial hardship in and around, but not restricted to, High Wycombe
- advancement of education
- advancement of religion
- advancement of scientific and medical research
- conservation and protection of the natural environment and endangered plants and animals
- relief of natural and civil disasters
- general charitable purposes.

In the first accounting period, to 30 June 2000, the trust had an income of £7.6 million, mostly from a donation but containing £58,000 generated from assets, suggesting that during a full year the generated income will be slightly higher. From this income, £7 million was transferred to assets and £552,000 was given in grants.

Two substantial grants were made during the year, these were £200,000 to Trent Vineyard and £100,000 to Jubilee 2000 Coalition. National Star Centre and YMCA each received £50,000. Other large grants were £20,000 each to Disaster Emergency Committee and Stepping Stones Trust, £15,000 to USPG and £10,000 to CARE International.

Other grants included £7,000 to Church Army, £6,000 each to BTCV and Marlow Pastoral Foundation, £5,500 to Children's Country Holidays and Rescue Foundation, £5,000 each to Action for Blind People, British Wireless for the Blind, Elimination of Leukaemia, Fauna and Flora International, Prince's Trust

and Young Minds, £3,500 to Greening Brill School and £2,500 to National Missing Persons Helpline.

Applications In writing to the correspondent. The trustees meet quarterly, in March, June, September and December.

The Vincent Wildlife Trust

Wildlife, environmental conservation

£431,000 (2000)
Beneficial area UK.

3–4 Bronsil Courtyard, Eastnor, Ledbury, Herefordshire HR8 1EP

Tel. 01531 636441 **Fax** 01531 636442

Email vwt@vwt.org.uk

Website www.vwt.org.uk

Correspondent Dr Johnny Birks, Secretary

Trustees *Hon. Vincent Weir, Chair; Ronald Yarham; Terence O'Connor.*

CC Number 270679

Information available Full accounts were on file at the Charity Commission.

General The trust's objectives are the promotion of the study, research and education about wildlife conservation and the establishment, control, development and maintenance of nature reserves.

Most of the trust's funds are spent carrying out its own work researching mammals and conservation, publishing survey reports and species leaflets, and purchasing reserves where available. Funding to other organisations is centred around three organisations, The Herpetological Conservation Trust, The British Butterfly Conservation Society and Plantlife.

In 2000 the trust had an income of £1.1 million, including £150,000 in donations received. Total charitable expenditure was £1.2 million, including £431,000 given in four grants. Assets totalled £20 million.

The three core charities were all supported, receiving £232,000 (Herpetological Conservation Trust), £132,000 (British Butterfly Conservation Trust) and £50,000 (Plantlife). The other grant was £17,000 to Nottingham University, which has also been supported in previous years.

Applications In writing to the correspondent. It appears unlikely that applications from charities without a relationship with the trust will be successful.

The William and Ellen Vinten Trust

Industrial education, training and welfare

£70,000 (2000/01)

Beneficial area UK, but mostly Bury St Edmunds.

Greene & Greene Solicitors, 80 Guildhall Street, Bury St Edmunds, Suffolk IP33 1QB

Correspondent D J Medcalf, Chair

Trustees *D J Medcalf, Chair; J V Crosher; M Shallow; A C Leacy; P M Tracey; A Grigg.*

CC Number 285758

Information available Accounts were on file at the Charity Commission, but without a list of grants.

General The 2000/01 accounts stated: 'During the year the trust was bringing to a close its five-year project of grants and initiatives to achieve enhancement and expansion in local upper schools of education towards careers in industry. The final parts of this project should be concluded in the next year.

'The trust continued industrially-related higher education grants and scholarships. The first phase of a major project supervised by Bury St Edmunds County Upper School, to introduce "Successmaker" computerised mathematics teaching into all of the Bury St Edmunds area local authority middle schools, was implemented.

'Exploratory work was begun upon possible new projects for industrial training and industrially-related school bursaries.

'The policy of the trust continued to be the pursuit of proactive projects related to industry.'

In 2000/01 the trust had assets of £1.8 million and an income of £83,000. Grants totalled £70,000. No grants information was listed in the accounts.

Applications This trust states that it is a proactive charity that does not seek unsolicited applications.

The Scurrah Wainwright Charity

Social reform, root causes of poverty and injustice

£196,000 (2001/02)

Beneficial area Preference for Yorkshire, South Africa and Zimbabwe.

16 Blenheim Street, Hebden Bridge, West Yorkshire HX7 8BU

Tel. 01422 845085

Email kerry@waintrust.fsnet.co.uk

Correspondent Kerry McQuade, Administrator

Trustees *J M Wainwright; H A Wainwright; M S Wainwright; T M Wainwright; P Wainwright; H Scott; R Bhaskar.*

CC Number 1002755

Information available Information was provided by the trust.

General The trust supports a wide range of charitable projects with an emphasis on social reform and tackling the root causes of poverty and injustice. Applications from the north of England, particularly Leeds and Yorkshire, will generally be given strong priority; the trustees also have an interest in Zimbabwe. In exceptional cases, the trust may make a personal award to an individual in recognition of some outstanding personal commitment relevant to the trust's interests.

Grants have ranged from less than £100 to over £25,000, but there is no minimum or maximum. Support may be given in stages, for example a £30,000 grant over three years via three annual payments of £10,000. A brief progress report must be sent within a year of receiving a grant.

In 2001/02 the trust had assets of £1.5 million and an income of £62,000. A total of £196,000 was given in 19 grants.

Grants included £30,000 over three years to Chapeltown and Harehills Assisted Learning Computer School, £9,400 to Big Issue in the North for the Big Futures Programme, £7,000 to People and Planet,

£6,000 each to YMCA Leeds and GIPSIL, £4,500 to Bradford Community Project, £3,000 each to Future Outlook and Liberatarian and Education Research and £1,000 to The Right Track (BMX) Foundation.

Exclusions No grants for individuals, buildings, medical research or the welfare of animals.

Applications In writing to the correspondent. Applicants are expected to provide background information about themselves and/or their organisation, the work they wish to pursue and their plans for its practical implementation, which will involve an outline budget and details of any other sources of finance. The most recent income and expenditure and balance sheets should be included.

Trustees meet in March, July and November. Applications should be received by the first day of the preceding month.

Wallington Missionary Mart and Auctions

Overseas Christian Mission

£186,000 (2001)

Beneficial area Overseas.

99 Woodmansterne Road, Carshalton Beeches, Surrey SM5 4EG

Tel. 020 8643 3616

Website www.wallingtonmissionary.org.uk

Correspondent B E Chapman, Company Secretary

Trustees *Council of Management: V W W Hedderly, Chair; B E Chapman; Mrs S P Collett; H F Curwood; D C Lewin; Mrs S M Symes; Mrs F L Willey; G C Willey.*

CC Number 289030

Information available Information was provided by the trust.

General This trust supports UK-registered Christian charities for missionary work overseas. It gathers its income from selling goods that are donated to the trust, either through its shop in Wallington or at the two-day auctions that are held six times a year. Donors can nominate when giving items to the trust which mission agency they wish the proceeds to go to if they wish. The trust is willing to sell any items people wish to donate, and as such is often asked to perform house clearances.

In 2001 the trust had an income of £269,000, including £168,000 in sale receipts and £98,000 in auction receipts. Assets totalled £170,000. Grants were made to 198 organisations totalling £186,000.

The largest donations were £17,000 in 11 grants to OMF International (UK) and £10,000 in 15 grants to Crusaders. Other large payments went to All Nations Christian College and Tearfund (£8,200 in 3 and 8 grants respectively), SIM-UK (£7,700 in 9 grants), Heath Evangelical Trust (£7,200 in 7 grants), CORD (£6,700 in 4 grants), Mission Aviation Fellowship (6,500 in 7 grants), South American Mission Society (£6,000 in 5 grants) and FEBA Radio (£5,900 in 6 grants).

Other beneficiaries included Baptist Missionary Society (£4,600 in 10 grants), Youth with a Mission (£3,100 in 9 grants), Mercy Ships (£2,500 in 4 grants), Holy Trinity Wallington (£2,100 in 8 grants), Eau Vive Mission (£1,800 in 1 grant) and Middle East Christian Outreach (£1,000 in 1 grant).

Exclusions Only registered charities may receive support. Applications from individuals are only considered if funds will go to a missionary society or Christian charity.

Applications In writing to the correspondent, with an sae. The trustees meet to consider grants throughout the year.

Warbeck Fund Ltd

Jewish, the arts, general

£179,000 (2000/01)
Beneficial area UK and overseas, with a preference for London.

2nd Floor, Pump House, 10 Chapel Place, Rivington Street, London EC2A 3DQ
Tel. 020 7739 2224 **Fax** 020 7739 5544
Correspondent The Secretary
Trustees Michael Brian David; Jonathan Gestetner; Neil Sinclair.
CC Number 252953
Information available Accounts were on file at the Charity Commission.

General This fund has general charitable purposes, with preferences for Jewish, Israeli and arts organisations. The grants list indicates a preference for London, especially the West End.

In 2000/01 the fund had assets of £189,000. Total income was £257,000, of which £250,000 came from donations received. Management and administration costs amounted to just £1,800. Grants totalling £179,000 were made to 129 organisations, just under half of which were also supported in the previous year.

The largest grants were £26,000 to Westminster Society for People with Learning Difficulties and £21,000 each to Royal National Theatre and United Jewish Israel Appeal.

Other large grants were £10,000 each to British ORT and Hampstead Theatre Trust, £7,000 to British Friends of Haifa University, £6,900 to West London Synagogue and £5,300 to Wiezmann Institute Foundation.

Other London beneficiaries included London Symphony Orchestra (£2,500), Heritage of London Trust (£1,000), Friends of Covent Garden (£750), Worshipful Company of Information Technologists (£250) and Chelsea and Westminster Hospital and West London Action for Children (£25 each).

Smaller grants included those to Chicken Shed Theatre Company (£4,300), Red Hot Aids Charitable Trust (£1,300), British Friends of the Art Museums of Israel and International Centre for Child Studies (£1,000 each), Jewish Museum (£570), Scopus Jewish Educational Trust (£500), Tibet Foundation (£430), English National Opera (£350), After Adoption (£150), Chamber Orchestra of Europe and Macmillan Cancer Relief (£100 each), Friends of Tate Gallery (£60), Jewish Historical Society of England (£30) and National Coastwatch Institute (£15).

Exclusions No grants to individuals or non-UK registered charities.

Applications According to the correspondent, it may not be worth writing to the trust as unsolicited applications tend to be unsuccessful.

The Ward Blenkinsop Trust

Medicine, social welfare, general

£220,000 to organisations
(1999/2000)
Beneficial area UK, with a special interest in Merseyside and surrounding counties.

PO Box 28840, London SW13 0WZ
Tel. 020 8878 9975
Correspondent Charlotte Blenkinsop, Trustee
Trustees A M Blenkinsop; J H Awdry; S J Blenkinsop; C A Blenkinsop; A F Stormer; H E Millin.
CC Number 265449
Information available Full accounts were on file at the Charity Commission.

General The trust currently supports charities in the Merseyside area and charities of a medical nature, but all requests for funds are considered.

In 1999/2000 the trust had an income of £238,000 and gave grants to: 50 charities totalling £220,000; 15 ex-employees totalling £7,200; and £4,400 in Christmas boxes for people of pensionable age.

Two-thirds of all grants are given to organisations in the Merseyside area for general charitable purposes, including Clatterbridge Cancer Research Trust (£45,000). Grants were given to other organisations in north west England including Cheshire County Council, which received £25,000 for its Youth Art Initiative, and £20,000 for its South Africa Initiative. Other beneficiaries were Wade Deacon High School (£12,000), Manchester Youth Theatre (£6,000) and Robson Street Clinic District Nurses (£3,000).

UK groups were supported with a preference for medical charities, especially those connected with cancer. Beneficiaries in the previous year included Royal Academy of Dancing Special Needs Programme (£17,000), International Spine Research Trust (£5,000), St John Ambulance (£4,000), National Asthma Campaign (£3,000), Roy Castle Lung Cancer Foundation (£1,500), Age Concern and British Polio Fellowship (£750 each) and Cancer Research Campaign (£50).

Exclusions No grants to individuals.

Applications In writing to the correspondent.

Mrs Waterhouse Charitable Trust

Medical, health, welfare, environment, wildlife, churches, heritage

£288,000 (2000/01)

Beneficial area UK, with an interest in Lancashire.

25 Clitheroe Road, Whalley, Clitheroe BB7 9AD

Correspondent D H Dunn, Trustee

Trustees *D H Dunn; E Dunn.*

CC Number 261685

Information available Full accounts were on file at the Charity Commission, with a useful summary and breakdown of grants.

General Support is given to organisations working in the Lancashire area or UK-wide. It mostly makes small recurrent grants towards core costs of small organisations to enable them to maintain and improve their services. Larger grants can also be made towards capital projects.

In 2000/01 the trust had assets of £6.4 million, which generated an income of £288,000. Grants were made to 71 organisations, including 59 recurrent grants from the previous year. They totalled £288,000, including £112,000 to Lancashire charities and £61,000 to Lancashire branches of UK-wide organisations. Grants were broken down as shown below:

	No of grants	Total
Medical and health		
– general	15	£69,000
– research	12	£63,000
– children	8	£27,000
Welfare in the community		
– children	9	£26,000
– people who are deaf or blind	5	£19,000
– general	8	£19,000
Environment and wildlife	8	£35,000
Church and heritage	6	£30,000

The largest grants were £15,000 to Whalley Abbey Restoration Fund and £10,000 each to Christie Hospital NHS Trust, East Lancashire Hospice Fund, National Trust for the Lake District Appeal and RSPB. Marie Curie Cancer Care and Macmillan Cancer Relief both received £8,000 while grants of £5,000 each were made to 20 organisations included Arthritis Research Campaign, British Diabetics Association and National Eczema Society.

Beneficiaries of smaller grants included Accrington and District Blind Society, East Lancashire Scout Council, I Can, Farming and Wildlife Advisory Group, Friends of the Lake District, Mencap, Mires Beck Nursery, Salvation Army – Blackburn Citadel, Whalley Pre-school Playgroup and Whizz–Kidz.

Exclusions No grants to individuals

Applications In writing to the correspondent. There is no set time for the consideration of applications, but donations are normally made in March each year.

G R Waters Charitable Trust 2000

General

£186,000 (1999/2000)

Beneficial area UK. Also North and Central America.

Finers Stephens Innocent, 179 Great Portland Street, London W1W 5LS

Tel. 020 7323 4000 **Fax** 020 7344 7689

Correspondent Michael Lewis

Trustees *G R Waters; A Russell.*

CC Number 1091525

Information available Full accounts (for the previous trust) were on file at the Charity Commission.

General This trust was registered with the Charity Commission in 2002, replacing Roger Waters 1989 Charitable Trust (Charity Commission number 328574), which transferred its assets to this new trust. (The 2000 in the title refers to when the declaration of trust was made.) Like the former trust, it receives a share of the Pink Floyd's royalties as part of its annual income. It has general charitable purposes throughout the UK, as well as North and Central America.

The following financial information (as well as the list of trustees) refer to the former, now extinct, trust. As the new trust stated that it will work in exactly the same manner as the one it has replaced, it can be assumed it is typical of how this trust will operate.

In 1999/2000 the trust had assets of £734,000. Total income was £68,000, including £45,000 as a share of the band's

income. Grants were made to 20 organisations totalling £186,000.

The largest grant was £100,000 to Rhys Daniels Trust, a regular beneficiary. Ovingdean Hall School received £25,000. Other large grants were US$10,000 each to Barbados Welfare Charities, Millennium Kids Foundation and Robin Hood Foundation and £5,000 each to Chicks, Dove Cottage Day Hospice, Happy Days Children's Charity, NSPCC and React.

Other beneficiaries included Croydon Playcare Company (£3,000 in three grants), Lambourn Open Day and Racing Welfare Charities (£2,000 each), Louise Gibson Medical Fund (£1,800), Morley School (£1,000) and Young Vic Company (£500).

Applications In writing to the correspondent.

Blyth Watson Charitable Trust

Humanitarian causes in the UK

£103,000 (2000/01)

Beneficial area UK.

50 Broadway, Westminster, London SW1H 0BL

Tel. 020 7227 7000

Correspondent Miss Helen Abbey, Administrator

Trustees *Edward William Nicholas Brown; Ian Hammond McCulloch.*

CC Number 1071390

Information available Full accounts were on file at the Charity Commission.

General The trustees will consider applications from UK-based causes that may broadly be described as humanitarian in nature. Their preference is for UK-registered charities. Grants are usually between £1,000 and £5,000, with one or two larger grants being made at the trustees' discretion.

In 2000/01 it had assets of £3.4 million its income was £96,000. Its management and administration costs totalled £23,000. The 25 grants made exceeded the income, totalling £103,000 and ranging from £1,000 to £7,300.

Beneficiaries included Seaford College (£7,300), Alzheimer's Society, Brain Research Trust, Cancer BACUP,

Deafblind UK, Development Foundation and Society for the Relief of Distress (£5,000 each), RUKBA (£3,500), Brent Adolescence Centre and English Concert (£2,500 each), Leukaemia Research London Bikeathon (£1,000) and Princes Trust (£800).

Applications The trust will consider applications for grants at meetings usually held in June and December each year. The trustees will respond to a letter of application indicating the purpose for which the grant is sought. They do not generally require to see formal accounts.

In order to save administration costs the trustees will not respond to applications that do not contain a reply paid envelope, unless the cause is awarded a grant.

Applications may be addressed to the trustees or to Miss Helen Abbey, the administrator.

The Weavers' Company Benevolent Fund

Young people at risk from criminal involvement, young offenders and rehabilitation of prisoners and ex-prisoners

£165,000 (2001)
Beneficial area UK.

The Worshipful Company of Weavers', Saddlers' House, Gutter Lane, London EC2V 6BR

Tel. 020 7606 1155 **Fax** 020 7606 1119

Email charity@weaversco.co.uk

Correspondent John Snowdon, Clerk

Trustees *The Worshipful Company of Weavers.*

CC Number 266189

Information available Full accounts and a detailed report and grants list were made available by the trust, along with a copy of their Guidelines for Applicants.

General This benevolent fund was set up in 1973 with funds provided by the Worshipful Company of Weavers, the oldest of the City of London Livery Companies.

The company has selected three particular areas of need which it wishes to support and grants are mainly restricted to projects working within these categories. These are:

- young people who for any reason are at risk from criminal involvement
- young offenders
- the rehabilitation of prisoners and ex-prisoners.

The following advice is given to applicants:

- it only supports specific projects
- it does not provide long-term funding to any one organisation, and it would wish to be assured that all other possible sources of finance had been explored and that efforts were being made to obtain long-term funding from statutory and voluntary sources
- it prefers to support small or new, community-based organisations rather than long-established, large or national organisations, and to support projects where the company's grant would form a substantial part of the funds required
- it is particularly interested in innovative projects that are trying to get off the ground, that would be evaluated and that could act as a catalyst for other similar projects elsewhere
- it is willing to consider applications for equipment and capital projects, as well as salaries and running costs, subject to the overall policy not to provide long-term funding.

Grants ordinarily range from £5,000 to £15,000, but the trust states that it welcomes applications for smaller amounts from small or new organisations.

The trust received 350 applications in 2001 and supported 57 charities. It was decided in 2000 that the size of individual grants should be increased up to £15,000, leading to a smaller number of organisations being supported. It was also agreed that, where appropriate, as funds allowed and subject to satisfactory reports, grants towards salaries could be for two years, rather than one.

During the year, the second Shared Experience conference was held, sponsored by the company. This interesting initiative brought together the charities it has supported which concentrate on drug abuse, offenders and ex-offenders. This highlighted 'the vital need for the interchange of information, experience and ideas'.

The trust report states 'major grants were awarded to a wide range of organisations within the fund's chosen areas of work, breaking down into two main categories:

support for projects working with young people who might be at risk from criminal involvement and for those working with convicted young offenders.

'Inevitably there is some overlap, and a constantly changing emphasis, as different projects are developed to meet changing needs, sometimes reflecting the availability of statutory funding. This year, the trustees have seen an increase in the establishment of youth cafes to try to address the problems of under-age and excessive drinking, and the lack of safe meeting places for young people.'

There were 23 major grants made in the year totalling £150,000. HMYOI Portland received £15,000 towards resettlement workshops, and three grants of £10,000 each went to Christ Church – Upper Armley for youth clubs, drop-in facilities and detached work, Sobriety Project for a training project for women prisoners and St Peter's Community & Advice Centre for drugs education and outreach work. Smaller grants included those to Bourne Trust (£1,800 for mentoring for people leaving prison), Portobello Trust (£5,000 for Holland Park School exclusion project), Streets Youth Project (£6,000 for computers) and Youth Alive & Connections (£5,000 for the Foundry Project – youth cafe).

Exclusions No grants to individuals, or to non-registered charities – unless they are intending to apply for charitable status. Grants are not normally made in response to general appeals from large, well-established charities whose work does not fall within one of the company's chosen areas of interest.

It does not often support central or umbrella bodies, but prefers assisting projects directly working in its chosen fields.

It is not the company's policy to provide for running costs or deficit funding for established projects, nor to provide grants to replace start-up funding provided by other statutory or charitable funds.

Applications Detailed Guidelines for Applicants are available from the trust and applicants are urged to obtain these before making any appeal.

Applicants should write in the first instance to the correspondent with details of their requirements and include a set of their most recent accounts. If an application is accepted for further consideration, an application form will be issued. Before an application goes to the trustees an assessment visit is always made. The company uses its own members, who live throughout the country, to do this. The trustees meet three times a year in February, June and October. Applications may be submitted at any time and will be put to the next appropriate committee. 'Applicants should take into account the time it takes to process an application, raise queries and organise an assessment visit.'

Successful applicants are required to provide regular reports on progress.

The Mary Webb Trust

General

£135,000 (2000/01)

Beneficial area UK and overseas.

Cherry Cottage, Hudnall Common, Berkhamsted HP4 1QN

Correspondent Mrs C M Nash, Trustee

Trustees *Martin Ware; Mrs Jacqueline Fancett; Mrs Cherry Nash.*

CC Number 327659

Information available Accounts were provided by the trust.

General The trust states that it generally supports only smaller charities and will continue to do so. In 2000/01 the trust had assets of £817,000 generating an income of £50,000. Grants, which appear to have been paid from the income and the assets, were given to 153 organisations and totalled £135,000. The majority of grants (129) were for less than £1,000. Of the remaining 24, four were for £5,000 or more.

The trust broke down its grant giving as follows (1999/2000 figures in brackets):

Philanthropic	£46,000	(£10,000)
Environment	£26,000	(£35,000)
Health	£22,000	(£44,000)
Social services	£18,000	(£62,000)
International	£10,500	(£31,500)
Culture & recreation	£6,000	(£7,000)
Religion	£4,000	(£8,000)
Education & research	£2,500	(£11,000)
Development & housing	£1,500	(nil)

The trust made two large grants to The National Trust (£35,000) and RNLI (£10,000), with two grants of £5,000 each being given to Fenland Archeaological Trust and The Royal Agricultural Benevolent Institute.

Other beneficiaries included The Soil Association (£3,000), Friedrich's Ataxia Group, London Zoo and NSRA

Apeldoorn Blind Shooting (£2,000 each) and Arthritis Research Campaign, John Grooms, RAF Benevolent Fund, Sue Ryder Foundation and The Woodland Trust (£1,500 each).

Organisations receiving £1,000 each were CICRA Children with Crohns & Colitis, Council for National Parks, Leukaemia Research Trust, Mousehole Wild Bird Hospital & Sanctuary, National Hospital for Neurology & Neurosurgery, Orbis, Friends of St Lawrence Parish Church, The Mayapur Trust, National Endometriosis Society, Prostate Cancer Charity and Wildfowl & Wetlands Trust.

Exclusions No grants to individuals or non-registered charities.

Applications The trust's annual report says that the trustees are 'concerned by the large number of appeals received during the year. They prefer to make their own enquiries and find it difficult to handle the large volume of documents and unsolicited accounts sent to them'.

Trustees normally meet quarterly, in March, May, August and December; applications need to be received by the month prior to the trustees' meeting.

The Weinberg Foundation

General

£178,000 (2000/01)

Beneficial area UK and overseas.

138 Park Lane, London W1K 7AS

Tel. 020 7436 6667

Correspondent N A Steinberg

Trustees *N H Ablitt; C L Simon.*

CC Number 273308

Information available Accounts were on file at the Charity Commission, but without a list of grants or a narrative report.

General In 2000/01 the trust had assets of £2.5 million, which generated an income of £97,000. Grants were made totalling £178,000.

As in recent years, the accounts provided no details about the size of the grants made, who they were given to or any information about the foundation's grant-making policies. The last accounts to contain such information were those for 1996, when grants ranged from £150 to £10,000, although they were mostly for

£500 or less. The grants list showed many health and welfare charities as well as numerous Jewish charities amongst its varied beneficiaries.

Applications In writing to the correspondent.

The Weinstein Foundation

Jewish, medical, welfare

£117,000 (1999/2000)

Beneficial area Worldwide.

32 Fairholme Gardens, Finchley, London N3 3EB

Tel. 020 8346 1257

Correspondent M L Weinstein, Trustee

Trustees *E Weinstein; Mrs S R Weinstein; M L Weinstein; P D Weinstein; Mrs L A F Newman.*

CC Number 277779

Information available Full accounts were on file at the Charity Commission.

General This trust mostly supports Jewish organisations, although it does have general charitable purposes and supports a wide range of other causes, notably medical-related charities.

In 1999/2000 it had assets of £1.6 million which generated an income of £55,000. Grants were made to 172 organisations totalling £117,000. Management and administration costs were high at £9,800, although this could have been due to the large number of grants made.

The largest grants were £21,000 to Menorah Primary School and £11,000 to Lubavitch Foundation.

Other large grants included £6,600 to Norwood, £5,000 to National Jewish Chaplaincy Board, £4,800 to Menorah Grammar School Trust, £3,700 to Gateshead Seminary, £2,800 to Kisharon, £2,300 to Jewish Care; £2,200 to Kupas Tzedaka Vochesed, £2,000 to Chrevas Ezras Nitzrochim, £1,700 to London Academy of Jewish Studies, £1,200 to Jewish Child's Day and £1,000 to Chesed Charitable Trust.

Most of the grants were for amounts of less than £1,000. Beneficiaries included Joint Jewish Charitable Trust (£900), North West London Jewish Day School (£500), Hospital Kosher Meals (£330), Craven Walk Charitable Trust (£270), Slabodka Yeshiva Trust (£200), English

National Opera (£180), Child Resettlement Trust (£140), Children with Leukaemia (£100), Age Concern England (£50), Zion Orphanage (£36), National Autistic Society (£25) and B'eer Shimuel Ltd (£18).

Exclusions No grants to individuals.

Applications In writing to the correspondent.

The James Weir Foundation

Welfare, education, general

£165,000 (2000)

Beneficial area UK, with a preference for Ayrshire and Glasgow.

84 Cicada Road, London SW18 2NZ

Tel. 020 8870 6233 **Fax** 020 8870 6233

Correspondent Louisa Lawson, Secretary

Trustees *Simon Bonham; William J Ducas; Elizabeth Bonham.*

CC Number 251764

Information available Full accounts were on file at the Charity Commission.

General The foundation has general charitable purposes, giving priority to schools and educational institutions; Scottish organisations, especially local charities in Ayrshire and Glasgow; and charities with which either James Weir or the trustees are particularly associated. These preferences, however, do not appear to be at the expense of other causes, UK-wide charities or local organisations outside of Scotland. The following six charities are listed in the trust deed as potential beneficiaries:

The Royal Society
The British Association for Advancement of Science
The RAF Benevolent Fund
The Royal College of Surgeons
The Royal College of Physicians
The University of Strathclyde.

In 2000 the trust had assets of £6.3 million and an income of only £190,000. The administration costs were very high at £51,000, including £38,000 spent on investment management charges. Grants ranging from £500 to £3,000 were made to 90 organisations and totalled £165,000.

The largest grants were for £3,000 each, given to the six organisations listed in the trust deed and to Royal Star and Garter

Home. Grants of £2,000 each went to 63 organisations, including Cot Death Society, Counsel and Care, Divert, Donaldson's Development Project, Epilepsy Association of Scotland, Guild of Disabled Homemakers, Haemophilia Society and David Tolkien Trust for Stoke Mandeville.

Exclusions Grants are given to recognised charities only. No grants to individuals.

Applications In writing to the correspondent. Distributions are made twice-yearly in June and November when the trustees meet. Applications should be received by May or October.

The Earl & Countess of Wessex Charitable Trust

General

£158,000 (2000/01)

Beneficial area Worldwide.

Farrer & Co, 66 Lincoln's Inn Fields, London WC2A 3LH

Tel. 020 7242 2022

Correspondent Jenny Cannon

Trustees *Mark Foster-Brown; Abel Hadden; Denise Poulton; Sir Henry Boyd-Carpenter; Malcolm Cockren.*

CC Number 1076003

Information available Accounts and an information leaflet were provided by the trust.

General This trust was established by Prince Edward and Sophie Rhys-Jones shortly after their marriage in 1999 and was initially named The Bagshot Park Charity after their Surrey home. It has general charitable purposes, although there are preferences for organisations working with young people, self-help organisations, applications that will open extra fundraising opportunities to the charity, as well as where the Earl or Countess of Wessex have a personal connection or interest. Most grants are one-off, although substantial grants may be made for up to five years.

In 2000/01 the trust had assets of £363,000. Total income was £118,000, of which £94,000 came from a trading subsidiary that holds the intellectual

property rights of the wedding of the Earl and Countess of Wessex. Grants to 16 organisations totalled £158,000.

Beneficiaries were A R C Addington, Delta, East Anglia's Children's Hospices 2000, Family Heart Association, Four Lanes Regeneration Group, International Care and Relief, Learning for Life, London Narrow Boat Project, Northwick Park Hospital Children's Centre Appeal, Michael Palin Centre for Stammering Children, Royal Liverpool Philharmonic Society, Rural Stress Network, Saddler's Wells Trust, St Georges School – Windsor Castle and Side by Side.

The accounts stated: 'The Charities {sic} Commission has been supplied with details of amounts given to each charity together with an explanation of the reasons for the non-disclosure of individual amounts in the financial statements.' Non-disclosure of grants information should only be made where the information being made public may be potentially harmful to the trust or its recipients; failing to disclose information without providing an explanation in the public sphere may prompt unjustified speculation about the grants made.

Exclusions No grants are made to:

- non-registered charities or causes
- individuals, including to people who are undertaking fundraising activities on behalf of a charity
- organisations whose main objects are to fund or support other causes
- organisations whose accounts disclose substantial financial resources and that have well-established and ample fundraising capabilities
- fund research that can be supported by government funding or that is popular among trusts.

Applications In writing to the correspondent in the first instance. A response will be made within two weeks in the form of an application form and guidelines to eligible applicants or a letter of rejection if more appropriate. Completed forms, which are not acknowledged upon receipt, need to be submitted by 1 May or 1 November, for consideration by the end of the month. Clarity of presentation and provision of financial details are among the qualities which impress the trustees. Successful applicants will receive a letter stating that the acceptance of the funding is conditional on an update being received before the next meeting. The trust's criteria state other correspondence cannot be entered into, and organisations cannot reveal the size of any grants they receive.

259

The Westcroft Trust

International understanding, overseas aid, Quaker, Shropshire

£108,000 (2000/01)

Beneficial area Unrestricted, but with a special interest in Shropshire – causes of local interest outside Shropshire are rarely supported.

32 Hampton Road, Oswestry, Shropshire SY11 1SJ

Correspondent Mary Cadbury, Managing Trustee

Trustees *Mary C Cadbury; Richard G Cadbury; James E Cadbury; Erica R Cadbury.*

CC Number 212931

Information available Information was provided by the trust. Full accounts were on file at the Charity Commission.

General Currently the trustees have five main areas of interest:

- international understanding, including conflict resolution and the material needs of the third world
- religious causes, particularly social outreach, usually of the Society of Friends (Quakers) but also for those originating in Shropshire
- development of the voluntary sector in Shropshire
- needs of people with disabilities, primarily in Shropshire
- development of community groups and reconciliation between different cultures in Northern Ireland.

Medical education is only helped by support for expeditions overseas that include pre-clinical students. Medical aid, education and relief work in developing countries is mainly supported through UK-registered organisations. International disasters may be helped in response to public appeals.

The trust favours charities with low administrative overheads and that pursue clear policies of equal opportunity in meeting need. Grants may be one-off or recurrent; recurrent grants are rarely made for endowment or capital projects.

In 2000/01 the trust had assets of £2.3 million, which generated an income of £123,000. Grants were made to 125 organisations totalling £108,000, broken down as follows:

Religious Society of Friends

Central Committees – 1 grant of £5,700
This went to Britain Yearly Meeting.

Meeting houses – 5 grants totalling £2,200
Heswall Preparative Meeting received £500 and Derby Preparative Meeting received £450. Grants of £400 each went to Newcastle upon Tyne Preparative Meeting, South Belfast Friends Meeting and Workingham Building Appeal Fund.

Other funds, institutions and appeals – 13 grants totalling £11,000
The largest grants were £2,800 to Friends World Committee for Consultation in two payments, £2,200 to Northern Friends Peace Board and £1,000 to Woodbrooke. Other recipients included The Retreat – York (£890), Quaker Peace Centre – Cape Town (£680), Leaveners (£650) and Quaker Bolivia Link (£350).

Shropshire

Social service in the community – 23 grants totalling £17,000
The largest grants were £5,000 to Silo Central Youth Project, £1,500 to Homeless in Oswestry Action Project in two payments and £1,000 each to Shropshire Youth Adventure Trust and Home-start North Shropshire and Oswestry. Other beneficiaries included Community Council of Shropshire (£910), Axis Counselling and NSPCC (£750 each), Oswestry and Border Citizens Advice Bureau (£500), Willowdene Farm (£400), Telford Christian Council (£300) and Shrewsbury Prison Chaplaincy (£150).

Education – 2 grants totalling £490
These went to Second Chance (£380) and Shropshire Playbus (£120).

Disability, health and special needs – 14 grants totalling £11,000
Derwen College received £3,000, while £1,000 each went to Marie Curie Cancer Care – Herefordshire and Shropshire, Ellesmere Community Care Centre Trust, Hamar Multiple Sclerosis Group and Shropshire and Mid Wales Hospice. Amongst the other beneficiaries were AssistU (£880), Hope House (£500), RNIB for Condover School (£240) and No Panic (£160).

Other Oswestry causes – 1 grant of £250
This went to St Oswald's Fabric Fund.

Medical and surgical

Research – 4 grants totalling £2,500
Recipients were Institute of Orthopaedics (£800), REMEDI (£780), Liverpool School of Tropical Medicine (£600) and Pain Relief Foundation (£350).

National

Health – 1 grant of £1,000
This went to the West Midlands branch of Marie Curie Cancer Care.

Disabilities and special needs – 7 grants totalling £4,000
British Epilepsy Association received £1,800. Other beneficiaries included Staffordshire University (£490), Re-Solv (£430), SANDS (£360) and Cancer Bacup (£250).

Social service (England, Scotland and Wales) – 11 grants totalling £5,200
Hoxton Hall received £1,700. Other recipients included London Connection (£550), Campus Cambridge (£450), Liverpool One Parent Families (£440 in two payments), Prisoners of Conscience Appeal Fund (£350) and Walton Prison Chaplaincy (£200).

Social service (Northern Ireland) – 3 grants totalling £1,300
Grants ranging from £250 to £500 went to Corrymeela Community, Positive Ethos Trust and Total Outdoor Experience.

Overseas

Medical aid – 19 grants totalling £16,000
Large grants went to Orbis International and Uganda Development Services (£3,000 each), Tropical Health and Education Trust (£1,500) and Christian Solidarity Worldwide (£1,000). Others to benefit included SSI (£550), Palawan Trust (£390), Hamlin Churchill Childbirth Injuries Trust (£380) and Bethesda Leprosy Hospital (£290).

Education – 12 grants totalling £7,900
Beneficiaries included Budiriro Trust (£1,400), Canon Collins Trust (£1,200), Jamia Masjid Quba (£1,000), Action Village – India (£750), National Council for Welfare of Prisoners Abroad (£500), World University Service (£310) and Mkauzaeneni Primary School – Bulawayo (£300).

Relief work – 17 grants totalling £12,000
Grants included £2,000 to DEC India Earthquake Appeal, £1,800 to Oxfam, £1,000 each to Christian Aid and International Care and Relief for the El Salvador earthquake, £950 to Miriam Dean Trust, £600 to Find your Feet, £550 to Save the Children, £350 to Seeds for Africa, £330 to UNICEF and £310 to Calcutta Rescue Service.

International understanding – 10 grants totalling £9,500
Beneficiaries included University of Bradford's Department of Peace Studies (£4,000), Alternatives to Violence (£2,000), Development Education Project (£600), Lampens (£530), Richardson Institute (£460) and Anti-Slavery International (£200).

Other

Unclassified – 1 grant of £680
This went to Medical Foundation for the Care of Victims of Torture.

Exclusions Grants to charities only. No grants to individuals or for medical electives, sport, the arts (unless specifically for people with disabilities in Shropshire) or armed forces charities. Requests for sponsorship are not supported. Annual grants are withheld if recent accounts are not available or do not satisfy the trustees as to continuing need.

Applications In writing to the correspondent. There is no application form or set format but applications should be restricted to a maximum of three sheets of paper, stating purpose, overall financial needs and resources together with previous years' accounts if appropriate. Printed letters signed by 'the great and good' and glossy literature do not impress the trustees, who prefer lower-cost applications.

Applications are dealt with about every two months. No acknowledgement will be given. Replies to relevant but unsuccessful applicants will be sent only if a self-addressed envelope is enclosed. As some annual grants are made by Bank Telepay, details of bank name, branch, sort code, and account name and number should be sent in order to save time and correspondence.

The Whitaker Charitable Trust

Education, environment, music, personal development
£212,000 (2000/01)
Beneficial area UK, but mostly east Midlands, Northern Ireland and Scotland, particularly Bassetlaw.

c/o Currey & Co., 21 Buckingham Gate, London SW1E 6LB

Tel. 020 7828 4091
Correspondent Edward Perks, Trustee
Trustees *Edward Ronald Haslewood Perks; David W J Price; Lady Elizabeth Jane Ravenscroft Whitaker.*
CC Number 234491
Information available Accounts were on file at the Charity Commission.

General The trust has general charitable objects, although with stated preferences for music education, agricultural and silvicultural education, countryside conservation, spiritual matters and prison-related charities.

Grants are made to UK-wide organisations and local organisations in Scotland, Northern Ireland and Nottinghamshire and the east Midlands, with a large number of grants made in Bassetlaw.

In recent years most of the funds have been given to two organisations, United World College of the Atlantic and Koppel Goodman Project. Grants to other organisations ranged from £500 to £15,000, although usually at the lower end of the scale.

In 2000/01 the trust had assets of £5.8 million, which generated an income of £211,000. Grants to organisations totalled £212,000.

A substantial grant of £100,000 was made to Atlantic College, although no analysis of this was made in the trust's accounts. The next largest grants were £15,000 to Marlborough College and £10,000 each to Koppel Goodman Family Housing for a family support project and Queen Margaret's School.

Beneficiaries in Bassetlaw included Bassetlaw Hospice and Focus on Young People in Bassetlaw (£2,000 each) and local branches of Mencap (£2,000) and Home-Start (£500). Other grants in the east Midlands included £5,000 to Harworth PCC, £2,000 to Bramcote School Limited, £1,500 to FWAG Nottinghamshire, £1,000 each to Lincoln Cathedral Fund, Nottinghamshire Hospital Concert 2000, Retford and District Scouts and St Mary's Church – Harrington for the bell appeal and £500 to Nottinghamshire Scouts.

Scottish and Northern Irish beneficiaries included Leith School of Art (£3,000), Game Conservancy Scottish Research Trust (£2,000), Royal Highland Education Trust (£1,000) and £500 each to Aberdeen International Youth Festival, Belfast Central Mission, East Glasgow Music School and East Kilbride Befriending Project.

Recipients elsewhere included Portland College and Royal Forestry Society (£5,000 each), Game Conservancy (£3,000), Prison Phoenix Trust (£1,500), STA and Soul of Women (£1,000 each), with £500 each to Association of General Practitioners of Natural Medicine, Campaigners, Drake Music Project, Fourth World ADT, Inside Out Trust, Macmillan Cancer Relief, NSPCC, Prince's Trust, Prison Arts Foundation, Royal Humane Society, Trees for Life and Youth at Risk.

Exclusions Support is given to registered charities only. No grants are given to individuals or for the repair or maintenance of individual churches.

Applications In writing to the correspondent. Trustees meet half-yearly. Applications should include clear details of the need the intended project is designed to meet plus a copy of the latest accounts available and an outline budget. If an acknowledgement of the application, or notification in the event of the application not being accepted, is required, an sae should be enclosed.

The Simon Whitbread Charitable Trust

Education, family welfare, medicine, preservation
£127,000 (2000/01)
Beneficial area UK, with a preference for Bedfordshire.

Dawsons, 2 New Square, Lincoln's Inn, London WC2A 3RZ
Fax 020 7421 4850
Correspondent E C A Martineau, Administrator
Trustees *Mrs H Whitbread; S C Whitbread; E C A Martineau.*
CC Number 200412
Information available Full accounts were on file at the Charity Commission.

General The trust supports general causes in Bedfordshire, and education, family welfare, medicine, medical research and preservation UK-wide.

In 2000/01 the trust had assets of £2.4 million. Total income was £139,000. Grants were made to 56 organisations totalling £127,000.

261

The largest grants were £30,000 to Bedford Hospitals Charity and £15,000 to Maytree.

Other beneficiaries in Bedfordshire included Mencap – Luton and Bedfordshire (£5,000), Relate Bedford (£3,500), Bedford Charity for Anna Varezhkina and New Bedfordshire Training Project (£2,000 each), Bedfordshire County Music Service (£1,500), Bedfordshire Housing Aid Centre (£1,200 in two grants), Bedford Open Door and Victim Support – Bedfordshire (£1,000 each) and Luton Shopmobility and WRVS Club Goldington (£500 each).

Other grants elsewhere included those to British Brain and Spine Foundation and Canine Partners for Independence (£5,000 each), Countryside Foundation for Education (£3,300), Mencap and RUKBA (£3,000 each), Pearson Holiday Fund and Telephones for the Blind (£2,000 each), Age Concern and National Playing Fields Association (£1,000 each), Mayday Trust (£710) and Guild of Disabled Homeworkers and Family Holiday Association (£500).

Exclusions Generally no support for local projects outside Bedfordshire.

Applications In writing to the correspondent. Acknowledgements are not given. Please do NOT telephone.

The Colonel W H Whitbread Charitable Trust

Health, welfare, general

£252,000 (2001)

Beneficial area UK, with an interest in Gloucestershire.

Winckworth Sherwood, 35 Great Peter Street, London SW1P 3LR

Tel. 020 7593 5000 **Fax** 020 7593 5099

Correspondent R H A MacDougald

Trustees *M W Whitbread; J J Russell; R H J Steel; H F Whitbread.*

CC Number 210496

Information available Full accounts were on file at the Charity Commission.

General This trust has general charitable purposes in the UK. Although the trust does not have a stated policy, there is a particular emphasis on supporting

applications from Gloucestershire. To keep administration costs low, the minimum grant the trust makes is £1,000. In some instances, more than one grant is made to an organisation in a year.

In 2001 the trust had assets of £5.3 million, which generated an income of £190,000. Grants were made to 60 organisations totalling £252,000.

By far the largest grant was £100,000 to ARC Addington Fund. Other recipients of larger grants were £7,000 each to Animal Health Trust and Child Health Research Appeal Trust (in two and three payments respectively), £6,000 in two payments to Countryside Foundation for Education and £5,000 each to Household Cavalry Museum Appeal, Hunt Servants Fund and Oval House Christchurch (Oxford) United Clubs (£5,000) and St John Ambulance.

Other grants in Gloucestershire included £4,000 each to Gloucestershire Multiple Sclerosis Information and Therapy Centre and in two payments to Tewkesbury Old People's Welfare Committee, £3,000 to Gloucestershire Historic Churches Trust, £2,000 each to Britsh Red Cross Gloucester Branch, Cathedral and Abbey Church of St Alban, Gloucestershire Hussars Museum and Slimbridge Wildfowl and Wetlands Centre and £1,000 each to Gloucestershire Disabled Afloat Riverboats Trust and Samaritans Gloucester.

Other grants included £4,000 in three payments to Riding for the Disabled, £3,000 in two payments each to Kate's Carers and Noah's Ark, £2,000 each to Battersea Dogs Home, DEBRA, Gurhka Welfare Trust, Lincoln Diocese Trust for Irnham Church, Mark Davies Injured Riders Fund, Mencap and RNLI and £1,000 each to Bristol Cancer Help Centre, CLIC, Douglas House, Macmillan Cancer Relief, National Trust for Scotland, Salvation Army, SSAFA and Willow Trust.

Applications In writing to the correspondent. Trustees meet quarterly. Please note, successful applicants must cash their cheques within three months of receipt or, unless there are special circumstances, it is the trust's policy to cancel the cheque.

The Norman Whiteley Trust

Evangelical Christianity, welfare, education

£237,000 to organisations
(2000/01)

Beneficial area Worldwide, although in practice mainly Cumbria.

23 Brow Crescent, Windermere, Cumbria LA23 2EY

Correspondent D Foster

Trustees *Mrs B M Whiteley; P Whiteley; D Dickson; J Ratcliff.*

CC Number 226445

Information available Full accounts were on file at the Charity Commission.

General This trust supports the furtherance of the Gospel, the relief of poverty and education. Grants are made worldwide, although the grants list shows many beneficiaries working in Cumbria and the surrounding areas.

In 2000/01 the trust had assets of £2.2 million. Total income was £189,000, including £54,000 in donations received. Grants were made to 26 organisations totalling £237,000, and to eight individuals totalling £43,000.

The largest grants were £44,000 to Baptistenge, £34,000 to Bethsan Sheltered Housing Association and £30,000 to Luis Palau Lakes 2000.

Other beneficiaries in Cumbria included Millom Methodist Church (£13,000), Lakes Christian Centre and Sports Reach (£10,000 each), New Life Church (£4,000), Don't Imagine Believe (£2,500), Maryport Christian Centre (£1,500), Breakthrough Team (£1,200), Kendal Methodist Church, Bootle Church and Skelton Methodist (£1,000 each).

Recipients elsewhere included Kindersingkrien (£16,000), Koinonia (£12,000), Alpha Osterreich (£11,000), The Potteries Trust (£10,000), India Earthquake Appeal and Salvation Army (£500 each).

Exclusions Whilst certain overseas organisations are supported, applications from outside of Cumbria are not accepted.

Applications In writing to the correspondent. Trustees meet to consider applications twice a year.

The Whitley Animal Protection Trust

Protection and conservation of animals and their environments

£262,000 (2000)

Beneficial area UK and overseas, with a preference for Scotland.

Edgbaston House, Walker Street, Wellington, Telford, Shropshire TF1 1HF

Tel. 01952 641651 **Fax** 01952 247441

Email info@gwynnes.com

Correspondent Paul Rhodes

Trustees *E Whitley, Chair; Mrs P A Whitley; E J Whitley; J Whitley.*

CC Number 236746

Information available Full accounts were on file at the Charity Commission.

General This trust supports the prevention of cruelty to animals and the promotion of their conservation and environment. Grants are made throughout the UK and the rest of world, with about 20% of funds given in Scotland.

In 2000 the trust had assets of £9.4 million, which generated a low income of £304,000. Management and administration costs for the year were high at £32,000. Grants totalling £262,000 were made to 21 organisations, just over half of which were also supported in the previous year.

Two substantial grants were made during the year: £85,000 to Whitley Awards Foundation and £50,000 to Hawk and Owl Trust. Other large grants went to IPE – Brazil (£17,000), The Tweed Foundation for the Riparian Habitats Project and the Wildlife Conservation Research Unit of the University of Oxford's Department of Zoology – Oxford WILDCRU (£15,000 each), with £10,000 each to Edinburgh Zoo, Fauna and Flora International and Tusk Trust.

Grants of £5,000 each went to Fisheries Trusts in Awe, Lochaber and District, West Galloway, West Sutherland, Wester Ross and Western Isle. Other beneficiaries were Spey Research Trust for the Findhorn habitat survey (£5,000), Orangutan Foundation and Shropshire Wildlife Trust (£3,000 each), Scottish Wildlife Trust (£2,000) and National Birds of Prey and Plantlife (£1,000 each).

Exclusions No grants to non-registered charities.

Applications In writing to the correspondent. The correspondent stated: 'The trust honours existing commitments and initiates new ones through its own contacts rather than responding to unsolicited applications.'

The Felicity Wilde Charitable Trust

Children, medical research

£90,000 (2001/02)

Beneficial area UK.

Barclays Bank Trust Company Ltd, Executorship & Trustee Service, PO Box 15, Northwich, Cheshire CW9 7UR

Tel. 01606 313173

Correspondent Miss M Bertenshaw

Trustees *Barclays Bank Trust Co Ltd.*

CC Number 264404

Information available Accounts were on file at the Charity Commission.

General The trust supports children's charities and medical research, with particular emphasis on research into the causes or cures of asthma.

In 2001/02 grants were made to 42 organisations totalling £90,000. National Asthma Campaign received £40,000, paid in two equal grants. Grants of £5,000 each went Children's Hospital Appeal Trust and Royal Alexandra Hospital for Sick Children for the Rocking Horse Appeal. Children Action Rocket Enterprise received two grants totalling £2,000.

The remaining 38 grants were all for £1,000 each. Beneficiaries included Bobath – Glasgow, Breast Cancer Campaign, Cystic Fibrosis Trust, The Drama Practice, Derbyshire Children's Holiday Centre, I Can, The Inspire Foundation, Jessie May Trust, Martin House Children's Hospice, National Meningitis Trust, North West Cancer Research Fund, React, Refuge, Scotland Yard Adventure Centre, Scottish Adoption Association, Starlight Children's Foundation, Tower Hamlets Education Business Partnership, WellBeing and Wirral Autistic Society.

Exclusions No grants to individuals or non-registered charities.

Applications In writing to the correspondent at any time. Applications are usually considered quarterly.

The Williams Family Charitable Trust

Jewish, medical

£230,000 (1998/99)

Beneficial area Worldwide.

8 Holne Chase, London N2 0QN

Correspondent The Trustees

Trustees *Shimon Benison; Arnon Levy.*

CC Number 255452

Information available Accounts were on file at the Charity Commission, but without a narrative report.

General In 2000/01 this trust had an income of £60,000 and a total expenditure of £179,000. This information was taken from the Charity Commission database, unfortunately no further details were available.

In 1998/99 the trust had assets of £1.6 million and an income of £114,000. After modest management charges of £2,400, grants to 115 organisations totalled £230,000. Only a quarter of these grants were of more than £1,000.

The largest were £65,000 to HaGemach Al-Shem Nahiem Zeev Williams, £20,000 to Amutat El-Ad – Jerusalem and £18,000 to Yeshivat Hahesder Kiryat Arba. Other beneficiaries included Child Resettlement Fund (£10,000), Joint Jewish Charitable Trust (£5,000), Ariel Mifalei Torah (£4,000), Seeing Eyes for the Blind (£2,000), Beit Haggai Youth Village (£1,000), Cambridge University (£500), Victims of Arab Terror (£400), Jewish Aid Trust (£250), Elz Hayim (£200), Operation Wheelchairs (£100) and Israel Society for the Deaf (£50).

Applications In writing to the correspondent.

Please note, in January 2003 the trust stated that the correspondent was likely to change in the near future.

Dame Violet Wills Charitable Trust

Evangelical Christianity

£114,000 (2000/01)

Beneficial area UK and overseas, but there may be a preference for Bristol.

Ricketts Cooper & Co., Thornton House, Richmond Hill, Bristol BS8 1AT

Tel. 0117 973 8441

Correspondent H E Cooper, Secretary and Treasurer

Trustees *D G Cleave, Chair; H E Cooper; A J G Cooper; S Burton; Dr D M Cunningham; J R Dean; Miss J R Guy; R Hill; G J T Landreth.*

CC Number 219485

Information available Full accounts were on file at the Charity Commission.

General The trust's 2000/01 accounts stated: 'During her lifetime, Dame Violet Wills was intensely interested in all forms of Christian work, especially of an Evangelical nature. She gave liberally of her money to this end. In 1954, arrangements commenced towards the setting up of a charitable trust to maximise the monies available for this work. The trust deed was signed on 2nd December 1955. She remained personally interested in the trust until her death.

'The Bristol Evangelical Centre Trust has very similar objectives to those of the Dame Violet Wills Charitable Trust. For a number of years, the two trusts operated in parallel. During 1995, the trustees of the Bristol Evangelical Centre Trust decided to transfer their funds to the Dame Violet Wills Charitable Trust.

'The trust continues to operate within the original terms of reference, supporting evangelical Christian activities both within the UK and overseas. It is not the practice of the trustees to guarantee long-term support to any work, however worthy. The trust does not make a practice of supplying funds to individuals. The grants made are usually small but tailored to provide encourgament to the organisations concerned.

'Current categories of Christian work for trustee consideration are:

Training and bursaries
Mission – UK
Missions – other countries
Literature
Broadcasts

'Whilst a vast number of appeals are received each year, grants are more likely to be made to those which are personally known to one or more of the trustees.'

Grants generally range from £100 to £2,500, and the grants list suggests that a preference for Bristol remains.

In 2000/01 the trust had assets of £1.6 million, which generated an income of £106,000. Grants were made to 115 organisations totalling £114,000.

The largest grant was £14,000 to Western Counties and SWE Trust for the Evangelists Fund, which also received £800 on behalf for an individual. Other large grants went to Echoes of Service at Bristol Missionaries (£6,400), Overseas Council (£5,000), Philip Street Chapel for Evangelist's house (£3,500) and Christian Ministries for general purposes (£3,000).

Some organisations received more than one grant during the year, such as Scripture Union, which received £1,800 as well as £400 each for work in Freetown and Sierra Leone and £300 for school fees for Zimbabwean field workers.

Other beneficiaries in the Bristol/ Gloucestershire area included Bristol International Students Centre and Open Air Campaigners – Bristol (£2,500 each), Ministry Amongst Asians in Bristol (£750), Bristol Crusaders (£300) and IVP Books for the Methodist College in Bristol (£200).

Other beneficiaries elsewhere included Living Waters Radio Ministry (£2,500), FEBA Radio (£2,000), AWM Media (£1,700), All Nations for a bursary fund for overseas students (£1,600), Counties (£1,500), Brass Tracks and London Institute for Contemporary Christianity for a bursary (£1,000 each), European Christian Mission (£750), Africa Evangelical Fellowship and Zagoma Bible Seminary – Poland (£500 each), Langham Research Scholarships (£400), City Eagles and Don Summers Evangelical Association – Mexico (£300 each), Narsapur Hostel – India for a building fund (£200) and Christian TV Association (£90).

Exclusions Grants are not given to individuals.

Applications In writing to the correspondent. The trust states 'whilst a vast number of appeals are received each year, grants are more likely to be made to those which are personally known to one or more of the trustees.' Trustees meet in March and in September; applications need to be received by January or June.

The Wixamtree Trust

General

£228,000 (2000/01)

Beneficial area Primarily Bedfordshire.

c/o CCAS, 80 Croydon Road, Elmers End, Beckenham, Kent BR3 4DF

Tel. 020 8658 8902 **Fax** 020 8658 3292

Email wixamtree@ccas.globalnet.co.uk

Correspondent Paul Patten, Administrator

Trustees *S C Whitbread; Mrs J M Whitbread; H F Whitbread; C R Skottowe.*

CC Number 210089

Information available Full accounts were on file at the Charity Commission.

General This trust, following a policy review in 2000/01, now funds: social welfare, medicine and health in Bedfordshire; education, environment/ conservation and the arts in Bedfordshire and ocasionally further afield.

In 2000/01 the trust had assets of £3.6 million and an income of £112,000. After management and administration costs of £21,000, grants were made totalling £228,000 (£74,000 in 1999/2000).

The accounts listed the largest 20 grants, by far the largest of which was £70,000 to Moggerhanger House Preservation Trust. Other larger grants included £21,000 to NSPCC and £20,000 each to Home Farm Trust, Lambeth Partnership and St Albans Cathedral.

The remaining listed grants were in the range of £1,000 to £6,000 and included those to All Saints Preservation Trust (£6,000), Priory Methodist Church (£5,000), Cardington PCC (£3,000), St Luke's Hospital for the Clergy (£2,600), Sue Ryder Palliative Home Care (£2,000), Lambeth Partnership (£1,500) and Ammerdown Centre, Cape Children's Trust and Constable Trust (£1,000 each).

Smaller unlisted grants totalled £47,000.

Exclusions No grants to non-registered charities, individuals or overseas projects

Applications On a form available from the correspondent, for consideration throughout the year. The trustees meet in January, April, July and October. An application form is available by e-mail and all requests for support must be accompanied by a current report and accounts, where available.

The Maurice Wohl Charitable Foundation

Jewish, health and welfare

£651,000 (2000/01)
Beneficial area UK and Israel.

1st Floor, 7–8 Conduit Street, London W1S 2XF

Tel. 020 7493 3777

Correspondent J Houri

Trustees *Maurice Wohl; Mrs Vivienne Wohl; Mrs Ella Latchman; Prof. David Latchman; M D Paisner.*

CC Number 244519

Information available Accounts were on file at the Charity Commission.

General This foundation has general charitable purposes in the UK and Israel, with a preference for Jewish charities. A wide range of causes are supported, includeing medical treatment and research, education, disability and older people's organisations, sheltered accommodation, the arts, relief of poverty and so on.

In 2000/01 the foundation had assets of £18 million which generated an income of £914,000. Despite sharing its offices and certain administration services with two connected charities, administration costs for the year were high at £97,000. Grants were made to 29 organisations totalling £651,000.

Substantial grants were £175,000 to The Royal Academy and £143,000 to Kings College. Other large grants were £83,000 to JFS, £67,000 to Bikur Cholim Hospital and £50,000 each to Friends of Bar-Ilan University, Lord Jakobovits Centre and UCL.

Other grants of £5,000 or more went to Yeshivat Hakotel (£17,000), Medical Aid Trust (£12,000), Jewish Care and Joint Jewish Charitable Trust (£10,000), Jerusalem Great Synagogue (£6,800), Yeshivath Meor Hatalmud (£6,600) and FMRCU Charitable Trust and Helensea Charities (£5,000 each).

Other beneficiaries included Israel Museum (£2,100), Kisharon Day School (£1,000), Ohel Torah Beth David and TAL (£680 each), Holocaust Educational Trust (£500), British Friends of the Needy of Jerusalem (£250) and Brainwave and Chicken Shed Theatre Company (£100 each).

Exclusions The trustees do not in general entertain applications for grants for ongoing maintenance projects. The trustees do not administer any schemes for individual awards or scholarships and they do not, therefore, entertain any individual applications for grants.

Applications In writing to the correspondent. The trustees meet regularly throughout the year.

The Maurice Wohl Charitable Trust

Health, welfare, arts, education

£40,000 (2000/01)
Beneficial area UK and Israel.

1st Floor, 7–8 Conduit Street, London W1S 2XF

Tel. 020 7493 3777

Correspondent J Houri

Trustees *Maurice Wohl; Mrs Vivienne Wohl; Mrs Ella Latchman; Prof. David Latchman; Martin Paisner.*

CC Number 244518

Information available Full accounts were on file at the Charity Commission.

General This foundation has general charitable purposes in the UK and Israel, with a preference for Jewish charities. A wide range of causes are supported, including medical treatment and research, education, disability and older people's organisations, sheltered accommodation, the arts, relief of poverty and so on.

In 2000/01 the trust had assets of £2.6 million, which generated an income of £147,000. Grants were made to 59 organisations totalling £40,000. After spending £25,000 on administration charges, there was a surplus for the year of £89,000.

The largest grant was £9,900 to Communauté Israelite de Genève. Other large grants were £3,500 each to Mecial Aid Trust and Society of Friends of the Torah, £2,100 to Yad Sarah, £2,000 in two grants to Yesodey Hatorah School, £1,800 to Helensea Charities, £1,400 to Re'uth; £1,300 in two grants to Western Marble Arch Synagoge and £1,000 each to Achisomoch Aid Co., Friends of the Sick,

Institute for Jewish Policy Research, Keren Klita and Orthodox Jewish Aid Society.

Other beneficiaries included British Friends of the Council of Beautiful Israel (£680), Conference of European Rabbis (£500), Talmud Torah Moriah School (£340), Notzer Chesed Trust (£300), British Friends of Israel Guide Dog Centre (£250), with £100 each to ASBAH, Headway, Jewish Marriage Council, Mind, National Eczema Society and Zion Orphanage, £75 to Kollel Rabinow, £50 each to Invalids at Home and Law of Truth Talmudical College and £25 to Friends of Sanhedria Boy's Home.

Exclusions The trustees do not administer any schemes for individual awards or scholarships, and they do not, therefore, entertain any individual applications for grants.

Applications To the correspondent in writing. Applications are regularly considered throughout the year.

The Woo Charitable Foundation

Education in the arts

£368,000 (2000/01)
Beneficial area UK.

277 Green Lanes, London N13 4XS

Tel. 07974 570475 **Fax** 020 7383 5004

Correspondent The Administrator

Trustees *Nelson Woo, Chair; Countess Benckendorff; Nigel Kingsley; Michael Trask; Jackson Woo.*

CC Number 1050790

Information available Accounts were provided by the trust.

General 'The Woo Charitable Foundation was established for the advancement of education through supporting, organising, promoting or assisting the development of the arts in England, together with the specific aim of helping children, young people and those less able to help themselves.'

In autumn 2000 the trust introduced a bursary scheme giving £5,000 each to artists who have finished formal education but are yet to establish meaningful careers. The first bursary awards were made in autumn 2000 with two further awards made in 2001. It is likely that the bursary scheme will become the main funding focus of the foundation.

In 2000/01 the trust had an income of £406,000 mostly from voluntary income and donations. After administration expenses of £25,000, grants were made totalling £368,000. The trust largely funds smaller projects that aim to restore arts education. Grants ranged between £800 and £15,000.

Grants over £10,000 included: £15,000 to Chicken Shed Theatre; £12,000 to Serpentine Gallery for educational activities focusing on the under-12 age group; £11,000 to the Royal Academy towards intensive education projects based on a specific exhibition; and £10,000 each to London Academy of Music and Dramatic Art for the student hardship fund, Greenwich Chinese School towards providing five extra teachers and classes and Opera North towards workshops in primary and secondary schools.

Beneficiaries of smaller grants included: Citizens Theatre towards its youth group (£8,500); Centre for Arts and Disability towards the salary of a sculptor tutor (£7,500); The Orchestra towards expenses for volunteers, New Addington Musical Project, Poetry Archive and SPEC Jewish Youth & Community Orchestra (£5,000 each); Stagecoach Youth Theatre (£1,000); and The Cedar Foundation (£800).

Exclusions No grants for travel, building work and fundraising activities, especially abroad. Support is very rarely given to individuals, but note the above.

Applications In writing to the correspondent.

Woodlands Green Ltd

Jewish
£183,000 (1998/99)
Beneficial area Worldwide.

19 Green Walk, London NW4 2AL
Correspondent A Ost, Trustee
Trustees *A Ost; E Ost; D J A Ost; J A Ost; A Hepner.*
CC Number 277299
Information available Accounts were on file at the Charity Commission, but without a list of grants.

General The trust's objectives are the advancement of the orthodox Jewish faith and the relief of poverty. It mostly gives large grants to major educational projects being carried out by orthodox Jewish charities.

In 2000/01 the trust had an income of £251,000 and a total expenditure of £217,000. These figures are similar to those in 1998/99, when grants were made totalling £183,000.

Exclusions No grants to individuals, or for expeditions or scholarships.

Applications In writing to the correspondent.

The Woodroffe Benton Foundation

General
£152,000 (2002)
Beneficial area UK.

16 Fernleigh Court, Harrow, London HA2 6NA
Tel. 020 8421 4120
Email alan.king3@which.net
Correspondent Alan King
Trustees *James Hope; Kenneth Stoneley; Colin Russell; Miss Celia Clout; Peter Foster; Tony Shadrack.*
CC Number 1075272
Information available Information was provided by the trust.

General This trust makes grants towards:

- people in need, primary care of people who are sick or elderly or those effected by the results of a local or national disaster
- promotion of education
- conservation and improvement of the environment

The trust rarely donates more than £2,000 and does not normally make more than one grant to the same charity in a 12 month period.

In 2002 the foundation had assets of £4.5 million and an income of £181,000. Grants were made totalling £152,000.

In the previous year £101,000 was given in ongoing grants to 19 organisations and £101,000 in 149 one-off grants. Charities

receiving ongoing grants included Calibre, Community Links, Queen Elizabeth's Grammar School – Ashbourne and Victim Support.

Exclusions Grants are not made outside the UK and are only made to registered charities. No grants to individuals. Branches of UK charities should not apply as grants, if made, would go to the charity's headquarters.

Applications On a form available from the correspondent. Full guidance notes on completing the form and procedures for processing applications, are sent with the form.

The Fred & Della Worms Charitable Trust

Jewish, education, arts
£187,000 (2001/02)
Beneficial area UK.

23 Highpoint, North Hill, London N6 4BA
Tel. 020 8342 5360 **Fax** 020 8342 5359
Email fred@worms5.freeserve.co.uk
Correspondent The Trustees
Trustees *Mrs D Worms; M D Paisner; F S Worms.*
CC Number 200036
Information available Full accounts were on file at the Charity Commission.

General In 2001/02 the trust had assets of £2 million, which generated an income of £86,000. After low administration fees of just £1,000, grants were made totalling £187,000.

The largest grants were £65,000 to British Friends of the Art Museums of Israel, £26,000 to Joint Jewish Charitable Trust, £21,000 to British Friends of the Hebrew University and £17,000 each to British Friends of Rabbi Steinsaltz and Moccali Union.

Other organisations receiving £1,000 or more were Child Resettlement Fund (£7,000), B'nai B'rith Hillel Foundation, and European Jewish Publication Society (£5,000 each), Jewish National Fund (£1,300), United Synagogue Hampstead Garden Suburb (£1,200) and Duke of Edinburgh Award and Jewish Literacy Trust (£1,000 each).

Exclusions No grants to individuals.

Applications In writing to the correspondent. The trust stated that its funds are fully committed.

The Worshipful Company of Chartered Accountants General Charitable Trust

(also known as CALC – Chartered Accountant Livery Charity)

General, education

£114,000 (2000/01)

Beneficial area UK.

Oak House, 38 Botley Road, Chasham, Buckinghamshire HP5 1XG

Tel. 01494 783402 **Fax** 01494 793306

Email michael_hardman@bigfoot.com

Correspondent M R Hardman

Trustees *D P J Ross; M N Peterson; J M Renshall; Sir Jeremy Hanley; Miss M A Yale; M J Richardson; A M C Staniforth; W I D Plaistowe.*

CC Number 327681

Information available Full accounts were on file at the Charity Commission.

General In general, the trust supports causes advancing education and/or benefiting disadvantaged people. It has a tendency to focus on a particular theme each year, as well as making grants to other causes and organisations of particular relevance to members of the company.

In 2000/01 the trust had assets of £933,000 and an income of £123,000, including £77,000 from donations received. Grants totalling £114,000 were made to 40 organisations.

Under the heading '2001 Charitable Project', five grants were made totalling £50,000. These went to The Place to Be (£20,000), Beacon Community Cancer Palliative Care Centre (£10,000), Jubilee Primary School (£9,000), Royal Albert Dock Trust (£6,200) and Foxhill and Birley Carr Live at Home Scheme (£5,000).

Under the heading '2000 Educational Project', grants of £1,000 to £2,600 were given to 23 schools in England and Wales, mostly in Cumbria, Kent and Surrey. Grants included £2,600 to Wildlesham Village Infant School (Surrey) and £2,500 each to Chieveley Primary School (Berkshire), Crofton Infant School (Kent), Dorton House School (Kent), Robert Ferguson Primary School (Cumbria) and St Peters C of E Primary School (Newport).

Outside of these categories, Guildhall School of Music received £9,000 towards scholarships and VSO (£3,300), Chartered Accountants in the Community (£3,000) and Lord Mayor's Appeal (£2,500) were also supported. A total of £3,900 was given in seven smaller donations and £1,600 was awarded in prizes.

Applications Applications must be sponsored by a liveryman of the company.

The Worwin UK Foundation

General

£320,000 (2000/01)

Beneficial area UK and overseas.

6 St Andrew Street, London EC4A 3LX

Tel. 020 7427 6400

Correspondent D J M Ward, Trustee

Trustees *William Hew John Hancock; Brian Moore; Mark Musgrave; Andrew Jonathan Hughes Penney; David John Marcus Ward.*

CC Number 1037981

Information available Accounts were on file at the Charity Commission, but without a list of grants or a full narrative report.

General This foundation has general charitable purposes. In 2000/01 it had assets of £15,000 and a total income of £364,000, almost entirely from donations received. Grants were made totalling £320,000. As in recent years, the accounts contained no mention of the type or size of grants made, or details of the beneficiaries, which makes understanding how trust operates very difficult.

Management and administration costs were high at £52,000, due to the extra administration and legal costs involved in making grants to overseas beneficiaries.

These payments included £18,000 to a firm of solicitors in which two of the trustees are partners. Whilst wholly legal, these editors always regret such payments unless, in the words of the Charity Commission, 'there is no realistic alternative'.

Applications The foundation makes its own arrangements for making grants and does not seek applications.

The Matthews Wrightson Charity Trust

Caring and Christian charities

£91,000 to organisations (2001)

Beneficial area UK and some overseas.

The Farm, Northington, Alresford, Hampshire SO24 9TH

Correspondent Adam Lee, Secretary & Administrator

Trustees *Miss Priscilla W Wrightson; Anthony H Isaacs; Guy D G Wrightson; Miss Isabelle S White.*

CC Number 262109

Information available Full accounts were provided by the trust.

General This trust has general charitable purposes, favouring innovation, Christian work and organisations helping disadvantaged people. Most grants are of £400 and go to smaller charities or projects seeking to raise under £25,000. Large UK charities and those seeking to raise in excess of £250,000 are not generally supported, unless they have received funds in previous years.

In 2001 the trust had assets of £1.6 million, which generated an income of £68,000. Management and administration expenses for the year were high at £9,700, partly due to processing the large number of applications the trust received. Grants were made to 168 organisations totalling £91,000, with a further £6,300 given to individuals. Grants were broken down as follows.

	No. of grants	grant total
Art causes	11	£19,000
Christian	22	£11,000
Disability	34	£15,000
Individuals	15	£6,300

Medical	13	£5,200
Older people	4	£1,600
Rehabilitation	17	£8,900
Worldwide	17	£8,100
Youth	45	£20,000
Miscellaneous	5	£2,000

By far the largest grant was £14,000 to Royal College of Arts for the Hardship and Industrial Production Awards.

The only other grants of amounts other than £400 were: £1,200 each to Children's Family Trust, Demand, Mongolian Street Children Project, and Peper Harrow Foundation; £1,000 to Edinburgh Academy; £800 each to ITDG, New Bridge, Penrose Housing Association, Premier Christian Radio, Procorda, Southampton District Scouts Community Development Project, Turntable Furniture Project and Yeldall Christian Centres; £500 to Wells Museum Appeal Fund; and £200 to Weston Young Mums Club.

Over 90% of the grants were of £400, with beneficiaries including Bag Books, Calibre, Cambodia Trust, Dream Holidays, Explosion! Museum of Naval Firepower, Guideposts Trust, Huddersfield Gymnastics Club, Live Music Now!, LSW Prison Project, Jessie May Trust, Network Youth Essex, Relate branches in South East Sussex and Wolverhampton, ScripNet, Sense, Tools for Self-Reliance and Write Away.

Exclusions No support for individuals (other than visitors from abroad) seeking education or adventure for personal character improvement. No support for unconnected local churches, village halls, schools and animal charities. Charities with a turnover of over £250,000 are generally not considered, most grants are to organisations seeking, or with a turnover of less than, £25,000. Individuals seeking funding for 'self-improvement' education are not favoured.

Applications In writing to the correspondent. No special forms are used, although latest financial accounts are desirable. One or two sheets (usually the covering letter) are circulated monthly to the trustees, who meet every six months only for policy and administrative decisions. Replies are only sent to successful applicants; allow up to three months for an answer. Please include an sae if an answer to an unsuccessful application is required.

The trust receives over 1,000 applications a year; 'winners have to make the covering letter more attractive than the 90 others received each month'.

Wychdale Ltd

Jewish
£111,000 (2000/01)
Beneficial area UK.

4–6 Windus Mews, Windus Road, London N16 6UP
Correspondent The Secretary
Trustees C D Schlaff; J Schlaff; Mrs Z Schlaff.
CC Number 267447
Information available Full accounts were on file at the Charity Commission.

General The objects of this charity are the advancement of the Orthodox Jewish religion and the relief of poverty. The charity stated in its 2000/01 accounts that it 'supports religious educational institutions in London, the provinces and further afield.'

In 2000/01 the trust had assets of £280,000. Total income was £49,000, including £25,000 in donations received. Grants were made totalling £111,000.

The largest grants were £50,000 to Bobover Yeshiva Bnei Zion, £19,000 to UTA and £15,000 to Breslov Yeshiva.

Other organisations receiving £1,000 or more were Kollel Bobover (£8,000), Slabodke Yeshiva Trust and Yetv Lev Jerusalem (£4,000 each), Yetev Lev Synagogue (£2,000), Yeshiva Shaar Hasomayim (£1,700) with £1,000 each to Achdut, Bayit Lepletot, Beis Nadvorne and Friends of Bais Abraham. Smaller donations totalled £3,300.

Exclusions Non-Jewish organisations are not supported.

Applications In writing to the correspondent.

Wychville Ltd

Jewish, education, general
£167,000 (2000/01)
Beneficial area UK.

44 Leweston Place, London N16 6RH
Correspondent Berisch Englander, Governor
Trustees B Englander, Chair; Mrs S Englander; E Englander; Mrs B R Englander.
CC Number 267584
Information available Accounts were on file at the Charity Commission, but without a list of grants.

General This trust support educational, Jewish and other charitable organisations. In 2000/01 it had an income of £174,000, of which £171,000 came from donations received. Grants were made totalling £167,000. No further information was available.

Applications In writing to the correspondent.

The Wyseliot Charitable Trust

Medical, welfare, general
£93,000 (2001/02)
Beneficial area UK.

17 Chelsea Square, London SW3 6LF
Correspondent J H Rose, Trustee
Trustees E A D Rose; J H Rose; A E G Raphael.
CC Number 257219
Information available Accounts were provided by the trust, but without a narrative report.

General In 2001/02 the trust had assets of £2.1 million, which generated an income of £89,000. Grants were made to 33 organisations totalling £93,000.

The largest grants were £5,000 each to Avenues Youth Project, Cystic Fibrosis Trust and Prostate Cancer Charity. Other grants were in the range of £1,000 to £4,000 and included those to: Enham Trust, St Mungo's Trust and Time and Talents Association (£4,000 each); Notting Hill Housing Trust (£3,500); Earls Court Homeless Families Trust, Queen Elizabeth Foundation for the Disabled, Trinity Hospice and Winged Fellowship (£3,000 each); Hackney Quest, Home Start, Musicians Benevolent Fund and Runnymede Trust (£2,000 each); and London Bereavement Network, Professional Classes Aid Council and Woodlarks Workshop (£1,000 each).

Exclusions Local charities are not supported. No support for individuals.

Applications In writing to the correspondent, however note that the trust states that the same charities are supported each year, with perhaps one or two changes. It is unlikely new charities sending circular appeals will be supported and large UK charities are generally not supported.

The Yamanouchi European Foundation

Medical

US$265,000 (2000/01)
Beneficial area Worldwide.

Yamanouchi House, Pyrford Road, West Byfleet, Surrey KT14 6RA

Tel. 01932 345535

Correspondent D Ferguson, Trustee

Trustees *Dr Toichi Takenaka, Chair; Yasuo Ishii; Philippe Ballero; Masayoshi Onoda; Joseph F Harford; Dudley H Ferguson; Prof. Peter van Brummeley; Toshinari Tamura; Dr Nick Matthews.*

CC Number 1036344

Information available Full accounts were on file at the Charity Commission.

General The objects of the foundation are:

- committing long-term support to basic medical and related scientific programmes through organisations such as the SIU (Société Internationale D'Urologie).
- supporting selected short- medium- and long-term projects, aimed at integrating basic science and clinical research through interdisciplinary projects.
- providing facilities, promoting or sponsoring the exchange of ideas and views through lectures and discussions of an educational or cultural nature.
- promoting, assisting or otherwise supporting charitable institutions aimed at serving good causes.

The 2000/01 annual report stated: 'It is the long-term goal of the foundation to provide support for programmes and cultures that contribute to the advancement of an increasingly healthy society.

'The foundation's trustees believes this is best accomplished by providing funding for basic scientific research, for the examination of public health and environmental policy issues, and for the support of educational and cultural exchange programmes.'

The foundation administers The Yamanouchi Award and The Yamanouchi Lectureship, which are of US$30,000 given every three years to reward people significantly contributing to the medical and medicinal disciplines. The Yamanouchi Fellowship is a

scholarship to people studying these disciplines worth up to US$150,000 as a two-year support programme, with people supported being eligible to reapply to a maximum of three years.

In 2000/01 the trust had assets of US$12 million, which generated an income of US$774,000. Direct scientific supported totalled US$194,000, with a further US$75,000 donated to charities.

The largest grants were both of US$75,000 as half of a US$150,000 two-year grant, to Dipartimento di Medicina Interna Università di Pisa and the Department of Oncology at Helsinki University Central Hospital.

Other grants included US$10,000 each to Brauninger Stiftung GmbH Online Mouse Projekt, Connaître Les Syndromes Cérébelleux and Chase Children's Hospice and US$7,500 each to Foundation Sance at the Department of Hematooncology in Pediatric Faculty Hospital – Olomouc; Associacao De Amigos Da Criança E Da Familia for 'Chão Dos Meninos', Dyadis, Stichting VTV, Archipelago Cooperativa Sociale r.1. and Comitato Maria Letizia Verga.

Applications In writing to the correspondent.

The Yapp Charitable Trust

Social welfare

£299,000 (2000/01)
Beneficial area UK.

47a Paris Road, Scholes, Holmfirth HD9 1SY

Tel. 01484 683403 **Fax** 01484 683403

Email info@yappcharitabletrust.org.uk

Website www.yappcharitabletrust.org.uk

Correspondent Mrs Margaret Thompson, Administrator

Trustees *Revd Timothy C Brooke; Peter R Davies; Peter G Murray; Miss Alison J Norman; Peter M Williams.*

CC Number 1076803

Information available Information was provided by the trust.

General The Yapp Charitable Trust was formed in 1999 from the Yapp Welfare Trust (two thirds share) and Yapp Education and Research Trust (one third share). However, rather than combining the criteria for the two trusts, the trustees

decided to focus on small charities, usually local rather than UK charities. The trust now accepts applications only from small charities and organisations with a turnover of less than £75,000 in the year of application. The objects are restricted to registered charities in the UK and cover work with:

1. older people
2. children and young people
3. people with disabilities or mental health problems
4. moral welfare – people trying to overcome life-limiting problems such as addiction, relationship difficulties, abuse or a history of offending
5. education and learning (including lifelong learning) and scientific or medical research.

Applications from outside these areas cannot be considered. Grants are given towards running costs and salaries but not for capital equipment.

The trust is proactive in ensuring its grants are made evenly across the areas of work and the UK. In 2002, for instance, it used targeted publicity to increase its funding in Northern Ireland and Wales as well as to older people's organisations to increase funding in these areas. As such, its priorities are continually revised – current priorities and exclusions are publicised on the trust's website.

In 2000/01 the trust had assets of £5.3 million generating an income of £319,000. Grants ranged between £800 and £12,000, although most were for about £2,000, and were made to 101 organisations totalling £299,000. Most grants are for one year, but recurrent grants for up to three years will be considered.

Examples of grants are broken down as follows:

Children and young people 36 grants £92,000 31%

The largest grant in this category was £12,000 over three years to Three Churches Youth Project in Coventry. Other organisations receiving funding over three years were Liveline, UK East African Women and Children Group and Youth-Link (around £7,000 each). Other beneficiaries included One-to-One Youth Befriending Service and Wickham Youth Action Group (£3,000 each), Denny and Dunipace YMCA, Family Focus and Nuneaton Club for Young People (£2,000 each) and Filey Sea Cadets (£1,500). There were seven grants of £1,000 or less totalling £6,500.

Disability 26 grants £72,000 26%

Coventry Refugee Centre received £9,000

over three years, with Adur Special Needs Project, Rochdale Citizen Advocacy, Special Needs Activity Club – Thurrock and St Barnabas Counselling Centre also receiving funding over several years amounting to around £5,000 to £6,000 each. Other beneficiaries included Bradford and District Autistic Support Group and Stepping Stones Nottinghamshire (£3,000), Kinloch Church of Scotland and MIND North Warwickshire (£2,000 each) and Shopmobility Furness (£1,500). Three organisations not listed received £1,000 each.

Education 14 grants £48,500 14%

The largest grant was £7,000 over three years to African People's Link. Other organisations which received grants over two or three years were Sahara Communities Abroad and Soundabout (£6,000 each), Centre for Specialist Educational Assistance and Silo Central Youth Project (£4,500 each) and The Garden Science Trust (£4,000). Other beneficiaries included Daneford Trust (£3,000), Abbey Access Centre (£2,000) and South Island Workshop (£1,500).

Elderly people 10 grants £33,000 11%

Funding of £6,000 each over two or three years went to Faith in Elderly People – Leeds, Moor Allerton Elderly Care and Strathfoyle Community Association. Other beneficiaries included Age Concern Orkney (£3,000) and ACE Resource Centre (£2,000).

Moral welfare 9 grants £31,000 10%

The largest grant went to Rape and Abuse Line, which received £6,000 over three years. Relate Keighley and Craven and Marriage Care Hallam both received £5,000 over two and three years respectively. Other beneficiaries included Link-Up Association Nuneaton (£4,000), Mediation Dorset and Outside Edge Theatre Company (£2,000 each).

Scientific and medical research 2 grants £7,500 3%

The two grants were £4,000 to Child and Family Trust and £3,500 over three years to The SHE Trust.

Four beneficiaries received grants covering several categories, these were Agape Family Support Group - Leigh (£6,000 over two years), Ystradgynlais Volunteer Centre (£2,000), Weston Council for Voluntary Services (£1,500) and Newbiggin Hall Community Minibus (£800).

Exclusions Grants are only made to organisations with charitable status. The following are not supported:

- individuals, including students undertaking research, expeditions or gap year projects and charities raising funds to purchase equipment for individuals
- groups that do not have their own charity registration number or exemption – students' hostels and youth hostels are therefore usually not eligible
- fundraising groups raising money to benefit another organisation such as a hospital or school.

In March 2002 the trust introduced the following exclusions due to a large number of applications. The trust hopes to lift these in the future:

- work with under-five's
- childcare
- holidays and holiday centres
- core funding of general community facilities such as community centres and village halls
- capital expenditure, such as buildings, renovations, extentions, furnishings, equipment or minibuses.

Applications On a form available from the administrator. Applicants may request a form by e-mail in Word 97 format if preferred, although all applications must be sent by post. The only document that will be read by all the trustees is the application form. It is therefore important that applicants complete every section. Applicants uncertain whether they are eligible or how to complete the form should contact the administrator for advice.

Applications must include most recent accounts, and annual reports and newsletters are also appreciated, although the trust does not like bulky reports or specialist or technical documents.

Closing dates for applications are 31 January, 31 May and 30 September for consideration about six weeks later, and notification around two weeks after this. Applications are all acknowledged, and all applicants hear the outcome after the trustees' meeting. In the case of successful applicants, this normally takes about two weeks as the letters are accompanied by grant cheques which take a little time to prepare and circulate for signature. Late applications will be considered at the following meeting.

The William Allen Young Charitable Trust

General

£135,000 (2000/01)

Beneficial area UK, with a preference for south London.

The Ram Brewery, Wandsworth, London SW18 4JD

Tel. 020 8875 7000

Correspondent J A Young, Trustee

Trustees J A Young; T F B Young; J G A Young.

CC Number 283102

Information available Full accounts were on file at the Charity Commission.

General The trust supports humanitarian causes, with a large number of health organisations supported each year. Grants are made to local and national organisations throughout the UK, although there appears to be a preference for south London.

In 2000/01 the trust had assets of £3.7 million, which generated an income of £114,000. Grants were made to 90 organisations totalling £135,000. Other expenditure totalled just £6.

The largest grant was £21,220 to National Hospital Development Foundation, which also received £1,000 for the John Young Ward. Other large grants were £11,000 to St George's Ophthalmic Research Fund, £10,000 to British Benevolent Fund of Madrid and £9,000 to West Sussex Doctors on Call.

Other beneficiaries of £1,000 or more included Brain Research Trust and St John Ambulance Somerset (£5,000 each), National Hospital for Neurology and Neurosurgery (£3,500), St George's Hospital for the Eye Department Research Fund (£3,000), RNLI Taunton (£2,000), Wandsworth Council (£1,800), Scope (£1,300) and Greater London Fund for the Blind and Royal Star and Garter Home (£1,000 each).

Recipients of smaller grants included Merton Nurses (£750), Mitcham Parish Church (£600), Coopers Livery Housing Fund and Shooting Star Trust (£500), Wandsworth Special Olympics (£300), Battersea Scouts and St Catherine's Hospice (£100) and Chelsea Arts Club AGBI (£50).

Applications The trust does not support unsolicited applications as funds are already committed.

Elizabeth & Prince Zaiger Trust

Welfare, health, general

£306,000 (2000/01)

Beneficial area UK, some preference for Somerset.

6 Alleyn Road, Dulwich, London SE21 8AL

Correspondent D W Parry, Trustee

Trustees *D W Parry; P J Harvey; D G Long.*

CC Number 282096

Information available Information was provided by the trust.

General As well as supporting general charitable causes, the trust has the following objects:

- relief of older people
- relief of people who are mentally and physically disabled
- advancement of education of children and young people
- provision of care and protection for animals.

In 2000/01 the trust's assets were £9.5 million and its income was £293,000 from invesments and interest. Administration fees were £9,700 and grants totalling £306,000 were made to 102 organisations.

The largest grant was £30,000 to the Variety Club of Great Britain. The rest of the grants ranged between £60 and £25,000.

Grants to disability organisations included: £25,000 to St Margaret – Somerset Hospice, £13,000 to British Institute for Brain-Injured Children, £5,000 each to Cystic Fibrosis Trust, Juvenile Diabetes Foundation and Royal Hospital for Neuro-disability, £4,000 each to Association for Spina Bifida and Hydrocephalus, Down's Syndrome Association and Royal National Institute for the Blind, £3,000 each to Mencap and National Association for Mental Health, and £2,000 to Association of Wheelchair Children.

Organisations for older people that were supported included Queen Alexander Hospital Home (£3,000) and Cheshire Home – South London (£2,000).

Animal causes supported included £4,000 to National Animal Welfare Trust.

Other grants included: £5,000 to British Heart Foundation, £3,500 to Marie Curie Cancer Care, £3,000 to King George's Fund for Sailors and £1,000 each to Salvation Army and Samaritans.

Applications The trust does not respond to unsolicited applications, stating 'we have an ongoing programme of support for our chosen charities'.

The I A Ziff Charitable Foundation

General, education, Jewish, arts, youth, older people, medicine

£131,000 (2000/01)

Beneficial area UK, with a preference for Yorkshire, especially Leeds and Harrogate.

Town Centre House, The Merrion Centre, Leeds LS2 8LY

Tel. 0113 222 1234 **Fax** 0113 242 1026

Correspondent B Rouse, Secretary

Trustees *I Arnold Ziff; Marjorie E Ziff; Michael A Ziff; Edward M Ziff; Ann L Manning.*

CC Number 249368

Information available Full accounts were on file at the Charity Commission.

General This trust likes to support causes that will provide good value for the money donated by benefiting a large number of people, as well as encouraging others to make contributions to the work. This includes a wide variety of schemes that involve the community at many levels, including education, public places, the arts and helping people who are disadvantaged. Capital costs and building work are particularly favoured by the trustees, as they feel projects such as these are not given the support they deserve from statutory sources.

In 2000/01 the trust had assets of £2 million, which generated an income of £248,000. Grants were made totalling £131,000.

The 2000/01 trustees' report stated the current policies as follows:

'1. The University of Leeds. Funding has been agreed for a further five-year project to refurbish the fabric of certain buildings within the university to continue to provide the students with a sound working environment.

'2. A project to recreate gardens from seven different countries of the world. These gardens are located at the Canal Gardens Roundhay, which is the site of the already renowned Tropical World, attracting nearly one million visitors annually. The gardens project is supported by this charity and Leeds City Council and the second tranche of the charity's commitment will be paid when the council has made further progress with the project.

'3. The refurbishing of the main display room of the Leeds Art Gallery to improve the quality of the air conditioning and lighting in order to better preserve the valuable works on display. The release of funding has been delayed whilst Leeds City Council undertake necessary repairs to the roof of the art gallery.

'4. The Queenshill Estate Leeds. A five-year project to contribute to the refurbishment of the Queenshill Day Centre in Leeds.

'5. The Jewish Education Trust. A commitment to fund education for Jewish children in their own language and tradition.'

The largest grant paid during the year was £50,000 to University of Leeds for the project mentioned above.

A number of grants were made to Jewish organisations in Yorkshire, particularly Leeds. Leeds Jewish Welfare Board received £7,600, while other beneficiaries included, Leeds Jewish Blind Society (£1,300), Leeds Lubavitch Centre (£550), Leeds Education Board (£100), Harrogate Hebrew Congregation (£60), Leeds Jewish Ex-Servicemen and Women (£50) and Leeds Jewish Representative Council (£25).

Leeds International Piano Competition received £6,300 while National Eye Research Centre – Yorkshire received £4,000. Other recipients in the Leeds area included Yorkshire Association of Boys Clubs (£2,000), Leeds City Council (£1,100), Leeds Civic Trust (£900), Harrogate Community House Trust Ltd (£60), Yorkshire Cancer Research and Yorkshire Kidney Research Fund (£50 each) and Friends of Leeds International Pianoforte Competition (£15).

Joint Jewish Charitable Trust received £13,000. Other Jewish organisations to benefit included United Jewish Israel Appeal (£3,000), United Hebrew Congregation (£2,100), The Jewish Museum (£800), Magen David Adom UK (£1,500), Norwood (£100), Jewish Marriage Council (£50) and Jewish Women's Week (£20).

Almshouse Association, Nepal Charity Fund and St Gemma's Hospice each received £2,000. Other beneficiaries included Gateways Educational Trust and The Zone (£500 each), NSPCC (£190),

Marie Curie Cancer Care (£65) and Army Benevolent Fund (£50).

Exclusions No grants to individuals.

Applications In writing to the correspondent. Initial telephone calls are welcome, but please note the above comments.

Subject index

The following subject index begins with a list of categories used. These are very wide-ranging to keep the index as simple as possible. *The Grant-making Trusts CD-ROM* and *www.trustfunding.org.uk* website have a much more detailed search facility on categories. There may be considerable overlap between some of these categories – for example, children and education, or older people and social/moral welfare.

The list of categories is followed by the index itself. Before using the index please note the following:

How the index was compiled

1. The index aims to reflect the most recently recorded grant-making practice. It is therefore based on our interpretation of what each trust has actually given to, rather than what its policy statement says or its charitable objects allow it to do in principle. For example, where a trust states that it has general charitable purposes, but its grants list shows a strong preference for welfare, we index it under welfare.

2. We have tried to ensure that each trust has given significantly in areas where it is indexed (usually at least £15,000). Thus small, apparently untypical grants have been ignored for index purposes.

3. The index has been compiled from the latest information available to us.

Limitations

1. Policies may change

2. Sometimes there will be a geographical restriction on a trust's grant giving which is not shown up in this index, or a trust may not give for the specific purposes you require under that heading. It is important to read each entry carefully. You will need to check:
   (a) The trust gives in your geographical area of operation.
   (b) The trust gives for the specific purposes you require.
   (c) There is no other reason to prevent you making an application to this trust.

3. We have omitted the General category as number of trusts included would make it unusable. It is also worth noting that some categories list over half the trusts included in this guide.

Under no circumstances should the index be used as a simple mailing list. Remember that each trust is different and that often policies or interests of a particular trust do not fit easily into given categories. Each entry must be read individually before you send off an application. Indiscriminate applications are usually unsuccessful. They waste time and money and greatly annoy trusts.

Categories are as follows:

Arts and culture *page 274*

A very wide category including performing, written and visual arts, crafts, theatres, museums and galleries, heritage, architecture and archaeology.

Children and young people *page 275*

Mainly for welfare and welfare-related activities.

Community and economic development *page 275*

This includes employment.

Disadvantaged people *page 276*

This includes people who are:
- socially excluded
- socially and economically disadvantaged
- unemployed
- homeless
- offenders
- victims of social/natural occurrences, including refugees and asylum seekers.

Education and training *page 276*

Environment and animals *page 277*

This includes:
- agriculture and fishing
- conservation
- animal care
- environmental education
- transport
- sustainable environment.

Housing *page 278*

Ill or disabled people *page 278*

This includes people who are ill, or who have physical or mental disabilities, learning difficulties, or mental health problems.

Medicine and health *page 279*

This excludes medical research, which is listed separately.

Medical research *page 280*

Older people *page 280*

Religion general *page 281*

This includes inter-faith work and religious understanding

Arts and culture

ADAPT Trust
Altajir Trust
AM Charitable Trust
Viscount Amory's Charitable Trust
Ove Arup Foundation
Ashworth Charitable Trust
Richard Attenborough Charitable Trust
Aurelius Charitable Trust
Lord Barnby's Foundation
Benham Charitable Settlement
Charlotte Bonham-Carter Charitable Trust
Harry Bottom Charitable Trust
A H & E Boulton Trust
Bowerman Charitable Trust
Bowland Charitable Trust
British Record Industry Trust
Britten-Pears Foundation
Roger Brooke Charitable Trust
Bulldog Trust
Arnold James Burton 1956 Charitable Settlement
R M 1956 Burton Charitable Trust
Edward & Dorothy Cadbury Trust (1928)
Charities Advisory Trust
J A Clark Charitable Trust
Francis Coales Charitable Foundation
John Coates Charitable Trust
Gordon Cook Foundation
Coppings Trust
Duke of Cornwall's Benevolent Fund
Sidney & Elizabeth Corob Charitable Trust
Craignish Trust
Daiwa Anglo-Japanese Foundation
David Charitable Trust
Gwendoline & Margaret Davies Charity
Leopold De Rothschild Charitable Trust
Duke of Devonshire's Charitable Trust
Dyers' Company Charitable Trust
Edinburgh Trust, No 2 Account
Englefield Charitable Trust
Equity Trust Fund
Alan Evans Memorial Trust
Sir John Fisher Foundation
Marc Fitch Fund
Timothy Franey Charitable Foundation
Jill Franklin Trust
Gordon Fraser Charitable Trust
Frognal Trust
Garrick Charitable Trust
Gibbs Charitable Trusts
Golden Charitable Trust
Jack Goldhill Charitable Trust
Golsoncott Foundation
Nicholas & Judith Goodison's Charitable Settlement

Great Britain Sasakawa Foundation
Grimmitt Trust
R J Harris Charitable Settlement
Hawthorne Charitable Trust
Hobson Charity Ltd
Holst Foundation
P H Holt Charitable Trust
Idlewild Trust
Inland Waterways Association
Inverforth Charitable Trust
Ireland Fund of Great Britain
Ironmongers' Quincentenary Charitable Fund
J P Jacobs Charitable Trust
James Pantyfedwen Foundation
John Jarrold Trust
Jungels-Winkler Charitable Foundation
Anton Jurgens Charitable Trust
Michael & Ilse Katz Foundation
Kobler Trust
Kohn Foundation
Neil Kreitman Foundation
Christopher Laing Foundation
Lambert Charitable Trust
R J Larg Family Charitable Trust
Raymond & Blanche Lawson Charitable Trust
Lawson-Beckman Charitable Trust
Leche Trust
Leverhulme Trade Charities Trust
Lynn Foundation
Sir Jack Lyons Charitable Trust
Mageni Trust
Michael Marks Charitable Trust
Marsh Christian Trust
Sir George Martin Trust
Mayfield Valley Arts Trust
Anthony and Elizabeth Mellows Charitable Settlement
Nigel Moores Family Charitable Trust
National Manuscripts Conservation Trust
Normanby Charitable Trust
Odin Charitable Trust
Ofenheim & Cinderford Charitable Trusts
Old Possum's Practical Trust
Ouseley Trust
Late Barbara May Paul Charitable Trust
Polden-Puckham Charitable Foundation
John Porter Charitable Trust
Nyda and Oliver Prenn Foundation
Prince of Wales's Charitable Foundation
Quercus Trust
R V W Trust
Radcliffe Trust
Ragdoll Foundation
Rainford Trust
Peggy Ramsay Foundation

Cliff Richard Charitable Trust
Helen Roll Charitable Trust
Audrey Sacher Charitable Trust
Dr Mortimer and Theresa Sackler Foundation
St James' Trust Settlement
Basil Samuel Charitable Trust
Coral Samuel Charitable Trust
Peter Samuel Charitable Trust
Scouloudi Foundation
N Smith Charitable Trust
Stanley Smith UK Horticultural Trust
Roama Spears Charitable Settlement
Jessie Spencer Trust
Swan Trust
Charles and Elsie Sykes Trust
C B & H H Taylor 1984 Trust
Van Neste Foundation
Warbeck Fund Ltd
Mrs Waterhouse Charitable Trust
Mary Webb Trust
James Weir Foundation
Westcroft Trust
Whitaker Charitable Trust
Wixamtree Trust
Fred & Della Worms Charitable Trust
Matthews Wrightson Charity Trust
I A Ziff Charitable Foundation

Children and young people

Access 4 Trust
Adint Charitable Trust
Sylvia Aitken Charitable Trust
Alchemy Foundation
Viscount Amory's Charitable Trust
Armourers and Brasiers' Gauntlet Trust
Ashe Park Charitable Trust
Balcombe Charitable Trust
Beaverbrook Foundation
Birmingham Hospital Saturday Fund Medical Charity & Welfare Trust
Bowerman Charitable Trust
Bowland Charitable Trust
David Brooke Charity
Bulldog Trust
Burden Trust
Clara E Burgess Charity
Bill Butlin Charity Trust
Edward & Dorothy Cadbury Trust (1928)
D W T Cargill Fund
Thomas Sivewright Catto Charitable Settlement
Children's Research Fund
Chownes Foundation
CLA Charitable Trust
Cleopatra Trust
Clover Trust
John Coates Charitable Trust

Gordon Cook Foundation
Augustine Courtauld Trust
David Charitable Trust
Dawe Charitable Trust
Peter De Haan Charitable Trust
Richard Desmond Charitable Trust
Duke of Devonshire's Charitable Trust
Dorus Trust
Dumbreck Charity
Dyers' Company Charitable Trust
Sir John Eastwood Foundation
Gilbert & Eileen Edgar Foundation
Edinburgh Trust, No 2 Account
Vernon N Ely Charitable Trust
Emmandjay Charitable Trust
Epigoni Trust
Finnart House School Trust
Football Association National Sports Centre Trust
Timothy Franey Charitable Foundation
Gordon Fraser Charitable Trust
Joseph Strong Frazer Trust
Charles S French Charitable Trust
Frognal Trust
Garrick Charitable Trust
Gough Charitable Trust
Reginald Graham Charitable Trust
Constance Green Foundation
Grimmitt Trust
Handicapped Children's Aid Committee
Haramead Trust
R J Harris Charitable Settlement
Hawthorne Charitable Trust
Haymills Charitable Trust
Christina Mary Hendrie Trust for Scottish & Canadian Charities
Charles Littlewood Hill Trust
Homelands Charitable Trust
Miss Agnes H Hunter's Trust
Hyde Charitable Trust
Worshipful Company of Innholders General Charity Fund
Inverforth Charitable Trust
Irish Youth Foundation (UK) Ltd
J P Jacobs Charitable Trust
Jewish Child's Day
Joanna Herbert-Stepney Charitable Settlement
Lillie Johnson Charitable Trust
Anton Jurgens Charitable Trust
David Laing Foundation
Langdale Trust
R J Larg Family Charitable Trust
Rachel & Jack Lass Charities Ltd
Edgar E Lawley Foundation
Lawlor Foundation
Lister Charitable Trust
London Law Trust
Lotus Foundation
C L Loyd Charitable Trust
Luck-Hille Foundation

Lyndhurst Settlement
Lynn Foundation
Lyons Charitable Trust
Madeline Mabey Trust
Robert McAlpine Foundation
D D McPhail Charitable Settlement
Marsh Christian Trust
Jim Marshall Charitable Trust
Sir George Martin Trust
Masonic Trust for Girls and Boys
Anthony and Elizabeth Mellows Charitable Settlement
Peter Minet Trust
George A Moore Foundation
Music Sound Foundation
Noel Buxton Trust
Late Barbara May Paul Charitable Trust
Prince of Wales's Charitable Foundation
Princess Anne's Charities
Priory Foundation
Ragdoll Foundation
Ratcliff Foundation
REMEDI
St James' Trust Settlement
St James's Place Foundation
Salters' Charities
Basil Samuel Charitable Trust
Ayrton Senna Foundation
Shipwrights Company Charitable Fund
Leslie Smith Foundation
Philip Smith's Charitable Trust
South Square Trust
W W Spooner Charitable Trust
Stoller Charitable Trust
Charles and Elsie Sykes Trust
Tajtelbaum Charitable Trust
C B & H H Taylor 1984 Trust
Towry Law Charitable Trust
Toy Trust
Truemark Trust
Bernard Van Leer Foundation
Mrs Waterhouse Charitable Trust
Weavers' Company Benevolent Fund
Felicity Wilde Charitable Trust
Woo Charitable Foundation
Matthews Wrightson Charity Trust
Yapp Charitable Trust
Elizabeth & Prince Zaiger Trust
I A Ziff Charitable Foundation

Community and economic development

Armourers and Brasiers' Gauntlet Trust
AS Charitable Trust
Barclays Stockbrokers Charitable Trust
Burdens Charitable Foundation

Disadvantaged people

Education and training

Environment and animals

Housing

Ill or disabled people

Medicine and health

Medical research

Older people

Chownes Foundation
David Charitable Trust
Duke of Devonshire's Charitable Trust
Dumbreck Charity
Sir John Eastwood Foundation
Gilbert & Eileen Edgar Foundation
W G Edwards Charitable Foundation
Football Association National Sports
 Centre Trust
Joseph Strong Frazer Trust
Charles S French Charitable Trust
Frognal Trust
Constance Green Foundation
Grimmitt Trust
Helen Hamlyn 1989 Foundation
Christina Mary Hendrie Trust for
 Scottish & Canadian Charities
Hudson Foundation
Miss Agnes H Hunter's Trust
Inman Charity
Inverforth Charitable Trust
J P Jacobs Charitable Trust
Dorothy Jacobs Charity
Anton Jurgens Charitable Trust
Edgar E Lawley Foundation
Lyndhurst Settlement
Lynn Foundation
Robert McAlpine Foundation
D D McPhail Charitable Settlement
Marsh Christian Trust
Sir George Martin Trust
Peter Minet Trust
George A Moore Foundation
Morris Charitable Trust
Late Barbara May Paul Charitable
 Trust
REMEDI
Violet M Richards Charity
Riverside Charitable Trust Limited
Cecil Rosen Foundation
Bassil Shippam and Alsford Trust
Philip Smith's Charitable Trust
Sovereign Health Care Charitable Trust
Stanley Foundation Ltd
C B & H H Taylor 1984 Trust
Towry Law Charitable Trust
Truemark Trust
Van Neste Foundation
Mrs Waterhouse Charitable Trust
Wixamtree Trust
Matthews Wrightson Charity Trust
Yapp Charitable Trust
Elizabeth & Prince Zaiger Trust
I A Ziff Charitable Foundation

Religion general

Sylvia Aitken Charitable Trust
Alexandra Rose Day
Benham Charitable Settlement
Edward & Dorothy Cadbury Trust
 (1928)

Chapman Charitable Trust
Alice Ellen Cooper-Dean Charitable
 Foundation
Duke of Cornwall's Benevolent Fund
Gilbert & Eileen Edgar Foundation
Englefield Charitable Trust
Joseph Strong Frazer Trust
Inlight Trust
C L Loyd Charitable Trust
Gerald Palmer Trust
Sir James Roll Charitable Trust
Sir Sigmund Sternberg Charitable
 Foundation
Roger Vere Foundation
Mary Webb Trust

Christianity

All Saints Educational Trust
Almond Trust
Viscount Amory's Charitable Trust
Andrew Anderson Trust
Archbishop of Canterbury's Charitable
 Trust
AS Charitable Trust
Ashburnham Thanksgiving Trust
Barber Charitable Trust
Barnabas Trust
Beaufort House Trust
Bisgood Charitable Trust
A H & E Boulton Trust
P G & N J Boulton Trust
Bowerman Charitable Trust
Bowland Charitable Trust
Buckingham Trust
Burden Trust
Burdens Charitable Foundation
D W T Cargill Fund
Joseph & Annie Cattle Trust
Childs Charitable Trust
Mansfield Cooke Trust
Augustine Courtauld Trust
Cross Trust
Dyers' Company Charitable Trust
Ebenezer Trust
Vernon N Ely Charitable Trust
Emmandjay Charitable Trust
Englefield Charitable Trust
Farthing Trust
Fulmer Charitable Trust
Gibbs Charitable Trusts
Golden Charitable Trust
Gough Charitable Trust
Grace Charitable Trust
Harnish Trust
Gay & Peter Hartley's Hillards
 Charitable Trust
May Hearnshaw's Charity
Highmoor Hall Charitable Trust
Hinchley Charitable Trust
Stuart Hine Trust
Homelands Charitable Trust

Sir Harold Hood's Charitable Trust
Hope Trust
J P Jacobs Charitable Trust
James Pantyfedwen Foundation
Joanna Herbert-Stepney Charitable
 Settlement
H F Johnson Trust
Langdale Trust
Lindale Educational Foundation
Lyndhurst Trust
M N R Charitable Trust
Maranatha Christian Trust
Marsh Christian Trust
Charlotte Marshall Charitable Trust
Sir George Martin Trust
Anthony and Elizabeth Mellows
 Charitable Settlement
Millfield Trust
Millhouses Charitable Trust
Morgan Williams Charitable Trust
Oliver Morland Charitable Trust
Moss Charitable Trust
National Catholic Fund
National Committee of Women's
 World Day of Prayer for England,
 Wales, and Northern Ireland
Norwood & Newton Settlement
Ogle Christian Trust
Panahpur Charitable Trust
Princess Anne's Charities
Cliff Richard Charitable Trust
River Trust
Saint Sarkis Charity Trust
Salamander Charitable Trust
Salters' Charities
Seedfield Trust
Seven Fifty Trust
Shanti Charitable Trust
Bassil Shippam and Alsford Trust
Shipwrights Company Charitable Fund
SMB Trust
Albert & Florence Smith Memorial
 Trust
South Square Trust
W F Southall Trust
Jessie Spencer Trust
Sylvanus Charitable Trust
C B & H H Taylor 1984 Trust
Thornton Trust
Tolkien Trust
Tory Family Foundation
Truemark Trust
Tufton Charitable Trust
Van Neste Foundation
Wallington Missionary Mart and
 Auctions
Mrs Waterhouse Charitable Trust
Westcroft Trust
Norman Whiteley Trust
Dame Violet Wills Charitable Trust
Wixamtree Trust
Matthews Wrightson Charity Trust

Sport and recreation

Voluntary sector management and development

Women

Geographical index

The following index aims to highlight when a trust gives preference to, or has a special interest in, a particular area: county, region, city, town or London borough. Please note the following:

1. Before using this index please read the following and the introduction to the subject index. We emphasise that this index:
   (a) should not be used as a simple mailing list, and
   (b) is not a substitute for detailed research.

When you have identified trusts, using this index, please read each entry carefully before making an application. Simply because a trust gives in your geographical area does not mean that it gives to your type of work.

2. Most trusts in this list are not restricted to one area; usually the geographical index indicates that the trust gives some priority to an area or areas.

3. Trusts which give throughout the UK have been excluded, as have those which give worldwide, unless they have a particular interest in one or more locality.

4. Each section is ordered alphabetically according to name of trust.

The categories for overseas and UK indexes are as follows:

England

We have divided England into following six categories:

The trusts are listed as follows:

(a) Trusts giving throughout a whole region or in several counties within it (or throughout London).

(b) Trusts giving in a particular county (or a particular borough in London).

(c) A trust may be listed under (b) as well as (a), if it has a particular interest in a town or county within a region where it also gives more widely.

These are listed in alphabetical order of continent, and within each continent by country where appropriate.

The Middle East has been listed separately. Please note that all of the trusts listed are primarily for benefit of Jewish people and advancement of Jewish religion.

England

North East

Gay & Peter Hartley's Hillards
  Charitable Trust
Lyndhurst Trust
Normanby Charitable Trust
Penny in Pound Fund Charitable Trust
Patricia and Donald Shepherd Trust

Cleveland

Anglian Water Trust Fund

East Yorkshire

Joseph & Annie Cattle Trust

North Yorkshire

Sir George Martin Trust

South Yorkshire

May Hearnshaw's Charity
Mayfield Valley Arts Trust
Hugh & Ruby Sykes Charitable Trust

West Yorkshire

Emmandjay Charitable Trust
Constance Green Foundation
Linden Charitable Trust
Sir George Martin Trust
Shanti Charitable Trust
L H Silver Charitable Trust

Yorkshire general

Harry Bottom Charitable Trust
Arnold James Burton 1956 Charitable
  Settlement
R M 1956 Burton Charitable Trust
Earl Fitzwilliam Charitable Trust
Barry Green Memorial Fund
George A Moore Foundation
W W Spooner Charitable Trust
Samuel Storey Family Charitable Trust
Charles and Elsie Sykes Trust
Scurrah Wainwright Charity
I A Ziff Charitable Foundation

North West

Bowland Charitable Trust
Eventhall Family Charitable Trust
Gay & Peter Hartley's Hillards
  Charitable Trust
William Geoffrey Harvey's
  Discretionary Settlement
M A Hawe Settlement
Penny in Pound Fund Charitable Trust
Patricia and Donald Shepherd Trust

John Slater Foundation
Steinberg Family Charitable Trust
Ward Blenkinsop Trust

Cumbria

Sir John Fisher Foundation
Sir George Martin Trust
Norman Whiteley Trust

Greater Manchester

Beauland Ltd
George Elias Charitable Trust
Jack Livingstone Charitable Trust
M B Foundation
Mole Charitable Trust
Oizer Charitable Trust
Searchlight Electric Charitable Trust
Stanley Charitable Trust
Stoller Charitable Trust
Treeside Trust

Lancashire

Florence's Charitable Trust
Barry Green Memorial Fund
Riverside Charitable Trust Limited
Mrs Waterhouse Charitable Trust

Merseyside

Sir John Fisher Foundation
P H Holt Charitable Trust
J P Jacobs Charitable Trust
Nigel Moores Family Charitable Trust
Mushroom Fund
Duncan Norman Trust Fund
Cecil Pilkington Charitable Trust
Sir Harry Pilkington Trust
Rainford Trust
Eleanor Rathbone Charitable Trust

Midlands

Anglian Water Trust Fund
Dumbreck Charity
GNC Trust
May Hearnshaw's Charity
Patrick Charitable Trust
Ratcliff Foundation
Whitaker Charitable Trust

Derbyshire

Harry Bottom Charitable Trust
Duke of Devonshire's Charitable Trust
Hugh & Ruby Sykes Charitable Trust

Herefordshire

E F Bulmer Benevolent Fund
Hawthorne Charitable Trust
Clive Richards Charity Ltd

Leicestershire

Haramead Trust
Joanna Herbert-Stepney Charitable
  Settlement (also known as Paget
  Charitable Trust)
Florence Turner Trust

Northamptonshire

Benham Charitable Settlement
Francis Coales Charitable Foundation
Earl Fitzwilliam Charitable Trust
Macdonald-Buchanan Charitable Trust
Constance Travis Charitable Trust

Nottinghamshire

Sir John Eastwood Foundation
Thomas Farr Charitable Trust
Charles Littlewood Hill Trust
Lady Hind Trust
Linmardon Trust
Jessie Spencer Trust
Whitaker Charitable Trust

Shropshire

Millichope Foundation
Westcroft Trust

Warwickshire

Wilfrid & Constance Cave Foundation

West Midlands

Birmingham Hospital Saturday Fund
  Medical Charity & Welfare Trust
George Cadbury Trust
Edward & Dorothy Cadbury Trust
  (1928)
Grimmitt Trust
Lillie Johnson Charitable Trust
Langdale Trust
Edgar E Lawley Foundation
Limoges Charitable Trust
Millichope Foundation
M K Rose Charitable Trust
Roughley Charitable Trust
Saintbury Trust
W F Southall Trust
C B & H H Taylor 1984 Trust

Worcestershire

Hawthorne Charitable Trust

South West

J A Clark Charitable Trust
Clifton Charitable Trust
Hyde Charitable Trust
Leach Fourteenth Trust
Norman Family Charitable Trust

Asia

India

Matliwala Family Charitable Trust
J B Rubens Charitable Foundation

Japan

Daiwa Anglo-Japanese Foundation
Great Britain Sasakawa Foundation

Pakistan

J B Rubens Charitable Foundation

Sri Lanka

J B Rubens Charitable Foundation

Australasia

Australia

J B Rubens Charitable Foundation

New Zealand

J B Rubens Charitable Foundation

Europe

Allavida
Fidelity UK Foundation
Sylvanus Charitable Trust

Ireland

Hospital Saturday Fund Charitable
  Trust
Inland Waterways Association
Ireland Fund of Great Britain
Graham Kirkham Foundation
Lawlor Foundation
Ouseley Trust
C B & H H Taylor 1984 Trust

Middle East

Israel

Acacia Charitable Trust
Bear Mordechai Ltd
Beauland Ltd
Bertie Black Foundation
A Bornstein Charitable Settlement
Arnold James Burton 1956 Charitable
  Settlement
R M 1956 Burton Charitable Trust
Carlee Ltd
Vivienne & Samuel Cohen Charitable
  Trust

Craps Charitable Trust
Elman Charitable Trust
Friends of Wiznitz Limited
J E Joseph Charitable Fund
Bernard Kahn Charitable Trust
Stanley Kalms Foundation
Kasner Charitable Trust
Neil Kreitman Foundation
Lambert Charitable Trust
Largsmount Ltd
Lauffer Family Charitable Foundation
M D & S Charitable Trust
Marbeh Torah Trust
Hilda & Samuel Marks Foundation
Melodor Ltd
Melow Charitable Trust
Morris Family Israel Trust
Ruth and Conrad Morris Charitable
  Trust
MYA Charitable Trust
John Porter Charitable Trust
M K Rose Charitable Trust
Rowanville Ltd
J B Rubens Charitable Foundation
Michael Sacher Charitable Trust
Ruzin Sadagora Trust
Annie Schiff Charitable Trust
Helene Sebba Charitable Trust
SEM Charitable Trust
Solo Charitable Settlement
Songdale Ltd
Cyril & Betty Stein Charitable Trust
Tajtelbaum Charitable Trust
Warbeck Fund Ltd
Williams Family Charitable Trust
Maurice Wohl Charitable Foundation
Maurice Wohl Charitable Trust

Alphabetical index